STUDIES IN THE BOOK OF ISAIAH

BIBLIOTHECA EPHEMERIDUM THEOLOGICARUM LOVANIENSIUM

CXXXII

STUDIES
IN THE BOOK OF ISAIAH

FESTSCHRIFT WILLEM A.M. BEUKEN

EDITED BY

J. VAN RUITEN AND M. VERVENNE

LEUVEN
UNIVERSITY PRESS

UITGEVERIJ PEETERS
LEUVEN

1997

ISBN 90 6186 817 3 (Leuven University Press)
D/1997/1869/31
ISBN 90-6831-926-4 (Uitgeverij Peeters)
D/1997/0602/35
ISBN 2-87723-336-7 (Peeters France)

Leuven University Press / Presses Universitaires de Louvain
Universitaire Pers Leuven
Blijde Inkomststraat 5, B-3000 Leuven-Louvain (Belgium)

© Uitgeverij Peeters, Bondgenotenlaan 153, B-3000 Leuven (Belgium), 1997

PREFACE

The present Festschrift marks two important occasions in the life and career of Professor W.A.M. Beuken; his sixty-fifth birthday on May 13th, 1996 and his retirement as Professor of Old Testament Studies at the Faculty of Theology of the Katholieke Universiteit Leuven. Both occasions have provided the editors with a most appropriate opportunity to honour our valued friend and colleague with the publication of this volume and its presentation at the 46th Colloquium Biblicum Lovaniense on July 31st, 1997.

Wim Beuken has dedicated much of his scholarly career to the study of one Old Testament book, the Book of Isaiah. Among his many publications on the topic, his commentaries on Deutero- and Trito-Isaiah in the series *De Prediking van het Oude Testament* have been welcomed as major contributions to the field of Isaianic studies. In addition to these, he is currently preparing a volume on Isaiah 13–39 in the series *Historical Commentaries on the Old Testament*. It seemed natural, therefore, that the present volume and its editors should honour Beuken's scholarly achievements with a collection of essays devoted to the Book of Isaiah and related topics.

The collection opens with a list of Beuken's publications and a survey of his academic career. The 28 contributions which follow are presented under four section headings. The first section contains a series of thematically oriented studies on the Book of Isaiah as a whole. The second section focuses on the so-called Proto-Isaiah and includes contributions dealing with PI as a whole together with contributions which have concentrated on specific portions thereof. The third section includes a number of articles which address issues related to specific themes and pericopes in Deutero- and Trito-Isaiah. The fourth and final section turns its attention to intertextual and *wirkungsgeschichtlich* questions: the Book of Isaiah's relationship with other Old Testament texts and its reception by early Judaism and by the gospel writers.

The editors are indebted to a great number of individuals for their generous support in the formation and realisation of this Festschrift. We are particularly grateful to drs. Brian Doyle and drs. Anthe Vrijlandt who provided essential assistance in the volume's overall preparation and to Dr. Bénédicte Lemmelijn and Dr. Hans Ausloos who compiled the indexes. Thanks are also due to the authors themselves who include a number of eminent specialists in the study of the Book of Isaiah. Their creativity and prompt submission of manuscripts is deserving of much praise. Our continued gratitude must be extended to the editor of the *Bibliotheca Ephemeridum Theologicarum Lovaniensium* series together with Leuven University Press and Uitgeverij Peeters who made the publication of this volume possible. Finally, the editors would like to express their appreciation for the efficient and accommodating coopera- tion which continues to exist with the staff of the *Orientaliste* who were responsible for the Festschrift's printing.

To conclude, the range, scope and number of the contributions pub- lished here are an eloquent testimony to the esteem in which Wim Beuken is held by biblical scholars throughout the world. It has been the privilege of many to have known and continue to know him as an extra- ordinarily considerate and faithful colleague: faithful to the *Societas Iesu*, faithful to his family, and faithful to the many friends who have encountered him along the way and experienced some of his passion for the Hebrew Scriptures and the exegesis of the hidden world contained therein, especially the Book of Isaiah.

Jacques VAN RUITEN
Marc VERVENNE

CONTENTS

BIBLIOGRAPHY OF W.A.M. BEUKEN
1960-1996

BOOKS AND ARTICLES

1960   Rond de chronologie van de passieweek. — *Bijdragen* 21 (1960) 377-385.

1961   Goddelijke lach. Een vergelijkend onderzoek van de antieke literatuur en de Bijbel. — *Bijdragen* 22 (1961) 117-132.

1967   *Haggai-Sacharja 1–8. Studien zur Überlieferungsgeschichte der frühnachexilischen Prophetie* (SSN, 10), Assen, 1967, XVII-350 p. (Dissertation).

1972   Mišpāṭ: The First Servant Song and Its Context. — *VT* 22 (1972) 1-30.

        Ezechiël 20: Thematiek en literaire vormgeving in onderling verband. — *Bijdragen* 33 (1972) 39-64.

        Ḥasid: gunstgenoot. Een verwaarloosde erfenis van de Statenvertaling. — *Ibid.*, pp. 417-435.

1973   Jes 50,10-11: Eine kultische Paränese zur dritten Ebedprophetie. — *ZAW* 85 (1973) 168-182.

1974   Isa. 55,3-5: The Reinterpretation of David. — *Bijdragen* 35 (1974) 49-64.

        The Confession of God's Exclusivity by All Mankind: A Reappraisal of Is. 45,18-25. — *Ibid.*, pp. 335-356.

        Isaiah LIV: The Multiple Identity of the Person Addressed. — J. BARR – W.A.M. BEUKEN – A. GELSTON et al., *Language and Meaning: Studies in Hebrew Language and Biblical Exegesis* (OTS, 19), Leiden, 1974, pp. 29-70.

        De vreugde om JHWH's Heerschappij. Een structuuranalyse van Ps 97. — M. BOERTIEN (ed.), *Verkenningen in een stroomgebied. Proeven van oudtestamentisch onderzoek ter gelegenheid van het afscheid van Prof. Dr. Martinus Adrianus Beek aan de Universiteit van Amsterdam*, Amsterdam, 1974, pp. 102-109.

1975   God's Presence in Salem: A Study of Psalm 76. — *Loven en geloven. Opstellen van collega's en medewerkers aangeboden aan Prof. Dr. Nic. H. Ridderbos ter gelegenheid van zijn vijfentwintigjarig ambtsjubileum als hoogleraar aan de Vrije Universiteit te Amsterdam*, Amsterdam, 1975, pp. 135-150.

1976   Twee visies op de laatste rechter. Opmerkingen bij I Samuël 12. — *Bijdragen* 37 (1976) 350-360.

1977   Ed.: *Proef en Toets. Theologie als experiment. Bijdragen bij gelegenheid van het tienjarig bestaan van de Katholieke Theologische Hogeschool te Amsterdam*, Amersfoort, 1977 (with H. GODDIJN and M. MARLET).

        1 Samuël 28: De profeet als heksenhamer. — *Ibid.*, pp. 10-24.

        Psalm 72: de koning en de armen. — *Communio* 2 (1977) 223-232.

1978   De vergeefse moeite van de knecht. Gedachten over de plaats van
        Jesaja 49:1-6 in de context. — *De Knecht. Studies rondom Deutero-
        Jesaja. Door collega's en oud-leerlingen aangeboden aan Prof. Dr.
        J.L. Koole*, Kampen, 1978, pp. 23-40.
        Psalm 39: Some Aspects of the Old Testament Understanding of
        Prayer. — *The Heythrop Journal* 19 (1978) 1-11.
        I Samuel 28: The Prophet as 'Hammer of Witches'. — *JSOT* 6 (1978)
        3-17.
1979   *Jesaja. Deel II A* (De Prediking van het Oude Testament), Nijkerk,
        1979, 335 pp.
1980   Psalm 16: The Path to Life. — *Bijdragen* 41 (1980) 368-385.
1981   Jeremiah 14,1–15,9: A Situation of Distress and Its Hermeneutics,
        Unity and Diversity of Form – Dramatic Development. — P.-M.
        BOGAERT (ed.), *Le livre de Jérémie. Le prophète et son milieu, les
        oracles et leur transmission* (BETL, 54), Leuven, 1981, ²1997, pp.
        297-342 (with H.W.M. VAN GROL).
        Psalm XLVII: Structure and Drama. — A.S. VAN DER WOUDE (ed.), *Re-
        membering All the Way* (OTS, 21), Leiden, 1981, pp. 38-54.
1983   *Jesaja. Deel II B* (De Prediking van het Oude Testament), Nijkerk,
        1983, 365 pp.
1984   *Trito-Isaiah: An Exhaustive Concordance of Isa. 56–66, Especially
        with Reference to Deutero-Isaiah. An Example of Computer Assisted
        Research* (Applicatio, 4), Amsterdam, 1984, 153 pp. (with J. BASTIAENS
        and F. POSTMA).
1985   Exodus 16.5,23: A Rule Regarding the Keeping of the Sabbath? —
        JSOT 32 (1985) 3-14.
        De hemelse herkomst van het manna en zijn betekenis. — *Brood uit de
        hemel. Lijnen van Exodus 16 naar Johannes 6 tegen de achtergrond
        van de rabbijnse literatuur*, Kampen, 1985, pp. 62-73.
        Mozes en het manna. — *Ibid.*, pp. 74-89.
1986   De redactiekritische methode. — A. S. VAN DER WOUDE (ed.), *Inleiding
        tot de studie van het Oude Testament*, Kampen, 1986, pp. 173-187
        Isa. 56:9–57:13: An Example of the Isaianic Legacy of Trito-Isaiah. —
        J.W. VAN HENTEN – H.J. DE JONGE – P.T. VAN ROODEN – J.W.
        WESSELIUS (eds.), *Tradition and Re-interpretation in Jewish and
        Early Christian Literature: Essays in Honour of Jürgen C.H.
        Lebram* (Studia Post-Biblica, 36), Leiden, 1986, pp. 48-64.
        *Abraham weet van ons niet (Jesaja 63:16). De grond van Israëls
        vertrouwen tijdens de ballingschap*, Nijkerk, 1986, 32 pp. (inaugural
        address, Katholieke Universiteit Nijmegen).
1987   Deuterojesaja en de val van Babel. Vervolgreferaat. — *Amsterdamse
        Cahiers* 8 (1987) 40-44.
        Trito-Jesaja: Profetie en schriftgeleerdheid. — F. GARCÍA MARTÍNEZ –
        C.H.J. DE GEUS – A.F.J. KLIJN (eds.), *Profeten en profetische
        geschriften*, Kampen - Nijkerk, 1987, pp. 71-85.
1988   Ten geleide: De waarheid en haar slachtoffers. — *Concilium* 1988/6
        (with S. FREYNE and A. WEILER).
1989   *Jesaja. Deel III A* (De Prediking van het Oude Testament), Nijkerk,
        1989, 282 pp.

Jesaja. Deel III B (De Prediking van het Oude Testament), Nijkerk, 1989, 178 pp.

Servant and Herald of Good Tidings: Isaiah 61 as an Interpretation of Isaiah 40–55. — J. VERMEYLEN (ed.), *The Book of Isaiah. Le livre d'Isaïe. Les oracles et leurs relectures. Unité et complexité de l'ouvrage* (BETL, 81), Leuven, 1989, pp. 411-442.

Does Trito-Isaiah Reject the Temple? An Intertextual Inquiry into Isa. 66.1-6. — S. DRAISMA (ed.), *Intertextuality in Biblical Writings: Essays in Honour of Bas van Iersel*, Kampen, 1989, pp. 53-66.

No Wise King Without a Wise Woman (I Kings iii 16-28). — A.S. VAN DER WOUDE (ed.), *New Avenues in the Study of the Old Testament* (OTS, 25), Leiden, 1989, pp. 1-10.

1990   The Main Theme of Trito-Isaiah: 'The Servants of YHWH'. — *JSOT* 47 (1990) 67-87.

Dood en leven in het Oude Testament: een andere taal. — J. LAMBRECHT – L. KENIS (eds.), *Leven over de dood heen. Verslagboek van een interdisciplinair Leuvens colloquium*, Leuven - Amersfoort, 1990, pp. 287-293.

1991   Ten geleide: De Bijbel en zijn lezers. — *Concilium* 1991/1 (with S. FREYNE and A. WEILER).

De trektocht van Abraham. — *Collationes* 21 (1991) 271-286

Jesaja: Gerechtigheid en vrede. — J. DE TAVERNIER – M. VERVENNE (eds.), *De mens: verrader of hoeder van de schepping?* (Nikè-reeks, 26), Leuven - Amersfoort, 1991, pp. 91-101.

Jesaja 33 als Spiegeltext im Jesajabuch. — *ETL* 67 (1991) 5-35.

Isaiah Chapters lxv–lxvi: Trito-Isaiah and the Closure of the Book of Isaiah. — J.A. EMERTON (ed.), *Congress Volume Leuven 1989* (SVT, 43), Leiden, 1991, pp. 204-221.

1991-92 Gen. 18:21: An Overview of the Problems of Interpretation and an Attempt at Translation. — *Jaarbericht van het Voorasiatisch-Egyptisch Genootschap Ex Oriente Lux* 32 (1991-92) 141-149.

1992   The Syntactical Structure of Isa. 4:2-6: A Computer Assisted Analysis. — E. TALSTRA – A.L.H.M. VAN WIERINGEN (eds.), *A Prophet on the Screen: Computerized Description and Literary Interpretation of Isaianic Texts* (Applicatio 9), Amsterdam, 1992, pp. 47-57.

Isaiah 34: Lament in Isaianic Context. — *Old Testament Essays* 5 (1992) 78-102.

Isa. 29,15-24: Perversion Reverted. — F. GARCÍA MARTÍNEZ – A. HILHORST – C.J. LABUSCHAGNE (eds.), *The Scriptures and the Scrolls: Studies in Honour of A.S. van der Woude on the Occasion of his 65th Birthday* (SVT 49), Leiden, 1992, pp. 43-64.

Psalm 96: Israël en de volken. — *Skrif en Kerk* 13 (1992) 1-10.

1993   The Book of Job. Colloquium Biblicum Lovaniense XLII (1993). — *ETL* 69 (1993) 509-511.

ראש I *rō'š*. — H.-J. FABRY – H. RINGGREN (eds.), *Theologisches Wörterbuch zum Alten Testament, Band VII*, Stuttgart, 1993, col. 271-282.

שכב *šākab* 'sich legen'. – *Ibid.*, col. 1306-1318.

Ten geleide: De messias in de geschiedenis. — *Concilium* 1993/1 (with S. FREYNE and A. WEILER).

Had Israël de Messias nodig? — *Ibid.*, pp. 14-23.

1994   Ed.: *The Book of Job* (BETL, 114), Leuven, 1994, X-462 pp.

Job's Imprecation as the Cradle of a New Religious Discourse: The Perplexing Impact of the Semantic Correspondences Between Job 3, Job 4–5 and Job 6–7. — *Ibid.*, pp. 41-78.

Special Column: Een nieuw document van de pauselijke bijbel-commissie over de uitleg van de bijbel in de kerk. — *Concilium* 1994/3, 148-151.

De boeken van Samuël in een nieuw licht. Een bespreking. — *Phoenix. Bulletin uitgegeven door het Vooraziatisch-Egyptisch Genootschap Ex Oriente Lux* 40 (1994) 109-116.

The Present State of Old Testament Studies in Europe and Foreseeable Directions for the Future. — *Old Testament Essays* 7 (1994) 25-32.

1995   Ten geleide: De Bijbel als culturele erfenis. — *Concilium* 1995/1 (with S. FREYNE).

Isaiah 28: Is It Only Schismatics That Drink Heavily? Beyond the Synchronic Versus Diachronic Controversy. — J. C. DE MOOR (ed.), *Synchronic or Diachronic? A Debate on Method in Old Testament Exegesis: Papers Read at the Ninth Joint Meeting of Het Oudtestamentisch Werkgezelschap in Nederland en België and the Society for Old Testament Study, Held at Kampen 1994* (OTS, 34), Kampen, 1995, pp. 15-38.

What Does the Vision Hold: Teachers or One Teacher? Punning Repetition in Isaiah 30:20. — *The Heythrop Journal* 36 (1995) 451-466.

De os en de ezel in Jesaja literair (Jes 1:3 en 32:20). — R. MICHIELS – H. SCHWALL (eds.), *Herinnering en hoop. Herman Servotte, aangeboden door de universitaire parochie van de K.U. Leuven*, Averbode, 1995, pp. 164-183.

1996   "Zij zijn dronken, maar niet van wijn" (Jes. 29:9). Beschouwingen over een tekst voor een *magister morum*. — *Magister Morum. Opstellen voor Jan Sanders*, Amsterdam, 1996, pp. 13-20.

Wie weet heeft van vergankelijkheid kan verzoening bewerken (2 Samuël 13:38–14:24). — R. BURGGRAEVE – J. DE TAVERNIER (eds.), *Terugkeer van de wraak? Een tijd verscheurd tussen revanche, vergelding en vergeving*, Averbode, 1996, pp. 234-252.

BOOK REVIEWS

Bijdragen. Tijdschrift voor filosofie en theologie

1960   K. Schubert, *Die Gemeinde vom Toten Meer*. — *Bijdragen* 21 (1966) 82.

1961   P. Winter, *On the Trial of Jesus*. — *Bijdragen* 22 (1961) 450.

1963   T.A. Burkill, *Mysterious Revelation: An Examination of the Philosophy of St. Mark's Gospel*. — *Bijdragen* 24 (1963) 435.

G.M. Landes, *A Student's Vocabulary of Biblical Hebrew Listed According to Frequency and Cognate*. — *Ibid.*, 460.

1966   B. Otzen, *Studien über Deuterosacharja*. — *Bijdragen* 27 (1966) 317-318.

J. Becker, *Gottesfurcht im Alten Testament*. — *Ibid.*, 318.

R. Knierim, *Die Hauptbegriffe für Sünde im Alten Testament.* — *Ibid.*, 427-428.

D. R. Hillers, *Treaty Curses and the Old Testament.* — *Ibid.*, 428.

1967 S. Hermann, *Die prophetischen Heilserwartungen.* — *Bijdragen* 28 (1967) 82-83.

M.A. Klopfenstein, *Die Lüge nach dem Alten Testament.* — *Ibid.*, 83-84.

J.P. Seierstad, *Die Offenbarungserlebnisse der Propheten Amos, Jesaja und Jeremia.* — *Ibid.*, 84.

E. Sellin – G. Fohrer, *Einleitung in das Alte Testament.* — *Ibid.*, 84-85.

1968 A. Gamper, *Gott als Richter in Mesopotamien und im Alten Testament.* — *Bijdragen* 29 (1968) 205.

J.L. Koole, *Haggaï.* — *Ibid.*, 205-206.

A.A. di Lella, *The Hebrew Text of Sirach.* — *Ibid.*, 206.

U. Kellermann, *Nehemia.* — *Ibid.*, 207.

J. Plöger, *Literarkritische, formgeschichtliche und stilkritische Untersuchungen zum Deuteronomium.* — *Ibid.*, 301.

A. van Selms, *Levend verleden.* — *Ibid.*, 301.

É. Lipiński, *Le poème royal du Psaume LXXXIX.* — *Ibid.*, 301-302.

J.A. Fitzmyer, *The Aramaic Inscriptions of Sefiri.* — *Ibid.*, 431.

1970 G. Fohrer, *Das Alte Testament* I. — *Bijdragen* 31 (1970) 90.

O. Kaiser, *Einleitung in das Alte Testament.* — *Ibid.*, 90.

T. Chary, *Aggée – Zacharie – Malachie.* — *Ibid.*, 91.

J.B. Pritchard (ed.), *The Ancient Near East.* — *Ibid.*, 334.

1971 L.I.J. Stadelmann, *The Hebrew Conception of the World.* — *Bijdragen* 32 (1971) 79.

A. Neubauer – S. R. Driver, *The Fifty-Third Chapter of Isaiah According to the Jewish Interpretation.* — *Ibid.*, 193.

J. M. Berridge, *Prophet, People, and the Word of Yahweh.* — *Ibid.*, 193.

G. Fohrer, *Das Alte Testament* II-III. — *Ibid.*, 194.

M. Buttenwieser, *The Psalms.* — *Ibid.*, 194.

L. Gorssen, *Breuk tussen God en mens.* — *Ibid.*, 194.

G. Fohrer, *Hebräisches und aramäisches Wörterbuch zum Alten Testament.* — *Ibid.*, 321.

Theologisches Wörterbuch zum Alten Testament, Band I, Lf. 1-2. — *Ibid.*, 320-321.

F. Stolz, *Strukturen und Figuren im Kult von Jerusalem.* — *Ibid.*, 321-322.

J. Lévêque, *Job et son Dieu.* — *Ibid.*, 323.

H. Orlinksy (ed.), *Notes on the New Translation of the Torah.* — *Ibid.*, 323-324.

1972 K. Baltzer, *The Covenant Formulary in the Old Testament.* — *Bijdragen* 33 (1972) 89.

R.N. Whybray, *The Heavenly Counsellor in Isaiah XI.* — *Ibid.*, 89.

C.P. Stuhlmueller, *Creative Redemption in Deutero-Isaiah.* — *Ibid.*, 89-90.

H.W. Wolff (ed.), *Probleme biblischer Theologie.* — *Ibid.*, 90-91.

Theologisches Wörterbuch zum Alten Testament, Band I, Lf. 3-4. — *Ibid.*, 337-338.

W. Richter, *Exegese als Literaturwissenschaft.* — *Ibid.*, 338.

W. Rudolph, *Joel – Amos – Obadja – Jona.* — *Ibid.*, 338-339.

1973   *Theologisches Wörterbuch zum Alten Testament*, Band I, Lf. 5-7. —
        Bijdragen 34 (1973) 319-320.
        O. Keel, *Die Welt der altorientalischen Bildsymbolik.* — *Ibid.*, 322.
        P.-E. Bonnard, *Le Second Isaïe.* — *Ibid.*, 322-323.
1974   *Theologisches Wörterbuch zum Alten Testament*, Band I, Lf. 8-9. —
        Bijdragen 35 (1974) 101.
        A. Schoors, *I am God your Saviour.* — *Ibid.*, 101-102.
        D. Eichhorn, *Gott als Fels, Burg und Zuflucht.* — *Ibid.*, 102-103.
        D. Barthélemy – O. Rickenbacher (eds.), *Konkordanz zum hebräischen
        Sirach.* — *Ibid.*, 103-104.
1975   C. A. Wahl, *Clavis librorum Veteris Testamenti apocryphorum philo-
        logica.* — *Bijdragen* 36 (1975) 208.
        Theologisches Wörterbuch zum Alten Testament, Band II, Lf. 1-2. —
        Ibid., 209-210.
1976   R. Lack, *La symbolique du Livre d'Isaïe.* — *Bijdragen* 37 (1976) 326-327.
        Theologisches Wörterbuch zum Alten Testament, Band II, Lf. 3-6. —
        Ibid., 203, 309.
        E. Camilo dos Santos, *An Expanded Hebrew Index for the Hatch-
        Redpath Concordance to the Septuagint.* — *Ibid.*, 429.
        T. Veijola, *Die ewige Dynastie.* — *Ibid.*, 429.
1978   *Theologisches Wörterbuch zum Alten Testament*, Band II, Lf. 7-9. —
        Bijdragen 39 (1978) 78-79.
        J. Cazeaux, *Critique du langage chez les prophètes d'Israël.* — *Ibid.*, 80.
        T. Veijola, *Das Königtum in der Beurteilung der Deuteronomistischen
        Historiographie.* — *Ibid.*, 79-80.
        L. Laberge, *La Septante d'Isaïe 28–33.* — *Ibid.*, 326-327.
        J.M. Vincent, *Studien zur literarischen Eigenart und zur geistigen
        Heimat von Jesaja, Kap. 40–55.* — *Ibid.*, 327.
        H.D. Preuß, *Deuterojesaja.* — *Ibid.*, 327-328.
1979   *Theologisches Wörterbuch zum Alten Testament*, Band III, Lf. 1-3. —
        Bijdragen 40 (1979) 78-79.
        C. Westermann, *Theologie des Alten Testaments in Grundzügen.* —
        Ibid., 325.
1980   *Theologisches Wörterbuch zum Alten Testament*, Band III, Lf. 4-5. —
        Bijdragen 41 (1980) 203.
        J.A. Fitzmyer, *An Introductory Bibliography for the Study of Scripture.*
        — *Ibid.*, 309.
        Theologisches Wörterbuch zum Alten Testament, Band III, Lf. 6-7. —
        Ibid., 309.
        E. Talstra, *Deuterojesaja: proeve van automatische tekstverwerking ten
        dienste van de exegese.* — *Ibid.*, 313-314.
        B. Lang, *Wie wird man Prophet in Israel?* — *Ibid.*, 315-316.
1982   C. Westermann, *Sprache und Struktur der Prophetie Deuterojesaja.*
        Bijdragen 43 (1982) 84-85.
        A. van der Wal, *Amos. Een systematische literatuurlijst.* — *Ibid.*, 206-207.
        Theologisches Wörterbuch zum Alten Testament, Band III, Lf. 8/9. —
        Ibid., 442.
        O. Kaiser, *Rechts- und Wirtschaftskunden: Historisch-chronologische
        Texte* (TUAT, I/1). — *Ibid.*, 443-444.
        T. Veijola, *Verheißung in der Krise.* — *Ibid.*, 84.

1983 *Theologisches Wörterbuch zum Alten Testament*, Band IV, Lf. 1/2. —
      Bijdragen 44 (1983) 442.
1984 *Theologisches Wörterbuch zum Alten Testament*, Band IV, Lf. 3/4. —
      Bijdragen 45 (1984) 59.
      O. Kaiser, *Rechts- und Wirtschaftskunden: Historisch-chronologische
      Texte* (TUAT, I/2). — *Ibid.*, 59.
      F. Postma – E. Talstra – M. Vervenne, *Exodus: Materials in Automatic
      Text Processing.* — *Ibid.*, 60-61.
      M. Greenberg, *Ezekiel 1–20.* – *Ibid.*, 62-63.
      Theologisches Wörterbuch zum Alten Testament, Band IV, Lf. 5. —
      Ibid., 431.
      O. Kaiser, *Rechts- und Wirtschaftskunden: Historisch-chronologische
      Texte* (TUAT, I/3). — *Ibid.*, 433.
1985 *Theologisches Wörterbuch zum Alten Testament*, Band IV, Lf. 8/9. —
      Bijdragen 46 (1985) 188.
      O. Loretz, *Der Prolog des Jesaja-Buches (1,1–2,5): Ugaritologische
      und kolometrische Studien.* — *Ibid.*, 189.
      Theologisches Wörterbuch zum Alten Testament, Band V, Lf. 1-4. —
      Ibid., 434-435.
      O. Kaiser, *Rechts- und Wirtschaftskunden: Historisch-chronologische
      Texte* (TUAT, I/4-5). — *Ibid.*, 435-436.
1986 O. Kaiser, *Rechts- und Wirtschaftskunden: Historisch-chronologische
      Texte* (TUAT, III). — *Bijdragen* 47 (1986) 436.
      B. van 't Veld, *De Klacht over de vergankelijkheid van het menselijk
      leven in het Oude Testament.* — *Ibid.*, 438.
      O.H. Steck, *Bereitete Heimkehr: Jesaja 35 als redaktionelle Brücke
      zwischen dem Ersten und dem Zweiten Jesaja.* — *Ibid.*, 439.
1987 M. Fishbane, *Biblical Interpretation in Ancient Israel.* — *Bijdragen* 48
      (1987) 206.
      Theologisches Wörterbuch zum Alten Testament, Band V, Lf. 5-8. —
      Ibid., 336-337.
      D. Barthélemy, *Critique textuelle de l'Ancien Testament, I Jos-Est.* —
      Ibid., 338.
1988 *Theologisches Wörterbuch zum Alten Testament*, Band V, Lf. 9/10. —
      Bijdragen 49 (1988) 90.
      A.J. Bjørndalen, *Untersuchungen zur allegorischen Rede der Propheten
      Amos und Jesaja.* — *Ibid.*, 91.
1990 M.A. Sweeney, *Isaiah 1–4 and the Post-Exilic Understanding of the
      Isaianic Tradition.* — *Bijdragen* 51 (1990) 85.
1992 W. Vogels, *Job.* — *Bijdragen* 53 (1992) 205.
      Vetus Latina (ed. R. Gryson), Vol. 12, Fasc. 4. — *Ibid.*, 212.

Ephemerides Theologicae Lovanienses

1990 B. Uffenheimer – H. Graf Reventlow (eds.), *Creative Biblical Exegesis.*
      — *ETL* 66 (1990) 395.
      R.C. van Leeuwen, *Context and Meaning in Proverbs 25–27.* — *Ibid.*,
      404.
      H.P. Nasuti, *Tradition History and the Psalms of Asaph.* — *Ibid.*, 403-
      404.

1991   D.J.A. Clines – S.E. Fowl – S.E. Porter (eds.), *The Bible in Three Dimensions*. — *ETL* 67 (1991) 146-147.
       D. Grossberg, *Centripetal and Centrifugal Structures in Biblical Poetry*. — *Ibid.*, 153.
       M. Goulder, *The Prayers of David (Psalms 51–72): Studies in the Psalter 2*. — *Ibid.*, 155-156.
       M. Gilbert (ed.), *La Sagesse de l' Ancien Testament*. — *Ibid.*, 156.
       M.C.A. Korpel, *A Rift in the Clouds: Ugaritic and Hebrew Descriptions of the Divine*. — *Ibid.*, 160-161.
       H. Brunner, *Das Hörende Herz. Kleine Schriften zur Religions- und Geistesgeschichte Ägyptens*. — *Ibid.*, 161-162.
1992   J. van Dorp, *Josia: De voorstelling van zijn koningschap in II Koningen 22–23*. — *ETL* 68 (1992) 414-415.
       R.N. Whybray, *Wealth and Poverty in the Book of Proverbs*. — *Ibid.*, 424-425.
1993   D.W. Cotter, *A Study of Job 4–5*. — *ETL* 69 (1993) 165-166.
       R. Murray, *The Cosmic Covenant*. — *Ibid.*, 167-168.
       J.W. Watts, *Psalm and Story*. — *Ibid.*, 409-410.
       E. Ulrich et al., *Priests, Prophets and Scribes*. — *Ibid.*, 410.
       E.F. Navarro, *El desierto transformado*. — *Ibid.*, 411-413.
       L. Neveu, *Au pas des Psaumes*. — *Ibid.*, 413-414.
       L.O. Eriksson, *"Come, children, listen to me!" : Psalm 34 in het Hebrew Bible and in Early Christian Writings*. — *Ibid.*, 414.
       F.-J. Steiert, *Die Weisheit Israels*. — *Ibid.*, 414-415.
       T.P. McCreesh, *Biblical Sound and Sense: Poetic Sound Patterns in Proverbs 10–29*. — *Ibid.*, 415-416.

Other Journals

1985   T.A. Mettinger, *A Farewell to the Servant Songs*. — *Nederlands Theologisch Tijdschrift* 39 (1985) 141-142.
1986   M. Oeming, *Gesamtbiblische Theologien der Gegenwart*. — *Tijdschrift voor Theologie* 22 (1986) 179-180.
1990   H. Hendricks, *Gedenk uw bevrijding: de profetische bijbelboeken van Deuteronomium tot Koningen. Een werkboek*. — *Streven* 57 (1990) 1043-1044.
1991   J. Koenig, *Oracles et liturgies de l'exil babylonien*. — *Bibliotheca Orientalis* 48 (1991) 635-637.
       S. Sekine, *Die tritojesajanische Sammlung*. — *Nederlands Theologisch Tijdschrift* 45 (1991) 145-146.
1992   R. Davidson, *Wisdom and Worship*. — *Louvain Studies* 17 (1992) 417-418.
1996   J. van Oorschot, *Exegese des AT und NT: Von Babel zum Zion, eine literarkritische und redaktionsgeschichtliche Untersuchung*. — *Theologische Revue* 92 (1996) 138.
       W. Lau, *Schriftgelehrter Prophetie in Jes 56–56*. — *Nederlands Theologisch Tijdschrift* 50 (1996) 331-332.

J.T.A.G.M. VAN RUITEN

CURRICULUM WILLEM ANDRÉ MARIA BEUKEN

1931	Born May 13th, in Helmond, The Netherlands. Son of Dr. Willem Hendrik Beuken and Philomena J.A. Spoorenberg
1943-1949	Municipal Gymnasium, Maastricht
1949	Entered the Dutch province of the Society of Jesus
1952-1955	Licentiate in Philosophy (PhL) at the Berchmanianum, Nijmegen
1955-1958	BA in classical languages at the University of Amsterdam
1958-1962	Licentiate in Theology (STL) at the Canisianum, Maastricht
1961	Ordained priest
1962-1963	Studies in spirituality in Paray-le-Monial, France
1963-1965	Candidatura ad lauream in Old Testament Exegesis at the Pontifical Biblical Institute, Rome
1965-1966	Individual research with Gerhard von Rad in Heidelberg
1967	Doctor in Theology (cum laude) at the University of Utrecht; promoter: Th.C. Vriezen
1967-1985	Reader and professor in ordinary of Old Testament Exegesis at the Katholieke Theologische Hogeschool Amsterdam. Chair of the Biblical Studies Research Group
1985-1989	Professor in ordinary of Old Testament Exegesis at the Katholieke Universiteit Nijmegen. Chair of the Biblical Studies Research Group
1989-1996	Professor in ordinary of Old Testament Exegesis at the Katholieke Universiteit Leuven. 1992-1996, Chair of the Department of Biblical Studies

Editing

Co-founder and member of *De Jesajawerkplaats* since 1980

Member of the Editorial Advisory Board of the *Journal for the Study of the Old Testament* (Sheffield) from 1980 to 1996

Member of the senior editorial board of the journal *Concilium* (Nijmegen) and editor for Old Testament Exegesis from 1985 to 1996. Member of the General Board of Advisors since 1996

Member of the editorial board of the series *Studia Semitica Neerlandica* (Assen) since 1989

Member of the editorial board of the journal *Skrif en Kerk* (South Africa) since 1992

Member of the *Formation of the Book of Isaiah Seminar*, *Society of Biblical Literature* since 1995

Censor of the Willibrord Vertaling 1995, Oude Testament, for the Belgian and Dutch Episcopal Conferences

Member of the *Pontifical Biblical Commission* since 1996

Study Residences and Visiting Lectureships

1969	Mundelein Seminary, Chicago, USA, one semester
1974	W.F. Albright School of Archaeology, Jerusalem, one semester
1976	Graduate Theological Union, Berkeley, USA, one semester
1987	Catholic University of Lublin, Poland, two weeks
1991	University of Pretoria (RSA), Faculty of Theology NG, two months, with visiting lectureships at UNISA, the University of Stellenbosch, the University of Kwa-Kwa and the Randafrikaans University
1995	University of Pretoria (RSA), Faculty of Theology NG, one month

ISAIAH AND HIS BOOK

ZION AS SYMBOL AND POLITICAL REALITY
A CENTRAL ISAIANIC QUEST

The fact that the book of Isaiah is presented as a literary unity, but that its component parts can be clearly identified as deriving from a period spanning at least two centuries and probably considerably more, raises fundamental issues concerning the nature of biblical prophecy in general. It is possible to maintain a wide variety of opinions as to what exactly this composite authorship implies. On one side those scholars who have believed that the tradition concerning authorship is sacrosanct and that, in spite of apparently conflicting evidence, an essential unity of authorship must be upheld, have been forced to argue that prophetic prediction might possibly explain even the presence of seemingly impossible details being disclosed long in advance of the events which rendered them meaningful[1]. It is possible on the other hand to defend the book's unity as primarily a literary fact, implying little at all regarding authorship, but which must nevertheless be respected since any attempt to unravel it, or to trace its emergence, becomes fraught with uncertainties[2]. Between such positions, less stringent approaches have noted that, like other prophetic texts, the book of Isaiah shows many characteristic features of being an anthology of material, drawn from different times but carefully edited into a whole. This necessarily raises major methodological problems regarding our ability to identify levels of tradition both within the smaller sections, and even more seriously within the larger framework of the whole[3].

1. INTERTEXTUALITY AND THE STRUCTURE OF ISAIAH

The present essay is an attempt to offer a contribution towards a better understanding of the relationship between Isa 1–39 and 40–66 by noting two neglected passages which have a bearing on the issue. Within any approach to the question of this relationship it is methodologically possi-

---

1. J.N. OSWALT, *The Book of Isaiah, Chapters 1–39* (NICOT), Grand Rapids, 1986; A. MOTYER, *The Prophecy of Isaiah,* Leicester, 1993, pp. 25-29.
2. Cf. the approach advocated by E.W. CONRAD, *Reading Isaiah* (Overtures to Biblical Theology), Minneapolis, MN, 1991, pp. 3-33.
3. Cf. C.R. SEITZ, *The Divine Council: Temporal Transition and New Prophecy in the Book of Isaiah*, in *JBL* 109 (1990) 229-247, esp. pp. 245-246.

ble to discern a measure of division of intent between the work of editors and the work of prophetic authors who have simply introduced fresh prophecies appropriate to new situations which nevertheless bear a relationship to what had already been preserved. The aim of the less prominent editors would have been to assist the reader in recognizing important points of transition. This they did by marking them with superscriptions or closures, and it is the presence of a significant number of such editorial aids that is a distinctive feature of the book of Isaiah. In many cases it must be assumed that major editorial restructuring became necessary in order to take account of events that had transpired after the original prophecies had been recorded. These events called for a substantial re-orientation of earlier sayings without necessitating their abandonment altogether. It would have been necessary in many instances to show that the foretold time of divine judgement was now ended and was soon to be replaced by renewal and restoration. A distinctive literary consequence of this is that, whereas the most pronounced message of the earliest prophets was one of threat and coming divine judgement, in their final form all the major prophetic books are broadly messages of hope for Israel's future[4]. This feature is especially relevant to understanding the division between Isa 1–39 and 40–66. The very nature of the book, and with it the understanding of the nature of prophecy, becomes very differently perceived once this connection between the two parts is broken.

A further aspect of the book of Isaiah lies in the presence within it of passages in which specific metaphors have been re-used and re-applied, frequently in sharply contrasted ways[5]. Thereby patterns of contrast and *inclusio* have been set up which help towards demonstrating the connection between distinct parts. The literary unity then becomes both theologically and artistically recognizable. The phenomenon of intertextual linkage within the book not only reveals important features about the manner of its origin, but is also relevant to the understanding of its overall message. It is true that in some cases repetition and *inclusio* appear as little more than artistic devices to hold together diverse sayings which have little in common other than their use of the same metaphor or theme. More generally, however, the use of such devices appears intended to reflect some deeper ideological level of unity.

4. Cf. R.E. CLEMENTS, *Patterns in the Prophetic Canon*, in G.W. COATS – B.O. LONG (eds.), *Canon and Authority: Essays in Old Testament Religion and Theology*, Philadelphia, 1977, pp. 42-55.

5. Cf. ID., *Patterns in the Prophetic Canon: Healing the Blind and the Lame*, in G.M. TUCKER – D.L. PETERSEN – R.R. WILSON (eds.), *Canon, Theology and Old Testament Interpretation*. FS B.S. Childs, Philadelphia, 1988, pp. 189-200.

There is an evident need, from the perspective of a methodological enquiry, to identify the larger structural patterns within a prophetic book, as well as the intertextual significance of recurrent themes and metaphors in the various parts of it. Continuity and discontinuity, unity and difference, are all present as recognizable features, making the identification of the different growth levels a complex proceeding. Since this intricate literary production is itself a reflection of the way that prophecy was interpreted and used as a means of encouraging, and holding together, a community suffering times of extreme stress and danger, a wider theological interest attaches to it. Prophecy served as a marker for community identity[6] and the various literary techniques and devices used in it bear testimony to the manner of its origin. The edited collections of prophecies were expected to shape the lives of the community to whom they were addressed. The extent to which recent research has shown how intricate, and often seemingly arbitrary, examples of literary word-play, are used alongside more familiar rhetorical and poetic devices of oral preaching shows that prophecy developed as a scribal, as well as a rhetorical, pursuit. Examination of the phenomenon of intertextuality has thereby given rise to a significant shift in the interpretation of prophecy by showing the extent to which its development was furthered by literary techniques and written preservation. The scribe could become a prophet by exploring his literary skills and artistry. From a broader biblical perspective it is arguable that it is this literary stage in the rise of prophecy which has given to it its most enduring influence. The particular situation of the preacher was extended and reshaped by written preservation into a more universal message of the scribe who could address not one age, but many ages. Through the creation of a book Isaiah of Jerusalem could address all humanity.

A major concern of the application of an intertextual methodology to the study of the book of Isaiah must therefore be, not simply to note the interconnections within it as a literary anthology, but to seek beneath its surface for its larger structure. It is behind these that we can hope to discover those factors which gave it momentum and which provide sufficient cohesive constraint to make the notion of unity a meaningful one. To a considerable extent the search for such factors could only really begin, once the mistaken belief in the unity of authorship of all sixty-six chapters was finally abandoned. That unity was explicable in terms of a single author became a dangerous device for failing to note the real basis of the book's unity. At the same time, the attempt to counter this by as-

---

6. Cf. P.D. HANSON, *The People Called: The Growth of Community in the Bible*, San Francisco, 1986, pp. 253-290.

suming that we are essentially dealing with two, or more probably three, separate and unconnected books of prophecy, with a corresponding trinity of authors, has also proved misleading.

It is then an exciting and stimulating advance of recent methodology to have begun the task of tracing carefully the basic motives and themes which give to the book its essential unity. In this research it is an immense pleasure to pay tribute to the rewarding and pioneering insights of a scholar whose commentaries have contributed richly towards the fulfilment of such a goal.

2. ISAIAH – ONE BOOK OR TWO?

We may set as a matter of first importance the question which undoubtedly stands as the most central of those which the book presents. This is whether we are seeking to interpret two books which have been joined together at some unknown point of time, or whether we are not seriously and essentially seeking to interpret one single book which has been built up and augmented in a manner unique to the nature of prophecy. It is this question which bears directly on the nature, and underlying assumptions, of the connection between chapters 1–39 and chapters 40–66. Already a substantial range of exegetical studies has drawn attention to the many intertextual connections which exist between the two parts[7]. These links and interconnections undoubtedly exist. The need is therefore to explain them in relation to the way in which prophecy was understood to provide an ongoing medium for revealing the will of God.

A point of immediate significance, which provides a central point of focus for the present study, concerns the nature and purpose of the connections between the original Isaiah call-narrative of Isa 6,1-13 and the opening address to Zion-Jerusalem in Isa 40,1-11[8]. That the latter has

---

7. Cf. R.E. CLEMENTS, *Beyond Tradition-History: Deutero-Isaianic Development of First Isaiah's Themes*, in *JSOT* 31 (1985) 95-113 [reprinted in R.E. CLEMENTS, *Old Testament Prophecy: From Oracles to Canon*, Louisville, 1996, pp. 78-92 and also in P.R. DAVIES (ed.), *The Prophets: A Sheffield Reader*, Sheffield, 1996, pp. 128-146]; now also esp. SEITZ, *The Divine Council* (n. 3); ID., *How Is the Prophet Isaiah Present in the Latter Half of the Book? The Logic of Chapters 40–66 within the Book of Isaiah*, in *JBL* 115 (1996) 219-240; H.G.M. WILLIAMSON, *The Book Called Isaiah: Deutero-Isaiah's Role in Composition and Redaction*, Oxford, 1994 and the extensive secondary literature cited by these scholars.

8. Cf. especially R. RENDTORFF, *Jesaja 6 im Rahmen der Komposition des Jesajabuches*, in J. VERMEYLEN (ed.), *The Book of Isaiah* (BETL, 81), Leuven, 1989, pp. 73-82; = *Isaiah 6 in the Framework of the Composition of the Book*, in R. RENDTORFF, *Canon and Theology* (Overtures to Biblical Theology), Minneapolis, MN, 1993, pp. 170-180; SEITZ, *The Divine Council* (n. 3), pp. 238-243.

been influenced by the former and makes clear and demonstrable allusions back to a number of its central assertions appears sufficiently evident as to be accepted as a datum. It then becomes important to explore the implications of this more fully.

It remains something of a legacy of the claim that we are primarily dealing with two distinct and identifiable prophetic individuals that the link between the two passages should be understood in terms of a prophetic call and the sense of a new call, or commission, by which a further message from God is to be added to that of Isaiah by a new prophet. Accordingly, as Isa 6 presents the story of the call of Isaiah of Jerusalem, so Isa 40,1-8 (11) has been viewed as the call-narrative of Deutero-Isaiah[9]. In this way something of the *persona* and sense of divine commissioning appropriate to the originating figure of Isaiah is taken up and renewed through the new prophet. Clearly there is a measure of validity for such an approach since different individuals undoubtedly stand behind the text. However, it is striking that, if the unit is taken as comprising 40,1-11 so that verses 9-11 are an integral part of it, the address is explicitly to Zion/ Jerusalem, rather than an individual prophetic figure. The city itself has become personified as the message-bearer of the good news. This links up with the form of the opening address to an unknown comforter in verses 1-2 who is bidden to "speak reassuringly" to Jerusalem. Seitz would see this as a prophetic employment of the form of a speech from within the heavenly council of Yahweh[10].

The case is strong, however, for regarding Jerusalem-Zion as the intended addressee throughout the passage, with a natural progression from a rhetorical appeal to an unspecified comforter for Jerusalem to one in which the city itself becomes the message-bearer whose changed fortunes constitute the good news of the new message. Since the content of the message is one of comfort and re-assurance for Jerusalem the different modes of address are simply different ways of drawing attention to this. It would seem that the idea of an extended form of call-narrative as the explanation of the unexpected form of 40,1-11 is largely occasioned by the conscious harking back to the call-narrative of Isa 6,1-13. In other respects it is not particularly significant since the new passage is emphatically concerned to demonstrate that what is now revealed is not wholly distinct, but is the essential continuation of the earlier message. It presents a call to declare the "new things" which are to replace the "former things" which have now been fulfilled.

9. Cf. SEITZ, *The Divine Council* (n. 3), pp. 231-232; WILLIAMSON, *The Book Called Isaiah* (n. 7), pp. 151-154.

10. SEITZ, *The Divine Council* (n. 3), pp. 229-233.

In reality the connection between chapters 1–39 and 40–66 can be fully understood in terms of the centrality of the theme of Zion-Jerusalem as the centre of divine rule and authority for the formation of the book of Isaiah[11]. The words of 40,1-11 take on a new significance once it is understood that, after the catastrophe of 587 BCE, the unanswered question which pervaded the entire *traditio* of Isaiah's prophesying was "What future can there be for Zion, now that the temple has been destroyed?". Against such a background the connection between the two major parts of the book becomes self-explanatory. A central part of our argument therefore is that, instead of seeking to follow out any sense of connection between 1–39 and 40–66 in terms of two sequential prophetic call experiences, we can find a more explicit linkage through the concern with Jerusalem-Zion as the central theme of the separate parts of the book.

3. ISAIAH – PROPHET OF ZION

A major change in the understanding of the relationship between the prophet Isaiah and the centrality of the Jerusalem temple traditions in the Psalter was brought about by S. Mowinckel in his *Psalmenstudien II*[12]. This change was based on the recognition that the Isaiah-narrative tradition of Isa 36–37 concerning Jerusalem's miraculous deliverance from the clutches of Sennacherib in 701 BCE has been shaped by the cult mythology of Mount Zion. This is shown by such psalms as 46 and 48 and reflects the belief in the protection afforded to Israel by Yahweh's choosing the sacred mountain as his dwelling-place. Accordingly the influence upon the entire Isaiah book from this Jerusalem psalmic background has been extensive, not only because the prophet himself was affected by it, but because the tradition of his sayings continued to be moulded by it.

The most extensive and far-reaching effect of this influence is to be seen in the way in which the story of what took place in 701 BCE was then given a revised presentation in the light of later events, most especially the disaster of Jerusalem's destruction in 587 BCE[13]. The wider

---

11. Cf. C.R. SEITZ, *Isaiah 1–66: Making Sense of the Whole*, in ID., *Reading and Preaching the Book of Isaiah*, Philadelphia, 1988, pp. 105-126, esp. pp. 115-116.

12. S. MOWINCKEL, *Psalmenstudien II. Das Thronbesteigungfest Jahwäs und der Ursprung der Eschatologie*, Kristiania, 1922; = Amsterdam, 1961, p. 65.

13. R.E. CLEMENTS, *Isaiah and the Deliverance of Jerusalem: A Study of the Interpretation of Prophecy in the Old Testament* (JSOT SS, 13), Sheffield, 1980; C.R. SEITZ, *Zion's Final Destiny: The Development of the Book of Isaiah*, Minneapolis, MN, 1991, esp. pp. 119-148.

perspectives of this revised presentation have then been incorporated extensively into the whole *traditio* of the sayings of First Isaiah. The story of the events of the years 705-701 BCE, and the reworking and editing of Isaiah's prophecies which this necessitated, provide the indispensable background for understanding the link between the so-called First and Second Isaiah. It is not only from a literary perspective that chapters 36–39 form a bridge to the fresh continuation of the message of Isaiah; they also provide an essential theological preparation for it. Our argument is that, once the effect of this edited presentation of Isaiah's prophecies is recognized, then the manner in which Isa 40,1-11 takes up the unresolved question of the Isaiah prophetic *traditio* becomes plain.

Mowinckel's own subsequent suggestions regarding the work of Isaiah's presumed "disciples" and the cult-prophets of Jerusalem would accord reasonably well with such a perspective[14]. Instead of looking for one or two major "authors" to explain the book, we can better recognize that a series of formative stages are present in it, largely determined by the events which befell Jerusalem between the eighth and fifth centuries BCE. Moreover, it has become evident from the extensive and detailed study of the narrative tradition of Isa 36–37 that this is not from a single literary source but has been built up from separate source materials and composed over a period of time by a specific circle of Jerusalem prophet-scribes. That these shared close links with the circles which produced the so-called Deuteronomistic History (Jos – 2 Kings) is also evident. Mowinckel's suggestion that the *traditio* of Isaiah's prophecies was maintained within a group of cult-prophets from Jerusalem would seem to be not far wide of the mark. We can therefore better grasp the nature of the growth of the book of Isaiah by recognizing the work of a plurality of authors from a Jerusalem temple circle than by endeavouring to focus on two individuals – the presumed First and Second Isaiahs.

Our contention is that it is this continuing relationship between the different parts of the scroll of Isaiah and the cult-tradition of Jerusalem that establishes its fundamental unity. Succeeding generations of cult-prophets working in the city, even after the temple's destruction in 587 BCE, can more readily be regarded as the authors of the book which bears Isaiah's name than any two individual figures. Moreover, it is the rise and fall, and subsequent re-establishing after 587 BCE, of the cult ideology of Jerusalem that explains the peculiar shifts and apparent incongruities in the book. Its shape has been brought about by the desire to uphold the central claims of Jerusalem as a religious and spiritual centre

14. S. MOWINCKEL, *Jesaja-disiplene. Profeten frå Jesaja til Jeremia*, Oslo, 1925.

first in a very positive and triumphalist manner in the wake of the events surrounding Sennacherib's capture of the city in 701 BCE, and then, more than a century later, after the further disasters of 598 and 587 BCE. Its message is clearly "Let Jerusalem live – even though the temple has been destroyed!".

Once we look away from the concern with individual authorship as a controlling principle and focus instead on the relationship between prophecy and Mount Zion, the site of the most central religious institution of Israel, we can make better sense of the complex shape which the book of Isaiah displays. It gives full weight to the strong evidence that a considerable number of authors and editors have taken a hand in producing the finished scroll. Far from the linkage between chapters 1–39 and 40–55 being a confusing and distorted one, such a connection can be seen to be essential for an understanding of the function which the emergent prophetic book fulfilled. It served to interpret and uphold the controlling authority of Jerusalem and its cultus as the primary religious institution of Judaism. In doing so it had to take account of events which appeared to discredit such a message of hope. Such a goal extended far beyond Jerusalem's original eminence as a national capital where the nation's ruling monarchs were enthroned. It affirmed its over-riding function as the sole legitimate place for sacrificial offerings and as the arbiter of power and truth in the worship of the God of the Jews. Once the first beginnings of the Jewish Dispersion began to emerge, initially exemplified by the fate of those deported to Babylon in 598 BCE, the need for re-establishing Jerusalem's claim to authority became stronger than ever. The existence of several such scattered communities begins to appear very strongly in Isa 40–55 and reveals their locations far beyond the relatively small community held in Babylon.

It is the concern to re-assert and re-establish this dominant position of Jerusalem and its religious significance as the holy mountain of God after the *débacle* of 587 BCE when the temple was destroyed which provides a key to understanding why there are necessary connections between Isa 1–39, 40–55 and 56–66. In a rather unexpected fashion it shows that even the seemingly anti-temple sentiment of Isa 66,1 is important to the theology of the book which strives to uphold that, even though the Jerusalem temple had at one time suffered physical destruction and lain in ruins, the status of Jerusalem as God's chosen centre was never imperilled.

4. THE REMNANT FROM JERUSALEM

In order to substantiate this claim concerning the central importance of Zion as a unifying theme, it is helpful to consider the function of two neglected passages within the book which illustrate the background to Isa 40,1-11.

The first of these passages in Isa 37, 30-32 occurs as the second of the prophecies attributed to Isaiah at the time when Jerusalem was threatened with siege and capture by Jerusalem. In reality it is undoubtedly the third, and latest, of the three such prophecies to have been composed. Since I have already elsewhere dealt extensively with the narratives concerning the confrontation between Hezekiah and Sennacherib and with these three prophecies attributed to Isaiah in particular[15] there is little need to do more than to reiterate my conclusions here. The prophecy reads:

> And this shall be the sign for you: This year eat what grows of itself, in the second year what springs from that; then in the third year sow, reap, plant vineyards, and eat their fruit. The surviving remnant of the house of Judah shall again take root downward, and bear fruit upward; for from Jerusalem a remnant shall go out, and from Mount Zion a band of survivors. The zeal of the LORD of hosts will do this. (Isa 37,30-32: NRSV translation)

By far the most striking aspect of the prophecy is to be found in the acknowledgement in verses 31-32 that the population of Judah will be reduced to a "surviving remnant" but that this remnant will again be securely rooted in its land. Most remarkably of all this surviving remnant is directly linked in verse 32 to the population of Jerusalem and Mount Zion. The historic Zion motif of the divine holy mountain, which clearly exercised a formative role in the composition and theology of the story of how Jerusalem was delivered from the clutches of Sennacherib in 701 BCE, is here linked with a newly devised "remnant motif", itself clearly drawn from the name of Isaiah's child Shear-jashub of Isa 7,3. The divine protection for Jerusalem made possible through God's presence on the holy mountain has become the basis for an assurance that a "band of survivors" will remain, and will flourish again in Jerusalem.

It is necessary to recall a number of widely recognized literary and historical conclusions regarding the setting of this prophecy for its importance to be understood. It is noteworthy that, although the narrative

---

15. R.E. CLEMENTS, *The Prophecies of Isaiah to Hezekiah concerning Sennacherib: 2 Kings 19:21-34//Isa 37:22-35*, in R. LIWAK – S. WAGNER (eds.), *Prophetie und geschichtliche Wirklichkeit im Alten Israel*. FS S. Herrmann, Stuttgart - Köln, 1991, pp. 65-78; = *Old Testament Prophecy: From Oracles to Canon*, Louisville, 1996, pp. 35-48.

sequence of Isa 36,1–39,8 shows affinities both with the Deutero-nomistic History of Jos-2 Kgs and an early collection of Isaianic proph-ecies, some measure of independence from both is also evident. Overall these narratives are concerned to show how and why Jerusalem was spared from Sennacherib in 701 BCE. They were clearly not contempo-rary compositions from Isaiah's time and, as is the case with this par-ticular prophecy, they show a degree of dependance upon a preserved collection of authentic Isaianic sayings. They have been composed no earlier than the time in the late seventh century when Assyrian control over Judah was waning. Taken collectively these narratives show signs of composite authorship and have reached their final form over an ex-tended period of time. Whether or not they formed any part of an origi-nal draft of the Deuteronomistic History appears doubtful. For under-standing the book of Isaiah their importance is that they show how Isaiah's message was being related to the interpretation of one of the most remarkable events of the prophet's lifetime at some interval after his death. They display a marked theological emphasis upon the power of Yahweh, God of Israel to defend Jerusalem for his own sake and that of the Davidic royal house that sat enthroned there (Isa 37,35//2 Kings 18,34)[16].

The survival of Jerusalem and its Davidic monarchy in the face of Assyrian oppression appeared as a self-evidencing fact of divine provi-dence which clearly reached a dangerous level of extravagance once that oppressive control began to wane[17]. It is this triumphalist perspective which has not only shaped the content which the narrative reports ex-press, but has brought substantial revision and addition to the collection of Isaiah's prophecies from the eighth century.

The prophetic saying of Isa 37,31-32 can confidently be attributed to a time after 587 BCE, when its reference to "a band of survivors" going out from Mount Zion took on a very specific and significant meaning. Virtually all of Judah had been reduced to a ruin by the prolonged Babylonian siege and the deliberate devastation of the land (cf. Deut 28,38-42; 29,22-3). The identification of the surviving remnant in Judah as the basis for hope of renewal and restoration is remarkable. All the more is this the case, since the regional administration was moved for a period to Mizpah (Jer 40,6-16; 41,1-10). The saying is little more than a

16. Cf. R.E. CLEMENTS, *The Politics of Blasphemy: Zion's God and the Threat of Im-perialism*, in I. KOTTSIEPER – J. VAN OORSCHOT – D. RÖMHELD – H.M. WAHL (eds.), *"Wer ist wie du. HERR, unter den Götter?" Studien zur Theologie und Religionsgeschichte Israels*. FS O. Kaiser, Göttingen, 1994, pp. 231-246.

17. Cf. C. HARDMEIER, *Prophetie im Streit vor dem Untergang Judas* (BZAW, 187), Berlin - New York, 1990.

clinging to the belief in the unique role of Mount Zion as a source of divine protection and blessing after events had seriously challenged its older and more comprehensive form.

It is not difficult to relate historically the situation presupposed by the prophecy of Isa 37,30-32 with that which pertained for a relatively brief period after the events of 587 BCE. Gedaliah's brief control as governor from Mizpah was brought dramatically to an end by his assassination (Jer 41,1-8). Eventually all expectation that any immediate return to a situation of stability and social normality, such as the words of Isa 37,30 reflect, proved to be impossible. We can readily see from the emphatic editorial assertions of Jer 25,1-11 and 27,1-11 that resignation to a time of chaos and destitution prevailed in Judah (so especially Jer 25,11). All hope subsequently came to be directed toward the community which had been taken to Babylon in 598 BCE (Jer 27,22; 29,10), eventually to be augmented by others who arrived there later. No doubt the presence of scions from the Davidic royal house in Babylon greatly strengthened such expectations. A return of the scattered remnants of the nation, most especially of that section of the nation which had been removed to Babylon, seemingly by an act of providential wisdom, gave a new focus to the idea of a remnant, no longer directly to be identified with survivors in Jerusalem. In the process the very concept of Israel called for substantial revision and extension. We can discern the same tensions and uncertainties well reflected in the latest stages of revision and addition that have been incorporated into the Deuteronomistic narrative of 2 Kings 25,27-30. In other passages too the shadow of the events of 587 BCE are to be seen (notably 1 Kings 8,46-53).

The recognition that the perspective offered by these Isaiah narratives marks a major formative stage in the literary development of the Isaiah tradition represents a considerable advance in understanding its overall theological shape. How the events of Isaiah's time, especially those surrounding Jerusalem's deliverance from destruction by Sennacherib, appeared in the light of the events of the next century became a matter of first importance. After the resurgence of Davidic fortunes under Josiah (639-609 BCE) Hezekiah's survival appeared to be have been a miracle! So, after the events of the next half century, the prophecy of Isa 37,31-32 reflects a sense that the tradition of Zion's unique role for the destiny of Israel remained valid. It was, nevertheless, compelled to undergo significant changes to take account of the realities of later events. We know that, in the political turmoil that followed the murder of Gedaliah, the governor of Judah, even this hope of a renewal arising from within the region did not last for long.

The acceptance that the land would lie desolate for a prolonged period
and that the restoration would have to come through a return of those
deported to Babylon became the normative expression of Jewish hope,
at least in approved official circles. The transition from a hope based on
renewal from within Judah and Jerusalem to one focused instead on a
return of the exiles from Babylon can be seen as a fundamental shift of
perspective in the tradition of Jeremiah's prophesying and also in that of
the final editing of the Deuteronomistic History. It is well to the fore
also in the preserved edition of Ezekiel's prophecies. The evidence provided by the narratives of Isa 36–39 in their relation to the formation of
the book of Isaiah reveals that a similar shift of perspective has deeply
influenced this process also[18].

Once the significance of the narrative tradition of Isa 36–39 as a mirror
of the reception history of Isaiah's prophesying is taken into account, then
the necessity for further explanation and understanding of the divine commitment to Mount Zion and its temple was urgently called for. Not only
do the narratives provide an important literary point of linkage between
the earliest written collection of Isaiah's prophecies and those which have
been added in chapters 40ff., but they also offer the necessary theological
basis for the connection. Isaiah's message had been recorded and shaped
so as to uphold the traditional mythological understanding of the divine
commitment to Mount Zion and its temple, and to the Davidic dynasty
which had been inseparably linked to this. The events of 587 BCE in
which the Jerusalem temple had been destroyed and the Davidic dynasty
removed from its royal throne had set in question all such belief in Mount
Zion's role as a place of refuge and a source of light and power to the nations. Could there be any credible feature left of the ancient holy mountain
mythology which would continue to command respect when no Davidic
king ruled from the city and no temple any longer stood amid its ruins?
The unique interest of the short prophecy ascribed to Isaiah in Isa 37,31-
32 lies in its contention that such a belief could be upheld and provide a
basis of hope for Judah's future:

> The surviving remnant of the house of Judah shall again take root down-
> ward and bear fruit upward: for from Jerusalem a remnant shall go out and
> from Mount Zion a band of survivors. (Isa 37,31-32)

In a number of respects it is worthwhile to note that this short prophetic saying expresses by its implications many of the same theological

18. Cf. P.R. ACKROYD, *Isaiah 36–39: Structure and Function,* in W.C. DELSMAN *et
al.* (eds.), *Von Kanaan bis Kerala.* FS J. van der Ploeg (AOAT, 211), Kevelaer, 1982, pp.
3-21; = *Studies in the Religious Tradition of the Old Testament,* London, 1987, pp. 105-
120.

characteristics which are to be found in Jer 3,15-16. This short Deuteronomistic reflection on the future role of Jerusalem, which marks a significant editorial gloss to Jeremiah's prophecies, is concerned to take
account of the events of 587 BCE, which are the most likely occasion
for the loss of the ark. Its message is clear that, even without such a re-
vered cult-object, Jerusalem, simply as a city, will provide God's earthly
throne. In a similar way the Isaianic prophecy that we have considered
faces the question: "What is left for Jerusalem once the temple has been
destroyed and the Davidic family taken into exile?". The answer is
given in terms of a remnant from which the new nation will arise. Israel's future is seen still to lie with the divine commitment to Mount Zion,
in spite of all the setbacks and humiliations that the Holy City had suffered.

It seems highly probable that another brief, and seemingly isolated,
passage in Isa 1–39 reflects the same situation and emanates from the
same general concern:

> What will one answer the messengers of the nation?
> "The LORD has founded Zion,
> and the needy among his people
> will find refuge in her". (Isa 14,32)

In this case the lack of any reference to a remnant, or any indication
that Judah had suffered a severe period of adversity and destruction
makes its chronological assignation difficult. Nevertheless it is the in-
sistence upon Zion being a place of refuge and protection for Yahweh's
people on account of its divine foundation that lends it special interest. If
it is to be dated after the events of 587 BCE then clearly it is further evidence that even these disasters had not finally put an end to the belief
that Jerusalem occupied a special place in the divine government and
protection of Israel. It did, however, necessitate a significant shift of emphasis away from the ark-throne theology of a temple sanctuary once the
temple had been destroyed. Instead it was necessary to insist that the
very location of Mount Zion, as Yahweh's chosen throne-foundation,
still fulfilled such a special role. We find many of the same theological
shifts to re-mint the traditional temple-divine presence theology emerg-
ing at this time in the Deuteronomic Movement[19].

It was, however, not only the desecration of the temple and its altars
which presented a problem for the retention of the belief in Jerusalem's
special position as a source of divine blessing and enlightenment after

---

19. Cf. T.N.D. METTINGER, *The Dethronement of Sabaoth: Studies in the Shem and Kabod Theologies* (CB OT, 18), Lund, 1982.

the Babylonian destruction. After Gedaliah's murder the rise of new leadership and vitality among the various settlements of scattered Jewish communities shifted Judah's geographical horizons much further afield to new, and in many instances, very distant locations. For these people too the importance of Jerusalem as the site in which all religious power and authority was vested had to be re-asserted. In a real measure the revival of Jerusalem's fortunes as a focus of religious leadership and worship became a paramount concern if the integrity and unity of Jewish worship of the one God Yahweh was to be meaningfully maintained. Jerusalem would have a very different role to play in the world after 587 BCE from that which it had previously fulfilled. Yet this new role was to be built on, and in part validated by, the older tradition of Mount Zion as the cosmic mountain on which Yahweh had settled for his abode.

5. GOOD NEWS FOR THE WATCHERS OF ZION

It is against such a historical and theological background that we can best understand the connection between Isa 40,1-11 and the prophecies and narratives which have preceded it. Once we recognize that, by the middle of the sixth century BCE, events had raised in a most dramatic fashion the question "What is to become of Jerusalem and Mount Zion?", then we can see that the new prophetic voice which speaks in Isa 40,1-11 addresses, not only Jerusalem as a city, but the precise question which the disasters that had befallen the city raised. The theme of Mount Zion's central role as a political centre and symbol of Jewish hope henceforth becomes the dominant one for the remainder of the book of Isaiah, especially in 49–55 and 60–62. In reality, however, it is not simply these chapters, but the final form of the book as a unified whole which exemplifies this.

A further major critical issue calls for careful re-examination in the light of this fact. The first of these concerns the location and setting of the prophetic materials contained in Isa 40–55. For too long the theory of "the unnamed prophet of the exile" has held sway as the majority viewpoint offering the most probable indication of the author's situation. The important references to Babylon, the rise of Cyrus as a threat to Babylon, and the impending downfall of Babylon as the city of oppression have seemed sufficient to support this. Yet a highly respected minority opinion has doubted such a conclusion, taking instead the many explicit forms of address to Jerusalem and Zion as indications that the author cannot have been located far from this city[20]. Moreover, the perspective adopted is that of an observer picturing from Jerusalem's walls the imminent return of lost and distant exiles from the city (Isa 49,18; 52,1-2; 7-9) like the homecoming of wandering children returning to their parents.

All such indications certainly favour the recognition of the location of the author of Isa 40–55 in Judah itself. It would then be the projections of the situation in Babylon which mark the more dramatic flights of poetic imagination. This contention deserves far fuller recognition than it has hitherto received in the light of the many strong indications that the entire book of Isaiah is a product that originated from within the Jerusalem cultic tradition, that it was preserved there, and that its final shape was primarily concerned to maintain the claims of this tradition over an ever-increasing number of scattered Jewish communities. The author's, or authors', strong familiarity with the traditions of Jerusalem psalmody would further favour such a perspective. Once the full impact of the book of Isaiah as a book of prophecies concerning the past, present and future of Jerusalem as a city of peace, splendour and truth is acknowledged then the frustrating pursuit of seeking to identify its many authors may appear less pressing and important. So far as Isa 40–55 is concerned too many premature assumptions concerning its presumed Babylonian setting call for careful revision. Even "the unnamed prophet of the exile" may eventually be brought home!

8 Brookfield Rd.   Ronald E. CLEMENTS
Coton
Cambridge CB3 7PT
United Kingdom

20. Cf. especially A.S. KAPELRUD, *Et Folk på Hjemferd. "Trøsteprofeten" – den annen Jesaja – og hans budskap*, Oslo, 1964; H.M. BARSTAD, *A Way in the Wilderness* (JSS Monograph, 12), Manchester, 1989.

»DIE FRAU ZION«

»Zion« ist in der Sprache jüdischer und christlicher Frömmigkeit zu einem kräftigen Symbol geworden. Die Aspekte wechseln und scheinen im christlichen Sprachgebrauch teilweise auseinanderzufallen: Da wird die Gemeinde als »(Tochter) Zion« angesprochen[1] oder es wird die »hochgebaute Stadt« in mancherlei biblisch vorgegebenen Farben vor Augen gestellt[2]. Das ist Sprache der Dichtung, und als solche will sie gelesen werden: Dichtung kann auch einander scheinbar widersprechende Bild-Motive in einem Text versammeln, wenn sie nur in der Gesamtsicht zusammenstimmen.

In deutlicher Ausprägung trifft man diese Bildwelt bei Deuterojesaja und in der ihm nachfolgenden Tradition an, daneben mit einem ganz anderen Akzent in den Threni. Von der »בַּת־צִיּוֹן« ist im Deuterojesajabuch allerdings nur einmal, in 52,2, die Rede, offensichtlich im Kontrast zur »בְּתוּלַת בַּת־בָּבֶל« in 47,1, dafür um so mehr von der Frau Zion; auch der Titel »Tochter« bezeichnet bekanntlich in dieser Verbindung die junge Frau und ist keine Verwandtschaftsbezeichnung[3]. Ob die Ziontexte bei Deuterojesaja zum Grundbestand gehören oder erst später hinzugewachsen sind, ist neuerdings wieder strittig[4], soll aber jetzt nicht weiter verfolgt werden, weil es im folgenden um einen poetischen Sprachgebrauch geht, den wir redaktionsgeschichtlich nicht differenzieren müssen: Zwar wird der Umgang mit bestimmten Metaphern seine Geschichte haben, aber in diesem Fall imponiert viel mehr die Vielzahl der Aspekte, die der Metapher in ein und demselben Text zukommen

---

1. Z.B. in dem Kirchenlied Friedrich Heinrich Rankes: »Tochter Zion, freue dich«.

2. Auch dafür sind Kirchenlieder der beste Beleg, so Johann Matthäus Meyfarts »Jerusalem, du hochgebaute Stadt« oder Philipp Nicolais »Wachet auf, ruft uns die Stimme«, wo es in der dritten Strophe heißt: »Von zwölf Perlen sind die Tore an deiner Stadt...«. Das zweite Lied ist aber instruktiv für die – gelungene – *Verknüpfung* unterschiedlicher Motive, die als biblisches Erbe in die Sprache der Liederdichter eingegangen sind.

3. Vgl. H. HAAG, Art. בַּת, *TWAT* I, pp. 867-872, 868-869.

4. Vgl. R.G. KRATZ, *Kyros im Deuterojesajabuch* (FAT, 1), Tübingen, 1991; J. VAN OORSCHOT, *Von Babel zum Zion* (BZAW, 206), Berlin - New York, 1993; zuvor K. KIESOW, *Exodustexte im Jesajabuch. Literarkritische und motivgeschichtliche Analysen* (OBO, 24), Fribourg - Göttingen, 1979. Aber obwohl eine Reihe von Ziontexten erst nachträglich hinzugewachsen ist, kann man den Themen- und Aspektwechsel von Jakob zur »Frau Zion« (als Repräsentationsgestalten des Gottesvolkes) nicht zum redaktionsgeschichtlichen Kriterium machen.

können und die nicht auf unterschiedliche Dichter zurückgehen, sondern gerade die Kraft einer Metapher erweisen.

Der Gestalt der Frau Zion hat O.H. Steck eine gründliche Studie gewidmet[5] und darin auf die deutliche Unterscheidung zwischen Zion als Gestalt und Bewohnern Jerusalems in deuterojesajanischen Texten aufmerksam gemacht; er schließt daraus auf eine gewisse Eigenständigkeit der »Frau Zion«, die als Mutter den Bewohnern der Stadt als ihren Kindern gegenübersteht und der Jahwe eine besondere Stellung, letzten Endes die Rolle des davidischen Königs in vorexilischer Zeit, zugewiesen hat. Das ist soweit nicht zu bestreiten und soll hier nur etwas weiter verfolgt werden, wobei umgekehrt noch einmal die Frage aufgenommen wird, wie denn das Verhältnis zwischen der Ziongestalt und der Bewohnerschaft näherhin gedacht und wodurch die so auffällige Differenzierung bedingt ist. Um das Verhältnis genauer in den Blick zu bekommen, muß man *vor* Deuterojesaja und den Threni einsetzen.

1. JESAJA

Der älteste Text, in dem die Stadt *Jerusalem* für unsere Kenntnis *in Person* erscheint, ist Jes 1,21-26[6]:

5. O.H. STECK, *Zion als Gelände und Gestalt*, in *ZTK* 86 (1989) 261-281; = ID., *Gottesknecht und Zion* (FAT, 4), Tübingen, 1992, pp. 126-145; mit Literatur. Neuere Arbeiten: J.F.A. SAWYER, *Daughter of Zion and Servant of the Lord in Isaiah: A Comparison*, in *JSOT* 44 (1989) 89-107; T. FRYMER-KENSKY, *In the Wake of the Goddesses: Women, Culture, and the Biblical Transformation of Pagan Myth*, New York, 1992, darin Kap. 15: Zion, the Beloved Woman, pp. 168-178; K. BALTZER, *Stadt-Tyche oder Zion-Jerusalem? Die Auseinandersetzung mit den Göttern der Zeit bei Deuterojesaja*, in J. HAUSMANN – H.J. ZOBEL (eds.), *Alttestamentlicher Glaube und Biblische Theologie*. FS H. Preuß, Stuttgart, 1992, pp. 114-119; H. SCHÜNGEL-STRAUMANN, *Mutter Zion im Alten Testament*, in T. SCHNEIDER – H. SCHÜNGEL-STRAUMANN (eds.), *Theologie zwischen Zeiten und Kontinenten*. FS E. Gössmann, Freiburg i.Br., 1993, pp. 19-30.

6. Natürlich wird auch die Echtheit dieses Textes neuerdings bestritten. J. VER-MEYLEN, *Du prophète Isaïe à l'apocalyptique*. Bd. I (EB), Paris, 1977, pp. 71-105, hält 1,21-26 für eine »deuteronomistische« relecture und sucht das wortstatistisch zu beweisen, sammelt aber ganz unverdächtige Wörter wie גַּנָּב »Dieb« (oder die Wurzel גנב) etc. O. KAISER, *Das Buch des Propheten Jesaja. Kap. 1–12* (ATD, 17), Göttingen, ⁵1981, nimmt bereits für den Teil 1,21-23a, den er auf Grund einer *metrischen* Analyse (über die man streiten müßte) für den ältesten hält, Abhängigkeit vom Deuteronomium und Entstehung im 5. Jh. an. Aber die Parallelen zum Deuteronomium beruhen auf gemein-orientalischem Rechtsgut und auf dem Vorkommen von סוֹרֵר »widerspenstig« und סֹבֵא »Säufer« in Dtn 21,18.20. Beide Vokabeln sind ganz untypisch für den Deuteronomismus, zudem handelt der Dtn-Text nicht von Beamten, sondern von einem widerspenstigen Sohn, der auch noch ein *Säufer* ist, während Jesaja hier nicht Säufer tadelt, sondern gepanschtes *Bier* (סֹבֵא) als *Metapher* für die Verdorbenheit der Stadt benutzt (parallel dem mit Schlacken durchsetzten Silber). Kurz: Das ganze ist nur eine pandeuteronomistische Konstruktion. Statt fragwürdiger Wörtervergleiche müßte man spezifisch deuteronomistische Wendungen vorweisen und darüber hinaus zeigen, wo denn das

21	Ach, wie ist zur Hure geworden	3+2
	die treue Stadt,	
	die voll war mit Recht,	2+3
	Gerechtigkeit wohnte darin, [jetzt aber Mörder].	
22	Dein Silber wurde zu Bleiglätte,	3+2
	dein Bier gepanscht [mit Wasser].	
23	Deine Beamten sind Widerspenstige	2+2
	und Diebsgenossen,	
	ein jeder liebt Bestechung	(3)2+2
	und jagt Geschenken nach,	
	die Waise richten sie nicht,	2+2+2
	und der Rechtsstreit der Witwe	
	kommt nicht vor sie.	
24	Darum der Ausspruch des Herrn	3+2[+2]
	Jahwe Zebaot,	
	[des Starken Israels]:	
	Ha, ich will mich letzen an meinen Gegnern	3+2
	und will Rache nehmen an meinen Feinden.	
25	[Und ich wende meine Hand gegen dich]	[3]
	und ich schmelze wie (mit?) Lauge deine Bleiglätte	3+2
	und entferne all deine Schlacken	
26	und mache deine Richter wie zu Anfang	3+2
	und deine Ratgeber wie zu Beginn.	
	Hernach wird man dich nennen:	2+2+2
	Gerechte Stadt,	
	treue Burg.	

Der Name der Stadt fällt in diesem Text nicht (erst *G* hat ihn in v. 21 zugefügt), aber es ist evident, daß Jerusalem oder der Zion[7] gemeint ist, wie das der spätere Kommentar in v. 27 auch ausdrücklich sagt. Es scheint, daß die Personifikation der Stadt in einer Frauengestalt an sich nichts Auffälliges hat: Auffällig ist vielmehr die gewählte Frauen*rolle* und der Stil des Leichenliedes. Von der »Tochter / jungen Frau Zion« ist bei Jesaja in zwei weiteren Texten die Rede (1,8; 10,32). Eine Personifikation des Volks (oder des verwüsteten Landes?[8]), offenbar in

Läuterungsgericht für Jerusalem im Deuteronomismus je eine Rolle gespielt hat. Die zwei nächstliegenden alttestamentlichen Beispiele bei Jeremia (6,27-30) und Ezechiel (22,17-22) stehen gerade *nicht* im deuteronomistischen Kontext; überdies scheint Ezechiel in der eigentümlichen Gestaltung seines Läuterungswortes – tatsächlich läuft es auf ein Vernichtungswort hinaus – bereits an Jesaja anzuknüpfen. – Auch die wenigen Glossen in Jes 1,21-26 (oben in eckigen Klammern) sind nicht spezifisch deuteronomistisch.

7. Beide Namen bezeichnen bei Jesaja einigermaßen die gleiche Größe, vgl. Jes 10,32, auch wenn er im Gebrauch unterscheidet: Z.B. wird nur von der Tochter *Zion* und in ursprünglichen Texten nur von den Bewohnern *Jerusalems* gesprochen; anders in späteren Texten des Jesajabuchs (Jes 10,24; 12,6; 30,19; vgl. 33,14; 4,3).

8. Vgl. H. WILDBERGER, *Jesaja* (BKAT, X/1), Neukirchen-Vluyn, ²1980, p. 25 z.St. (»der ›Leib‹ des Volkes … ist seinerseits Bild für das kriegsverwüstete Land«) und die Fortsetzung in v. 7.

einer männlichen Gestalt, ist Jes 1,5-6 vorausgesetzt, und der Übergang von der Anrede an die Glieder des Volkes zur Verkörperung in einer ausgepeitschten[9] Person vollzieht sich ganz zwanglos. Das zeigt, daß solche Personifikationen beliebt und nicht ungewöhnlich sind, wie in Jes 1,5 spontan eingeführt oder wie im Falle der »Tochter Zion« Jes 1,8 offenbar schon als bekannt vorausgesetzt werden können.

Die negative Rolle der »Frau Stadt« in Jes 1,21ff., im Bild der Dirne gezeichnet, kontrastiert mit ihrer einstigen Treue, und das verweist auf ihr Verhältnis zu Jahwe, nun auf ihre Abtrünnigkeit von ihm. Aber ganz anders als bei Hosea und beim jungen Jeremia konkretisiert sich das bei Jesaja nicht im Abfall zu fremden Göttern, sondern im mangelnden Recht: Die Beamten sind bestechlich und sorgen nicht für das Recht von Witwen und Waisen. Das bedeutet aber: Die Beamtenschaft ist ein integrierender Bestandteil der »Dirne Jerusalem«, wie sie einst zur treuen und gerechten Stadt gehörte und dereinst, nach Jahwes Gericht an Jerusalem, wieder dazu gehören wird. Im Läuterungsgericht wird Jerusalem von Menschen, d.h. eben von dieser ihr als Institution wesentlich zugehörigen Beamtenschaft, gereinigt, und die Stadt bleibt gewissermaßen bestehen. Aber an eine menschenleere Stadt als Ergebnis des Gerichts ist überhaupt nicht gedacht. In v. 25aβb und v. 26a stehen zwei Verszeilen parallel: Wenn Jahwe im Läuterungsverfahren Jerusalems Bleiglätte schmilzt und seine Schlacken entfernt (v. 25), macht er (zugleich) seine Richter und Räte wieder wie zu Anfang. Natürlich sind das nicht dieselben, die jetzt dort regieren und am Ende geläutert wären, aber die Formulierung zeigt, daß Jerusalem gar nicht ohne jene Institutionen der Rechtsgewährung und Rechtsherstellung vorgestellt werden kann. Jerusalem, auch die Frau Jerusalem, ist also eine komplexe Größe aus Mauern und Menschen, und nur so nimmt sie ihre Funktion wahr: als Jahwe treue und darum die Rechtsordnung wahrende Stadt – oder sie verfehlt sie in Gestalt der Hure. Die Frage, ob Jerusalem außer seiner Beamtenschaft (mit dem König an der Spitze, der hier nicht eigens erwähnt wird) nicht noch andere Bewohner hatte, tritt in diesem Text gar nicht näher in den Blick, weil das für die Beurteilung der *Rechts*schutz gewährenden (oder versagenden) Stadt nicht wesentlich ist.

Die beiden anderen Texte Jesajas, in denen die Stadt personifiziert erscheint, geben für die Frage nach dem Verhältnis der »Frau Stadt« und ihrer Bewohnerschaft nicht viel her: In Jes 1,8 bleibt die »Tochter

---

9. So wegen פֶּצַע und חַבּוּרָה v. 6, auch der Eingangswendung עַל מֶה תֻכּוּ עוֹד v. 5; anders WILDBERGER, *Jesaja* (Anm. 8), z.St.: מַכָּה = Schlag durch Krankheit wie Dtn 28,59 u.ö.; aber der traditionsgeschichtliche Hintergrund des Fluchs für *Bundes*bruch liegt bei Jesaja nicht nahe.

Zion« allein »übrig wie eine Wächterhütte im Weingarten«: Das bedeutet, nach der politischen Situation von 701 geurteilt, in die dieser Text gehört, daß mit der »Tochter Zion« Jerusalem mit seinem Umland gemeint ist, die Bevölkerung natürlich eingeschlossen.

H. WILDBERGER setzt den Rest der Tochter Zion mit dem Rest der Bewohnerschaft Jerusalems gleich[10], aber das geht nicht an: Es ist wieder die Gesamtgröße gemeint. Mit Recht weist er jedoch darauf hin, daß »Zion« der stärker religiös geprägte Begriff ist, vgl. bes. 8,18: Jahwe Zebaot wohnt auf dem Berg Zion; 28,16: Jahwe legt auf dem Zion den fest gegründeten Eckstein; schließlich der Sache nach – auch wenn die Herkunft von Jesaja nicht sicher ist – 14,32: »Jahwe hat den Zion gegründet«.

Wenn in Jes 10,32 vom »Berg der Tochter[11] Zion« als Angriffsziel der anrückenden Feinde gesprochen wird, soll damit die Tochter Zion nicht von ihrem Berg unterschieden werden: Ebenso wie im parallelen »Hügel Jerusalems« ist das eine veranschaulichende Umschreibung der Lage der Stadt, dem »Berg Zion« entsprechend (Jes 8,18; 31,4; sek. 10,12; 18,7; 28,8).

2. DIE KLAGELIEDER

Nur ein kurzer Seitenblick kann hier auf die Threni geworfen werden, weil darin – von Deuterojesaja abgesehen – die Personifikation Zion/ Jerusalems am deutlichsten hervortritt. Das betrifft (mit geringen Ausnahmen) aber nur Klgl 1; 2 und in geringerem Maß wohl auch Klgl 4; in Klgl 1 und 2 tritt die Frau Jerusalem/Zion selbst klagend auf. Die Bezeichnungen des personifizierten Jerusalem wechseln: Tochter Zion (1,6; 2,1.4.8.10.13.18; 4,22) steht neben einfachem Zion (1,4.17; 2,6; 4,2.11), Tochter Jerusalem (2,13.15), Jerusalem (1,7.8.17; 4,12), daneben erscheint der Vergleich mit der Witwenrolle (1,1) oder die Rolle der Herrscherin (1,1) und die der Mutter, die ihre Kinder verloren hat (1,5; 2,22). Bemerkenswert für unsere Frage ist, was der Frau Zion dabei zugeordnet werden kann. Sie hat Priester (1,4) und Älteste (2,10), Vorsteher (1,6), junge Frauen und Männer (1,4.18) etc., aber ebenso natürlich Mauern (2,8.18; vgl. 4,11) und Zugangswege, die ihrerseits trauern (also eine erneute Personifikation, 1,4; 2,8), und Tore, die verödet sind (1,4): kurz, die »Tochter Zion« ist oder war vielmehr eine richtige Stadt und als solche eine komplexe Größe, zu der Menschen und

---

10. *Ibid.*, p. 29.
11. So *Qᵉrē*, *Qᵃ* und die Versionen; *Kᵉtîb* hat בית, aber »Haus Zion« ist singulär und gibt keinen rechten Sinn, selbst wenn dabei schon an die Bewohnerschaft gedacht wäre.

Mauern gleichermaßen gehören. Vorerst nur zu notieren ist hier, daß von
der Mutterrolle der Frau Zion gegenüber den Bewohnern als ihren
Kindern dort die Rede ist, wo sie ihre Kinder verloren hat.

Nicht leicht zu beantworten ist die Frage nach der Beziehung zwischen Threni
und Deuterojesaja und hier insbesondere nach der Abhängigkeit, die – bei später
Ansetzung der Threni – ja gerne auch für eine Spätdatierung der Ziontexte
Deuterojesajas geltend gemacht wird. Da die Parallelen bei der Zeichnung der
»Tochter Zion« an einigen Stellen bis in Einzelheiten gehen, werden die Text-
gruppen schwerlich ganz unabhängig voneinander entstanden sein. So, wie die
Threni jetzt vorliegen, haben aber wahrscheinlich die deuterojesajanischen
Texte die Priorität, weil das Konzept hier viel geschlossener vorliegt und auf der
anderen Seite die Threni auch sonst von der Prophetie profitiert haben (besonders bekanntlich von Jeremia). Das schließt nicht aus, daß die Threni auf
eine ältere Tradition der Klage um Jerusalem und Juda nach 587 zurückgehen,
in der die ja schon ältere Frauenrolle der Stadt (und des Landes Juda!, wie
gleich noch zu erörtern) dramatisiert wurde; davon kann dann auch der Prophet
im Exil schon Kenntnis gehabt haben.

3. בת עמי – »DIE TOCHTER ›MEIN VOLK‹«

Ehe die deuterojesajanischen Zionpassagen zur Sprache kommen, ist
noch ein Problem zu erörtern, dessen Lösung zum Verständnis jener
Texte beitragen könnte. Schon bei Jesaja (22,4), dann häufig bei Jeremia
(4,11; 6,26; 8,11.19.21.22.23; 9,6?[12]; 14,17), schließlich mehrfach in
den Threni (2,11; 3,48; 4,3.6.10) ist von der בַּת עַם die Rede, immer in
der Form בַּת־עַמִּי. A. Fitzgerald deutet die Wendung »Tochter meines
Volks« auf die Hauptstadt[13], also Jerusalem, und der Kontext einer ganzen Reihe von Belegen, in dem jeweils Jerusalem erscheint oder gemeint
ist, scheint ihm Recht zu geben. Aber es ist schwer zu sehen, warum die
Hauptstadt ausgerechnet als »Tochter meines Volks« bezeichnet werden
sollte; die bloße »Zugehörigkeit zu … einem Land oder einem
Stamm«[14] wie in בנות חת oder בת לוי kommt als Bezeichnung der
Hauptstadt nicht in Betracht, und auch die »Tochterstädte« sind wegen
ihrer Abhängigkeit (von einer größeren Stadt)[15] oder wieder wegen ihrer
Zugehörigkeit zu einem Land so genannt, was für die eine Stadt an der
Spitze kaum in Frage kommt, vor allem nicht in der Form בת עמי. Für
die Bezeichnung בת als Titel einer Hauptstadt hat A. Fitzgerald über-

---

12. Mit unsicherem Text, vgl. W. RUDOLPH, *Jeremia* (HAT, I/12), Tübingen, ²1958,
und BHS z.St.

13. A. FITZGERALD, *BTWLT and BT as Titles for Capital Cities*, in *CBQ* 37 (1975)
167-183, dort 172-177; er versteht auch בַּת־כַּשְׂדִּים Jes 47,1 im gleichen Sinn.

14. H. HAAG, in *TWAT* I, 869.

15. *Ibid.*, 870.

haupt nur alttestamentliche Belege[16], so daß man diesen Sprachgebrauch nicht so selbstverständlich voraussetzen kann, wie er annimmt. Grammatisch ist die *unterschiedliche* Auffassung der Konstruktion dort, wo בת mit Stadtnamen dicht neben בת mit Volksbezeichnung erscheint (Jes 47,1; Jer 6,23/26; Klgl 2,10f.) – einmal als epexegetischer Genitiv oder (eher) als Apposition, dann als possessiver Genitiv – recht unwahrscheinlich, und es muß doch wohl dabei bleiben, daß בת עמי »Ausdruck ... für die Volksgemeinde« ist[17], also eine Personifikation des Volks[18] in einer Frauengestalt ausdrückt. Instruktiv ist schließlich Klgl 2, wo nach mehrfachem Wechsel zwischen »Tochter Zion«, »Israel«, »Jakob«, »Tochter Juda« in v. 11 alles zusammenfassend vom »Zusammenbruch der ›Tochter mein(es) Volk(es)‹« die Rede ist: Es handelt sich um den Zusammenbruch des gesamten umfassenden Gemeinwesens.

Wie sind dann die unmittelbaren Bezüge auf Jerusalem zu erklären, die schon Jes 22,4 gegeben sind, bei Jeremia an verschiedenen Stellen nahe liegen und auch in Klgl 2,11 im unmittelbaren Kontext erscheinen? Bei Jesaja kann man noch darauf verweisen, daß der »Zusammenbruch der Tochter ›mein Volk‹« ja zumindest äußerlich nicht Jerusalem, sondern Juda betroffen hat, und in den Jeremia-Texten ist Jerusalem die Spitze und das letzte Ziel des Angriffs durch den »Feind aus dem Norden«. Aber deutlicher ist Klgl 4,10, wo offensichtlich auf Verzweiflungstaten auf Grund der Hungersnot in einer belagerten Stadt angespielt wird, und vollends Klgl 4,6, wo die Schuld der »Tochter ›mein Volk‹« mit Sodoms Schuld verglichen wird.

Der sprachliche Befund[19] einerseits und die Kontextkonnotationen andererseits erlauben m.E. nur einen (ähnlich einmal bei Fitzgerald erwogenen) Schluß: Bereits in solchen Texten kann Zion/Jerusalem das Jahwevolk insgesamt repräsentieren. In Jes 22 ist Jerusalem und sein Umfeld gewissermaßen der Rest dessen, was von der בת עמי übrig blieb und was nun, weil es die ihm von Jahwe angewiesene Zeit verkannt und versäumt hat, auch noch untergehen muß. In dem Wort von der wie eine »Wachthütte im Weinberg« übrig gebliebenen

16. A. Fitzgerald, *The Mythological Background for the Presentation of Jerusalem as a Queen and False Worship as Adultery in the OT*, in CBQ 34 (1972) 403-416, zitiert eine fragliche Ausnahme p. 409 Anm. 31.

17. Haag, in *TWAT* I, 869; ähnlich GB; HAL; vgl. auch בתולת ישראל Am 5,2, GK §128k.

18. Wieweit Volk und Land als Einheit gesehen werden und das feminine Genus Israels sich damit erklärt, muß jetzt offen bleiben; für Jer 2,2 und daher eine Reihe von בת עמי-Belegen bei Jeremia empfiehlt sich das nicht.

19. Dazu gehört der negative Befund, daß es kein Beispiel für eine ausdrückliche Benennung Jerusalems als בת עמי gibt, also nirgends die Wendung: ירושלם בת עמי (oder umgekehrt), ebensowenig beide Bezeichnungen im Parallelismus membrorum.

»Tochter Zion« Jes 1,8, das aus der gleichen Zeit stammt, ist von solchem definitiven Ende nicht die Rede, aber es zeigt die gleiche Situation: Jerusalem ist alles, was von Volk und Land übrig blieb. Noch enger beieinander liegen die Dinge in Jeremias Gedichten vom »Feind aus dem Norden«. In Jer 4,11 kommt der Feind als »heißer Wüstenwind« über die בת עמי, aber das anschließende Mahnwort fordert die Frau Jerusalem auf: »Wasche von Bosheit dein Herz, Jerusalem, damit du gerettet wirst«. Umgekehrt hört man in Jer 6,23 von dem grausamen Feind, der gegen die »Tochter Zion« gerüstet ist, während gleich darauf die בת עמי zur Totenklage aufgefordert wird. In Jer 8,19 liest man:

> Sieh, das Hilfegeschrei der Tochter ›mein Volk‹
> > aus weitem Land:
> Ist Jahwe nicht in Zion
> > oder ihr König nicht in ihr?

Die zweite Verszeile bezieht sich auf die Ziontheologie, also eine Tradition, die herkömmlich von der Unverletzlichkeit des Zion, nicht des ganzen Landes sprach: Jetzt aber beruft sich die בת עמי darauf. Vollends zu Wechselbegriffen geworden sind (Tochter) Zion/Jerusalem und »Tochter ›mein Volk‹« in Klgl 4, aber immer noch so, daß das Jahwevolk gemeint ist, das sich nun in der Gestalt Zions darstellen kann.

Das ist, schon in jeremianischen Texten, die Jerusalemer Perspektive, die sich für ein klein gewordenes Land, mit allem Gewicht auf der Hauptstadt, nahelegt und vollends im Exil durchschlägt, zumal dann, wenn die Exulanten zu wesentlichen Teilen ihr Lebenszentrum einst in der Hauptstadt hatten. Es ist aber vorgegeben durch die wachsende Bedeutung Jerusalems als kultisches Zentrum des Jahwevolkes, wie es dann auch in verschiedenen exilischen »Verfassungsentwürfen«, bei Ezechiel und noch deutlicher in der Priesterschrift, zur Geltung gebracht wird: Israel, das Jahwevolk, ist das Volk, das um das Heiligtum versammelt ist, und dieses Heiligtum stand in Jerusalem und wird dereinst wieder dort stehen.

Die zentrale Bedeutung Jerusalems ist im Deuterojesaja-*Buch* ganz offenkundig, und ich halte es noch immer für Wüstenromantik, wenn man dem *Propheten* diesen Teil der Texte gänzlich bestreiten will. Aber wie dem auch sei: Die Frau Zion hat jetzt einen entscheidenden Platz im deuterojesajanischen Konzept der eschatologischen Heilswende: der Heimkehr des Jahwevolkes mit den umstürzenden Konsequenzen dieses Ereignisses für die ganze Welt. Wie ist die Rolle der Frau Zion / Jerusalem in diesen Texten zu verstehen?

4. DEUTEROJESAJA

Die repräsentative Rolle Jerusalems für das ganze Jahwevolk, von der
eben die Rede war, begegnet sogleich im Eingang des Buches. Die beiden anfänglichen Verszeilen sind ja nicht additiv zu verstehen, sondern
entsprechen einander im Parallelismus der Verszeilen[20]:

1 Tröstet, tröstet *mein Volk*,
      spricht euer Gott,
2 Redet zum Herzen *Jerusalems*
      und ruft ihr zu,
      daß ihr Frondienst erfüllt,
      daß ihre Schuld bezahlt ist …

Mit »zum *Herzen* Jerusalems reden« als anthropomorpher Wendung
für »trösten« wird Jerusalem von Anfang an als Person, und zwar als
Frauengestalt (vgl. וְקִרְאוּ אֵלֶיהָ) eingeführt. Ihr Frondienst und ihre
Schuld aber sind nichts anderes als Frondienst und Schuld »meines
Volkes« im Exil: Mit der Figuration »Frau Jerusalem« kann das
Jahwevolk angesprochen werden.

Noch im gleichen Text[21] trifft man auf eine andere schon bekannte
Konfiguration: Die Frau Zion/Jerusalem[22] und ihren Berg. Wenn die
Freudenbotin Zion[23] auf einen hohen Berg steigen soll, ist damit nur
ein anschaulicher Zug, ihre Lage als Stadt auf dem Berge,
dramatisiert und funktionalisiert: Von dort aus erreicht sie mit lauter
Stimme die Städte Judas. Zugleich aber wird darin von ferne etwas
anklingen von ihrem Wiederaufbau auf ihrem Berg, worüber andere
Texte sprechen sollen. Schließlich steht der *hohe* Berg nicht von
ungefähr: Der Zionberg ist ja der Berg in der Mitte der Welt, der
Gipfel des Zaphon (Ps 48,3), der dereinst an der Spitze der Berge
stehen soll (so der berühmte spätere Text von der Völkerwallfahrt
zum Zion, Jes 2,2-4) – auch bei Deuterojesaja verweist das auf eine
noch ausstehende, aber *jetzt* beginnende Realität, die spätere Texte
näher in den Blick nehmen.

---

20. Vgl. W.A.M. BEUKEN, *Jesaja II^A/II^B* (POT), Nijkerk, 1979/1983 z.St. – Kommen-
tare zu Deuterojesaja werden einmal mit vollem Titel, danach mit dem Namen des Autors
zitiert.

21. Die Einheit von Jes 40,1-11 ist mit C. WESTERMANN, *Das Buch Jesaja. Kap 40–66*
(ATD, 19), Göttingen, 1966; W.A.M. BEUKEN u.a. gegen K. ELLIGER, *Deuterojesaja* (BK,
XI/1), Neukirchen-Vluyn, 1978, festzuhalten.

22. Zion/Jerusalem sind hier Wechselbegriffe, wie der Parallelismus der Verse, die
gleiche Anrede als Freudenbotin und die notwendige Ergänzung der einen durch die andere Handlung (auf den hohen Berg steigen / laut rufen) zeigen.

23. Zur Konstruktion als Apposition oder epexegetischer Genitiv vgl. ausführlich
ELLIGER, *Deuterojesaja* (Anm. 21), p. 31.

Muß man dann nicht von einer eigenen, der Identifikation in v. 1f. entgegenstehenden Rolle Zion/Jerusalems sprechen? Sie wäre dadurch bedingt, daß die Ankunft Jahwes mit seinem Volk (im Bild der Herde) noch bevorsteht und durch Zion als Botin angekündigt werden soll. Hier besteht also eine zeitweilige und durch das Exil bedingte Differenz, aber natürlich kein Widerspruch zu v. 1f., wo die neu zu gewinnende ›Identität‹ vorweggenommen wird. Ein literarkritisches Argument ist daraus nicht zu gewinnen.

Es liegt am Aufbau des Deuterojesajabuches, daß Zion als Gestalt nur hier und dann erst wieder ab Jes 49,14ff. erscheint. Es gibt eine Ausnahme, die der Aufmerksamkeit des anordnenden Redaktors vielleicht entgangen ist, weil der Name der Stadt darin nicht fällt[24]: Jes 45,14-15. Die feminine Anrede und das Motiv der Völkerwallfahrt[25] machen aber deutlich, daß hier die Frau Zion angesprochen ist. Das Bekenntnis der Völker »Nur in dir ist Gott und ist keiner sonst« ist in Anknüpfung an die Ziontradition formuliert und durchaus lokal von der Präsenz Jahwes auf dem Zion zu verstehen. Daß die Stadt wieder von Jahwes Volk besiedelt ist, ist vorausgesetzt, spielt aber im Text selbst keine Rolle; nur im jetzigen Kontext wird in 45,13 der Wiederaufbau Jerusalems und die Heimkehr der Gola ausdrücklich genannt. Über das Verhältnis von Stadt und Bewohnerschaft kann man aus 45,14-15 also nur e silentio schließen, aber das ist bezeichnend genug: Hier, wo das Exil schon überholt ist, muß über eine Differenz von Stadt und Bewohnern nicht mehr nachgedacht werden; an die Stelle der Distanz tritt wieder die einheitliche, wenn auch in sich gegliederte Größe »Frau Zion«, und da jetzt auch Jahwes Präsenz in der Stadt wieder gegeben ist, bleibt nur über das Verhältnis der Stadt Jahwes zu den Völkern noch etwas zu sagen.

Darüber hinaus ist im ersten großen Hauptteil des Deuterojesajabuches bis 49,13 noch mehrfach die Jerusalemer Perspektive vorausgesetzt, obwohl man doch bis zum Beweis des Gegenteils davon ausgehen kann, daß der Prophet im Exil gewirkt hat. Aber ehe man das zum Echtheitskriterium macht[26], muß man fragen, was solche Perspek-

---

24. Es gibt aber auch positive Gründe, den Text hier unterzubringen: z.B. den Zug der Völker und ihre Einsicht in Jahwes Einzigkeit; sogar der zuvor erwähnte Wiederaufbau der »Stadt Jahwes« (45,13) könnte bedacht sein: Dann wäre doch die Völkerwallfahrt zum Zion Anordnungsprinzip.

25. Der Text ist nachträglich auf den *Reichtum*, der zum Zion strömt, zugespitzt worden, während die Völker noch in Ketten defilieren dürfen. Das entspricht hinsichtlich der Schätze späteren Ausprägungen des Völkerwallfahrtsmotivs; s. im einzelnen H.-J. HERMISSON, *Deuterojesaja* (BK, XI/7), Neukirchen-Vluyn, 1987, pp. 29-50.

26. Ein bekanntes Beispiel dafür ist das מִשָּׁם in 52,11.

tive auch im Exil bedeuten könnte. Der Jerusalemer Standpunkt ist deutlich in Jes 49,12 erkennbar – man hat den Vers sogar öfter umgestellt und dem folgenden Ziontext zugerechnet. Das besagt freilich nichts für Deuterojesaja, denn Jes 49,8-12 ist m.E. ein redaktioneller Text, der vom zweiten Gottesknechtslied zum ersten großen Zionorakel (49,14ff.) überleitet[27] – ob es sich um eine exilische Redaktion handelt, hängt davon ab, wie lange man das Exil dauern läßt. Aber schon in 41,9: »Du, den ich von den Enden der Erde gegriffen und von ihren Rändern berufen habe« als Anrede an Abraham-Jakob-Israel[28] im Heilsorakel – wird ein Jerusalemer oder wenigstens ein palästinensischer Standort eingenommen, denn für einen Babylonier liegt Ur in Chaldäa nicht an den Enden der Erde. Ähnliches gilt für die Heimkehr- und Sammlungsaussagen für Exulanten aus den vier Himmelsrichtungen[29] in 43,5f.: Der Zielpunkt für das »Herbeibringen« von ferne und aus den vier Himmelsrichtungen ist das Land Israel / Juda oder Jerusalem, ohne daß das ausdrücklich gesagt wird. Als ein drittes Beispiel kann man Jahwes Aufruf an die Völker, sich zu ihm zu wenden, und seinen Schwur, jedes Knie werde sich ihm beugen, in 45,22f. ansehen: Konkret verstanden zielt das wieder auf seine Präsenz in Jerusalem, aber erst spätere Texte bringen das so zur Sprache.

Kann man so im babylonischen Exil reden, und was trägt es zu unserer Fragestellung bei? Die Antwort auf beides heißt: So redet man auch in der Fremde, wenn man sich mit der »Mutterstadt Jerusalem« verbunden weiß, weil sie der eigentliche Ort des Gottesvolkes ist und dieses Volk repräsentiert.

Die »Mutterstadt Jerusalem«: Eine solche Bezeichnung beruht auf den umfangreichen Ziontexten im zweiten Teil des Deuterojesajabuches, in denen Zion bei Deuterojesaja am deutlichsten personifiziert und als Mutter von ihren Kindern getrennt ist. Auf diese Texte beruft sich O.H. Steck, wenn er die Frau Zion als eine eigene und von der Bevölkerung

---

27. Da v. 8 an v. 6 anknüpft, dürfte v. 7 später sein; er paßt auch nicht zu der Kyros-Deutung, die dem zweiten Gottesknechtslied durch v. 8-12 gegeben wird. R.G. KRATZ (s. Anm. 4), pp. 135-139, hält den Text ebenfalls für redaktionell, rechnet jedoch mit der Einheit 49,7-13 und sieht darin eine Deutung des Gottesknechtslieds auf den Ebed Israel.

28. Die geläufige Repräsentation Israels im Erzvater Jakob wird hier auf den Erzvater Abraham ausgedehnt: Zwar heißt das angesprochene Israel »Same Abrahams«, wird aber in v. 9a sogleich selbst in die Abrahamgeschichte und Abrahams Wanderung aus Mesopotamien verstrickt (»Du ... von den Enden der Erde«). Vgl. auch BEUKEN, *Jesaja* II[A] (Anm. 20), pp. 74f. z.St.

29. Ob man das zeitgeschichtlich deuten und *daher* den Text für sekundär erklären darf, ist zweifach fragwürdig: Einmal gab es um die Mitte des 6. Jh. eine nördliche, östliche und südliche »Gola«, zum andern darf man die dichterische Figur schwerlich auf die geographische Goldwaage legen.

der Stadt zu unterscheidende Gestalt ansieht. Nun ist gar nicht zu bestreiten, daß es da auch eine innere Beziehung zwischen der bergenden
(und daher mütterlichen) Stadt und der darin geborgenen Bevölkerung
gibt. Aber wie sich schon an dem ersten Jesaja-Beispiel zeigte, genügt
eine Aufteilung der Stadt auf Bauwerke und Menschen als die beiden
Elemente einer Stadt nicht. Eine menschenleere Stadt wäre ja alles andere als »bergend« oder »mütterlich« – sie wäre vielmehr ein Alp-
traum. Auch »Jahwes Gründung« (vgl. Jes 14,32) beschränkt sich nicht
auf die Immobilien, sondern sie stiftet ein Gemeinwesen, in dem er
selbst präsent ist und das durch sein Jahweverhältnis seine besondere
Rolle wahrnehmen kann. Die Trennung der Mutter von den Kindern
aber ist ein eindeutig defizitärer Zustand: eben das Exil, die zerstörte
und verlassene Stadt, die tief gebeugte, erniedrigte, im Staub sitzende
»Tochter Zion«. In dieser Situation muß auch von der Sünde der (ins
Exil verkauften) *Kinder* die Rede sein, weil sie ja von der »Mutterstadt«
getrennt leben und in der Tat das Geschick ihrer Stadt vor Jahwe
verschuldet haben: so daß nun also auch die Stadt von Jahwe getrennt ist
(Jes 50,2). Die Stadt aber, die dann wieder Gemahlin Jahwes und
Königin an seiner Seite sein soll, ist selbstverständlich die wiederauf-
gebaute und *bewohnte* Stadt.

Das läßt sich an dem ersten großen Zionorakel, Jes 49,14-21, am besten zeigen, weil hier der Zusammenhang von Wiederaufbau und
Wiederbesiedlung poetisch am dichtesten zur Sprache kommt[30]:

   14 Und Zion sprach: Verlassen hat mich Jahwe
          und der Herr mich vergessen.
   15 Vergißt denn eine Frau ihren Säugling,
          daß sie sich nicht erbarmt über den Sohn ihres Leibes?
       Auch diese mögen vergessen,
          ich aber werde dich nicht vergessen.
   16 Siehe, auf die Handflächen habe ich dich eingezeichnet,
          deine Mauern sind beständig vor mir.
   17 Es eilen deine 'Erbauer' 'mehr als deine Einreißer'[31],
          und deine Verwüster ziehen aus von dir.
   18 Erhebe rundum deine Augen und sieh,
          sie alle sammeln sich, kommen zu dir.

---

30. Eine literarkritische Analyse gibt R.P. MERENDINO, *Jes 49,14-26: Jahwes
Bekenntnis zu Sion und die neue Heilzeit*, in *RB* 89 (1982) 321-369; sein »Urtext«
umfaßt 49,14-17.19b.24-25 und gehört nicht mehr in die Zeit Deuterojesajas. Eine
Auseinandersetzung ist hier nicht möglich; doch passen m.E. die vv. 18-19a und 20-21
viel besser zum Text als die vv. 24-25 mit ihrer nicht ganz gelungenen Nachahmung des
Anfangs.

31. Der erste Stichos ist anders abzuteilen und zu punktieren; lg. בָּנַיִךְ (Q^a בוניך) und
מֵהֹרְסַיִךְ (Q^a מהורסיך). G οἰκοδομηθήσῃ ὑφ' ὧν.

' '32 Ja, sie alle wirst wie einen Schmuck du anziehen,
und sie umbinden wie eine Braut.
19 Ja, deine Trümmer und Wüsteneien und 'Ruinenstätten',
'so wahr ich lebe, Spruch Jahwes'33:
Fürwahr, jetzt wird's dir zu eng vor Bewohnern,
und ferne sind, die dich verschlingen.
20 Noch werden sie sagen in deine Ohren,
die Söhne deiner Kinderlosigkeit:
Zu eng ist mir der Raum,
mach mir Platz, daß ich wohnen kann!
21 Und du wirst sagen in deinem Herzen:
Wer hat mir diese geboren?
Ich war doch kinderlos und unfruchtbar [verbannt und abtrünnig]33,
diese aber – wer hat sie großgezogen?
Sieh, ich war übriggeblieben allein,
diese – wo waren sie?

Der Text besticht durch seine prägnante poetische Gestaltung. Da sind einmal die wechselnden Rollen der Frau Zion: Erscheint sie in der Antwort auf ihre eingangs zitierte Klage wie ein kleines Kind, so in v. 18 wie eine geschmückte Braut, schließlich als eine kinderlose Mutter, die zahllose Söhne hat. Zion ist also ganz und gar nicht auf eine bestimmte Rolle festgelegt: Die Figur bleibt beweglich und wird dem jeweiligen Bedürfnis angepaßt. Kunstvoll ist auch der Anfang mit dem Ende verknüpft: Die suggestiv-argumentierende Frage nach der unmöglichen Vergeßlichkeit von Müttern, wenn es um ihre Kinder geht, ist gezielt an die Mutter gestellt, die der Kinder beraubt war.

Noch wichtiger ist jetzt aber eine andere Engführung. Auf das Bild von Zion als dem kleinen Kind, das in *Jahwes* Erbarmen[34]

---

32. v. 18 + 19: v. 18b ist überfüllt, »so wahr ich lebe, Spruch Jahwes« gehört nicht an diese Stelle, der Rest schließt besser an v. 18a an. In v. 19a fehlt ein Prädikat; man sucht das zu beheben,

1., indem man in v. 19a statt der Nomina Verben liest (1.p.sg.) und ארץ streicht (mit *G*), s. BHS (prps); aber der Übergang zu v. 19b würde damit noch härter. Oder

2., indem man in v. 19b כִּי streicht und statt תֵּצְרִי: תֵּצַר liest, also die 3.p.fem. statt der 2. Das Verb bezöge sich nur auf »Land« in v. 19a.

Da v. 19b nicht zu beanstanden ist, bleibt das eine unbefriedigende Lösung. Überdies ist v. 19a auch dann nicht in Ordnung: Wörtlich müßte man übersetzen »das Land deiner Einreißung = dein eingerissenes Land«, was schwerlich richtig ist; das Verb wird sonst vom Niederreißen von Bauwerken gebraucht. Die *G* hat אֶרֶץ nicht gelesen; statt des Abstraktums הֲרִסֹת ist mit K°tîb הֲרִסֹת »Trümmer« zu lesen (vgl. *T*); אֶרֶץ ist mit *G* zu tilgen. Der verbleibende Text ist für eine Verszeile zu kurz; hier läßt sich das in v. 18b überschüssige »so wahr ich lebe: Spruch Jahwes« unterbringen. Der Satz v. 19aα bleibt ohne Prädikat; er ist als eine Art casus pendens aufzufassen: »was anbetrifft...«.

33. גָּלָה וְסוּרָה ist (nachträglich gedeutete) Dittographie oder von vornherein Deutung von וְגָלְמוּדָה.

34. Vgl. das מְרַחֵם in v. 15a, das aus dem steigernden Vergleich mit herübergenommen werden soll.

schon gar nicht vergessen werden kann, folgt als Konkretion der
Blick auf Zion als die wieder aufzubauende Stadt, deren Bauplan
Jahwe als ihr Architekt ständig vor Augen hat (v. 16). Die nächste Verszeile spricht, wenn die Textkorrektur zutrifft, von den Baumeistern,
die den Wiederaufbau schneller zustande bringen als die Feinde
einst die Zerstörung. In בֹּנַיִךְ »deine Erbauer« soll offensichtlich
schon anklingen, was am Ende herauskommt, hier aber poetisch
noch nicht am Platz ist: der Hinweis auf die Söhne בָּנַיִךְ, die zugleich
die Bauleute sind[35]. Denn schon die nächste Verszeile spricht von
der Sammlung und Heimkehr derer, die Zion wie einen Braut-
schmuck umlegen wird: eine anschauliche Imagination des wieder
besiedelten Stadthügels von Jerusalem, und hier sind natürlich keine
fremden Bauarbeiter gemeint. Am kräftigsten wird der Zusammenhang von Wiederaufbau und Wiederbesiedlung der Stadt durch das
Anakoluth in v. 19 dargestellt (wie immer man den Text zu korri-
gieren hat):

> 19 Ja, deine Trümmer und Wüsteneien und 'Ruinenstätten' –
>   'so wahr ich lebe, Spruch Jahwes':
> Fürwahr, jetzt wird's dir zu eng vor Bewohnern,
>   und ferne sind, die dich verschlingen.

Das verwüstete Zion ist ja menschenleer – sieht man von den
Zwingherren, die Zion »verschlingen«, ab[36]. – Wird's Zion nun zu eng
vor Bewohnern, so ist die Stadt keine Wüstenei mehr; so muß man das
Verhältnis des anakoluthischen, vielleicht als eine Art Ausruf zu
fassenden Vordersatzes in v. 19a zu v. 19b fassen: als eine totale
Umkehrung der Verhältnisse. Solche Umkehrung wird, wenn der Text
richtig wiederhergestellt ist, durch eine eidliche Verpflichtung Jahwes
angesagt.

Das Motiv von der Enge wird in v. 20 weiter ausgeführt: Da liegen
nun die Kinder der Mutter in den Ohren: »Schaff mir Platz[37], daß ich
wohnen kann«. Man soll sich das ganz plastisch vorstellen: Praktisch
geht es darum, daß die Mauern der Stadt erweitert werden müssen, weil
man in der umfriedeten Stadt keinen Raum mehr hat. Die drangvolle
Enge ist natürlich nicht als ein Mangel beschrieben, sondern als drasti-
sche Zeichnung eines Segensmotivs gewählt: Der Volksreichtum macht
eine Stadt groß und bedeutend.

---

35. Ein ähnliches Wortspiel wohl 54,13.
36. Vgl. Klgl 2,16: Die Feinde Jerusalems »rissen das Maul ... auf, höhnten und
knirschten mit den Zähnen, sprachen: ›Wir haben sie verschlungen‹«.
37. Zu dieser Bedeutung von נגש cf. Gen 19,9 גֶּשׁ־הָלְאָה »mach dich fort«.

Der Schluß des Textes malt nur die Reaktion Zions auf die Umkehrung der Verhältnisse in einer erstaunten Frage[38] und muß hier nicht näher vorgestellt werden.

Dieses wiedererbaute und volkreiche Zion wird dann die Königin und Weltherrscherin neben dem König Jahwe sein. Davon redet auf seine Weise schon der (jetzt sinnvoll hier angeschlossene) Text 49,22f., der die Völkerwallfahrt der Könige und Königinnen der Welt auf seine Weise mit der Heimführung der Israeliten und der Huldigung der Weltkönige vor Zion verbindet. Im großen theologischen Konzept kommt die Königinnenrolle deutlicher in dem sogenannten Imperativ-

---

38. Als echte Fragen, die Jahwe in v. 22-26 beantworte, versteht O.H. STECK, *Beobachtungen zu Jes 49,14-26* (1990), in ID., *Gottesknecht* (Anm. 5), pp. 47-59, dort p. 49, die Fragen Zions v. 21. Ähnlich hat C. WESTERMANN, *Sprache und Struktur der Prophetie Deuterojesajas*, in ID., *Forschung am Alten Testament* (TB, 24), München, 1964, pp. 92-170, dort 120f., den Text aufgefaßt, wenn er in v. 21 den Reflex einer *klagenden* Frage findet. Nun mag der Redaktor in v. 22ff. in der Tat die Antwort auf eine offene Frage gesehen haben, aber der Bezug der Fragen auf die Aussagen in v. 22-26 erscheint für einen ursprünglich zusammenhängenden Text zu gesucht. So wird die Frage: »Wer hat sie groß gezogen?« nicht mit dem Hinweis auf die *künftige* Wärter- und Ammenrolle der Könige und Königinnen beantwortet, und wenn, wie Steck meint, diese Rolle sich auf den Heimweg beschränken sollte, ist die Zeit für das גִּדֵּל reichlich knapp bemessen. Vollends wird »Wer hat sie geboren?« in v. 25 nicht beantwortet: Obwohl der Verfasser von v. 24-26 offenbar v. 14-21 (oder v. 14-23) voraussetzt und die Eingangswendung nachahmt, hat er ein anderes Problem: die Frage, ob Jahwe die Söhne wirklich heimbringen kann, die für die Frau Zion in v. 21 schon erledigt ist. Daß Zions Frage sich auf »Heimkehrer der zweiten oder späterer Generation« (a.a.O. 48f.) bezöge, setzt voraus, daß ein späterer Autor auf spätere Fragen antworten will; im Textverlauf von v. 14-21 könnte das höchstens an עוֹד in v. 20 anknüpfen und müßte eine zweite Heimkehrerwelle von Kleinkindern mit königlichem Transport im Sinn haben – dann aber hätte die kinderlose und unfruchtbare Frau Zion vergessen, nach der Herkunft ihrer Erbauer, die ebenso ihre Söhne sind, zu fragen. Wenn sie aber diese Heimkehrer meinte, dann hätte die Antwort statt der heimkehrenden Kinder besser die Könige für die Bauarbeiten anbieten sollen, und daß diese Könige vor einem Trümmerhaufen huldigen, paßt auch nicht ins Bild. Kurz: Sobald man beginnt, die Metapher von der Frau Zion allegorisch auf Einzelzüge festzulegen, gibt es überall Unstimmigkeiten; man muß dem Dichter die poetische Beweglichkeit der Metapher und das in v. 20 formulierte Paradox von den Söhnen der Kinderlosigkeit Zions als Ausdruck des Wunders lassen. Das gleiche Paradox findet sich 54,1f., ohne daß es einer Erklärung bedarf. Dann empfiehlt es sich, die Bilder in v. 14–21 und v. 22–23 trotz ihrer thematischen Berührungen zunächst je für sich stehen zu lassen: Man kann sie addieren, aber nicht logisch aufeinander beziehen, und sie sind viel selbständiger, als die Bilderfolge in v. 14ff. oder die wechselnden Rollen der Frau Zion in 54,1-6. Schließlich nimmt das futurische וְאָמַרְתְּ v. 21 das präteritale וַתֹּאמֶר des Anfangs in v. 14 auf und rundet den Text: Der *vergangenen klagenden* entspricht die *zukünftige verwunderte* Frage, und es wäre seltsam, wenn Jahwe jetzt schon auf solche Frage antworten sollte: Zion fragt ja nicht: »Wie soll das geschehen?«, sondern »Wie war das möglich?«, und die Frage nach dem geschehenen Wunder braucht keine Antwort. – Daß v. 21 nicht mit v. 14 und v. 24 in eine Reihe klagender Fragen gehört, habe ich gegen Westermann schon *EvT* 31 (1971) 665-680, dort p. 676 Anm. 32, zu zeigen versucht. V. 24 ist nicht mit v. 14 zu vergleichen, sondern mit v. 15a; v. 25 entspricht v. 15b.

gedicht[39], besonders in 52,1-2 zur Sprache, hier mit klarem Bezug auf den Sturz der Königin Babel nach Jes 47. Wie das miteinander zusammenhängt, ist bekannt und auch bei O.H. Steck ausgeführt; es gehört dazu der Herrschaftsantritt Jahwes auf dem Zion in 52,7-10 und die Bildrede von Zion als Jahwes (königlicher) Gemahlin (54,5): Einzelmotive, die nirgends zu einem Gesamtgemälde zusammengefügt werden, die aber in der Sache schlüssig sind auch da, wo die poetischen *Bilder* rasch wechseln und nicht untereinander zu verrechnen sind. Das ließe sich z.B. an den verschiedenen Frauenrollen in 54,1-6 zeigen, die doch alle auf dieselbe Sache, die Heilswende in ihren unterschiedlichen Aspekten, zielen.

Hier soll indes nur noch von Zion als Königin die Rede sein, weil darin ein zentraler Aspekt der zukünftigen Frau Zion angezeigt ist. Die künftige Königinnenrolle der Frau Zion ist, wie Steck mit Recht herausgestellt hat, als ein Erbe der Davidtradition zu verstehen: Zion rückt in die Rolle der davidischen Könige als Weltherrscher ein. Davon ist nun aber in einem Text die Rede, der die *Frau Zion* gar nicht nennt, obwohl er unabhängig von der Ziontradition nicht hinreichend zu verstehen ist:

> 3 Neigt euer Ohr und kommt zu mir,
>   hört, daß eure Seele lebe,
>   und ich will euch schließen einen ewigen Bund,
>   die Gnadenerweisungen an[40] David, die zuverlässigen.
> 4 Siehe, als Zeuge für die Völker habe ich ihn eingesetzt,
>   als[41] Fürst und Gebieter der Nationen;
> 5 Siehe, ein Volk, das du nicht kennst, wirst du rufen,
>   und Leute, die dich nicht kennen, werden zu dir laufen,
>   um Jahwes, deines Gottes willen,
>   und des Heiligen Israels, denn er verherrlicht dich.

Jes 55,3-5

---

39. Jes 51,9-10.17-23*; 52,1-2.(11-12).

40. Vgl. BEUKEN, *Jesaja* II[A] (Anm. 20), z.St. (mit Literatur p. 354 Anm. 23), gegen ID., *Isa. 55:3-5: The Reinterpretation of David*, in *Bijdragen* 35 (1974) 49-64. Für gen. obj. auch J.L. KOOLE, *Jesaja* II (COT), Kampen, Teil 1, 1985, Teil 2, 1990, z.St.

41. BEUKEN, *Jesaja* II[A] (Anm. 20), z.St., vgl. zuvor ID., *Reinterpretation* (Anm. 40), p. 55f. mit stilistischen Argumenten, übersetzt: »(ihn), den ...« und bezieht v. 4b nicht auf das Verb »einsetzen«, sondern auf das Suffix »ihn«. Die Wahl der grammatisch ebenso möglichen Übersetzung hängt mit seiner eindrücklichen Interpretation von v. 4-5 zusammen, in der das »Vorher / Nachher« in beiden Teilen des Vergleichs unterschieden und zudem die Unterschiede zwischen David und Israel stark unterstrichen werden. Obwohl ich dem im Ergebnis in vieler Hinsicht zustimme, möchte ich hier eine andere Auffassung vorschlagen, weil mir der Text das »Vorher / Nachher« nicht herzugeben scheint: Wodurch geschieht die Einsetzung Davids zum Zeugen, wenn nicht durch die Einsetzung in die Herrschaft? Auch Ps 18,50, worauf Beuken verweist (*Reinterpretation*, p. 60), ist »Davids« Lobpreis unter den Völkern die Konsequenz seiner Rettung und Einsetzung über die Völker. – M.E. knüpft auch תִּקְרָא v. 5aα an מִצְוָּה v. 4b an. Stilistisch dürfte v. 4 eher ein synonymer als ein synthetischer Parallelismus vorliegen.

Der Text, von dem hier nur der zweite Teil zitiert wurde, setzt in Jes 55,1-2 mit einer höchst plastischen Erweiterung des »Aufrufs zum Hören« ein, deren Sätze das Stichwort »umsonst« hervorheben: Das angebotene Leben kostet nichts, man muß es nur in Empfang nehmen, *essen* und *hören*. Jahwes anfängliche Einladung zum Mahl hat einen besonderen Bezug, denn das Lebensangebot konkretisiert sich im Angebot eines Bundesschlusses, zu dem traditionell ein Bundesmahl gehört. Der Inhalt der Bundesverpflichtung Jahwes ist die Erneuerung oder Bestätigung eines längst bestehenden Bundes: der Hulder- weisungen an David, die nicht hinfällig geworden sind, sondern נֶאֱמָן »zuverlässig« bleiben, die sich aber nun in neuer Gestalt realisieren sol- len. Obwohl der Text damit an die Nathanweissagung von 2 Sam 7 anknüpft, nimmt er doch nicht Bezug auf deren spezifische Zusage, daß da immer ein Nachkomme Davids auf seinem Thron sitzen werde, sondern er verweist auf die *Weltherrschaft* Davids[42] und des davidischen Königs nach den Königspsalmen, indem er diese Herrschaft zugleich von ihrer Funktion her in den Blick nimmt. Darin bestehen für Deuterojesaja die חַסְדֵי דָוִד הַנֶּאֱמָנִים, und so werden sie sich jetzt in der neuen Zusage an Israel erneut erfüllen. Allerdings gibt es da Unter- schiede: Wenn Davids Weltherrschaft *anschaulich* zum Zeugnis für Jahwe wurde – was hat Israel zu bieten? Wie David als Völker*gebieter* Zeugnis gab, wird auch Israel einen *gebietenden* Ruf in die Völkerwelt ausgehen lassen, aber worin besteht dieser Ruf, und was ist seine gebietende Kraft, daß die Völker ihm folgen? Das sagt erst die folgende Zeile: »um Jahwes willen«, und vor allem: »denn er verherr- licht dich«. Es geht also um das »passive« Zeugnis Israels, um eine von Jahwe gestiftete anschauliche Realität – wie einst das Weltreich Davids.

Aber was hat das mit unserer Frage nach Zion zu tun? Weder fällt der Name, noch ist eine Frau angeredet: Vorherrschend ist die 2. Pers. masc. plur., nur am Ende in v. 5 steht der kollektive Singular, offenbar durch die Übertragung von David auf das Volk bedingt; der Adressat ist durchweg »Israel«, das Jahwevolk. Dennoch erscheint Israel gewisser- maßen in Ziongestalt oder, vorsichtiger gesagt, unter der Jerusalemer Perspektive. W.A.M. Beuken hat auf Jes 46,13 hingewiesen, wo Israel als Jahwes תִּפְאֶרֶת in Zion Heil findet, und wenn jener Text wohl auch einer anderen Schicht des Deuterojesajabuches angehört, spricht er doch von der gleichen Sache. H. Spykerboer sieht in Jes 55,1-5 geradezu

---

42. Beuken weist treffend darauf hin, daß an die Stelle des נָגִיד עַל עַמִּי עַל יִשְׂרָאֵל von 2 Sam 7,8 das נָגִיד ... לְאֻמִּים getreten ist.

>eine Einladung, in das Neue Jerusalem zu kommen<[43] und verweist
dafür auf die anfängliche Einladung und den Überfluß, der da ge-
schildert wird. Eindeutiger sind zwei weitere seiner Beobachtungen:
Jahwe ruft (Israel) *zu sich* (v. 3); auf Israels »Ruf« kommen die Völker.
Das letztere ist formuliert auf dem Hintergrund der Völkerwallfahrt zum
Zion, wie sie bei Deuterojesaja in 49,22f. und in 45,14f. angedeutet war
und in Texten wie Jes 60 vollends ausgemalt wird, am eindrücklichsten
in Jes 2: Immer ist es die Verherrlichung oder die Erhöhung des Zion,
die die Völker herbeiströmen läßt. Schließlich gehört zur Übernahme der
königlich-davidischen Rolle der Ort, an dem sie ausgeübt wird.

Ältere Texte der Königstradition kennen jene Wallfahrt der Völker
vor allem als Zug zur Huldigung vor dem Weltherrscher als dem
Stellvertreter Jahwes. In unserem Text wird kräftig unterstrichen, daß sie
um Jahwes willen geschieht, aber um des Jahwe willen, der Israels Gott
ist und es in Gestalt des neuen Jerusalem verherrlicht. Und hier ist nun
allerdings weitaus mehr als bei David. W.A.M. Beuken unterstreicht,
daß David als Zeuge eingesetzt und in Dienst genommen wurde. Wenn
Gott Israel verherrlicht, geschieht mehr: ›Glanz/Herrlichkeit ist eigentlich das, was Er für sich selbst in diesem neuen Plan mit Israel erwirbt
(44,23; 49,3), aber das steht in Israel als Heil zur Verfügung (46,13), so
daß die Stadt selbst den Glanz Jahwes als ihren eigenen Schmuck betrachten darf<[44].

Gewiß, von Zion als (junger) Frau ist hier nicht mehr ausdrücklich die
Rede. »Sie« tritt jetzt vielmehr unter dem Aspekt ihrer Bewohnerschaft
in den Blick, gibt dem Jahwevolk eine bestimmte Gestalt. Eine
Unterscheidung ist nicht mehr nötig, wenn Jahwe zu diesem »ewigen
Bund« einlädt, und man kann fragen, ob die Gestalt nicht nur da ins
Rampenlicht treten mußte, wo ein defizitärer Zustand oder seine
Überwindung zu schildern war. Auch O.H. Steck erwägt, »ob das Her-
vortreten der personalen Jerusalem-Vorstellung im Alten Testament erst
ab der exilischen Zeit … mit der Erfahrung der Katastrophe Jerusalems
ursächlich zusammenhängt« und vermutet einen Zusammenhang mit der
alten mesopotamischen Tradition der Stadtklage. Und man kann mit A.
Fitzgerald[45] durchaus überlegen, ob die Anregung zu solchen Personifi-

43. H. SPYKERBOER, *Isaiah 55:1-5: The Climax of Deutero-Isaiah: An Invitation to
Come to the New Jerusalem*, in J. VERMEYLEN (ed.), *The Book of Isaiah / Le livre d'Isaïe*
(BETL, 81), Leuven, 1989, pp. 357-359.
44. BEUKEN, *Jesaja* II[A] (Anm. 20) zu 55,1-5, original: »›Luister‹ is eigenlijk datgene
wat Hij voor zichzelf in dit nieuwe plan met Israël verwerft (44:23; 49:3), maar het staat
in Sion als heil ter beschikking (46:13), zodat de Stad zelf de luister van YHWH als haar
eigen tooi mag beschouwen« (287).
45. Vgl. dazu FITZGERALD, *Background* (Anm. 16).

kationen der Stadt nicht von ursprünglich westsemitischen, dann auch in Mesopotamien heimisch gewordenen Vorstellungen ausgegangen ist, in denen die Stadt als göttliche Königin erscheint oder durch die Stadtgöttin repräsentiert wird.

Nur: Was bedeutet eigentlich die Vergöttlichung der Stadt in bestimmten Bereichen des Alten Orients? Da es die Exklusivitätsforderung des Jahweglaubens dort nicht gab – ist sie mehr als ein figurativer Superlativ? Was wäre der Sinn kultischer Verehrung der königlich-göttlichen Stadt, wenn es das – abgesehen von der Verehrung der Stadtgöttin, deren Verhältnis zur göttlichen Stadt nicht ganz deutlich ist[46] – gegeben hat? Die Fragen sind hier nicht zu beantworten, aber es ist evident und von O.H. Steck nachdrücklich herausgestellt worden, daß göttliche Sinngebungen für die israelitische Rede von der Frau Zion nicht in Frage kommen[47]. Es bleibt die Rolle der Königin nach dem Modell der Jerusalemer Königstradition, aber bezeichnenderweise kann dabei von einer Mittlerrolle der Stadt zwischen Jahwe und ihren Bewohnern keine Rede sein[48]; solche Mittlerrolle hat sie als ganze gegenüber den Völkern. Wenn Zion metaphorisch als Jahwes Gemahlin gezeichnet wird, mag das Modell von der Stadtgöttin als Gemahlin des Stadtgottes im Hintergrund stehen, bleibt aber ein Kontrastmotiv, das nur mit entschiedener Abwandlung übertragbar ist[49]. Wenn Deuterojesaja den hybriden göttlichen Anspruch der Königin Babel mit dem אֲנִי וְאַפְסִי עוֹד von Jes 47 andeutend in Konkurrenz zu Jahwe zeichnet, so ist das gerade das negative Gegenbild zur Königin Zion. Vielleicht muß man die Anregung zu solcher Kontrastierung schon in der älteren prophetischen Tradition suchen, etwa bei Hosea, der sein Bild von der Frau Israel als untreuer Gemahlin Jahwes auch im Gegenzug zu einer religionsgeschichtlichen Gegebenheit seiner Welt gestaltet hat. Daß Deuterojesajas farbenprächtige Kontrastierung von Babel und Zion da-

46. Vgl. STECK, *Gottesknecht* (Anm. 5), p. 139. Die Stadtgöttin kann eine weitergeführte, verselbständigte Personifikation sein, sie kann der Stadt aber auch »von außen« zugewachsen sein.

47. Vgl. auch FRYMER-KENSKY, *In the Wake* (Anm. 5), p. 178; BALTZER, *Stadt-Tyche* (Anm. 5), pp. 118f.

48. Etwas anders in den Klagen der Threni, aber da ist das klagende Zion nur eine Stimme neben anderen. Bei Jeremia ist die klagende Frau Zion/Jerusalem eine prophetisch-dichterische Imagination im Zusammenhang seiner antizipatorischen Gerichtsschilderung (vgl. Jer 4,31 den Todesschrei der Tochter Zion; andere Texte wie 6,26 und 8,19 haben als Subjekt der Klage die בת עמי in großer Nähe zu Zion, s. dazu oben Abschn. 3).

49. BALTZER, *Stadt-Tyche* (Anm. 5) sieht unter Verweis auf einige emblematische Züge der Stadt-Tyche, die vielleicht in der Götzenpolemik des Deuterojesajabuchs wiederkehren, in der Zion-*Gestalt* geradezu eine Gegendarstellung zum paganen Stadtkonzept der Zeit.

nach eine beträchtliche Wirkungsgeschichte gehabt hat bis hin zur Hure Babel einerseits, zum edelstein- und perlengeschmückten neuen Jerusalem[50] andererseits, ist nicht verwunderlich.

Aber den genetischen Problemen wie der weiteren Wirkungsgeschichte kann hier nicht mehr nachgegangen werden. Es ging in diesen Überlegungen vorrangig um die Frage, ob Zion als Gestalt, als die »junge Frau Zion«, eine von ihrer Bewohnerschaft unabhängige Rolle zu spielen hat. Zusammenfassend darf man vielleicht sagen: In der Tat gibt es eine innere Relation zwischen der Stadt und ihren Bewohnern, aber sie kommt im Normalfall in den Texten kaum zur Sprache und ist auch nicht zu verstehen als Relation zwischen Immobilien einerseits und Bewohnern andererseits. Wo Jahwe ein negatives oder ein positives Verhältnis zur Stadt hat, sind die Bewohner immer einbezogen – mit ihren Freveln (Jes 1,21ff.) wie mit ihrer Gerechtigkeit (Jes 1,26) oder schließlich mit ihrer Teilhabe am Heil und ihrem Anteil an der »Herrlichkeit«, die Jahwe der Stadt Jerusalem als ganzer, mit ihren Mauern und ihren Bewohnern, gibt. Eine wirkliche Trennung und Verselbständigung der Stadt in Texten Deuterojesajas und in den Threni bezeichnet einen defizitären Zustand: Trümmer und Menschenleere, das Elend der Mutter und die Ferne der Kinder. Eine Stadt ohne Menschen ist – wie in unserem Sprachgebrauch – immer eine tote Stadt, oder in den Bildmotiven der Frauengestalt: גַּלְמוּדָה und עֲקָרָה. Das sind zwei Begriffe für »unfruchtbar«, die man nach der Etymologie vielleicht einmal als »versteinert« und »wurzellos« umschreiben darf. Der späte Text Jes 51,16 vollzieht nicht erst die Identifizierung von Stadt und Volk, sondern setzt sie voraus: Er betont nur, daß Jahwe zu Zion wieder *mein* Volk sagt. Zion als Gestalt ist keine mythologische[51] Figur, sondern eine Stadt mit Mauern und Menschen, und nur so Jahwes Stadt und Königin, die er an seiner Verherrlichung teilhaben läßt. »Zion« ist als solche eine kräftige Metapher, in der die Bewohnerschaft mitsamt der Stadt als ihrem Lebensgrund und mit ihrem Jahweverhältnis als Ganzheit aufgehoben ist und angesprochen werden kann. Mutatis mutandis entspricht diese Metapher in ihrer Funktion der Gestalt des Erzvaters bei Deuterojesaja, der auch die Gesamtheit Israel in Person repräsentiert. Auch dort kann die Gesamtgemeinschaft, die im Erzvater angesprochen wird, sich differenzieren, indem sie gleichzeitig als

---

50. Vgl. schon den (späten) Text Jes 54,11-17.

51. D.h.: kein Wesen der göttlichen Welt, auch kein Zwischenwesen. Versteht man indes Mythos in einem weiteren Sinn als erzählend-veranschaulichende religiöse Rede, dann sind Mythos und Metapher als Elemente der Dichtung gar nicht weit voneinander entfernt.

Nachkommenschaft des Erzvaters angeredet wird: »Du« und »dein Same« in Jes 43,5 meinen keine verschiedenen Generationen[52]. »Zion« ist nur eine komplexere Größe, daher ist die Metapher viel variabler und stärker auszugestalten, auch nach der defizitären Seite hin. Sie ist als Metapher in der Dichtung bis in unsere Tage lebendig und für die Anschauung des Glaubens unverzichtbar geblieben.

Stauffenbergstraße 11   Hans-Jürgen HERMISSON
D-72074 Tübingen

---

52. Ebenso ist in Jes 44,3 nicht erst eine kommende Generation gemeint, sondern die Fruchtbarkeit des gegenwärtigen Israel, dem die Verheißung gilt.

THE RECONCEPTUALIZATION OF THE
DAVIDIC COVENANT IN ISAIAH

I

The past two decades have seen tremendous advances in the study of the book of Isaiah; scholars have come to recognize the importance of considering Isaiah as a coherent literary whole as well as a composite text with a literary history of some four or more centuries[1]. Such work has revolutionized critical study of Isaiah in that scholars are now able to explore the interrelationships of the various blocks of the text, identified by Duhm as Proto-, Deutero-, and Trito-Isaiah, that were previously treated as completely separate literary works that had little to do with one another[2]. Indeed, the complexities of the interrelationships between the various parts of the present form of Isaiah and the variegated history of its composition have led scholars to conclude that it is no longer desirable or even possible to treat First, Second, and Third Isaiah as completely separate literary works; rather, any treatment of Isaiah must examine its various texts not only in relation to their immediate literary contexts within the book, but in relation to the book as a whole.

Willem Beuken's work has been particularly important in this endeavor, in that he has pointed especially to the hermeneutics of inner-biblical exegesis as an essential aspect in the reconstruction of the compositional history of Isaiah and in the interpretation of its present literary form. In his commentaries on Isaiah 40–66 and in a series of studies on various texts from Trito-Isaiah and more recently from Proto-Isaiah, Beuken demonstrates that the authors of these compositions draw heavily on earlier texts from the Isaianic tradition in order to articulate their understanding of Isaiah's message and to apply it to the needs of their own later times[3]. Especially important in this regard is his study of

---

1. For a survey of current research on the book of Isaiah as a whole, see M.A. SWEENEY, *The Book of Isaiah in Recent Research*, in *Currents in Research: Biblical Studies* 1 (1993) 141-162.

2. B. DUHM, *Das Buch Jesaia* (HKAT, III/1), Göttingen, 1892.

3. W.A.M. BEUKEN, *Jesaja Deel II A* (POT), Nijkerk, 1979; *Jesaja Deel II B* (POT), Nijkerk, 1983; *Jesaja Deel III A/B* (POT), Nijkerk, 1989; *Isa. 56:9–57:13 – An Example of the Isaianic Legacy of Trito-Isaiah*, in J.W. VAN HENTEN et al. (eds.), *Tradition and Reinterpretation in Jewish and Early Christian Literature.* FS J.C.H. Lebram, Leiden, 1986, pp. 48-64; *Trito-Jesaja: Profetie en Schriftgeleerdheid*, in F. GARCÍA MARTÍNEZ et

the main theme of Trito-Isaiah which he identifies as "the servants of YHWH"[4]. Noting that Deutero-Isaiah speaks exclusively of a single "servant of YHWH" until Isa 54,17, he argues that Isaiah 56–66 employ *aposiopesis* or a deliberate rhetorical silence to identify the "servants of YHWH" as the primary concern of these chapters. Trito-Isaiah speaks explicitly of "the servants of YHWH" only in 56,6; 63,17; 65,8.9.15; 66,13.14, but develops this theme in association with the notions of the "seed" or "offspring" who will inherit the covenant of YHWH and the "righteousness" of the servants who will be vindicated when YHWH's sovereignty is manifested in Zion. In this regard, Trito-Isaiah develops the image of the servant in Isa 53,10 who will ultimately see his off-spring prosper.

Important questions remain, however, concerning the identity of these anonymous servants of YHWH and the role that they play in relation to the book as a whole. One might hesitate to address this question in that a great deal of ink has been spilled on attempts to identify or characterize the servant of Deutero-Isaiah to little avail[5]. Whether the servant of Deutero-Isaiah is intended to be a royal figure, either a Davidic figure or Cyrus, or the people of Israel in some form or another is immaterial for the present purposes. Clearly, a shift in perspective takes place in Trito-Isaiah, in which the servant of Deutero-Isaiah no longer serves as the major focal point for the realization of YHWH's plans for the future. Rather, the servants of YHWH presented in Trito-Isaiah are considered to be the righteous and prosperous offspring that the servant in Isa 53,10 will ultimately see.

Recognition of this shift points to several additional dimensions of this issue that are related to recent study of the book of Isaiah as a whole. The first is the literary context in which this theme appears. Within the structure of the book of Isaiah as a whole, Trito-Isaiah is in-troduced by Isaiah 55, which redefines the Davidic covenant as an eter-nal covenant applied to the people of Israel at large, not simply to the house of David[6]. Given Proto-Isaiah's presentation of several oracles

---

al. (eds.), *Profeten en Profetische Geschriften*, Kampen - Nijkerk, 1987, pp. 71-85; *Serv-ant and Herald of Good Tidings: Isaiah 61 as an Interpretation of Isaiah 40–55*, in J. VERMEYLEN (ed.), *The Book of Isaiah – Le livre d'Isaïe* (BETL, 81), Leuven, 1989, pp. 411-442; *Servant and Herald of Good Tidings: "The Servants of YHWH"*, in *JSOT* 47 (1990) 67-87; *Isaiah Chapters LXV–LXVI: Trito-Isaiah and the Closure of the Book of Isaiah*, in J.A. EMERTON (ed.), *Congress Volume Leuven 1989* (SVT, 43), Leiden, 1991, pp. 204-221; *Jesaja 33 als Spiegeltext in Jesajabuch*, in *ETL* 67 (1991) 5-35.

4. *JSOT* 47 (1990) 67-87.

5. For a full survey of research on the Servant of YHWH in Deutero-Isaiah, see H. HAAG, *Der Gottesknecht bei Deuterojesaja* (EdF, 233), Darmstadt, 1993.

6. For discussion of the place of Isaiah 55 within the structure of the book of Isaiah as

concerning the future establishment of a righteous Davidic monarch (i.e., Isa 9,1-6; 11,1-16; cf. 32,1-20), such a shift has tremendous implications for understanding the hermeneutics employed in reading the book of Isaiah that point to the continued development of the book and reflection on its meaning in relation to the social and political realities of the post-exilic Jewish community. The second is Trito-Isaiah's explicit use of earlier Isaianic textual traditions, particularly the oracle concerning the nations' recognition of the restoration of Judah and Israel under the rule of the righteous Davidic monarch in Isaiah 11,1-16, to portray the people of Israel as a priestly people in relation to the nations. Isaiah 11,1-16 appears in various manifestations throughout the framework of Trito-Isaiah[7], and, together with other Isaianic texts, it is especially influential in Isaiah 60–62 and 65–66, which portray the nations' return of the exiled Jews to Zion and their presentation of offerings. Particularly important in this regard is the articulation of this priestly role to the nations in the context of the "eternal covenant" established between YHWH and the people of Israel in Isa 61,8-9. Finally, these observations must be considered in relation to the overall identification of YHWH's reign with the rule of the Persian empire throughout the book of Isaiah, especially in relation to the oracles against the nations in Isaiah 13–23 and the designation of Cyrus as YHWH's anointed in Deutero-Isaiah.

Overall, these factors combine to define the role of "the servants of YHWH" in the context of a reconceptualized Davidic covenant in the book of Isaiah. Given the demise of the Davidic dynasty and the subsequent rise of the Persian empire articulated in the book of Isaiah, the people of Israel will continue to represent YHWH's eternal covenant in the world at large as a priestly people who serve YHWH at Zion. In this regard, Zion will serve as the holy center or sanctuary of YHWH's new creation and the people of Israel will serve as the priesthood to the nations in relation to the establishment of YHWH's sovereignty over the entire world. Given the keen interest in the Davidic tradition throughout the book of Isaiah, this would suggest that this reconceptualization of the Davidic covenant in Trito-Isaiah permeates the book as a whole and constitutes a major aspect of the book's overall perspective on YHWH's

whole, see M.A. SWEENEY, *Isaiah 1–4 and the Post-exilic Understanding of the Isaianic Tradition* (BZAW, 171), Berlin - New York, 1988, pp. 27-95, esp. pp. 87-92.

7. Cf. B.D. SOMMER, *Allusions and Illusions: The Unity of the Book of Isaiah in Light of Deutero-Isaiah's Use of Prophetic Tradition*, in R.F. MELUGIN – M.A. SWEENEY (eds.), *New Visions of Isaiah* (JSOT SS, 214), Sheffield, 1996, pp. 156-186; cf, Y. KAUFMANN, *The Babylonian Captivity and Deutero-Isaiah*, translated by C.W. EFROYMSON, New York, 1970, pp. 183-204, esp. p. 189.

relationship with Israel, Zion, David, and the world at large. The various dimensions of these observations constitute the balance of this paper.

II

One of Beuken's fundamental observations is that Isaiah 54,17 introduces the first plural reference to the "servants of YHWH", which contrasts markedly with the portrayal of a singular servant throughout Deutero-Isaiah[8]. He sees it as an important literary clue, introduced in the context of Deutero-Isaiah, which anticipates the cardinal theme of Trito-Isaiah. By this means, the statement in Isa 54,17b, "'this is the heritage of the servants of YHWH, and their righteousness from Me', oracle of YHWH", presents the "servants of YHWH" as the righteous seed that the servant will ultimately see prosper in Isa 53,10. The theme is then extensively elaborated throughout Trito-Isaiah.

Beuken correctly notes the thematic role that Isaiah 54,17b plays in introducing the major concerns of Trito-Isaiah, but the generic character of this statement must also be considered in that it points to the overall role and function of this statement within the structure of the book of Isaiah. Isaiah 54,17b is an example of the "summary-appraisal form", which is employed extensively throughout Isaiah as well as in other prophets and the wisdom literature[9]. It is a didactic form that is characterized by an introductory demonstrative pronoun (e.g., *zeh*, *zō't*, "this") and its function as a summary and appraisal of preceding material. In the present instance, Isaiah 54,17b concludes chapter 54, which proclaims the restoration of the covenant or marriage between YHWH and Zion, here portrayed as a wife and mother whose husband and children have returned to her[10]. The chapter is formulated as the prophet's announcement to Zion of her restoration, and comprises five major sub-units or addresses directed by the prophet to Zion. First, the prophet calls upon Zion to rejoice in v. 1 because the formerly barren woman will have a multitude of children. Second, the prophet calls upon Zion to enlarge her

8. *JSOT* 47 (1990) 67-68.

9. For discussion of the summary-appraisal form, see B.S. CHILDS, *Isaiah and the Assyrian Crisis* (Studies in Biblical Theology, 2/3), London, 1967, pp. 128-136; J.W. WHEDBEE, *Isaiah and Wisdom*, Nashville, 1971, pp. 75-79; M.A. SWEENEY, *Isaiah 1–39, with an Introduction to Prophetic Literature* (Forms of the Old Testament Literature, 16), Grand Rapids - Cambridge, 1996, p. 539.

10. Cf. J.F.A. SAWYER, *Daughter of Zion and Servant of the L-rd in Isaiah: A Comparison*, in *JSOT* 44 (1989) 89-107; P. T. WILLEY, *The Servant of YHWH and Daughter Zion: Alternating Visions of YHWH's Community*, in E.H. LOVERING, Jr. (ed.), *Society of Biblical Literature 1995 Seminar Papers*, Atlanta, 1995, pp. 267-303.

tent or dwelling in vv. 2-3, because her children will spread out and possess nations and cities. Third, the prophet announces a salvation oracle
for Zion in vv. 4-6 that proclaims YHWH's decision to redeem or marry
Zion and thereby to put an end to her shame and despair. Fourth, the
prophet conveys YHWH's "covenant of peace" to Zion in vv. 7-10 that
compares YHWH's restored relationship with Zion to the covenant
made with Noah. Finally, the prophet conveys YHWH's promise to
adorn and protect Zion in vv. 11-17 so that Zion will be established with
righteousness and never be threatened again. The summary-appraisal of
v. 17b identifies this promise of YHWH's covenant and eternal protection for Zion as the heritage of the servants of YHWH.

But in considering the role of this statement, it must be recognized that
it functions not only in relation to the promise of Zion's restoration in
Isaiah 54, but in relation to a major theme of Deutero-Isaiah and indeed of
the book of Isaiah as a whole up to this point. Isaiah 54 appears at the conclusion of a major block of material in Isaiah 49–54 that takes up the restoration of Zion/Jerusalem by presenting complementary images of the
servant of YHWH and the Daughter of Zion[11]. On the one hand, the servant is commissioned from the womb to bring Jacob or Israel back to
YHWH, and the Daughter of Zion is presented as the restored bride to
whom Jacob or the children are returned. These chapters draw upon a variety of images from biblical tradition, including the motif of YHWH's
marriage to the bride Israel in the wilderness from Hosea and Jeremiah,
the image of the barren Sarah who finally bears a child with her husband
Abraham, YHWH's defeat of the chaos monster Rahab to restore or create
order in the world and to redeem the people of Israel from Egyptian bond-
age, and the transformation of the wilderness into the garden of Eden
where the first human couple originally were placed in creation. Clearly,
the marriage motif permeates Isaiah 49–54 and points to the restoration of
the bride and mother Zion as the ultimate goal of this section.

In this regard, it must be noted that Isaiah 49–54 take up similar motifs from other parts of the book. For example, following the announcement that Cyrus is the messiah of YHWH and the builder of YHWH's
temple in Isa 44,24–45,8, Isaiah 46 portrays the weakness of Babylon's
gods, and Isaiah 47 portrays Babylon as a defeated and humiliated
woman who has been deposed from her throne and who will sit as a
widow who has lost her children. Isaiah 48 then calls upon Jacob to go
forth from Babylon and to return to Zion as articulated in Isaiah 49–54.
In this context, the restoration of the bride Zion is clearly contrasted
with the fall of the "bride" Babylon. Furthermore, the theme of a Zion

11. See WILLEY, *The Servant* (n. 10).

as a restored bride whose children return is not confined to Deutero-Isaiah, but appears in earlier parts of Isaiah as well[12]. Thus, Isaiah 3,25–4,1 portrays Jerusalem as a mother who has lost her sons in defeat, and Isaiah 5,1-7 portrays YHWH's dissatisfaction with his beloved vineyard, a common metaphor for a woman in the ancient world. Other images in Isaiah likewise build upon the theme. The portrayal of YHWH's defeat of Babylon in Isaiah 13 employs the language of labor and childbirth to portray a new creation, and Isaiah 26 employs similar language prior to portraying YHWH's restored vineyard in Isaiah 27. In this regard, Isaiah 54,17b summarizes and appraises the heritage of YHWH's servants not only in relation to the restoration of the bride Zion in chapter 54, but in relation to a long process of restoration that is articulated throughout the book of Isaiah. The servants of YHWH are those who will continue the relationship with YHWH as presented in the book of Isaiah. Insofar as earlier materials in Isaiah anticipate the emergence of a remnant of Israel that will continue (e.g., Isa 6,13), the "servants of YHWH" in Isaiah 54,17b constitute that remnant.

The summary-appraisal form of Isaiah 54,17b must also be considered in relation to the following material in Isaiah 55[13]. Insofar as Isaiah 54,17b concludes the preceding material, it also points to the introductory character of what follows. Scholars have generally viewed Isaiah 55 as a part of Deutero-Isaiah, but they have generally overlooked its rhetorical function within the literary structure of the book of Isaiah as an introduction to the Trito-Isaiah material in Isaiah 56–66[14]. In this instance, the role of the literary-historical character of the text in its interpretation must give way to the role of literary context. Although Isaiah 55 may originally have been composed in relation to the writings of Deutero-Isaiah in Isaiah 40–55, the placement of the writings of Trito-Isaiah immediately following Isaiah 55 radically changes its literary function[15]. Isaiah 55 is formulated as the prophet's

12. For discussion of the feminine and childbirth imagery in Isaiah, see K.P. DARR, *Isaiah's Vision and the Family of G-d*, Louisville, 1994; cf. SWEENEY, *Isaiah 1–39* (n. 9), *ad loc.*

13. See W.A.M. BEUKEN, *Isaiah 55,3-5: The Reinterpretation of David*, in *Bijdragen* 35 (1974) 49-64.

14. See for example, C. WESTERMANN, *Isaiah 40–66: A Commentary*, translated by D.M.G. STALKER (OTL), Philadelphia, 1969, pp. 280-292; P.-E. BONNARD, *Le second Isaïe. Son disciple et leurs éditeurs, Isaïe 40–66* (EB), Paris, 1972, pp. 298-311; R.F. MELUGIN, *The Formation of Isaiah 40–55* (BZAW, 141), Berlin - New York, 1976, pp. 82-87, 169-175 (but compare pp. 175-178 on the relation to First Isaiah); R.N. WHYBRAY, *Isaiah 40–66* (NCBC), London - Grand Rapids, 1981; R.J. CLIFFORD, *Fair Spoken and Persuading: An Interpretation of Second Isaiah*, New York, 1984, pp. 188-194; P.D. HANSON, *Isaiah 40–66* (Interpretation), Louisville, 1995, pp. 177-183.

15. See SWEENEY, *Isaiah 1–4* (n. 6), pp. 87-88.

exhortation to join in YHWH's eternal covenant; vv. 1-5 invite the audience of the text to join in YHWH's eternal covenant, and vv. 6-13 constitute the exhortation proper in that they provide the reasons why the audience should join, i.e., YHWH is near, YHWH's thoughts and ways are higher than those of the audience, YHWH's word will accomplish its purpose, peace and new creation will result. Although many have argued that Isaiah 55 was composed as a conclusion to Deutero-Isaiah[16], Isaiah 54,17b already fills a concluding role in relation to Deutero-Isaiah. With the inclusion of Isaiah 56–66, Isaiah 55 anticipates the theme of the eternal covenant articulated in Isa 59,21 and 61,8; the everlasting sign and name that will not be cut off for those who hold fast to that covenant in 56,5; and the role of the righteous who seek YHWH throughout Isaiah 56–66.

The introductory role of Isaiah 55 is especially important to the present issue in that it presents a preliminary redefinition of the Davidic covenant. Isaiah 55,3-5 states, "Incline your ears and come to Me, hear that you may live and I will make for you an eternal covenant (bĕrît 'ôlām), the secure steadfast love of David. Behold, I appointed him as a witness for the peoples, a leader and commander for the peoples; behold you will call a nation that you do not know, and a nation that does not know you will run for the sake of YHWH your G-d and for the Holy One of Israel for he has glorified you". This passage has been extensively discussed[17], and scholars have recognized several essential features. Most importantly, it redefines the concept of the Davidic covenant in that the Davidic king is no longer the primary recipient of YHWH's steadfast love, but the people who accept the covenant are now the recipients of that relationship instead. This is particularly important in relation to the preceding statements that YHWH has named the Persian monarch Cyrus as messiah and Temple builder. Obviously, a Davidic figure will no longer fill that role, but the Davidic promise still stands secure. Now, it is the people of Israel who receive that promise. This is highlighted by the statement that the people will call upon a nation that they do not know and that nation will run to them for the sake of YHWH. In context, the Persian empire and its monarch Cyrus fill the royal role formerly occupied by the Davidic dynasty as expressed in the royal oracles of Proto-Isaiah (Isa 9,1-6; 11,1-16; 32,1-20). The people of Israel will continue the Davidic covenant by accepting this new reality as the purpose of YHWH. Apart from generalized statements of ad-

16. See note 14 above.
17. For bibliography on Isaiah 55, see J.D.W. WATTS, *Isaiah 34–66* (WBC, 25), Waco, TX, 1987, pp. 240-241.

herence to YHWH, however, Isaiah 55 does not define what it means by accepting the eternal covenant other than to accept the role of this foreign people (and their ruler). Otherwise, the role of the people is not defined in this chapter. Nevertheless, Isaiah 55 clearly sets the agenda for what is to follow. A new conceptualization of the Davidic covenant that redefines the relationship between YHWH and Israel has been announced. Isaiah 56–66 defines how that reconceptualization is to be understood.

III

The recent interest in the literary form and formation of the book of Isaiah as a whole has influenced the study of Trito-Isaiah in that scholars are no longer treating this material in isolation, but they are asking how this material relates to the earlier portions of the book. Beuken has already demonstrated how much of the material in Trito-Isaiah employs themes and texts from Deutero-Isaiah, especially as they relate to the theme of the "servants of YHWH"[18]. He has likewise demonstrated how Isaiah 65–66 forms the conclusion not only to Deutero- and Trito-Isaiah, but points to a relationship with Isaiah 1 as well that has implications for understanding Trito-Isaiah in relation to the book as a whole. Indeed, other scholars have likewise raised this issue. Rendtorff, for example, points to key terms such as "the glory of YHWH" (kĕbôd yhwh), "the Holy One of Israel" (qĕdôš yiśrā'ēl), and "righteousness" (ṣĕdāqâ) from Trito-Isaiah that permeate the entire book and demonstrate that Trito-Isaiah plays a role in binding the entire book together[19]. Likewise, Steck argues that Isaiah 56–66 do not represent a self-standing textual block, but constitute the redactional continuation of the earlier material in Isaiah from the 6th through the 3rd centuries[20]. My own studies have pointed to the role of Isaiah 56–66 within the structure of the book of Isaiah as a whole, and to the citation and reinterpretation of earlier texts and themes from Proto-Isaiah in Isaiah 65–66[21].

18. See the studies listed in n. 3 above.
19. R. RENDTORFF, Zur Komposition des Buches Jesajas, in VT 34 (1984) 295-320; Jesaja 56,1 als Schlüssel für die Komposition des Jesajabuches, in Kanon und Theologie. Vorarbeiten zu einer Theologie des Alten Testaments, Neukirchen-Vluyn, 1991, pp. 172-179.
20. O.H. STECK, Bereitete Heimkehr. Jesaja 35 als redaktionelle Brücke zwischen dem Ersten und dem Zweiten Jesaja (SBS, 121), Stuttgart, 1985; Tritojesaja im Jesajabuch, in VERMEYLEN (ed.), The Book of Isaiah (n. 3), pp. 361-406 = Studien zu Tritojesaja (BZAW, 203), Berlin - New York, 1991, pp. 3-45.
21. SWEENEY, Isaiah 1-4 (n. 6); On umesos in Isaiah 8.6, in D.J.A. CLINES - P.R. DAVIES (eds.), Among the Prophets: Language, Image, and Structure in the Prophetic Writings (JSOT SS, 144), Sheffield, 1993, pp. 42-54; Prophetic Exegesis in Isaiah 65-66, in C. BROYLES - C. EVANS (eds.), Writing and Reading the Scroll of Isaiah: Studies in an Interpretive Tradition, Leiden (forthcoming).

Overall, this recent interest in the interrelationship between Isaiah 56–66 and the book of Isaiah as a whole has tremendous implications for defining the role of Beuken's "servants of YHWH" in relation to the entire Isaianic tradition. Among other concerns, it points to a new understanding of the Davidic covenant in these chapters that accounts for the realities of Persian rule and the demise of the house of David. This is especially noteworthy in that the following discussion shows that Isaiah 11,1-16, the oracle concerning the establishment of a righteous Davidic monarch over a reconstituted and reunited Israel, plays a particularly prominent role in the message of Trito-Isaiah.

When read in relation to Isaiah 55, the Trito-Isaiah material in Isaiah 56–66 defines the requirements for those who will be included in YHWH's covenant as articulated in the book of Isaiah[22]. In this regard, it functions as substantiation for the exhortation to adhere to YHWH's covenant in Isaiah 55. Generically, these chapters constitute prophetic instruction concerning the reconstituted covenant community in Jerusalem that comprises three major sections. The first is Isaiah 56–59, which take up the issue of proper observance of YHWH's covenant. The basic criterion in Isa 56,1-8 for "those who hold fast to my covenant" (Isa 56,4.6) is Shabbat observance, which may be undertaken by converts to Judaism or by eunuchs who were mutilated for imperial service[23]. This is expanded in Isa 58,1-14 in an admonition to repent that calls upon the people to act in a socially responsible manner by releasing captives, feeding the hungry, clothing the naked, giving shelter to the homeless, and observing the Shabbat. Overall, these criteria are articulated in the context of attempts to convince the audience to become a part of the righteous who will join in YHWH's covenant. Isa 58,14 states that those who do so will feed on the heritage of Jacob (cf. Isa 54,17b), and Isa 59,20-21 argues that those who turn from transgression will share in YHWH's covenant. The second is Isaiah 60–62, which constitute a prophetic announcement of salvation for the reconstituted covenant community in Jerusalem. Overall, this section employs the imagery of light to portray the reconstitution of Jerusalem and the pilgrimage of the nations who will come to Jerusalem to give honor to YHWH and to restore the city and its exiled inhabitants. Again, YHWH's covenant is granted to the restored community (Isa 61,8). Finally, Isaiah 63–66 provides instruction in the process by which the identity of the reconstituted community is established. Basically, it argues that those who are righteous

22. For detailed discussion of the form-critical issues treated here, see SWEENEY, *Isaiah 1–4* (n. 6), pp. 87-92.
    23. See below.

will be included in the community whereas those who are wicked will be destroyed. It likewise portrays YHWH as the ruler of a new heaven and earth and the nations processing to Jerusalem in order to return exiled Jews and to recognize YHWH's sovereignty.

There are several key texts within these chapters that play important roles, not only in defining the character of the "servants of YHWH" in the reconstituted covenant community, but also in defining the reinterpretation of the Davidic covenant that stands as the basis of the renewed relationship between YHWH and the "servants". Isaiah 65–66 must be considered because it portrays YHWH in royal terms as the sovereign of a new heavens and earth who presides over the restoration of the exiles to Zion, brought by the nations who come to recognize YHWH's sovereignty. In keeping with the understanding of the Davidic covenant articulated in Isaiah 55, no Davidic figure appears within this material, but the people of Israel will serve as priests within YHWH's new creation[24]. Likewise, Isaiah 60–62 portrays the nations' return of exiles to Zion, and posits that the people will become priests. These chapters take up the theme of "light" that plays so important a role in the royal thanksgiving song of Isaiah 9,1-6, and they present a figure whom YHWH has anointed (61,1). Isaiah 56,1-8 must also be considered. Although this text does not point to a royal figure, its assertion that foreigners can join in the covenant of YHWH has obvious implications for understanding the interrelationship between Jews and Gentiles as presented in Isaiah 60–62 and 65–66 and thus for the overall theme of the "servants of YHWH". In this regard, it is noteworthy that Isaiah 56,1-8 and 65–66 constitute the introductory and concluding literary framework for Trito-Isaiah, and Isaiah 60–62 constitute its core.

I have already treated Isaiah 65–66 in detail elsewhere[25]. Overall, these chapters constitute the conclusion to the book of Isaiah. They are presented as a report of YHWH's response to the community that YHWH will requite the evil and reward the righteous in a new creation centered around Zion. Within this context, Isa 65,1-7 report YHWH's announcement that evil will be requited; Isa 65,8-25 report YHWH's address to the wicked that the seed of Jacob will be restored; and Isa 66,1-24 report YHWH's address to the righteous that they will be restored at Zion. In presenting this scenario of punishment of the wicked

24. See B. SCHRAMM, *The Opponents of Third Isaiah: Reconstructing the Cultic History of the Restoration* (JSOT SS, 193), Sheffield, 1995, pp. 172-173, who demonstrates that the statement in Isa 66:21, 'and also from them I will take for priests (and) for Levites, says YHWH', refers to the exiled Jews whom the nations return, and not to the nations themselves.

25. SWEENEY, *Prophetic Exegesis* (n. 21).

and restoration of the righteous, Isaiah 65–66 draw heavily on a number of texts from Proto-Isaiah that focus especially on the imagery of trees and seed. Among them are Isaiah 1 and Isaiah 6, which portray the destruction of the wicked as rotten trees that will be felled in part due to their own rottenness, and Isaiah 11 and 37,30-32 which portray the restoration of the righteous remnant of Israel as new shoots that will grow anew and result in the restoration of the exiles to Zion. Likewise, Isaiah 2–4 presents an image of the nations' "flowing" to Zion to learn YHWH's Torah, and the image of Assyrian waters that inundate and "rape" the land of Judah in Isaiah 8,6-8 are reversed in Isa 66,10-16 to portray the exultation of mother Zion. Altogether, the use of texts and themes from Proto-Isaiah stands behind the imagery of restoration of the righteous, and plays a role in redefining the Davidic covenant in these chapters. In contrast to the claims of Davidic rule in Isaiah 11,1-16, which is explicitly quoted in Isa 65,25[26], YHWH will be king and will preside over the paradisial new creation envisioned in the oracle from Proto-Isaiah. The people of Israel will serve as priests to the nations who, in keeping with the perspective of Isaiah 11,10-16, will return the exiles of Israel to Zion as part of their procession to acknowledge YHWH's world-wide sovereignty.

Isaiah 56,1-8 must also be considered in that it constitutes Trito-Isaiah's programmatic introduction to YHWH's covenant (cf. Isa 56,4.6). Overall, it points to Shabbat observance as the overriding concern, which is developed more fully in subsequent chapters as indicated above. Generically, it is a prophetic instruction concerning the inclusion of observant foreigners and eunuchs in the Temple community. The basic instruction appears in v. 1, in which the prophet conveys YHWH's instructions to do justice and righteousness. The prophet then elaborates on this instruction in vv. 2-8 by pointing to the inclusion of foreigners and eunuchs in vv. 2-3 and by reporting YHWH's explicit instructions for the inclusion of foreigners and eunuchs in vv. 4-8. Many scholars have seen this passage as a warrant for the inclusion of foreigners in the covenant that overturns explicit instructions to avoid foreigners in the Torah, but more recent discussion has established that these chapters do not provide an overall warrant for the blanket inclusion of the nations in YHWH's covenant[27]. Isaiah 56,1-8 merely takes up the issue of Gentiles

26. See O.H. STECK, »... *ein kleiner Knabe kann sie leiten*«, in J. HAUSMANN – H.-J. ZOBEL (eds.), *Alttestamentlicher Glaube und Biblische Theologie*. FS H.D. Preuß, Stuttgart, 1992, pp. 104-113; J.T.A.G.M. VAN RUITEN, *The Intertextual Relationship between Isaiah 65,25 and Isaiah 11,6-9*, in F. GARCÍA MARTÍNEZ et al. (eds.), *The Scriptures and the Scrolls*. FS A.S. van der Woude (SVT, 49), Leiden, 1992, pp. 31-42.

27. See G.I. EMMERSON, *Isaiah 56–66* (Old Testament Guides), Sheffield, 1992, pp.

who would convert to Judaism, here expressed as those would observe the Shabbat. Likewise, the concern with eunuchs envisions a place for those Jews who were mutilated for government service, either by the Babylonians or by the Persians, in keeping with common practices of the times. Scholars have noted that this passage constitutes interpretation of various aspects of the Torah tradition[28], but it also interprets passages from Isaiah. Lau demonstrates that Isa 56,1 builds on Isa 46,13, which states that YHWH's salvation will not tarry[29]. Both Fishbane and Lau note that Isaiah 56,8 employs language and imagery from Isaiah 11,12[30]. Thus, the reference to YHWH as one "who gathers the outcasts of Israel (*mĕqabbēṣ nidhê yiśrā'ēl*)" and who states, "I will gather yet others to him (i.e., to Israel) besides those already gathered (*'ôd 'ăqabbēṣ 'ālāyw lĕniqbāṣāyw*)", takes up language from Isa 11,12, "and he (i.e., YHWH) will raise an ensign to the nations, and he will gather the outcasts of Israel (*wĕ'āsap nidhê yiśrā'ēl*), and the dispersed of Judah he will gather (*ûnĕpuṣôt yehûdâ yĕqabbēṣ*) from the four corners of the earth". Likewise, the reference to "my holy mountain" (*har qodšî*) in Isa 56,7 employs the same language from Isa 11,9. Obviously, Isa 56,1-8 is presented in relation to the Davidic oracle of Isa 11,1-16, but it does not envision the restoration of Davidic rule. Rather, it focuses on the statements in Isa 11,10.12 that the nations will respond to the ensign of YHWH by seeking the root of David and the resting place of his glory, i.e., Zion, and that they will return the outcasts of Israel to Zion. In this regard, those from the nations who convert to Judaism and the return of the eunuchs respond to that call.

The use of Isaiah 11,1-16 in the concluding verse of Isaiah 56,1-8 is noteworthy in that it signals the ingathering of the outcasts of Israel within the covenant, including converted foreigners and eunuchs, as a major motif of Trito-Isaiah. The motif appears again in Isaiah 59,21, which concludes the lament that calls for repentance on the part of the nation and completes the instructions concerning covenant observance in Isaiah 56–59. The lament ends with statements to the effect that YHWH will repay enemies with wrath and come to Zion as the redeemer for

62-63; SCHRAMM, *Opponents* (n. 24), pp. 115-125; P.A. SMITH, *Rhetoric and Redaction in Trito-Isaiah: The Structure, Growth & Authorship of Isaiah 56–66* (SVT, 62), Leiden, 1995, pp. 54-60, for summaries of this discussion and contributions to it.

28. W. LAU, *Schriftgelehrte Prophetie in Jes 56–66* (BZAW, 225), Berlin - New York, 1994; R.D. WELLS, Jr., *Isaiah as an Exponent of Torah: Isaiah 56:1-8*, in E. LOVERING, Jr. (ed.), *Society of Biblical Literature 1994 Seminar Papers*, Atlanta, 1994, pp. 883-896. A revised version of this essay appears in R.F. MELUGIN – M.A. SWEENEY (eds.), *New Visions of Isaiah* (JSOT SS, 214), Sheffield, 1996, pp. 140-155.

29. LAU, *Schriftgelehrte Prophetie* (n. 28), pp. 262-279, esp. pp. 264-265.

30. M. FISHBANE, *Biblical Interpretation in Ancient Israel*, Oxford, 1985, p. 498, n. 103; LAU, *Schriftgelehrte Prophetie* (n. 28), p. 278.

those in Jacob who return from rebellion (cf. Isa 1,2-4.27-28). The prophet reports YHWH's statement in v. 21, "As for me, this is my covenant with them, says YHWH, my spirit which is upon you and my word which I have placed in your mouth shall not move from your mouth and from the mouth of your seed and from the mouth of the seed of your seed, says YHWH, from now and until forever". Overall, this verse expresses an important hermeneutical principle of the book of Isaiah, viz., that the covenant and the word of YHWH will not depart from the people, but will stand throughout the generations. In this regard, it is analogous to statements in Isaiah 40,8 that the word of G-d shall stand forever, Isaiah 55,11 that word of YHWH will accomplish what YHWH intends, and Isa 34,16-17 that commands one to read the book of Isaiah in order to see the realization of YHWH's statements. Once spoken, the word of YHWH will achieve its purpose.

This is particularly important when considered in relation to the use of earlier Isaianic statements from throughout the book of Isaiah in Trito-Isaiah, but especially in relation to the present context. Isaiah 59,21 employs several texts from Proto-Isaiah to make its point. First, it refers to YHWH's covenant mentioned already in Isa 54,10; 55,4; and 56,4.6. Second, it notes that YHWH's word is placed in the mouth of the righteous, i.e., the servants of YHWH as understood by Beuken, and their succeeding generations. This statement calls to mind the imagery of Isaiah 6, in which YHWH's word is given to Isaiah after his mouth was purified (Isa 6,7) in order to see to the eventual emergence of the "holy seed", or the remnant of the people who survive YHWH's punishment of the land. Finally, the reference to the "spirit" (*rûaḥ*) that is upon the people calls to mind the spirit that fills the righteous Davidic monarch of Isaiah 11,1-16 prior to the restoration of the exiles by the nations, and the spirit of Isa 32,15 that is poured upon the people prior to the restoration of the destroyed city and justice in the wilderness. Again, earlier Isaian texts have been employed to convey the constancy of YHWH's word and the promise of restoration based upon earlier texts that portray restoration of Jerusalem, the people, and the Davidic monarchy. Nevertheless, no Davidic monarch is evident here.

Finally, Isaiah 60–62 must be considered. Overall, many scholars point to these chapters as the core of Trito-Isaiah[31]. They constitute a

---

31. E.g., WESTERMANN, *Isaiah 40–46* (n. 14), p. 296; EMMERSON, *Isaiah 56–66* (n. 27), p. 20; STECK, *Tritojesaja im Jesajabuch* (n. 20), pp. 373-379; see also K. PAURITSCH, *Die neue Gemeinde: Gott sammelt Ausgestossene und Arme (Jesaia 56–66)* (AnBib, 47), Rome, 1971, pp. 241-244; S. SEKINE, *Die Tritojesajanische Sammlung (Jes 56–66) redaktionsgeschichtlich untersucht* (BZAW, 175), Berlin - New York, 1989, p. 182.

prophetic announcement of salvation for the reconstituted covenant community in Zion in which the prophet expresses this message by quoting or conveying the words of other figures. Thus, Isa 60,1-5 is the prophet's address to mother Zion to rise and see the return of her exiled children. The prophet conveys YHWH's words to Zion in Isa 60,6-22 in order to elaborate on the theme of the nations' return of Zion's exiles and the exaltation of Zion by the nations. Isa 61,1-4 presents the words of an anointed figure, who states a commission to release captives and to restore the ruined Zion. Isa 61,5-9 conveys YHWH's words to the people that they will serve as priests to the nations, and in Isa 61,10-11, the prophet rejoices over the restoration of YHWH's righteousness before the nations. In Isa 62,1-5, the prophet addresses Zion again that he will not rest until Zion's restoration is complete. In Isa 62,6-9, the prophet conveys YHWH's oath that foreigners will no longer take the grain and wine of Zion, but that Zion's own people will consume their produce before YHWH. Finally, the prophet calls for the return of the exiles to Zion in Isa 62,10-11.

Beuken and other scholars have recognized a host of references to material from Deutero-Isaiah in these chapters, but relatively little attention has been paid to their use of texts from Proto-Isaiah. Several key themes from Proto-Isaiah stand out, however. First is the imagery of light and darkness that permeates Isaiah 60. This language and imagery draws heavily on that of Isa 8,16–9,6. Thus, the prophet calls upon Zion to see the light or glory of YHWH that dissipates the darkness that covers the earth and the peoples in Isa 60,1-2. Such statements are comparable to those of Isa 8,22, in which the people (of Israel) see darkness throughout the land and Isa 9,1 in which the people see a great light shining that puts an end to the darkness in which they walk. The nations' recognition of this light in Isa 60:3 builds on the reference to "Galilee of the nations" in Isa 8,23, and more explicitly on Isa 2,2-4, which portrays the nations' pilgrimage to Zion to hear the instruction (tôrâ) and justice (mišpāṭ) of YHWH (cf. Isa 8,16, 19 [tôrâ]; 9,6 [mišpāṭ]). The portrayal of the pilgrimage of the nations coming to YHWH's light in Isa 60,3-18 is especially important for establishing a relationship with texts from Proto-Isaiah in that Isa 2,2 employs the verb wěnāhǎrû to describe the nations' approach to Zion. The verb is generally taken to mean "to flow" as a river that flows to Zion, but it also means "to shine" and thereby reinforces the imagery of light that appears in Isaiah 60[32]. The command to Zion to "lift up your eyes round about and see" in Isa 60,2

---

32. See entries, נהר I and נהר II in F. BROWN et al., A Hebrew and English Lexicon of the Old Testament, Oxford, 1972, pp. 625-626.

likewise takes up the theme of the blinded people of Israel from Proto-Isaiah (see esp. Isa 6,9-10), who are finally able to open their eyes and see YHWH's new deeds in Isaiah 35 and in texts throughout Deutero-Isaiah. The motif of the nations' bringing wealth to Zion is anticipated in Isaiah 23,17-18 which states that Tyre's merchandise and food will be dedicated to those who dwell before YHWH and in Isaiah 18,7 which states that Egypt will bring gifts to YHWH at Zion. Finally, Isa 60,21 employs references to a number of Isaianic texts to convey an image of the righteous people who will possess the restored land, "and all of your people shall be righteous, forever they shall possess (the) land; the shoot of my planting (*nēṣer maṭṭāʿay*), the work of my hands (*maʿaśēh yāday*), is for my being glorified. The smallest shall be a thousand, and the youngest shall be a mighty nation; I am YHWH, in its time, I will hasten it (*ʾăḥîšennāh*)". First of all, the passage points to the realization of YHWH's promise in a manner analogous to that of Isa 59,21 as indicated above. Secondly, it employs language from Isaiah 11,1-16; "shoot" (*nēṣer*) is the same term applied to the righteous Davidic monarch in Isa 11,1. But the passage also employs the term, "work of my hands", a term that appears throughout the book of Isaiah in various capacities. For the present instance, the appearance of this term in Isa 5,12 is especially pertinent in that it expresses the refusal of the guilty to see the deed of YHWH or the "work" of YHWH's "hands". Likewise, the statement that YHWH will hasten the "work" in Isa 60,22 refers back to the statement of the guilty in Isa 5,19, "let him (YHWH) hurry, let him hasten (*yaḥîšāh*) his work so that we may see it, that the counsel of the Holy One of Israel may draw near and that it may come, and we will know it". The sarcasm of this statement is clear; consequently, Isa 60,21-22 employs it to demonstrate that the wicked will get exactly what they ask for and YHWH's word will be confirmed. In doing so, it points to the realization of the righteous monarch and the return of the people portrayed in Isaiah 11,1-16, but no Davidic monarch is evident in the present context.

Isaiah 61 is likewise filled with themes and textual citations from Proto-Isaiah. The statement that "the spirit of my L-rd YHWH is upon me" calls to mind the references to "the spirit of YHWH, the spirit of wisdom and understanding, the spirit of counsel and might, the spirit of knowledge and fear of YHWH" that descends upon the Davidic figure of Isaiah 11,1-2. The fact that the speaker of Isa 60,1 identifies as one anointed by YHWH reinforces the identification of this figure with the Davidic monarch portrayed in Isaiah 11. The references to the aliens (*zārîm*) who will feed the flocks and care for the fields and vineyards in

v. 5 reverse the imagery of the aliens (*zārîm*) who devour the land and leave it desolate in Isa 1,7. Likewise, the references to the desolations (*šōmĕmôt*) of the land in v. 4 (cf. Isa 62,4) employ the language of desolation from Isa 1,7 and 6,11 as well (*šĕmāmâ*). Verse 6 explicitly states that "you (Israel) shall eat the wealth of the nations" in contrast to the imagery of Isa 1,7. The reference to YHWH's granting an eternal covenant to the people in v. 8 contrasts with statements that the covenant is broken in Isa 24,5 and 33,8. The reference to the "seed" of the people that will be known among the nations and that will be blessed by YHWH in v. 9 compares with the "holy seed" (*zera' qōdeš*) that will survive the destruction outlined in Isa 6,11-13 and serve as the basis for restoration. Finally, the imagery of sprouting seed and righteousness in v. 11 draws upon the imagery of a blooming root of Jesse that produces righteousness in Isa 11,1, 4, although it employs vocabulary from Isa 4,2 that describes the "sprout of YHWH (*ṣemaḥ yhwh*)" (cf. the four uses of the root *ṣmḥ* in v. 11) in a restored Zion that will become "beautiful (*lĕtip'eret*)" (cf. "beauty, splendor [*pĕ'ēr*], v. 10).

Isaiah 62 likewise employs a number of themes and texts from Proto-Isaiah. The reference to the desolation of the land with the term *šĕmāmâ* in Isa 62,4 was alluded to above. The same term appears in Isa 6,11 to refer to YHWH's intention to destroy the land. Isa 6,12 immediately following employs the verb *'ăzûbâ*, "abandoned", for the same purpose, which stands behind the statements, "and it will no longer be said of you *'ăzûbâ* (abandoned) and for your land it will no longer be said *šĕmāmâ* (desolate)", in Isa 62,4 to refer to the restoration of Zion. The notice that Zion will be called Hephzi-bah (my will is in her) in v. 5 is noteworthy in that 2 Kings 21,1 indicates that Hephzi-bah was the mother of King Manasseh and therefore the wife of King Hezekiah. The use of the image of King Hezekiah in Isaiah 36–39, who turns to YHWH in faithfulness following the failure of his revolt, has long been recognized as a model of repentance and piety within the book of Isaiah. The images of Jerusalem as a married woman with rebuilt walls in v. 4-7 recalls the images of Isa 32,9-20 which portrays abandoned women in the midst of ruins (cf. the use of *'uzzāb*, "abandoned", in 32,14) "until the spirit is poured out upon us from on high" (cf. the use of *rûaḥ*, "spirit", in Isa 11,2 in reference to the righteous Davidic monarch). The references to YHWH's oath in vv. 8-9 that the people of Israel will consume their own grain and wine in the courts of YHWH's holy sanctuary (*haṣĕrôt qodšî*, "my holy sanctuary", v. 9) not only calls to mind the earlier imagery of aliens and enemies who devour the land (Isa 1,7), but YHWH's rejection of false worship in the Temple courtyards in Isa 1,10-17 (cf. *rěmōs ḥăṣērāy*, "trampling of my courts", in Isa 1,12).

Isaiah 62,10-12 deserve special consideration because Steck points to its role as a major redactional key that ties into earlier texts from Isa 11,11-16; 27,13; and 35,1-10 in order to constitute the goal of his proposed 6th century redaction of the "great Isaiah book"[33]. Overall, these verses highlight the interest in this redaction to portray the return of exiles and the restoration of Zion in this edition of Isaiah. In this regard, the references to Isaiah 11 in these verses are noteworthy. The command to build up "the highway" (*hamměsillâ*) in v. 10 employs the same term in relation to the return of the exiles from Egypt and Assyria in Isa 11,16. The reference to the "ensign" (*nēs*) over the nations in v. 10 employs the same term employed in Isa 11,10.12 for the signal given to the nations prior to the return of the exiles. Thus, Isa 62,10-11 employs references to Isa 11,1-16 to close the announcement of salvation to Zion in Isaiah 60–62 and to tie it to earlier texts in Proto-Isaiah (and Deutero-Isaiah, cf. Isa 40,3-5; 48,20-22).

Altogether, it appears that Isaiah 56–66 employs a great deal of material from Proto-Isaiah in articulating its understanding of the covenant with YHWH, the role of the righteous in that covenant, and the constancy of YHWH's word. Although various texts are employed, Isaiah 11,1-16 appears again and again in this material, especially at key points in the structure of Isaiah 56–66 as a whole (i.e., Isa 56,8; 59,21-22; 60,21; 61,1-4; 62,10-12; 65,25) where it expresses the general theme of restoration of the exiles to Zion, especially by the nations, and the institution of righteousness in YHWH's rule of the world. The major themes of this chapter, the spirit of YHWH, the ensign to the nations, the submission of the nations to YHWH's will, and the ingathering of the exiles, are present with the exception of the righteous Davidic monarch. It would seem that, given the interest in demonstrating the viability of YHWH's previous words through the prophet Isaiah, Trito-Isaiah presents a scenario in which the promises of Isaiah 11,1-16, and those of other texts from throughout Isaiah, are realized. The absence of the Davidic monarch in this scenario, however, points to the new realities of Jewish life in the Persian period; i.e., the restoration of the people to the land is taking place, but the restoration of the Davidic monarchy is not. YHWH's world rule is identified not with the Davidic monarchy as expressed in earlier texts, but with the rule of the Persian empire. In order to place this phenomenon in context, we must now turn to the entire

---

33. STECK, *Bereitete Heimkehr* (n. 20), pp. 60-68.

book of Isaiah and its expressions of the identification of the Persian empire with YHWH's rule.

IV

The preceding discussion demonstrates that the reconceptualization of the Davidic covenant presented in Isaiah 55 can no longer be read simply as an isolated expression of Deutero-Isaiah's perspectives concerning the theological significance of the fall of Babylon to Cyrus for the exilic Jewish community. Rather, the "democratization" of the Davidic covenant must be read in relation to the following material in Trito-Isaiah, which presents an overall scenario concerning the future of the servants of YHWH in the post-exilic community of a restored Jerusalem and Judah and in relation to the traditions in Proto-Isaiah. This is particularly true of those traditions concerning the idealized future monarch of Israel in Isaiah 11 and elsewhere, that point to the character and constitution of the restored community. When considered in this perspective, it is evident that a fundamental hermeneutical shift takes place within the book of Isaiah concerning the portrayal of the ideal king who will preside over a restored and purified community. In Proto-Isaiah, it is a Davidic monarch and in Deutero-Isaiah it is the Persian king Cyrus, but in Trito-Isaiah, it is YHWH. Obviously, the understanding of ideal royal authority and identity changes from Proto-Isaiah to Deutero-Isaiah and from Deutero-Isaiah to Trito-Isaiah in accordance with the historical realities presupposed in each[34]. Nevertheless, the book as a whole does not present itself as the product of three successive "historical prophets" or literary stages, but as the message of a single and consistent whole, in which the presentation of YHWH as world monarch at the end of the book is the natural outcome of the expectations of ideal monarchic rule articulated throughout the book.

This is especially evident when one considers the royal oracles of Proto-Isaiah (Isa 9,1-6; 11,1-16; 32,1-8) in relation to the oracles against the nations in Isaiah 13–23. As I have argued elsewhere, even though the oracles against the nations in Isaiah contain a great deal of material that apparently stems from the eighth century prophet Isaiah ben Amoz, the present form of the section addresses the realities of the Persian period in that all of the nations included in Isaiah

---

34. See M.A. SWEENEY, *On Multiple Settings in the Book of Isaiah*, in E.H. LOVERING, Jr. (ed.), *Society of Biblical Literature 1993 Seminar Papers*, Atlanta, 1993, pp. 267-273, which applies this principle to the interpretation of Isa 9,1-6.

13–23, i.e., Babylon (Isa 13,1–14,23); Assyria (Isa 14,24-27); Philistia (Isa 14,28-32); Moab (Isaiah 15–16); Damascus/Aram and northern Israel (Isaiah 17); Egypt (Isaiah 18–20); the Wilderness of the Sea/Chaldea/Elam (Isa 21,1-10); Duma (Isa 21,11-12); Arabia (Isa 21,13-17); the Valley of Vision/Jerusalem (Isaiah 22); and Tyre (Isaiah 23), were incorporated into the Persian empire during the late-6th through the 5th centuries B.C.E[35]. Furthermore, the special attention given to Babylon as the subdued head of the nations likewise highlights the Persian period setting of the present form of the oracles against the nations in that the fall of Babylon was the key to the establishment of Persian hegemony in the larger Near East. Given the absence of Persia in Isaiah 13–23, the portrayal of YHWH's judgment against the nations identified in these chapters, and the portrayal of YHWH's banquet for the nations on "his holy mountain" in Isaiah 24–27 following world-wide judgment, it becomes clear that the book of Isaiah as a whole, by means of Isaiah 13–23/24–27 in particular, identifies YHWH's world rule with that of the Persian empire[36]. This is evident also in the portrayal of YHWH as king in Isaiah 65–66 and in the processions of the nations to Zion evident in Isaiah 2,2-4; 11,10-16; 14,1-2; 25,6-12; 49,22-23; 60–62; and 66,18-24. In all cases, YHWH is acknowledged as king by the nations in a manner consistent with the tribute paid by subject nations to the Persian monarch from the time of Cyrus on[37].

This obviously has implications for understanding the role and identity of the servants of YHWH as articulated in Isaiah 56–66. First, it is clear that although the servants of YHWH are portrayed as the heirs to the eternal covenant of David, there will be no king among them other than YHWH. From the perspective of the present form of the book of Isaiah, Davidic kingship has come to an end as first Cyrus and later YHWH emerges as the righteous monarch who fulfills the various prophecies of an ideal royal figure in the first part of the book. Second, it is also clear that the servants of YHWH are to fulfill a priestly or cultic role in relation to the larger world order being established by YHWH at Zion. Overall, the servants of YHWH are presented as those who keep YHWH's covenant by observing Shabbat, as those who are born by the nations to Zion and who receive or manage the gifts brought by the nations for YHWH at

35. SWEENEY, *Isaiah 1–39* (n. 9), pp. 51-55, 212-217.
36. Cf. R.G. KRATZ, *Kyros im Deuterojesaja-Buch* (FAT, 1), Tübingen, 1991, who argues this point for a specific redactional stage in Deutero-Isaiah.
37. On the payment of tribute and later taxes to the Persian monarchs, see M.A. DANDAMAEV – V.G. LUKONIN, *The Culture and Social Institutions of Ancient Iran*, Cambridge, 1989, pp. 177-195, esp. pp. 180, 255-256.

Zion, and as those who serve as priests in relation to the nations[38]. Third, it is clear that in the perspective of the present form of the book, this role has not yet been realized. Isaiah 2,2-4 calls upon Jacob to join the nations in their pilgrimage to Zion to hear YHWH's Torah; Isaiah 60–62 points to the time when the nations will bring their wealth to Jerusalem where the people, i.e., YHWH's servants, will serve as priests; Isaiah 66,18-24 points to a similar procession of nations who bring the exiled Jews, some of whom will become priests and Levites, to Jerusalem and who present them as an offering (minḥâ) to YHWH on YHWH's holy mountain.

Altogether, the scenario presented here corresponds to the restoration program attempted by Ezra and Nehemiah in the latter half of the fifth century B.C.E[39]. Both Ezra and Nehemiah are appointed as officers of the Persian empire to fill official roles during a time of Persian rule when there is no realistic possibility of the restoration of Davidic rule. Nehemiah is appointed by the Persians as governor of the province of Yehud, and Ezra is appointed as priest and scribe skilled in the Torah of Moses, who is able to implement the local laws of a subject territory in keeping with Persian imperial policy[40]. Major elements of their reform programs include observance of the Shabbat, restoration of Jerusalem and support of the Temple, and the expulsion of foreign wives and children who might compromise the sacred character and Jewish identity of the community. In this regard, it is noteworthy that foreign men who have attached themselves to YHWH and observe the covenant are not expelled by Ezra and Nehemiah. Koch has already noted the effort to portray Ezra's return to Jerusalem as a "second Exodus" patterned after that of Deutero-Isaiah and the concern with establishing the "holy seed" as a remnant in Jerusalem in accordance with the statements of Isa 6,13[41]. Furthermore, Ezra's concern with establishing the Torah of Moses at the center of the reconstituted Jewish community corresponds with the concern for YHWH's Torah articulated throughout the book of Isaiah from the very beginning[42]. In sum, the book of Isaiah points to a priestly community restored in Zion as the "servants of YHWH", and the Ezra-Nehemiah traditions point to Isaiah as a major basis for the self-understanding of Ezra's restoration program.

---

38. Note that under Cyrus, subject nations were required to bring gifts to the Persian monarchs. Only later under Darius I, was a regular system of taxation instituted: cf. ibid., p. 178.

39. Cf. SWEENEY, Isaiah 1–39 (n. 9), pp. 52-55.

40. Cf. K.G. HOGLUND, Achaemenid Imperial Administration in Syria-Palestine and the Missions of Ezra and Nehemiah (SBL DS, 125), Atlanta, 1992.

41. K. KOCH, Ezra and the Origins of Judaism, in JSS 19 (1974) 173-197.

42. See M.A. SWEENEY, The Book of Isaiah as Prophetic Torah, in MELUGIN – SWEENEY (eds.), New Visions (n. 28), pp. 50-67.

Altogether, the identification of the "servants of YHWH" in the book of Isaiah with the priestly restoration program of Ezra and Nehemiah in the late-5th century opens any number of possibilities for future research. It breaks down the artificial distinction between priests and prophets or visionaries that has permeated the field and has pitted a priestly figure such as Ezra over against the prophetic book of Isaiah when in fact their perspectives, particularly their concerns for the Temple and the Torah of YHWH, are very similar[43]. It lays the groundwork for studies in the newly recognized phenomenon of "scribal prophecy" insofar as the book of Isaiah appears to be in large measure the product of writers who interpreted earlier material from the book of Isaiah and resignified it in relation to their own times and hermeneutical needs[44]. Finally, it provides a model for the formation of the book of Isaiah into its present form as the product of a community which took very seriously the claims of the book that YHWH was the author of their own historical experience. Such perspectives thereby point to the institutional or social context in which those claims could continue to form a major basis for the self-identity and continued life of the Jewish community in the post-exilic era.

School of Theology at Claremont   Marvin A. SWEENEY
1325 N. College Avenue
Claremont, CA 91711-3199
U.S.A.

43. Cf. SCHRAMM, *Opponents* (n. 24).
44. Cf. LAU, *Schriftgelehrte Prophetie* (n. 28).

BACK TO HISTORICAL ISAIAH
REFLECTIONS ON THE ACT OF READING

The act of reading is a dynamic process. The readers set the text in motion, given their own perception. However, the readers's creative mind is not out of boundaries; it is restricted to the text, which concretizes the act of reading. Thus W. Iser sheds light on the act of reading. He writes:

> ... the literary work has two poles, which we might call the artistic and the aesthetic: the artistic pole is the author's text and the aesthetic is the realization accomplished by the reader... This is not to deny the vital importance of each of the two poles – it is simply that if one loses sight of the relationship, one loses sight of the virtual work[1].

The point is that reading is stimulative, and works on the reader's creative mind. But there are borders to the reader's imagination: the reading is anchored in the concrete text.

The following text of Isaiah may demonstrate the act of reading in its artistic pole:

> Their land is full of silver and gold
>> there is no limit to their treasures,
> Their land is full of horses
>> there is no limit to their chariots.
> Their land is full of idols
>> they bow down to the work of their hands,
>> to what their own fingers have wrought[2]. (Isa 2,7-8)

For the artistic pole of the readers, this concrete text of Isa 2,7-8, which sets the boundaries for the readers, is an argumentative utterance. It presents an argument for the limits of human power. The utterance does not address the subject of the false human perception in abstract, as a general matter of principle. Rather a specific objective is referred to, alluded as "their". The use of those ("their") people concretizes the act of reading. The pronoun "they" ("their") denoting those who enjoy unlimited prosperity, unrestricted military means, worshipping gods that fill up their land, alludes to concrete people; a nation which overwhelms the addressees.

---

1. See W. Iser, *The Act of Reading*, Baltimore, 1978, p. 21.
2. The biblical citations are partially based on *The Book of Isaiah*. The Jewish Publications of America, Philadelphia, 1973.

The passage addresses an audience who are scared by the mighty power of a specific foreign nation. Thus, the repeated description of their ample physical power: silver and gold, treasures, horses, chariots and idols, is not presented to shock the already frightened addressees. On the contrary, the utterance seeks to present this cornucopia as nothing. Hence, the presentation of the meaningless human power is not provided as a mere statement, but is depicted in an argumentative manner. The utterance presents the argument of the ridicule, which might function as a sharp rhetorical means:

> Ridicule is a powerful weapon at the disposal of a speaker against those who might undermine his argument by refusing ... to accept some premise of his discourse. This is the weapon that must be used against those who take it into their heads to hold and persist in holding two incompatible points of view without trying to remove the incompatibility: Ridicule affects only the person who allows himself to be entangled in the system forged by his adversary. Ridicule is the penalty for blindness and is apparent only to those for whom this blindness is obvious[3].

The employment of the ridicule as a rhetorical strategy indicates that the text constitutes an argument between two sides: an addresser and its addressees. The addressees are effected by the power of the objective of the text, and the addresser argues against the impact of human power, compared to God.

The argument through the means of ridicule reveals that the speaker seeks to create a common argumentative ground with the audience in order to communicate with them through an accepted premise. The addresser intends therefore to establish a dialogue with the addressees. As a matter of fact, there are no texts which are proclaimed in a social vacuum. The dialogic nature of the text has been enlightened by M. Bakhtin as follows:

> Utterance is constructed between two socially organized persons, and in the absence of a real addressee, an addressee is presupposed in the person, so to speak, of a normal representative of the social group to which the speaker belongs. The word is oriented toward an addressee ... There can be no such thing as an abstract addressee ... Each person's inner world and thought has its stabilized social audience that comprises the environment in which reasons, motives, values, and so on are fashioned[4].

3. See Ch. PERELMAN – L. OLBRECHTS-TYTECA, *The New Rhetoric*, Notre Dame, 1969, p. 206.
4. See M. BAKHTIN, *Marxism and the Philosophy of Language*, cited in P. BIZZELL – B. HERTZBERG (eds.), *The Rhetorical Tradition*, Boston, 1990, pp. 932-933.

The speaker seeks communication with the audience through a dialogue based, given the example of Isaiah 2,6-8, on a common agreement between the addresser and the addressees: Human beings can not worship their own deeds (v. 8). This premise is the foundation for the dialogue between the utterance and its addressees:

> To make his discourse effective, a speaker must adapt to his audience. What constitutes this adaption, which is a specific requisite for argumentation? It amounts essentially to this: the speaker can choose as his point of departure only the theses accepted by those he addresses[5].

Given its dialogic character the text is shaped on the basis of its common social condition. That is to say, the social condition determines which term, which metaphor, and which form, and we may add, which argumentative strategy may develop in an utterance for reaching its communicative aim[6]. In other words, texts do not emerge in a social vacuum, texts emerge out of an immediate social situation. The social context regarding polemic texts is socio-cultural situation, which must be determined in order to read the texts as dialogues responding to that situation. Thus, explains Bitzer:

> The presence of a rhetorical discourse obviously indicates the presence of a rhetorical situation … it is the situation which calls the discourse into existence … It seems clear that rhetoric is situational … We need to understand that a particular discourse comes into existence because of some specific condition which invites utterance[7].

The argumentative discourse is a response to a situation that has caused the argument. Without seeing this rhetorical situation the essence of the text, its dialogical nature, is out of reach. Therefore, the interpreter of texts faces a hermeneutic goal: reconstructing the rhetorical situation.

The rhetorical situation, the social matrix, which initiates the text, is the subject of a historical determination. However, this reconstruction is not necessarily an historical task in the sense that the text is a factual document, constructed by "hard" historical data. The text of Isaiah 2,7-8, for instance, is a literary design, which maintains repetition ("Their land is full of…"), and hyperbole ("There is no limit…"). Those are rhetorical features rather than dry facts. Furthermore, the style determines the function of the text. As a rule, Isaiah's discourse is poetic, and poetry is a medium in itself: "Poetry expresses concepts and things by

---

5. See Ch. PERELMAN, *The Realm of Rhetoric*, Notre Dame, 1982, p. 21.
6. *Ibid.*, p. 34.
7. See, L.F. BITZER, *The Rhetorical Situation*, in W.R. FISHER (ed.), *Rhetoric: A Tradition in Transition*, Michigan, 1974, pp. 247-260.

indirection. To put it simply, a poem says one thing and means another"[8]. Aristotle has determined the function of poetry as follows:

> ... a poet's object is not to tell what actually happened but what could and would happen either probably or inevitably ... poetry tends to give general truths while history gives particular[9].

However, also the poetic texts are communication, and do not emerge in a social vacuum. Therefore, the critic who deals with poetic texts such as Isaiah is asked to read the texts in a sensitive manner, which pays close attention to the design of the text. This critic is not asked to reconstruct the hard facts: the shape of the chariots, or the amount of gold owned by this nation. The critic's task is to throw light on the socio-cultural context that gave birth to the text[10]. Searching for the rhetorical situation of Isaiah 2, one can not avoid noticing that the editors of the book seek to avoid a reading in a historical darkness. The superscription of the book (1,1) intends to lead a reading of Isaiah's utterances in a given historical context.

History in this regard does not mean a detailed, documentary investigation, *Quellenkritik*. The historical concern is to allude to the readers that the argument that they are facing through the act of reading, is not presented in a socio-cultural vacuum. That is to say, the editors seek to present the text against a certain historical context, submitting a point of departure that establishes the readers' artistic pole, and determine the rhetorical situation. The superscription of 1,1 reveals the editors' aim to present the argumentative utterance in the context of Assyria's invasion. The rhetorical situation is, therefore, a debate regarding Judah's foreign policy at the time: submitting to human power (the addressees), or relying on the belief in God, who determines the course of history (the addresser).

The following text may be read as a characteristic prophetic criticism:

> Hear, O heaven, and give ear, O earth,
> For the Lord has spoken:
> I reared children and brought them up –
> And they have rebelled against me! (Isa 1,2)

The intention of the superscription of 1,1 is to avoid the reading of the utterance, started at 1,2ff, as a matter of a routine prophetic accusation. The concern is to provide a reality, which establishes the rhetorical situation of the argument. The intention is to avoid a timeless criticism of

8. See M. RIFFATERRE, *Semiotics of Poetry*, Bloomington, IN, 1984, p. 1.

9. ARISTOTLE, *Poetics* (Loeb Classical Library), London, 1927, 1451b. For further discussion on the poetics of biblical prophecy, see Y. GITAY, *Oratorical Rhetoric*, in *ACEBT* 10 (1989) 72-83.

10. For the relationship between writing history and rhetoric, consult D. LACAPARA, *History and Criticism*, Ithaca, 1985, pp. 15-44.

Israel, causing a perpetual punishment. The situation may be changed, leading to a different relationship between God and Israel rather than sin and punishment. Thus, there is a need to confine the historical frame of the rhetorical situation of the utterance, and to direct the reading to the historical context, provided in the superscription, which is the days of the kings of Judah: Uzziah, Jotham, Ahaz and Hezekiah. The editors direct the artistic pole of the reader, seeking a concretized text.

The editors' attempt to avoid a timeless reading of the utterances, is reemphasized in the so-called Isaiah's memoir, started at chapter 6[11]. The historical reference at the head of the chapter: "In the year that king Uzziah died..." intends to establish the rhetorical situation. Isaiah resumes his prophetic mission under the new regime after Uzziah, reestablishing his prophetic authority. The form of the utterance, 6,1-13, is a vision, designed in the form of the genre of the prophetic call[12]. The question is the aim and function of the form in this context. The new political hour, following the death of Uzziah, has required the reestablishment of the prophetic authority. Thus, the first ascribed utterance under the new king of Judah is "dressed" with the conventional form of the prophetic call. That is to say, the utterance reports in public about God's direct revelation to the prophet in order to constitute his credibility as God's messenger, not just in Uzziah's days. Further, the utterance under the prophetic form of the prophetic call conveys the need to reassure the continuity of the prophetic divine message. It should be noticed that Isaiah's revelation is not placed at the head of the book, but is presented later on, given the need to reestablish the prophetic mission under the new period[13]. Moreover, the superscription of chapter 6 differs from the superscription of chapter 1, thus providing a chronological continuity. The editors' intention has been revealed: notifying the start of a new prophetic epoch. This is the social matrix, the artistic pole, which seeks to concretize the reading of the utterance of chapter 6.

Similarly, the prosaic passage of 8,1-4 is an autobiographical account regarding the birth of Isaiah's son, *Maher-Shalal-Hash Baz*. The name of the new born son signifies a disastrous message:

> For before the boy learns to call Father and Mother, the wealth of Damascus and the spoils of Samaria shall be carried off before the king of Assyria (v. 4).

---

11. For the question of the memoir and its literary structure, consult Y. GITAY, *Isaiah and His Audience*, Assen, 1991, pp. 117-127.

12. Consult *ibid.*, pp. 117-121.

13. For further detailed discussion of the place and the rhetorical function of Isa 6, consult my *Isaiah and His Audience* (n. 11), p. 119.

Mentioning by name the two faithful witnesses of God's message: the priest Uriah and Zechariah son of Jeberechiah (8,2), apparently well familiar to the audience, is intended to provide a reality for the literary account. Thus, the attachment of the following prophetic utterance to the prosaic account of 8,1-4, depicted in realistic colour, is sought to present the utterance in the historical context of Assyria's military threat. Hence, the reference of 8,18: "Here stand I and the children the Lord has given me, as signs and portents in Israel from the Lord of Hosts, who dwells on Mount Zion," is meant to orient the reading in the historical context of Isaiah's life. That is, the Assyrian period rather than to be conceived as a prophetic eschatological message.

Interestingly, the direct reference at chaps 44,28 and 45,1 to Cyrus does not share the chronological frame of the superscription of 1,1. A total new historical context has been established, and the Assyrian period of the beginning has been shifted to the Persian era. The prophetic utterance revolving around Cyrus creates the new historical context for the prophetic utterances. The change of periods, from Assyria to Persia, the new historical context, invites a new rhetorical situation of the given utterances.

However, it looks as though the strong historical orientation of the first part of the book of Isaiah has been dismissed at its second half. The historical and biographical superscriptions such as 1,1, 6,1 and 7,1 have disappeared. In response, and given the new holistic approach to the book of Isaiah, recent scholarship has renewed the discussion regarding the literary and theological integration of the book as well as the question of the prophetic persona, standing behind the utterances of chaps 40-66. This holistic approach is speculating about the meaning of the editorial process of the book of Isaiah[14]. It has been suggested that the editors intentionally sought to dismiss any specific identifiable character of the new period and its prophet in order to depict a coherent theological line of prophecy and its fulfilment between Isaiah son of Amoz and the prophecies to come. Thus, C. Seitz claims that the reason why no new prophet appears in the second half of the book is:

> that God is here referring Israel to what Isaiah had spoken beforehand and, alongside that, to what Israel's past history was intended to reveal, for its own sake and in conjunction with God's word to Isaiah...[15].

14. For the approach and the literature, consult D. CARR, *Reaching for Unity in Isaiah*, in *JSOT* 57 (1993) 61-80 and C.R. SEITZ, *How is the Prophet Isaiah Present in the Latter Half of the Book? The Logic of Chapters 40–66 within the Book of Isaiah*, in *JBL* 115 (1996) 219-240.

15. See SEITZ, *How is the Prophet Isaiah Present* (n. 14), p. 231.

However, the strong editorial emphasis on the historical references, ascribed to Isaiah son of Amoz at the first part of the book, reveals the
editorial effort to restrict the reading of those utterances to a specific historical frame: the days of kings Uzziah, Jotham, Ahaz and Hezekiah.
Are we asked to conclude that the utterances of chaps 40–66 must be
also read in the realm of the those Judean kings? The direct internal references to Cyrus, king of Persia, in 44,28 and 45,1, questions this historical tendency. For the artistic reading, anchored in the rhetorical situation of the text, an historical perception of the kings of Judah during the
First Temple period carried on while reading the utterances of Isa 40 and
its remainder is, indeed, a strange reading endeavour.

However, a close reading reveals that the text of 40,1ff furnishes its
readers with sufficient literary clues, which enable a contextual historical reading of the utterances. Already the utterance of 40,1-11 (1-8) refers, in fact, to the new epoch[16]. Scholars have drawn literary parallels
between the beginning of chapter 40 and the utterance of 6,1-13[17]. Both
utterances are presented in the form of the prophetic call[18]. Form is a
useful vehicle of communication. K. Burke sheds light on the effect of
the form upon the readers. He writes:

> Form is a creation of an appetite in the mind of the auditor, and the ad-
> equate satisfying of that appetite ... If, in a work of art, the poet says some-
> thing, let us say, about a meeting, and then, if he places that meeting before
> us – that is form ... Obviously, that is also the psychology of the audience,
> since it involves desires and their appeasements[19].

Form signifies, raises expectations. The readers respond to the conventional form, proclaimed in a new historical era. The readers realize
through the conventional literary code of the form that they are facing a
new period under new circumstances.

However, form itself is a tool for carrying a message, which differs from
Isa 6 to 40. The pessimistic tone of the unavoided punishment of chapter 6:

> I asked, how long my Lord? And he replied:
> Till towns lie waste without inhabitants
> and houses without people... (v. 11),

16. See Carr, *Reaching for Unity* (n. 14), p. 68, and the literature cited therein. For
my treatment of the literary unit, see Y. Gitay, *Prophecy and Persuasion*, Bonn, 1981,
pp. 63-80.
17. See, for instance, R. Rendtorff, *Jesaja 6 im Rahmen der Komposition des
Jesajabuches*, in J. Vermeylen (ed.), *The Book of Isaiah* (BETL, 81), Leuven, 1989, pp.
79-81. See, moreover, the literature cited in Carr, *Reaching for Unity* (n. 14), p. 68.
18. See, for instance, R.F. Melugin, *The Formation of the Book of Isaiah 40–55*
(BZAW, 141), Berlin - New York, 1976, pp. 82-86.
19. See K. Burke, *Counter-Statement*, Chicago, 1957, p. 31.

has been totally changed in chapter 40, starting as follows:

> Comfort, oh comfort my people,
> says your God,
> Speak tenderly to Jerusalem,
> And declare to her
> That her term of service is over,
> That her iniquity is expiated;
> For she has received at the hand of the Lord
> double for all her sins. (vv. 1-2)

The readers' artistic pole, which constitutes the rhetorical situation of chapter 40 and its literary context, has been dramatically transformed. The readers set the utterance in motion, concretizing their artistic reading given the new content. The explicit references to Cyrus in 44,28 and 45,1 further focuses the artistic pole of the readers, revealing the rhetorical situation of the given utterances.

Thus, Isa 40,12-31 is a polemic utterance against the foreign gods, aiming to reinstate God's control of the political situation. Foreign gods are powerless. The argumentative strategy is the ridicule[20]:

> To whom, then, can you liken God,
> what form compared to Him?
> The idol? A woodworker shaped it,
> And a smith overlaid it with gold,
> forging links of silver.
> As a gift, he chooses the mulberry –
> A wood that does not rot –
> Then seeks a skilful woodworker
> To make a firm idol,
> That will not topple. (vv. 18-20)

The ridicule is also the argument employed in 2,7-8 above. Are both utterances replaceable? The artistic reading, which is a contextual act, provides different rhetorical situations for each utterance. The utterance of 40,12-31 is presented as a dialogue. It starts with a series of questions such as: "Who measured ... who has plumbed ... whom did He consult ... who guided Him...?" (vv. 12-14) The text also uses the second personal direct approach: "To whom then can you liken God?" (v. 18), thus alluding to a specific audience. The employment of the rhetorical questions presupposes a common agreement between the addresser and the addressees. The utterance is communicative.

The comparison between the two polemic utterances, against foreign gods and for God's absolute domination, reveals that both use the same

---

20. See GITAY, *Prophecy and Persuasion* (n. 16), pp. 82-97.

form and the same rhetorical strategy for arguing the case. However, a close reading projects two different rhetorical situations, leading to different messages. The contextual reading of 2,7-8 reveals its rhetorical situation: the Assyrian campaign and its political implications on Judah. The message to the frightened audience is to ignore the military threats upon their land. However, the rhetorical situation of 40,12-31 corresponds to 40,1-11: there is neither military nor political danger for a fallen Judah, but a struggle against the people's scepticism–after the destruction of the Temple–regarding their political redemption (also see vv. 29-31)[21].

To conclude, the hermeneutical concern is the act of reading the book of Isaiah. The different historical circumstances create the rhetorical situations that give birth to the various utterances of the book. The various contextual and historical allusions guide the readers' artistic pole to the concrete texts.

The prophetic utterances respond to specific situations. Concrete references and literary formulations provide literary codes to a contextual, historical and social reading, which contradicts a timeless elaboration of the book. Literary texts have no existence in a vacuum. The critics' task is, therefore, to shed light on the rhetorical situations of the given utterances.

The holistic approach pays close attention to the editorial process of the book in order to present a unified thematic-theological composition. This supposed editorial process, in fact, negates the editorial intention of 1,1, which seeks to provide a confined historical framework. The superscription of 1,1 is an editorial work, which was not altered in the course of expanding the book beyond the time of Hezekiah (the last Judean king mentioned in the superscription). Thus, the historical superscription of 1,1 may be perceived as a deliberate attempt to avoid the reading of texts of the Persian period in the realm of the part of the book ascribed to the First Temple era. Actually, the act of combining texts, even sporadic texts, establishes in itself a composition[22]. Regarding the biblical text, the act of combining texts may appeal to the modern reader, given the stylistic similarities. However, the similarities are characteristic of the formulaic linguistic codes of the biblical literature[23], and the comparison between the similar form of Isa 6 and 40 is a demonstration.

---

21. Consult *ibid.*
22. See J. GOODY, *The Domestication of the Savage Mind*, Cambridge, 1977, pp. 74-112.
23. Consult my essay *Reflections on the Study of the Prophetic Discourse*, in *VT* 33 (1983) 207-221.

In short, the act of reading depends on the artistic pole of the readers. The texts, which constitute the present book of Isaiah, are basically polemic texts that are anchored in contextual-historical situations. Those rhetorical situations initiate the prophetic utterances.

Department of Hebrew and Jewish Studies   Yehoshua GITAY
Private Bag
University of Cape Town
Rondebosch 7700
South Africa

PROTO-ISAIAH

HISTORICAL INFORMATION IN ISAIAH 1–39

1. INTRODUCTION

In the final text of Isa 1–39 a few pericopes are dated, but the majority of the texts are not. If the dates are correct, we have a chance of situating those dated pericopes in their historical context or to cull from them historical information. We find the following introductory sentences that contain a date (translation taken from *RSV*):

> 1,1: The vision of Isaiah the son of Amoz, which he saw concerning Judah and Jerusalem in the days of Uzziah, Jotham, Ahaz, and Hezekiah, kings of Judah.
> 6,1: In the year that King Uzziah died I saw the Lord sitting upon a throne…
> 7,1: In the days of Ahaz the son of Jotham, son of Uzziah, king of Judah, Rezin the king of Syria and Pekah the son of Remaliah the king of Israel came up to Jerusalem to wage war against it, but they could not conquer it.
> 14,28: In the year that King Ahaz died came this oracle…
> 20,1-2: In the year that the commander in chief, who was sent by Sargon the king of Assyria, came to Ashdod and fought against it and took it, – at that time YHWH had spoken by Isaiah the son of Amoz…
> 36,1: In the fourteenth year of King Hezekiah, Sennacherib king of Assyria came up against all the fortified cities of Judah and took them.
> 38,1: In those days Hezekiah became sick and was at the point of death…
> 39,1: At that time Merodach-baladan the son of Baladan, king of Babylon, sent envoys with letters and a present to Hezekiah, for he had heard that he had been sick and had recovered.

Literary-critical analysis (in the sense of *Literarkritik*[1]) has discovered in Isa 1–39 more than one redactional layer from different periods. Only what can be attributed to Isaiah or his contemporaries is a direct source for the history of the final phase of the 8th century B.C. All later layers represent a later representation and appreciation of that period.

---

* It is a privilege and a pleasure to offer this short article as a modest tribute to W.A.M. Beuken, the prominent interpreter of the Book of Isaiah, whom I greatly appreciate as a competent and dedicated scholar and a friend.

1. In this article, the terms "literary criticism, literary-critical" are always used with this meaning.

2. ANALYSIS OF THE TEXTS WITH HISTORICAL INFORMATION

A few years ago J.H. Hayes and S.A. Irvine rejected almost the whole literary-critical work of the past and they have consistently exploited Isa 1–39 (except chapters 34–35) as a historical source written almost completely by Isaiah himself[2]. In their opinion, the material has been arranged chronologically in Isa 1–27, whereas chapters 28–33, which deal with the end of the kingdom of Northern Israel and therefore should be placed between chapters 18 and 19, have found their final place as a preparation to Isa 36–37. The prophetic legends in Isa 38–39 concern facts from 713-711 B.C. and belong to the same historical context as chapters 20–22. They received their present form and place as a literary preparation for the exile and the message of Deutero-Isaiah. The pericopes in Isa 1–33 relate to facts of the Israelite and Judean history as follows: chapters 1–6 date from the time of Uzziah and Jotham, 7–14 from the time of Ahaz and 15–33 from the time of Hezekiah. Only very few editorial additions, mostly glosses, are accepted. According to Hayes and Irvine the detailed historical situation of the pericopes looks as follows: the historical background of Isa 1,1-20 is the earthquake during the reign of Uzziah (Amos 1,1), and Isa 2,6-22 concerns the same event. Several details in Isa 5 point to the period of Menahem (2 Kings 15,17-22), whereas Isa 6 describes an experience of the prophet, which introduces a new period in his life. As a matter of course, Isa 7 and 8 deal with the Syro-Ephraimitic crisis. Isa 8,21–9,7 has its historical setting in Pekah's coup (2 Kings 15,25) and Ahaz's subsequent move to assert independence from the Northern Kingdom and the Syro-Ephraimitic coalition. Isa 10,27–12,6 constitutes a single speech delivered on the eve of the siege of Jerusalem by Rezin and Pekah. The oracle in chapter 13 belongs to the period of Tiglath-pileser's efforts to subdue a rebellion in Babylon (731-729). Isa 14,1-27 should be interpreted against the background of the international situation in the years 729-727, and the king of Babylon, whose death is announced, is Tiglath-pileser! In Isa 17,28-32 his death is already presupposed by verse 29, whereas chapters 15–16 indicate that Moab was part of an anti-Assyrian coalition in 728/7, against which Shalmaneser took action. According to Isa 17 Damascus and Israel were also part of the coalition. Chapter 18, in which the prophet condemns possible coalitions with the Ethiopian dynasty in Egypt, dates from the same period. The subjection of the

---

2. J.H. HAYES – S.A. IRVINE, *Isaiah, the Eighth-Century Prophet: His Times and Preaching*, Nashville, 1987.

Syro-Palestinian coalition by Sargon and the latter's new relationship to the Egyptians in 720 provide the background for Isa 19 and chapter 21 has Sargon's attack on southern Mesopotamia and Merodach-baladan and his allies as its background (713-709). The speech in Isa 22,1-14 "belongs to the occasion of celebration in Jerusalem, following the departure of the Assyrian army from southern Palestine in 711, after Sargon's forces had captured Ashdod and Gath and dissipated the anti-Assyrian coalition"[3]. The movement to participate in the revolt, without the support of king Hezekiah, had seriously divided Judean society, and in Isa 22,15-25 the prophet turns on the leader of the revolt Shebna and on his successor Eliakim, who is not any better. The occasion for the speech in Isa 23 is the reduction of Tyre's power in 709 because of the capitulation of the Phoenicians on Cyprus to Assyria and the alliance of Midas of Phrygia with Sargon. Isa 24–27, which Hayes and Irvine call a "Cantata of Salvation", belongs to the period of Judah's revolt against the Assyrians in 705. Chapters 28–33 reflect the last years of the Northern Kingdom and thus chronologically belong after Isa 18. Finally, Isa 36–37 deals with Sennacherib's campaign in 701. Chapters 38 and 39 have been added later and not at the correct chronological place. They center on events which occurred much earlier than Sennacherib's invasion and which should be related to the period of the anti-Assyrian rebellion in 714-711. Thus they have the same general historical background as Isa 20–22. Isa 34–35 is related to the later chapters 40–66 and has also been added afterwards. This exegesis is founded on a detailed introduction to the general historical background.

As a reaction against an excessive scepticism with respect to the Isaianic authenticity of many pericopes this analysis has its merits. I can agree with a number of their historical comments. But Hayes and Irvine carry their reaction too far and their historical explanations are often extremely hypothetical. This analysis is in opposition to a broad consensus which rightly ascribes large portions of the text to later redaction. This redactional edition and expansion is much more extensive than accepted by Hayes and Irvine. A literary-critical analysis, based on linguistic and literary indications and not only on possible historical allusions, is needed[4].

It is commonly accepted that the so-called Apocalypse of Isaiah (Isa 24–27), the "Small Apocalypse" (34–35) and chapters 36–39 (comp. 2 Kings 18,13.17–20,19) are later non-Isaianic collections. Also in the

---

3. HAYES – IRVINE, *The Eighth-Century Prophet* (n. 2), p. 277.
4. Cf. A. SCHOORS, *Neuere Literatur über das Buch Jesaja*, in *TR* 89 (1993) 441-454, p. 444.

prophecies against foreign nations (Isa 13–23) a later collection seems to have been inserted. For when the most probably authentic words, viz. against Assyria (14,24-27), the Philistines (14,28-32), Damascus-Samaria (17,1-6), Egypt (18,1–19,15*; 20) and Jerusalem (22,1-9)[5] are left aside, we obtain a collection of later oracles against foreign nations, which are all called משׂא "oracle"[6] (13,1; 15,1; 21,1.11.13; 23,1). This collection then includes 13,1-22 (against Babylon); 15,1-16,14 (Moab); 19,16-25 (Egypt); 21,1-17 (the wilderness of the sea); 23,1-14 (Phoenicia: Isaianic?). There is, however, a problem, because the Isaianic units 17,1-6 and 19,1-15 also begin with such a heading. It is possible that these headings have changed places or have been added, when the Isaianic and the non-Isaianic collections were assembled. If the collection "*massa*" really existed, it has been enriched with a few later additions: e.g. 16,13-14; 19,16-25; 21,16-17; 23,15-18. Next to these larger collections there are also several shorter later additions which have been inserted between the Isaianic units: 3,10-11; 4,2-6; 10,20-23.24-27a.33-34; 11,6-9.10-16; 12; 22,24-25; 28,5-6; 29,17-24; 30,18-26; 32,6-8; 33. From the outset I should remark that in the latest edition of his commentary O. Kaiser considers practically all the pericopes which I am going to discuss, as non-Isaianic[7].

According to the heading of the book (Isa 1,1) Isaiah was active during the reigns of the Judean kings Uzziah, Jotham, Ahaz and Hezekiah, and this is historically correct. But already the first chapter is not simply a speech by the prophet. It consists of short units, of which only 1,4-9 can be historically situated with some probability: it may date from the time during or immediately after the siege of Jerusalem, when Sennacherib had abandoned the flat country to the Philistine princes (comp. v. 7)[8]. In poetic language the general bad situation is described without historical particulars. J. Vermeylen's analysis, in which he ascribes this pericope rather to the time of Jeremiah and the Deuteronomic school, is not convincing and the author is aware of it, since he admits

5. Cf. F. HUBER, *Jahwe, Juda und die anderen Völker beim Propheten Jesaja* (BZAW, 137), Berlin, 1976, pp. 3, 27.

6. P.A.H. DE BOER, *The Meaning of* maśśā', in *OTS* 5 (1948) 197-214; H.P. MÜLLER, in *TWAT* V, col. 23-25.

7. O. KAISER, *Das Buch des Propheten Jesaja. Kapitel 1–12* (ATD, 17), Göttingen, [5]1981.

8. H. DONNER, *Israel unter den Völkern. Die Stellung der klassischen Propheten des 8. Jahrhunderts v.Chr. zur Außenpolitik der Könige von Israel und Juda* (SVT, 11), Leiden, 1964, pp. 120-121; W. DIETRICH, *Jesaja und die Politik* (BEvT, 74), München, 1976, p. 191; S. NIDITCH, *The Composition of Isaiah 1*, in *Bib* 61 (1980) 509-529, extends the Isaianic authorship to the whole of 1,4-20.

that the inauthenticity cannot be proven[9]. H. Wildberger rightly defends the authenticity but he is perhaps somewhat naive, when he asserts that it is undisputed[10]. In its present form, however, chapter 1 can be ascribed to a later, according to Vermeylen dtr, redactor. J.T. Willis, however, explains the whole of vv. 2-20 in the context of Sennacherib's campaign[11]. Isa 1,21-26 is an authentic prophecy which cannot be connected with an historical event, but it reflects a situation of decay of the legal order in Jerusalem (cf. v. 26).

Isa 2,6-22 is a later composition, partly deuteronom(ist)ic (cf. Deut 18,9-15), partly post-exilic, in which Isaianic material has been preserved. Therefore it is hard to decide whether the description in vv. 6-8 alludes to the religious situation in Isaiah's days either in Samaria or in Judah: "they are full of diviners (from the east?) and soothsayers like the Philistines, and they swarm with foreigners. His (Jacob's) land is filled with silver and gold, and there is no end to his treasures; his land is filled with horses, and there is no end to his chariots. His land is filled with idols; they bow down to the works of their hands, to what their own fingers have made." According to Wildberger the authenticity of the vv. 7-9 is hardly doubted and one can agree with that statement[12]. H. Barth also is of the opinion that vv. 2,7-17 are words of Isaiah, which have been adopted in the so-called "Assur-Redaction", which he dates at the end of the 7th century B.C. during the reign of King Josiah[13]. This would mean that in Isaiah's days idolatry together with wealth and military equipment were imported from abroad. According to G. Pettinato everything in these verses is religious: gold and silver here signify the idols, and horses and chariots are the symbols of the solar cult in Judah (2 Kings 23,11; Hos 14,4; Micah 5,9-14)[14]. On the contrary, in Kaiser's opinion 2,6-8 is a bridging text which connects the central poem vv. 10.12-17 with the extension vv. 2-5, and all the conditions for considering even the central poem as an Isaianic fragment are lacking[15]. According to R. Kilian, however, vv. 8-9 have their origin in dtr circles[16]. H. Cazelles distinguishes between an Isaianic layer (vv. 6.7b-8a.9b.10-19),

9. J. VERMEYLEN, *Du prophète Isaïe à l'apocalyptique*, I, Paris, 1977, pp. 50-57.

10. H. WILDBERGER, *Jesaja 1–12* (BKAT, X/1), Neukirchen-Vluyn, 1972, p. 20.

11. J.T. WILLIS, *The First Pericope in the Book of Isaiah*, in *VT* 34 (1984) 63-77.

12. WILDBERGER, *Jesaja* (n. 10), p. 100.

13. H. BARTH, *Die Jesaja-Worte der Josiazeit* (WMANT, 48), Neukirchen-Vluyn, 1977, pp. 311-312.

14. G. PETTINATO, *Is 2,7 e il culto del sole in Giudea nel sec. VIII av.Chr.*, in *OrAnt* 4 (1965) 1-30.

15. KAISER, *Jesaja* (n. 7), p. 75.

16. R. KILIAN, *Jesaja 1–12* (NEB), Würzburg, 1986, p. 31.

directed against the pride of Samaria, which, with the help of Damascus, Tyre, the Philistines and even Egypt, tries to force Jerusalem into the anti-Assyrian coalition, and a later edition (vv. 7a.8b-9a.20-21)[17]. Verse 16 "against all the ships of Tarshish" belongs to the oracle 2,12-17, which is generally recognized as Isaianic[18]. Jehoshaphat made such ships at Ezion-geber (1 Kings 22,48) and since according to 2 Kings 14,22; 2 Chron 26,2 Azariah (Uzziah) built Elath and restored it to Judah, he may have done the same.

Many scholars date Isa 3,1-12, which announces anarchy in Jerusalem, to the beginning of Ahaz's reign[19]. But the description does not offer concrete information which would allow a precise date. The authenticity of the oracle against the haughty daughters of Zion (3,16-24) is almost uncontested, except for a later insert in vv. 18-23. But there is no specific information about when these words were pronounced[20]. They show, however, that the prophet condemned not only the men of the higher classes but also their ladies with their luxury. In 5,13; 6,12; 11,12-16; 27,8-13 Isaiah seems to know an exile and therefore many scholars have considered these texts as non-Isaianic. A. Niccaci, on the other hand, has concluded from these verses that there was a Judaic exile in Assyria after 701 (Sennacherib)[21]. With regard to 11,12-16 and 27,8-13 the literary-critical researchers are right: they belong to a (post-) exilic redaction, and also 6,12 is quite exilic. But in 5,13, under the impression of the Assyrian threat, Isaiah himself may have expected a future exile. In 5,26-28 the prophet draws a picture of the military might of Assyria.

The so-called *Denkschrift* (memoirs) of Isaiah (7,1-9,6 or 7,1-8,18) poses a special problem. In the footsteps of K. Budde[22], the historical value of this *Denkschrift* is highly regarded in large circles of historical-critical research, since Isaiah himself supposedly wrote it shortly after the Syro-Ephraimitic war. But from a literary-critical point of view, the shift from the third (chapter 7) to the first person (chapter 8) renders the original unity of the memoirs suspect. Furthermore, the repeated use of

17. H. CAZELLES, *Qui aurait visé, à l'origine, Isaïe II 2-5?*, in *VT* 30 (1980) 409-420, pp. 413-416.

18. Cf. R.B.Y. SCOTT, *The Book of Isaiah. Chapters 1–39* (Interpreter's Bible, 5), Nashville, 1956, p. 185; WILDBERGER, *Jesaja* (n. 10), p. 105.

19. According to G. FOHRER, *Das Buch Jesaja. 1. Band* (ZBK), Zürich, 1966, pp. 62-63, the vv. 10-11 reflect a later redaction.

20. WILDBERGER, *Jesaja* (n. 10), p. 137: "... über die Zeit, daß Jesaja das Wort über die stolzen Zionstöchter gesprochen hat, läßt sich nichts ausmachen".

21. A. NICCACI, *Un profeta tra oppressori e oppressi*, Jerusalem, 1989, p. 137.

22. K. BUDDE, *Jesaja's Erleben. Eine gemeinverständliche Auslegung der Denkschrift des Propheten*, Gotha, 1928.

the formula וְהָיָה בַּיּוֹם הַהוּא "in that day", especially in the Book of
Isaiah, points to a later redaction and the borrowing of 7,1 from 2 Kings
16,5 confirms this[23]. According to W. Dietrich, these hinge joints and a
few additions (e.g. in 7,17.20; 8,6-7) betray redactional work, and that,
as it seems, from the same hand. "With his additions the redactor works
towards a double goal: to form the disparate material he has at his disposal into a whole and to anchor this whole in a certain historical situation"[24]. In his opinion, the redactor has built a series of very small units
into the present literary unit by means of transpositions and redactional
additions. Other scholars also find here quite complicated redactional interventions. Thus for example C. Dohmen, who distinguishes three layers in Isa 7,1-17: a basic layer (vv. 3-8a.9a.10-13 [וַיֹּאמֶר].14*.16-17), a
first adaptation (vv. 1-2.8b) and a second adaptation (vv. 9b.13*.14
[לָכֶם].15)[25]. Also E. Haag distinguishes three layers of tradition, but his
literary criticism is, if possible, even more complicated and operates with
a completely different basic layer. He draws the following redaction-
critical picture: basic layer: 1a.2a.3aα.b.4a.bβ.5b.6.7b.8a.9a.10.17aα.b;
old redactional layer: 2b.3aβ.4aβ.9b.11-13.14b.15a.16a.17a; younger redactional layer: 1aβ.b.5a.7a. 16b.17aβ; and in addition a couple of glosses
(4b.8b.15b). The old redactional layer is rooted in the (post-)exilic interpretation of Nathan's prophecy in 2 Sam 7, as it appears especially in Isa
54–55, and therefore this redaction may be dated in the (post-)exilic
period. The younger redactional layer is then post-exilic in any case[26].
Barth considers Isa 6,1-8,18* as a collection which Isaiah himself wrote
down, and he associates 7,2-20; 8,1-8a.11-18 with this original collection, which was adapted by the "Assur-redaction", whereas 8,9-10 and
8,23b–9,6 have been added by this redaction[27]. Kilian ascribes the
Denkschrift (Isa 6,1–8,18) to a dtr redactor and also according to Kaiser
the real creator of the *Denkschrift* wrote in the shadow of deuteronomic
theology, after which eschatological redactions further elaborated the
text[28]. Our concern is the value of the texts in the Book of Isaiah as his-

---

23. A. LAATO, *Who is Immanuel? The Rise and the Foundering of Isaiah's Messianic Expectations*, Åbo, 1988, pp. 118-119.

24. DIETRICH, *Jesaja und die Politik* (n. 8), pp. 63-65, esp. p. 65: "Mit seinen Zusätzen verfolgt der Redaktor ein doppeltes Ziel: das ihm vorliegende, disparate Mate-rial zu einem übergreifenden Zusammenhang zu formen und das so entstandene Ganze in einer bestimmten historischen Situation zu verankern".

25. C. DOHMEN, *Das Immanuelzeichen. Ein jesajanisches Drohwort und seine inner-alttestamentliche Rezeption*, in *Bib* 68 (1987) 305-329, pp. 307-313.

26. E. HAAG, *Das Immanuelzeichen in Jesaja 7*, in *TTZ* 100 (1991) 3-22.

27. BARTH, *Jesaja-Worte* (n. 13), pp. 317-320.

28. KILIAN, *Jesaja* (n. 16), p. 47; KAISER, *Jesaja* (n. 7), pp. 118-119. In this respect C.H.W. BREKELMANS, *Deuteronomic Influence in Isaiah 1–12*, in J. VERMEYLEN (ed.),

torical sources, and therefore we do not have to follow the redaction-critical analysis in all details. As we have seen, for the most part 7,1 is a later borrowing from 2 Kings 16,5. The aim of this verse is the historical anchoring of the Immanuel pericope and, although added later, this anchoring in the Syro-Ephraimitic crisis is plausible. Isa 7,2-17 has been adapted in vv. 4b.5b.8b.15 and 17. In 4b.5b and 8b we have explicative or interpretative glosses. Verse 15 interrupts the connection of the naming in v. 14 with its justification, introduced with כי in v. 16. It is an insert that has been created by combining 16a and 22b, which is confirmed by the *scriptio plena* of the two infinitives מאוס and בחור in contrast with the orthography in v. 16. In v. 17 "the king of Assyria" is a gloss which makes an announcement of doom out of an ambiguous verse. In my opinion, the sign of Immanuel can only be a promise of salvation, and therefore one should understand v. 17 without the gloss in that sense: the days which YHWH will bring upon Judah mean a period of welfare such as Israel has experienced no more since the time that the kingdom of David and Solomon broke up into the kingdoms of Israel and Judah. If the verse is to be understood as an announcement of doom, it cannot be part of the same layer as vv. 14.16. The vv. 18-25 as a whole must be ascribed to a later redaction, although in 18-20 Isaianic material may have been incorporated and so these verses may have been adopted in the "Assur-redaction"[29].

Isa 8,1-4, the Isaianic authenticity of which is practically undisputed, announces the approaching destruction of Damascus and Samaria by the Assyrians in the Syro-Ephraimitic crisis. In this connection the Prophet announces doom for Judah too (8,5-8): the mighty waters of the Euphrates, i.e. the Assyrians, will also sweep on into Judah, "because this people has refused the waters of Shiloah that flow gently", i.e. YHWH. The expression "waters of Shiloah" does not allude to the Siloam tunnel made under King Hezekiah, but to the older conduit which ran, largely as an open-air channel, through the Kidron valley. Dietrich prefers to situate this pericope rather in the crisis of 705-701: only the redactional additions vv. 6b.7ab contain clear references to the Syro-Ephraimitic war. G. Brunet recognizes here the expression of resistance against the digging of the Siloam tunnel, which was achieved later under Hezekiah and also Dietrich sees here an allusion to this enterprise[30]. But according

The Book of Isaiah (BETL, 81), Leuven, 1989, pp. 167-176, has rightly warned against pandeuteronomism.

29. BARTH, *Jesaja-Worte* (n. 13), p. 318.

30. DIETRICH, *Jesaja und die Politik* (n. 8), pp. 158-160; G. BRUNET, *Essai sur l'Isaïe de l'histoire*, Paris, 1975, pp. 171-183.

to Donner it is better to relate the pericope to the state of affairs at a certain moment during the Syro-Ephraimitic border war[31]. If it is correct to consider vv. 6b.7ab and 8b as glosses, Dietrich may be right. Vv. 9-10 are not easily conected with their context and their historical background is not very clear. Because of the literary context we tend to relate them to the anti-Assyrian coalition of 734/733 and to situate them perhaps in the period before the Syro-Ephraimitic expedition in 733[32]. But because of the broad address to the nations, they fit better in the period of the threat by Sennacherib (705-701) or, what is even more probable, they are a later redactional addition ("Assur-redaction")[33]. According to Isa 8,11-15 the Prophet and, as may appear from the plural forms, also his circle are urged to move away from their fellow Judeans. The threat can be situated in the Syro-Ephraimitic crisis. In vv. 16-18 we can see some sort of conclusion: "The prophet draws a line under a certain period of his activity, and if not everything deceives us, it was the period of his hard struggle to be heard during the Syro-Ephraimitic war"[34]. The extremely difficult verses 19-23aα date from the Exile and are partly under Deuteronomistic inspiration. K. Jeppesen prefers to see in vv. 21-22 the expression of Isaiah's frustration[35].

The authenticity of the pericope Isa 8,23aβ-9,6 is disputed. Barth counts it with his "Assur-redaction" and also Vermeylen prefers this date[36]. Others, like J. Vollmer, Fohrer or Kaiser, take the view that the pericope is post-exilic, either because of the vocabulary or because of the contents which betray the post-exilic eschatological prophecy[37]. According to T. Lescow the pericope reflects Sennacherib's retreat and originated in the circles of court prophecy in Jerusalem[38]. It is hard to settle these discussions. There are no decisive linguistic arguments against Isaianic authorship of Isa 9,1-6. If the pericope is Isaianic, the historical context must be an Assyrian oppression: it is not an accident

31. DONNER, *Israel unter den Völkern* (n. 8), p. 24.

32. *Ibid.*, pp. 26-27.

33. BARTH, *Jesaja-Worte* (n. 13), p. 319; HUBER, *Jahwe, Juda und die anderen Völker* (n. 5), pp. 69-82.

34. WILDBERGER, *Jesaja* (n. 10), p. 344: "Der Prophet zieht einen Schlußstrich unter eine gewisse Periode seiner Wirksamkeit, und zwar, wenn nicht alles täuscht, unter die Zeit seines harten Ringens um Gehör während des syrisch-efraimitischen Krieges".

35. K. JEPPESEN, *Call and Frustration: A New Understanding of Isaiah viii 21-22*, in *VT* 32 (1982) 145-157.

36. BARTH, *Jesaja-Worte* (n. 13), pp. 141-177; VERMEYLEN, *Du prophète Isaïe* (n. 9), p. 245.

37. J. VOLLMER, *Zur Sprache von Jes 9,1-6*, in *ZAW* 80 (1968) 343-350; FOHRER, *Jesaja* (n. 19), p. 138; KAISER, *Jesaja* (n. 7), pp. 207-208.

38. T. LESCOW, *Das Geburtsmotiv in den messianischen Weissagungen bei Jesaja und Micha*, in *ZAW* 79 (1967) 172-207, pp. 187-188.

that the prophet uses the Assyrian loan-word סאון "boot", when he alludes to the enemy (v. 4). A. Alt was of the opinion that 8,23b was the
original introduction to the poem and that it alluded to Tiglath-pileser's
campaigns in Galilee and to the annexation of northern and eastern Israel in 732 (cf. 2 Kings 15,29)[39]. In that case, Isaiah promises here a
"day of the Lord", which will liberate Northern Israel by the intervention of a Davidic king. But the meaning of 8,23 is not clear. The traditional translation (e.g. *RSV*) can hardly be correct: the point is not the
contrast between a former time and a later, future, time. A literal translation may rather be: "Now the former one brought the land of Zebulun
and the land of Naphtali into contempt and the latter one treated harshly
the Way of the Sea, the land beyond the Jordan, Galilee of the nations".
It seems impossible to me to establish who are the former one and the
latter one: Assyrian kings? Israelite kings? The verse may mean, for
example, that Tiglath-pileser treated Northern Israel relatively mildly in
732, whereas Shalmaneser V liquidated it completely. Against Alt we
must stick to the redactional character of 8,23b: the verse offers a later
historical interpretation. Thus the poem Isa 9,1-6 cannot offer us reliable
historical information. According to Barth, the *terminus a quo* is the retreat of the Assyrians from the occupied northern part of Western Palestine in the last third of the 7th century, and the king who is the subject of
the poem is Josiah[40].

The beginning of the poem Isa 9,7–10,4 is addressed to Northern Israel (Ephraim in v. 8). The strophe 8-11 recalls the earthquake which
struck Palestine during the reign of Uzziah (cf. Amos 1,1). The prophet
mentions hostilities with Aram and the Philistines. The name Rezin in v.
10 cannot be original, since he was Ephraim's ally. It is not clear at all
which wars between Israel on the one hand and Aram and Philistia on
the other the prophet has in mind. As far as Aram is concerned, it can
only be hostilities from the time before the treaty between Rezin of Damascus and Pekah of Samaria, e.g. under Jehoahaz (2 Kings 13,22). We
do not know which difficulties with the Philistines are meant, but Aram
and Philistia were probably now and then allies. Also Amos 1,6-8 still
reflects an oppression by the Philistines. With Wildberger we can say
that the prophet seems to look back onto a more remote past[41]. In the
second strophe (vv. 12-16) v. 14 is a secondary interpretation and also

---

39. A. ALT, *Jesaja 8,23–9,6. Befreiungsnacht und Krönungstag*, in W. BAUMGARTNER
(ed.), *Festschrift Alfred Bertholet zum 80. Geburtstag*, Tübingen, 1950, pp. 29-36.

40. BARTH, *Jesaja-Worte* (n. 13), pp. 141-177.

41. WILDBERGER, *Jesaja* (n. 10), p. 212: "Der Prophet blickt also wohl tiefer in die
Geschichte zurück".

the authenticity of 15-16a is not wholly undisputed. The prophet has in mind here the revolutions which follow one another rather fast: Shallum, Menahem and Pekah (2 Kings 15,10.14.25), and perhaps particularly Jehu's revolution (2 Kings 9–10). In 17-20 it is again hard to know the concrete historical data which are alluded to. According to Donner they are the tribal strife around the accession to the throne of the usurper Hoshea about 732/731 (2 Kings 15,30)[42]. But in 2 Kings 15,30 there is no explicit statement about strife between the tribes on this occasion. With Hayes & Irvine we can as well suggest that the point is the conflict around the accession of Pekah[43]. Isa 10,1-4, which was originally connected with 5,8-20, is an accusation of injustice in Jerusalem. In its totality we owe the poem 9,7–10,4, which mostly has in mind events from the time before or at the beginning of Isaiah's career, to a later redaction, such as the "Assur-redaction". This redaction must also have brought about the transpositions between chapter 5 and 9,7–10,4.

Isa 10,5-15 is a woe-oracle against the arrogance of Assur, in which the prophet imitates the style of the Assyrian boast literature. Verse 12 undoubtedly is an insert but also vv. 10-11 are considered as secondary by a number of exegetes[44]. They appear to have the dtr Version of the speeches of the Rabshake as their example (comp. 2 Kings 18,33-35; 19,11-13). If vv. 10-11 are original, the pericope can be dated in the time of Sennacherib's invasion of Judah. If, however, it is a dtr insert, than we lack all tangible connection with Jerusalem and the pericope perhaps originated in the time when Sargon II (722-705) consolidated his rule in Northern Israel. Dietrich thinks he can fit it into the period of time in which Hezekiah had to make his choice between participation in the rebellion planned by Ashdod and his loyalty as a vassal of the Assyrian king, thus before 713[45].

Isa 10,27-32 seems to have been taken from a war report. In 701 Sennacherib marched on Jerusalem by the coastal plain and thus from the south-west. If the pericope is related to Sennacherib's invasion, then the route of the march, as it is described here, is imaginary and not a description *post eventum*. But the context in the Book of Isaiah suggests an earlier invasion. We do not learn, however, who the aggressor is. Rightly Wildberger asserts that the redactor who placed the pericope

42. DONNER, *Israel unter den Völkern* (n. 8), p. 73.
43. HAYES – IRVINE, *Isaiah, the Eighth-Century Prophet* (n. 2), p. 188.
44. Cf. WILDBERGER, *Jesaja* (n. 10), p. 392.
45. DIETRICH, *Jesaja und die Politik* (n. 8), p. 118; cf. R.E. CLEMENTS, *Isaiah and the Deliverance of Jerusalem: A Study of the Interpretation of Prophecy in the Old Testament* (JSOT SS, 13), Sheffield, 1980, pp. 36-39.

here, after the Assur prophecies of chapter 10, thought that in vv. 27b-32 too, the enemy was Assyria. And since Sennacherib drops out, we may think of the rebellion of Ashdod in 713-711, on which Sargon reports in a number of inscriptions[46]. From these inscriptions we learn that Judah also participated in the rebellion, and according to Isa 20 the Prophet warned against this participation. The details, however, are completely unknown and there are no decisive indications that 10,27b-32 has anything to do with that episode. An alternative is offered by the Syro-Ephraimitic war and in that case, the enemies are the allied Syrian and Northern Israelite forces[47], or Sargon's campaign in the West in 720, when, after his victory on the Syrian rebels at Qarqar, he marched through Judah in order to defeat the Egyptians and the Philistines near Raphia[48].

In the prophecies against foreign nations (Isa 13–23) authentic Isaianic pieces have been redactionally linked with later oracles. When we look at the authentic words separately, we see a planned sequence: East (Assyria; 14,4-20) – West (Philistines; 14,28-32) – North (Damascus and Samaria; 17,1-6) – South (Egypt; 18; 20) – Centre (Jerusalem; 22,1-19). The Isaianic origin of Isa 14,4-20 is disputed. In the poem there are no indications which can be related to Babylon with certainty. The connection with a king of Babylon in the present text is secondary. Wildberger has rejected the authenticity on the ground of theological and linguistic arguments. H.L. Ginsberg, however, has presented good arguments in favour of a connection with Sargon II[49]. Barth agrees but he regards vv. 20b-21 as redactional and he is of the opinion that 14,4b-21in its redactional form should be dated in the last years before the collapse of the Assyrian empire[50]. Isa 14,24-27 is a threat against Assur which is often explained in the framework of Sennacherib's invasion of Judah. But concrete points in support of an unequivocal historical context are lacking. According to R.E. Clements the pericope is a midrashic elaboration of Isaianic themes and Barth reckons it with his "Assur-redaction"[51]. Isa 14,28-32 is explicitly dated in the year of Ahaz's death

46. *AOT*, p. 351; *TUAT* I, p. 381; *ANET*, p. 287; cf. WILDBERGER, *Jesaja* (n. 10), pp. 427-428.

47. H. DONNER, *Der Feind aus dem Norden. Topographische und archäologische Erwägungen zu Jes 10,27b-34*, in *ZDPV* 84 (1968) 46-54; S.A. IRVINE, *Isaiah, Ahaz, and the Syro-Ephraimitic Crisis* (SBL DS, 123), Atlanta, 1990, pp. 278-279.

48. M.A. SWEENEY, *Sargon's Threat against Jerusalem in Isaiah 10,27-32*, in *Bib* 75 (1994) 457-470.

49. H. WILDBERGER, *Jesaja 13–27* (BKAT, X/2), Neukirchen-Vluyn, 1978, pp. 541-542; H.L. GINSBERG, *Reflexes of Sargon in Isaiah after 715 B.C.E.*, in *JAOS* 88 (1968) 47-53.

50. BARTH, *Jesaja-Worte* (n. 13), p. 141.

51. CLEMENTS, *Isaiah and the Deliverance of Jerusalem* (n. 45), pp. 45-46; BARTH,

and in the threat the prophet speaks of the joy of the Philistines, "that the rod which smote you is broken" (*RSV*). The two pieces of information are not easily connected. The rod which smote the Philistines should be an Assyrian king. In Isaiah's time three Assyrian kings died, and in exegetical literature 29-32 has been connected with each of these dates: Tiglath-pileser III in 727, Shalmaneser V in 722 and Sargon II, who was succeeded by Sennacherib, in 705. Obviously, "the messengers of the nation" in v. 32 are Philistine ambassadors who try to gain support for an action against Assyria in Jerusalem. Then, we can again think of the Ashdodite rebellion, which was beaten down by Sargon in 711. It is conceivable that the embassadors came to Jerusalem already at the beginning of Hezekiah's reign, i.e. in the year of Ahaz's death (about 716). Then the date given in v. 28 would be correct. However, v. 29 seems to allude to Sargon's death and then the oracle should be situated rather in the context of the Philistine ambassadors in the days of the next rebellion in which Hezekiah participated and which eventually led to Sennacherib's invasion. In this case the redactional date is wrong and should be ascribed to a redactor who transposed the metaphors of v. 29 to Ahaz because of the events that are narrated in 2 Kings 18,8. Yet, an early date of the year of Ahaz's death can allow another solution. If, with Pavlovsky & Vogt and others, we date the year of Ahaz's death in 728/727, then the rod of v. 29 means Tiglath-pileser, who died in the same year and treated the Philistines harshly (cf. *ANET*, p. 283). According to Dietrich the whole pericope is a later imitation, but his linguistic and aesthetic arguments are not convincing[52].

The threat against Damascus and Israel in Isa 17,1-6 is undoubtedly to be situated in the time of the Syro-Ephraimitic war, shortly before the intervention of Tiglath-pileser in 733[53]. Verses 17,12-14, the Isaianic authenticity of which is in any case much debated, may refer to Sennacherib's invasion in 701. But the content of the oracle is so general that a precise dating is impossible and the expression "the thunder of many peoples", i.e. the idea of the roaring of the nations against Zion, is rather in the line of post-exilic eschatological prophecy[54]. According to Barth it belongs to the "Assur-redaction".

Jesaja-Worte (n. 13) pp. 103-119; cf. A.K. JENKINS, *The Development of the Isaiah Traditions in Isaiah 13–23*, in VERMEYLEN (ed.), *The Book of Isaiah* (n. 28), pp. 240-241.

52. DIETRICH, *Jesaja und die Politik* (n. 8), pp. 208-209.

53. DONNER, *Israel unter den Völkern* (n. 8), p. 41; WILDBERGER, *Jesaja 13–27* (n. 49), p. 647.

54. FOHRER, *Jesaja* (n. 19), p. 218; HUBER, *Jahwe, Juda und die anderen Völker* (n. 8), pp. 69-82.

In chapter 18, verse 7 is a later conclusion which in an eschatological perspective announces the conversion of the Nubians (Cush is the region south of Egypt: Nubia, Sudan, Ethiopia), and v. 3 apparently has been inserted by the same editor. Since in Isaiah's days Egypt had come under the rule of a Cushitic (Greek: Ethiopian) dynasty (the 25th), the prophet here means Egypt under Cushitic rule. During Hezekiah's reign, the Egyptians sought to induce the small states of Syria-Palestine, and among them also Judah, to a rebellion against Assyria. The efforts of the Philistines to which Isa 14,28-32 alludes, are to be seen in the same context. It is just not clear whether Isa 18 should be situated at the beginning of these efforts or later, after the succession of Sargon by Sennacherib (703), when relations between Hezekiah and Pharao were particularly close. Dietrich prefers the earlier period, about 713-711, but according to Donner and W. Zimmerli the later period is more convenient, since Hezekiah then sought to get into contact with Egypt and was quite actively involved in the anti-Assyrian movement[55]. The Isaianic authenticity of chapter 19 is generally rejected by the literary-critical scholars. Only with respect to vv. 1-4.11-14 does a possible Isaianic authorship deserve consideration[56]. If it is Isaianic, the word is older than Chapter 18, as Cush is not mentioned and therefore Egypt is not under the rule of the 25th dynasty. It would then belong in the troubled days of the end of the 22nd dynasty. Isa 20 reports a symbolic act by Isaiah. The chapter has not been written by Isaiah himself but it may have been taken from a collection of stories about Isaiah similar to Isa 7. Nevertheless, it offers reliable information on an action of the prophet in the period of the Ashdodite rebellion (713-711), as is commonly accepted[57].

As for the oracle Isa 22,1-14, the Isaianic authenticity of vv. 1-4.12-14 is almost generally accepted, whereas that of vv. 5-11 is disputed and rejected e.g. by Kaiser, Fohrer, Vermeylen and Clements. The authentic part would be better dated shortly after Sennacherib's retreat from Jerusalem in 701. According to Donner, 9b-11a is a very old addition which comes from a well informed source and is close to the historical facts, but Clements is of the opinion that 8b-11 is an interpretation which has

---

55. DIETRICH, *Jesaja und die Politik* (n. 8), pp. 128-130; DONNER, *Der Feind aus dem Norden* (n. 47), pp. 123-126; W. ZIMMERLI, *Jesaja und Hiskia*, in H. GESE – H.P. RÜGER (eds.), *Wort und Geschichte*. FS K. Elliger, Kevelaer, 1973, pp. 199-208, esp. pp. 206-208.

56. Cf. JENKINS, *Isaiah 13–23* (n. 51), pp. 244-245.

57. Cf. HUBER, *Jahwe, Juda und die anderen Völker* (n. 5), pp. 107-113; JENKINS, *Isaiah 13-23* (n. 51), pp. 245-246; differently O. KAISER, *Der Prophet Jesaja Kapitel 13–39* (ATD, 18), Göttingen, 1973, pp. 92-97: post-exilic.

been added after the fall of Jerusalem in 587[58]. The mention of works at the water supply and at the fortifications has a parallel in 2 Chron 32,2-5 and seems to be borrowed from a reliable source. The oracle against Shebna (22,15-25) is certainly not homogeneous. The main part of vv. 15-19 is Isaianic, but it is hard to fix the moment of their origin. Occasionally they are dated before Sennacherib's campaign in 701, because in 2 Kings 18,18 (= Isa 36,3) Schebna is called secretary (סֹפֵר) and therefore had already been dismissed from his function of steward or prime minister (סֹכֵן, אֲשֶׁר עַל־הַבָּיִת). In the same texts Eliakim the son of Hilkiah is already steward. Therefore I have the impression that Isa 22,20-23 was added later in order to harmonize vv. 15-19 with 36,3, and 22,24-25 is a still later addition in prose. Chapter 23 contains an oracle against Phoenicia (1-14), to which a few verses in prose have been added later (15-18). There is no longer any doubt that this addition is post-exilic but the authenticity and date of 1-14 is amply debated and opinions are quite divided. The pericope is not a prediction but a retrospection on a great affliction which hit Phoenicia. It is not Isaianic, but may have originated in the Late Assyrian Period and may have the punitive expeditions of Esar-haddon (681-669) against Phoenicia as its historical background[59].

After the so-called Apocalypse of Isaiah (chapters 24-27) follows a collection of prophecies about Israel and Judah (28-33). In 28,1-13, the redactor has included an older word against the leaders of Samaria (vv. 1-4) and applied it to the leadership of Jerusalem (vv. 7-13). The Isaianic word can best be dated in the period between the Syro-Ephraimitic war (733/732) and the siege of Samaria by Shalmaneser (725/724). The announcement of salvation in vv. 5-6 is a post-exilic insert. By means of v. 7a a collector of Isaianic words has connected the oracle 7b-13 with the preceding one. Also 28,14-22, an oracle against alliances with Egypt, is basically Isaianic and can best be understood as originating in the days of the rebellion against Sennacherib[60]. In the Ariel-oracle (29,1-8) only vv. 1-4a are Isaianic, while 4b is a transitional doublet and 5-8 are in literary and contentional contradiction with 1-4. Vv. 5-8 consist of gradual additions which perhaps as *vaticinia ex eventu* look back at the events of 701 in their legendary

---

58. DONNER, *Israel unter den Völkern* (n. 8), p. 128; CLEMENTS, *Isaiah and the Deliverance of Jerusalem* (n. 45), p. 33; cf. ID., *The Prophecies of Isaiah and the Fall of Jerusalem in 587 B.C.*, in *VT* 30 (1980) 421-436, pp. 429-432; JENKINS, *Isaiah 13–23* (n. 51), pp. 247-248.

59. *ANET*, pp. 290-291; cf. WILDBERGER, *Jesaja 13–27* (n. 49), pp. 862-866.

60. *Ibid.*, p. 1072.

version (cf. Isa 36–37)[61]. The authentic Ariel-oracle can be dated
shortly before the siege of 701. Dietrich is of the opinion that, to all
appearances, in 29,13-14 Isaiah expresses himself at a liturgy of supplication which took place in 701, and Wildberger agrees with him[62].
In my opinion, indications to this effect are extremely vague. Also
29,15-16 probably has to do with Hezekiah's rebellion in 705-701 and
more in particular with the attempts of the Judeans to keep YHWH, i.e.
the Prophet, away from their plans. Isa 30,1-5 originates from the same
situation and also opposes the attempt to conclude an alliance with
Egypt, and 30,6-7, too, can be counted with the words against this
policy of alliances. Fohrer connects sections 30,8-14 and 15-17 with
Hezekiah's rebellion against Assyria and his alliances with Egypt[63],
but, apart from the fact that most of the sections in chapters 28–31 belong to such a context, there are in the text of 30,8-17 no direct indications of that historical background and thus these verses may have
originated in a different moment of Isaiah's career. The authenticity of
30,27-33 has been strenuously debated and the historical connection of
this heavily edited text is not at all clear. According to F.J. Gonçalves,
29,5-7; 30,27-33 and 31,5.8-9 belong to the same redactional layer
while Barth includes 30,27-33 and 31,5.8b-9 with his "Assur-
redaction"[64]. In chapter 31 vv. 1-3 constitute a coherent word against
the alliance with Egypt, which belongs to the same period as 30,1-5.
Of the remaining verses of the chapter only 4-5.8a are Isaianic and it is
debatable whether v. 4 is a threat or a word of salvation. In the former
case v. 5 can only be a secondary interpretation which changes v. 4
into a word of salvation. As we have said, Barth ascribes vv. 5.8b-9 to
the "Assur-redaction. Fohrer considers Isa 32,9-14, an utterance
against the frivolous women, as Isaiah's last pronouncement[65]. The
Isaianic authenticity, however, is questionable and is rejected by Kaiser and Wildberger, whereas Barth includes the pericope with the
Isaianic texts of his "Assur-redaction".

The Proto-Isaianic part of the Book of Isaiah concludes with chapters
36–39, which are almost completely parallel to 2 Kings 18,13.17–20,19.
The material of these chapters first circulated on their own and the
Isaiah-Hezekiah-stories were inserted first in 2 Kings and adopted from

---

61. DONNER, *Israel unter den Völkern* (n. 8), pp. 154-155; DIETRICH, *Jesaja und die Politik* (n. 8), pp. 188-189.
62. *Ibid.*, p. 174; WILDBERGER, *Jesaja 13–27* (n. 49), p. 1120.
63. G. FOHRER, *Das Buch Jesaja. 2. Band* (ZBK), Zürich, 1967, p. 96.
64. F.J. GONÇALVES, *L'expédition de Sennacherib en Palestine dans la littérature hébraïque ancienne* (EB), Paris, 1986, p. 307; BARTH, *Jesaja-Worte* (n.13), pp. 334-335.
65. FOHRER, *Jesaja 2* (n. 63), p. 127.

there into the Book of Isaiah. The text underwent some minimal changes in order to make Hezekiah an even more ideal king than he already was in 2 Kings. An opposite opinion is defended by K.A.D. Smelik and C.R. Seitz: the original purpose of the stories was to function as an editorial bridge between the two major parts of the Book of Isaiah, and only later were they added to 2 Kings because of Hezekiah's exceptional role in these stories, but this position has been refuted convincingly by A.H. Konkel[66]. Anyhow, apart from 2 Kings 18,13-16, of which only v. 13 has been adopted in the Book of Isaiah (36,1), these legends contain no reliable historical information, but lack of space prevents a more detailed analysis of this problem[67].

3. RESULTS

On the politicial scene Isaiah's action is primarily related to the Syro-Ephraimitic crisis, the Ashdodite rebellion (713-711) and the rebellion against Sennacherib (705-701). The relation of many of Isaiah's utterances to these historical facts has, however, to be detected through interpretation, since the facts that occasioned the prophetic word are mostly not explicitly mentioned.

From Isa 7,6 we learn, that the main purpose of the Syro-Ephraimitic campaign against Jerusalem was to replace the king by a certain Tabe-el[68]. It was therefore a threat for the Davidic dynasty. In this situation Isaiah heartened the king on condition that he trust exclusively in YHWH, and he announced the ruin of the coalition (7,5-17*; 8,1-4; 17,1-6). The Isaianic texts do not confirm the report in 2 Kings 16,7-9 that Ahaz called in Tiglath-pileser and that renders the report very dubious, because Isaiah would certainly have protested against such an appeal to the Assyrians. The prophet supported Ahaz in his neutrality between Damascus and Assyria and hence in his opposition to the Syro-Ephraimitic coalition. S.A. Irvine appears to be right when he states that Isaiah was not against the king's policy but against that of the people (8,12 העם הזה "this people"), who were in favour of the anti-

---

66. K.A.D. SMELIK, *Distortion of Old Testament Prophecy: The Purpose of Isaiah XXXVI and XXXVII*, in *OTS* 24 (1986) 70-93, p. 74; C.R. SEITZ, *Zion's Final Destiny: The Development of the Book of Isaiah: A Reassessment of Isaiah 36–39*, Minneapolis, 1991, pp. 51-61; A.H. KONKEL, *The Sources of the Story of Hezekiah in the Book of Isaiah*, in *VT* 43 (1993) 462-482.

67. Cf. A. SCHOORS, *Die Königreiche Israel und Juda im 8. und 7. Jahrhundert v.Chr. Die assyrische Krise* (Biblische Enzyklopädie, 5), Stuttgart, (in the press).

68. MT טָבְאַל is a tendentious deformation of an original טָבְאֵל; comp. LXX ταβεηλ.

Assyrian coalition[69]. This does not mean that we can agree with all the details of his historical interpretation of Isaiah's utterances. In 8,16-18 the prophet seems to retreat temporarily because of the opposition of the people.

It is often hard to distinguish between utterances from the time of the Ashdodite rebellion and those from the period of the rebellion against Sennacherib. On both occasions the prophet warned against alliances with Egypt and against Assyria: the acted prophecy in chapter 20 is to be situated in the time of the Ashdodite rebellion, whereas 18; 28,14-22; 29,1-4a.15-16; 30,1-7; 31,1-3 are most probably connected with plans of a coalition with Egypt against Sennacherib. Nowhere is it said that Isaiah condemned the breakaway from Assyria. On the contrary, in 10,5-19 he clearly said what opinion he had of the expansionism of the Assyrians: he certainly condemned Sennacherib's campaign and he wished the victory for Jerusalem (30,15). However, he rejected Hezekiah's defensive measures as a lack of faith in YHWH (22,8b-11; 30,16). He also opposed alliances, be it with Egypt or with other nations such as the Philistines. Dietrich has aptly summarized this: "Isaiah here reproaches his countrymen with that wrong orientation which they have had all over the years: watching for the Egyptian armed forces and the own possibilities of defense instead of watching for the one who wanted first to protect and then to punish his people and whom they neither need to support militarily nor can keep away"[70]. Isaiah wished victory for his people and in the end he was sure of it. However, Judah suffered a heavy defeat but in their frivolity the people celebrated Sennacherib's retreat as a victory (22,12-13). A number of texts in the Book of Isaiah allude to the events of 701 and, in accordance with the narratives in Isa 36-37//2 Kings 18,17-19,34, interpret them as a victory over the enemies of Zion, but they are not of Isaianic origin or they have at least been reworked later on. Gonçalves would ascribe them to a redaction in Josiah's days and Barth also includes these verses with his "Assur-redaction"[71]. In this redactional layer the historical data of Isaiah's time are interpreted anew by contemporaries of Josiah (about 620-614 B.C.): YHWH is right and the wisdom of his planning and intervention is expounded in the composition 2,1–14,27* (cf. 14,24-26) as well as in the parable 28,23-29,

69. IRVINE, *Isaiah, Ahaz, and the Syro-Ephraimitic Crisis* (n. 47), pp. 278-279.

70. DIETRICH, *Israel unter den Völkern* (n. 8), p. 158: "Was Jesaja seinen Landsleuten hier zum Vorwurf macht, ist jene falsche Blickrichtung, die sie die ganzen Jahre über beibehalten haben: das ›Hinblicken‹ zu der ägyptischen Kriegsmacht und zu den eigenen Verteidigungsmöglichkeiten – statt zu dem, der sein Volk zuerst schützen und nun strafen wollte, und den man militärisch weder zu unterstützen brauchte noch fernhalten konnte".

71. GONÇALVES, *L'expédition* (n. 64), p. 540; BARTH, *Jesaja-Worte* (n. 13), *passim*.

which is some sort of commentary on 28,21, YHWH's strange deed and alien work. In God's plan for history the role of the Assyrians as an instrument of punishment against his people is limited. The "Assur-redaction" posits that "in the general framework of YHWH's plan, the judgment executed by the Assyrians is a – necessary – intermediate stage. But with the removal of all the opposing factors, not least the criminal Assyrian oppression, YHWH's action aims beyond that stage: the achievement of comprehensive salvation for his people"[72]. And this people is here Israel in its totality of the Davidic *Doppelmonarchie*.

It is rather strange that no words of Isaiah about the fall of Samaria have been handed down. True, the pericopes 9,7-10,4 and 28,1-4 are threats against Ephraim but they are quite vague, and according to 8,4 the prophet announced that "the spoil of Samaria will be carried away before the king of Assyria", but this was part of a threat which was also against Damascus. In any case, we have no further utterances of the prophet which could have explained this important event.

As for the social situation in Judah, Isaiah turned against injustice, oppression of the poor, bribery and unjust administration of justice in a context of exaggerated luxury (1,17; 3,13-15.16-24; 5,8-24*; 10,1-3), which means that in his days social injustice was a bitter reality. This is confirmed by utterances of Amos, Hosea and Micah, and by such texts as the book of the Covenant (Ex 21–23) and the legal corpus of Deuteronomy, which underwent an important editing in those days and partly reflect the same concern as the prophets[73].

Departement Oosterse en Slavische Studies   Antoon SCHOORS
Blijde-Inkomststraat 21
B-3000 Leuven

72. *Ibid.*, p. 269: "daß im Gesamtzusammenhang des Planes JHWHs das von den Assyrern vollzogene Gericht eine – notwendige – Zwischenstation war, JHWHs Handeln aber unter Aufhebung aller dem entgegenstehenden Gegebenheiten, nicht zuletzt der frevlerischen assyrischen Bedrückung, darüber hinauszielt: auf die Realisierung umfassenden Heils für sein Volk".

73. Cf. SCHOORS, *Die Köningreiche Israel und Juda* (n. 67).

HYPOTHÈSES SUR L'ORIGINE D'ISAÏE 36–39

Les chap. 36–39 du livre d'Isaïe proposent un récit en trois épisodes: l'invasion de Sennachérib et la délivrance miraculeuse de Jérusalem en l'an 701 (chap. 36–37), la maladie et la guérison d'Ézéchias (chap. 38), et enfin l'ambassade du fils du roi de Babylone à Jérusalem (chap. 39). Le prophète Isaïe intervient dans chacun des trois récits, et ses interventions forment d'ailleurs leur point commun le plus évident. À la seule exception du cantique d'Ézéchias (Is 38,9-20, propre à Isaïe), cet ensemble est presque identique à 2 R 18,13–20,19. Il est généralement présenté comme un appendice tiré du livre des Rois, de la même manière que Jr 52 est une reprise secondaire de 2 R 24,18–25,30. Dans cette perspective, Is 36–39 apparaît comme une pièce rapportée – on pourrait presque dire: un corps étranger – à l'intérieur du livre. D'autre part, l'exégèse du récit de l'invasion de Sennachérib (2 R 18,13–19,37, par. Is 36–37) reste largement tributaire de l'hypothèse proposée il y a plus d'un siècle par B. Stade[1]: il faudrait y distinguer trois récits indépendants aujourd'hui combinés[2]. Ces théories, acceptées par le plus grand nombre, n'ont cependant jamais fait l'unanimité. Dans un article paru en 1986, K.A.D. Smelik a fait valoir une série d'arguments en faveur de la priorité d'Is 36–39 sur le livre des Rois[3], et cette hypothèse a été prolongée par d'autres auteurs[4]. S'il a raison, ces chapitres ont été écrits en fonction du

* Je dédie ces pages au professeur W.A.M. Beuken, grand connaisseur du livre d'Isaïe, en gage de respectueuse et cordiale estime.

1. B. STADE, *Anmerkungen zu Kö. 15-21*, dans *ZAW* 6 (1886) 173-183.

2. À la suite de B. Stade, on distingue le plus souvent un récit A (2 R 18,13-16), un récit B1 (2 R 18,17–19,9a.36–37* par. Is 36,2–37,9a.37-38*) et un récit B2 (2 R 19,9b-35* par. Is 37,9b-36*). Sur les réactions à cette hypothèse et son adoption par le plus grand nombre des exégètes, voir F. GONÇALVES, *L'expédition de Sennachérib en Palestine dans la littérature hébraïque ancienne* (Publications de l'Institut Orientaliste de Louvain, 34), Louvain-la-Neuve, 1986, pp. 351-354. La délimitation précise des trois récits et l'ampleur des éléments secondaires restent discutées.

3. K.A.D. SMELIK, *Distortion of Old Testament Prophecy: The Purpose of Isaiah xxxvi and xxxvii*, dans COLL., *Crises and Perspectives: Studies in Ancient Near Eastern Polytheism, Biblical Theology, Palestinian Archaeology and Intertestamental Literature* (OTS, 24), Leiden, 1986, pp. 70-93. L'auteur a encore exposé sa théorie en reprenant les mêmes arguments dans *King Hezekiah Advocates True Prophecy: Remarks on Isaiah XXXVI and XXXVII / II Kings XVIII and XIX*, dans ID., *Converting the Past: Studies in Ancient Israelite and Moabite Historiography* (OTS, 28), Leiden, 1992, pp. 93-128, spéc. pp. 97-101.

4. En particulier C.R. SEITZ, *Zion's Final Destiny: The Development of the Book of Isaiah. A Reassessment of Isaiah 36–39*, Minneapolis, 1991. Voir aussi J.H. HAYES – S.A.

livre d'Isaïe, et la «théorie documentaire» proposée par Stade devient difficile à tenir. Je voudrais donc reprendre ici le dossier, avec ses deux volets. Je vérifierai tout d'abord la priorité d'Is 36–39; ceci me permettra d'élaborer ensuite quelques éléments de *Redaktionsgeschichte* de ce texte.

I. Is 36–39 et 2 R 18,13–20,19

Is 36–39 et 2 R 18,13–20,19 proposent, on le sait, des textes presque identiques[5]. Comment expliquer ce phénomène? Trois solutions simples peuvent, a priori, être envisagées: la priorité du récit de 2 Rois[6], la priorité d'Is 36–39[7] et la dépendance commune par rapport à un texte indépendant[8]. Cette troisième hypothèse apparaît cependant comme théorique, car il est impossible de déterminer la teneur et la finalité d'un tel document, ou même d'en établir l'existence. Restent les deux premiè-

IRVINE, *Isaiah. The Eighth-Century Prophet: His Time and His Preaching*, Nashville, 1987, p. 372; Claire R. MATHEWS, *Defending Zion: Edom's Desolation and Jacob's Restoration (Isaiah 34–35) in Context* (BZAW, 236), Berlin – New York, 1995, pp. 171-178.

5. On trouve une présentation synoptique des deux textes dans H. WILDBERGER, *Jesaja* (BKAT, 10), t. 3, Neukirchen-Vluyn, 1982, pp. 1484-1493.

6. Le premier à avoir suggéré cette solution semble avoir été J.G. EICHHORN, *Einleitung ins Alte Testament*, t. 3, Leipzig, ²1787, p. 74. Aujourd'hui, cette hypothèse est encore retenue par le plus grand nombre des exégètes; voir par exemple L. CAMP, *Hiskija und Hiskijabild. Analyse und Interpretation von 2 Kön 18–20* (Münchener Theologische Abhandlungen, 9), Altenberge, 1990, pp. 53-61; P. HÖFFKEN, *Das Buch Jesaja Kapitel 1–39* (Neuer Stuttgarter Kommentar. Altes Testament, 18/1), Stuttgart, 1993, pp. 18, 241. Certains commentaires du Proto-Isaïe vont même jusqu'à omettre les chap. 36–39, à l'exception du cantique d'Ézéchias; ainsi L.A. SNIJDERS, *Jesaja deel I* (POT), Nijkerk, 1979.

7. Pour l'exégèse traditionnelle, l'auteur ne peut être qu'Isaïe. Avant Smelik, on peut signaler parmi les partisans modernes de cette hypothèse: A.T. OLMSTEAD, *The Earliest Book of Kings*, dans *The American Journal of Semitic Languages and Literatures* 31 (1915) 169-214; P.R. ACKROYD, *Isaiah 36–39: Structure and Function*, dans W.C. DELSMAN *et al.* (éd.), *Von Kanaan bis Kerala*. FS J.M.P. van der Ploeg (AOAT, 211), Kevelaer - Neukirchen-Vluyn, 1982, pp. 3-21, repris dans P.R. ACKROYD, *Studies in the Religious Traditions of the Old Testament*, London, 1987, pp. 105-120, puis dans R.P. GORDON (éd.), *"The Place Is Too Small for Us": The Israelite Prophets in Recent Scholarship*, Winona Lake, 1995, pp. 478-494. Je citerai cet article à partir du recueil de 1987. Voir encore dans le même sens J.N. OSWALT, *The Book of Isaiah Chapters 1–39* (The New International Commentary on the Old Testament), Grand Rapids, 1986, pp. 699-703; R.E. CLEMENTS, *The Prophecies of Isaiah to Hezekiah Concerning Sennacherib 2 Kings 19.21-34 // Isa. 37.22-35*, dans R. LIWAK – S. WAGNER (éd.), *Prophetie und geschichtliche Wirklichkeit im alten Israel*. FS S. Herrmann, Stuttgart, 1991, pp. 65-78 (spéc. p. 69); C.R. SEITZ, *Isaiah 1–39* (Interpretation), Louisville, 1993, pp. 9, 243-244.

8. Cette hypothèse a été proposée notamment par W.M.L. DE WETTE, *Lehrbuch der historisch-kritischen Einleitung*, Berlin, ⁷1852, p. 287. Voir aujourd'hui dans ce sens A. LAATO, *Who Is Immanuel? The Rise and Foundering of Isaiah's Messianic Expectations*, Åbo, 1988, pp. 271-296, spéc. 203-204.

res[9]. Examinons les différentes pièces du dossier, et en particulier les arguments invoqués en faveur de chaque hypothèse.

1. La comparaison attentive des deux textes montre une série de différences, dont la plupart peuvent être qualifiées de minimes. Après un examen attentif du TM – et sans tenir compte de 2 R 18,14-16 comme d'Is 38,9-20, passages propres à un seul texte –, F. Gonçalves observe au total 146 différences, dont 38 «plus» de 2 Rois et 21 «plus» d'Isaïe[10]. Il ajoute que ces derniers ne dépassent jamais un mot et n'affectent guère le sens du texte, tandis que les «plus» de 2 Rois comportent des propositions[11] et des incises[12] de quelques mots. A priori, ces observations sont nettement favorables à la priorité du texte d'Isaïe, car le mouvement habituel n'est pas celui de l'abréviation, mais au contraire celui de l'expansion[13]. Cependant les choses ne sont pas si simples: il faut tenir compte de la possibilité d'ajouts postérieurs au dédoublement du texte[14]. Tel est, presque certainement, le cas du «cantique d'Ézéchias» ajouté en Is 38,9-20, et un phénomène semblable peut avoir affecté 2 R 18–20. L'observation des différences entre les deux textes ne peut donc prouver la priorité de l'un d'entre eux[15]. Il n'empêche qu'elle va plutôt dans le sens de la dépendance du texte de 2 Rois par rapport à celui d'Is 36–39.

9. Il faut aussi tenir compte avec la possibilité de théories plus complexes. Ainsi, SEITZ, *Zion's Final Destiny* (n. 4), pp. 186-191, estime qu'Is 36–38 livre le texte de base des récits de la délivrance de Jérusalem et de la guérison d'Ézéchias, mais que le récit de la visite de Mérodach-Baladan à Jérusalem a au contraire son texte original en 2 R 20,12-19.

10. GONÇALVES, *L'expédition* (n. 2), p. 331.

11. Is 18,17bαß.18aα.28bα.32aα.ß.bα; 19,20bß.35aα; 20,4a.5b.7b.8aγ.9aα.9b-11a.

12. 18,17a.34a; 20,5aα.6bßγ.8b. Cette liste, comme celle de la note précédente, provient de GONÇALVES, *L'expédition* (n. 2), p. 331.

13. C'est ce que rappelle notamment WILDBERGER, *Jesaja* (n. 5), t. 3, p. 1372. L'auteur souligne, par exemple, que le rédacteur d'Is 36 n'avait aucune raison de supprimer au v. 2 la mention du général en chef (*tartan*) et du grand eunuque (*rab-sarîs*), qui figurent en 2 R 18,17. Il relève cependant que, dans quelques cas au moins, le texte de 2 Rois paraît primitif par rapport à celui d'Is.

14. WILDBERGER, *Jesaja*, (n. 5), p. 1373; GONÇALVES, *L'expédition* (n. 2), p. 348. De plus, il faut tenir compte des manuscrits de la Mer Morte et des versions anciennes. Ainsi, A.H. KONKEL, *The Sources of the Story of Hezekiah in the Book of Isaiah*, dans *VT* 43 (1993) 462-481, s'appuie sur le témoignage de la recension καιγε de la LXX pour confirmer la priorité du texte de 1 R 18–20; en fait, les choses ne sont pas simples, et Konkel lui-même écrit: «There are also indications that the Hezekiah story was related to Isaianic materials before being incorporated in Kings» (p. 477).

15. C. HARDMEIER, *Prophetie im Streit vor dem Untergang Judas. Erzählkommunikative Studien zur Entstehungssituation der Jesaja- und Jeremiaerzählungen in II Reg 18–20 und Jer 37–40* (BZAW, 187), Berlin - New York, 1990, p. 125, estime que le texte d'Is 36–39 se caractérise par une plus grande uniformité du vocabulaire et un meilleur style; en vertu du principe *lectio difficilior potior*, nous aurions ainsi un indice de la priorité du texte de 2 R 18–20. L'auteur ne donne cependant aucun exemple concret à l'appui de cette affirmation.

2. Le «plus» de 2 R 18,14-16 forme un cas particulier, invoqué à l'appui des deux hypothèses principales. Ces versets, qui relatent la soumission d'Ézéchias et la livraison d'un important tribut à Sennachérib, sont écrits dans le style des sources de l'école deutéronomiste et fournissent sans doute des renseignements de grande valeur historique[16]. Comment expliquer leur omission dans le livre d'Isaïe? Les uns y voient le signe de l'antériorité d'Is 36–39[17]; d'autres rétorquent que le rédacteur d'Is 36–39 a pu omettre ce passage soit par accident[18], soit consciemment, parce que ce passage peu glorieux ne concernait directement ni le prophète ni le sort de Jérusalem[19]. Pour Gonçalves[20], le problème revient surtout à se demander si le v. 13 (par. Is 36,1) a été écrit comme introduction à cet épisode ou plutôt comme introduction à celui de l'envoi du grand échanson (Is 36,2ss, récit B1). Après discussion, l'auteur tranche en faveur de la première hypothèse[21], et je pense qu'il faut, en effet, admettre cette opinion comme la plus vraisemblable[22]. Caractérisé par l'emploi de titres officiels, mais aussi par sa concision et l'absence de toute dimension légendaire, 2 R 18,13-16 se présente comme un récit ancien, qui reproduit sans doute un document officiel[23]. Ceci étant acquis, aurions-nous ici un indice probant de la priorité du texte de 2 R 18–20 sur celui d'Is 36–39? Il faut répondre par la négative. En effet, le cas trouve un parallèle remarquable dans la reprise presque littérale de 2 R 16,5 en Is 7,1[24]. Chaque fois, le rédacteur isaïen reprend l'assaut par le

16. E. RUPRECHT, *Die ursprüngliche Komposition der Hiskia-Jesaja-Erzählungen und ihre Umstrukturierung durch den Verfasser des deuteronomistischen Geschichtswerkes*, dans *ZTK* 87 (1990) 33-66, p. 35, objecte qu'il n'y a pas concordance avec les sources assyriennes: Sennachérib s'y vante d'avoir «enfermé Ézéchias comme un oiseau dans une cage», ce qui supposerait un siège en bonne et due forme. Mais les documents assyriens sont-ils nécessairement plus objectifs sur ce point que le récit biblique? GONÇALVES, *L'expédition* (n. 2), p. 117, écrit d'ailleurs avec raison: «Le récit de *II Rois*, XVIII,13-16 et la partie du récit des annales de Sennachérib concernant ses hostilités avec Juda présentent certes quelques différences, mais s'accordent pour l'essentiel».

17. Ainsi, SEITZ, *Zion's Final Destiny* (n. 4), pp. 51-61; ID., *Account A and the Annals of Sennacherib: A Reassessment*, dans *JSOT* 58 (1993) 47-57.

18. B.S. CHILDS, *Isaiah and the Assyrian Crisis* (Studies in Biblical Theology, Second Series, 3), London, 1967, pp. 69-70, n. 1, pense que l'omission est due au passage accidentel du *wayyišlaḥ* du début du v. 14 à celui du début du v. 17.

19. Ainsi, GONÇALVES, *L'expédition* (n. 2), pp. 347-348; HARDMEIER, *Prophetie im Streit* (n. 15), pp. 108-117, 125.

20. GONÇALVES, *L'expédition* (n. 2), pp. 344-345.

21. *Ibid.*, pp. 356-361.

22. Malgré les observations faites par RUPRECHT, *Die ursprüngliche Komposition* (n. 16), p. 36.

23. GONÇALVES, *L'expédition* (n. 2), pp. 367-372.

24. Voir SMELIK, *Distortion* (n. 3), p. 73. Le texte d'Isaïe est légèrement différent: la mention d'«Achaz fils de Yotam» et «roi de Juda» semble provenir de 2 R 16,1, qui appartient au fond pré-deutéronomiste du livre; la mention d'Ozias pourrait avoir été suggé-

roi ennemi avec son résultat, mais il omet l'épisode suivant (ancien), qui parle de l'envoi d'émissaires auprès du roi d'Assyrie et du versement d'un tribut[25]. En Is 7, le rédacteur ajoute le v. 2 (terreur de la «maison de David» et du peuple)[26], puis il introduit les oracles d'Isaïe qui annoncent l'échec des envahisseurs (vv. 3-17)[27]: les événements de l'année 734 sont ainsi présentés dans la ligne de l'inviolabilité de Jérusalem. Or nous avons le même phénomène aux chap. 36–37: la capitulation honteuse d'Ézéchias est remplacée par un long texte faisant état de l'intervention d'Isaïe, puis de la délivrance miraculeuse de Jérusalem. L'analogie des procédés rédactionnels[28] et de la tendance théologique plaide en faveur de la priorité d'Is 36–39 par rapport à 2 R 18–20, même s'il est vrai que 2 R 18,13-16 est plus ancien qu'Is 36,1.

rée par Is 6,1, le rédacteur voulant ménager un lien entre les chap. 6 et 7. D'autre part, Is 7,1 omet les mots *wayyasurû 'al-'āḥāz*, «Ils assiégèrent Achaz». On a fait remarquer le caractère peu usuel de cette dernière expression: le siège est en principe dirigé contre une ville, et non contre un roi. Mais «assiéger quelqu'un» est encore attesté en 2 S 20,15, et l'expression convient bien au contexte historique: les assaillants ne veulent pas conquérir Jérusalem, mais ils s'en prennent au roi qui refuse d'entrer dans leur coalition. Il n'y a donc pas lieu de corriger le texte de 2 R 16,5; voir dans ce sens M. COGAN – H. TADMOR, *II Kings* (AB, 11), New York, 1988, p. 186. L'omission de l'expression en Is 7,1 va de pair avec celle des vv. 6-9 et montre que celle-ci ne tient pas seulement à des raisons de chronologie (l'intervention du prophète aurait eu lieu avant l'ambassade auprès de Senna-chérib): le rédacteur a tendance à supprimer ce qui porte ombrage à Jérusalem et à son roi.

25. SEITZ, *Zion's Final Destiny* (n. 4), p. 57, relève combien 2 R 16,5.7-9 et 18,13-16 sont parallèles. 2 R 16,5-9 est généralement reconnu comme matériau pré-deutérono-miste, au moins en substance; voir par exemple G.H. JONES, *1 and 2 Kings* (NCBC), t. 2, Grand Rapids - London, 1984, p. 532.

26. Le v. 2, qui n'a pas d'équivalent en 2 R 16, parle d'événements antérieurs à ceux que raconte la finale du v. 1 («mais il ne put l'attaquer»); il n'est plus question de Resîn et de Peqah, mais d'Aram et d'Éphraïm. En conséquence, de nombreux auteurs pensent que ce verset constitue – éventuellement avec les mots *wayᵉhî biméy 'āḥāz*, «au temps d'Achaz» (v. 1aα), l'introduction primitive du chap. 7. Cette solution ne s'impose pas: sans le v. 1, le début du récit serait abrupt, car le lecteur ignorerait le cadre historique. Les différences avec le v. 1 trouvent une autre explication: alors que ce dernier reproduit en substance un document plus ancien, le v. 2 est rédactionnel: il interprète la finale de ce v. 1 en un sens nouveau, en fonction du v. 4 («Ne crains pas»): ce n'est pas l'échec de la coalition, mais une halte de l'armée syrienne en Éphraïm, d'où la panique d'Achaz. L'ex-pression *béyt dāwid*, «maison de David», a pu être inspirée par le v. 13, comme la men-tion du «cœur» (*lébab*) d'Achaz a pu l'être par le v. 4.

27. Telle est la teneur actuelle du texte, qui souligne en particulier la fin d'Éphraïm (vv. 8b-9) et l'abandon de la terre dont «les deux rois jettent (Achaz) dans l'épouvante» (v. 16b, avec une référence au v. 2). Ce message ne correspond cependant pas à la teneur originelle des oracles d'Isaïe. L'oracle de l'Emmanuel, notamment, avait dans la bouche du prophète une portée avant tout menaçante; par l'addition du v. 16bß, il a été relu dans un sens de promesse en faveur de Jérusalem; voir dans la même ligne la reprise du nom d'«Emmanuel» en 8,8b,10.

28. Notons aussi la présence parallèle du signe de l'Emmanuel (7,14-17) et du signe de la récolte lors de la troisième année (37,30).

3. Smelik relève le silence de l'«histoire deutéronomiste» à propos des prophètes «classiques» dont les oracles ont été recueillis dans les livres qui portent leurs noms[29]. En revanche, on peut observer que le livre d'Isaïe comporte aussi des récits (chap. 7 et 20). Tout ceci convient à l'hypothèse de la priorité d'Is 36–39, mais il faut avouer que l'argument du silence est toujours fragile, et qu'il n'a pas valeur de preuve.

4. E.W. Conrad[30] souligne le parallélisme entre Is 7 («histoire d'Achaz») et Is 36–39 («histoire d'Ézéchias»), deux histoires royales écrites l'une et l'autre à la troisième personne. Il ne fait guère référence à la discussion sur 7,1 et 36,1, mais il note les points suivants:

– Les deux récits s'ouvrent par l'invasion par une armée étrangère (7,1-2; 36,2);
– La menace sur Jérusalem est exprimée chaque fois «près du canal de la piscine supérieure, sur le chemin du champ du foulon» (7,3; 36,2);
– Le roi de Juda est saisi d'une grande frayeur (7,2; 37,1);
– Face à cette situation, Isaïe délivre un «oracle de guerre», qui s'ouvre par l'appel à ne pas craindre (*'al-tîrā'*) et annonce la défaite ennemie (7,4-9; 37,6-7);
– Chaque fois, le prophète donne au roi un signe (*'ôt*), destiné à confirmer l'accomplissement de l'oracle (7,10-16: 37,30-32);
– Les deux récits racontent comment Jérusalem est épargnée, mais ils s'achèvent par l'annonce d'une nouvelle catastrophe (7,15-17.20; 39,6-7).

Même si le rapprochement est plus évident pour certains points que pour d'autres[31], la parenté entre l'«histoire d'Achaz» et l'«histoire d'Ézéchias» est réelle. Conrad relève aussi des différences significatives; en particulier, Ézéchias est bien plus actif qu'Achaz: il se rend de lui-même au temple, sollicite la prière d'Isaïe, prie lui-même, et la délivrance de Jérusalem a un retentissement bien plus grand qu'au chap. 7. Ajoutons que le contraste entre Achaz et Ézéchias porte aussi sur la foi manquante du premier (cf. 7,9b et 10-13) et sur la foi réelle du second (voir en particulier 37,16-20). Il semble donc que les chap. 7 et 36–37 forment système. En d'autres termes, l'«histoire d'Ézéchias» a été, au moins par-

29. SMELIK, *Distortion* (n. 33), p. 72. Sur la question du silence de l'«histoire deutéronomiste», voir K. KOCH, *Das Prophetenschweigen des deuteronomistischen Geschichtswerks*, dans J. JEREMIAS – L. PERLITT (éd.), *Die Botschaft und die Boten*. FS H.W. Wolff, Neukirchen-Vluyn, 1981, pp. 115-128.

30. E.W. CONRAD, *The Royal Narratives and the Structure of the Book of Isaiah*, dans *JSOT* 41 (1988) 67-81.

31. Le dernier élément, en particulier, apparaît comme faible, car l'annonce du sac du Temple (39,6-7) appartient à un autre récit.

tiellement, rédigée en fonction du chap. 7. Encore une fois, cet élément est favorable à la thèse de la priorité d'Isaïe.

5. Plusieurs autres éléments du récit sont empruntés ou tout au moins apparentés à la tradition isaïenne. Mentionnons les exemples les plus saillants:

– 2 R 18,18.26 par Is 36,3.11: on retrouve ici, associés, les noms des maîtres du palais Élyaqim fils de Hilqiyyahu (Is 22,20) et Shebna (Is 22,15), alors qu'en Is 22 le second est destitué au profit du premier;
– L'expression *'éṣāh ûgbûrāh*, «conseil et force» (2 R 18,20 par. Is 36,5) est également attestée en Is 11,2 et peut lui avoir été empruntée;
– Le verbe *baṭaḥ*, «avoir confiance», utilisé en 2 R 18,19.20.21a.21b. 22.24.30 par. Is 36,4.5.6a.6b.9.10.15 (la confiance des Judéens en Pharaon ou en YHWH), ainsi qu'en 2 R 19,10 par. Is 37,10 (la confiance d'Ézéchias en YHWH), fait écho à Is 30,15 (les Judéens n'ont pas eu confiance); 31,1 (les Judéens mettent leur confiance dans l'armée égyptienne) et 32,9.10.11 (les femmes de Jérusalem avec leur prétention, alors que la ville sera ruinée, vv. 12-14);
– Le motif des chars (*rèkèb*) et des cavaliers (*pārāšîm*) d'Égypte (2 R 18,24 par. Is 36,9) paraît emprunté à Is 31,1 (mêmes mots, associés au même verbe *bāṭaḥ*);
– La prétention de Sennachérib d'avoir été envoyé par YHWH (2 R 18,25 par. Is 36,10) correspond à Is 10,5-6;
– La vantardise de Sennachérib, qui se flatte d'avoir vaincu les dieux des nations et diverses villes, dont Hamat, Arpad et Samarie (2 R 18,33-34 par. Is 36,18-19; voir aussi 2 R 19,12-13 par. Is 37,12-13) peut être rapprochée d'Is 10,9-11, où le roi d'Assyrie se voit reprocher son orgueil d'avoir pris Hamat, Arpad, et Samarie avec leurs idoles;
– Le thème du «reste» (*šeʾérît*, 2 R 19,4.30.31 par. Is 37,4.32) apparaît fréquemment dans le livre d'Isaïe (*šeʾérît*, Is 14,30; 15,9; 46,3; *šeʾār*, Is 10,19.20.21.22; 11,11.16; 14,22; 16,14; 17,3; 21,17; 28,5);
– L'expression *qedôš yiśrāʾél*, «le Saint d'Israël» (2 R 19,22 par. Is 37,23) est caractéristique du livre d'Isaïe[32]; en revanche, l'apposition du mot *ṣebāʾôt* – autre caractéristique isaïenne[33] – au nom divin n'est attestée qu'en Is 37,16.32 et 39,5 et non dans le texte parallèle de 2 R[34];
– Le discours prêté à Sennachérib en 2 R 19,23-24 par. Is 37,24-25 est comme l'écho du discours orgueilleux du roi de Babylone en Is 14,13-14;

32. L'expression est utilisée 25 fois en Is, pour 6 fois dans reste de la Bible hébraïque.
33. Voir Is 1,9.24; 2,12; 3,1.15; etc.
34. Sinon en 2 R 19,31 Q; nous avons ici un cas particulier, car la phrase est identique à Is 9,6b. Dans les trois cas, le «plus» d'Isaïe peut relever d'une activité rédactionnelle postérieure au redoublement.

– La locution *ḥattû wābōšû*, «ils tremblent et sont honteux» (2 R 19,26
par. Is 37,27) connaît sa seule autre occurrence en Is 20,5;
– Le motif du signe (2 R 19,29 par. 37,30; 2 R 20,8.9 cf. Is 38,7.21)
renvoie au signe de l'Emmanuel (Is 7,14; voir aussi 8,18);
– 2 R 19,31b par. Is 37,32b est identique à Is 9,6b; H.G.M. Williamson[35] relève en outre que la première partie du même verset est
construite d'une manière semblable à Is 2,3b;
– La protection dont YHWH fait bénéficier Jérusalem (2 R 19,32-34
par. Is 37,33-35) est un thème récurrent dans le livre d'Isaïe; voir en
particulier Is 31,5, où l'on retrouve le même verbe *ganan*, «protéger»
(2 R 19,34; 20,6 par. Is 37,35; 38,5); l'annonce de la délivrance anticipe, par ailleurs, le thème majeur de la consolation de Sion/Jérusalem
en Is 40–66.

Nous constatons donc des liens multiples et souvent précis avec Is 1–35,
alors que les mêmes motifs sont le plus souvent absents du reste de l'histoire deutéronomiste. Ces liens supposent une grande familiarité avec le
Proto-Isaïe en voie de formation[36]; ils s'expliquent au mieux dans le cadre du livre d'Isaïe, alors qu'ils ne s'expliquent guère dans l'hypothèse
de la priorité du récit du livre des Rois.

6. P.R. Ackroyd[37] souligne qu'Is 36–39 prépare la perspective de la
restauration de Sion, qui sera développée à partir du chap. 40: le récit
serait comme une préface à la seconde partie du livre. Si l'on prend l'ensemble du livre d'Isaïe, tant la délivrance de Jérusalem attaquée par Sennachérib (chap. 36–37) que la guérison d'Ézéchias (chap. 38) préfigu-
rent, en effet, la consolation de Sion; la visite du babylonien
Mérodach-Baladan à Jérusalem (chap. 39), de son côté, annonce les événements de 587, et cet épisode prépare ainsi, par contraste, le chap. 40[38].

35. H.G.M. WILLIAMSON, *The Book Called Isaiah: Deutero-Isaiah's Role in Composition and Redaction*, Oxford, 1994, p. 193.
36. C'est ce que reconnaît Williamson (*ibid.*, pp. 193-194), bien qu'il refuse l'hypothèse de la priorité d'Is 36–39.
37. ACKROYD, *Isaiah 36–39* (n. 7), pp. 109,119; voir déjà avant lui R.F. MELUGIN,
The Formation of Isaiah 40–55 (BZAW, 141), Berlin - New York, 1976, pp. 176-178.
38. Pour ACKROYD, *Isaiah 36–39* (n. 7), pp. 106-109, l'ordre des chap. 36–39 n'est
explicable que par cette volonté d'offrir une transition vers la seconde partie du livre;
voir déjà ID., *An Interpretation of the Babylonian Exile: A Study of 2 Kings 20*, dans
ScotJT 27 (1974) 329-352, repris dans P.R. ACKROYD, *Studies in the Religious Traditions
of the Old Testament*, London, 1987, pp. 152-171 (spéc. p. 160). En effet, les récits ne
suivent pas l'ordre chronologique; cet argument est également souligné par SMELIK,
Distortion (n. 3), pp. 73-74, ainsi que par MATHEWS, *Defending Zion* (n. 4), pp. 171-174.
WILLIAMSON, *The Book Called Isaiah* (n. 35), pp. 208-209, répond en deux temps: d'une
part, l'épisode de la visite de Mérodach-Baladan à Jérusalem prépare aussi 2 R 24,12-16;
d'autre part, le lien est loin d'être idéal. J'ajouterais pour ma part que l'ordre d'Is 36-39

Les récits concernant Ézéchias et Isaïe assurent ainsi une certaine transition entre les deux grandes parties du livre[39]. Rien, pourtant, ne permet de penser que ces chapitres aient été composés dans ce but. En effet, les points de contact entre les chap. 36–39 et 40–66 sont assez peu nombreux, peu précis et concentrés dans une seule section du texte (37,23-29)[40]. Williamson[41], qui cherche pourtant à montrer comment le Deutéro-Isaïe a été influencé par la prédication du prophète du VIIIᵉ siècle et qu'il a utilisé le recueil de ses oracles comme première partie de sa propre œuvre, en arrive à conclure que les contacts se réduisent ici à peu de choses: le lien thématique (mais sans contact particulier au niveau du vocabulaire) entre les chap. 39 et 40, la similitude de 37,26 avec plusieurs textes deutéro-isaïens[42], et enfin la locution *lᵉma'anî*, «à cause de moi» (cf. 43,25; 48,9; 55,5) en 37,35. Il est donc improbable que les chap. 36–39 aient été écrits comme «pont» entre les deux grandes parties du livre d'Isaïe. L'effet de transition peut être expliqué dans le cadre des deux hypothèses envisagées ici. D'une part, les chap. 40–66 ont été d'autant plus facilement joints à la première partie du livre (ou écrits en ayant cette première partie sous les yeux) que le livre se terminait par des perspectives de salut et par des allusions à l'oppression babylonienne; il faut d'ailleurs compter avec une rédaction en plusieurs étapes, certaines d'entre elles étant postérieures à la formation du «grand» livre d'Isaïe avec ses deux volets principaux. D'autre part, dans l'hypothèse de la priorité de 2 R 18–20, on aura d'autant plus volontiers inséré ce matériau dans le livre d'Isaïe qu'il permettait de ménager une transition entre ses deux grandes parties[43].

peut s'expliquer par l'histoire de la rédaction du texte, comme je le montrerai plus loin. La théorie de RUPRECHT, *Die ursprüngliche Komposition* (n. 16), pp. 33-66, selon laquelle l'ordre du récit primitif (guérison d'Ézéchias, ambassade de Mérodach-Baladan, puis siège et délivrance de Jérusalem) a été renversé par Dtr pour permettre l'interprétation de la visite du trésor du Temple comme annonce des événements de 598 (cf. 2 R 24,13), me paraît peu vraisemblable: une telle interprétation était également possible dans l'ordre supposé primitif.

39. Voir par exemple OSWALT, *The Book of Isaiah Chapters 1–39* (n. 7), pp. 672-673; S.H. WIDYAPRANAWA, *The Lord Is Savior: Faith in National Crisis. Isaiah 1–39* (International Theological Commentary), Grand Rapids - Edinburgh, 1990, p. 229; SEITZ, *Isaiah 1–39* (n. 7), p. 14.

40. Les principales similitudes sont relevées par J.W. GROVES, *Actualization and Interpretation in the Old Testament* (SBL DS, 86), Atlanta, 1987, pp. 198-199.

41. WILLIAMSON, *The Book Called Isaiah* (n. 35), pp. 195-197.

42. 40,21; 41,4.26; 44,7-8; 45,21; 46,9-11; 48,3-5; 51,9-10. L'auteur fait cependant remarquer que la première partie de 37,26 – celle qui apparaît la plus «deutéro-isaïenne» – manque dans le Vaticanus, témoin le plus ancien de la LXX; il faut donc se demander si la phase ne constitue pas une addition très tardive.

43. Remarquons toutefois que les chap. 33–35 fournissent une transition meilleure encore.

7. L'analogie avec le cas de Jr 52 parallèle à 2 R 24,18–25,30 est souvent invoquée en faveur de la priorité de 2 R 18–20[44], car ici le doute n'est pas permis: la notice de Jr 51,64 («Jusqu'ici les paroles de Jérémie») montrent bien que le chap. 52 est une addition. Cependant les deux cas ne sont pas identiques, car Jr 52 ne dit pas un mot de Jérémie et n'entretient aucun lien particulier (thématique ou de vocabulaire) avec le reste du livre. Au contraire – nous l'avons vu –, les liens entre Is 36–39 et 1–35 sont importants. Autre différence significative: les «plus» sont, cette fois, du côté de Jr 52. Il ne paraît donc pas possible de tirer argument de Jr 52 pour affirmer la priorité de 2 R 18–20[45].

8. Gonçalves relève un autre élément apparemment favorable à la priorité du texte de 2 R 18–20: «si l'on excluait *II Rois*, XVIII,13-XX,19 des récits relatifs à Ézéchias, il faudrait en retrancher aussi *II Rois*, XVIII,5-6.7b et 9-12»[46]. En effet, le jugement positif que le rédacteur deutéronomiste porte sur le règne d'Ézéchias paraît aller de pair avec le récit de la délivrance miraculeuse de Jérusalem, qui récompense la bonne conduite du roi. En fait, l'argument n'est pas décisif. Imaginons que l'auteur deutéronomiste ignore la tradition de l'intervention divine lors de la campagne de Sennachérib en Palestine, ou qu'il la refuse comme trop liée à la théologie de l'inviolabilité de Sion. N'aurait-il pu écrire les vv. 5-12? Je pense que rien ne s'y oppose: le jugement favorable sur le roi est motivé par sa réforme religieuse (v. 4) et trouve sa récompense dans sa victoire sur les Philistins (v. 8); quant au rappel de la prise de Samarie, déjà racontée au chap. 17, il s'explique par la volonté d'atténuer l'impact des événements de 701, rapportés aux vv. 13-16. Juda a été envahi, Ézéchias a dû payer un lourd tribut, mais Jérusalem n'a pas subi le sort de Samarie: elle n'a pas été assiégée, n'a pas été prise par la force, et sa population n'a pas été déportée. En d'autres termes, Samarie a subi en 722/720 le sort qui sera celui de Jérusalem sous Nabuchodonosor, à causse de son infidélité, mais la Jérusalem d'Ézéchias est restée intacte. Il me paraît donc impossible de prouver que l'écriture de 2 R 18,1-12 suppose la connaissance de la délivrance de la ville, racontée à partir de 18,17.

9. Williamson rapporte encore, à l'appui de la priorité de 2 R 18–20, les importantes divergences qui affectent le récit de la guérison d'Ézé-

---

44. Voir par exemple WILDBERGER, *Jesaja* (n. 5), t. 3, p. 1370.
45. Voir dans la même ligne ACKROYD, *Isaiah 36–39* (n. 7), p. 108.
46. GONÇALVES, *L'expédition* (n. 2), p. 346.

chias (2 R 20,1-11 par. Is 38)[47]. Il y a tout d'abord le «psaume d'Ézéchias» (Is 38,9-20), qui ne figure pas dans le texte de 2 R. Comme Ackroyd[48] l'a montré, ce psaume utilise une série de métaphores qui, dans les livres de Jérémie et des Lamentations, se réfèrent à la situation de l'Exil. Le psaume interprète donc la guérison d'Ézéchias dans un sens métaphorique: il s'agit en réalité de la restauration de la communauté, comme le confirme d'ailleurs le v. 20, avec l'apparition soudaine du «nous» et du motif du Temple. Williamson ajoute: comme l'histoire deutéronomiste est réticente à l'idée d'une telle restauration, on comprendrait que le psaume ait été ajouté au moment du transfert de l'histoire d'Ézéchias dans le livre d'Isaïe[49]. Surtout, l'ordre actuel des récits s'expliquerait par la priorité de 2 R 20,1-11. On y trouve, en effet, deux épisodes juxtaposés: les vv. 1-7 forment une unité littéraire complète, qui s'achève par la guérison du roi; ensuite seulement, Ézéchias demande et obtient un signe de sa prochaine guérison (vv. 8-11)! Logiquement, la demande du signe aurait dû évidemment venir avant la guérison. Or, l'ordre logique est précisément rétabli dans le récit d'Is 38, où l'annonce de la guérison (vv. 5-6) est immédiatement suivie par celle du signe (vv. 7-8)! Cette opération littéraire a cependant introduit une nouvelle difficulté: le discours juxtapose désormais le «je» divin (vv. 5b-6) et la mention de YHWH à la troisième personne (v. 7)[50]. En d'autres termes, l'auteur d'Is 38 a voulu corriger le texte déficient de 2 R 20[51]. Mais cette explication s'impose-t-elle?

Si l'on ne tient pas compte du «cantique d'Ézéchias», qui forme une pièce ajoutée tardivement, le récit du livre des Rois est sensiblement plus long que celui du livre d'Isaïe, et ses «plus» s'expliquent au mieux comme autant de développements secondaires. Ainsi, 2 R 20 ajoute au v. 4a: «Isaïe n'était pas encore sorti de la cour[52] centrale»; le rédacteur souligne ainsi l'exceptionnelle rapidité de la réponse divine, qui correspond à la fidélité tout aussi exceptionnelle du roi. De même, au v. 5b, il ajoute: «Je vais te guérir: dans trois jours, tu monteras au Temple de YHWH»; on retrouve ici les deux mêmes préoccupations: la rapidité de l'intervention divine (il ne s'agit plus seulement d'ajouter quelques an-

---

47. WILLIAMSON, *The Book Called Isaiah* (n. 35), pp. 202-208; ces pages ont été reprises avec quelques modifications sous le titre *Hezekiah and the Temple*, dans M.V. FOX et al. (éd.), *Texts, Temples, and Traditions*. FS M Haran, Winona Lake, 1996, pp. 47-52. Voir dans le même sens COGAN – TADMOR, *II Kings* (n. 24), pp. 256-257.

48. ACKROYD, *An Interpretation* (n. 38), pp. 165-166.

49. WILLIAMSON, *The Book Called Isaiah* (n. 35), p. 203.

50. Ceci a été relevé par C. JEREMIAS, *Zu Jes. xxxiii 21f.*, dans *VT* 21 (1971) 104-111.

51. WILLIAMSON, *The Book Called Isaiah* (n. 35), pp. 204-205.

52. Il faut probablement suivre 1QIs[a], certains manuscrits hébreux et les versions, et lire *hèḥāṣér* au lieu de *hā'îr* (TM).

nées à la vie du roi, mais aussi de le guérir immédiatement) et la piété d'Ézéchias, attaché au Temple[53]. De même encore, la version de 2 R 20 souligne le caractère miraculeux du recul de l'ombre, ce qui apparaît clairement comme un développement secondaire[54].

Le récit d'Is 38 peut s'expliquer sans recours à celui de 2 R 20. Au v. 5, Isaïe répond très exactement à la situation décrite au v. 1, ainsi qu'à la prière formulée par Ézéchias aux vv. 2-3. Le v. 6, en revanche, introduit un élément nouveau, qui s'explique seulement par le rapprochement de l'épisode avec les événements racontés aux chap. 37–38: la délivrance de la ville, de la main du roi d'Assyrie; la formulation du verset est d'ailleurs partiellement empruntée à 37,35. La vie prolongée d'Ézéchias devient signe de la survie de Jérusalem. Cet élément, commun aux deux versions du récit, est cependant antérieur au redoublement. Le v. 21, enfin, formait la conclusion originelle de l'épisode[55]; le témoignage du livre des Rois montre qu'il suivait immédiatement le v. 6. En revanche, le don du signe (vv. 7-8), qui fait concurrence avec l'application du pain de figues (v. 21)[56], est secondaire; il a pu être suggéré par 37,30 ou inséré en parallèle avec ce verset. Le v. 22, enfin, est sans doute une glose marginale inspirée par 2 R 20,8. Le passage du «je» divin (vv. 5-6) à la mention de «YHWH» (v. 7), dans le discours d'Isaïe, s'explique par le fait que le «je» du v. 8 est celui du prophète[57].

Il reste à expliquer pourquoi 2 R 20,1-11 place le don du signe après la guérison d'Ézéchias, survenue au v. 7. La difficulté est réelle, quelle que soit l'idée qu'on se fait du rapport à Is 38: même si l'on affirme que les vv. 8-11 forment un élément secondaire, comment a-t-on pu le placer après le v. 7? Dans l'hypothèse d'une dépendance par rapport à Is 38, on peut tenter l'explication suivante. La concurrence entre le signe surnaturel (vv. 7-8) et le remède naturel, qui suivait immédiatement (v. 21) a dû être ressentie comme une difficulté. C'est pourquoi les deux éléments ont été intervertis et ré-interprétés dans 2 R 20, comme s'ils faisaient référence à des réalités différentes: la survie d'abord, la guérison rapide de l'ulcère ensuite. En Is 38,21, l'application du pain de figues n'était

---

53. Voir WILDBERGER, *Jesaja* (n. 5), t. 3, p. 1446. La référence au Temple correspond au point de vue longuement exprimé en 2 Ch 29-31.

54. Voir en ce sens *ibid.*, p. 1452; RUPRECHT, *Die ursprüngliche Komposition* (n. 16), p. 40. Le miracle est plus éclatant encore qu'à Gabaôn, quand YHWH avait arrêté le soleil (Jg 10,12-13): cette fois, il l'a fait reculer!

55. Au contraire du v. 22, rien n'indique que ce verset doive être considéré comme une addition tardive; voir V. HOFFER, *An Exegesis of Isaiah 38.31*, dans *JSOT* 56 (1992) 69-84.

56. À quoi bon le signe de l'ombre qui recule, si l'application du pain de figues guérit l'ulcère? La guérison elle-même atteste la véracité de la promesse.

57. WILDBERGER, *Jesaja* (n. 5), t. 3, p. 1452.

qu'ordonnée, avec la promesse $w^e y è h î$, «et il vivra»; ainsi se terminait le récit, auquel il manquait la réalisation effective de la promesse. 2 R 20,7 rapporte l'exécution de l'ordre et note son résultat[58], en reprenant le même verbe et la même forme consonantique, mais avec une vocalisation différente: $wayyèhî$, que l'on peut traduire ici par: «et il survécut». Le rédacteur interprète ensuite le signe de l'ombre comme annonce de la guérison ($yirpā'$, v. 8), thème absent d'Is 38 mais déjà introduit en 2 R 20,5b et lié à la présence au Temple au bout de trois jours. Tout ceci s'inscrit sans trop de difficulté dans le cadre de la relecture d'ensemble opérée par le rédacteur de 2 R 20,1-11.

Malgré les observations de Williamson, la balance penche donc, encore une fois, du côté de la priorité d'Is 36–39[59].

10. Les 15 années de 2 R 20,6 par. Is 38,5 s'expliquent à partir de la chronologie de 2 R, et non à partir du livre d'Isaïe. Pour Gonçalves[60], on peut y reconnaître le résultat de la soustraction de deux chiffres: le nombre des années de règne d'Ézéchias (29 ans; 2 R 18,2) et celui de la date l'invasion de Sennachérib (14e année, 2 R 18,13). En effet, cet élément ne s'accorde pas avec la mention insistante des «dix degrés» qui mesurent le recul de l'ombre. La précision des quinze années résulte donc sans doute de la volonté de faire correspondre la maladie et la guérison d'Ézéchias avec l'expédition de Sennachérib[61]. Comme ceci ne s'explique qu'à partir de la chronologie de 2 R, cet élément est favorable à l'hypothèse de la priorité de ce dernier récit sur celui d'Is 36–39. On ne peut cependant y voir une preuve irréfutable, car il faut compter avec la possibilité d'une correction harmonisante tardive apportée à Is 38,5[62].

11. Que faut-il conclure de ce premier volet de mon enquête? Établissons un bref bilan:

Plusieurs arguments invoqués dans un sens ou dans l'autre paraissent en réalité très faibles. Ainsi, Is 36–39 n'a pas été rédigé comme «pont»

---

58. Le rédacteur comble ainsi une lacune. L'absence de réalisation de la promesse est peu compréhensible en Is 38, si le récit dépend de 2 R 20.

59. Voir en ce sens P. AUVRAY, *Isaïe 1–39* (SB), Paris, 1972, p. 315. Se prononcent, en revanche, pour la priorité du récit de 2 R 20: O. KAISER, *Der Prophet Jesaja Kapitel 13–39* (ATD, 18), Göttingen, 1973, pp. 317-318; OSWALT, *The Book of Isaiah Chapters 1–39* (n. 7), p. 673; P. HÖFFKEN, *Das Buch Jesaja Kapitel 1–39* (Neuer Stuttgarter Kommentar Altes Testament, 18/1), Stuttgart, 1993, p. 254; R. KILIAN, *Jesaja II 13–39* (Die Neue Echter Bibel), Würzburg, 1994, p. 211.

60. GONÇALVES, *L'expédition* (n. 2), pp. 336,345.

61. *Ibid.*, pp. 357-359. L'auteur écarte avec raison l'hypothèse selon laquelle la date de 2 R 18,13 serait secondaire par rapport à celle de 20,6.

62. Une telle correction est plus «nécessaire» en ce qui concerne les chiffres, dont la discordance saute aux yeux, que dans des domaines plus flous (théologie, éléments narratifs).

entre les deux grandes parties du livre; de même, on ne peut rien conclure du silence de l'«histoire deutéronomiste» sur les «grands prophètes», de l'analogie supposée avec Jr 52 ou du jugement porté sur Ézéchias en 2 R 18,1-12.

En faveur de l'hypothèse classique (priorité de 2 R 18–20), on peut
retenir avant tout le motif des 15 ans de survie d'Ézéchias, qui suppose
le cadre chronologique du livre des Rois.

Et enfin, d'autres observations sont favorables à la priorité d'Is 36–
39: le nombre et la qualité des «plus» de ce texte (notamment dans
l'épisode de la guérison d'Ézéchias); l'analogie de la reprise de 2 R
18,13 en Is 36,1 avec celle de 2 R 16,5 en Is 7,1 et, plus largement, le
parallélisme entre Is 7 et Is 36–37; plus globalement encore, la reprise
en Is 36–39 de nombreux éléments de la tradition isaïenne

Tout ceci donne à penser que les récits concernant Isaïe et Ézéchias
sont insérés d'une manière bien plus profonde dans le contexte du livre
d'Isaïe que dans celui de 2 R[63]. Il paraît donc raisonnable d'accorder la
priorité à Is 36–39, au moins comme hypothèse de travail. Ceci ouvre la
voie à une nouvelle démarche: tenter de voir clair dans la *Redaktionsgeschichte* de ces chapitres. Si l'hypothèse de travail est valable, il faudrait pouvoir retrouver en Is 36–39 des rédactions qui affectent le reste
de l'ouvrage.

II. Éléments pour une *Redaktionsgeschichte* d'Is 36–39

Is 36–39 comprend donc trois éléments: l'histoire de la campagne de
Sennachérib (chap. 36-37), celle de la guérison d'Ézéchias (chap. 38) et
celle de la visite de Mérodach-Baladan au Temple (chap. 39). On distingue généralement à propos du premier épisode trois récits soit, d'après
l'ordre chronologique de leur rédaction: 36,1 (extrait du récit A, qu'on
trouve en 2 R 18,13-17); 36,2–37,9a.37-38 (B1); Is 37,9b-36 (B2). Rap-
pelons les résultats auxquels parvient Gonçalves, au terme d'une analyse
fouillée: A est un document ancien, qui reproduit sans doute une pièce
d'archive[64]; B1 est une composition ancienne, elle aussi, qui remonte au
milieu du VIIe siècle environ et reste encore proche du message d'Isaïe[65];
B2, enfin, dépend de B1 et est l'œuvre d'un rédacteur de l'époque
exilique[66]; les textes comptent en outre un certain nombre d'additions

---

63. Contrairement à ce que déclare GONÇALVES, *L'expédition* (n. 2), p. 346.
64. *Ibid.*, pp. 367-370.
65. *Ibid.*, pp. 441-442.
66. *Ibid.*, pp. 478-480. On retrouve la même interprétation de B2 comme relecture de
B1 dans HARDMEIER, *Prophetie im Streit* (n. 15), pp. 427-431, ainsi qu'en RUPRECHT, *Die*

post-exiliques. Cette explication est représentative du courant dominant de l'exégèse de ces chapitres[67].

La taille et la complexité du texte invitent à une longue enquête. Je ne pourrai ici qu'aller à l'essentiel, en esquissant un certain nombre de propositions sans entrer dans tous les détails.

1. Commençons par l'histoire de la campagne de Sennachérib. La notice de 36,1 est indispensable au récit, car elle seule en donne le contexte: la prise des villes de Juda par le roi assyrien. Tenons pour établi que ce verset est repris à 2 R 18,13 ou, plus exactement, à la source ancienne de ce texte, alors que la suite du récit ne dépend pas de 2 R. Une telle opération littéraire n'a aucun sens si elle ne permet pas d'introduire de nouveaux développements; c'est d'ailleurs ce que confirme l'analogie avec 7,1. Ce dernier verset s'inscrit sans doute dans le cadre d'une rédaction ancienne du livre, qui interprète les oracles du prophète en opposant les sorts respectifs de Samarie et de Jérusalem, en insistant sur la protection que YHWH accorde à cette dernière[68]. Ce motif, on le trouve aussi bien en B1 qu'en B2, mais celui-ci le met davantage en valeur, et c'est lui seul qui l'expose dans un oracle du prophète (37,33-35). Sa formulation la plus typique se trouve dans ce qui a sans doute été la finale de ce discours: $w^e gannôtî$ 'al-$hā$'$îr$ $hazzô$'t $l^e hôšî$'$āh$, «Je protégerai cette ville, et je la sauverai» (v. 35a)[69]. Or, on observera que le verbe

---

ursprüngliche Komposition (n. 16), pp. 61-63; ces auteurs tiennent cependant B2 pour une composition de l'époque perse.

67. Certains auteurs distinguent plusieurs rédactions en B1; voir par exemple CAMP, *Hiskija und Hiskijabild* (n. 6), pp. 108-170.

68. J'attribue à cette rédaction les éléments suivants. Tout d'abord dans le «livre de l'Emmanuel»: 7,1-3aα.4b.5b.8b-9a.16bß.17b.20b; 8,4bß*.6b.7aß.8b-10.15. Ces additions n'ont pas pour but de donner des renseignements historiques, mais elles interprètent les événements des années 734-732 (guerre «syro-éphraïmite») à la lumière de la chute de Samarie (722-720) et, sans doute, de la campagne de Sennachérib (701). Le rédacteur insiste sur la défaite d'Éphraïm, qui a voulu s'emparer de Jérusalem, tandis que l'oracle de l'Emmanuel est interprété comme une promesse de protection accordée à cette dernière. On note, en outre, une tendance à comprendre l'offensive contre Jérusalem comme un assaut de tous les peuples de la terre contre la cité de YHWH. Cette relecture du «livre de l'Emmanuel» n'est pas isolée, et des remaniements comparables sont discernables en 5,26.30; 9,8a.10; 10,27b-34; 14,28-32*; 17,1-6*.12-14a; 23,1-14*; 28,14-18*.21; 29,5-7; 31,5; 33,3-4. Ceci recoupe partiellement l'hypothèse de H. BARTH, *Die Jesaja-Worte in der Josiazeit. Israel und Assur als Thema einer produktiven Neuinterpretation der Jesajaüberlieferung* (WMANT, 48), Neukirchen-Vluyn, 1977; cependant le rédacteur me semble plus attaché à l'inviolabilité de Sion qu'à la condamnation d'Assur comme telle, et je pense qu'il écrit plutôt à l'époque de Manassé qu'à celle de Josias. Sur tout ceci, voir J. VERMEYLEN, *Du prophète Isaïe à l'apocalyptique. Isaïe, I–XXXV, miroir d'un demi-millénaire d'expérience religieuse en Israël* (EB), t. 2, Paris, 1978, pp. 678-688.

69. Le v. 35b introduit une motivation, ce qu'on ne trouve jamais ailleurs à ce niveau rédactionnel. En outre, la phrase est apparentée à des éléments récents du livre. La locu-

gānan n'est attesté dans la Bible hébraïque que dans quelques textes: notre passage et ses reprises secondaires (Is 38,6; 2 R 19,34; 20,6), en Is 31,5 (bis) et dans deux textes très tardifs (Za 9,15; 12,8). Ceci confirme l'hypothèse de l'appartenance d'Is 37,33-35* à la même strate littéraire pré-exilique soulignant l'inviolabilité de Jérusalem.

2. Peut-on étendre cette hypothèse à l'ensemble du récit B2? Il me semble que oui, à condition de reconnaître certains passages comme des additions postérieures, en particulier la plus grande partie du discours d'Isaïe à Ézéchias (37,21b-32)[70]. Quelques observations vont en ce sens:

Si B2 est l'élément le plus ancien d'Is 36–39, la section 37,9b-35* forme la suite originelle de 36,1. Ceci ne fait aucune difficulté: 37,9b donne une suite très naturelle à 36,1. Bien plus, l'introduction secondaire de *wayyāšob*, qui marque l'idée du recommencement, dans le texte parallèle de 2 R 19,9b ainsi qu'en 1QIsᵃ, montre bien que la difficulté de la succession des deux récits B1 et B2 a été ressentie. L'absence de *wayyāšob* en Is 37,9b[71] donne à penser que, dans un état antérieur du texte, la seule ambassade auprès d'Ézéchias était celle de B2.

Le motif de la confiance (*bāṭaḥ*) d'Ézéchias en son Dieu (v. 10) peut avoir été suggéré par l'emploi du même verbe en 31,1 (bis) et 32,9.10.11. Ces textes, qui remontent à la prédication du prophète lui-même, parlent d'une confiance mal placée, qui se fonde sur les moyens humains, alors que les Judéens ne se sont pas tournés vers YHWH (31,1). Ici encore, Sennachérib parle d'une confiance mal placée (à ses yeux!) d'Ézéchias, mais le thème est mis au service de la théologie de Sion inviolable.

E. Ben Zvi a montré que la liste des peuples vaincus par les rois assyriens en 37,12-13 (par. 2 R 19,12-13) s'explique à partir de la tradition de la déportation de Samarie (cf. 2 R 18,11) et de l'installation de colons

tion *lᵉmaʿanî*, «à cause de moi», n'est utilisée (outre notre péricope et ses reprises secondaires en 2 R 19,34; 20,6) qu'en Is 43,25 et 48,11. D'autre part, l'expression *lᵉmaʿan dāwid ʿabdî*, «à cause de mon serviteur David» est attestée en 1 R 11,13.34.36 (ainsi qu'au v. 32, où elle est inversée) et en 2 R 8,19; elle y est liée au thème de l'élection de Jérusalem, ce qui renvoie encore une fois à de nombreux passages d'Is 40–55; voir aussi le Ps 132, post-exilique.

70. Ceci rejoint l'opinion exégétique courante, confirmée par l'analyse de GONÇALVES, *L'expédition* (n. 2), pp. 450-452. Un détail n'est pas clair: des deux introductions au discours d'Isaïe (vv. 21b et 33aα), il est difficile de déterminer laquelle appartenait déjà au texte original et laquelle a été introduite par le deuxième rédacteur.

71. Voir *ibid.*, pp. 380-382, avec un aperçu plus complet du problème textuel. Il rapproche 2 R 19,9b (*wayyašob wayyišlaḥ*) du v. 7: *wayyašob* appartenait primitivement au récit B1, et il fallait le lire dans son sens verbal de «il retourna». L'auteur n'explique pas, cependant, son absence en Is 37,9b; sa théorie ne tient que dans la perspective de la priorité de 2 R 18–20.

étrangers dans la même ville (cf. 2 R 17,24)[72]. C'est donc une manière indirecte d'opposer les destins respectifs de Jérusalem et de Samarie. Or nous avons vu que cette préoccupation a marqué la rédaction pré-exilique qui souligne la protection accordée par YHWH à Jérusalem.

Le récit utilise plusieurs fois l'expression *mèlèk 'aššur*, «le roi d'Assyrie» (37,10.21[73]; voir encore 37,11.17, au pluriel). Certes, l'expression est banale et correspond au titre officiel, mais on remarquera qu'elle est aussi employée avec insistance par le rédacteur pré-exilique; voir Is 7,17b.20a*; 8,7aß.

Tant les messagers de Sennachérib (37,11-13) qu'Ézéchias dans sa prière (37,16-20) soulignent que la souveraineté de YHWH sur tous les royaumes est en cause. Ceci rejoint les perspectives de 8,9; 14,26; 17,12; 29,7; 33,3: Jérusalem n'est pas attaquée par l'armée assyrienne seulement, mais par «les peuples», «toutes les nations». Il est possible cependant que le texte d'Is 37 soit, sur ce point, surchargé par des additions plus récentes[74].

La finale du récit (v. 36; peut-être faut-il y ajouter le v. 37) parle de l'action de l'Ange de YHWH, qui «frappe» (*wayyakkèh*, v. 36a) le camp assyrien[75], comme YHWH avait «frappé» (*hikkāh*) les premiers nés du pays d'Égypte au cours de la nuit (Ex 12,29); ce parallèle confère à la défaite assyrienne une dimension «mythique», qu'on retrouve sous d'autres formes dans des passages comme Is 8,8b-10 ou 17,12. Surtout, la disparition du danger ennemi «au lever du matin» (v. 36b) correspond à 17,14a et, implicitement, à 29,7.

Même si les observations rassemblées ci-dessus n'ont pas toutes le même poids, il semble donc raisonnable d'attribuer le récit B2 au rédacteur pré-exilique attaché à l'idée de la protection de Jérusalem par YHWH[76]. Le récit aurait été placé en finale d'un «livre d'Isaïe» encore

---

72. E. BEN ZVI, *Who Wrote the Speech of Rabshakeh and When?*, dans *JBL* 109 (1990) 79-92, pp. 89-91. Voir dans le même sens LAATO, *Who Is Immanuel?* (n. 8), pp. 289-290.

73. 37,33aα forme probablement un raccord rédactionnel postérieur.

74. GONÇALVES, *L'expédition* (n. 2), pp. 464-468, relève les affinités de plusieurs phrases avec le Deutéronome, Is 40–55 et d'autres textes récents; c'est d'ailleurs essentiellement sur cette base qu'il situe la rédaction B2 à l'époque exilique (pp. 478-480).

75. CLEMENTS, *The Prophecies* (n. 7), pp. 66-67, souligne que le massacre dépasse de loin ce qui avait été annoncé par Isaïe en 37,14-20; il en déduit que le v. 36 forme un élément ajouté tardivement au récit. Ceci est peut-être vrai pour le nombre des victimes (185000 hommes!), mais rien ne permet d'affirmer que l'ensemble du verset est tardif; d'ailleurs l'extermination de l'armée assyrienne répond, d'une certaine manière, au rappel des massacres opérés par la même armée assyrienne (v. 18).

76. S. DE JONG, *Het verhaal van Hizkia en Sanherib. 2 Koningen 18,17–19,37/Jesaja 36–37 als narratieve reflectie op de Ballingschap*, dans *ACEBT* 10 (1989) 57-91, p. 65, attire l'attention sur le fait que l'expression *'ᵉlōhéy ḥay*, «le Dieu vivant» n'est utilisée

assez court, qui devait s'ouvrir avec le chap. 6[77]. Cette place est logique, car les chap. 29-32 annonçaient les événements de l'année 701 : en 29,1-4 ; 30,1-5 ; 31,1.3 et 32,9-14, en particulier, le prophète avait dénoncé la politique judéenne et annoncé une catastrophe ; le rédacteur pré-exilique avait complété ces oracles en parlant d'un sauvetage inattendu de Jérusalem (29,5-7 ; 31,5 ; 33,3-4). Il restait à raconter les événements, en montrant comment la cité avait, effectivement, bénéficié de la protection divine[78]. Notons, par ailleurs, qu'on ne trouve aucune trace d'une rédaction présentant les mêmes caractéristiques dans les livres des Rois, ni même dans l'ensemble de l'«histoire deutéronomiste». Ceci confirme donc l'hypothèse de la priorité du texte d'Isaïe.

3. Qu'en est-il alors de B1 (Is 36,2–37,9a.38*)? Gonçalves[79] a montré que B1 et B2 ont la même structure, utilisent une série d'éléments communs et ne peuvent être tenus pour indépendants l'un de l'autre. Je pense cependant que B1 s'appuie sur B2, et non l'inverse.

Si l'on met entre parenthèses les additions récentes, B2 est nettement plus court que B1. Celui-ci développe plusieurs éléments du texte ; on comparera en particulier 37,9b-13 et 36,2-22.

Le scénario de B1 est plus complexe, avec le message du grand échanson délivré d'abord aux princes, puis au peuple, puis enfin au roi.

Si l'on compare 36,19-20 (B1) à 37,13 (B2), on voit que le rôle des rois est transféré aux dieux ; il est plus difficile d'expliquer une éventuelle «politisation» du récit.

Si B2 forme la suite immédiate de 36,1, il n'y a aucun envoi de troupe par Sennachérib à Jérusalem, mais seulement l'envoi de messagers. Ceci reste beaucoup plus proche du scénario de l'ancien récit A. B1 dramatise le récit lorsqu'il transforme l'envoi d'émissaires en expédition militaire commandée par le Rabshaqé.

Dans l'hypothèse du récit B1 indépendant de B2, l'annonce du retour de Sennachérib dans son pays en 37,7 pose problème. En effet, ce retour est motivé par une nouvelle que le roi d'Assyrie recevra. Au v. 9, en ef-

---

avec le verbe *ḥārap*[h], «dire des insultes» qu'en 1 S 17,26.36, texte reconnu comme très ancien.

77. La section 5,24-30 devait se lire à la fin du chap. 9 (même refrain) et a été déplacée plus tard.

78. SEITZ, *Zion's Final Destiny* (n. 4), pp. 100-101, propose une hypothèse analogue : il faudrait compter avec une rédaction du livre d'Isaïe datant de l'époque de Manassé et culminant avec l'histoire d'Ézéchias. L'auteur considère cependant que B1 et B2 forment un récit homogène.

79. GONÇALVES, *L'expédition* (n. 2), pp. 449, 479. Je ne puis discuter ici la thèse de SMELIK, *Distortion* (n. 3), pp. 74-85, et de SEITZ, *Zion's Final Destiny* (n. 4), pp. 66-72, qui considèrent B1 et B2 comme un seul récit substantiellement homogène.

fet, Sennachérib apprend que le Pharaon Tirhaqa est parti en guerre contre lui[80]. Mais, au lieu de retourner chez lui, le roi d'Assyrie quitte
Lakish pour aller assiéger Libna! La localisation précise de ce dernier
site reste discutée, mais, quoi qu'il en soit, la cité n'est pas distante de
Lakish de plus de 10 km! En d'autres termes, un tel déplacement n'a
guère de sens, dans le contexte de l'offensive égyptienne[81]. En revanche,
il s'explique littérairement: il sert à justifier l'envoi d'une deuxième
ambassade auprès d'Ézéchias, et donc à introduire B1[82]. Quant au v. 7, il
a pu être inspiré par le v. 37, qui formait sans doute la finale du récit B2.

4. Le récit B1 établit un double parallèle entre Ézéchias et Achaz,
d'une part, entre Ézéchias, Josias et Yoyaqim, de l'autre.

Le parallèle avec Achaz est souligné en particulier par la reprise du
lieu de la rencontre de l'année 734 («près du canal de la piscine supérieure, sur le chemin du champ du foulon», 7,3 et 36,2)[83]. Mais là où
Achaz a manqué de foi (cf. 7,9b,13), Ézéchias manifeste au contraire
une grande confiance. Ce thème, déjà présent en B2 (*bāṭaḥ*, 37,10) est
considérablement développé en 36,19-24.30.

D'autres éléments du texte s'expliquent dans le cadre d'un autre parallèle, avec Josias et Yoyaqim cette fois. Ainsi, la mention d'Èlyaqim
fils de Hilqiyyahu, de Shebna et de Yoah fils d'Asaph (le nom des deux
premiers personnages provient du chap. 22) est parallèle à celle des princes du temps de Josias[84] et du temps de Yoyaqim[85]. Comme en Jr 36
(texte sans doute l'origine deutéronomiste[86]), le message est transmis à

---

80. Malgré les efforts déployés par plus d'un pour montrer le contraire, la mention de
Tirhaqa – qui ne monta sur le trône qu'en 690 environ – doit sans doute être considérée
comme un anachronisme; l'auteur écrit donc assez longtemps après 701.

81. C'est ce que note AUVRAY, *Isaïe 1–39* (n. 59), p. 307: «on ne voit pas bien comment l'annonce d'une attaque égyptienne aurait décidé Sennachérib à aller assiéger la
ville de Libna».

82. L'annonce de l'offensive du Pharaon interrompant le siège, inconnue des sources
anciennes, a pu être inspirée par l'attaque de Hophra en 588 (cf. Jr 37,5-11). Certes, Sennachérib a vaincu une armée égyptienne à Elteqé, mais cet événement se situe avant la
prise d'Eqrôn, dans une phase précédente de la campagne assyrienne.

83. Pour J. WERLITZ, *Studien zur literarkritischen Methode. Gericht und Heil in
Jesaja 7,1-17 und 29,1-8* (BZAW, 204), Berlin - New York, 1992, p. 141, la localisation
est mieux en place en 36,2 qu'en 7,3, et ce serait donc ce dernier texte qui dépendrait du
premier. En fait, ce jugement est subjectif et ne peut s'appuyer sur aucun argument irréfutable.

84. Le prêtre Hilqiyyahu, le secrétaire Shaphan, ainsi que Ahiqam, Akbor et Asaya (2
R 22,8-14).

85. Mikayehu fils de Gemaryahu fils de Shaphan, Élishama, Delayahu fils de
Semayahu, Elnatan fils d'Akbor, etc. (Jr 36,11-12).

86. Voir notamment T. RÖMER, *Y a-t-il une rédaction deutéronomiste dans le livre de
Jérémie?*, dans A. DE PURY et al. (éd.), *Israël construit son histoire. L'historiographie*

trois auditoires: les princes, puis le peuple (assis sur les remparts, et qui comprend![87]), et enfin le roi; le récit du livre de Jérémie montre Yoyaqim déchirer et faire brûler le rouleau des oracles du prophète, qu'il tente d'ailleurs d'arrêter. Ici, au contraire, Ézéchias déchire ses vêtements, se couvre d'un sac et se rend au Temple (37,1), puis il fait demander au prophète Isaïe d'intercéder auprès de YHWH (vv. 3-4). Cette attitude rejoint celle de Josias, rapportée en 2 R 23: à la lecture du «livre de la Loi» trouvé au Temple, le roi déchire ses vêtements (v. 11) et envoie ses collaborateurs consulter YHWH par l'intermédiaire de la prophétesse Hulda (vv. 12-20). Le parallèle avec Josias est encore souligné en 36,7: le grand échanson explique qu'Ézéchias «a supprimé les hauts lieux et les autels en disant aux gens de Juda et de Jérusalem: 'C'est devant cet autel que vous vous prosternerez'»; le roi aurait donc ordonné une réforme religieuse qui anticipe celle de l'an 622 (cf. 2 Rois 23,4-14)[88]. Pour l'auteur du récit B1, Ézéchias agit comme le pieux roi Josias, mais à l'inverse des rois impies Achaz et Yoyaqim[89].

Cet ensemble de parallélismes, qui commande les modifications apportées au scénario du récit, interprète celui-ci dans la ligne morale de l'école deutéronomiste[90]. La pierre de touche du jugement, c'est l'attitude de confiance envers YHWH, par opposition aux dieux des nations (36,18-20). D'autre part, nous avons en 36,17 une allusion assez évidente à la déportation. Comme d'autres observations le confirment[91], il

deutéronomiste à la lumière des recherches récentes (Le Monde de la Bible, 34), Genève, 1996, pp. 419-441, spéc. pp. 439-441. SEITZ, Zion's Final Destiny (n. 4), pp.106-109 souligne les points communs à Is 36-37 et aux sections en prose, généralement considérées comme deutéronomistes, du livre de Jérémie; en fait, la ressemblance repose avant tout sur B1, comme l'indique la liste des détails communs proposée par Seitz lui-même (p. 108).

87. Il est historiquement peu vraisemblable que le grand échanson de Sennachérib ait été capable de tenir un discours en langue judéenne, comme le dit pourtant 36,13. Ce motif appartient plutôt aux stéréotypes deutéronomistes de la parole reçue aux différents niveaux de pouvoir, et notamment par le roi (voir aussi Jr 26).

88. H. WILDBERGER, Die Rede des Rabsake vor Jerusalem, dans TZ 35 (1979) 35-47, pp. 38-39, explique que le v. 7b ne correspond pas à la réforme d'Ézéchias comme 2 R 18,4-5 la présente et n'a sans doute aucun fondement historique. De cette observation, il tire cependant une conclusion indue: le v. 7b formerait une addition dans le discours.

89. Voir dans le même sens SEITZ, Zion's Final Destiny (n. 4), p. 109, qui parle cependant de Yoyaqim et Sédécias comme anti-types d'Ézéchias.

90. Il me paraît difficile de souscrire au jugement formulé par LAATO, Who Is Immanuel? (n. 8), p. 285: «It is certainly evident that Rabshakeh's speech has preserved the historical situation and spiritual atmosphere of the year 701». Ce discours est, tout au contraire, une composition théologique deutéronomiste, qui s'appuie sur les renseignements historiques fournis par B1 et d'autres éléments du livre d'Isaïe.

91. Il faudrait ici analyser le vocabulaire et les attaches littéraires du texte. Voici un seul exemple: Isaïe déclare, au nom de YHWH: «Voici que je vais mettre en lui (Ézéchias) un esprit et, sur une nouvelle qu'il entendra, il retournera dans son pays»; le don

faut sans doute attribuer cette rédaction à l'école deutéronomiste du temps de l'Exil[92]: non l'historien principal de Josué-Rois, mais un rédacteur plus récent, apparenté à celui que d'aucuns appellent DtrP[93]. Ézéchias est resté fidèle à son Dieu, et YHWH a délivré Jérusalem: c'est ce qui se serait passé en 587 si Sédécias et ses prédécesseurs avaient eu la même attitude. L'addition du récit B1 s'inscrit ainsi dans le cadre d'une rédaction deutéronomiste qui affecte l'ensemble du Proto-Isaïe[94].

    5. Le récit primitif de la guérison d'Ézéchias (38,1-5) insiste sur la juste rétribution divine: c'est parce que le roi s'est conduit fidèlement (v. 2), qu'il obtient la guérison. Encore une fois, nous retrouvons donc ici la préoccupation morale de l'école deutéronomiste[95]. Le lien entre cet épisode et les deux chapitres qui précèdent est assuré par le v. 6, où la guérison d'Ézéchias est liée à la délivrance de Jérusalem; ce v. 6 reprend à 37,35a la locution *wᵉgannôtî 'am-hā'îr hazzô't*, «et je protégerai cette ville», mais il comprend aussi l'expression *hiṣîl miyyad* («délivrer de la main de...»), comme en 36,19-20 B1. Autres points communs avec B1: au v. 3, Isaïe reçoit le titre de *nābî'* (cf. 37,2), et Ézéchias est idéalisé comme souverain fidèle à YHWH. La visite de Mérodach-Baladan (chap. 39) est motivée par la guérison du roi (v. 2), et elle est ainsi liée au récit précédent[96]. Peut-être ce chapitre s'appuie-t-il sur le souvenir d'une ambassade babylonienne, qui s'inscrivait dans le con-

de cet esprit peut être rapproché de 1 R 22 Dtr, où l'Esprit va tromper Achab, de telle sorte qu'il meure à Ramot de Galaad. BEN ZVI, *Who Wrote the Speech of Rabshakeh* (n. 72), pp. 85-88, relève un certain nombre d'expressions du discours qui trouvent leur meilleur parallèle dans des textes réputés deutéronomistes ou apparentés (comme la «source C» de Jérémie); il pense cependant que ces deutéronomismes sont le fait d'additions (voir surtout p. 92).

    92. Tel est aussi l'avis de DE JONG, *Het verhaal van Hizkia en Sanherib* (n. 76), p. 68; l'auteur ne distingue cependant pas entre B1 et B2.

    93. Cette rédaction s'intéresse particulièrement au prophétisme. Pour ma part, cependant, je préfère parler de Dtr560, car je pense que le prophétisme n'est qu'un centre d'intérêt parmi d'autres.

    94. Voir VERMEYLEN, *Du prophète Isaïe à l'apocalyptique* (n. 68), t. 2, pp. 693-709. Je devrais cependant revoir la question, en tenant compte notamment des remarques critiques formulées par C. BREKELMANS, *Deuteronomistic Influence in Isaiah 1–12*, dans J. VERMEYLEN (éd.), *The Book of Isaiah. Le livre d'Isaïe. Les oracles et leurs relectures. Unité et complexité de l'ouvrage* (BETL, 81), Leuven, 1989, pp. 167-176.

    95. Voir WILDBERGER, *Jesaja* (n. 5), t. 3, p. 1448: «Das Bild, daß er vom König zeichnet, steht dem Ideal nicht fern, an welchem der Deuteronomist die Herrscher Judas gemessen hat».

    96. Comme tel, le récit de la maladie d'Ézéchias annonce la guérison sans la déclarer réalisée, et les commentateurs s'en étonnent. Mais si les deux récits sont l'œuvre de la même rédaction, cet élément est bien présent, en 39,2, et le rédacteur n'a sans doute pas jugé utile de le répéter. Sur le lien ainsi assuré entre les deux épisodes, voir RUPRECHT, *Die ursprüngliche Komposition* (n. 16), p. 42.

texte de la fronde anti-assyrienne des années 705-701[97]. Quoi qu'il en soit, le récit a pour fonction d'annoncer les événements tragiques du début du VIe siècle (vv. 6-7), tout en les opposant au sort personnel – favorable – d'Ézéchias (v. 8)[98]. Le souverain est personnellement récompensé pour sa bonne conduite, mais la nation coupable sera sévèrement châtiée en 598 et 587; ceci correspond à ce que Dtr dit de Josias en 2 R 22,20. On reconnaît donc à nouveau les préoccupations de l'école deutéronomiste. Rien n'empêche le double récit des chap. 38–39 d'avoir été composé, sur base de traditions anciennes[99], par la même rédaction que B1[100].

6. Le grand oracle d'Isaïe sur l'échec de Sennachérib est complété, à l'époque perse, par la section 37,21b-32*. Ce discours paraît homogène, à l'exception cependant du v. 30, qui forme un commentaire postérieur[101]; la condamnation du blasphémateur est encadrée, en contraste, par la perspective du triomphe de Sion/Jérusalem (vv. 22 et 31-32). L'addition interprète et prolonge le discours ancien d'Isaïe aux vv. 33-35a (le v. 35b est peut-être de la même main); plus précisément, le v. 29 reprend au v. 34 l'annonce du retour du roi d'Assyrie sur le chemin par lequel il est venu. L'auteur reprend aussi (vv. 23-24) les motifs des blasphèmes et insultes, qu'il a trouvés respectivement au v. 6 et aux vv. 4.17. D'autre part, l'introduction de ces versets s'inscrit dans le cadre d'une vaste opération littéraire, sans doute celle qui vit la constitution du «grand livre d'Isaïe», du chap. 1 au chap. 66[102]. Notons quelques connexions significatives:

97. L'utilisation d'une tradition plus ancienne permet d'expliquer pourquoi le v. 6 s'achève par ce qui indique en principe la fin d'un discours prophétique (*'āmar YHWH*).

98. On a souvent paraphrasé ce verset par «après moi le déluge». Un tel commentaire ne me paraît pas approprié, parce qu'il met l'accent sur l'attitude psychologique d'Ézéchias, alors que le texte doit se lire avant tout dans la perspective d'une théologie de l'histoire.

99. RUPRECHT, *Die ursprüngliche Komposition* (n. 16), pp. 43-44, a bien montré que les paroles d'Isaïe (vv. 5-7) ne peuvent être comprises comme *vaticinia ex eventu*: Yoyaqim n'avait pas d'enfant lorsqu'il a été déporté, et ceux de Sédécias ont été égorgés sous ses yeux. Mais peut-être est-il excessif de parler de «traditions anciennes»: en fait, des réminiscences suffisent; nous observons le même phénomène en B1, à propos de Tirhaqa (37,9), par exemple.

100. Rien ne permet de penser que les chap. 38–39 aient jamais précédé les chap. 36–37, comme l'imposerait pourtant la logique chronologique; SEITZ, *Zion's Final Destiny* (n. 4), pp. 151-152, a montré les difficultés rencontrées par la théorie de l'inversion.

101. On observera le changement de personne: le «tu» du v. 30 ne s'adresse plus à Sennachérib, mais sans doute à Jérusalem. Les vv. 31-32, en revanche, se lisent sans difficulté à la suite des vv. 22-29.

102. Voir à ce sujet J. VERMEYLEN, *L'unité du livre d'Isaïe*, dans ID. (éd.), *The Book of Isaiah* (n. 94), pp. 11-53.

Pour le v. 22 (*bat ṣiyyôn*): Is 1,8; 10,32; 16,1; 52,2; 62,11; voir encore, par opposition, la «fille de Babylone» humiliée (47,1).

Les vv. 23-29, qui soulignent l'orgueil mégalomane du souverain, présentent des analogies avec la satire sur le roi de Babylone (14,4-21); voir aussi 10,12, et on rapprochera le v. 24 de 10,33-34[103]. Au-delà de Sennachérib, l'auteur semble songer davantage à Babylone, qui avait humilié Jérusalem et soumis le monde entier

Pour les vv. 31-32a: Is 4,2-3; 10,21-22a; 28,5.

Le v. 32b est identique à Is 9,6b.

L'oracle d'Isaïe s'inscrit ainsi dans le cadre d'une vaste relecture du livre, qui inclut désormais les chap. 1 à 66. En revanche, on ne trouve aucune rédaction comparable dans l'«histoire deutéronomiste». Ceci confirme, une fois de plus, les conclusions de la première partie de mon enquête.

7. Is 37,30 et 38,7-8, secondaires dans leurs contextes respectifs, s'ouvrent par la même formule *wᵉzèh-lᵉkā hā'ôt*, «et voici pour toi le signe»; 37,30 commente les vv. 31-32 (les nouveaux fruits produits à l'avenir par le reste de Jérusalem sont annoncés par les fruits de la récolte), comme 38,7-8 commente les vv. 5-6[104]. L'identité du procédé semble indiquer que les deux additions proviennent du même rédacteur. La présentation d'un signe est un motif important du livre d'Isaïe, qui remonte à la prédication du prophète (7,11.14; 8,18; cf. 20,3), mais trouvera des prolongements dans les rédactions tardives de l'ouvrage (19,20; 66,19).

8. Les éléments les plus récents sont postérieurs à la transposition du récit en 2 R: le cantique d'Ézéchias (38,9-20)[105] et quelques additions mineures, comme 38,22. L'introduction du cantique d'Ézéchias est parallèle à celui des cantiques de Moïse (Ex 15,1-18; Dt 32), d'Anne (1 S 2,1-10), de David (2 S 22) et de Jonas (Jon 2,2-10), qui paraissent provenir de l'«école d'Esdras».

---

103. Pour un aperçu plus complet des contacts de vocabulaire entre les vv. 22-29 et le reste du Proto-Isaïe, voir WILDBERGER, *Jesaja* (n. 5), t. 3, pp. 1428-1429.

104. L'addition a pu être inspirée par 36,9, où le roi d'Assyrie met Ézéchias au défi de faire reculer un seul de ses serviteurs.

105. Sur le cantique et son insertion dans son contexte narratif, voir J.W. WATTS, *Psalm and Story. Inset Hymns in Hebrew Narratives* (JSOT SS, 139), Sheffield, 1992, pp. 118-131.

CONCLUSION

Ces pages trop rapides demandent compléments et vérification soigneuse. Il semble cependant que la théorie classique selon laquelle Is 36–39 forme un appendice dérivé de 2 R 18–20 doive être abandonnée. Au contraire, les récits mettant en scène Ézéchias et Isaïe ont été écrits en liaison étroite avec le livre d'Isaïe en voie de formation. On peut y reconnaître plusieurs rédactions qui s'étagent de la période royale (époque de Manassé?) au milieu de la période perse environ; ces rédactions s'inscrivent sans difficulté dans l'histoire littéraire de l'ouvrage, alors que certaines d'entre elles (la rédaction responsable du récit B2, par exemple) n'ont pas d'équivalent dans l'ensemble Josué-Rois. D'autre part, contrairement à la théorie reçue, le récit B2 est en fait plus ancien que le récit B1, qui l'interprète dans la ligne moralisante de l'école deutéronomiste; ni l'un ni l'autre, cependant, ne doit être considéré comme une source historique fiable.

156, avenue H. Conscience   Jacques VERMEYLEN
B-1140 Bruxelles

ISAIAH 6,13 AND 1,29-31

The translation and interpretation of the last verse of Isaiah 6 have been disputed from the earliest days for which we have documentary evidence. In a lengthy and detailed article, Emerton has surveyed in full the history of this debate, with attention to the ancient versions, the medieval Jewish commentators, and subsequent translations, commentaries and other discussions down to the present day[1]. It is not my purpose here to repeat this discussion, nor to propose a new rendering for so fiercely contested a passage. Rather, the present aim is considerably more modest. Emerton introduced the survey part of his article with the words, "The earliest evidence (other than the text from Qumran) for Jewish interpretation of the verse is found in the ancient versions" (p. 88). That is, of course, correct in terms of translation and explicit commentary. I should like here to suggest, however, that in the broader sense generally intended by the rubric "inner-biblical interpretation" it is possible that there is a still earlier interpretation of the verse embedded within the text of the book of Isaiah itself, namely at 1,29-31. I shall first establish the connection between the two passages and what it means for the way 6,13 was understood, then discuss the direction of dependence, and finally reflect briefly upon the implications of the results for the interpretation of chapter 1.

We may begin by noting the incidences of shared vocabulary and ideas[2]. In 6,13 those who survive the first wave of destruction will be destroyed[3] "like a terebinth and like an oak ..." (כאלה וכאלון). In 1,30 this same comparison (כאלה) is drawn in association with the judgment of the "transgressors and sinners ... and those that forsake the Lord" (verse 28) who have indulged in illicit cultic practices (verse 29). This relatively rare word occurs nowhere else in the book of Isaiah, though there is clearly a close connection between it and the related form אילים

---

1. J.A. EMERTON, *The Translation and Interpretation of Isaiah vi.13*, in J.A. EMERTON – S.C. REIF (eds.), *Interpreting the Hebrew Bible*. FS E.I.J. Rosenthal, Cambridge, 1982, pp. 85-118.

2. Long after I had worked out the main line of argument in this article I discovered that H.-P. Müller had also observed these same connections; see *Sprachliche und religionsgeschichtliche Beobachtungen zu Jesaja 6*, in ZAH 5 (1992) 163-85, p. 183. Müller himself seems to have been unaware of Emerton's article, though he covers some of the same ground.

3. For the interpretation of בער, see further below.

in the previous verse. There, it is said of the condemned that they will be ashamed of the אילים and of the "gardens" (גנות) which they have chosen. Since in verse 30 their destruction is compared to that of an אלה and of a גנה, it looks as though the writer considered אילים to be the plural of אלה. As we shall see later, this introduces the possibility of a connection with 57,5, where the variant spelling אלים is used[4].

The difficult word שלכת in 6,13 has been variously interpreted over the centuries. Emerton (p. 87) maintains reasonably that it is more likely to be a noun than a unique form of the infinitive construct *pi'el* of שלך. The verb occurs in the *hiph'il* and *hoph'al*, but nowhere in the *pi'el*, whereas nouns of this formation are often abstract in sense[5]. Usually, the verb means "to throw, cast down", but Emerton maintains several times (see pp. 87, 90, 106) that it is also used of a tree shedding its leaves (though he himself favours the rendering "when they have been felled" at this point, in common with most modern commentators). He does not justify this rendering, however, and apart from the possibility that this is its meaning in the present verse I have not been able to find any passage where the verb has this precise sense. The closest (indeed, so far as I can see, the only) parallel is Job 15,33: "and shall cast off his flower (... וישלך נצתו) like the olive". This may be sufficient to allow the rendering "to shed (of leaves)", but given the facts that, unlike in Job, no object is expressed and, at best, that this meaning is extremely rare, it would not have been surprising if it had never been proposed for Isa 6,13. It is, therefore, of particular interest to note that there was a firm tradition in antiquity for rendering it in this way. It is first attested by Symmachus (ητις αποβαλουσα [τα φυλλα])[6], and is clear in the Targum (מיתר טרפיהון), which in turn was followed by both Rashi and Kimhi as well as much later by, for instance, Calvin and the English Great Bible and AV. Now, we have already noted that אלה occurs in Isaiah only in this verse and in 1,30. It seems unlikely to be a pure coincidence, therefore, that 1,30 continues with a description of the terebinth as נבלת עלה, "whose foliage withers"[7]. (The LXX uses the same verb here as Symmachus did

---

4. IQIsaᵃ also has the spelling אלים at 1,29. The close connection between verses 29 and 30 indicates that the LXX's rendering "idols" (plural of אל) at both 1,29 and 57,5 is mistaken, or interpretative at best; for further discussion, see the references cited by H. WILDBERGER, *Jesaja, 1. Teilband. Jesaja 1–12* (BKAT, X/1), Neukirchen-Vluyn, ²1980, p. 69.

5. The name of a temple gate in 1 Chron 26,16 (שער שלכת), to which a few commentators have referred, sheds no light on the present use.

6. See conveniently J. ZIEGLER, *Isaias*, Göttingen, ³1983, p. 144.

7. For the construction, see G.B. GRAY, *A Critical and Exegetical Commentary on the Book of Isaiah I–XXVII* (ICC), Edinburgh, 1912, pp. 39-40, who compares עם כבד עון in 1,4 (cf. W. GESENIUS – E. KAUTZSCH, *Hebräische Grammatik*, Leipzig, ²⁸1909, §128x).

at 6,13.) It appears that the same image is being developed in a comparable manner. I shall return below to a possible consequence of this conclusion for the interpretation of 6,13 after first drawing attention to another point of correspondence between these two passages.

The meaning of the *pi'el* infinitive construct לבער at the end of the first line of 6,13 has also been disputed. The verb commonly means "to kindle, burn", and hence by extension "to consume, destroy". In addition, there have been a few both in antiquity and more recently who have favoured the sense which may have developed from the meaning "consume", namely "graze"[8]. This interpretation, which may already lie behind the rendering in the LXX[9], is found in Symmachus (εἰς καταβοσκησιν) and Saadya, as well as being advocated in more recent times by, for instance, Budde[10], Procksch[11], Seierstad[12], Kaiser[13], and Wildberger. Those who adopt this approach vary over the question whether the image is one of destruction (even the shoots which sprout after the first destruction will be nibbled away) or of potential hope for the future. The latter approach seems to be excluded by the fact that even where "graze" is a possible (though even then not certain) rendering, the emphasis is always on the resulting destruction. This is already the case in the most convincing example (Exod 22,4), let alone in those passages in Isaiah where this meaning has been more questionably proposed (e.g. 3,14; 5,5). One way or the other, as Emerton has convincingly demonstrated, Isa 6,13a describes destruction. Nevertheless, the precise form that this destruction will take remains ambiguous.

The ambiguity concerns only the *pi'el* of the verb(s). The *qal* consistently refers to kindling or burning, and it is interesting to note, therefore,

The fact that the LXX does not translate the suffix on עלה suggests that it read the same consonantal text as MT (as does 1QIsa[a]), so that we should not follow those Hebrew manuscripts which read עליה (*contra* WILDBERGER, *Jesaja* [n. 4], p. 69).

8. More recently there has been a tendency to identify separate roots for these different meanings; so, for instance, *HAL* I, pp. 139-140; H. RINGGREN, *TWAT* I, cols. 727-731; *DCH* 2, pp. 242-243. For discussion, see H. CAZELLES, *Les sens du verbe b'r en hébreu*, in *Semitica* 23 (1973) 5-10; F.C. FENSHAM, *The Root b'r in Ugaritic and in Isaiah in the Meaning "To Pillage"*, in *JNSL* 9 (1981) 67-69. It makes little difference for our purposes whether we are choosing between two roots or two somewhat different meanings of the same root.

9. Cf. U.F.C. WORSCHECH, *The Problem of Isaiah 6:13*, in *AUSS* 12 (1974) 126-138, p. 129.

10. K. BUDDE, *Jesaja's Erleben. Eine gemeinverständliche Auslegung der Denkschrift des Propheten (Kap. 6,1–9,6)*, Gotha, 1928, p. 27.

11. O. PROCKSCH, *Jesaia I* (KAT, 9), Leipzig, 1930, p. 59.

12. I.P. SEIERSTAD, *Die Offenbarungserlebnisse der Propheten Amos, Jesaja und Jeremia*, Oslo, 1946, pp. 107-109.

13. O. KAISER, *Das Buch des Propheten Jesaja, Kapitel 1–12* (ATD, 17), Göttingen, [5]1981, pp. 121 and 134.

that we find the *qal* in 1,31, a verse which continues the description of the judgment of the sinners from the previous verse. And if any lingering doubts should remain, the concluding "with no one to quench them (ואין מכבה)" puts the matter beyond question. Even on the assumption that the present vocalization is correct (the MT could equally be pointed as a *pi'el*, of course), it still seems very likely, in view of the connections which we have already noted between these two passages, that this is a further point of verbal association[14].

Even before we move on to consider the direction of dependence between these two related passages, it will be worth pausing at this point to consider one possible consequence for the rendering of 6,13. As has already been mentioned, virtually all studies of this verse in the modern period are agreed that שלכת refers to the felling of trees rather than to their loss of foliage[15]. There are probably two reasons for this. The first is conscious, and may be summarized in Emerton's words (p. 106): "such a meaning seems too weak as a figure of speech for the disaster that has just been described". The other may be less conscious, but has probably also played a part: it is noteworthy that in the various renderings from antiquity which have taken this line it is always associated with what we may term the hopeful interpretation of the verse – an interpretation which it nowadays seems difficult to share.

In the light of our comparison with 1,29-31, however, neither argument seems necessarily to be justified for a writer of antiquity. Isa 1,30 seems to regard the withering foliage as a token of the drying out of the

14. MÜLLER, *Sprachliche und religionsgeschichtliche Beobachtungen zu Jesaja 6* (n. 2), p. 183, adds as a separate argument the suggestion that the two passages are associated by virtue of the fact that they both relate to the desacralization of a sacred grove, and adds, "die Vorstellung eines heiligen Heims haftet dabei, deutlicher als in 6,13 und mit 17,10b.11 vergleichbar, an *hagannôt* 'die (einzelnen) Gärten' 1,29b und *gannā/* '(einzelner) Gärten' V. 30b". If justified, this would not really be an independent argument so much as an amplification of the comparison already inherent in כאלה, but in any case it is based upon a particular interpretation of 6,13 which is not universally shared. As we shall see, on the assumption that 1,29-31 is based on 6,13, it may be that the introduction of "the gardens" indicates something of the way in which the author *interpreted* 6,13, but it cannot legitimately be used for establishing dependence in the first place. For that, we should have required a mention of "gardens" or the like in 6,13 itself. For a sustained attempt to justify a cultic interpretation of 6,13, see G.K. BEALE, *Isaiah vi 9-13: a Retributive Taunt against Idolatry*, in *VT* 41 (1991) 257-278. Part of Beale's argument is that 6,13 stands after 1,29-31 in the book, so that it should be interpreted in its light. Whether or not this can be justified in terms of a "final-form" reading, the argument can hardly be admitted in terms of an historical reading of the text unless and until it has been established that 6,13 is dependent on (or presupposes) 1,29-31 rather than *vice versa*.

15. I refer, of course, to those who retain the MT at this point. A minority of scholars has suggested various emendations, but it seems unnecessary to pursue that route in the present context.

tree, which makes it more combustible, a point reinforced by the parallel phrase (with reference to the garden), "which has no water". There then follows a reference to "the strong" being made like tow (נערת), a word which on its only other occurrence in the Hebrew Bible (Judg 16,9) is again said to be particularly vulnerable to fire, and in parallel with this "his work"[16] will become like a spark. The passage then concludes with a description of the unquenchable burning as a climax to the paragraph in which this destruction is advanced in amplification of the complete devastation announced in verse 28 (יכלו and שבר). Fallen leaves thus seem to be part of a process that renders the tree tinder dry. (For desiccation as a prelude to combustion, see, for instance, Ezek 19,12-14.) It is thus not clear that this notion would be unsuitable or weak in 6,13, and it is emphatically not the case that some notion of hope is inherent in it. This does not, of course, necessarily mean that it is the best way of rendering שלכת, only that it should not be discounted on the basis of the arguments which have generally been advanced against it. Whether it is in fact to be preferred rests on considerations which go beyond our present concern.

It is now time to consider the direction of dependence between these two related passages. It will have been apparent from the start that in my opinion 1,29-31 is an interpretation of 6,13 rather than the other way about; in the nature of the case, it has proved difficult to present the data in a completely neutral manner. Nevertheless, this opinion needs to be justified, not least because there are those who argue or imply that the first part of the book of Isaiah is arranged in broadly chronological order[17], while, as mentioned in n. 14 above, Beale in particular has argued trenchantly that 6,13 presupposes 1,29-31, at least at the literary level.

One possible approach to this question should be eliminated at the outset. It might be held that since Isaiah 6 describes Isaiah's call, everything else in the book must have been written (or at least spoken) after it. However, quite apart from the fact that I am not necessarily persuaded that it is correct to label Isaiah 6 as the prophet's initial call, there are many commentators who argue that verses 12-13 are in any case a later

---

16. The vocalization has sometimes been thought to indicate "its maker" (taking חסן as a reference to an idol); see, for instance, GRAY, *Book of Isaiah I–XXVII* (n. 7), p. 40, following Kimhi. This is unnecessary, however; cf. GK §93q and Joüon §96Aj. There is a probable additional example of this vocalization at Mic 2,1 (apparently overlooked by the grammarians); cf. W. RUDOLPH, *Micha – Nahum – Habakuk – Zephanja* (KAT, 13/3), Gütersloh, 1975, pp. 51-52. The variations in the versions over the rendering of the suffix in Isa 1,31 are doubtless secondary.

17. E.g. J.H. HAYES – S.A. IRVINE, *Isaiah, the Eighth-Century Prophet: His Times and his Preaching*, Nashville, 1987; Y. GITAY, *Isaiah and his Audience: The Structure and Meaning of Isaiah 1–12* (SSN, 30), Assen, 1991.

addition to the original narrative. This is not the place to argue the merits or otherwise of that opinion, but it clearly means that the relationship with 1,29-31 ought to be settled on its own merits.

On purely internal grounds, we have noted that two of the three strongest points of connection between the passages are ambiguous in 6,13, namely the significance of בער and of שלכת. The equivalents of both words in 1,30 and 31 are unambiguous, however. Since it is normally the purpose of interpretation to make plain what may be obscure or open to misunderstanding, it is probable that 1,29-31 is an interpretation of 6,13 rather than the reverse.

Secondly, there can be little doubt that 1,29-31 is an expression of judgment for rather specific cultic malpractice[18], whereas the possible cultic allusions in 6,13, which in any case are not accepted by all commentators, are more allusive at best. Once again, it is more probable that a general statement is being applied to a specific situation in 1,29-31 than that 6,13 has deliberately emptied an earlier condemnation of its particular content.

These initial considerations bring us naturally to the question of the date of 1,29-31, over which there is little consensus. In common with many others, I have argued elsewhere[19] that Isaiah 1 as a whole is best regarded as a compilation of mainly Isaianic fragments, assembled late in the process of the development of the book as a whole in order to serve as an introduction to the (more or less) completed work[20]. This means that (i) in principal any part of it may have been composed by Isaiah, (ii) that we must be alert to the possibility that the redactor of the chapter as a whole may have intervened in order in particular to make a coherent whole out of the parts which he assembled, and (iii) that any part which on normal critical grounds we are inclined to ascribe to Isaiah

18. Against Budde's attempt to empty these verses of any cultic reference (K. BUDDE, *Zu Jesaja 1–5*, in *ZAW* 49, 1931, 16-40, pp. 35-39), see K. NIELSEN, *There is Hope for a Tree: The Tree as Metaphor in Isaiah* (JSOT SS, 65), Sheffield, 1989, pp. 202-210. Without reference to Budde, a comparable non-cultic interpretation has been advanced by J. HØGENHAVEN, *Gott und Volk bei Jesaja. Eine Untersuchung zur biblischen Theologie* (AThDan, 24), Leiden, 1988, pp. 186-187, but he expresses himself so cautiously that he seems hardly to have persuaded himself. For discussion of the practices in question, see (in addition to the commentaries) S. ACKERMAN, *Under Every Green Tree: Popular Religion in Sixth-Century Judah* (HSM, 46), Atlanta, 1992, esp. pp. 186-188; of possible relevance too is J.E. TAYLOR, *The Asherah, the Menorah and the Sacred Tree*, in *JSOT* 66 (1995) 29-54.

19. H.G.M. WILLIAMSON, *Synchronic and Diachronic in Isaian Perspective*, in J.C. DE MOOR (ed.), *Synchronic or Diachronic? A Debate on Method in Old Testament Exegesis* (OTS, 34), Leiden, 1995, pp. 211-226.

20. See most recently M.A. SWEENEY, *Isaiah 1–39, with an Introduction to Prophetic Literature* (FOTL, 16), Grand Rapids, 1996, pp. 63-87.

himself must have been moved from its original location elsewhere among the oracles of the prophet[21].

An impressive attempt to deal with 1,29-31 under this third point has been made by Nielsen[22]. She first demonstrates that these verses have a parallel in both message and imagery in the refrain passage 9,7-20 + 5,26-29, and then proposes that 1,29-31 would fit well following 9,20, their refrain element and a further stanza being now found in 5,25c + 5,26-29. Originally, "both of them together" (1,31) would have referred to the kings of Israel and Aram (see especially 7,4), for which the way was partly prepared by 9,20. The use of כי at the start of 1,29 has a parallel in the opening of the supposed previous stanza at 9,17, while יחדו in 1,31 may also indicate a link with the previous stanza at 9,20. The overall length of 1,29-31 + 5,25c matches the length of the other stanzas in the poem, and the variations in metre are not sufficient (in view of our uncertainties about metre in Biblical Hebrew generally) to rule out the suggestion.

There is, however, one serious difficulty which confronts this otherwise attractive proposal, and that is that the refrain poem is couched consistently in the third person, whereas 1,29-31 is predominantly second-person plural. Nielsen sees in this fact evidence that the passage has been adapted to its new context by the redactor of chapter 1, but that he did not see his work through consistently: she uses her hypothesis to explain the awkward (indeed, harsh) third-person introduction to the paragraph (כי יבשו) as well as its not-so-difficult third-person conclusion. While this is, of course, a possibility, I note against it that earlier in the chapter the redactor has *retained* the person and number of the passages he has moved to their new location and indeed, as I have tried to show in the article cited in n. 21, this is one of the best clues to tracing their original location. At the least, therefore, he would be acting out of character had he here followed the procedure which Nielsen proposes. Nonetheless, I regard Nielsen's discussion as the best approach for a defence of Isaianic authorship[23].

21. Cf. H. BARTH, *Die Jesaja-Worte in der Josiazeit. Israel und Assur als Thema einer produktiven Neuinterpretation der Jesajaüberlieferung* (WMANT, 48), Neukirchen-Vluyn, 1977, pp. 217-220; R.E. CLEMENTS, *Isaiah 1–39* (NCB), Grand Rapids - London, 1980, p. 28. Preliminary research on the pre-redactional form of verses 2-9 has persuaded me that it is perfectly possible to advance reasonable hypotheses to meet this third point; see my *Relocating Isaiah 1:2-9*, in C.C. BROYLES – C.A. EVANS (eds.), *Writing and Reading the Scroll of Isaiah: Studies of an Interpretive Tradition* (forthcoming).

22. NIELSEN, *There is Hope for a Tree* (n. 18), pp. 211-214.

23. There have not been lacking, of course, others who in recent times have similarly maintained Isaianic authorship, but they do not advance the kind of positive arguments

The alternative main approach to these verses is by way of an analysis of their vocabulary in comparison with usage elsewhere in the book of Isaiah, as well as, to a lesser extent, their setting within the present form of chapter 1 as a whole. The result of such studies is usually to ascribe the paragraph to a much later period than Isaiah himself, and in particular to find parallels with the closing chapters of the book. A good representative recent example is Smith. Smith believes that Isaiah 56–66 developed in two main stages (TI[1,2]), and he notes the following connections of theme and vocabulary between 1,27-31[24] and his TI[2]: "Yahweh's saving of the repentant in Zion (cf. שוב [1:27; 59:20]); illicit cults in gardens (cf. אילים [1:29; 57:5] and גנה/גן [1:29-30; 65:3; 66:17]); the people choosing these things (cf. בחר [1:29; 65:12; 66:4]); the forsakers of Yahweh (cf. עזבי יהוה [1:28; 65:11]); and shame for these activities (cf. בוש [1:29; 65:13; 66:5])"[25]. These observations may be linked with the repeatedly observed associations generally between Isaiah 1 and 65–66, on which Professor Beuken has himself written with commendably more caution than some[26]. Such connections can be explained in different ways: the author(s) of Isa 56–66 may have been influenced by the earlier parts of the book (something which is demonstrably the case in some instances), or the later editor(s) of the

found in Nielsen. They content themselves rather with observing that the paragraph is fragmentary and that there is nothing against ascribing it to Isaiah; see, e.g., WILDBERGER, *Jesaja* (n. 4); SWEENEY, *Isaiah 1–39* (n. 20), p. 87, with an unacknowledged change of mind from M.A. SWEENEY, *Isaiah 1–4 and the Post-Exilic Understanding of the Isaianic Tradition* (BZAW, 171), Berlin, 1988, p. 130.

24. It is well-nigh universally agreed that 1,27-28 are part of the work of the final redactor of chapter 1.

25. P.A. SMITH, *Rhetoric and Redaction in Trito-Isaiah: The Structure, Growth and Authorship of Isaiah 56–66* (SVT, 62), Leiden, 1995, p. 186. For similar summaries, cf. J. VERMEYLEN, *Du prophète Isaïe à l'apocalyptique. Isaïe, I–XXXV, miroir d'un demi-millénaire d'expérience religieuse en Israël*, I (EB), Paris, pp. 105-108; BARTH, *Die Jesaja-Worte* (n. 21), p. 292; O. LORETZ, *Der Prolog des Jesaja Buches (1,1–2,5)* (UBL, 1), Altenberge, 1984, p. 59; B. GOSSE, *Isaïe 1 dans la rédaction du livre d'Isaïe*, in *ZAW* 104 (1992) 52-66. It was noted long ago by Marti that Isaiah never uses בחר in the sense it has here, nor אילים or גנות, but that, as seen above, they occur more than once in Trito-Isaiah; cf. K. MARTI, *Das Buch Jesaja* (KHAT, 10), Tübingen, 1900, p. 22.

26. W.A.M. BEUKEN, *Isaiah Chapters lxv–lxvi: Trito-Isaiah and the Closure of the Book of Isaiah*, in J.A. EMERTON (ed.), *Congress Volume, Leuven 1989* (SVT, 43), Leiden, 1991, pp. 204-221. General studies of these links include L.J. LIEBREICH, *The Compilation of the Book of Isaiah*, in *JQR* 46 (1955-56) 259-277, and 47 (1956-57) 114-138; R. LACK, *La symbolique du livre d'Isaïe. Essai sur l'image littéraire comme élément de structuration* (AnBib, 59), Rome, 1973; SWEENEY, *Isaiah 1–4* (n. 23), pp. 21-24 (with particular attention to 1,29-31); A.J. TOMASINO, *Isaiah 1.1–2.4 and 63–66, and the Composition of the Isaianic Corpus*, in *JSOT* 57 (1993) 81-98. Some important reservations about overpressing the consequences of these observations, linked to considerations about the constraints under which late redactors of the book will have worked, are rightly voiced by D. CARR, *Reaching for Unity in Isaiah*, in *JSOT* 57 (1993) 61-80.

first part of the book may have been influenced by what, *ex hypothesi*, they knew was to follow, or they may be identified with each other or have moved in closely related circles. Without going into the kind of detail that would be needed to settle this matter with regard to each individual passage, however, I regard as probable at least the minimum represented by the last of these possibilities. This conclusion is based on the likelihood, already seen, that the compilation of Isa 1 in its present shape is relatively late, that 1,29-31 witnesses the kind of interpretation of 6,13 which is more likely to be the work of a later editor (as elsewhere in Isa 1–39) than of the prophet himself, and that, being joined closely (כי) with the generally accepted redactional passage 1,27-8, it may well also have been written by the same redactor for its present setting. The kind of links to which Smith and others have drawn attention seem to find their most natural explanation on this hypothesis. Although we cannot at present rule out absolutely the possibility that an earlier fragment has here been reworked or in some other way incorporated into chapter 1, the distinctive overlap of practices condemned here and in 65,3 and 66,17, in particular, makes their approximate contemporaneity more probable.

If this position is justified (and I am conscious that it has not been possible to argue for it fully here), then we may draw an interesting conclusion for our appreciation of the work of the redactor in chapter 1 as a whole. As others have argued recently[27], the purpose of this chapter is not so much to introduce the book (whether Isa 1–39 or 1–66) by way of a summary of its main themes, as was once thought, but rather to invite the reader to adopt a responsive attitude to all that is to follow. It exposes the past sin of the people and the judgment which has come upon them in consequence (1,2-9), exhorts them to a changed way of life (10-17) in the confidence that the past slate can be wiped clean if only they will now demonstrate obedience (18-20), and then finally draws fuller attention to the blessings of obedience (21-27, amplifying 19) and the disastrous perils of disobedience (28-31, amplifying 20). In emphasizing this last point, it is noteworthy that the redactor has chosen to take up the saying which concluded the ominous oracle in chapter 6, and has interpreted it for his post-exilic contemporaries in a way which challenges them in a manner which the final chapters of the book show to have been very much to the point. The influence of Isaiah 6 on the rest of the book in all of its main historical and redactional layers was pervasive[28],

27. See especially the works of Carr and Sweeney, already cited.
28. See my *The Book Called Isaiah: Deutero-Isaiah's Role in Composition and Redaction*, Oxford, 1994, pp. 30-56.

and it is perhaps not surprising that it should be prominent in this introductory section as well. But by focussing on its last and most severe
word of judgment, and by presenting it in terms which will have been so
relevant to his first readers, he has demonstrated both a fine literary and
rhetorical appreciation of the work which he was introducing, and a pas-
sionate pastoral concern for his readers which matches the solemnity of
the message which both Isaiah himself and he in his own later time were
called upon to deliver.

Christ Church   H.G.M. WILLIAMSON
Oxford, OX1 1DP
United Kingdom

JESAJA 8,19-23A ALS LITERARISCHE EINHEIT

Der Abschnitt Jes 8,19-23a gehört zu den Texten, die man als spätere Zusätze zur Denkschrift Jesajas (6,1–8,18) zu betrachten pflegt. Es handelt sich um ein Teilstück, dessen Erklärung nicht geringe Schwierigkeiten bereitet und dessen literarische Einheit in der Regel bestritten wird. Wir wenden uns im folgenden den vom Text aufgegebenen Problemen zu und möchten mit unseren Überlegungen den mittels der vorliegenden Festschrift geehrten Freund und Kollegen grüßen, dessen in der Reihe *De Prediking van het Oude Testament* erschienener Kommentar zu Deutero-Jesaja zu den hervorragendsten Arbeiten gehört, die je zur Klärung von Jes 40–66 verfaßt worden sind.

Bekanntlich betrachten die meisten Kommentatoren Jes 8,19-20 als späteren Zusatz von 8,16-18[1], beurteilen 8,21-22 als redaktionelle Bildung bzw. als Bruchstück eines Textes, dessen Anfang im überlieferten Text fehle[2], und sehen 8,23a als überleitende Glosse zu 8,23b–9,6 an[3]. Diese literarische Zersplitterung der Verse dürfte jedoch unnötig sein. Die nachfolgenden Überlegungen versuchen diese Sicht der Dinge

---

1. Vgl. B. DUHM, *Das Buch Jesaja*, Göttingen, ⁵1968, p. 86; A. BENTZEN, *Jesaja*. Bd. I: *Jes 1-39*, København, 1944, pp. 74-75; G. FOHRER, *Das Buch Jesaja*. Bd. I (ZBK), Zürich - Stuttgart, 1960, pp. 121-122 [Vs. 20 Zusatz]; H. WILDBERGER, *Jesaja* (BKAT, X/1), Neukirchen-Vluyn, 1972, pp. 343, 349; H. BARTH, *Die Jesaja-Worte in der Josiazeit* (WMANT, 48), Neukirchen-Vluyn, 1977, pp. 152-153; R.E. CLEMENTS, *Isaiah 1–29* (NCBC), Grand Rapids, MI, 1980, p. 101. Dagegen befürworten G.R. DRIVER, *Isaianic Problems*, in G. WIESSNER (ed.), *Festschrift für Wilhelm Eilers: ein Dokument der Internationalen Forschung zum 27. September 1966*, Wiesbaden, 1967, pp. 43-49 und J. VERMEYLEN, *Du prophète Isaïe à l'apocalyptique* I, Paris, 1977, pp. 228-229 die literarische Einheit von 8,19ff., vgl. auch A. SCHOORS, *Jesaja* (BOT, 9A), Roermond, 1972, p. 80. O. KAISER, *Das Buch des Propheten Jesaja. Kapitel 1-12* (ATD, 17), Göttingen, ⁵1981, p. 194 fragt sich, ob »der Abschnitt 8,19ff. nicht doch als eine Einheit zu werten ist«. O. PROCKSCH, *Jesaja I* (KAT, 4), Leipzig, 1930, p. 138-139 betrachtet 8,18.16-17.19 (*sic*) als literarische Einheit und Vs. 20 als Zusatz (vgl. G. Fohrer). E. JACOB, *Esaïe 1–12* (CAT, 8a), Genève, 1987, p. 131-132 behandelt 8,16-18 in direktem Zusammenhang mit 8,19-20. Nach K. MARTI, *Das Buch Jesaja* (KHAT, 10), Tübingen - Freiburg i.B. - Leipzig, 1900, p. 89 zeigen die Verse 19, 20 und 23 die Hand des Redaktors.

2. Vgl. PROCKSCH, *Jesaja* I (Anm. 1), p. 142; DUHM, *Jesaja* (Anm. 1), p. 86, FOHRER, *Jesaja* I (Anm. 1), p. 122; WILDBERGER, *Jesaja* (Anm. 1), pp. 355ff.; CLEMENTS, *Isaiah 1–29* (Anm. 1), p. 102; BARTH, *Jesaja-Worte* (Anm. 1), p. 153; JACOB, *Esaïe 1–12* (Anm. 1), p. 133.

3. MARTI, *Jesaja* (Anm. 1), p. 90 [Glosse]; DUHM, *Jesaja* (Anm. 1), p. 68; FOHRER, *Jesaja* (Anm. 1), p. 122 [Zusatz]; KAISER, *Jesaja* (Anm. 1), p. 194; CLEMENTS, *Isaiah 1–29* (Anm. 1), p. 103. PROCKSCH, *Jesaja* I (Anm. 1), p. 142 verbindet Vs. 23a direkt mit 8,21-22 und JACOB, *Esaïe 1–12* (Anm. 1), pp. 136-137 sieht jenen Versteil als Anfang der Prophetie 8,23–9,6 an.

zu begründen. Des besseren Verständnisses unserer Ausführungen halber
schicken wir unseren Erwägungen eine Übersetzung der einschlägigen
Verse voran, die sich einerseits bemüht, dem Grundtext gerecht zu werden, andererseits dazu anleiten möchte, die literarische Einheit von Jes
8,19-23a plausibel zu machen.

> 19 Und wenn man zu euch spricht:
>   Fragt an bei den Toten- und Wahrsagegeistern,
>   die da zirpen und murmeln!
>   Soll nicht ein Volk bei seinen »Göttern« anfragen,
>   zugunsten der Lebenden bei den Toten?,
> 20 (so antwortet:) Zur Weisung und zum Zeugnis!
>   Wenn man nicht diesem Wort gemäß spricht,
>   fürwahr, es (= das Volk) hat keine Morgenröte.
> 21 Man wird bedrückt und hungrig durch sie (= die Stadt)
>   hindurchziehen
>   und wenn man hungert, wird man in Wut geraten
>   und seinen König und seinen Gott verfluchen.
>   Man wird sein Antlitz nach oben wenden
> 22 oder zur Erde blicken, –
>   aber siehe, (nur) Not und Finsternis ohne Glimmer,
>   Bedrängnis und Dunkel ohne »Glanz«.
> 23a Fürwahr, nicht gibt es einen Schimmer
>   für den, der dadurch bedrängt wird.

Der Verfasser des Textes setzt voraus, daß es Personen geben wird,
die in der Notzeit dazu anregen, mittels Nekromantie[4] Auskunft und
Geleit für die Zukunft von den »wissenden«, hier als אלהים bezeich-
neten Totengeistern zu erlangen. Diesen Israels religiöse Tradition
mißachtenden Leuten gegenüber sollen die Angesprochenen, die ebensowenig wie die Sprechenden identifiziert werden[5], nachdrücklich auf die
prophetische Weisung und Predigt als einziges zuverlässiges Wort
hinweisen. Wenn das Volk diese göttliche Offenbarung in den Wind
schlägt, wird es nicht einen Schimmer von Hoffnung erleben, sondern
verzweifelt in schwarzgrauer Finsternis herumirren.
Man soll den schwierigen Vs. 20 nicht als einen an Stelle der
ursprünglichen Antwort Jesajas auf den Vorschlag von Vs. 19 hinzugefügten Zusatz[6], sondern als notwendige Fortsetzung des Konditional-
satzes dieses Verses betrachten. Unserer Meinung nach gibt es weder

---

4. Zur Nekromantie in Israel vgl. jetzt J. TROPPER, *Nekromantie. Totenbefragung im
Alten Orient und im Alten Testament* (AOAT, 223), Kevelaer - Neukirchen-Vluyn, 1989.
Weil Procksch אלהיו als Gott (Israels) interpretieren möchte, fand er in 8,19b einen
Nachsatz mit einer Gegenrede des Propheten.

5. Daß hier mit den Angesprochenen die Jünger des Propheten gemeint sein sollten,
ist recht unwahrscheinlich.

6. So FOHRER, *Jesaja* (Anm. 1), pp. 121-122.

einen guten Grund die Termini תורה und תעודה als Eidesinstanz[7] zu interpretieren noch den אם לא-Satz von 8,20b als Schwurformel zu beurteilen[8]. Denn die Verwendung der Präposition ל zur Einführung einer Eidesinstanz ist im Alten Testament sonst nicht belegt[9] und sachlich eignen sich »Zeugnis« und »Weisung« nicht als solche: nicht, wenn damit auf das schriftlich niedergelegte Prophetenwort angespielt sein sollte, und vollends nicht, wenn damit die mündliche Botschaft Jesajas gemeint ist. Den אם לא-Satz kann man einfach übersetzen: »Wenn man nicht diesem Wort gemäß spricht«, d.h. nicht nach dem in der Weisung und dem Zeugnis des Propheten verkündeten Wort Gottes (für die Verwendung von דבר im Sinne des zukunftgestaltenden Gotteswortes vgl. 9,7). Allerdings bereiten die Schlußworte von 8,20 bei dieser Übersetzung neue Probleme, besonders אשר und שחר. Was אשר anbelangt, – wir haben vor vielen Jahren die Meinung vertreten, daß die hebräischen Demonstrativpronomina זה, זאת und אלה sowie אשר ursprünglich als deiktische Interjektionen zu betrachten sind und daß die ihnen von alters her inhärente Funktion noch an bestimmten Stellen des Alten Testaments erhalten geblieben ist[10]. Daher möchten wir auch in Jes 8,20 אשר als »fürwahr« deuten und folglich schließen, daß der Verfasser des Textes hervorheben wollte, daß Leute, die der göttlichen Weisung bzw. dem prophetischen Zeugnis nicht gehorchen, keinen Schimmer von Hoffnung haben. Dann aber bedeutet שחר wohl nicht, wie manchmal vorgeschlagen worden ist, »Zauber«[11], sondern im Einklang mit der Übersetzung der Vulgata (matutina lux) »Morgenröte« als Metapher für einen Schimmer von Hoffnung. Diese Erklärung von 8,20 wird nicht dadurch beeinträchtigt, daß לו (Singular) auf den Plural יאמרו Bezug nimmt, weil man לו leicht auf das vorhin erwähnte »Volk« beziehen[12] oder allenfalls distributiv deuten kann.

Was dem Volk, das der Weisung und dem Zeugnis nicht gehorchen will, bevorsteht, wird u.E. in den folgenden Versen ausgeführt. Das Perfectum consecutivum ועבר bestätigt diese Deutung. Es wäre wohl

---

7. Wie BARTH, *Jesaja-Worte* (Anm. 1), p. 153, Anm. 75 mit Recht bemerkt, sind »Weisung« und »Zeugnis« als Eidesinstanz sachlich problematisch.

8. So H.-P. MÜLLER, *Das Wort von den Totengeistern*, in *Welt des Orients* 8 (1975) 65-76, bes. pp. 72-73 und BARTH, *Jesaja-Worte* (Anm. 1), p. 153.

9. So mit Recht BARTH, *Jesaja-Worte* (Anm. 1), p. 153, Anm. 75 gegen H.-P. MÜLLER, *Totengeistern* (Anm. 8), pp. 67-68 und TROPPER, *Nekromantie* (Anm. 4), p. 272.

10. *Das Hebräische Pronomen Demonstrativum als hinweisende Interjektion*, in *Jaarbericht Ex Oriente Lux* 18 (1964) 307-313. Vgl. z.B. 2 Sam 2,4 und Micha 6,12.

11. So z.B. dem Hinweis von DRIVER, *Isaianic Problems* (Anm. 1), pp. 43-49 folgend, WILDBERGER, *Jesaja* (Anm. 1), p. 352; MÜLLER, *Totengeistern* (Anm. 8), pp. 73-74 und TROPPER, *Nekromantie* (Anm. 4), p. 276. »Zauber, Macht« paßt aber nicht als Kennzeichnung des Wortes V. 19: cf. BARTH, *Jesaja-Worte* (Anm. 1), p. 153, Anm. 78.

12. So VERMEYLEN, *Isaïe* (Anm. 1), p. 230.

kaum gewählt worden, wenn die Verse 21-22 nicht die Fortsetzung des
Vorangehenden bildeten, und es wäre kaum beibehalten, wenn der
Abschnitt (wie oft angenommen) ein Bruchstück eines ursprünglich
längeren Textes, dessen Anfang verschollen ist, sein sollte. Das Volk
wird »bedrückt und hungrig durch sie hindurchziehen«. Mit »sie« kann,
wie H. Barth nachgewiesen hat[13], nur die Stadt Jerusalem gemeint sein,
auf die ohne vorangehendes Beziehungswort auch an anderen jesajanischen Stellen hingedeutet wird[14]. Vorausgesetzt scheint eine Belagerung der Stadt zu sein, die bedrückend ist und allenthalben Hungersnot
hervorgerufen hat. Das Motiv kann im Rahmen eines der Gedenkschrift
hinzugefügten Abschnitts nicht wundernehmen, weil eben sie einen
feindlichen Angriff auf Jerusalem und eine Überschwemmung Judas
durch den assyrischen König (8,7) voraussieht. In völliger Verzweiflung
und vom Hunger gequält wird man den König, der nicht helfen kann,
und Gott, der nicht helfen will, für die hoffnungslose Situation
verantwortlich machen und sie verfluchen[15]. Nach oben oder nach unten
blickend findet man nichts als unentrinnbare Bedrängnis und Finsternis.
Es ist verlockend, in Vs. 22b מעוף als מֵעִיף, »ohne Glimmer«, zu lesen
und מנדח entweder als מִנְדֹּחַ, »ohne Entrinnen«, aufzufassen[16], oder in
מְנֻגַּה, »ohne Glanz« (vgl. LXX), zu ändern. Aber auch wenn man den
Vers anders emendieren bzw. übersetzen möchte[17], bliebe die Beschreibung einer aussichtslosen Lage behalten.

Noch schwieriger als bei den vorangehenden Versen lassen sich der
Sinn und die Funktion von Jes 8,23a bestimmen. Die unterschiedlichen
Deutungen der Stelle machen einen fast mutlos[18]! Immerhin dürfte die
Übersetzung: »Fürwahr, nicht gibt es einen Schimmer für den, der
dadurch bedrängt wird«, nicht abwegig sein. לה bezieht sich auf die im
vorigen Vers genannte Not, Finsternis, Bedrängnis und das Dunkel, vgl.
GK, §135p. Daß man die Stelle stilistisch, formgeschichtlich und inhaltlich nicht als ursprünglichen Bestandteil des Vorangehenden betrachten
könne[19], leuchtet nicht ein: daß die vorausgesagte Finsternis ohne Glimmer und Glanz sich auf eine Belagerung Jerusalems durch die Assyrer

13. *Ibid.*, p. 153.
14. Vgl. Jes 3,25-26; 5,14.
15. Daß »König« hier einen Götzen andeute und das folgende Substantiv mit »seine
Götter« zu übersetzen sei – so C.F. WHITLEY, *The Language and Exegesis of Isaiah 8: 16-
23*, in *ZAW* 90 (1978) 28-43, pp. 32-33 – ist unwahrscheinlich, weil im Kontext weder
von diesen noch vom jenem die Rede ist.
16. So DRIVER, *Isaianic Problems* (Anm. 1), p. 46 und KAISER, *Jesaja* (Anm. 1), p. 193.
17. Vgl. die von WHITLEY, *Language and Exegesis* (Anm. 15), p. 33 gebotene Über-
sicht der Textänderungsvorschläge.
18. Vgl. *ibid.*, pp. 33-34.
19. So BARTH, *Jesaja-Worte* (Anm. 1), p. 154.

beziehen kann, ist im Einklang mit der jesajanischen Prophetie[20]. Als *überleitende* Glosse ist 8,23a (wenn unsere Übersetzung das Richtige trifft) kaum zu betrachten, weil im Folgenden von einer *Rettung* aus der Finsternis (9,1, vgl. auch 8,23b-c) die Rede ist. Hätten wir tatsächlich mit einer überleitenden Glosse zu tun, dann müsste in ihr wenigstens eine Heilsperspektive durchklingen. Daß aber ist offenkundig nicht der Fall. So bleibt 8,23a durchaus dem *vorangehenden* Text verhaftet. Formgeschichtlich läßt sich nicht recht einsehen, weshalb in diesem Textteil nicht eine Schlußfolgerung aus der vorangehenden Beschreibung vorliegen könnte, die dem Propheten zuzuschreiben wäre, vgl. 2,22; 3,7c.

Obgleich Barth[21] Jes 8,19-23a nicht als literarische Einheit betrachtet und 8,21-22 offenbar als ursprünglich nicht mit 8,19-20 zusammengehörigen Text ansieht, hebt er dennoch mit Recht hervor, daß die Annahme eines Fragments immer eine problematische Notauskunft ist. Daß 8,21-22 als von den zwei vorangehenden Versen unabhängiger Text zu beurteilen sei, geschweige denn, daß der Anfang dieses Abschnitts fehle, ist aufgrund unserer oben zur Sprache gebrachten Erwägungen mindestens zu bezweifeln. Es gibt u.E. keinen genügenden Grund 8,21-22 von 8,19-20 zu trennen, weil der Inhalt jener Verse sich vorzüglich als Beschreibung der verzweifelten Lage, in die sich die Leute, die wegen ihrer Mißachtung der jesajanischen Weisung und seines Zeugnisses keinen Schimmer von Hoffnung haben, versetzen. Hinzu kommt, daß die Aussage, daß es keinen Schimmer geben wird (8,23a), vorzüglich zum Schluß von Vs. 20 paßt. In angstvoller Zeit hilft keine Nekromantie, nur Vertrauen auf das Wort Gottes und das Zeugnis seines Propheten: »Wenn ihr nicht glaubt, so werdet ihr nicht bleiben« (Jes 7,9c)! Die sich inhaltlich an Jes 8,16-18 und an das Hauptanliegen der jesajanischen Denkschrift anschließenden Verse entsprechen der Tendenz der Botschaft des Propheten des achten Jahrhunderts v. Chr. und könnten daher von ihm stammen, umsomehr weil Metrum, Stil und Vokabular durchaus für Jesaja sprechen. Zwar weckt 8,16-18 den Eindruck einer abschließenden Aussage. Das bedeutet aber nicht, daß der Prophet seiner Denkschrift nicht nachträglich eine Betrachtung hinzugefügt haben kann. Manche Kommentatoren möchten »Weisung« in 8,20 als *schriftlich* niedergelegten Nachlaß der prophetischen Bewe-

---

20. Wenn Jes 5,30 tatsächlich sekundär ist und teilweise aus 8,22 »geborgt ist« – DUHM, *Jesaja* (Anm. 1), p. 63 –, läßt sich die Authentizität von Jes 8,21-23 dennoch vertreten, weil sonst in 5,30 mit einer Sekundärverwendung eines sekundären Textes zu rechnen wäre.

21. *Ibid.*, p. 153.

gung verstehen. Weil aber »Zeugnis« offenbar synonym mit »Weisung« gebraucht wird, der Gebrauch von תורה für die schriftlich niedergelegte Weisung eines Propheten geradezu nicht charakteristisch ist und »Zeugnis« ebenfalls auf mündlich vermitteltem Unterricht hinzuweisen scheint, dürfte trotz der gegenüber 8,16 vorgenommenen Umkehrung der beiden Wörter in 8,20 nicht ein schriftlich fixiertes Dokument gemeint sein. Weil aus sprachlichen Gründen nichts gegen die jesajanische Verfasserschaft von 8,19-23a spricht, dürfte also weder der eine noch der andere Einwand durchschlagend sein und könnten also »Weisung und Zeugnis«, wie immer man auch 8,16 deuten will, in 8,20 die jetzt in seiner Denkschrift aufgezeichnete *Predigt* des Propheten meinen, deren Inhalt nicht nur dem König, sondern auch anderen (vgl. 8,12) bekannt war. Auf jeden Fall bietet der Text keinen ausreichenden Grund ihn in die Zeit, in der Jerusalem von Nebukadnessar II. erobert wurde, anzusetzen. Wegen der Erwähnung des Königs (8,21) und der vorausgesetzten angstvollen Zeit sowie des sprachlichen Kolorits sollten wir die Verse 8,19-23a dem Propheten Jesaja also nicht vorschnell absprechen. Vielmehr erläutern sie auf konkrete Weise den Tenor seiner Denkschrift. So dürfte Jes 8,19-23a nicht nur eine literarische Einheit bilden, sondern auch von Jesaja stammen.

Diese Datierung wäre unausweichlich, wenn man den Ausführungen von Whitley folgen könnte, der 8,23b-c literarisch nicht (wie üblich) von 8,23a trennen möchte, sondern jenen Versteil als Begründung der Aussage von 8,23a auffaßt[22]: Tiglathpilesers Eroberung der nördlichen Gebiete Israels und seine Eroberung der westlichen Küstenebene, des Ostjordanlandes und Galiläas seien der beste Beweis dafür, daß auch Jerusalem vom mächtigen Assyrer gefährdet sei[23]. Aber seine Deutung von הכביד im Sinne von »Er hat eine schwere Last auferlegt»[24] läßt sich kaum aufrechterhalten, weil der explizite oder implizite Gebrauch von כבד Hiph. im Zusammenhang mit קלל Hiph. die Deutung von הכביד im Sinne von »er hat zu Ehren gebracht« nahelegt: vgl. Jes 23,9, wo davon die Rede ist, daß man »diejenigen, die auf Erden geehrt sind« (נכבדי ארץ) »verächtlich macht« (להקל), und Ez 22,7, wo es heißt, daß man »Vater und Mutter in dir (= in der Blutstadt Jerusalem) verächtlich behandelt« (הקלו) unter Mißachtung des Rechtsgebots, das die Ehrung der Eltern fordert (כבד; Ex 20,12; Dt 5,16). Dann aber bringt 8,23b-c eine Heilswende zum Ausdruck und kann dieser Textteil literarisch nicht unmittelbar mit dem Vorangehenden verbunden werden. Die Frage, ob die Worte ursprünglich zur Prophetie 9,1-6 gehören oder vielmehr als

22. *Ibid.*, pp. 34ff.
23. *Ibid.*, pp. 41-42.
24. *Ibid.*, pp. 36-37.

redaktionelles Brückenglied, das 9,1-6 mit 8,21-23a bzw. 8,19-23a verbindet, zu betrachten sind, wird verschiedentlich beantwortet, ist aber im Hinblick auf Datierungsprobleme auch im Zusammenhang mit unseren Überlegungen nicht unwichtig. Auf jeden Fall soll betont werden, daß die traditionelle Übersetzung von 8,23b-c, die הקל perfektisch, הכביד jedoch futurisch interpretiert, grammatikalisch nicht statthaft ist[25]. Deswegen kann nur gemeint sein, daß, nachdem über das Land Sebulon und das Land Naphtali ehemals Schande gebracht wurde, diesen Gebieten *jetzt* Ehre verliehen worden ist. Man kann darüber streiten, ob in 8,23c auf die Bildung dreier assyrischer Provinzen (*du'ru* = Meerstraße; *magidu* = Völkerkreis; *gal'azu* = Ostjordanland) in der Regierungszeit Tiglatpilesers III. angespielt wird[26], oder ob, dem Gebiet von Sebulon und Naphtali entsprechend, vielmehr an die von Damaskus zum Mittelmeer führende Straße[27], das Gelände des Jordans[28] und Galiläa gedacht ist. Wie immer man auch dieses Problem zu lösen gedenkt, klar ist, daß davon geredet wird, daß die nördlichen Gebiete des ehemaligen nordisraelitischen Königtums neulich (offenbar von Gott selber) wieder »zu Ehren gebracht« worden sind. Diese Aussage stammt kaum anders als aus der Zeit Josias, der imstande war dieses Land seinem Königreich einzuverleiben, und läßt sich schwerlich mit einer nachexilischen Situation vor der Hasmonäerzeit vereinbaren. Daß 8,23b-c literarisch von 9,1-6 zu trennen sei, wie eine Anzahl von Kommentatoren denkt, mutet als Notauskunft an, weil der 9,3 erwähnte Midianitertag uns ebenfalls nach Nordisrael versetzt (Richt 7,1) und Sebulon und Naphtali sich an dem Sieg über die Midianiter beteiligten (Richt 6,35). Die erwähnte Befreiung vom feindlichen Joch, die Thronnamen und die Nominalsätze von 9,6a, die keine futurische Übersetzung nahelegen, sprechen entschieden dafür, 9,1-6 mit H. Barth und Vermeylen der josianischen statt der nachexilischen Zeit zuzuweisen und den Text von 8,23b-c, der offenbar ebenfalls aus jener Epoche stammt, als Anfang des betreffenden Abschnitts zu betrachten. Denn die Bezugnahme auf Sebulon und Naphtali stellt die Freude über die Wiederherstellung des Umfangs des davidischen Reiches heraus und bei nachexilischer Abfassung hätten, wie schon Greßmann[29] hervorgehoben hat, »ganz an-

---

25. Wie J.A. EMERTON, *Some Linguistic and Historical Problems in Isaiah VIII.23*, in *JSS* 14 (1969) 157-158 mit Recht betont hat.

26. So besonders A. ALT, *Jesaja 8,23–,9,6. Befreiungsnacht und Krönungstag*, in W. BAUMGARTNER (ed.), *Festschrift Alfred Bertholet zum 80. Geburtstag*, Tübingen, 1950, pp. 29-49 (= *Kleine Schriften* II, pp. 206-225) und viele andere Kommentatoren nach ihm.

27. Dazu BARTH, *Jesaja-Worte* (Anm. 1), pp. 159-160.

28. Vgl. B. GEMSER, *Be'eber hajjarden. In Jordan's Borderland*, in *VT* 2 (1952) 349-355, bes. p. 354.

29. H. GRESSMANN, *Der Messias*, Göttingen, 1929, p. 244; vgl. BARTH, *Jesaja-Worte* (Anm. 1), p. 172.

dere Tatsachen« betont werden müssen. In exilischer und erst recht in nachexilischer Zeit »sind weder eine Situation noch ein Motiv auszumachen, aus denen heraus gerade das in 8,23b in Blick genommene nordisraelitische Territorium von Interesse wäre«[30]. Fraglich ist, ob die Vorstellungen vom Königtum, wie wir sie in den Thronnamen antreffen, in nachexilischer Zeit so lebendig waren, daß einer damit hätte rechnen können, von seinen Hörern oder Lesern verstanden zu werden[31]. Vor allen Dingen fällt aber ins Gewicht, daß die Gestalt von 9,5-6 ein aktuell-gegenwärtiger, vorfindlicher Jerusalemer König ist[32]. Die Bemerkung, daß 9,1-6 aus dem (jesajanischen) Entweder-Oder vom Umkehr oder Gericht ein zeitliches Vorher-Nachher geworden ist (erst Gericht, dann Heil), führt nicht notwendig zu der Schlußfolgerung, daß wir mit einem exilischen bzw. nachexilischen Text zu tun haben[33]. Denn auch die Verse 8,23b-c, die kaum anders als aus josianischer Zeit herrühren können, setzen dieselbe Wandlung voraus. So läßt sich schließen, daß 8,23b–9,6 eine literarische Einheit bildet, die vorexilisch, wenn auch nicht jesajanischer Herkunft ist.

Wenn die vorhergehenden Betrachtungen das Richtige treffen, ist es wahrscheinlich, daß wir das vom Danklied her zu verstehende[34] Heilswort 8,23b–9,6 als Gegenstück von 8,19-23a aufzufassen haben. Denn die Notschilderung dieser Verse ist dem Text von 8,23b–9,6 kaum *nachträglich* hinzugefügt worden, vor allen Dingen nicht in exilischer oder nachexilischer Zeit. Vielmehr antwortet 8,23b–9,6 im jetzigen Zusammenhang auf die düstere Prophetie von 8,19-23a mit einem Heilszeugnis, das der josianischen Zeit entstammt. Somit muß der Abschnitt 8,19–23a chronologisch dem Inhalt von 8,23b–9,6 vorangehen und steht nichts im Wege, jene Verse dem Propheten Jesaja zuzuschreiben.

So dürfte die gangbare Aufsplitterung der rätselhaften Verse 8,19-23a mehr Probleme hervorrufen als sie zu lösen vermag. Bis auf bessere Belehrung halten wir dafür, daß man die literarische Einheit der Perikope und seine jesajanische Herkunft mit guten Gründen befürworten kann. Die These erscheint zwar angesichts der bisherigen Forschung als ziemlich verwegen, läßt sich aber aufgrund der angestellten Analysen dennoch nicht unterdrücken.

Domela Nieuwenhuislaan 57   Adam S. VAN DER WOUDE
NL-9722 LJ Groningen

---

30. BARTH, *Jesaja-Worte* (Anm. 1), p. 172.
31. So mit Recht WILDBERGER, *Jesaja* (Anm. 1), p. 369.
32. Vgl. BARTH, *Jesaja-Worte* (Anm. 1), p. 173.
33. Wie J. VOLLMER, *Zur Sprache von Jes 9,1-6*, in ZAW 80 (1968) 343-350 und R. KILIAN, *Jesaja 1–39* (EdF, 200), Darmstadt, 1983, pp. 9-10 meinen.
34. Vgl. BARTH, *Jesaja-Worte* (Anm. 1), p. 148ff.

DIE VERHEISSUNG JESAJA 11,1-10
UNIVERSAL ODER PARTIKULAR?

I

Jes 11,1-10 gilt als einer der »großen« Texte des Ersten Testaments[1]. Er wird einerseits gerne in der Zusammenschau mit Jes 7,10-17 und Jes 9,1-6 messianisch bzw. christologisch gelesen; deshalb hat der Abschnitt in der christlichen Liturgie seinen »Sitz« in der Advents- und Weihnachtszeit. Andererseits spielt der Text wegen des in ihm gegebenen Zusammenhangs von Gerechtigkeit (11,1-5) und Schöpfungsfrieden (11,6-8) in der theologischen Ökologiediskussion eine bedeutsame Rolle; er scheint die im konziliaren Prozeß entwickelte Programmatik »Gerechtigkeit – Friede – Bewahrung der Schöpfung« klassisch zusammenzufassen[2] und wird deshalb gerne zitiert.

Blickt man in die exegetische Landschaft, macht der Text eher Schwierigkeiten, insbesondere was das Verständnis des Abschnitts über den sog. Tierfrieden angeht.

Von nicht wenigen Exegeten wird bezweifelt, daß 11,1-5 und 11,6-8 eine ursprüngliche Einheit bildeten. Auch wenn 11,6-8 als eine spätere kommentierende Fortführung von 11,1-5 begriffen werden könne, seien hier zwei Themen zusammengestellt worden, die *eigentlich* nicht zusammenpassen[3]. Gegen die These, die beiden Teile 11,1-5 und 11,6-8 bildeten

---

1. Meist wird, vor allem mit Blick auf eine christologische Perspektive, der Text mit 11,1-9 abgegrenzt; auf der Ebene der Endkomposition muß 11,10 in jedem Fall hinzugenommen werden. Der Anfang der Perikope wird unterschiedlich bestimmt. Ob man die Perikope schon mit 10,27b – so z.B. K. KOCH, *Die Profeten I. Assyrische Zeit*, Stuttgart, ³1995, p. 241 – oder mit 10,33 – so z.B. H. BARTH, *Die Jesaja-Worte in der Josiazeit. Israel und Assur als Thema einer produktiven Neuinterpretation der Jesajaüberlieferung* (WMANT, 48), Neukirchen-Vluyn, 1977, pp. 54-76 – oder eben mit 11,1 – so z.B. H. SEEBASS, *Herrscherverheißungen im Alten Testament* (Biblisch-Theologische Studien, 19), Neukirchen-Vluyn, 1992, pp. 19-21 – beginnt, hängt nicht unwesentlich davon ab, ob man 10,27-34 im Kontext von 10,5-34 als Gerichtsankündigung gegen Assur oder 10,27-34 als Gerichtsankündigung gegen Juda bzw. das davidische Königshaus versteht.

2. Vgl. SEEBASS, *Herrscherverheißungen* (Anm. 1), pp. 37-39.

3. H.-J. HERMISSON, *Zukunftserwartung und Gegenwartskritik in der Verkündigung Jesajas*, in EvT 33 (1973) 54-77, p. 59: »Vielfach rechnet man auch V. 6-8 zum ursprünglichen Textbestand. Es fällt aber auf, daß hier ein neues Thema angeschlagen wird … Man hat nun demgegenüber darauf hingewiesen, daß ›Gerechtigkeit‹ (das Thema von 3-5) und ›Naturheil‹ seit alters zusammenhängen. Aber dieser Hinweis ist nicht

eine originäre Einheit, werden nicht nur traditionsgeschichtliche Überlegungen geltend gemacht, sondern auch der Textbefund selbst: »Dem
Ductus von 11,1-5 hätte entsprochen, daß die wilden Tiere wie die Gewalt-
menschen in 11,4 gemäß Lev 26,6; Ez 34,25-28 ausgerottet werden«[4].

Vor allem erweist sich das genauere Verständnis von 11,6-8 bzw.
11,6-9 als schwierig. Es gibt allegorische, metaphorische, mythische
Deutungen und Mischungen dieser Interpretationen unter stärkerer oder
schwächerer Berücksichtigung der innerbiblischen Intertextualität[5].

Dezidierte Vertreter der allegorischen Auslegung sind in neuerer Zeit
M. Rehm und *M. Buber*. Rehm stellt zunächst gegen alle Versuche, den
Text wörtlich zu verstehen, fest: »Der Prophet spricht vom Frieden, der
die Tiere miteinander und mit dem Menschen verbindet. Es kann nun
nicht Zufall sein, daß gerade solche Arten aufgezählt werden, zwischen
denen in der Natur eine Freundschaft unmöglich ist. Der Löwe kann sich
nicht vom Stroh ernähren und der Bär nicht Gras fressen, da ihnen die
dazu erforderlichen Organe fehlen. Ebensowenig können Lämmer und
Kälber friedlich mit Löwen, Panthern und Wölfen zusammenleben, da
die kleinen Tiere den großen Raubtieren von der Natur als Nahrung
bestimmt sind. Diese müssen daher töten, um überhaupt überleben zu
können. Naturnotwendig wird deswegen die Nähe eines Löwen eine
Schafherde in jähen Schrecken versetzen und die Tiere zu wilder Flucht
auseinandertreiben, so daß kein Hirt, erst recht kein Kind, imstande ist,
sie ruhig zu leiten. Von Natur aus empfindet eine Schlange und jedes im
Freien lebende Tier die Berührung durch einen Menschen als Bedrohung
und versucht daher zu fliehen oder sich zu wehren. Die Behauptungen
des Propheten widersprechen allen Gesetzen der Natur und ihre Verwirk-
lichung würde eine gänzliche Umwandlung der bestehenden Ordnung
und eine Änderung in den Organen und der Lebensweise der Tiere
bedeuten«[6]. Rehm schlägt deshalb eine konsequente allegorische
Deutung vor und findet ihre Begründung im biblischen Text: »Ent-

exakt. Wohl weiß die Königsideologie Israels wie des alten Orients von den Segens-
wirkungen, die vom König ausgehen, zu berichten, und solcher Segen erstreckt sich
durchaus auf den Bereich der Natur und der Welt. Aber m.W. erscheint in diesem
Zusammenhang nirgends das Thema ›Tierfrieden‹. Das Thema ist in der Königsideologie
auch gar nicht zu erwarten, weil die Darstellungen des Königsheils bei allem Überschwang durchaus im Bereich (potentiell) *realer* Erfahrungen bleiben«.

4. O.H. STECK, »... *ein kleiner Knabe kann sie hüten«. Beobachtungen zum Tierfrieden in Jesaja 11,6-8 und 65,25*, in J. HAUSMANN – H.-J. ZOBEL (eds.), *Alttestamentlicher Glaube und Biblische Theologie*, Stuttgart, 1992, pp. 104-113, p. 107.

5. Vgl. den Überblick bei M. REHM, *Der königliche Messias im Licht der Immanuel-
Weissagungen des Buches Jesaja* (Eichstätter Studien NF, 1), Kevelaer, 1968, pp. 210-
218, 228-234.

6. *Ibid.*, p. 210.

scheidend ist... der Wortlaut des Spruchs selbst. ›Sie tun nichts Böses und handeln nicht verderblich auf meinem ganzen heiligen Berg; denn das Land ist voll von Erkenntnis Jahwes‹. Die Aussage folgt auf die Bemerkung über die Tiere. Die Sätze aber sind so miteinander verbunden und 11,9 setzt 11,8 so unmittelbar fort, daß unmöglich ein Wechsel des Subjekts angenommen werden kann. Jene, die nichts Böses tun und nicht verderblich handeln, müssen daher die gleichen sein, von denen vorher die Rede war. Daß Tiere als Vollbringer des Bösen und Verderblichen bezeichnet werden, ist ungewöhnlich. Auf keinen Fall kann ihnen ›Erkenntnis Jahwes‹ zugeschrieben werden. Der Prophet begründet aber das Fehlen böser und verderblicher Handlungen damit, daß ›das Land voll ist von Erkenntnis Jahwes‹. Da nun Träger der Gotteserkenntnis nur Menschen sein können, muß in der Schilderung des Tierfriedens eine Beschreibung menschlicher Verhältnisse gegeben sein. Dies ist aber nicht so zu verstehen, als würden durch die einzelnen Tiere bestimmte Typen von Menschen bezeichnet. Der Prophet will vielmehr die Vorzüge nennen, die unter der Herrschaft des erwarteten Königs eintreten. Durch das friedliche Zusammensein von Wolf und Lamm, Panther und Böcklein, Löwe und Kalb, das in der Natur nicht möglich ist, ... wird gelehrt, daß tief eingewurzelte Feindschaften, die von Natur geschaffen zu sein scheinen, im Reich dieses Königs aufhören. Durch das Bild von der Bärin, die auf die Weide geht, und dem Löwen, der sich von Stroh ernährt, was in der Natur niemals geschehen kann, wird ausgesprochen, daß gewalttätige, wilde Menschen sich unter diesem König zu friedsamer Tätigkeit herbeilassen. Durch das ruhige Verhalten des Kalbes und des Masttieres in der Gegenwart eines Löwen und durch die Sorglosigkeit, mit der ein Kind am Schlupfloch der Natter spielt und nach der jungen Schlange greift, wird ausgedrückt, daß unter der Herrschaft dieses Königs alle Gefahren verschwinden und die Menschen frei von Furcht leben können. Mit den Bildern aus der Tierwelt zeichnet also der Prophet die glücklichen Verhältnisse, die im Reich des erwarteten Königs eintreten werden. Es handelt sich um eine Allegorie. Sie umschreibt, was in 9,5 durch den Namen ›Friedensfürst‹ ausgedrückt war, und verdeutlicht, was in der Aussage vom ›Frieden ohne Ende‹ enthalten war«[7].

Buber deutet die Schilderung des Tierfriedens in V. 6-8 als Allegorie des Weltfriedens. »Es will mich bedünken, daß dieses Idyll, wo die wilden Tiere bei den zahmen ›gasten‹, nur ein Sinnbild des Völkerfriedens sein soll, vielleicht gar eins, in dem man unter den Namen der Wildlinge bestimmte

7. *Ibid.*, pp. 216-218.

Nationen erkannte. Die Schilderung steht ja zwischen der Darstellung des
gerechten Waltens des Zukunftsherrschers und der Ansage (V. 9), es werde
nichts Böses und Verderbliches mehr geübt werden ›auf dem ganzen Berg
meines Heiligtums‹, weil die Erde ›der Erkenntnis JHWHs voll‹ sei – nicht
mehr bloß der Ausstrahlung Gottes also, wie im Wechselgang der Seraphen,
sondern auch der menschlichen Wahrnehmung, der menschlichen An- und
Aufnahme seines Wirkens. In diesen Zusammenhang paßt der Völkerfriede
weit eher als der Tierfriede – zumal wenn man bedenkt, daß der Berg des
Heiligtums eben der ist, zu dem als dem höchsten der Heiligtümer in einer
anderen messianischen Weissagung (2,1-5) die Völker ›strömen‹, um dort
von Gott in seinen Wegen unterwiesen zu werden und seinen Schiedsspruch
zu empfangen, der all ihre Streitigkeiten schlichtet»[8].

Zu dieser Art der allegorischen Deutung von V. 6-8 hat *H. Groß* kri-
tisch angemerkt, daß hier keine bloße Tierallegorie vorliege, sondern
daß in dem Text auch menschliche Figuren auftreten. »Bezöge sich die
Weissagung nur allegorisch oder symbolisch auf verschiedene Men-
schenklassen oder Völker, so wäre sicher ein menschliches Wesen in ihr
selber nicht erwähnt. Wenn auch nicht alle Einzelzüge der Verheißung
sich dinglich ereignen werden, so ist es dennoch unberechtigt, in den
Tieren nur symbolische Größen zu sehen. Im Gegenteil: in dem ...
Zusammenhang mit der Urzeit (Gen 1,29f) hat die Stelle sicher auch den
realen Inhalt, daß am Ende der Zeit die ursprüngliche Harmonie
zwischen Tier und Tier, zwischen Tier und Mensch auf wunderbare
Weise wieder in Erscheinung treten wird«[9]. Der Text sichert dem
Menschen zu, »daß er im Frieden der Endvollendung des Glücksgutes,
das die Tierwelt darstellt, nicht zu entbehren braucht. Der Inhalt dieser
neuen Realität wird allerdings nicht in natürlichen und geschichtlichen
Kategorien aufgehen, sondern der verwandelten Endzeit zugehören, sie
wird mithin eine ›ideale Realität‹ sein«[10]. Was diese Kategorie meint,
erläutert Groß in einer Anmerkung folgendermaßen: »Mit ›idealer
Realität‹ sei einmal das Bleibende der geschöpflichen Dinge, dann aber
auch ihre Entwicklung bis in die Endvollendung hin ausgedrückt, die sie
dem Endzustand überhaupt wird homogen werden lassen«[11].

Auf der Linie dieser »realen« Deutung liegt auch die Interpretation
von *R. Bartelmus*, der sein »reales« Verständnis zugleich »symbolisch«
nennt und dies folgendermaßen erläutert: »Da ich den Text mit vielen

8. *Der Glaube der Propheten*, Zürich, 1950, pp. 215-216.
9. *Die Idee des ewigen und allgemeinen Weltfriedens im Alten Orient und im Alten Testament* (Trierer Theologische Studien, 7), Trier, 1956, p. 92.
10. *Ibid.*, pp. 92-93.
11. *Ibid.*, p. 93 Anm. 75.

anderen Exegeten von der Paradiesgeschichte her lese – und zwar von der bereits mit Gen 1 verbundenen Paradiesgeschichte her – kann ich in ihm nur Anspielungen auf konkrete Tiere erkennen, auf Tiere allerdings, die sich anders verhalten als es der menschlichen Erfahrung entspricht. Das symbolische Element liegt für mich nicht darin, daß die geschilderten Relationen zwischen Raubtieren und Haustieren, zwischen Schlange und Kind auf etwas anderes hinweisen wollten – seien es Völker, sei es eine abstrakte Vorstellung. Symbolisch ist der Text vielmehr insofern, als hier nach dem Prinzip *pars pro toto* Einzelaspekte angesprochen werden, die als Hinweis auf die gesamthafte Wiederherstellung des paradiesischen Urzustandes zu verstehen sind – die geschilderten Einzelaspekte meinen nichts anderes, sondern mehr als das, was sie unmittelbar ansprechen. Wenn die gesamte Tierwelt im Einklang mit Gen 1,29f wieder zur vegetarischen Ernährung zurückkehrt, wenn also die zwischentierische Aggression aufgehoben ist, wenn der Fluch von Gen 3,15 nicht mehr gilt, nach dem zwischen Mensch und Schlange ewige Feindschaft bestehen soll, dann sind diese Fakten zunächst im Wortsinn so zu verstehen, wie sie dastehen. Die symbolische Bedeutung ergibt sich daraus, daß die angesprochenen Fakten von einem Kontext her bekannt sind, den nicht nur wir unschwer als den paradiesischen Urzustand erkennen können, der durch das hybride Verhalten des Menschen zerstört wurde. Indem einzelne Aspekte dieses Gesamtentwurfs explizit angesprochen werden, die dem Autor als besonders typisch erscheinen, wird der paradiesische Urzustand selbst heraufbeschworen, dessen eschatologische Wiederherstellung der Text ankündigen will«[12]. Dadurch daß diese eschatologisch-universalistische Schau von Jes 11,6-8 nun in 11,1-10 mit dem partikularistisch-messianischen Konzept 11,1-5.9-10 (sekundär) verbunden wurde, sei der ursprünglich auf den Zion bezogene Messiasgedanke ausgeweitet worden und zur »Basis einer nicht mehr national gebundenen Religion« gemacht worden; damit aber sei der »Weg ins NT gewiesen«[13].

Daß die Vision von Jes 11,6-8, gerade wenn sie schöpfungstheologisch verstanden wird, nicht die Aufhebung der geschaffenen Naturordnung meint, daß der Text also nicht »real« gelesen werden darf, wird von einer ganzen Reihe von Autoren ausdrücklich betont. So faßt *G.J. Botterweck* seine Deutung so zusammen: »Nach Jes 11,6-8

---

12. *Die Tierwelt in der Bibel II. Tiersymbolik im Alten Testament exemplarisch dargestellt am Beispiel von Dan 7, Ez 1/10 und Jes 11,6-8*, in B. JANOWSKI – U. NEUMANN-GARSOLKE – U. GLESSMER (eds.), *Gefährten und Feinde der Menschen. Das Tier in der Lebenswelt des alten Israel*, Neukirchen-Vluyn, 1993, pp. 283-306, bes. pp. 304-305.

13. *Ibid.*, p. 306.

findet das kommende Friedensreich des Heilskönigs auch darin seinen sichtbaren Ausdruck, daß die Schöpfung wieder ihre uranfängliche Schöpfungsordnung, die Harmonie zwischen Menschen und Tieren und damit auch ihre Sicherheit zurückerhält... Will der Prophet für die kommende Friedenszeit eine reale Umwandlung der Tiernaturen und -instinkte aussagen, daß der Löwe wirklich Strohhäcksel frißt? Kaum! Entscheidend ist die Verheißung des totalen Friedens, dessen kosmischen Umfang die Schilderung des Tierfriedens veranschaulichen soll«[14]. Und *R. Kilian*, der den Text ähnlich versteht, kommentiert folgendermaßen: »Der endzeitliche Friede ist demnach die Rückkehr zum Paradies. Endzeit und Urzeit entsprechen sich. In [6-8] äußert sich menschliche Sehnsucht, die ziel- und sinngerichtet ist, auch wenn sie in unzulänglichen, nicht realistischen Bildern zur Darstellung gelangt. Es geht nicht um biologische Fakten, die als solche ganz anders sind, sondern um eine letzte Harmonie, die der Autor dadurch zum Ausdruck bringt, daß er alles in dieser Welt Störende negiert. Er will in [3-8] aufzeigen, was Friede wirklich ist: das Ende von Unterdrückung, Ungerechtigkeit und gewaltsamem Tod. In [9] faßt er sein Anliegen und seine Botschaft zusammen: Das Böse in der Welt wird überwunden sein!«[15]. In dieser Perspektive ist der Text dann geradezu problemlos christologisch aktualisierbar, insofern »das NT ... Jesus Christus als den endgültigen und alleinigen Messias ausweist, der auf seine Weise all das birgt, was in [1-8] angedeutet ist«[16].

Gegen alle bislang skizzierten Formen kosmischer und universaler Interpretation von Jes 11,6-8 hat nun *O.H. Steck* massiven Einspruch erhoben: »Das gängige Stichwort ›Tierfriede‹ verleitet dazu, mit V. 6-8 das umfassende Bild einer wieder friedlichen Natur zu verbinden, in der alle Tiere und Menschen ohne Bedrohung und Angst zusammenleben ... So generell kann die Thematik im Alten Testament durchaus gesehen werden – in der Nahrungszuweisung innerhalb der göttlichen Ur-Setzung der Schöpfung Gen 1,29f., der die vorfindliche Welt auch in ihrer göttlichen Lebensordnung im Sinne der Priesterschrift freilich nicht mehr entspricht (Gen 9,1-7; Ps 8). Im exegetischen Bestreben, Jes 11,6-

---

14. Art זאב *zeʾeb*, in *TWAT* II, pp. 501-509, bes. p. 508.

15. R. KILIAN, *Jesaja 1–12* (Neue Echter Bibel, 17), Würzburg, 1986, p. 90. – Vgl. ähnlich SEEBASS, *Herrscherverheißungen* (Anm. 1), pp. 23 und 34: »... kann schließlich die höchste Steigerung erreicht werden: die Wiederkehr der Urzeit. Dabei hat man V. 6-8 als Bild/Mythos für etwas zu fassen, was als Realität ja nicht beschrieben werden kann. Die Beschreibung gilt einer Zukunft, wie sie der Weltordnung (in Ägypten: Maat) entspräche ... das Ziel der Weissagung ist eine Gewaltfreiheit, die in einer nur mythisch sagbaren Weise auch die Tierwelt erfaßt«.

16. KILIAN, *Jesaja 1–12* (Anm. 15), p. 89.

8 ebensoweit zu dimensionieren, erscheint hingegen der Wunsch oder die Utopie der Vater des Gedankens. Genau genommen ist hier die Perspektive jedoch anders. Man sieht es schon daran, daß unter den gefährdeten Lebewesen kein einziges Tier der freien Wildbahn genannt ist – nicht Gazelle, Wildesel, Strauß, Steinbock, Reh, Damhirsch, o.ä. V. 6-8 ist vielmehr ... im Grunde menschenorientiert«[17]. Genauer gesprochen: V. 6-8 ist israelorientiert. Der Abschnitt handelt »nicht universell von Natur, Tierwelt im ganzen, sondern von Tiergefährdungen für Israel im Land als Strafe, deren Wende in unüberbietbarer Weise hier angekündigt wird... Die todbringenden Tiere werden sich so verhalten, wie es die Haus- und Nutztiere jetzt schon tun, so daß im Blick auf Tiere und Menschen mit besonderem Augenmerk auf das Kleine, Wehrlose, Schwache (vgl. 11,1-5!) ein ungefährdetes Zusammenleben gegeben sein wird. Der leitende Sachaspekt ist also die menschliche Lebens- und Versorgungswelt mit den besonders bedrohten Herdentieren und Menschen; für Israel in seinem Lande wird sich die empirische Tierwelt gleichsam in eine allumfassende Haustierwelt verändern, so daß für das ganze Heilsland in V. 9 auch in dieser Hinsicht das Résumé gezogen werden kann: ›Nicht wird man Schaden anrichten/ übelhandeln und nicht wird man Verderben wirken auf meinem ganzen heiligen Berge‹, weil die Jahweerkenntnis das ganze Land überzieht und auch die todbringenden Tiere (vgl. schon 1,3) einschließen wird«[18].

Mit diesen Präzisierungen hat Steck zweifellos dem Text seinen Israel-Bezug zurückgegeben. Gleichwohl ist zu fragen, ob der Text nicht doch *zugleich* eine schöpfungstheologische Perspektive hat, vor allem wenn der Text in seiner *Gesamtmetaphorik* bedacht und wenn diese noch stärker, als Steck dies tut, im Kontext der Komposition Jes 1–12 gedeutet wird. Dazu sollen im Folgenden einige Beobachtungen zusammengestellt werden.

II

Auf der Ebene der Endkompsition von Jes 1–12 gehört Jes 11,1-10 zu dem Komplex Jes 10,5–12,6, der sich zusammen mit dem Komplex Jes 1,2–4,6 um den Mittelteil Jes 5,1–10,4 legt. Während 10,5-34 das Gericht über Assur und damit die Rettung Zions vor äußerer Bedrohung ankündigt, entfaltet 11,1-10 die Rettung Israels vor innerer Bedrohung und die dadurch ausgelöste Wallfahrt der Völker zu diesem Ort der

17. *Beobachtungen* (Anm. 4), pp. 109-110.
18. *Ibid.*, pp. 111-112.

Offenbarung des כבוד. Zu diesem Ort strömt der »Rest seines Volkes« (11,11-20) und singt das Danklied der Rettung durch den endgültigen Exodus (Jes 12).

Der Abschnitt 11,1-10 weist vielfältige Bezüge bzw. Entsprechungen zu 1,2–4,6 auf:

(1) Daß der neue Trieb aus dem abgehackten Baumstumpf Isais sich zuinnerst von צדק und אמונה leiten läßt (11,5), entspricht dem Wesen Zions/Jerusalems gemäß 1,21.26.

(2) Daß der neue Baum »Recht schafft« (שפט) und »schlichtet« (יכה hi.), wie 11,3 hervorhebt, entspricht dem Wirken JHWHs in Zion, wie es Jes 2,4 beschreibt.

(3) Daß nun »Erkenntnis JHWHs« und »Einsicht« (vgl. 11,2.9) um sich greift, ist Aufhebung des in 1,3 beklagten Zustandes, daß Israel keine Erkenntnis und JHWHs Volk keine Einsicht hat. Es ist auch eine Aufhebung des in Jes 6,9f als Gericht über Israel/Zion verhängten Zustandes.

(4) Daß der neue Trieb »Frucht bringt« (11,1), korrespondiert der Verheißung von 4,2. Die dann in 11,1-5 beschriebene »Fruchtbarkeit« des Baumes ist die Funktion des Königs als Lebensbaum (vgl. Ri 9,7-15; Ez 31; Dan 4)[19].

(5) Daß auf dem heiligen Berg nichts Böses mehr getan wird (רעע) und daß nicht mehr verderbt gehandelt wird (שחת), beendet, wie die Stichwortbezüge unterstreichen, das in 1,4 beklagte schuldhafte Handeln[20].

(6) Die in 4,2-6 dem Zion verheißene Qualität, Ort des כבוד zu sein (4,2.5), wird dem Zion auch in 11,10 zugesprochen[21].

(7) Wie in 2,1-5 das auf dem Zion sich vollziehende Geschehen »die Völker« (גוים) und »die Nationen« (עמים) zur Wallfahrt dorthin bewegt, so geschieht dies auch gemäß 11,10.

Was aber ist es, das die Völker und die Nationen gemäß Jes 11,1-10 auf dem Zion »erfragen« und als eine Art Gottesorakel (11,10: דרש) lernen können bzw. sollen?

---

19. Vgl. H. GENGE, Zum »Lebensbaum« in den Keilschriftkulturen, in Acta Orientalia 33 (1971) 321-334; K. NIELSEN, There is Hope for a Tree: The Tree Metaphor in Isaiah (JSOT SS, 65), Sheffield, 1989, pp. 79-85. Der König als Lebensbaum hat im übrigen mehrfach eine Schutz- und Ordnungsfunktion für die Tierwelt: vgl. schon Ez 31 und Dan 4.

20. Jes 1,4: זרע מרעים בנים משחיתים.

21. Zur Interpretation des Abschnitts Jes 4,2-6 in Korrespondenz zu Jes 2,1-5 vgl. besonders I. FISCHER, Tora für Israel – Tora für die Völker. Das Konzept des Jesajabuchs (SBS, 164), Stuttgart, 1995, pp. 24-36.

Unter Beachtung der intertextuellen Bezüge und der Gesamtmetaphorik von Jes 11,1-10 muß die Antwort auf diese Frage lauten: Die
Völker sollen *auf dem Zion* erfahren und lernen, *daß* und *wie* die
Schöpfung als Ort der Gottesherrschaft und als Haus des Lebens zu
jener Vollendung kommt, die in Gen 1–9 entworfen ist. Sie sollen
lernen, daß und wie die eschatologische Erneuerung der Schöpfung in
und mit der messianischen Zionsgemeinde beginnt – »an jenem Tag«
(11,10) bzw. »in der Zeitenwende« (2,2).

Daß die universale schöpfungstheologische Perspektive des am Zion
partikular beginnenden Geschehens in der Sicht von Jes 11,1-10
konstitutiv bleibt, unterstreicht zunächst einmal 11,9a. Dieser Halbvers
hat, worauf Steck aufmerksam gemacht hat[22], die Funktion, die beiden
Abschnitte 11,3b-5 und 11,6-8 zusammenzufassen. Zugleich aber ist
nicht zu übersehen, daß der Halbvers auf die biblische Sintfluterzählung
anspielt. Was in Gen 6,5 bzw. in Gen 6,11f als Auslöser der Flut
genannt wird[23] und (auf der Ebene der Priesterschrift) zur Modifikation
der Schöpfungsordnung in Gen 9,1-3 («Schreckensherrschaft der
Menschen über die Tiere«) führt, findet gemäß Jes 11,9 »auf dem ganzen heiligen Berg« sein Ende. Das aber heißt doch nichts anderes, als
daß nun – wenigstens auf dem Zion – das in Gen 1,26-31 intendierte
Schöpfungsziel »endgültig« erreicht ist[24]. Diesen Aspekt unterstreicht
11,9b mit der Feststellung, daß dann das ganze Land Israel erfüllt ist mit
Erkenntnis JHWHs und eben nicht, wie Gen 6,12 beklagte, erfüllt ist mit
חמס, an dem כל־בשר (d.h. Mensch *und* Tier) beteiligt sind. Genau dazu
aber entwirft 11,3-8 das Gegenbild. Die Welt auf dem »ganzen heiligen
Berg« ist eine Welt ohne חמס – vermittelt durch den neuen »königlichen« Trieb aus dem Baumstumpf Isais.

---

22. *Beobachtungen* (Anm. 4), p. 106 Anm. 14.

23. Gen 6,5: רע; Gen 6,11-12: שחת ni. und hif. Während Gen 6,5 nur das böse
Handeln der Menschen betont, ist in Gen 6,11-12 das verderbte Handeln von כל בשר =
Mensch *und* Tierwelt im Blick.

24. Da nun Gen 6,11-12 zurückgenommen ist, findet auch der in Gen 9,1-3 vom
Schöpfergott konzedierte »Krieg« der Menschen gegen die Tiere ein Ende. Damit
kann die »königliche« Menschheit gemäß Gen 1,26-30 ihr friedliches Leitungsamt in
Vertretung des Schöpfergottes wahrnehmen. Zu diesem Verständnis von Gen 1,26-28
vor dem Hintergrund der neuassyrischen *Königsideologie* vgl. besonders B.
Janowski, *Herrschaft über Tiere. Gen 1,26-28 und die Semantik von* רדה, in G.
Braulik – W. Gross – S. McEvenue (eds.), *Biblische Theologie und gesell-
schaftlicher Wandel*. FS N. Lohfink, Freiburg, 1993, pp. 183-198. Da, wie vielfach
herausgearbeitet, das Verhältnis der Menschen zu den Tieren in Gen 1,26-28 eine
königstheologische Metapher ist, ist die Verbindung von Königsideologie und
Beziehung Mensch – Tier, insbesondere unter dem Aspekt der Hirtentätigkeit (Jes
11,7!), nicht so ungewöhnlich wie unterstellt wird: vgl. oben Hermisson, *Zukunftserwartung* (Anm. 3).

Auch wenn Jes 11,1-10 gezielt alle Königs- und Herrschertitulatur vermeidet, ist die Metaphorik des *ganzen* Abschnitts, was bei Steck etwas zu kurz kommt, königstheologisch bestimmt:

(1) Das in 11,3-5 im Hintergrund stehende Bild vom König als dem Kämpfer für Recht und Gerechtigkeit wird in 11,6-7 kollagenartig fortgeführt mit dem Bild vom königlichen Hirten, der autoritativ das Zusammenleben der Wild- und Haustiere als »König/Herr der Tiere« ordnet[25]. In Jes 11,6-7 geht es ja nicht einfach darum, daß nur die Bedrohung des Landes durch die Raubtiere zu Ende ist, sondern daß sie von einem kleinen Knaben »geleitet« (נהג) werden. Der sog. Tierfriede stellt sich nicht einfach ein, sondern ist Folge dieser »Hirtentätigkeit«[26].

(2) Im Hintergrund von 11,6f könnte auch die besonders in der assyrischen, persischen und hellenistischen Königsideologie entfaltete Vorstellung von den königlichen *paradeisoi*-Parks stehen, die geradezu als »Realsymbole« der königlichen Vollmacht, die göttliche Schöpfungsordnung an ihr Reich zu vermitteln, betrachtet bzw. präsentiert wurden[27].

(3) Das Motiv des Gottesgartens, in dem gottgestifteter Friede herrscht, dürfte auch im Hintergrund von Jes 11,8 stehen.

(4) Daß sich schließlich das Bild von dem aus dem abgehackten Baum neu nachwachsenden »Königsbaum« am urzeitlichen »Baum des Lebens« der Paradiesgeschichte inspiriert, ist möglich, aber nicht sicher.

25. Neben die Vorstellungslinie, daß Ruhe und Frieden nur durch die Vernichtung der Feinde und der feindlichen Tiere hergestellt werden können (z.B. Lev 26,6-7), tritt hier (wie in Jes 2,1-5) die Vorstellung, daß die Feinde und die feindlichen Tiere von ihrer zerstörerischen Feindschaft lassen – weil sie im Kraftfeld der רוח יהוה leben, die sich vom »neuen Sproß« aus ausbreitet. Vgl. J. EBACH, *Ende des Feindes oder Ende der Feindschaft? Der Tierfrieden bei Jesaja und Vergil*, in DERS., *Ursprung und Ziel. Erinnerte Zukunft und erhoffte Vergangenheit*, Neukirchen-Vluyn, 1986, pp. 75-89, bes. p. 78. – Zum Motiv vom »Herrn der Tiere« als einer autoritativen Ordnungsgestalt für das Zusammenleben der Tiere bzw. zur Begründung einer heilvollen Welt vgl. besonders O. KEEL, *Jahwes Entgegnung an Ijob. Eine Deutung von Ijob 38–41 vor dem Hintergrund der zeitgenössischen Bildkunst* (FRLANT, 121), Göttingen, 1978, pp. 86-125 sowie dort besonders Abb. 67 und Abb. 69.
26. In der Komposition 11,6-7 bildet die »Hirtennotiz« 11,6bβ die Mitte und muß auf die ganze Komposition bezogen werden. Das Verbum נהג für die Hirtentätigkeit unterstreicht die autoritative Leitungsfunktion. Daß mit נער קטן auf Jes 7,14-15 und Jes 9,5-6 angespielt wird, ist m.E. durchaus möglich.
27. Diese »Gärten« waren »Miniaturen« der ganzen Natur. Vgl. dazu vor allem W. FAUTH, *Der königliche Gärtner und Jäger im Paradeisos. Beobachtungen zur Rolle des Herrschers in der vorderasiatischen Hortikultur*, in *Persica* 8 (1979) 1-53. Auf Zusammenhänge zwischen Gen 1 und der paradeisos-Vorstellung weist auch C. UEHLINGER, *Vom dominium terrae zu einem Ethos der Selbstbeschränkung. Alttestamentliche Einsprüche gegen einen tyrannischen Umgang mit der Schöpfung*, in *Bibel und Liturgie* 64 (1991) 59-74, p. 70 hin.

Die besondere Pointe von Jes 11,1-10 liegt nun aber darin, daß zumindest von 11,10 her und in Korrespondenz zu Jes 2,1-5; 4,2-6 der »königliche« Fruchtbaum, der als Anfang der »neuen Schöpfung« auf dem Zion wächst und die Völker anzieht, nicht eine Einzelgestalt ist, sondern die erneuerte Zionsgemeinde, auf der die schöpferische רוח יהוה ruht[28]. Daß die רוח יהוה den Lebensort Israels in einen urgeschichtlichen Garten des Friedens und der Gerechtigkeit für Mensch und Tier verwandelt, ist im übrigen auch die in Jes 32,15-20 entworfene Vision. Es ist eine partikulare Vision, die gleichwohl universale Relevanz hat.

Weder müssen »real« auf dem Zion Schmiedewerkstätten errichtet werden, damit dort Schwerter zu Pflugscharen und Lanzen zu Winzermessern umgeschmiedet werden, noch müssen dort in Labors die Raubtiere genetisch zu Haustieren verändert werden. Entscheidend ist, daß dort eine Pflanzung von Recht und Gerechtigkeit wächst. Das ist die Pointe, der schöpfungstheologisch *und* königstheologisch inspirierten Verheißung Jes 11,1-10: Wenn auf dem Zion die Unterdrückten und Armen endlich zu ihrem Lebensrecht kommen, bricht an diesem Ort der Schöpfung die Gottesherrschaft an. Dieser Ort lohnt dann wirklich, daß die Völker sich dort kundig machen[29].

Israel und die Kirche beanspruchen, daß sie sich von Jes 11,1-10 konstituieren lassen. Ob beide wenigstens darunter leiden, daß sich diese Vision in ihnen *beiden* noch nicht erfüllt hat?

Seminar für Zeit- und Religionsgeschichte   Erich ZENGER
des Alten Testaments der WUU Münster
Johannisstraße 8-10
D-48143 Münster

---

28. Auf der Ebene der Endkomposition muß 11,1-9 von 11,10 her gelesen werden; das wird auch durch den Rückbezug von 11,1 nach 6,13 bestätigt. Diese Sicht setzt im übrigen voraus, was hier nicht weiter diskutiert werden kann, daß zumindest 11,6-9 bzw. 11,1-9 als kompositionelle Einheit nachexilisch ist. Zur Kollektivierung der Davids- bzw. der Königstheologie im Jesajabuch vgl. vor allem Jes 55,3-5.

29. Mit diesem kleinen Beitrag grüße ich den liebenswürdigen Kollegen Wim Beuken: in Erinnerung an seine faszinierende Gastvorlesung in Münster und mit großer Hoffnung für den Jesaja-Kommentar, den er für die von mir herausgegebene Reihe HThKAT übernommen hat: עד מאה ועשרים שנה.

ISAIAH 12,1-6
A DOMAIN AND COMMUNICATION ANALYSIS

In recent years, the use of *domains*[1] to describe a text has been introduced into Old Testament exegesis from modern linguistics[2]. The main concept of a domain analysis is the idea that a text consists of a basis domain with dependent sub-domains. The basic domain is made up of the whole of the text(fragment) to be analyzed, i.e. the (textual) reality of the *narrator*. Within this basis domain, subordinated domains may occur, in which, even though linguistically dependent on the basis domain, other, new (textual) realities may occur which, by definition, need not coincide with the basis domain.

The advantage of such a method of analysis is that transitions between narration and discourse and between direct speech and forms of indirect speech can be demonstrated and described in a more adequate manner, as well as shifts within one and the same domain. Domains analyzed in such a way, give shape to both the communication pattern in a text and to the communication between text and reader.

A number of linguistic observations play an important role here[3]:

1. The verbal tense marks the two communicative worlds of *narration* and *discourse*[4]. *Tempus-Übergänge* indicate shifts in or in relation to these two worlds[5].

1. The following names occur: "primarily intentional domain" and "intentional subdomain", cf. G.H. RIGTER, *Intentional Domains and the Use of Tense, Perfect and Modals in English*, in *Journal of Semantics* 1 (1982) 95-145; "mental base space" and "mental subspace", cf. G. FAUCONNIER, *Mental Spaces: Aspects of Meaning Construction in Mental Language*, Cambridge, ²1994 (¹1985); ID., *Domains and Connections*, in *Cognitive Linguistics* 1 (1990) 151-174; "discourse domain", cf. P. SEUREN, *Discourse Semantics*, New York, 1985; "perspective domain", cf. W. SPOOREN, *Some Aspects of the Form and Function of Global Contrastive Coherence Relations*, Nijmegen, 1989; "partitioned representation", cf. J. DINSMORE, *Partitioned Representations*, Dordrecht, 1991; "linguistic world", cf. A. PALACAS, *Attribution Semantics: Linguistics World and Point of View*, in *Discourse Processes* 16 (1993) 239-277.

2. See in particular: L.J. DE REGT, *Tempus in het Bijbels Hebreeuws*, in *Glot* 6 (1983) 247-275; J.M. SANDERS, *Perspective in Narrative Discourse*, Tilburg, *s.a.* [= 1994], esp. pp. 82-113 about the "Garden of Eden" and "Solomon's Judgement"; L.J. DE REGT, *Domains and Subdomains in Biblical Hebrew Discourse*, in E. TALSTRA (ed.), *Narrative and Comment*. FS W. Schneider, Amsterdam, *s.a.* [= 1995], pp. 147-161.

3. See also A.L.H.M. VAN WIERINGEN, *The Reader in Genesis 22:1-19*, in *EstBíb* 53 (1995) 291-296.

4. See also: H. WEINRICH, *Tempus. Besprochene und erzählte Welt*, Stuttgart, ³1977 (¹1964), p. 33 and W. SCHNEIDER, *Grammatik des biblischen Hebräisch. Völlig neue*

2. The *verba dicendi* as well as other verbal and prepositional phrases function as linguistic signs which open new sub-domains[6].

3. The linguistic categories *person*, *number* and *gender* are decisive for the *referential centre* in and between the domains[7].

4. Furthermore, the deictic elements indicate the *deictic centre* in and between the domains[8].

In the present contribution, I would like to describe and analyze the text of Isa 12,1-6[9] by means of domains, based on linguistic observations.

Work Translation of Isaiah 12

To lay out the text of Isa 12,1-6, I will make use of a form in which each *clause(-atom)* is connected to another *clause(-atom)*. The *brackets* indicate which *clause(-atom)s* are connected and when. The double *brackets* mark the direct speech. On principle, no more than two units are ever connected to each other[10]. The asterisk * marks the ending of the *clauses/clause-atoms*.

Bearbeitung der »Hebräischen Grammatik für den akademischen Unterricht« von Oskar Grether, München, [7]1989 ([1]1974), pp. 183-193; E. TALSTRA, *Text Grammar and Biblical Hebrew: The Viewpoint of Wolfgang Schneider*, in *Journal of Translation and Textlinguistics* 5 (1992) 269-297.

5. See also WEINRICH, *Tempus* (n. 4), pp. 164-221 and SCHNEIDER, *Grammatik* (n. 4), pp. 193-200; DE REGT, *Domains* (n. 2), pp. 148-150, 159-160.

6. See also SCHNEIDER, *Grammatik* (n. 4), pp. 195, 201.

7. See also SANDERS, *Perspective* (n. 2), p. 42. Here, the phenomena of "pronominalization" and "renominalization" are important, too. Cf. SCHNEIDER, *Grammatik* (n. 4), pp. 235-237.

8. See also SANDERS, *Perspective* (n. 2), p. 42 and SCHNEIDER, *Grammatik* (n. 4), pp. 237-240.

9. Especially since L. ALONSO SCHÖKEL, *Is 12: De duabus methodis pericopam explicandi*, in *Verbum Domini. Commentarii de re Biblica* 34 (1956) 154-160, this chapter is at the centre of interest, in particular from the viewpoint of redaction criticism. See, moreover, W.S. PRINSLOO, *Isaiah 12: One, Two or Three Songs?*, in K.-D. SCHUNCK – M. AUGUSTIN (eds.), *Goldene Äpfel in silbern Schalen. Collected Communications to the XIIIth Congress of the International Organization for the Study of the Old Testament, Leuven 1989* (BEATAJ, 20), Frankfurt - Berlin - Bern - New York - Paris - Wien, 1992, pp. 25-33; H.-P. MATHYS, *Dichter und Beter. Theologen aus spätalttestamentlicher Zeit* (OBO, 132), Freiburg - Göttingen, 1994, pp. 181-200; H.G.M. WILLIAMSON, *Isaiah XI 11-16 and the Redaction of Isaiah I–XII*, in J.A. EMERTON (ed.), *Congress Volume Paris 1992* (SVT, 61), Leiden - New York - Köln, 1995, pp. 343-357. Cf. also W.A.M. BEUKEN, *The Prophet Leads the Readers into Praise: Isa 25:1-10a in Connection with Isa 24:14-23 Seen Against the Background of Isaiah 12*, which will appear in the monograph on Isaiah 24–27 on behalf of the *Jesaja Werkplaats* (1997).

10. A.F. DEN EXTER BLOKLAND, *In Search of Text Syntax: Towards a Syntactic Text Segmentation Model for Biblical Hebrew* (Applicatio, 14), Amsterdam, 1995, pp. 135-200; H. LEENE, *Unripe Fruit and Dull Teeth (Jer 31,29; Ez 18,2)*, in TALSTRA (ed.), *Narrative* (n. 2), pp. 84-87. The tabulation does not indicate levels, whereas the brackets mark grammatical connections.

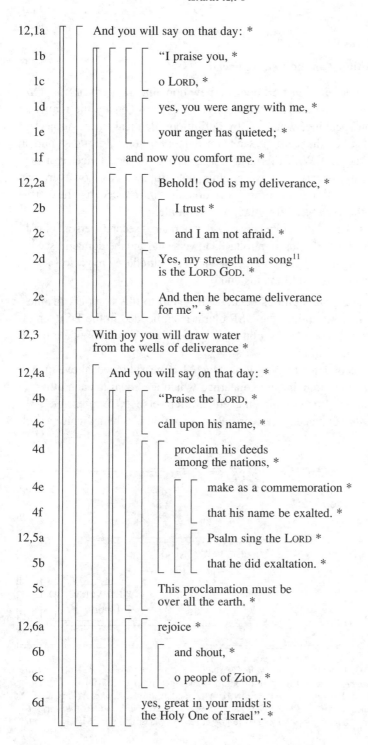

12,1a	And you will say on that day: *
1b	"I praise you, *
1c	o LORD, *
1d	yes, you were angry with me, *
1e	your anger has quieted; *
1f	and now you comfort me. *
12,2a	Behold! God is my deliverance, *
2b	I trust *
2c	and I am not afraid. *
2d	Yes, my strength and song[11] is the LORD GOD. *
2e	And then he became deliverance for me". *
12,3	With joy you will draw water from the wells of deliverance *
12,4a	And you will say on that day: *
4b	"Praise the LORD, *
4c	call upon his name, *
4d	proclaim his deeds among the nations, *
4e	make as a commemoration *
4f	that his name be exalted. *
12,5a	Psalm sing the LORD *
5b	that he did exaltation. *
5c	This proclamation must be over all the earth. *
12,6a	rejoice *
6b	and shout, *
6c	o people of Zion, *
6d	yes, great in your midst is the Holy One of Israel". *

I. DOMAIN ANALYSIS OF ISAIAH 12

1. The Positions of the *Verba Dicendi*

The *verbum dicendi* אמר opens a new domain: the verb אמר is a *domain builder*. The clauses dependent on this verb convey the reality of the person speaking, which is, by definition, identical to the subject of אמר. In Isa 12, the verb אמר occurs twice: in verse 1a וְאָמַרְתָּ and in verse 4a וַאֲמַרְתֶּם. With this, a direct speech is opened twice as a new domain. This observation is certainly not problematic. However, two connected questions concerning the domains introduced by the verbal forms of the verb אמר, are much more complex:

– What is the relationship between the domain "second person plural" (henceforth: DSP plural) introduced in verse 4a, and the domain "second person singular" (henceforth: DSP singular) introduced in verse 1a?
– And where do both domains end?

Two reading possibilities occur with regard to this complex of questions. In the first option, the DSP plural is embedded in the DSP singular[12]. The scheme of this option is as follows. The abbreviation *DB* means *domain builder*.

In the second reading option, which I have followed above in my translation, two domains are concerned which are equal to each other. In this option, the first domain ends either after verse 2[13] or after verse 3[14]. If the caesura is placed after verse 2e, this option is schematically as follows.

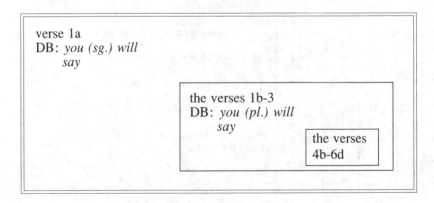

verse 1a
DB: *you (sg.) will say*

the verses 1b-3
DB: *you (pl.) will say*

the verses 4b-6d

11. Cf. D. BARTHÉLEMY, *Critique Textuelle de l'Ancien Testament*. Vol. 2: *Isaïe, Jérémie, Lamentations*, (OBO, 50), Fribourg – Göttingen 1986, pp. 87-90.

12. This reading option is followed by H. WILDBERGER, *Jesaja. Kapitel 1–12* (BKAT, X/1), Neukirchen-Vluyn, ²1980 (¹1965-1972), p. 479; Y. GITAY, *Isaiah and His Audience: The Structure and Meaning of Isaiah 1–12* (SSN, 30), Assen - Maastricht *s.a.* [= 1991], p. 230.

However, if the caesura is placed after verse 3, this option is the following.

---

verse 1a
DB: *you (sg.) will say*

the verses 1b-2e

verse 3
DB: *you (pl.) will say*

the verses 4b-6d

---

13. This reading option is followed by: B. DUHM, *Das Buch Jesaia* (HAT, III/1), Göttingen, 1892, p. 88; A. CONDAMIN, *Le Livre d'Isaïe. Traduction critique avec notes et commentaires* (EB), Paris, 1905, p. 93; G.B. GRAY, *A Critical and Exegetical Commentary on the Book of Isaiah* (ICC), Edinburgh, 1912, p. 230; A. VAN HOONACKER, *Het Boek Isaias: Vertaald uit het hebreeuwsch en in doorloopende aanteekeningen verklaard*, Brugge, 1932, pp. 85-86; W. EICHRODT, *Der Heilige Israel. Jesaja 1–12* (Die Botschaft des Alten Testaments, 17/1), Stuttgart, 1960, pp. 146-147; I.W. SLOTKI – A.J. ROSENBERG, *Isaiah: Hebrew Text & English Translation with an Introduction and Commentary* (Soncino Books of the Bible), London - New York, ²1983 [= 1987] (¹1949), pp. 60-61; O. KAISER, *Das Buch des Propheten Jesaja. Kapitel 1–12* (ATD, 17), Göttingen, ⁵1981 (¹1950), p. 254. Compare also: F. DELITZSCH, *Commentar über den Buch Jesaia* (Biblischer Commentar über das Alte Testament, III/1), Leipzig, 1889, p. 199; R.B.Y. SCOTT – G.G.D. KILPATRICK, *The Book of Isaiah: Chapters 1–39* (The Interpreter's Bible, 5), New York - Nashville, 1956, p. 253; J.D.W. WATTS, *Isaiah 1–33* (WBC, 24), Waco, TX, 1985, p. 181; J. OSWALT, *The Book of Isaiah. Chapters 1–39* (NICOT), Grand Rapids, MI, 1986, p. 294.
14. This reading is followed by J.A. ALEXANDER, *Commentary on the Prophecies of Isaiah*, s.l., 1875²; = Grand Rapids, MI, 1976, p. 263; E. KAUTZSCH – A. BERTHOLET (eds.), *Die heilige Schrift des Alten Testaments*, Tübingen, 1922, p. 611; E.J. KISSANE, *The Book of Isaiah: Translated from a Critically Revised Hebrew Text with Commentary*, Vol. I: *i–xxxix*, Dublin, 1941, p. 147; V. HERNTRICH, *Der Prophet Jesaja. Kapitel 1–12* (ATD, 17), Göttingen, 1950, p. 220; ALONSO SCHÖKEL, *Is 12* (n. 9), pp. 156, 158; G. FOHRER, *Das Buch Jesaja. I Kapitel 1–23* (ZBK), Zürich - Stuttgart, 1960, p. 158; L.A. SNIJDERS, *Jesaja I* (POT), Nijkerk, ²1979 (¹1969), p. 153; R.E. CLEMENTS, *Isaiah 1–39* (NCB), London - Grand Rapids, 1980 (= 1982), pp. 128-129. R. SCHEDL, *Rufer des Heils in heilloser Zeit. Der Prophet Jesajah Kapitel I–XII*, Paderborn, 1973, p. 358 and PRINSLOO, *Isaiah 12* (n. 9) place the caesura after verse 3, but, nevertheless, they give verse 3 a special status as *Überleitung*.

```
┌─────────────────────────────────────────────────────────────┐
│                                                               │
│    verse 1a                                                   │
│    DB: you (sg.) will say                                     │
│                                         ┌───────────────────┐ │
│                                         │  the verses 1b-3   │ │
│                                         └───────────────────┘ │
│                                                               │
│    verse 4a                                                   │
│    DB: you (pl.) will say                                     │
│                                         ┌───────────────────┐ │
│                                         │  the verses 4b-6d  │ │
│                                         └───────────────────┘ │
│                                                               │
└─────────────────────────────────────────────────────────────┘
```

The essence of this question is the connection of the verbal form וַאֲמַרְתֶּם in verse 4a to the preceding clauses. In the first reading option, וַאֲמַרְתֶּם is connected to אוֹדְךָ in verse 1b. For only then can the direct speech, introduced in verse 4a, be embedded within the direct speech introduced in verse 1a. In that case, however, the problem of the connection of the verbal form וּשְׁאַבְתֶּם in verse 3 to the preceding clauses arises.

The two verbal forms וּשְׁאַבְתֶּם and וַאֲמַרְתֶּם are linguistically identical: a second person plural *weqatal* form. This excludes a caesura between the verses 3 and 4[15].

The main tense in the discursive world is the *yiqtol* tense and the *q^etal* tense[16]. The *yiqtol* tense occurs in the verses 1a-2e several times. The introduction to this direct speech, however, consists of the *weqatal* form וְאָמַרְתָּ in verse 1a. It is obvious, therefore, to connect the *weqatal* forms in the verses 3-4a to that in verse 1a; after all, a connection of verse 3 to the verses 1b-2e would cause a double grammatical shift.

As a consequence, there are two parallel domains concerned here: a DSP singular in the verses 1b-2e, introduced by verse 1a, and a DSP plural starting from verse 4b, introduced by the verses 3-4a.

In respect to the demarcation of the second domain, it is also important as to how far the clauses starting from verse 4b, are dependent on

---

15. SNIJDERS, *Jesaja* I (n. 14), p. 153, therefore, asks himself in regard to his chosen structure – in fact, with due reason – why in verse 3 the phrase *you* (pl.) occurs and not the phrase *we*. E.J. YOUNG, *The Book of Isaiah: The English Text, with Introduction, Exposition, and Notes*, Vol. I: *Chapters 1 to 18*, Grand Rapids, MI, 1965 [reprint: 1993], p. 405 silently introduces this "we" into verse 3. ALONSO SCHÖKEL, *Is 12* (n. 9), p. 154 interprets וּשְׁאַבְתֶּם as *hauriam*, a first person singular. In fact, verse 3 is connected to *gratias ago* in verse 1b in this way.

16. SCHNEIDER, *Grammatik* (n. 4), pp. 184, 188; TALSTRA, *Text Grammar* (n. 4), pp. 276-279.

the verbal form וַאֲמַרְתֶּם in verse 4a. The main tense in this domain is the *qᵉtol* tense. Because of this, the following chain arises: הוֹדוּ in verse 4b; קִרְאוּ in verse 4c; הוֹדִיעוּ in verse 4d; הַזְכִּירוּ in verse 4e; and זַמְּרוּ in verse 5a.

With the form צַהֲלִי in verse 6a, number and gender change. Because the verbal tense of verse 5a is continued, verse 6a itself offers insufficient syntactic signs which could mark a new domain[17].

In order to determine the extension of the DSP plural completely, an evaluation of verse 5c has to be undertaken: is verse 5c to be connected to verse 4a, so that a new domain will begin in verse 6a? Or to verse 4d, in order that verse 6 belong to the same domain as the verses 4b-5? Because verse 5c is a nominal clause, the verbal tense perspective is taken from the preceding clause(s), so that, in the case of an absence of an own verbal indication about the closing or opening of a domain, a continuation of the actual domain may be supposed. Moreover, verse 5c contains the deictic element זֹאת, which refers to the own reality of the DSP plural. If verse 5c were meant to be connected to verse 4a, the form (הַ)הִיא "that (proclamation)" would be used, instead of the word זֹאת "this (proclamation)"[18].

This also implies that an inclusion between the verses 4d and 5c arises within the DSP plural: the root ידע occurs in verse 4d in the verbal form הוֹדִיעוּ and in verse 5c in the noun מִידַעַת[19], while the term בְּכָל־הָאָרֶץ in verse 5c resumes the notion בָּעַמִּים from verse 4d.

2. Direction Shifts

(a) Direction Shift within the Domain "Second Person Singular" (DPS-singular)

With the expression וְאָמַרְתָּ, a domain comes into being in which a "you" (sg.) becomes a speaking "I". In de verses 1b-2e, this speaking can be divided into two parts: the verses 1b-f and the verses 2a-e. In the verses 1b-f, the I-figure is speaking to a "you" (sg.). This "you" (sg.) is made explicit in verse 1c with the vocative יהוה. There is a relation between the "I", present in the verbal form אוֹדְךָ (verse 1b) and the suffixa

---

17. *Pace* P.D. MISCALL, *Isaiah* (Readings: A New Biblical Commentary), Sheffield, 1993, p. 46.

18. Cf. K. EHLICH, *Verwendungen der Deixis beim sprachlichen Handeln. Linguistisch-philologische Untersuchung zum hebräischen deiktischen System* (Forum Linguisticum, 24), Frankfurt, 1979, pp. 769-775.

19. The word מִידַעַת may be read as מוּדַעַת with the Qere, a participle hof'al of the verb ידע, or, as מְיֻדַּעַת, a participle pu'al also of ידע, with Qumran, the Septuagint and the Vulgate. In both cases, a substantivized participle with the meaning "proclamation" is meant. See also ALEXANDER, *Isaiah* (n. 14), p. 265; GRAY, *Isaiah* (n. 13), pp. 231-232; WATTS, *Isaiah 1–13* (n. 13), p. 181.

of the prepositional phrase בִּי (verse 1d) and of the verbal form וּתְנַחֲמֵנִי (verse 1f).

This communication situation changes from verse 2a on. Because the verses 2a-e belong to the same domain, the I-figure is still speaking. This "I" is expressed in the text in the verbal forms אֶבְטַח (verse 2b) and אֶפְחָד (verse 2c) and in the suffixes to the nomina יְשׁוּעָתִי (verse 2a) and עֻזִּי (verse 2d) and the suffix of the prepositional phrase לִי (verse 2e). However, the addressed "you" (sg.) from the verses 1b-f has changed into a third person, present in the nominal expressions אֵל (verse 2a) and יָהּ יְהוָה (verse 2d) and in the verbal form וַיְהִי (verse 2e).

Whereas God is spoken *to* in the verses 1b-f, God is spoken *about* in the verses 2a-e[20]. This brings about a direction shift; in other words: by changing the direction of speech, only the direction changes, but the vantage point still remains in the same domain.

In the first part, the present moment is central to the communicating figures, indicated by the *yiqtol* forms אוֹדְךָ in verse 1b and וּתְנַחֲמֵנִי in verse 1f. The first form indicates the relation of the I-figure towards the addressed "you" (sg.). This relation consists of *praising*. The second *yiqtol* form indicates the relation of the addressed "you" (sg.) towards the I-figure. This relation consists of *comforting*. The two clauses in between discuss the reason for the relation *praising – comforting*: the addressed "you" (sg.) was angry, but the anger is over[21].

---

20. See also WILDBERGER, *Jesaja* (n. 12), p. 481 who points out the difference between *berichtende Lob* and *beschreibende Lob* from a *formgeschichtlich* viewpoint and WATTS, *Isaiah 1–33* (n. 13), p. 183 who supposes that the prayer turns to confession of faith. Only the verses 1b-f are directed to God. The thesis of FOHRER, *Jesaja* (n. 14), p. 159 that the verses 4b-6d are directed to God as well, is not tenable. Fohrer's view is also due to the fact that the *Gattungsforschung* wants to see one or more "Songs of Thanksgiving" in Isa 12 at every turn, whereas such a determination of the genre does not fit here. See also CLEMENTS, *Isaiah* (n.14), p. 128.

21. The verbal form יָשֹׁב in verse 1e is thought to be problematic. The form is a iussive of the verb שׁוּב. Several solutions may be used.
1. The *yiqtol*-form יָשֹׁב belongs to the main tense as a modal form. The translation should be: "that your anger may turn away". Thus HERNTRICH, *Jesaja* (n. 14), p. 219; EICHRODT, *Der Heilige Israel* (n. 13), p. 146; WILDBERGER, *Jesaja* (n. 12), p. 477. See also WATTS, *Isaiah 1–33* (n. 13), pp. 181, 182 who also interprets the form וּתְנַחֲמֵנִי as modal, under the influence of the modal יָשֹׁב. Such a modal form is not really in harmony with the past perspective of the *qatal*-form אָנַפְתָּ in verse 1d. Moreover, it causes a semantic problem: why should someone be about to praise, if the anger has not yet turned away?
2. The iussive יָשֹׁב is simply interpreted as a past tense. Thus VAN HOONACKER, *Isaias* (n. 13), p. 86; CLEMENTS, *Isaiah* (n. 14), p. 128; GITAY, *Isaiah* (n. 12), pp. 230, 267. See also YOUNG, *The Book of Isaiah* (n. 15), p. 402.
As a consequence of the fact that the iussive form might have the function of an imperfect, other people translate the three verbal forms אנף, שׁוב and נחם as if they were something like three *qatal*-forms. Thus DELITZSCH, *Commentar* (n. 13), p. 199; DUHM, *Jesaia* (n. 13), p. 88; H. RENCKENS, *De profeet van de nabijheid Gods. Schriftlezing uit*

In the second part, the I-figure is speaking about God in the present moment. By means of the *wayyiqtol* form וַיְהִי in verse 2e, this discursion switches to the telling of a *Sproß-Erzählung*[22] about how God has become יְשׁוּעָה for the I-figure. Thus, an inclusion of the noun יְשׁוּעָה arises within verse 2.

The addressed person in verse 2 is not any longer God, but (an) unknown person(s). This/these unknown person(s) is/are not made explicit in the text. This shift between the verses 1f and 2a is marked by the *Aufmerksamkeitserreger* הִנֵּה at the beginning of verse 2a[23]. The deictic element הִנֵּה does not mark a domain shift here, but a direction shift.

(b) Direction Shift within the Domain "Second Person Plural" (DSP-plural)

In the DSP plural, the verses 4b-6d, a direction shift occurs as well. The chain of seven *qetol* forms can be divided into two parts: the verbal forms הוֹדוּ (verse 4b), קִרְאוּ (verse 4c), הוֹדִיעוּ (verse 4d), הַזְכִּירוּ (verse 4e) and זַמְּרוּ (verse 5a) are plural masculine, whereas the forms צַהֲלִי (verse 6a) and וָרֹנִּי (verse 6b) are singular feminine.

The direction shift, marked by the change in the categories *gender* and *number*, is supported by the concluding nominal clause in verse 5c, which forms an inclusion with verse 4d.

Isajas (Jesaja). Hoofdstukken 1–12 (Woord en Beleving), Tielt - Den Haag, 1961, pp. 42, 228; SNIJDERS, *Jesaja* (n. 14), p. 153. See also KISSANE, *The Book of Isaiah* (n. 13), pp. 147-149; SCOTT – KILPATRICK, *The Book of Isaiah* (n. 13), p. 253; FOHRER, *Jesaja* (n. 14), p. 157; R. LACK, *La symbolique du Livre d'Isaïe. Essai sur l'image littéraire comme élément de structuration* (AnBib, 59), Rome, 1973, p. 57; SLOTKI – ROSENBERG, *Isaiah* (n. 13), p. 60.

3. The form יֹשֵׁב is emendated in the form וַיָּשָׁב: the speaker switches to telling a short story about the turning away of the anger by means of a *wayyiqtol*-form. Thus ALEXANDER, *Commentary* (n. 14), p. 264; C. VON ORELLI, *Der Prophet Jesaia* (Kurzgefaßter Kommentar zu den heiligen Schriften Alten und Neuen Testamentes, IV/1), München, ³1904 (¹1887), p. 55.

As a continuation of the proposed emendation, some people read a *wayyiqtol*-form וַתְּנַחֲמֵנִי in verse 1f instead of the *weqatal*-form וּתְנַחֲמֵנִי. Thus GRAY, *Commentary* (n. 13), p. 231; KAUTZSCH – BERTHOLET, *Die heilige Schrift* (n. 14), p. 611; KAISER, *Jesaja* (n. 13), p. 254. See also OSWALT, *The Book of Isaiah* (n. 13), p. 290.

4. CONDAMIN, *Le Livre d'Isaïe* (n. 13), p. 93 reads the *qatal*-form שָׁב. Moreover, he reads a *wayyiqtol*-form וַתְּנַחֲמֵנִי in verse 1f instead of the *weqatal*-form וּתְנַחֲמֵנִי.

5. With a little alteration of the vocalization, one may read the verbal form יָשַׁב, a *qatal*-form of ישׁב with past perspective which can be literally rendered as "your anger has set down", i.e., "has quieted".

6. It is possible to consider the *yiqtol*-form יֵשֵׁב as a direct speech engaged with the past, supported by the asyndetic clause connection. Thus the form אָנַפְתָּ in verse 1c should be translated as a simple past tense and the form יֵשֵׁב in verse 1d as a simple present perfect. Cf. also SCHNEIDER, *Grammatik* (n. 4), p. 196 about *engagiertes Erzählen*.

The issue of the form יֹשֵׁב is not dealt with by BARTHÉLEMY, *Critique textuelle* (n. 11).

22. SCHNEIDER, *Grammatik* (n. 4), p. 200.

23. Cf. *ibid.*, p. 262. *Pace* YOUNG, *The Book of Isaiah* (n. 15), p. 402 who lets the particle הִנֵּה transgress domain borders.

It is striking, that the "you" (pl.) in verse 4a, which starts the direct speech, does not become a "we" anywhere in the direct speech. Neither are the persons addressed by the implicit "we", made explicit in the first part, the verses 4b-5c. In the second part, the verses 6a-d, they are made explicit: the nominal phrase יוֹשֶׁבֶת צִיּוֹן functions as a vocative in verse 6c.

The entire domain is enclosed by an indication of God: לַיהוָה in verse 4b and קְדוֹשׁ יִשְׂרָאֵל in verse 6d. God, however, is not spoken to in the DSP plural, but God is spoken *about* to the addressees.

3. Embedded Domains within the Domain "Second Person Plural" (DSP-plural)

In the first part of the DSP plural, the verbs ידע hif'il, זכר and זמר create three new domains, which can be said to be embedded in this domain. Therefore the verbs ידע hif'il, זכר and זמר are *domain builders*. Each time, that which has to be proclaimed by the addressees to the עַמִּים, is at issue. Here, the shift to a new domain is hardly not marked by a syntactical sign, but mainly by a semantic sign.

The content of the first embedded domain is expressed in verse 4d with the direct object עֲלִילֹתָיו. Concerning the verses 4e en 5a the following: each time a dependent subordinate clause, introduced by כִּי, forms the content of the new domains. These domains are considered as a consequence of the עֲלִילֹתָיו concerning the theme *exaltation*, expressed in two synonyms: God is exalted (the verb שׂגב in verse 4f) and his deeds are exalted (the noun גֵּאוּת in verse 5b).

4. The Domain of the *Narrator*

Domains are always embedded in a basis domain. The basis domain is the standard domain of the *narrator* and contains the entire text. Concerning Isa 12, the two domains, the verses 1b-2e and 4b-6d, are embedded in the total domain, the verses 1a-6d. This domain is characterized by second person verbal forms: with respect to the verses 1a-2e a second person singular and with respect to the verses 3-6d a second person plural. However, a second person supposes a first person who initiates the contact. This implies that the domain formed by the verses 1a-6d, is not directly the basis domain of the *narrator*, but belongs to a speaker who is not made explicit[24].

This anonymous speaker is silently installed by the *narrator* in order to say the verses 1a-6d, including the various domains in those verses.

---

24. That is why the utmost left bracket in the work translation scheme on p. 151 is a double bracket.

5. Domain Structure of Isaiah 12

The analysis above leads to the following structure of Isa 12 composed of domains.

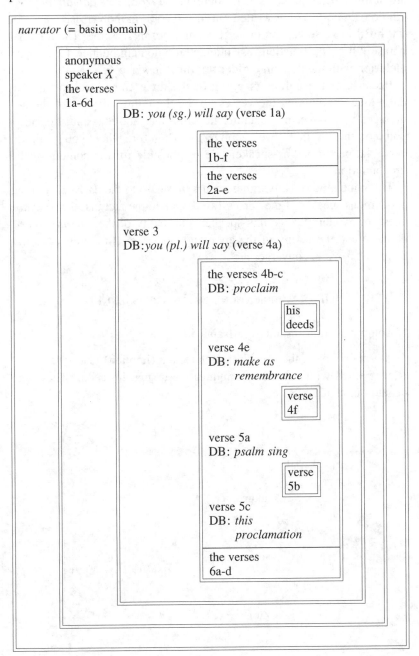

The domains are bordered by double lines. Direction shifts within a domain, namely the switches between the verses 1b-2e and 3-6d, between the verses 1b-f and 2a-e, and between the verses 4b-5c and 6a-d, are outlined by single lines. The abbreviation *DB* means *domain builder*. All domain builders are written out in full: אמר in the verses 1a and 4a, ידע hif'il in verse 4c, זכר in verse 4e and זמר in verse 5a. The nominal phrase מידעת זאת functions as an anaphoric domain builder, forming an inclusion with the domain builder ידע hif'il in verse 4c.

Because of the indirect shaping of the three embedded domains in the domain containing the verses 4b-5c, the points of view of the addressees who have to proclaim one thing and another, and the viewpoint of the implicit "we", converge. Therefore, the "you" (pl.) in verse 4a, performed as speaker, are responsible for the content of the proclamation.

The same kind of converging occurs in regard to the *narrator* and the anonymous speaker of the verses 1a-6d. Due to the fact that the *narrator* does not explicitly stage this speaker, the reality of the *narrator* (basis domain) and the reality of the anonymous speaker (first embedded domain), as it were, converge.

II. COMMUNICATION ANALYSIS OF ISAIAH 12

1. Communication Instances in Isaiah 12

As appears from the domain structure, the (implicit) reader of Isa 12 is confronted with several communicative textual instances. These can be laid out as follows.

In this scheme, the textual communicative instances are indicated by a number in *brackets* in *superscript*, which I will use henceforth, when refering to this scheme. The *N* means *narrator*, the *X* the anonymous speaker of Isa 12, and the *R* the *(implied) reader* of Isa 12.

If the *narrator* [no. 1] and the *reader* [no. 12] are not included in the number of communicative instances, Isa 12 contains ten instances. Only a few textual instances are filled in: the first addressee in the verses 1b-f, namely God [no. 5]; the first addressees of the implicitly addressed "we" in the verses 4d.4e-f.5a-b, namely the nations [no. 10]; the address of praise, namely the Lord, in verse 4b [no. 9]; the address of psalm singing, namely the Lord, in verse 5a [no. 11]; and the second addressee, addressed by the implicit "we" in the verses 6a-d, namely Zion [no. 8]. These communicative instances are underlined in the scheme above.

Not only does the textsyntax contribute to the structure of a text, but also the textsemantics, within the framework built by the textsyntax[25]. In this light, two addressees from the group of five unidentified communicative participants can be identified in more detail.

The anonymous speaker [no. 2] makes the (implied) I-figure [no. 3] use the word יְשׁוּעָה in verse 2 in his speech to the unspecified addressee(s) [no. 6], forming an inclusion. Next, the word יְשׁוּעָה is used in the domain of the anonymous speaker via percolation from the DSP singular, namely in verse 3. There the noun יְשׁוּעָה is used to describe the "you" (pl.) [no. 4]. This observation implies that the verses 2a-e can be understood as addressed to the "you" (pl.) of verse 3. Otherwise formulated: the textual communicative instances [no. 6] en [no. 4] are identical. Thus the communication structure arises that the I-figure, introduced by the anonymous speaker, first speaks to God and after that to the implicit "we" introduced subsequently by the same anonymous speaker.

2. Towards a Filling in of the Communication Instances in Isaiah 12

The majority of the exegetes considers the "you" (sg.) [no. 3] and the "you" (pl.) [no. 4] as identical[26], both namely as an indication of the

---

25. WEINRICH, *Tempus* (n. 4), pp. 29-30; E. TALSTRA, *Text Grammar and Hebrew Bible. II: Syntax and Semantics*, in *BO* 30 (1982) 35-36; VAN WIERINGEN, *The Reader* (n. 3), pp. 291, 296.

26. Thus DELITZSCH, *Commentar* (n. 13), p. 199; DUHM, *Jesaia* (n. 13), p. 88; VON ORELLI, *Der Prophet Jesaia* (n. 21), p. 59; VAN HOONACKER, *Het Boek Isaias* (n. 13), p. 86; HERNTRICH, *Der Prophet Jesaja* (n. 14), p. 221; LACK, *La symbolique* (n. 21), p. 57; SNIJDERS, *Jesaja* (n. 14), p. 153; CLEMENTS, *Isaiah* (n. 14), p. 128; R. KILIAN, *Jesaja 1–12*

congregation[27]/people of Israel. Snijders, moreover, explicitly indicates this group as the congregation of Zion[28]. Reading this way, an identification with the communicative instance Zion [no. 8] arises. Watts also identifies the "you" (sg.) [no. 3] and the "you" (pl.) [no. 4] as (parts of) Zion: the singular masculine of the instance [no. 3] refers to the city of Zion[29], the plural masculine [no. 4] to the (male) inhabitants of Zion (presumably the priests), and the feminine indication יוֹשֶׁבֶת צִיּוֹן [no. 8] to the female inhabitants of Zion[30].

Since the instances [no. 6] en [no. 4] have proved to be identical, the only possibility that remains is that these members of the congregation speak to each other, which entails: "you" (sg.) [no. 3] = "you" (pl.) [no. 4] = instance [no. 6] addressed to by the I-figure = Zion [no. 8]. With such a reading, the text is made one-dimensional.

Wildberger, however, tries to explain the difference between the "you" (sg.) [no. 3] and the "you" (pl.) [no. 4] by subdividing the congregation of Israel into a core group and the other members. The first group he calls: Israel κατὰ πνεῦμα; the second: Israel κατὰ σάρκα[31]. I believe the text does not give the faintest cause for an allusion to Rom 8,1-17; Gal 6,8.

The communicative instance [no. 7] is noticed by only a few exegetes. Without saying, the text is usually understood in such a way that the "you" (pl.) [no. 4] proclaim to the nations [no. 10], which makes the unspecified addressees [no. 7] diasappear even more completely. Snijders, however, suggests interpreting this instance [no. 7] as foreigners who are temporarily staying in the city of Jerusalem and who apparently are allowed to participate in the celebration[32]. Other exegetes suggest an identification of instance [no. 7] with the "you" (pl.) [no. 4][33]. Here, verse 4a is freely translated with: "In that day,

(Die Neue Echter Bibel, 17), Würzburg, 1986, pp. 92-93. GRAY, *Commentary* (n. 13), pp. 230-231 speaks about "Israel" and "the restored Israelites".

27. SCOTT – KILPATRICK, *Isaiah* (n. 13), p. 253 use the term "church".

28. SNIJDERS, *Jesaja* (n. 14), p. 156.

29. It would be very strange if the text refers to Zion by means of the masculine form וְאָמַרְתָּ (verse 1a), instead of using a feminine form, all the more because Zion is addressed by means of feminine forms in verse 6. Cf. also SLOTKI – ROSENBERG, *Isaiah* (n. 13), p. 61.

30. WATTS, *Isaiah 1–33* (n. 13), pp. 181, 183-184.

31. WILDBERGER, *Jesaja* (n. 12), p. 480.

32. SNIJDERS, *Jesaja* (n. 14), p. 155.

33. *Pace* M. FRIEDLÄNDER, *The Commentary of Ibn Ezra on Isaiah: Edited from Mss. and Translated, with Notes, Introduction, and Indexes*, New York, 1873, p. 63; ALEXANDER, *Isaiah* (n. 14), pp. 264-265; KISSANE, *Isaiah* (n. 14), p. 147; SLOTKI – ROSENBERG, *Isaiah* (n. 13), p. 61; A.L.H.M. VAN WIERINGEN, *Jesaja 6–12: die Vegetationsbildsprache*

you will say <u>to each other</u>". This interpretation also leads to the problem that two communicative instances distinguished in the text, are
made to converge in the interpretation of the text. Moreover, the Qal of
אמר has no reflexive meaning.

(a) First Reading Option: *X* [no. 2] = Isaiah

Taking into account these comments, I wish to come to a concrete filling in of the textual communicative instances, as presented in the domain and communication analysis above.

I begin with the anonymous speaker *X* [no. 2]. Only a very few
exegetes tackle this instance. If they do so, it is nearly always filled in
with the prophet Isaiah[34]. If the prophet speaks to a "you" (sg.) [no. 3]
and to a "you" (pl.) [no. 4], it is obvious to see the people in at least one
of these two instances. If a reference is made to Isa 11, it is logical to
refer to, for example, the verses 11 and 16 שְׁאָר אַמּוֹ[35].

The communication poles "you" (sg.) [no. 3] and "you" (pl.) [no. 4]
have to be filled in as various instances. In my opinion, the ideal king
and his people are at issue. They are portrayed by the prophet throughout Isa 6–12 in contrast with the failing king and in particular they are
expressed in the images of the Immanu-El (Isa 7–8), of the Child (Isa 9),
and of the Trunk of Jesse (Isa 11). The king [no. 3], as leader of the people[36], is first addressed by the prophet [no. 2] to praise God. In his turn,
he [no. 3], as an exemplary king, speaks to his people [no. 6].

Some textsemantic lines support this view. The ideal king speaks
about not being afraid any more. This creates a contrast with the king
from Isa 7,1-17[37]. There, the king was afraid: וַיָּנַע לְבָבוֹ (verse 2); and his
people as well: וּלְבַב עַמּוֹ (verse 2 again). The call of the prophet not to
be afraid (Isa 7,4 אַל־תִּירָא וּלְבָבְךָ אַל־יֵרַךְ), but, on the contrary, to trust

---

und die prophetische Struktur, in J. VERMEYLEN (ed.), *The Book of Isaiah. Le Livre
d'Isaïe. Les oracles et leurs relectures unité et complexité de l'ouvrage* (BETL, 81),
Leuven, 1989, p. 206; cf. also J.-P. SONNET, «*Tu diras ce jour là...*» *(Is 12,1)*, in R.
LAFONTAINE – P. PIRET – J.N. ALETTI *et al.*, *L'Écriture âme de la théologie* (Collection
Institut d'Études Théologiques, 9), Bruxelles, 1990, p. 182.

34. Thus DELIZTSCH, *Commentar* (n. 13), p. 200; SNIJDERS, *Jesaja* (n. 14), p. 152;
SLOTKI – ROSENBERG, *Isaiah* (n. 13), p. 60; GITAY, *Isaiah* (n. 12), p. 229. WATTS, *Isaiah
1–33* (n. 13), pp. 181, 183-184 speaks about "Herald". YOUNG, *The Book of Isaiah* (n.
15), pp. 401, 403, 407 makes no difference between the anonymous speaker *X* of verse 1a
[no. 2] and the addressee, addressed with "you" (sg.), in vers 1a [no. 3], both of which he
identifies with the prophet Isaiah.

35. Thus KAISER, *Jesaja* (n. 13), p. 255. See also DELITZSCH, *Commentar* (n. 13), p.
200; WATTS, *Isaiah 1–33* (n. 13), p. 183.

36. WATTS, *Isaiah 1–33* (n. 13), p. 181 fills in this communicative instance [no. 3] as
"Zion"; elsewhere, however, he refers to a king's prayer (pp. 183-184).

37. For this textsemantic line, cf. OSWALT, *The Book of Isaiah* (n. 13), p. 293.

(the verb אמן twice in Isa 7,9), was put aside by the king at that time[38]. This fear excludes a relationship with God: King Ahaz refuses flatly to call the Lord אֱלֹהַי _my_ God in Isa 7,11-17. In contrast with this, the ideal king [no. 3] uses the expressions בטח[39] (verse 2b) and לֹא פחד[40] (verse 2c). The ideal image of the Trunk of Jesse is characterized by the יִרְאַת יְהוָה (Isa 11,2.3). The ideal king [no. 3], therefore, can also confess: אֵל יְשׁוּעָתִי (verse 2a). Thus the אַף from the refrain verse in Isa 9,7–10,19 is reversed; as already announced in 10,25.

Just as king and people can be distinguished, for instance in Isa 7,2, so can the ideal king [no. 3] and his people [no. 6 = no. 4] be distinguished as well. This people speaks first to the nations [no. 10] via an intermediate instance [no. 7]. I indicate this intermediate instance as the entire people [no. 7]. Here, the idea is that the ideal people, as a remnant, will grow again. This is already expressed in the term זֶרַע קֹדֶשׁ in Isa 6,13[41], but also in the growth of the גּוֹי לֹא _non-people_ in 9,2[42]. Next, the people [no. 4] speaks to Zion [no. 8] itself.

Before the "you" (pl.) [no. 4] starts speaking, the prophet [no. 2] says in verse 3 that they will draw water from the wells of deliverance. The noun יְשׁוּעָה combines the ideal king and his people. Moreover, the water contrasts the people of the ideal king with the people in Isa 8,7 that is flooded by mighty waters[43].

Analogous to the first verb in the domain of the ideal king [no. 3] in verse 1b, the verb ידה (verse 4b) occurs in the domain of his people [no. 4] as first verb as well[44]. Likewise, the verb זמר (verse 5a) appears parallel to the nominal expression זִמְרָת in verse 2d in the DSP plural [no. 4]. Further, the entire people [no. 7] is charged to call upon, to make known and to commemorate. The act ידע hif'il creates a contrast with the ignorant people in Isa 6,9.10. The verb קרא, used in Isa 6,3 as well as in 12,4c, may play a role here.

---

38. The noun אַף occurs in Isa 7,4 as well as in 12,1d.

39. *Pace* WILDBERGER, *Jesaja* (n. 12), p. 1660 who is of the opinion that the verb חטב is always used in a negative context.

40. Cf. also *THAT* I, col. 412 [H.P. STÄHLI].

41. See also A.L.H.M. VAN WIERINGEN, *Jes 6,13: een structuuronderzoek*, in *Bijdragen* 48 (1987) 33; K. NIELSEN, *There is Hope for a Tree: The Tree Metaphor in Isaiah* (JSOT SS, 65), Sheffield, 1989, pp. 149-150; A.L.H.M. VAN WIERINGEN, *Jesaja 6: aankondiging van noodlot of oproep tot heil? Een communicatieve lezing*, in P. VAN TONGEREN (ed.), *Het lot in eigen hand? Reflecties op de betekenis van het (nood)lot in onze cultuur*, Baarn, 1994, p. 117.

42. See also A.L.H.M. VAN WIERINGEN, *Het volk dat in het donker wandelt*, in *Heraut* 124 (1993) 331.

43. For this textsemantic line, cf. LACK, *La symbolique* (n. 21), p. 247.

44. Cf. PRINSLOO, *Isaiah 12* (n. 9), p. 26.

The deeds of God have to be proclaimed to the nations. Here, a parallel movement is indicated as in Isa 11,9, in contrast with the acts of Assur in 10,13-14. God's deeds are explicitly narrated using the verb עשׂה (verse 5b) in Isa 9,6 as well.

Subsequently, Zion [no. 8] is specifically addressed. She is explicitly introduced with the status constructus structure יוֹשֶׁבֶת צִיּוֹן (verse 6c). An allusion to יוֹשֵׁב in Isa 6,11, to יוֹשֵׁב יְרוּשָׁלַ͏ִם in 8,14, to יֹשְׁבֵי בְאֶרֶץ צַלְמָוֶת in 9,1 and to אַמִּי צִיּוֹן יֹשֵׁב in 10,24 seems to be evident here. This Zion is allowed to rejoice and shout[45], because God is in her midst. On the one hand, the phrase of location בְּקִרְבֵּךְ in verse 6d creates a contrast with the place of devastation in Isa 6,12; 10,23. On the other hand, it continues with the place of preservation of life in 7,22[46], as does the combination of God with the root קדשׁ in 10,17.20[47].

This first reading option results in the following schematic filling in.

```
                          God[5]
                        ↗
           ideal
           king[3]
        ↗              ↘
                          people
                          of the
                          ideal
                          king[6]

N[1]→Isaiah[2]                                        ↔ R[12]
                                God[9]
                              ↗
                          entire
                          people[7]
              ↘        ↗           ↘
           people              nations[10] →  God[11]
           of the
           ideal
           king[4]
                    ↘
                   Zion[8]
```

In this scheme, the *N* means *narrator* and the *R* the *(implied) reader*. Further, the same numbering of communicative instances is used as above.

---

45. The verb צהל in verse 6a may again take up the line of no longer being afraid, in contrast with Isa 11,30.

46. See also VAN WIERINGEN, *Jesaja 6–12* (n. 33), p. 207.

47. See also *THAT* II, col. 599-600 [H.P. MÜLLER]; VAN WIERINGEN, *Jesaja 6–12* (n. 33), pp. 206-207.

(b) Second Reading Option: *X* [no. 2] = God

Presupposition of the first reading option is that the ideal images actively take part in the text of Isa 6–12 as "actants". The ideal images
are, as it were, not only identification figures for the characters in the
text, but also characters themselves. Such a utilization of the ideal images is necessary because of the option to identify the anonymous
speaker [no. 2] with the prophet Isaiah.

However, it is possible to arrive at another filling in. For that, I start
again with the anonymous speaker *X* [no. 2]. The addressed "you" (sg.)
in verse 1a becomes an "I" within the domain of the addressee (verse
1b). As a result, the relation between speaker and addressee, between
"I" and "you", is a fact. Likewise, an "I" outside the DSP singular,
constituted by the "you" (sg.) in verse 1a, corresponds with the "you"
(sg.) inside the domain (the suffix second person singular masculine in
verse 1b). Because this instance is identified with יהוה within the domain
to which verse 1b belongs, it is obvious that the implicit "I" in verse 1a
should be יהוה as well. In this second reading option, I thus identify the
anonymous speaker *X* [no. 2] with the *character* God[48].

God first speaks to a second person singular masculine [no. 3], and
secondly to a second person plural masculine [no. 4]. In view of the
positive relation between God and the prophet Isaiah in Isa 6–12, it is
obvious to identify the second person singular masculine [no. 3] with the
prophet Isaiah. The addressees addressed by the prophet [no. 6], and the
persons plural masculine addressed by God [no. 4], have proved to be
identical. From the fact that they are addressed by the prophet as well as
by God himself, it may be concluded that they also have a positive relation with these characters. Therefore, I identify them with the circle
round the prophet Isaiah which has appeared to be ready to accept Isaiah's message and which is distinguished from the entire people. This is
the case in Isa 7 too, where the proclamation of the Immanu-El was not
accepted by Ahaz and his people, but only by a small group, called up in
verse 9[49], and present as an individual in verse 21 (אִישׁ *a single man* =
[only] a few). This distinction is also clear in Isaiah's speech to his followers in Isa 8,11-23b. A group does exist which does not go the way of
הָעָם־הַזֶּה (Isa 8,11) and which is addressed with the second person plural

---

48. This identification is almost absent in Old Testament exegesis. However, cf.
HERNTRICH, *Jesaja* (n. 14), p. 219.

49. C. HARDMEIER, *Gesichtspunkte pragmatischer Erzähltextanalyse. »Glaubt ihr
nicht, so bleibt ihr nicht«. Ein Glaubensappell an schankende Anhänger Jesajas*, in *Wort
und Dienst* 15 (1979) 40-41; VAN WIERINGEN, *Jesaja 6* (n. 41), p. 118. Cf. also
WEINRICH, *Tempus* (n. 4), p. 97.

masculine (8,12vv.). This group grows out to become the entire people [no. 7] via the returning remnant, which is subsequently addressed by the group round the prophet Isaiah. This group subsequently calls to the nations [no. 10]. Next, this group round the prophet Isaiah speaks to Zion [no. 8] as well.

As in the first reading option, this second reading option is supported by some textsemantic observations. God [no. 2] has at his disposal the יוֹם *day*[50] which he announces. With this, the character God makes a connection with the vision in Isa 6. There, the prophet asked how long (verse 11 עַד־מָתַי), admitting that God disposes over the time span concerned. In his speech, this time span is expressed in chapter 12 with a double בַּיּוֹם הַהוּא (the verses 1a en 4a)[51].

The prophet Isaiah [no. 3] is identifiable by the use of the root ישׁע, which occurs in his name יְשַׁעְיָהוּ and forms the noun יְשׁוּעָה in the verses 2a.e as well[52]. This address by God does not any longer evoke fear, as seeing the Lord did in the vision in Isa 6 causing the exclamation אוֹי לִי (verse 4)[53]. His fear is not any longer that which the people has as object of fear (Isa 8,12). Isaiah's confidence in God is evident. Because of that confidence, he is able to call on other people to have confidence as well, as in Isa 7,9, expressed with the verb אמן[54]. The *hapax legomenon* בטח in Isa 6–12 in verse 2b causes no surprise. In Isa 12,2, this idea is used to call on other people to have confidence, for this verse is directed at the textual instance [no. 6]. Isaiah was the only one, who up until now called upon the Lord as his God in Isa 6,5. Isa 7,11 makes clear, that Isaiah sees the Lord as his God, but that Ahaz, addressed by Isaiah, does not.

The group round the prophet [no. 6] is called on by the prophet in Isa 8,11-23b to follow his behaviour; this also happens in 12,2. This group [no. 4] is addressed by God now, after having told them to draw water from the wells of deliverance[55]. With the percolating noun יְשׁוּעָה in verse

---

50. Cf. also the use of the word יום in Isa 7,17; 9,3.13; 10,3.17.

51. For the back reference function of הַהוּא, cf. EHLICH, *Verwendungen* (n. 18), p. 756-757.

52. Cf. L. ALONSO SCHÖKEL – J.L. SICRE DIAZ, *Profetas. Introducciones y comentario* (Nueva Biblia Española), Vol. 1: *Isaías, Jeremías*, Madrid, 1980, p. 113; KAISER, *Jesaja* (n. 13), p. 255; KILIAN, *Jesaja 1–12* (n. 26), p. 93; MATHYS, *Dichter und Beter* (n. 9), p. 188.

53. Cf. *THAT* I, col. 475 [E. JENNI].

54. HARDMEIER, *Gesichtspunkte* (n. 49), pp. 40-41; VAN WIERINGEN, *Jesaja 6* (n. 41), p. 118.

55. Cf. the contrasting text based upon the nouns מַיִם and מָשׂוֹשׂ/שָׂשׂוֹן in Isa 8,6-7. For this, see also LACK, *La symbolique* (n. 21), p. 247.

3, the relation between the prophet and his benevolent audience is supported. Further, this is underlined by the parallel verb ידה (the verses 1b and 4b) and the analogy between the noun זִמְרָת and the verb זמר (the verses 2d and 5a). They are also directly addressed by God, just as they were indirectly addressed by God in Isa 8,11-12vv. This group [no. 4] is further ordered to charge, to call upon, to make known to and to commemorate the people [no. 7]. The activities ידע hif'il and קרא create a contrast with Isa 6,3.9.10. God's deeds (cf. Isa 9,6) have to be proclaimed to the nations [no. 10]. A parallel with Isa 11,9 and a contrast with 10,13-14 may both play a role here.

Next, Zion [no. 8] is explicitly addressed. Her introduction reminisces of Isa 6,11; 8,14; 9,1; 10,24. Zion's rejoicing and shouting lie continuation in the fact that God is in her midst. A continuation from Isa 7,22 (cf. also 10,17.20) and a contrast with 6,12; 10,23 probably play a role.

This second reading option results in the following schematic filling in.

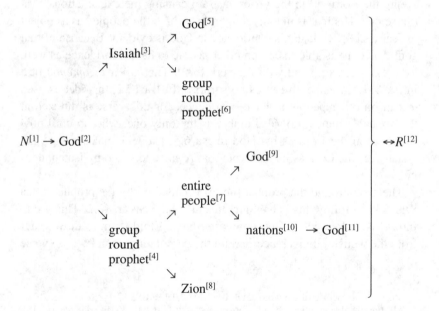

In this scheme, the *N* means the *narrator* and the *R* the *(implied) reader* again. Further, the same numbering of the communicative instances is used once more.

3. The (Implied) Reader [no. 12] in Isaiah 12

From the analysis above, it is clear that the (implied) reader is confronted with a poly interpretable text because of the great number of textual communicative instances. What is the effect of this text on the implied reader?

It is a matter of course that no *actual reader* can be forbidden to identify himself with any one of the communicative instances I have described, whatever the reading option may be. Nevertheless, it is not obvious to identify the *implied reader* either with the "you" (sg.) (verse 1a) or with the "you" (pl.) (verse 4a)[56]. For these two second persons are not described in asides in the text, but they are text bound instances with their own domain.

The reader's communication does not just happen via identification with a character[57], but via the experience of being addressed from the text. Here, the point of address in the nations [no. 10] is very important. The text offers a chain of addressees to the reader. This chain is the most extensive in the second reading option. This chain can be schematically outlined as follows.

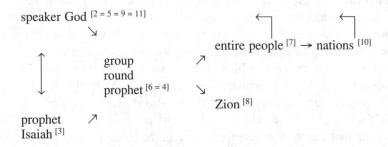

By joining up with the nations[58], the reader enters, as it were, into the chain of callings as the final destination. The beneficial message of God is also destined for the reader.

The reliability of the proclamation is increased by the manner in which the domains in this chain of addressees are shaped. Because of the indirect domain building, ascending from the small group [no. 4] to that which the people [no. 7] has to proclaim to the nations [no. 10], the reality of the people [no. 7] coincides with the reality of the small faithful group [no. 4]. Because this textual instance is not characterized by an explicit "we", the reality of the small group [no. 4] converges with the one who speaks to her [no. 2]. In other words: the domains of the nations [no. 10] are indirectly built and are possessed by the nations [no.

---

56. *Pace* GITAY, *Isaiah* (n. 12), pp. 229-230 who lets the reader enter the text via the "you" (sg.) as well as via the "you" (pl.).

57. Cf. also VAN WIERINGEN, *The Reader* (n. 3), p. 300.

58. It is striking here, that verse 4c uses the word עַמִּים, not the word גּוֹיִם.

10] as well as by the addressees [no. 7]. It is left to the reader to complete the filling in of these domains.

The starting point of the chain is also of interest here. The text can be
read as starting with the prophet Isaiah as the filling in of the anonymous
speaker *X* [no. 2] as well as starting with God. Whatever choice is made,
the concretization of the communication pole [no. 2] itself is installed by
the *narrator* [no. 1]. Because this installation is only indirectly present
in the text, a blending takes place between the reality of the communicative instance [no. 2] with the reality of the *narrator* [no. 1]. Because of
this, it is suggested to the reader that either the prophet Isaiah or God is
the *narrator*. Such a merging has already taken place in the *Ich-Berichte*
in Isa 6–12, namely between the I-figure (= the prophet Isaiah) and the
narrator. Chapter 12 either makes a connection with this, in the case that
X [no. 2] is the prophet Isaiah, or can be understood as a further evolu-
tion, in the case that *X* [no. 2] is God.

In the event that the prophet is the primary speaker [no. 2], as in the
first reading option, the reader is confronted, on the one hand, with a
communication, especially for the ideal king [no. 3], directed at God.
On the other hand, the reader is confronted with a communicative line,
initiated by this character, in which other people are told about God. In
the event that God is the primary speaker [no. 2], as in the second
reading option, the reader is confronted, on the one hand, with a closed
communicative circuit, in which God speaks to the prophet and the
prophet, in his turn, to God (as represented in the scheme above)[59]. On
the other hand, an extension of this circuit is created by telling other
people about God. In both cases, a break of the communication lines to
third parties is concerned, with the *implied reader* as final destination.
God is not only able to be approached by the prophet and to be re-
joiced by Zion, but also by even more people. The expression of (the
realization of) this is beyond the text of Isa 12, but is open towards the
reader.

This break is given a point in time with בַּיּוֹם הַהוּא (the verses 1a and
4a). Here also, there is an opening into the text for the implied reader.
The point of time is a present moment within the domains embedded
in the domain of the initiating speaker *X* [no. 2]. But in the domain of

---

59. In this, the specific aspect of the function of Isaiah *as a prophet* may be seen. He
is called and sent to the people in the name of God. See also Isa 6,8-9 ־קוֹל אֲדֹנָי אֹמֵר אֶת;
מֵעִם יְהוָה צְבָאוֹת in 8,18. In מִי אֶשְׁלַח וּמִי יֵלֶךְ־לָנוּ וָאֹמַר הִנְנִי שְׁלָחֵנִי וַיֹּאמֶר לֵךְ and the expression
the form of a direct speech, God speaks only directly to Isaiah. In my view, Isa 7,10 has
to be understood, because of the hif'il form וַיּוֹסֶף, as "the Lord made the speaking to Ahaz
continue", sc. via Isaiah: cf. VAN WIERINGEN, *Jesaja 6* (n. 41), p. 119. See also Deut
18,15-20.

the speaker [no. 2] himself, the point of time is still in the future[60]. In the text of Isa 12,1-6, this future moment nowhere becomes reality. This invites the implied reader to get involved in this textual future point of time[61]. all the more so because the realization of the communication chain, even back to God, is beyond the point of time of the בַּיּוֹם הַהוּא[62].

From this reflection on Isa 12, Isa 6 can also be re-read. There, the Seraphim were calling to each other, by which a closed communication circuit arose[63]. Its content is the *trishagion* in Isa 6,3. The end of the Immanu-El book Isa 6–12 is formed by a break of this closedcircuit into an open chain[64] towards the reader and, after that, towards God again[65].

As for the content, an important development is involved in this framing in the Immanu-El-book. In both texts, God is called קָדוֹשׁ[66]. From Isa 6,3, it is clear that God's holiness has a programmatic[67] relation to כָּל-. הָאָרֶץ Isa 12,5-6 makes clear that, when כָּל-הָאָרֶץ has heard the proclamation of the *magnalia Dei*, God dwells in Zion as קְרוֹשׁ יִשְׂרָאֵל.

*

This reflection on Isa 12 is dedicated to Wim Beuken in great gratitude. He has always showed the openness that biblical texts have, and

---

60. The future perspective is also indicated by the w^{e}qatal-form: cf. TALSTRA, *Text Grammar* (n. 4), pp. 276-279.

61. *Pace* HERNTRICH, *Der Prophet Jesaja* (n. 14), p. 220 who, without saying, moves the now-moment of the embedded DSP-singular and the now-moment of the DSP-plural to the now-moment of the actual reader; P.A. MUNCH, *The Expression Bajjôm Hāhū': Is It an Eschatological Terminus Technicus?* (Avhandlinger utgitt av Det Norske Videnskap-Akademi i Oslo, 2/1936, 2), Oslo, 1936, p. 8.

62. Cf. MUNCH, *The Expression* (n. 61), p. 50.

63. VAN WIERINGEN, *Jesaja 6* (n. 41), p. 115.

64. As a matter of course, a chain of callings also evokes the opening text of the Second Isaiah, Isa 40,1-11. I would like to suggest here, that the communication line of Isa 12, which forms a new development in regard to chapter 6, is continued there in one way or another. Cf. A.L.H.M. VAN WIERINGEN, *Jesaja 40,1-11: eine drama-linguistische Lesung von Jesaja 6 her*, in *BN* 49 (1989) 82-93.

65. *Pace* VAN WIERINGEN, *Jesaja 6–12* (n. 33), p. 206 who does not recognize the shift from a formula introducing a direct speech, *with* the expression זֶה אֶל-זֶה in Isa 6,3, to a formula *without* such an expression in 12,1a.4a, and thus wrongly suggests that a closed communication circuit arises in *both* texts.

66. Cf. OSWALT, *The Book of Isaiah* (n. 13), p. 295.

67. VAN WIERINGEN, *Jesaja 6* (n. 41), p. 115.

* I am greatly indebted to Mr. Maurits J. Sinninghe Damsté (Amsterdam, The Netherlands) for his correction of the English translation of this article.

the pleasure of exegesis. May God bless him, in this Isaianic communicative line, with many fruitful years, until *that day*.

Katholieke Universiteit Nijmegen   Archibald L.H.M. VAN WIERINGEN
Faculteit der Godgeleerdheid
Postbus 9103
NL-6500 HD Nijmegen

A LITERARY ANALYSIS OF ISAIAH 25,10A

1.1 *The Centrality of Metaphor in the Bible*

A glance at recent publications on the use and significance of metaphors in biblical texts will reveal that the topic has experienced something of a boom in recent years and continues to do so[1]. In his thorough

---

1. Fairly recent publications devoted exclusively to studies on metaphor are illustrative of the complexity of the topic: W.A. SHIBLES, *Metaphor: An Annotated Bibliography and History*, Whitewater, 1971; J.P. VAN NOPPEN *et al.* (eds.), *Metaphor: A Bibliography of Post-1970 Publications*, Amsterdam - Philadelphia, 1985; J.-P. VAN NOPPEN – E. HOLS (eds.), *Metaphor II: A Classified Bibliography of Publications 1985-1990*, Amsterdam, 1990. Articles and monographs tend to fall into a number of distinct camps: (i) dealing with metaphors on a book-specific basis: for example, A.J. BJØRNDALEN, *Untersuchungen zur allegorischen Rede der Propheten Amos und Jesaja*, Berlin - New York, 1986 (cf. pp. 7-103); D. BOURGUET, *Des métaphores de Jérémie* (EB, 9), Paris, 1987; H. JAUSS, *Tor der Hoffnung. Vergleichnisformen und ihre Funktion in der Sprache der Psalmen* (EurHS XXIII, 412), Frankfurt a.M - Bern - New York - Paris, 1991; H.-P. MÜLLER, *Vergleich und Metapher im Hohenlied*, Göttingen, 1984; F. LANDY, *In the Wilderness of Speech: Problems of Metaphor in Hosea*, in *Biblical Interpretation* 3 (1995) 35-59; B. SEIFERT, *Metaphorisches Reden von Got im Hoseabuch*, Göttingen, 1996; G. EIDEVALL, *Grapes in the Desert: Metaphors, Models and Themes in Hosea 4–14* (CB OT, 43), Stockholm, 1996; J. MCINLAY, *Bringing the Unspeakable to Speech in Hosea*, in *Pacifica* 9 (1996) 121-134; (ii) focus on a particular metaphor and its application in various biblical texts: for example, M. BRETTLER, *God is King. Understanding an Israelite Metaphor* (JSOT SS, 76), Sheffield, 1989; ID., *Images of YHWH the Warrior in Psalms*, in *Semeia* 61 (1993) 135-65; M.C.A. KORPEL, *A Rift in the Clouds: Ugaritic and Hebrew Descriptions of the Divine*, Münster, 1990; N. STIENSTRA, *YHWH is the Husband of His People: Analysis of a Biblical Metaphor with Special Reference to Translation*, Kampen, 1993; (iii) focus on a single metaphor within a specific biblical text: for example, K. NIELSEN, *There is Hope for a Tree: The Tree as Metaphor in Isaiah* (JSOT SS, 65), Sheffield, 1989. A small number of monographs and articles exist with reference to the images and metaphors employed in Isaiah as such: e.g. R. LACK, *La symbolique du Livre d'Isaie. Essai sur l'image literaire comme élément de structuralisme* (AnBib, 59), Rome, 1973; K. NIELSEN, *op. cit.*; P.D. MISCALL, *Isaiah: The Labyrinth of Images*, in *Semeia* 54 (1991) 103-121; (iv) A growing number of authors are focusing on biblical metaphors from a feminist perspective: e.g., N. DELBECQUE, *Images and Metaphors in a Feminist Perspective*, in J.-P. VAN NOPPEN (ed.), *Metaphor and Religion: Theolinguistics 2* (Study Series of the Vrije Universiteit Brussel, 12), Brussels, 1983, pp. 231-250; C.V. CAMP, *Woman Wisdom as Root Metaphor: A Theological Consideration*, in K.G. HOGLUND *et al.* (eds.), *The Listening Heart: Essays in Wisdom and the Psalms in Honor of Roland E. Murphy* (JSOT SS, 58), Sheffield, 1987; P. BIRD, *"To Play the Harlot": An Inquiry into an Old Testament Metaphor*, in P.L. DAY (ed.), *Gender and Difference in Ancient Israel*, Minneapolis, 1989, pp. 75-94; R.J. WEEMS, *Gomer: Victim of Violence or Victim of Metaphor?*, in *Semeia* 47 (1989) 87-104; C.V. CAMP, *Metaphor in Feminist Biblical Interpretation: Theoretical Perspectives*, in *Semeia* 61 (1993) 3-36; G.A. YEE, *By the Hand of a Woman: The Metaphor of the Woman Warrior in Judges 4*, in *Semeia* 61 (1993) 99-

exposition on the use of metaphor in the bible, Peter W. Macky[2] partly accounts for the popularity of the topic by highlighting the central place metaphors enjoyed among the literary resources at the disposal of the biblical author. For Macky, the biblical authors did not only intend to appeal to their readers'/listeners' intellects (cognitive purpose), they also, and perhaps more importantly, endeavoured to move their audience and transform their faith (rhetorical purpose). One of the central methods employed by the biblical authors to this end was the use of what Macky calls "profound metaphors"[3], metaphors which invite the reader/ listener to imaginatively explore the depths of an image, uniting their personal experience with a literary expression for which there is no adequate "more literal" substitute. Since the bible itself deals substantially with non-corporeal realities – the divine sphere [God, salvation etc.] & the inner-human sphere [faith, trust, fear etc.] – profound metaphors offered an ideal resource for the biblical author to engage his audience in the exploration of such realities. For Macky, such supersensible realities ultimately require the use of metaphor. Metaphor is the essential "way of meaning" when we, and the biblical authors, attempt to explain mystery[4]. While not immediately evident on the surface, it remains my contention that Isa 25,10a contains just such a profound metaphor.

Although there is an ongoing discussion with regard to the ultimate purpose of metaphor[5], we will subscribe for the time being to Macky's definition – to which we will return below – and inclusive approach to the topic, accepting that the biblical authors had more than one pur-

---

132; M. BAL, *Metaphors He Lives By*, in *Semeia* 61 (1993) 185-207; F. LANDY, *On Metaphor, Play and Nonsense*, in *Semeia* 61 (1993) 219-237 (a critique especially of C.V. Camp); F. VAN DIJK-HEMMES, *The Metaphorization of Women in Prophetic Speech: An Analysis of Ezekiel 2*, in A. BRENNER (ed.), *A Feminist Companion to the Latter Prophets* (The Feminist Companion to the Bible, 8) Sheffield, 1995, pp. 244-255.

2. P.W. MACKY, *The Centrality of Metaphors to Biblical Thought: A Method for Interpreting the Bible* (Studies in the Bible and Early Christianity, 19), Lewiston - Queenston - Lampeter, 1990.

3. MACKY, *Centrality* (n. 2), p. 2.

4. *Ibid.*, p. 27.

5. The tendency is to move towards one of two poles and "reject" or at least "devalue" the other: Rhetorical: P. RICŒUR, *La métaphore vive*, Paris, 1975 (= *The Rule of Metaphor*, R. CZERNY (tr.), London, 1978); BOURGUET, *Des métaphores de Jérémie* (n. 1); J.M. SOSKICE, *Metaphor and Religious Language*, Oxford, 1985, etc.; Cognitive: G. LAKOFF – M. JOHNSON, *Metaphors We Live By*, Chicago, 1980; E.F. KITTAY – A. LEHRER, *Semantic Fields and the Structure of Metaphor*: in *Studies in Language* 5 (1981); cf. also E. KITTAY, *Metaphor: Its Cognitive Force and Linguistic Structure*, Oxford, 1987; E.R. MACCORMAC, *A Cognitive Theory of Metaphor*, Cambridge, MA, 1985; S. MCFAGUE, *Speaking in Parables: A Study in Metaphor and Theology*, Philadelphia, 1975; ID., *Metaphorical Theology: Models of God in Religious Language*, London, 1982; STIENSTRA, *Husband* (n. 1), etc.

pose in mind when they used metaphors and accepting also that on some occasions they had no other option than to use metaphorical speech[6].

1.2 *The Centrality of Metaphors in Isaiah*

The use of image and metaphor abounds in the prophetic literature and its presence has also been recognised as a "structuring" feature of the book of Isaiah (BI) as a whole[7]. Peter D. Miscall has noted, however, that most studies on Isaiah tend to subordinate metaphor to meaning, seeing it as a means for conveying meaning (usually with respect to historical processes and figures) and not as a "textual element in its own right"[8]. The present contribution intends to follow Miscall's lead and move forward on the basis of two premises: 1) avoid the historical/theological and emphasise the literary/theological and 2) give priority to metaphor over meaning. He further proposes that tracing an image throughout the entire book of Isaiah will create a labyrinth of corridors into the meaning of the text, thereby implying that as there are many images there are also many ways to approach meaning and interpretation of the text. Miscall enters into the labyrinth of Isaiah via the image of "light" but soon finds himself in a maze of adjoining corridors which extend and expand and even reverse his original starting point. Our entry into the labyrinth will be via the metaphor in Isa 25,10a. Within the labyrinth of metaphors, however, it is our intention to look "... more to the workings and to the meanings of Isaiah as it stands, not as a mirror of the history of ancient Israel"[9]. Once inside the Isaiah's labyrinth our endeavour will be to allow the "door" metaphor to be our guide rather than trying to discover a pathway based on some pre-conceived conceptual notions about history and prophecy. For Miscall, Isaiah is primarily a vision "... in the sense of a text that presents something to be seen and imagined rather than just thought of and conceptualized ... 'vision' in the broader sense of the realm of the imagination ... a panorama of God and world and, against this backdrop, ... a way of life that is God's way and an ideal community that dwells on God's holy mountain"[10].

---

6. Cf. MACKY, *Centrality* (n. 2), Chapter VI (pp. 163-187) and his proposed "critical metaphoricalism".

7. LACK, *La symbolique* (n. 1).

8. MISCALL, *Labyrinth* (n. 1), p. 103.

9. *Ibid.*, p. 105.

10. ID., *Isaiah* (Readings: A New Biblical Commentary), Sheffield, 1993, p. 12.

1.3 *The Context*

The unanswered or disputed questions from the history of exegesis of
Isa 24–27 will have been thoroughly rehearsed elsewhere and, as promised, the present contribution will endeavour to avoid them and focus on
the text as a literary/theological work[11]. In spite of the divisions proposed by Duhm[12] or the somewhat contrived liturgical structures proposed by Hylmö[13], Lindblom[14], Fohrer[15] and March[16], Isa 24–27 in its
present form can confidently be spoken of as a distinct and ordered
compositional unity[17]. Without further ado, Sweeney characterises the
chapters as having a universal focus[18], widening the national focus of the
oracles against the nations in Isa 13–23 to include the entire earth. Such
an approach requires a judgement as to the meaning of the word ארץ
(and its parallels) in the text, a significance which remains a matter of
dispute. For the present contribution I prefer to leave ארץ untranslated
and thus suspend judgement on its meaning. Sweeney is certainly correct in distinguishing words of punishment and their human consequences directed towards ארץ and words of blessing and their human
consequences directed towards ארץ, which together constitute the broad
lines of unity which hold these chapters together[19]. I believe he is also
correct in assigning the overall title of "a prophecy of salvation for Israel at Zion"[20] to Isa 24–27, but to follow such a statement any further
would be to stray from our purpose.

The author of Isa 24–27 employed words/phrases/statements to express two primary realities: disaster and salvation. A glimpse at the
opening verses of chapter 24, however, will reveal that, for the poet, two

11. A succinct yet thorough overview can be found in D.G. JOHNSON, *From Chaos to
Restoration: An Integrative Reading of Isaiah 24–27* (JSOT SS, 61), Sheffield, 1988, pp.
11-17; cf. also W.H. MILLAR, *Isaiah 24–27 and the Origin of Apocalypse* (HSM, 11),
Missoula, MT, 1976, esp. pp. 1-22; H. WILDBERGER, *Jesaja 13–27* (BKAT, X/2),
Neukirchen-Vluyn, 1978, esp. pp. 893-896.

12. B. DUHM, *Das Buch Jesaia*, Göttingen, 1892.

13. G. HYLMÖ, *De s.k. profetishka liturgiernas rytm, stil och komposition* (Lunds
Universitets Arsskrift N.F. Avd. 1. Bd. 25. Nr. 5), Lund, 1929.

14. J. LINDBLOM, *Die Jesaja-Apokalypse, Jes. 24–27* (Lunds Universitets Arsskrift
N.F. Avd. 1. Bd. 34. Nr. 3), Lund, 1938.

15. G. FOHRER, *Der Aufbau der Apokalypse des Jesajabuchs, Jes. 24–27*, in *CBQ* 25
(1963) 34-45.

16. W.E. MARCH, *A Study of Two Prophetic Compositions in Isaiah 24:1–27:1*, Dissertation, Union Theological Seminary, New York, 1966.

17. JOHNSON, *Chaos* (n. 11), p. 15; M.A. SWEENEY, *Isaiah 1–39, with an Introduction
to Prophetic Literature* (FOTL, 16), Grand Rapids, MI – Cambridge, U.K., 1996, pp.
316-317.

18. SWEENEY, *Isaiah 1-39* (n. 17), p. 312.

19. *Ibid.*

20. *Ibid.*, p. 313-315.

always means three. The three primary actants throughout the piece are YHWH, ארץ and its inhabitants who are mutually involved and are mutually obligated. In order to express and underline that relationship and its disintegration/re-integration, the poet employed a variety of literary techniques (cf. sections 2.2 & 2.3 below) one of which was metaphor. According to Sweeney's overall division, Isa 24,1-23 constitute a prophetic announcement of punishment by YHWH and 25,1-12 an expression of YHWH's blessing of ארץ at Zion[21]. Within the latter division there is a statement (25,10a) which can act, in a sense, as the turning point between disintegration and re-integration, a phrase which combines a "retired" *métaphorisé*[22] ("the *hand* of YHWH") with an unusual *métaphorisant*[23] ("... *rests* on this mountain"), thereby bringing the *métaphorisé* out of retirement to present a particular view of Israel's blessing and restoration This colon is, therefore, something of a key, a doorway into the labyrinth of metaphors used/restored/created by the author which allows us to explore the relationship between an angry, destructive deity who is ultimately restored to his sinful people.

Before proceeding to the metaphor as such, let us situate Isa 25,10a in its immediate literary context.

2. DELIMITATION OF PERICOPE CONTAINING THE PHRASE

Consensus is lacking among scholars on the exact limits of the pericope within which 25,10a is located. Sweeney[24] lists two factors which suggest that 25,1-12 can be envisaged as a distinct unit: (i) 25,1 lacks any syntactical connection with 24,23; (ii) the introductory ביום ההוא in 26,1 indicates the beginning of a new unit. The further division of 25,1-12, however, reveals a considerable variety of opinion[25]. The

---

21. *Ibid.*, pp. 325, 333.
22. Terminology taken from D. BOURGUET, *Des métaphores de Jérémie* (n. 1), p. 12.
23. *Ibid.*
24. SWEENEY, *Isaiah 1–39* (n. 17), pp. 333-334. J.D.W. WATTS, *Isaiah 1–33* (WBC, 24), Waco, TX, p. 327 begins the first pericope with 24:23 and ends it with 25,8.
25. WATTS, *Isaiah 1–33* (n. 24), p. 327: 24,23–25,8; 25,9-12; C.J. BREDENKAMP, *Der Prophet Jesaja*, Erlangen, 1887, p. 151: 1-5; 6-9; 9-12; F. DELITZSCH, *Biblical Commentary on the Prophecies of Isaiah*, Edinburgh, 1875, pp. 436-443: 1-8; 9-12; A. CONDAMIN, *Le livre d'Isaïe. Traduction critique avec notes et commentaires*, Paris, 1905, pp. 168-170: [1-5 after 26,6] 6-8; 9-12; A. SCHOORS, *Jesaja*, Roermond, 1972, pp. 150-152; R. KILIAN, *Jesaja II. 13–39*, Würzburg, 1994, pp. 147-150; P. HÖFFKEN, *Das Buch Jesaja, Kapitel 1–39* (Neuer Stuttgarter Kommentar – Altes Testament, 18/1), Stuttgart, 1993, pp. 181-184; WILDBERGER, *Jesaja, 13–27* (n. 11), pp. 942-974; L. ALONSO SCHÖKEL – J.L. SICRE DIAZ, *Profetas I, Isaías & Jeremías* (Nueva Biblia

majority of scholars seem to agree that vv. 1-5 constitute a unity (a "hymn of thanksgiving') while disagreeing on what to do with the remaining verses. Sweeney basically divides the chapter into two major sections (1-5 & 6-12) with further subdivisions – 6-8 = blessings; 9-10a = response; 10b-12 –, although he notes that all the subdivisions are clearly connected. For the sake of simplicity, therefore, we will follow Sweeney's calculations. 25,10a is thus located within subdivision vv. 6-12 which Sweeney describes as an "Announcement of YHWH's blessings of peoples and [Israel's] response"[26]. The statement contained in 25,10a is more precisely situated in the smaller subdivision made up of vv. 9-10a and constitutes a response on Israel's part to her awareness of new blessing after a period of affliction and, more importantly, of divine alienation. In 25,10a Israel confesses that YHWH has been restored to His city and His people[27]. Johnson[28] follows Lindblom[29] in placing a division after v. 10a because of the inclusion formed by the repeated הזה בהר here and in v. 6. Wildberger also draws a line at v. 10a – seeing the colon as a song of thanksgiving – but he is equally aware that the text as we have it links v. 10a with v. 10bff. by way of a conjunctive (perhaps appositional) ו forcing us to read what follows the ו in the light of what precedes it, i.e. to contrast salvation for Zion with downfall for Moab[30]. Certainly from the stylistic perspective it is important to read vv. 9-12 as a piece as we shall see.

Española, Comentario), Madrid, 1980, p. 204; J.A. MOTYER, *The Prophecy of Isaiah*, Leicester, 1993, pp. 207-210: 1-5; 6-8; 9-12; P. AUVRAY, *Isaïe 1–39* (SB), Paris, 1972, pp. 229-231: 1-5; 25,6–26,6; LINDBLOM, *Die Jesaja-Apokalypse* (n. 14), pp. 30-40: 1-5; 6-10a; 10b-12; E.J. KISSANE, *The Book of Isaiah*, Vol. 1, Dublin, 1941, pp. 284-287: 1-2; 3-5; 6-7; 8-9; 10-12; MILLAR, *Origin* (n. 11), pp. 38-45: 1-4c; 6-8; 9; 10-12; W.E. MARCH, *A Study of Two Prophetic Compositions in Isaiah 24:1–27:1*, Dissertation, Union Theological Seminary, New York, 1966, pp. 81-105; D.J. LEWIS, *A Rhetorical Critical Analysis of Isaiah 24–27*, Dissertation, Southern Baptist Theological Seminary, 1985, pp. 99-121: 1-5; 6-10a; [10b-12]; SWEENEY, *Isaiah 1–39* (n. 17), pp. 333-335: 1-5; 6-12; etc.

26. SWEENEY, *Isaiah 1–39* (n.17), p. 333.

27. We agree with JOHNSON *Chaos* (n. 11), pp. 62-64 here that the particularisation of Zion need not exclude an otherwise universalistic interpretation of the text.

28. *Ibid.*, p. 61.

29. LINDBLOM, *Die Jesaja-Apokalypse* (n. 14), p. 34.

30. WILDBERGER, *Jesaja 12–17* (n. 11), p. 972. Cf. SCHOORS *Jesaja* (n. 25), p. 152 who argues convincingly that vv. 10b-12 are probably an interpolation and do not belong to the original text which would then have ended with v. 10a; cf. also MARCH, *Two Prophetic Compositions* (n. 25), p. 103. Although the poetic elements of these verses may be obscure we cannot agree that they have been completely prosaized as MILLAR, *Origin* (n. 11), p. 44 and others would claim. Evidence of poetic features will be presented below.

2.1 *Colometry & Translation of Isa 25,9-10a [10b-12]*

9a   And a person will say on that day:

b   "Behold, our God is this.^{a}
c   We waited^b for him and he saved us.^{c}
d   Here is YHWH:$^{a'}$ we waited$^{b'}$ for him.
e   Let us rejoice and be glad in his salvation."$^{c'}$

10a   *For it rests, the hand of YHWH, on this mountain.*

10b   But it will be trodden down,^{a} Moab,^{b} in its place,^{c}
c   as it is trodden,$^{a'}$ a heap of straw,$^{b'}$ into the water of a dung pit.$^{c'}$

11a   And it will extend^a its hands in the midst of it,^{b}
b   as a swimmer extends$^{a'}$ [hands] to swim.$^{b'}$

c   But it will be made humble,^{a} its pride,^{b}
d   in spite of the cleverness$^{a'}$ of its hands.$^{b'}$

12a   The lofty fortifications^a of your walls$^{a'}$ he will make humble,^{b}
b   he will cause [them] to bend,$^{b'}$ let touch the earth,^{c} even the dust.$^{c'}$

The unit vv. 9-12 consists of an opening formulaic monocolon followed by a tetracolon exhibiting a complex parallel pattern ($^{a-b-c}$ // $^{a'-b'-c'}$)[31] followed by a climactic monocolon in 25,10a. In a certain sense this climactic monocolon draws the unit to a close, offering an explicative reason for the rejoicing of the previous colon which itself constitutes the climax of the manifold affirmations of God's presence accumulated in the tetracolon. It is within this climactic monocolon[32] that we find the metaphor of "the hand of YHWH resting". Clearly its climactic position, affirming salvation from God, indicates its importance to the author of the text. Our examination of the metaphor will further reveal the content of that salvation and how it might be understood within the labyrinth of metaphors running through the text. Lewis divides the text into word units (as opposed to cola?) some of which are synonymously parallel but comes up with the same basic pattern as we have suggested[33]. He describes the parallelism of vv. 9a-10a as follows:

31. ^{a} – affirmation of God's presence; ^{b} – waiting; ^{c} – salvation // $^{a'}$ – affirmation of YHWH's presence; $^{b'}$ – waiting; $^{c'}$ salvation + rejoicing
32. W.G.E. WATSON, *Classical Hebrew Poetry: A Guide to its Techniques* (JSOT SS, 26), Sheffield, 1984, ^{2}1995, p. 170.
33. LEWIS, *Rhetorical* (n. 25), pp. 112-113.

9a	ואמר ביום ההוא
9b	הנה אלהינו זה
9c	קוינו לו ויושיענו
9d	זה יהוה קוינו לו
9e	נגילה ונשׂמחה בישׁועתו
10a	כי־תנוח יד־יהוה בהר הזה

Lewis also notes that v. 10a is longer than the surrounding verses, further affirming our belief that it has a climactic/emphatic function. Johnson, to conclude, points out that the deictic particle כי further strengthens the exhortatory character of the concluding phrase of the pericope[34].

With regard to vv. 10b-12, Lewis points out that the conjunctive ו and the repetition of the term יד are strong reasons to suggest that we need to read these verses in the light of what precedes them. 10bc, therefore must be seen, according to Lewis, as the consequence of 10a. 10bc, 11ab, 11cd and 12ab all constitute bicola in synthetic parallelism[35].

2.2 *Text Critical Notes*

While it has been noted that practically every word of the text complex Isa 24–27 can be discussed and disputed at a text critical level, nothing of major significance exists with regard to our pericope or, in particular, the specific monocolon which constitutes the focus of our study[36]. I agree with Wildberger (and most others) with respect to one point and disagree on another, both of which deserve to be noted here if only to defend my English translation of the Hebrew text. In IQIsa[a] and Syr., the opening verb of v. 9 (MT ואמר) is in the 2nd person ואמרת. Wildberger (and others) see no referent for the second person and treat the MT as a sort of impersonal third person (German *"man"*), hence our translation "a person will say...". The *ketib* of MT 25,10b reads במי while the *qere* reads במו, the former being supported by 1QIsa[a], Sym. (εις πηλον) and Targ. (בטינא), the latter by LXX (εν αμαξαις), Pesh. (*'rgrgb*) and Vulg. (*in plaustro*). Two possible lines of interpretation can be discerned, therefore, the first following the *qere* and providing an

---

34. JOHNSON, *Chaos* (n. 11), p. 67.
35. 10b: [a]//[a'] – trodden // trodden; [b] // [b'] – Moab // straw; [c] // [c'] – location // location; 11ab: [a] // [a'] – extending; [b] // [b'] – hands; 11cd: [a] // [a'] – humbled // cleverness negated; [b] / / [b'] – pride // hands; 12ab: [a] // [a'] – fortifications // walls, [b] // [b'] – humble // bend; [c] // [c'] – earth // dust.
36. For a detailed text critical analysis of vv. 9-12 cf. WILDBERGER, *Jesaja 12–27* (n. 11), pp. 970-971.

image of the threshing of straw with some kind of instrument (a thresh-ing wagon of some kind), the second following the *ketib* and envisaging a sort of pit containing straw and water. On this question Wildberger opts for the *qere* arguing that it is simply a fairly well attested alternative for simple בְּ "in". The context, however, would seem to argue for the presence of water (*ketib*), both to support the metaphor of the swimmer which follows in v. 11 and to allow the straw to ferment in the dungheap. We opt, therefore, for the *ketib*[37]. A final point relates to the translation of the verb פרש. Most frequently this verb is rendered "to spread (the hands)" for swimming. In a recent note, however, J. Ellington has pointed out the lack of logic involved in such an interpretation, given that swimmers cup/extend their hands for swimming rather than "spread" them out like a fork[38]. He notes in addition that RSV has opted for the translation of פרש as "extend/stretch out" in several other places[39]. Our translation reflects his recommendations.

2.3 *Further Stylistic Features*

Millar points out that from Isa 24,1–25,9 we have an "excellent ex-ample of Hebrew poetry"[40]. From v. 10 onwards, however, he feels that the text has been prosaized to such an extent that poetic features are hard to trace although he does point out some evident residue of poetry. Much of Millar's difficulties lie with the fact that from v. 10 onwards there is metrical imbalance. Notwithstanding the fact that the text may be corrupt at this point[41] one should look further than the much disputed element of meter in order to establish whether a text is poetic or not[42]. We already noted some of the aspects of parallelism when we estab-lished the colometry of our pericope. Further analysis shows that the au-thor used assonance through repetition + anaphora (v. 9 וִיוֹשִׁיעֵנוּ ,קִוִּינוּ לוֹ זה, – // בִּישׁוּעָתוֹ; v. 10 – דוֹשׁ; v. 11 – פרש), consonance alliteration (10c – מַתְבֵּן בְּמֵי מַדְמֵנָה) possible punning (מַדְמֵן – being a town in Moab מַדְמֵנָה a dungheap)[43]. Perhaps the most intriguing feature of the text, however, is its sense of movement (or its absence): v. 9cd – waiting (stasis); v. 9e – rejoicing (up); v. 10a – resting hand (stasis); v. 10b – treading foot

37. Cf. LINDBLOM, *Die Jesaja Apokalypse* (n. 14), p. 38; AUVRAY, *Isaïe 1–39* (n. 25), pp. 232-233: "dans l'eau du fumier"; ALONSO SCHÖKEL – SICRE DIAZ, *Profetas* (n. 25), p. 211: "en el agua del muladar".

38. J. ELLINGTON, *A Swimming Lesson (Isaiah 25:11)*, in BTrans 47 (1996) 246-247.

39. Exod 9,29.33; 1 Kgs 8,38; 2 Chron 6,29; Job 11,13; Jer 4,31; Lam 1,10.12.

40. MILLAR, *Origin* (n. 11), pp. 43-45.

41. LEWIS, *Rhetorical* (n. 25), p. 119.

42. Cf. Watson's discussion of the topic in *Classical Hebrew Poetry* (n. 32), pp. 91-113.

43. Cf. WILDBERGER, *Jesaja 12–27* (n. 11), p. 971.

(down further); v. 11 – swimmer's hands/clever hands/pride (up); v. 12 – humbling to the earth/dust (down as far as you can go!). Contrastive images are everywhere and are supported by this pattern of movements: the person who waits (trustfully קוה) is rewarded with "a gesture of benediction"[44]; the person who attempts to rise by the cleverness of his own hands is rewarded by being trodden into a dungheap. Moab's hands are paralleled with those of the swimmer in v. 11ab and constitute a metaphor for human pride/cleverness which is further related by external parallelism to the lofty fortifications and walls of v. 12a. Sweeney, perhaps unhappy about the idea of a swimmer "spreading" his hands, misinterprets the metaphor of the swimmer, suggesting that he is spreading his arms "to portray Moab's demise"[45]. The context, however, seems to relate the idea of the swimmer's hands to self-sufficient pride (rising to the top by one's own devices) in contrast with patient trust ("waiting" for YHWH)[46]. Thus the hands of Moab and hand of YHWH are also set in contrast. YHWH's hand rests, but his "feet" appear to be more than active in the contrast between v. 10a and 10b. Finally, v. 12 contains a beautiful extended metaphor taking the *hiphil* forms of שחח, שפל and נגע, normally related to "bringing down" persons[47], and applying them to inanimate lofty walls/fortifications.

The most powerful poetic device employed in this pericope is the metaphor of "YHWH's hand resting". The said metaphor will constitute the focus of our study for the remainder of this contribution.

3. The Metaphorical Use of "YHWH's Hand"

3.1 *Speaking Metaphorically About God*

So far we have rather uncritically taken for granted that the expression "YHWH's hand" is metaphorical. Before going on to examine some aspects of the theory and function of metaphor with regard to 25,10a as a whole, however, a word or two needs to be said about the matter of speaking metaphorically about God in the bible. First of all we need to ask whether it is possible to speak literally about God? In his discussion on the use of literal and metaphorical speech with regard to unobservable realities – inner states, emotions, the supernatural, the divine –,

44. MOTYER, *The Prophecy of Isaiah* (n. 25), p. 211.
45. SWEENEY, *Isaiah 1–39* (n. 17), p. 335.
46. Cf. MOTYER, *The Prophecy of Isaiah* (n. 25).
47. Cf. F. BROWN – S.R. DRIVER – C.A. BRIGGS (eds.), *The New Brown – Driver – Briggs – Gesenius Hebrew and English Lexicon* (henceforth NBDB), Peabody, MA, 1979, 7817, 8213, 5060.

Macky admits that the possibilities of literal speech in this context are limited and that our only means of exploring, understanding and describing such realities is metaphor[48]. On the question of speaking literally about God, Macky continues, William Hordern[49] suggests that it is in the nature of theological speech that it must begin with analogy and then erode that initial analogy with further qualifications which simply underline the fact that such speech is inaccurate and approximate in the first place as an expression of truth about God. It would appear that the limitations of human speech and thinking and the transcendent and infinite nature of God are incompatible and that we can only speak about God using finite concepts and terms which are derived of necessity from our imperfect human world and applied to God as ultimately "inadequate" analogous terms. Even when we employ a speech act which describes the divinity in terms of a particular analogy, the very fact that we have to qualify the analogy reminds us that it is inadequate and that there can be no literal speech about God.

Humphrey Palmer[50] points out a number of weaknesses in this position. Firstly, it tends to assume that because the human world is finite and imperfect then our concepts and speech are also finite and imperfect. This is not necessarily the case since, for example, we can think and speak of numbers etc. in a perfect way. Secondly, our speech about the infinite need not be brushed aside as inadequate. There seems to be confusion between comprehending a reality such as infinity and having an adequate concept thereof. The former may be difficult if not impossible for humans but the latter need not be. Thirdly, the argument that proposes that our speech and thought about God must be inadequate tends to confuse the term "inadequate" with the term "metaphorical". There are many simple, observable realities which our human categories are inadequate to describe, but that does not mean that literal speech about such realities is impossible. All our speech is inadequate to the reality it attempts to describe but that does not mean that we are unable to speak literally even to the smallest extent about reality, whether observable or unobservable. It would appear from Palmer's criticism, therefore, that the idea that all speech about God must be metaphorical and not literal is inaccurate as a universal theory.

48. MACKY, *Centrality* (n. 2), pp. 163-187.

49. W. HORDERN, *Speaking of God: The Nature and Purpose of Theological Language*, New York, 1964, pp. 125f.

50. H. PALMER, *Analogy: A Study of Qualification and Argument in Theology*, New York, 1973, pp. 26-27.

Macky employs the arguments of Charles Hartshorne[51] whose position allows us to come close to literal speech about God. Hartshorne proposed that of universally applicable positive/negative pairs of concepts one or the other can be applied literally. With respect to conceptual pairs such as relative/absolute, mortal/immortal, finite/infinite etc., everything is either one or the other – if not one then the other. When speaking of God, then, we can say that if he is not literally finite, relative and mortal then God must be literally infinite, absolute and immortal. The procedure, therefore, is to find a positive/negative pair at least one of which is applicable to the subject and we are looking at literal speech. Where both apply to the subject we may be dealing with metaphor but the context will help us decide which is being used literally (best fitting the context) and which not. Macky goes on to argue on the basis of Hartshorne's axiom that it is plausible that the biblical writers were speaking literally when they made certain assertions about God. His analysis need not delay us here. Suffice to say that his arguments affirm the possibility of speaking literally about God and that it is necessary to distinguish this usage from metaphorical speech[52].

Stienstra likewise affirms such a possibility, making an important distinction between anthropomorphism as such and anthropomorphic metaphors. The "titular metaphor" which constitutes the focus of her study "YHWH is the husband of his people" clearly has an anthropomorphic dimension in that what she calls the donor field (*métaphorisant*, secondary subject) refers to the human institution of marriage. Theological language-use tends to be highly anthropomorphic for obvious reasons although some have shown themselves to be uncomfortable with this fact. Nevertheless, anthropomorphic metaphors referring to God or to inanimate objects have been recognised as common for many centuries. Caird notes, in fact, that "anthropomorphism in all its variety is the commonest source of metaphor"[53]. While none of this will come as much of a surprise it remains important to recognise the significance of Stienstra's distinction before we move on to our analysis of the content of 25,10a As she notes, not all biblical anthropomorphism is metaphorical. She il-

51. C. HARTSHORNE, *Creative Synthesis and Philosophic Method*, Lanham, MD, 1983, pp. 152-153.

52. Cf. the summary of the discussion between Lakoff/Johnson and Earl A. MacCormac with regard to the sense of "literal" and the possibility of a speech act being literal in one sense and non-literal in another in G.A. LONG, *Dead or Alive? Literality and God-Metaphors in the Hebrew Bible*, in *JAAR* 62 (1994) 509-537.

53. G.B. CAIRD, *The Language and Imagery of the Bible*, London, 1980, p. 173. Caird, it should be noted, grants both an expressive and a cognitive function to our metaphorical language about God.

lustrates her point with an example from the book of Genesis in which God is described as walking in the garden and as one who speaks and can be hidden from (Gen 3,8-10). Stienstra describes such talk as real anthropomorphism, allegorical perhaps, but nevertheless describing the deity in purely human, literal and non-metaphorical terms. She notes that it is impossible to boil this and similar stories[54] down to a metaphorical concept and reminds us of the fact that they are presented as narratives of events which were considered to have really happened. One aspect missing from Stienstra's analysis is the use of human limbs[55] (and face) in reference to YHWH. The analysis of Isa 25,10a will reveal that such usage must be classified under anthropological metaphor and is not intended to be a literal anthropomorphism[56].

According to G.A. Long, "the writers of the Hebrew Bible were aware that they used language we today call figurative and, to be more specific, figures of speech we call metaphors"[57]. While it is true that, from the perspective of the modern reader, God is anthropomorphised, anthropopathised, theriomorphised and physiomorphised[58] it seems clear that the same authors intended certain language about God to be understood literally and that it is usually fairly easy to distinguish between the two. It remains somewhat chauvinistic to state that the biblical authors were simply mistaken in *thinking* that they were being literal when speaking about the deity and that we are correct in stating that they were *always* being metaphorical.

Is "YHWH's hand" a literal anthropomorphism or an anthropomorphic metaphor? The fact that we are dealing with an anthropomorphism is beyond dispute – YHWH does not have hands. The question remains: is the expression literal or metaphorical? In order to attempt an answer to this question we need to take a look at the usage of the expression in the bible and in proto-Isaiah (henceforth PI).

---

54. E.g. Gen 18,20-21.

55. Particularly "hands" and "feet"; cf., however, KORPEL, *Rift* (n. 1), pp. 108-116.

56. Literal anthropomorphism, according to Stienstra, tends to be restricted to Genesis and Exodus. The story of Jacob wrestling with God in Gen 32, for example, a text with which exegetes and biblical translators have struggled in their efforts to tone down the anthropomorphic element, is mentioned later in Hos 12,4-5 at a time when metaphor had largely taken over from literal anthropomorphism. Hosea himself tones down the literal anthropomorphism by placing YHWH on a par with the angel of YHWH which was clearly an acceptable procedure at his time of writing. Later appearances of YHWH in the OT, however, tend to be more veiled, presented in the form of dreams or visions, presented in fact as anthropomorphic metaphors.

57. LONG, *Dead or Alive?* (n. 52), p. 523.

58. *Ibid.*, p. 521.

3.3 *"YHWH's Hand" in the Bible and in PI*

According to Bourguet's theory of metaphor[59] we are clearly dealing with metaphor here since we have a simple juxtaposition of two terms stemming from quite distinct isotopes, one divine (the divine name)[60] one human, the cross-reference or metaphorical core of which lies in the positive analogy between divine power and the power/strength of the human hand. Even Macky would have to accept that the expression "YHWH's hand" is metaphorical or figurative because at the bottom line it is dependant speech, a speech act dependant on our knowledge of the strength of human hands[61].

Besides the ordinary, non-theological and unequivocally literal usage of יד[62] in the OT as a whole[63], the term is frequently[64] employed to express the notion of human/military power or strength (Gen 31,29; 41,35; 49,24; Dt 28,32; Josh 8,20; Ps 89,26; Dan 8,25; Job 34,20 etc.). Where the divinity is concerned, however, the vast majority of usages appear to be related to power of various kinds both negative and positive: divine power in general: Job 30,21; creative power: Isa 41,20; 45,12; 48,13; 66,2; Ps 95,4; protective power: 1 Kgs 18,36; Ezra 8,22; 1 Chron 4,10; Ps 37,24; with suggestion of hostile military power (both positive and negative to Israel): Exod 3,19; 13,3; 15,12; Num 20,20; Isa 9,11 etc.; deliverance from and into alien control: Exod 3,8; Dt 32,39; 7,8; Ps 49,16; 106,10; 107,2; Jer 31,11; Neh 1,10 etc. A significant number of references point to hostile divine power: with enemy as (God's) agent: Dt 19,12; Josh 2,24; Jgs 2,14; 1 Sam 30,15; with reference to God:

59. BOURGUET, *Des métaphores de Jérémie* (n. 1), pp. 7-71, esp. pp. 10, 59.
60. Although see also his discussion of the isotope of the divine *ibid.*, pp. 20-22.
61. MACKY, *Centrality* (n. 2), pp. 36-39.
62. As "hand", "wrist" or "arm" (Gen 24,22 etc.), as "holding" (Gen 22,6; 40,11; Num 22,23; Josh 8,18; 2 Kgs 11,8; 1 Chron 11,23 etc. [the extended sense of "having in one's control" (Exod 22,3; 1 Sam 21,4) emerges in a number of texts while the literal sense dominates in others (e.g. Exod 32,4; Prov 6,17)]; for "gestures of various kinds' (Prov 11,21; Job 17,3; Lev 5,21; Ezek 17,18; Gen 38,28; Exod 6,8; Ps 28,2; 134,2 etc.), cf. *TDOT* V, 393-427 (Bergman, von Soden, Ackroyd).
63. Cf. also ימין which is similar in meaning and when associated with יד also takes on the figurative implications of power and strength (Ps 74,11; 89,14; 138,7; 139,10; Isa 48,13 etc.). In the theological context, however, it would appear that ימין is more associated with YHWH's positive power, laying foundations/creating (Isa 48,13), protecting/upholding (Ps 63,9; 139,10), supporting (Ps 18,36), a source of righteousness (Ps 48,11); cf. *TDOT* VI, 99-104 (Soggin/Fabry).
64. The *Interpreter's Dictionary of the Bible* II, pp. 520-521 (Dentan) suggests that the majority of uses are thus intended: "Most numerous are those in which it [יד] occurs as a picturesque symbol of 'power'". Other less common metaphorical usage includes "portion" or "share" (Gen 47,24; Jer 6,3; II Sam 19,44; "debt" (Neh 10,32); "monument" (Isa 56,5; 1 Sam 15,12; 1 Chron 18,3); "sexual"/"genital" references are fairly frequent but may also be related to power and vitality (Dt 23,13; Isa 57,8.10; Cant 5,4f. etc.).

Exod 9,3; 14,31; Dt 2,15; Jgs 2,15; Ruth 1,13; 1 Sam 17,46; Ps 31,9; 109,27; Isa 8,11; Jer 15,17; 16,21; Ezek 3,14 etc[65]. Johnson notes that is used frequently in the Isaianic tradition to denote YHWH's power, both in the negative and positive sense. With respect to PI, the expression is found in Isa 1,25 (hostile); 11,11 (deliverance); 11,15 (hostile); 19,16 (hostile); 31,3 (hostile); 34,17 (hostile)[66]. We agree with him that in Isa 25,10a the expression clearly has to do with promised deliverance but what is the content of that deliverance? Is it just a bald statement of YHWH's ability to deliver or does it go deeper than that?

It would appear then that "YHWH's hand" is a conventional metaphor[67]; one might even call it a lexicalised, "retired" or even "dead" metaphor, a notion to which we will return below. Long might call it a conventional literal expression[68]. Given the frequency of occurrences being related to the firmly lexicalised understanding of "hand of God" as hostile divine power (especially in PI) it would be reasonable to suggest that such usage would, at the very least, not have created much metaphorical tension[69]. In any case, the phrase appears to have shaken off its dependant character and taken on an independence of its own through frequent use and ultimate lexicalisation. For Macky, then, it would have to be viewed as non-figurative. Bourguet would probably confirm such a claim on similar grounds: "La particularité des métaphores morts c'est que leur lexicalisation entraîne leur emploi sans intentionnalité"[70]. On its own, therefore, the biblical authors probably did not intend "YHWH's hand" to be understood metaphorically. Said

65. *TDOT* V, 393-426 (Bergman, von Soden, Ackroyd); HAL II, 386-388. In some of these cases, certain translations simply render יד as "power" or "might" or "great work": e.g. NRSV – Exod 14,31; Jer 16,21.

66. JOHNSON, *Chaos* (n. 11), p. 67; cf. his footnote 97, p. 127: Isa 1,25; 11,11.15; 19,16; 31,3; 34,17 etc.

67. Cf. LONG, *Dead or Alive?* (n. 52), pp. 523-524.

68. *Ibid.*, p. 511.

69. E.A. MACCORMAC, *Metaphor and Myth in Science and Religion*, Durham, NC, 1976, p. xi: "… a metaphor can be best characterised by the "tension" or surprise it causes in the hearer by means of its absurdity" (= the so-called "tension theory of metaphor").

70. BOURGUET, *Des métaphores de Jérémie* (n. 1), p. 19. His claim that lexicalisation as an indicator for discerning "dead" metaphors is only valid for living languages (cf. footnote 14, same page) might be countered by Macky's assertion that it is still possible to distinguish "common" (conventional) and "uncommon" (perhaps metaphorical) usage on the basis of frequency and, of course, a little common sense. He offers the example of the more than 50 uses of the term ראש meaning "head" or "high point" to be taken literally (e.g. head of a road: Ezek 16,25.31; 21,19.21; 42,12; top of a mountain: Exod 19,20; Num 14,40; Josh 15,8; 1 Sam 26,13; Isa 2,2; Hos 4,13 etc.) and the few examples where it is probably not meant literally (e.g. Joel 3,47; Obad 15; Ps 7,16; Judg 9,57).

authors and their audience simply understood it as "power" without referring to the notion of human power.

What makes it "YHWH's hand" in Isa 25,10a so interesting as a focus
of study, however, is the verb of which it is the subject, namely נוח "to
rest".

3.4 *The Uniqueness of "YHWH's Hand Resting" in PI and OT*

Wildberger is among the few to note that the expression "the hand of
YHWH rests on this mountain" is unique in the OT. Watts makes a similar statement, agreeing with Wildberger that the phrase is kin to the Zion
Theology of the Psalms[71]. Neither author makes much of the fact that the
expression is unique, particularly in the combination of יד and נוח.
Ackroyd points out that the phrase as a whole may suggest divine protection[72]. In the same place, however, he points out that Ps 38,3 parallels
the combination of נחת and יד with נחת and הץ. His reason for doing so
is apparently to suggest that via a possible word-play on נחת and נוח the
expression "the hand of YHWH rests" might be given a hostile interpretation. My suspicion that this suggestion is unconvincing is confirmed by
Motyer who points out that the *qal* of נוח never expresses violent action[73]. We will return to the positive meaning of this verb below. Suffice
to say that Motyer understands the phrase as a gesture of divine benediction[74] but the question remains: what is the content of that benediction?

The unique combination of יד יהוה and נוח suggests a specific kind of
protection/security/benediction by "YHWH's hand" informed by the term
נוח at the level of metaphor. Looked at from Bourguet's perspective, a
"new" metaphor is being created here, one in which a familiar expression – YHWH's hand – becomes the *métaphorisé* and the unexpected
"rest" becomes the *métaphorisant*. We are forced to re-interpret our assumptions about the significance of the *métaphorisé* – יד יהוה – in the
light of what we know about the *métaphorisant* – נוח. The same is true
from Macky's perspective given that "YHWH's hand" is placed in a dependant relationship with the verb "rest"[75]. Thus, using Macky's termi-

---

71. WATTS, *Isaiah 1–33* (n. 24), p. 335; Wildberger actual says the following: "In
10a formuliert der Verfasser eigenständig; daß die Hand Jahwes »auf diesem Berg« ruht,
wird sonst so nicht gesagt, entspricht aber durchaus der Ziontheologie. »Hand« ist Symbol für Stärke, Macht; es geht um den absoluten Schutz, den Israel auf dem Gottesberg
finden kann". cf. *Jesaja 12–28* (n. 11), p. 972.

72. Cf. *TDOT* v, 409 (Ackroyd).

73. MOTYER, *The Prophecy of Isaiah* (n. 25), p. 710.

74. *Ibid.*, p. 711.

75. Although authors such as Janet Soskice (there can be only one "subject") disagree
with the possibility of what Macky calls "dual-direction" metaphors, it seems at least

nology, one reality, namely the Subject (יד יהוה), is depicted in terms that are more commonly associated with a different reality, namely the Symbol (נוח). For both authors, however, the two realities in question have to be related to one another at some level: for Macky by positive or negative analogy; for Bourguet by cross-reference or isotopic intersection.

We have already looked in some detail at the "content" of the *méta-phorisé* or subject of our metaphorical statement. Before we can further unpack the significance of the entire metaphorical statement, however, it is important that we examine the *métaphorisant*. What is the meaning and usage of the verb נוח in OT and PI?

3.5 נוח *in OT and PI*

The *qal* of נוח in OT primarily means "to settle (on)" or "to rest". One can divide the (±) 35 OT occurrences of the *qal* into three types or categories: (i) more literal – Gen 8,4; Exod 10,14; Num 10,36; II Sam 17,12; 21,10; Isa 7,2.19 (ii) more abstract – (wisdom) Prov 14,33; Qoh 7,9; (the spirit of YHWH) Num 11,25f.; II Kgs 2,15; Isa 11,2; (iii) fuller/more comprehensive – (being at rest) Isa 14,7; Job 3,13.26; (nuance of death as rest) Job 3,16; Prov 21,16; (rest from one's enemy) Isa 23,12; Est 9,16.22; Neh 9,28[76]. Evidently there is nothing particularly unusual about the usage of the term in the OT as a whole or in PI in particular. As we noted above, however, what makes the expression in Isa 25,10a unique is the combination of terms. If we were to understand the use of נוח in 25,10a as belonging to type (i) then the expression would mean nothing more than it says, YHWH's hand would settle on "this mountain" like a bird settling on the branch of a tree. Similarly, if we were to place it under category (iii), the reference would focus us on the subject: YHWH's hand would be experiencing rest, be at sleep, be free from its enemies. In line with Stolz, therefore, we understand the significance of נוח in Isa 25,10a to be more abstract, "like wisdom settling on the hearts of the wise" or like "the spirit of YHWH resting on the prophets or the king" and entering therein. Such an interpretation allows a clearer insight into the function of the combination of terms at the metaphorical level.

What then is the specific meaning of נוח in 25,10a? The full answer to this question can only emerge if we look at the term in its context, the context of the metaphorical statement: כי־תנוח יד־יהוה בהר הזה.

---

possible that the present metaphor can function in the opposite direction: יד יהוה informing our understanding of נוח; cf. SOSKICE, *Metaphor and Religious Language* (n. 5), p. 49; MACKY, *Centrality* (n. 2), p. 60.

76. Cf. *THAT* II, 43-46 (Stolz); HAL II, 678-679; *TWAT* V, 298-307 (Preuß).

4. EXAMINATION OF THE MEANING OF THE METAPHOR IN ITS CONTEXT

4.1 *Definitions and Indicators*

Even the briefest perusal of the relevant literature will show that there are almost as many theories of metaphor and how it functions as there are writers on the topic, although it is possible to establish some broader categories. The present contribution has followed the definitions of Daniel Bourguet who underlines the distinction between the (at least) two distinct isotopes involved in a metaphorical speech act and Peter W. Macky who stresses the dependant nature of figurative/ metaphorical language. In a certain sense then we can say that dependant speech and contrasting isotopes are among the primary indicators of the presence of metaphor. For Bourguet, what makes the metaphor function as such is the core of cross-reference between the two (or more) terms from distinct isotopes, corresponding to a point of resemblance upon which the metaphor is based, the seat or core of the metaphor. Macky describes the same thing in terms of analogy which can be both positive, negative and neutral. We have already conceded the fact that in speaking about God (and other incorporeal realities) the use of metaphor is necessary. In the present context we have also noted that part of the metaphorical statement contained in Isa 25,10a is a "retired" metaphor – the hand of YHWH –, one which through frequent use (and ultimate lexicalisation) has come to mean the power of God, often bearing hostile overtones. Seen as a whole, however, it would appear that the metaphorical statement is not confined to the retired metaphor "YHWH's hand". The introduction of the notion of "resting" and its connotations insinuates a new dimension to our understanding of the hand of YHWH, one which brings it out of retirement. It is clearly possible to see two distinct isotopes at work in the statement, one powerful and perhaps even hostile, the other gentle and protective, bringing security. Thus our understanding of "YHWH's hand" is made dependant on our understanding of the content of the term נוח. The uniqueness of this combination of terms in the OT suggests that the author was quite aware that he was reactivating a "retired" metaphor and that his "audience" would have been jarred by the unusual character of the combination into reflecting on the profundity of the reality it was attempting to describe, namely that there is salvation for Israel and that said salvation had a specific content which is revealed in the complexity of the "reactivation". The author employs his creative skill to transform a retired metaphor into a novel metaphor.

4.2 *Three Way Re-birth*

It is at this point that we can enter further into the metaphor (and into the labyrinth)[77] and endeavour to explore some of its depths.

(i) At the first, and perhaps most obvious level, the association of נוח with the hand of YHWH constitutes a cessation of the negative power being meted out by YHWH in the first part of the text complex Isa 24–27. At the same time, the destructive power of YHWH's hand is not only at rest, it is now a source of protection and benediction.

(ii) As we move further into the labyrinth we are confronted with further associations. In his commentary on the book of Lamentations, J. Renkema argues that the phrase לא מצאה מנוח in Lam 1,3 does not signify the Deuteronomistic "rest" of a safe and peaceful lifestyle in the land of the promise (cf. Dt 3,20; 12,9f.; 25,19; 28,65)[78] but should be associated with the idea of rest and security provided by marriage. The use of the concept in the Book of Ruth helps point us in a direction which fits much more appropriately in the present context. "Naomi is in search of 'rest' for Ruth. As events turn out it would appear that she finds it by urging her daughter-in-law to enter into a new marriage, through which she will be relieved of her widowhood. Naomi had already expressed such a wish in 1,9. A woman finds 'rest', therefore, in the house of her husband who obliges himself to care for her needs and protection. When a woman becomes a widow, however, she forfiets her 'rest'. It is evident from Ruth 1,9 and 3,1 that such 'restlessness' is a fact of widowhood"[79]. The metaphor of widowhood in Lamentations is applied to both Jerusalem (1,1) and Judah (1,3; cf. also 5,3). Both widows sit restlessly: both have lost house and husband. Thus the metaphorical statement of Isa 25,10a can be understood as bringing a term which would be at home in the isotope of widowhood[80] in contact with a retired

---

77. For Miscall, one creates the labyrinth by entering it. It does not already exist. Its corridors are made up of images, terms, metaphors. It has no single entrance and is not already mapped out. Thus our interpretation of a text will depend on the direction we follow as we enter and explore the labyrinth of Isaiah. Cf. *Labyrinth* (n. 1), pp. 117-118.

78. Having said this, he insists that the Deuteronomist's later theological formulations with respect to "redemptive rest" may already be present here in embryonic form. Indeed, as part of the metaphor, the restlessness of widow Judah corresponds at its deepest level with the rupture in the relationship between YHWH and Judah's inhabitants, which turned out for them to mean loss of house and home, peace and security.

79. J. RENKEMA, *Klaagliederen*, Kampen, 1993, pp. 77-78.

80. The remaining context may be further enlightened by such an association. The "banquet" (25,6), the "removal of the veil" (25,7) the "swallowing up of death" (25,7), the "wiping away of tears" (25,8), the "removal of disgrace" (25,8) etc. may all be associated with the notion of widowhood and would deserve further investigation. This is unfortunately beyond the scope of the present contribution. Cf. also the image of women birthing only "wind" in Isa 26,16ff.: without her husband, Zion is unable to procreate.

anthropomorphic metaphor from the isotope of the divine, restoring its vitality. Throughout the book of Lamentations YHWH's hand is turned against Lady Jerusalem and Daughter Zion[81]. Throughout the first part of the text complex Isa 24–27 we are witness to YHWH's hostile dealings and then to his absence (there is no wine?). In 25,10a his hand rests on "this mountain" as a sign of the restoration of a widow's rest, his hand rests as a husband's hand, he has come back.

(iii) If one ventures even further into the labyrinth, further metaphorical associations emerge. Marjo Korpel describes the idea of the city personified as a woman as a kind of root metaphor upon which others are based, i.e. the city as widow[82]. Here it is Daughter Zion who is seen as a woman and a widow. As such, the restoration of YHWH as husband signifies the presence of what Nelly Stienstra calls a "titular metaphor" (or a metaphorical concept), namely "YHWH is the husband of his people"[83]. Although she does not think there are references to YHWH as husband in PI she is clearly mistaken[84]. "YHWH's hand rests on this mountain" can be reduced to metaphorical concept: YHWH is the husband of his people.

5. CONCLUSIONS

Isa 25,10a is a unique combination of images, a reactivated retired metaphor opening up an entrance to the complex labyrinth of metaphors employed by the author(s) of Isaiah and allowing as to explore the depths of that labyrinth. The "resting hand of YHWH" can be understood as a symbol of restoration out of chaos[85], the restoration of YHWH to his people as husband and the reversal of their widowhood. In this sense, Isa 25,10a is a unique metaphor for salvation. It invites its "reader" to imaginatively explore and re-evaluate his or her relationship with God[86]. In the context of Isa 24–27 as a whole it is equal in contrastive power to the many violent words found in these chapters. In former times, YHWH's hand was turned against Israel's enemy and was a source of protection for Zion. After a time of destruction and destruction and a period of widowhood, YHWH's hand once again offers protection and thus "rest"

---

81. For the personification of the city as a woman and a widow, cf. RENKEMA, *Klaagliederen* (n. 79), pp. 61ff.; C. COHEN, *The Widowed City*, in *JANES* 5 (1973) 75-81; P.L. DAY, *Whence Shall Help Come to Me? The Biblical Widow*, in P.L. DAY (ed.), *Gender and Difference in Ancient Israel*, Minneapolis, MN, 1989, pp. 125-141.

82. KORPEL, *Rift* (n. 1), p. 261.

83. STIENSTRA, *Husband* (n. 1), p. 9, and n. 1, p. 12.

84. *Ibid.*, p. 162.

85. Cf. JOHNSON, *Chaos* (n. 11), especially Chapter 2.

86. MACKY, *Centrality* (n. 2), pp. 260-263: "Relational metaphors".

is restored to "restless" Zion[87]. Read in the light of 26,6 with which בהר הזה constitutes an inclusion, the full expression serves as a climax of blessing, a sign of complete restoration: the table is set and Zion's husband is at home for the feast.

To have been invited to contribute to this celebratory volume is for me a unique honour, not only because Wim Beuken has been an imposing "mountain" in my studies and fledgling exegetical career but also because it places me in such illustrious, and somewhat humbling, company. It has been obvious to me, however, – and here I take the liberty of mixing my metaphors – that "the hand of YHWH" has been at rest on this particular mountain for many a decade. Long may it continue to bring creative insight and "rest" to my respected teacher and friend.

Jozef II-straat 7   Brian DOYLE
B-3000 Leuven

---

87. ... and his foot is turned against the enemy (25,10b).

ISAIAH 27,10-11:
GOD AND HIS OWN PEOPLE

Er zijn velen die de stem maken,
maar weinigen die hem horen[1].

To write an article for Wim Beuken is rather special. He saw my beginnings in biblical scholarship. He showed a lot of care and warmth. He
was a father to me. Certainly not a 'God-father' (like the one in this article), but still, it is difficult for a son like me to live up to his expectations. He knows the ins. I will always remember El-Azariye: sitting on a
balcony with Wim, reading Jeremiah 14–15, talking and reading a whole
week[2]. It was paradise. Thank you!

This article is about Isaiah 27,10-11. Two verses from the 'Isaiah
apocalypse'[3]. Some attention is paid to the verse structure of the poem,
and a lot of attention to interpretation, that is the meaning of images, inner coherence, and textual nuances, especially in the light of parallels in
the book of Isaiah.

The exegetical literature on this passage is occupied mostly with questions of reference. Where on earth and in history can that fortified city
be found? Is it Jerusalem? The 'pagan' city of Samaria? A 'Weltstadt'[4]?
I will not play that game. My thesis will be that the way the text speaks

1. Bert SCHIERBEEK, interview in *Trouw* 04-05-1996.
2. W.A.M. BEUKEN – H.W.M. VAN GROL, *Jeremiah 14,1–15,9: A Situation of Distress and its Hermeneutics. Unity and Diversity of Form-Dramatic Development*, in P.-M.
BOGAERT (ed.), *Le Livre de Jérémie. Le prophète et son milieu. Les oracles et leur transmission* (BETL, 54), Leuven, 1981, pp. 297-342.
3. Isaiah 24–27 is object of research in the *Jesaja Werkplaats* these years. The Jesaja
Werkplaats was founded by Prof. Koole in Kampen and taken over – later on, after some difficult years – by W. Beuken and H. Leene in Amsterdam. It has flourished since then. Mem-
bers are on the moment, May 1996: Prof. Dr. W.A.M. Beuken (Leuven), Prof. Dr. A. van der
Kooij (Leiden), Prof. Dr. H. Leene (Amsterdam), Prof. Dr. E. Talstra (Amsterdam); Dr.
H.W.M. van Grol (president, Utrecht), Dr. J. Holman (Tilburg), Dr. K.D. Jenner (Leiden), Dr.
D. Ryou (Seoul), Dr. A.L.H.M. van Wieringen (Nijmegen); and R. Abma, J. Beckers, H.J.
Bosman, B. Doyle, H. van Laarhoven, J. Loete, P. Lugtigheid, M. van der Meer, N. Rosier,
W. van Stiphout, P. van der Voort, A. Vrijlandt, H.J.M. van der Woude (secretary).
4. See e.g. O. KAISER, *Der Prophet Jesaja. Kapitel 13–39* (ATD, 18), Göttingen,
1973, pp. 183-185; H. WILDBERGER, *Jesaja. 2. Teilband* (BKAT, 10, 2), Neukirchen-
Vluyn, 1978, pp. 1015-1018; J.N. OSWALT, *The Book of Isaiah. Chapter 1–39* (NICOT),
Grand Rapids, MI, 1986, pp. 496-497.

about this city, especially the choice of words, makes very clear that this people is described as something special to God, his own people, and certainly not a pagan people. It could live in Samaria, but it is seen as his own people.

1. *Text*

\ ונעזב כמדבר	כי עיר בצורה בדד \ נוה משלח	10a
\ וכלה סעפיה	שם ירעה עגל \ ושם ירבץ	10b
\ מאירות אותה	ביבש קצירה תשברנה \ נשים באות	11a

11b   כי לא עם־בינות הוא \ על־כן לא־ירחמנו עשהו \ ויצרו לא יחננו

10a   Yes, the fortified city is desolate,
        the pasture is driven away
        and deserted like the desert.
10b   There the bullcalf grazes
        and there it lies down
        and it finishes up its twigs.
11a   Dried out, its branches break off
        women coming,
        setting them alight.

11b   Yes, this is not a people with intelligence,
        therefore he has no compassion on it, he who made it,
        and he who formed it, shows no mercy to it.

2. *Verse structure*

Our poem consists of two strophes, vv. 10-11a and 11b. The first one has three tricolic verse lines and describes the destruction of a city, the second one has a single tricolon and offers background information, an account of the destruction[5]. Both strophes start with כי. They have no other words in common. The first strophe has a very regular rhythm with 3+2+2 metrical units in each verse line, the second 3+3+2.

I will give some attention to the inner unity of the four separate verse lines. The first verse line states the desolation of a city. The three cola of v. 10a correspond to three clauses. Each colon contains a geographical term (עיר בצורה; נוה, metaphor for עיר[6]; מדבר, in a simile) and a predi- cate stating desolation in one way or another (נעזב; משלח; בדד). These parallel terms are first lineary arranged and then chiastically:

---

5. The poem may be compared with a prophetic oracle and its two parts, accusation (v. 11b) and announcement (vv. 10-11a).
6. See §3.

כמדבר	ונעזב	משלח	נוה	בדד	בצורה	עיר
A''	B''	B'	A'	B	A	

Note the alliterations:

כמדבר	ונעזב	משלח	נוה	בדד	בצורה	עיר

The three cola of the second verse line, v. 10b, correspond to three clauses, all presenting an activity of a bullcalf, introduced in the first colon. The other words are referring to the city in the preceding line: 2× שם and the suffix in סעפיה – all three words start with /s/. The arrangement is again first linear and then chiastic:

סעפיה	וכלה	ירבץ	ושם	עגל	ירעה	שם
A''	B''	B'	A'		B	A

The third verse line, v. 11a, is about dried out branches. They are introduced in the first colon, קצירה, and referred to in the third, אותה. Apart from the infinitive ביבש, there are three clauses, corresponding to three cola. The verbs are placed in the same linear/chiastic pattern:

אותה	מאירות	באות	נשים	תשברנה	קצירה	ביבש
B''		B'		B		

Note the phonetic play with /-ot/ in the last three words of the verse line: באות \ מאירות אותה.

The three verse lines belong together by being description of one event. The suffixes in סעפיה and קצירה refer to עיר בצורה; they connect the three lines.

The fourth verse line exchanges עיר for עם. The three cola of v. 11b correspond to three clauses. All clauses have the negation לא and end with הוא and corresponding suffixes (/hu, -hu, -nu/). Again predicates (A) and subjects (B) are placed in a linear/chiastic pattern:

לא יחננו	ויצרו	עשהו	על־כן לא־ירחמנו	הוא	כי לא עם־בינות
A''	B''	B'	A'	B	A

The semantic parallelism between the second and third colon is evident.

3. *Verse line 10a:*   כי עיר בצורה בדד \ נוה משלח \ ונעזב כמדבר

עיר בצורה, "the fortified city", is a normal technical term and it is found many times, mostly in the plural[7]; only Isa 25,2 and 27,10 have the singular. The plural term is referring to cities in Judah, Israel or Trans-Jordan, never to cities abroad[8]. So, if we would like to identify this city, we would have to look for it in the land itself. The two passages with a singular term, Isa 25,2 and 27,10, both belong to the 'Isaiah apocalypse'. Therefore, the city of 27,10 could be or has to be that of 25,2. In Isa 25,2 the phrase is split up over two cola: "Yes, you (God) have turned the *city* into a rubble heap[9], / the *fortified* town into a ruin... ". Isa 27,10 combines the two words again[10]. Isa 27,10 could be a comment on the destruction of the city in 25,2[11].

This fortified city is בדד, "desolate". The only other desolate city in the Bible is that of Lam 1,1, Jerusalem: "How *lonely* she sits, / this city, once full of people!". The city becomes personified in the word בדד. Elsewhere, it is only used for people or animals[12]. They are or live physically isolated, on themselves. The term itself is neutral, sometimes parallel to לבטח, "safe"[13]. But when the isolation is not self chosen, things are different[14]. In Lam 1,1 the isolation is worked out in several directions: 1) the people in the city have left it; 2) the city itself is like a widow, in the midst of peoples and nations, no power any more, a slave; 3) the city is a woman left by its lovers (v. 2). Reality, simile and metaphor are combined in one complex picture. What could this mean for Isa 27,10? Is our city a woman left by its husband?

---

7. 18x plural, phrase or clause: Num 13,28; Deut 1,28; 3,5; 9,1; Josh 14,12; 2 Sam 20,6; 2 Kings 18,13; 19,25; Isa 36,1; 37,26; Ezek 36,35; Hos 8,14; Zeph 1,16; 2 Chron 17,2; 19,5; 32,1; 33,14; Neh 9,25.

8. 2 Kings 19,25 / Isa 37,26 is rather general, inclusive.

9. The only other collocation with גל: Isa 37,26 / 2 Kings 19,25.

10. The phrase קריה בצורה of Isa 25,2 is unique and exists thanks to the splitting up of the usual phrase עיר בצורה.

11. Within the scope of this article, it is not possible to go into Isa 25,2 and parallel passages of the 'Isaiah apocalypse'. Compare G. FOHRER, *Der Aufbau der Apokalypse des Jesajabuchs (Is 24–27),* in *CBQ* 25 (1963) 34-45. He gives a sketch of "die mehrfache, aber der Bedeutung nach unterschiedliche Erwähnung der ›Stadt‹" (pp. 40-42).

12. Animals: the verb בדד in Hos 8,9 and Ps 102,8; the adjective for Yhwh in Deut 32,12 and Ps 4,9.

13. Num 23,9; Deut 33,28; Jer 49,31.

14. Lev 13,46; Isa 27,10; Micah 7,14; Jer 15,17; Ps 102,8 (בודד); Lam 1,1; 3,28. H.-J. ZOBEL argues rightly that in Isa 27,10; Micah 7,14 and Lam 1,1 we find "eine aus dem individuellen Bereich auf eine gesellschaftliche Größe übertragene Redeweise" (*TWAT* I, p. 516).

Parallel to עיר בצורה בדד a second statement is made: נוה משלח, "the pasture is driven away". A strange statement. No other pasture ground in the Bible is ever said to be driven away. נוה could stand for the small cattle on the נוה, like קן, "nest", stands for the birds in Isa 16,2: קן משלח, "scattered nestlings" (NEB[15])[16]. But small stock is not an object of such a שלח anywhere[17]. It seems there is something more going on.

נוה משלח makes more sense if it is a matter of personification again, as in עיר ... בדד. The pi'el/pu'al of שלח is used a.o. in the case of divorce[18]. שלח pi'el is used in the immediate context of our passage, exactly in this meaning: "*by driving her away* you contended with her" (Isa 27,8). In Isa 50,1 Yhwh speaks about Sion, the city, like about a mother (wife) he repudiated[19].

The two personifications בדד and משלח are both fitting in the image of divorce: "sitting alone" and "driven away". This is said of the city and of the pasture. What does the combination of city and pasture allude to? What does the pasture add to the city? There are three options: (1) The city becomes a pasture. (2) The text speaks about a city and its pasture grounds. (3) The city is called "pasture".

The first option is based upon an event many other texts speak about: a city left by its inhabitants and destroyed becomes a pasture ground. Human beings are replaced by (small) cattle or more exotic animals[20]. But this well known picture does not match our text. Ringgren translates: "Sie ist ein 'Weideplatz', entvölkert, verlassen wie die Wüste"[21], but this translation is impossible: משלח (masc.) does not refer to "city" (fem.) but to "pasture" (masc.). And it would be strange to say that the city has become or is a depopulated pasture. That would be two disasters in one: first the city becomes a pasture, then the pasture is left by its people and cattle. Of course this is possible[22], but it will certainly not be said in one phrase.

The second option is based upon the reality that each city has its pasture grounds. The pasture fills out the image of desolation. Not only the city is left by its people, but also the pasture by its cattle. Compare the

---

15. *The New English Bible*, Oxford, 1970.
16. Metonymy: W. Bühlmann – K. Scherer, *Stilfiguren der Bibel. Ein kleines Nachschlagewerk* (BibB, 10), Fribourg, 1973, p. 69.
17. שלח with צאון as an object: Gen 38,17; Job 21,11 in a positive sense, "send", and therefore incomparable. Apart from that, שלח pi'el is found with עיר as an object, but only in the expressions שלה אש ב + עיר: Hos 8,14, and שלח עיר באש: Judg 1,8; 20,48.
18. Deut 21,14; 22,19.29; 24,1.3.4; Isa 50,1; Jer 3,1.8; Mal 2,16.
19. Comp. W.A.M. Beuken, *Jesaja. Deel IIB* (POT), Nijkerk, 1983, pp. 70-72.
20. H. Ringgren, *TWAT* V, p. 294.
21. *Ibid.*
22. The deserted pasture is a motive itself: *ibid.*

prophecy of hope in Jer 33,12-13[23]: "In this place, desolate and without men or animals – in all its towns there will again be pastures for shepherds to rest their flocks. In the towns of the hill country, of the western foothills and of the Negev, in the territory of Benjamin, in the villages around Jerusalem and in the towns of Judah, flocks will again pass under the hand of the one who counts them" (NIV[24]). But if the pasture in Isa 27,10 was the pasture of the city, why would this pasture not be called "*her* pasture" or "her pasture ground*s*"? I am missing a suffix and a plural form[25].

This leaves us with the third option: The city is called "pasture". The pasture is metaphorical and pointing to the city itself. The city is described as a pasture. We find this in Isa 33,20, where Jerusalem is mentioned a.o. קריה and נוה: "Look upon Zion, the city of our festivals; your eyes will see Jerusalem, a peaceful *abode*, a tent that will not be moved" (NIV). In this way, Zobel translates Isa 27,10: "Die 'feste Stadt' Jerusalem ist 'allein'..., 'eine entvölkerte Stätte'..., 'verlassen wie die Wüste'"[26]. This means that עיר ... בדד and נוה משלח are parallel statements, נוה being a metaphor for עיר. But what does this metaphor add? As a semi-nomadic word for place-to-live, it is opposite to עיר בצורה[27]. Secondly, it helps the composition of this tricolic verse line: נוה ,עיר and מדבר are parallel. עיר is the only concrete term, נוה is metaphor and מדבר is comparison. Semantically, נוה stands midway between city and wilderness. Thirdly, נוה points, maybe, to the cited text, Isa 33,20, bringing Isa 27,10-11 in opposition to that text[28].

The pasture is not only משלח, "driven away", but also ונעזב כמדבר, "deserted like the desert". An unique statement again[29]. Nowhere else in the Bible a pasture is said to be deserted. In fact, נעזב belongs together with the other two predicates, בדד and מלשח, and the verb ע.ז.ב. is used with עיר a lot of times. נעזב prolongs the personification and contributes to the image of divorce[30]. The verb ע.ז.ב. *qal/nif'al* in the meaning man-

---

23. There are only four verses in MT with a collocation of נוה and עיר: 2 Sam 15,25; Isa 27,10; Jer 31,23; 33,12.

24. *The Holy Bible. New International Version*, Grand Rapids, MI, ⁹1979.

25. Comp. the Babylonian expression: RINGGREN, in *TWAT* V, p. 293.

26. ZOBEL, *TWAT* I, p. 514; OSWALT, *Isaiah* (n. 4), p. 496 translates "a habitation deserted"; O. PROCKSCH, *Jesaia I* (KAT, 9), Leipzig, 1930, p. 336: "preisgegebene Flur"; F. DELITZSCH, *Isaiah* (COT, 7), Grand Rapids, MI, 1978 (reprint), p. 459: "a dwelling given up".

27. Compare Lam 2,2: את כל־נאות יעקב \\ מבצרי בת־יהודה. Both cola are referring to the same reality. RINGGREN, in *TWAT* V, p. 295 ("vielleicht").

28. Comp. Isa 32,18.

29. The verb ע.ז.ב. and the noun מדבר are not found connected elsewhere in the meaning that the desert itself is deserted.

30. Comp. E.S. GERSTENBERGER, in *TWAT* V, p. 1205.

abandons-wife has a strong presence in Isaiah, first in 9,14 and 54,6-7 and later on in 60,15 and 62,4.12. Our text refers to this discussion about divorce and takes up the language of the last mentioned text, 62,12: עיר לא נעזבה. Both the noun עיר and the verb .ע.ז.ב. *nif'al* are found here[31].

The city is a woman sitting alone, repudiated and abandoned. The metaphor of divorce is enriched by the simile כמדבר. Why? The desert is used in a simile, but it appeals to the plain sense of city and pasture. In this way, the wilderness is the end result of the transformation described. But, maybe, there is more. Is it an allusion to the great prophet of divorce, Hosea: ושמתיה כמדבר \ ושתה כארץ ציה, "I will make her like a desert, / turn her into a parched land" (2,5; NIV)? Or is it an allusion to Isa 64,9: "Your sacred cities have become a desert; even Zion is a desert, Jerusalem a desolation" (NIV)?[32]

4. *Verse lines 10b-11a:*   שם ירעה עגל \ ושם ירבץ \ וכלה סעפיה
                           ביבש קצירה תשברנה \ נשים באות \ מאירות אותה

The city is deserted by its inhabitants like the desert. The modifier of place שם points back to that city. On that place other things which make the destruction complete, will take place.

Firstly, on that place a bullcalf will graze and lie down. That means that the city is deserted and ruined and that it has become a place to graze, that is a נוה. The city that was called נוה, has become a נוה. Bitter irony.

A bullcalf is introduced. עגל certainly has a plural meaning. But why bullcalfs and not, for example, sheep? Nowhere in the Bible bullcalfs are grazing, nowhere they are associated with doom, like here. Of course, "Um die Verwüstung ... zu veranschaulichen, sagt Jes 20,10 [sic!], daß dort Kälber weiden werden"[33], but why calfs? I have three options: (1) Bullcalfs are better equipped to eat twigs (v. 10b''') than sheep, physically. (2) The bullcalf creates an ironic contrast with Isaiah 11,6. (3) The bullcalf is an ironic allusion to the golden calf.

The first option is the most convenient, plain like the rest of vv. 10b-11a. Bullcalfs can be expected to strip bushes and trees. Sheep are smaller and have less strength.

---

31. Other collocations of עיר and .ע.ז.ב. *qal/nif'al*, but not speaking about divorce: Josh 8,17; 1 Sam 31,7; Isa 17,2.9; 32,14; Jer 4,29; 48,28; 49,25; Ezek 36,4; I Chron 10,7. There are strong parallels between Isa 17,9 (and context) and our text in motives and words; see note 41.

32. Other collocations of עיר and מדבר: Isa 14,17; Jer 4,26; 22,6.

33. H. RINGGREN, in *TWAT* V, p. 1058.

The second option is based on the facts that the only other bullcalf in Isaiah is found in 11,6 and that the word pair רעה \ רבץ can be found nearby in 11,7[34]. Moreover, רעה and the word pair רעה \ רבץ are used "meist metaphorisch für das unangefochtene Leben von Mensch und Tier in dem erhofften Friedensreich"[35]. Our bullcalf finds its paradise on the ruins of the city. But that irony is part of our text itself and of comparable texts and does not need Isa 11,6[36]. For the moment, I do not see compositional reasons to stress the ironic contrast between Isa 11,6 and 27,10.

In the third option, the bullcalf is an ironic allusion to the golden calf or better to bull worship in general. עגל is used as a word for idol in more than half of the texts, so one has to think of it: "The use of 'calf' rather than cattle or flocks is suggestive here. Note that it is used as a diminutive to mock bull worship elsewhere (Exod. 32:4; 1 K. 12:28; etc.). Perhaps the prophet is saying that because the people of the world worship 'calves,' real calves will graze on their cities"[37]. "Perhaps" is a nice way of saying there are no confirmations of this allusion in the immediate context.

In the third colon, our bullcalf becomes a real instrument of destruction: "it finishes up its twigs". What does it eat? Twigs of a ruined city? Most interpreters take this literally, but there is a metaphorical option too. Mostly, one thinks of ruins taken over by bushes and trees or of neglected pasture grounds with bushes and trees[38].

I prefer another literal option: The calf eats the twigs of the fruit-trees of the city[39]. After the abandonment by the people and the transformation of the city into ruins and pasture grounds, the only left sign of culture are the fruit-trees. They are destroyed now. This option is more meaningful than the first one, which speaks of a destruction of wild bushes. But there is another reason to think of fruit-trees. סעיף is used only twice in the Bible. And that other text, Isa 17,6, speaks of סעפיה פריה, "the twigs of the fruit-tree"[40]. This may be taken seriously, be-

34. The word pair רעה \ רבץ: Isa 11,7; 14,30; 27,10; Ezek 34,14f; Zeph 2,7; 3,13; Cant 1,7.

35. G. WALLIS, in *TWAT* VII, p. 567.

36. Compare Isa 5,17; 14,30; 17,2; Zeph 2,7.

37. OSWALT, *Isaiah* (n. 4) , p. 496, n. 4.

38. The scenario of Dalman: Cultivation stops and woodland increases at the expense of cultivated land (Isa 27,10; Jer 26,18; Micah 3,12; Hos 2,14). Then, this new forest area in turn is threatened by grazing calves and women looking for firewood; G. DALMAN, *Arbeit und Sitte in Palästina. Band I*, Gütersloh, 1928, pp. 87-88. WILDBERGER, *Jesaja* (n. 4), p. 1020 speaks of bushes. So many others.

39. PROCKSCH, *Jesaja* I (n. 26), p. 342 refers to 2 Kings 3,25.

40. *BHS*: סעפי הפריה.

cause there are more connections between Isa 17 and 27,10-11 (and context), although difficult to interpret[41].

As said, there is a metaphorical option too. Oswalt says: "that once mighty city becomes a pasture field (v. 10), or a once-spreading tree whose limbs are now stripped and dead (vv. 10b, 11a; cf. Ezek. 31; Dan. 4:13-26)"[42]. If I supposed a metaphor, I would not refer to Ezek 31 and Dan 4, but I would prefer the vine: Ezek 15 and especially Ps 80. Israel is compared to a vine in Ps 80,9ff. Verse 12 speaks of קציר, verse 14 of grazing (רעה) and verse 17 of burning, all like Isa 27,10b-11a. But there is no metaphor. If the city was a tree in vv. 10b-11a, the suffixes in סעפיה and קצירה would be explained well, but the repeated שם would be a problem: where would be 'there' if the city was not a place but a tree? Moreover, I prefer to read vv. 10-11a as a coherent text, giving one picture of the city in stead of two.

And then v. 11a gives the next momentum, which makes the destruction complete. The fruit-trees stripped of their green foliage will drie out, branches will break off and will be gathered by women to be used as firewood. So, everything that belonged to the life of the city is destroyed: people, buildings, fruit-trees.

What does קציר mean? According to Dalman: סעפים means "twigs", while it seems probable that קציר points to the "Gesamtheit des Gezweigs", or the "crown"[43]. More important, קציר is used as the opposite of roots[44]. If the branches are dried out and broken off, there are still roots that can sprout: a symbolic way of saying there is room for compassion – refused in v. 11b[45]. Or are the roots dried out too, if the קציר dries out: is this the ultimate image of a total lack of compassion?[46]

5. *Verse line 11b:* כי לא עם־בינות הוא \ על־כן לא־ירחמנו עשהו \ ויצרו לא יחננו

The reproach כי לא עם־בינות הוא has a unique way of putting it. The plural בינות is found only here. The plural form is "evidently intended to

---

41. Isa 17,5 comp. 27,12: כמלקט שבלים; 17,6 comp. 24,13: עוללת כנקף זית; 17,7 comp. 27,11: עשהו, "his maker"; 17,8 comp. 27,9: האשרים והחמנים, "sacred poles and incense-altars"; 17,1-3.9 comp. 27,10: the abandonment (עזב) and destruction of fortified cities (מבצר), including grazing flocks (רבץ).

42. OSWALT, *Isaiah* (n. 4), p. 499.

43. G. DALMAN, *Arbeit und Sitte in Palästina*. Band IV, Gütersloh, 1935, pp. 167 and 169.

44. WILDBERGER, *Jesaja* (n. 4), p. 1020: Job 14,9; 18,16; 29,19.

45. Comp. Isa 6,13; the tree is cut down, not dried out.

46. Job 18,16 (יבש).

intensify the idea of the stem (plural of amplification)"[47]. But what does this reproach mean? What is the point? What kind of insight?

Wildberger says: "בינה muß hier, dem Zusammenhang gemäß, religiös verstanden werden: Es geht diesem Volk, alttestamentlich gesprochen, Gotteserkenntnis und Gottesfurcht ab. Die Bewohner der Stadt verstehen Gottes Wege nicht und haben für seine Verheißungen kein Sensorium"[48]. More close to the text: there has to be a relation between יצרו \ עשהו and עם־בינות. God expects from this people that it recognizes that he created it, and that it has an understanding of the nature of such a relation.

Other texts confirm that בינות means relational insight[49]. In Deut 32,6 the reproach is the following:

> Is this the way you repay the LORD,
>> O foolish and unwise people (עם נבל ולא חכם)?[50]
> Is he not your Father, your Creator,
>> who made you (עשׂך) and formed you? (NIV)

The Song of Moses makes clear that this foolishness becomes apparent in idolatry (vv. 15-18) and permits only one reaction: destruction (vv. 26-28)[51].

Hos 4,14 says in conclusion: ועם לא־יבין ילבט – "a people without understanding will come to ruin!" (NIV). Although a lack of דעת אלהים leads to a wide range of crimes (4,1-3)[52], if it is about insight, fornication and adultery are emphasized, that is idolatry (vv. 11-14).

The beginning of the book Isaiah itself gives a nice parallel to the start of the Song of Moses. The relational nature of the foolishness under discussion is elaborated (Isa 1,2-3; NIV):

> Hear, O heavens!
>> Listen, O earth!
>> For the LORD has spoken:
> "I reared children and brought them up,
>> but they have rebelled against me.
> The ox knows his master,
>> the donkey his owner's manger,
> but Israel does not know,
>> my people do not understand (עמי לא התבונן)".

---

47. GK §124e: "keen understanding".
48. WILDBERGER, *Jesaja* (n. 4), p. 1020.
49. The form of the clause is important too. The clause לא עם־בינות הוא brings in mind the clause לא עמי אתם (Hos 2,1; comp. 1,9). The insight of Isa 27,11b (בינות) has the same syntactical position as the suffix 1sg of Hos 2,1!
50. In the context, we find forms of the stem בין: 32,7.28.29.
51. Comp. the same motifs in Deut 4,3ff (v. 6: עם חכם ונבון).
52. Comp. Jer 4,22.

Here too a father-son relationship ("children"). If Israel abandons Yhwh (v. 4), that is incredible foolishness. Even an animal has a better understanding of relations and behaves accordingly.

The insight of God is mentioned at the end of Isa 29,16:

> You turn things upside down,
>> as if the potter (היצר) were thought to be like the clay!
> Shall what is formed say to him who formed it (יאמר מעשה לעשהו),
>> "He did not make me (לא עשני)"?
> Can the pot say of the potter (ויצר אמר ליוצרו),
>> "He does not understand" (לא הבין)?[53].

This insight is about relations again. According to the people, God has a lack of understanding, that is he thinks he made the people. And that is a false representation of things, the people says. Therefore, the reproach is mutual. There are some points in common between our passage, Isa 27,11, and the last two mentioned texts. In Isa 1,2-3 the subject is called עם. We find the negative לא and a form of the stem בין[54]. In Isa 29,16 we find the role עם (v. 14), the negative לא and the three stems בין, עשה and יצר; the last two in the same form and meaning: עשהו and יוצרו. And of course, these three texts all suppose that the relation between God and this people is a relation between creator and creature (potter and pot), father and son. And again and again, the reproach is that this people does not accept, does not understand this relationship.

In the scope of this article the compositional relations between Isa 1,2-3; 27,11 and 29,16 can not be studied, but one thing may be clear: the interpretation of 27,11 has to reckon with these two other texts.

We return to Wildberger. He continues his passage about בינה as follows: "Es ist aber doch auffallend, daß der vornehmlich im Bereich der Weisheit beheimatete Begriff בינה gewählt wurde und eben nicht von דעת אלהים oder יראת יהוה die Rede ist. – בינה kann von jedem Menschen erwartet werden; wer sich ihr verschließt, ist ein Tor. Die Bewohnerschaft von Samaria bestand von alters her nicht nur aus Israeliten..., Alexander der Große setzte die Tradition fort und siedelte in der Stadt mazedonische Veteranen an. ... Da aber Jahwe und kein anderer Gott Schöpfer ist, ist auch von solchen Bevölkerungsgruppen בינה zu erwarten"[55].

In the foregoing, Wildberger was a little bit too verbose: "Gotteserkenntnis", "Gottesfurcht", "Gottes Wege" and "Verheißungen"[56]. Now he is

---

53. NIV, apart from the last colon; there it has: "He knows nothing".
54. I like the phonetic resemblance between הָתְבּוֹנָן and the once-only form בִּינוֹת.
55. WILDBERGER, *Jesaja* (n. 4), pp. 1020f.
56. Also H. RINGGREN, in *TWAT* I, p. 627, mentions the ways of God as an object of

too quick in his conclusions. He sees the use of the word בינה as evidence of his thesis that the city of Isa 27,10-11 is Samaria. Apart from the historical data, he has one argument. Even if he was right to record that בינה mainly belongs to wisdom terminology[57], it would not be right to state that, therefore, this בינה may be expected from every human being. Is the Israelite wise man of the opinion that his wisdom is universal, that it is granted to everybody, and that it may be demanded from everyone? That seems a crass statement to me, transcultural as Israelite wisdom may be.

So, is the relational insight of Isa 27,11 something that may be expected from non-Israelites? The texts that are close to Isa 27,11 in genre and theme, make clear that the insight that God is creator, has not a universal nature, but concerns the relationship between God and his people Israel. Moreover, Wildberger takes no notice of the immediate, literary connections (Isa 1,2-3; 29,16). These contradict his thesis: both texts concern Jerusalem and its people.

There is one more reason to reject Wildberger's view. He speaks about Yhwh as a creator in a 'dogmatic' way, that is not context-sensitive but generalizing[58]. In Isa 27,11 Yhwh is the creator of a people. I would not ask whether Yhwh is the creator (יוצר) of one and all, but where he is called the creator of a people, as in Isa 27,11. Is יצר used with עם or a synonym for it or a name of a people, while it concerns another people than Israel?

There is a small number of important texts outside of the book of Isaiah. In Ps 2,9 and Lam 4,2 we find the breaking of pottery. In Ps 2,9 the pots stand for peoples in general – the anointed king is the one who breaks; in Lam 4,2 for the sons of Zion. In Jer 19,1.11 Jeremiah performs a symbolic act: the breaking of a pot, image of God breaking "this people and this city" (Jerusalem). These texts concentrate on the breaking and not on the process of creation, so that they are not very relevant to the interpretation of Isa 27,11.

We find another image in Jer 18,1-12: the potter forms a pot and if the potting goes wrong, he uses the clay to form another pot. This crea-

---

בין: "Die Einwohner der zerstörten heidnischen Großstadt Jes 27,11 sind ein unverständiges Volk..., verstehen also nicht die Wege Gottes". These ways of God are mentioned nowhere in the context.

57. *Ibid.*, modifies: "בינה "Einsicht, Verstand" ist zum großen Teil, aber nicht ausschließlich ein Weisheitswort".

58. Comp. R. KILIAN, *Jesaja II. 13–39* (Die Neue Echter Bibel, 32), Würzburg, 1994, p. 157: "11b scheint zunächst auf Israel hinzudeuten (vgl. 1,3; 43,1), aber nachdem sich seit Deuterojesaja der Monotheismus in Israel durchzusetzen vermochte (vgl. 44,6-8; 45,18), konnten derartige Aussagen auch auf andere Völker angewandt werden". This is speculative reasoning and not to the point.

tive freedom is typical of God in his dealing with peoples: "If at any time I announce that a nation or kingdom is to be uprooted, torn down and destroyed, and if that nation I warned repents of its evil, then I will relent and not inflict on it the disaster I had planned. And if at another time I announce that a nation or kingdom is to be built up and planted, and if it does evil in my sight and does not obey me, then I will reconsider the good I had intended to do for it" (vv. 7-10; NIV). Jer 18,1-12 is about the creative process itself. The text may be compared with our text. God is creator of peoples, no matter which[59]. But this is not the whole picture. Even in Jer 18,1-12 this free creator-god is interested in only one people: "O house of Israel, can I not do with you as this potter does?... Like clay in the hand of the potter, so are you in my hand, O house of Israel!" (v. 6; NIV). Although this passage supposes that God is the creator of peoples and kingdoms, it actualizes this general view for only one people: Israel[60].

The book of Isaiah is even clearer. It mentions God as creator (יוצר) of one people, Israel: 29,16^2; 43,1.7.21; 44,2.21.24; 45,9^2.11; 64,7[61]. Other peoples are out of view. Within the book of Isaiah, Isa 27,11 has to relate to this Deutero-Isaianic tradition[62]. This relation is strengthened by the use of the participle *qal* of יצר and the combination with the verb עשׂה[63].

It is said of this Creator that he has no compassion on this people, shows no mercy to it. Apparently mercy and compassion go with creating. But this connection is made explicit only once. The verbs עשׂה and חנן are collocated in Prov 14,31:

He who oppresses the poor insults his Maker (עשׂהו);
he who is generous (חנן) to the needy honours him (NEB).

Three images are connected with רחם or רחמים in the book of Isaiah: the compassion of a woman on her child (Isa 49,10.13.15), that of a man

---

59. Comp. Ps 86,9: "all nations, which you made (עשׂית), will come and bow down..." (cf. *BHS*).

60. Therefore, the climactic statement of B. OTZEN, in *TWAT* III, p. 833 is incorrect: "Bei Jeremia aber liegt die Pointe im Verhältnis zwischen dem Schöpfergott JHWH und seinem erwählten Volk Israel, ja zwischen dem Weltgott JHWH und den anderen Völkern". Comp. p. 837.

61. *Ibid.*, pp. 835-836, says that in DI "das Verbum jāṣar beinahe ausschließlich in den Zusammenhängen vorkommt, wo von der Erschaffung (und Erwählung) Israels die Rede ist". See the commentary of W.A.M. BEUKEN, *Jesaja deel IIA* (POT), Nijkerk, 1979, *passim*, and *Jesaja deel IIIB* (POT), Nijkerk, 1989, p. 44.

62. So rightly W.H. SCHMIDT, in *THAT* I, p. 764.

63. The verbs יצר and עשׂה are collocated in: 2 Kings 19,25; Isa 22,11; 27,11; 29,16; 37,26; 43,7; 44,2.24; 45,7.9.18; 46,11; Jer 33,2; Amos 4,13; (Hab 2,18); Ps 95,5.

on his repudiated wife (Isa 54,(4-)7.8.10)[64], and that of a father on his children (Isa 63,7(.8).15(.16))[65]. In the last text the image of father is again combined with that of creator/potter (Isa 64,7; comp. Ps 103,8.13-14)[66]. The compassion of the father is highly self-evident[67]. That of the creator too. But this creator has no compassion on his creature. Such a behaviour is highly significant.

The word pair "to have compassion" / "to show mercy", רחם *pi'el* / חנן *qal*, is used for the relationship of God with his people and not with other peoples[68]. The word pair רחום וחנון is a liturgical formula, part of the name of God[69]. Jonah 4,2 seems an exception, but even that text is not about compassion on a people (that of Nineveh) or on peoples but on human beings (4,11; comp. Ps 145,8f).

In the book of Isaiah the word pair has been used in only one other place, Isa 30,18: "Yet the LORD longs to be gracious to you (לחננכם); he rises to show you compassion (לרחמכם) ... O people of Zion, who live in Jerusalem, ..." (NIV). If there is a redactional/compositional connection between this text and Isa 27,11, the point will be the contrast between the rejection by God in Isa 27,11 and his longing to show mercy in this text.

Why does the writer use this word pair? He calls up an important liturgical formula. In the normal use of this formula one detects a ten-

64. See for a good study of the internal complexity of the image(s) in Isa 54,4-10: W.A.M. BEUKEN, *Jesaja deel IIB* (POT), Nijkerk, 1983, pp. 250-254; and ID., *Isaiah liv: The Multiple Identity of the Person Addressed*, in J. BARR (ed.), *Language and Meaning: Studies in Hebrew Language and Biblical Exegesis* (OTS, 19), Leiden, 1974, pp. 29-70.

65. The verb חנן is hardly found in Isaiah: *qal*: Isa 27,11; 30,18.19; 33,2; *hof'al*: 26,10. It supposes a relation of master (king) and servant (H.J. STOEBE, in *THAT* I, p. 589 and 595; D.N. FREEDMAN – J. LUNDBOM, in *TWAT* III, p. 29). The verb רחם *pi'el* is more often found in Isaiah; with a negative: Isa 9,16; 13,18; 27,11; 49,15 and without a negative: Isa 14,1; 30,18; 49,10.13; 54,8.10; 55,7; 60,10; רחמים is found in Isa 47,6; 54,7; 63,7.15.

66. Working on this paper, I liked to see the prayer in Isa 63,7–64,11 as the final answer on the reproach in Isa 27,10-11 (in the book of Isaiah as we know it now). Comp. the compassion of a father on his children (63,7-8.15-16), the image of the creator/potter (64,7) and the collocation of עיר and מדבר (64,9).

67. H.J. STOEBE, in *THAT* II, p. 763 says with reference to Hos 1,6-8; 2,3.6.25: "Es handelt sich dabei nicht um eine im Emotionalen wurzelnde väterliche Zärtlichkeit, sondern eine willentliche Anerkennung (bwz. Ablehnung) der Vaterschaft mit den sich gegenüber dem Kind daraus ergebenden Pflichten der Lebenssicherung und des Schutzes".

68. רחם *pi'el* + חנן *qal*: Isa 27,11; Ps 102,14; חנן *qal* + רחם *pi'el*: Exod 33,19; 2 Kings 13,23; Isa 30,18. H. SIMIAN-YOFRE says: "Adressat der durch *rḥm pi* ausgedrückten Handlung ist normalerweise das Volk Israel als solches, oder im einzelnen Jakob. ... Nur Jer 12,15 sind die Nachbarvölker Israels Adressat von *rḥm*" (*TWAT* VII, p. 463; see also p. 465).

69. רחום וחנון: Exod 34,6; Pss 86,15; 103,8; חנון ורחום: Joel 2,13; Jonah 4,2; Pss 111,4; 112,4; 145,8; Neh 9,17.31; 2 Chron 30,9; רחם + חנון *pi'el*: Ps 116,5.

dency to stress God's mercy (against his justice)[70]. If the writer denies exactly this mercy[71], he brings out an enormous contrast: Yhwh showing no mercy…?!

Katholieke Theologische Universiteit   Harm W.M. VAN GROL
Heidelberglaan 2
NL-3584 CS Utrecht

70. SIMIAN-YOFRE, in *TWAT* VII, pp. 471-473 gives a sketch of the history of the formula. "War mit Ex 34,6f. ein Gleichgewicht zwischen Gnade und Gerechtigkeit erreicht, so ändert sich jenes in den anderen nachexil. Texten, die die Gnadenformel zitieren, zugunsten der Huld. Dabei wird der Gedanke einer Strafe für die Sünde unterdrückt (vgl. Ps 103,8) und die Aussage über die Barmherzigkeit Gottes verstärkt…" (473).

71. The word pair is supplied with negatives only here.

DEUTERO- AND TRITO-ISAIAH

WHO WAS SECOND ISAIAH?

1. *Introduction*

The canons of literary criticism demand that a book be read as a unity, and that the parts be first interpreted, not from their immediate external referents, but from the literary whole which contains them[1]. The application of this principle is always fruitful, and always challenging. Application to the book of Isaiah requires more complex considerations than, perhaps, any other major literary work in Western culture[2].

First, the historical frame for the whole book is given in 1,1. It invites us to interpret the whole book within the historical context from the time of king Uzziah to that of Hezekiah. And chapter 8 describes a sealed document of testimony involving the person of Isaiah and his children which together will provide a key to unlock meaning in subsequent history.

This strategy in writing, and in understanding, has profound consequences. It marks a great deal of biblical writing. It is found, for example, in writing a story about the anointing of David king in 1 Sam 16, thus creating a key to the rest of the David story up to the point where he actually becomes king; and it is found in the special events surrounding important births, notably Esau and Jacob, Moses, Samuel, Jeremiah, Jesus, John the Baptist. More generally, it is found in placing creation at the beginning of Genesis as an underlying insight which will enlighten all that follows; and in placing Deuteronomy and the covenant of Moab as key to the story of decline in the Deuteronomistic history; or again in the general strategy of understanding the Old Testament as fulfilled in the New, or understanding the Paschal mystery as key to all history in Christian belief. Our modern instincts for writing history run counter to this. In writing our national histories, we begin with those historical outcomes which form our present horizon and perspective, in order to identify and interpret the events which have led up to them. In writing ancient histories, where effects in the present are sketchy, we very cautiously look for clues of influence and hegemonies within and between eras, amid meticulously dated artefacts and texts.

---

1. Cf. for example N. FRYE, *The Great Code: The Bible and Literature*, Toronto, 1982, pp. 57-62.
2. For a survey and critique of recent studies concerning the unity of Isaiah, cf. D. CARR, *Reaching for Unity in Isaiah*, in *JSOT* 57 (1993) 61-88.

Isaiah, then, uses a different form of history in a special hermeneutic of imposing a perspective from the past in order to understand what unfolded from it. Moreover it unfolds, not only up to an editor's present national horizon, but beyond to an eschatological and universal horizon, which is identified from the start (cf. 2,1-4). This hermeneutic is not historical in our sense of causal relations, but rather it is an ancient theological method in action. More precisely it implies an ancient foundational theology, in the sense of choosing categories for interpretation and understanding[3]. The interpretative key for Isaiah is expressed in a narrative slogan which is found in the hymn which concludes the first collection, and expresses Isaiah's reading of his short history, "I give you thanks YHWH, because you were angry with me; your anger turns so that you comfort me" (12,1). The contents of the book markedly document a final end of Hezekiah at the end of chapter 39, and subsequent chapters refer discreetly but explicitly to historical reality centuries later. But this moment in history from Uzziah to Hezekiah, understood in this prophetic slogan, is made normative and is the equivalent of a theological doctrine of "the prophet".

Second, the book seems to be a prophetic book written by an individual, and certainly it has been named after, and is inevitably associated with, an historical person. A man named Isaiah is muscularly present as a distinct personality with a message through the first 39 chapters. Another Isaiah breaks through as a distinct personality only in a short sentence (40,6-7), though the style of this author is as distinctive almost as that of Pg. The author of chapters 56–66 never is seen, and it is not at all certain that it is one person. The strongest presence in the book is that of the Suffering Servant, whom one may understand as a literary persona for the corporate Isaiah[4]. This persona possesses an identity so unforgettably depicted and yet so completely mysterious that it has been easy for Christians to follow Jesus' reading of Isaiah in identifying the Suffering Servant as himself. In understanding "the book of Isaiah" then, as a literary unity, the perspective of the implied author is not only just hard to find, but rather it has to be imaginatively created respecting hard evidence of at least three different, but not disparate, perspectives.

3. Cf. B. LONERGAN, *Method in Theology*, London, 1971, especially ch. 11, "Foundations". Where the Bible chose narrative categories, Thomas Aquinas chose Aristotelian categories, classical biblical theologians chose historical categories, and Lonergan proposes consciousness categories.

4. Cf. W.A.M. BEUKEN, *The Main Theme of Trito-Isaiah 'The Servant of YHWH'*, in *JSOT* 47 (1990) 67-87. See also C.R. SEITZ, *How is the Prophet Isaiah Present in the Latter Half of the Book? The Logic of Chapters 40–66 within the Book of Isaiah*, in *JBL* 115 (1996) 219-240.

Third, as has been richly pointed out in recent literature, the interweaving of texts from the three distinct periods of the book's writing is such that it is no longer acceptable to interpret the book in three parts. All three parts are hermeneutically present in each part. This is complex literature, requiring complexity in the reader[5]. One result of this, as Prof. Seitz has pointed out, is that the vocation narrative of chapter 40 must be seen more as a comment on the continuity and change in the Word of God, rather than a personal history of an individual[6].

Still, there is a momentous change between chapters 1–39, where the official time frame of the book comes to an end historically, and where the prophet is seen as speaking directly to the king, or to his disciples or the public, and chapters 40ff. where, for eight and a half chapters at least, the prophetic voice becomes that of an anonymous commentator, with a very different style[7]. The notable exception is 40,6, where the speaker irrupts personally. Who is this person? Is this, after all, a personal vocation story? If we are to put together a composite image of the author of Isaiah, we must clarify as much as possible the few historical clues which the Isaiah editors have chosen to preserve. This article will attempt to add a tiny glimmer to the floodlight of research which has focused on what has been called the "vocation narrative" or "call narrative" of Second Isaiah over the years. It will argue that, just as the book

---

5. Cf. W.A.M. BEUKEN, *Isaiah Chapters LXV–LXVI: Trito-Isaiah and the Closure of the Book of Isaiah*, in J.A. EMERTON (ed.), *Congress Volume. Leuven 1989* (SVT, 43), Leiden - New York, 1991, pp. 204-221; R. RENDTORFF, *The Book of Isaiah: A Complex Unity. Synchronic and Diachronic Reading*, in *SBL 1991 Seminar Papers*, Atlanta, 1991, pp. 8-20. Cf. also A.-M. PELLETIER, *Le livre d'Isaïe et le temps de l'histoire*, in *NRT* 112 (1990) 30-43; J. VERMEYLEN, *Du prophète Isaïe et le temps de l'histoire*, Paris, 1977.

6. Cf. C.R. SEITZ, *The Divine Council: Temporal Transition and New Prophecy in the Book of Isaiah*, in *JBL* 19 (1990) 229-247, especially pp. 245-246. See also a further study of this article: R.F. MELUGIN, *The Servant, God's Call, and the Structure of Isaiah 40–48*, in *SBL 1991 Seminary Papers,* Atlanta, 1991, pp. 21-30. There is no need of repeating here, once again, all that has been successfully argued about this form. Cf., for example, W. RICHTER, *Die sogenannten Vorprophetischen Berufungsberichte*, Göttingen, 1970. I would point out that Seitz' way of formulating his position suggests that the divine council scene is a "literary form" in the same sense, and he argues about compliance or deviation from both these forms as though forms were formulated doctrines. I believe that forms operate at a more subliminal level, exercising great power because they are subliminal but allowing any variation because they are only a tool for organizing materials which the author knows. Moreover, the case for defining the literary form of divine council visions has yet to be made. The most obvious understanding of the relationships between I Kings 22, Isa 6, and Isa 40 is that of conscious reference, rather than literary form. Ps 82, dealing with the same experience of a heavenly court, does not share the same character of dialogue. The Job narrative is not about vocation.

7. As Seitz points out (*The Divine Council* [n. 6]) there is no trace of a speaker or hearer or messenger formula until 48,16b-17. And this speaker is addressing the scattered exiles, and in 49,1 the coastlands.

author was careful to leave historical clues (mention of Cyrus) about the Persian period within the Isaiah purview, so he was careful to leave clues to the fact that a woman wrote the "Second Isaiah" material; and that we are invited to understand the unfolding of history through the theology of a pre-exilic man of God, but equally to understand it all anew through the interpretation of an exilic woman.

Her influence is allowed to come to voice as early as 12,6. The speaker may be either man or woman, but s/he chooses to address the inhabitants of Zion in two feminine singular imperative verbs, and characterizes them with a feminine singular participle suggesting they all were women, or that women control public feeling in cases like this, or at least choosing to see them in the image of a single woman, commanding her to shout for joy because the holy one of Israel is in her midst[8]. We are in a women's world. And shouting for joy is, of course, just what Second Isaiah herself will do.

2. *The Turning Point in Isaiah*

The shift between chapters 39 and 40 is astonishing. We go from the court in Jerusalem to the heavenly court, without any warning or introduction. And we shift suddenly from narrative mode to drama, where no narrator intervenes between the reader and the direct speech of the players[9]. It is like a movie where we, the viewers, are watching some people inside a car for some moments, and then suddenly we find ourselves walking among clouds and hearing pervasive voices. We know right away that an accident has happened and we are now in heaven. Similarly in Isa 40, without a single introductory word, we move from 3rd person narrative to mysterious plural commands, and from a historical genre to a wholly different world. The most remarkable characteristic of this unit is the use of three unattached participles, which read like stage directions.

As the scene opens, we hear two imperative plurals "Comfort, comfort my people", picking up this programme word from 12,1, which one must understand as spoken by God in the heavenly court[10]. Then, successively, three other voices are introduced with participles,

8. The feminine participle *yoshevet* is explained as a "collective" meaning found in some feminine forms in P. Joüon – T. Muraoka, *A Grammar of Biblical Hebrew*, Rome, 1991, §134 o. Still it is worth noting that the masculine form is used in all other occurrences of this formula in Isaiah: 5,3; 8,14; 22,21. Joüon's position correctly identifies the referent as collective, but he offers no grounds to deny the feminine feel and colouring of the designation.

9. Cf. A. van Wieringen, *Jesaja 40,1-11, eine drama-linguistische Lesung von Jesaja 6 her*, in *BN* 49 (1989) 82-93.

10. For a solution based on different presuppositions about the experience of reading, see R.G. Kratz, *Der Anfang des Zweiten Jesaja in Jes 40,1f. und seine literarischen Horizonte*, in *ZAW* 105 (1993) 400-419.

"A voice crying out" (v. 3)
"A voice saying" (v. 6)
"She saying" (v. 6)[11]

None of the three is identified. The first two speak with supernal authority. The third seems to be a human response. What is the identity of this "she" who is "saying"? Although she is party to this heavenly dialogue, Petersen places her on earth and identifies her with the "bearer of good tidings" in v. 9 on the grounds that this is a unified vocation narrative. But then he fails to realize that his reading has implications about who the bearer of good tidings (herald) can be, and he goes on to leave unchanged the traditional interpretation according to which *mebasseret* remains identified with a collective Zion/Jerusalem[12]. This must be examined.

3. *The Call Narrative*

We shall first review the unit as a vocation narrative. Vv. 1-5 correspond to the "confrontation" in vocation narratives. Here it is the reader who feels confronted most directly since no other hearer is identified. But, as resuming the experience of Isa 6 (and recalling 1 Kings 22), it is understood that some one person, (perhaps in the Temple again, although this is not mentioned), will feel challenged by this confrontation. Certainly the relationship between Yahweh and Israel is clearly defined, punishment is over, and Yahweh's glory will be revealed to mankind. Then a heavenly voice in v. 6 issues a sharp command in a masculine singular imperative, "Call out". This corresponds to the "commission" in vocation narratives, and it is masculine because it is experienced as a sending of some one who is still unspecified, recalling the "Whom shall I send" of 1 Kings 22 and Isa 6[13]. There follows a woman's voice, im-

---

11. Following the Qumran manuscript. Grammatical discussion in D.L. PETERSEN *Late Israelite Prophecy: Studies in Deutero-Prophetic Literature and in Chronicles*, Missoula, 1977, pp. 46-47, note 15 (citing S.D. McBride). This reading is supported by the observation that it fits in a series of three parallel participles, with the same role of introducing unidentified voices in the heavenly court. Moreover, it is certainly the *lectio difficilior*, because the *qol* is not repeated this third time. Without "voice" the participle is surprising and is easily misread as a meaningless 1st pers. sing. cohortative and then emended. Such an emendation is easier to understand than an emendation in the opposite direction. Cf. also D. BARTHÉLEMY, *Critique textuelle de l'A.T. 2: Isaïe, Jérémie, Lamentations* (OBO, 50/2), Fribourg, 1986, pp. 278-279. He discusses various possible interpretations, but does not consider the possibility of a feminine participle form.

12. Cf. PETERSEN, *Late Israelite Prophecy* (n.11), p. 20.

13. See K. HOLTER, *Zur Funktion der Städte Judas in Jesaja XL,9*, in *VT* 46 (1996) 119-121. Holter shows extensive correspondence in vocabulary and structure between the vocation narratives in Isa 6 and 40.

plicitly acknowledging the call as addressed to herself, and expressing her "objection" as in all examples of the vocation narrative form. Her objection is among the most bitter lines in the Bible, comparable only to complaints of Job. And finally the "confirmation" is expressed in v. 8. As always in this narrative form, it does not argue or attempt to make things easier. It merely commissions anew, stating that the prophetic word will be with her always.

In vv. 9-11 there is no "sign" (and there is really no sign in the Jeremiah call as well, or in the Priestly version of the Moses call in Exod 6), but there is a second sending as in Jer 1,10 (11-19), and in Isa 6,11-12. Many commentators do not consider this to be a continuation of God's speech in 40,8, but rather a speech of the prophet to Jerusalem. Clearly Jerusalem is not addressed in vv. 1-8, and if one believes Jerusalem is addressed in v. 9 then one will conclude that it is the prophet who addresses Jerusalem. Against this reading is the fact that there is no editorial signal about such a radical switch of speaker and situation. But then editorial signals are uncertain throughout. Also against this is the weight of vocation narrative form, which looks for a "confirmation" after the "objection". And finally there is the continuation of the feminine forms from the individual who speaks in v. 6, and who is addressed directly in v. 9. As always, there will be no decisive proof one way or the other, but rather a conclusion about inter-related probabilities based on attentive and sensitive evaluation of the whole text.

4. *Who is the herald?*

What is the referent of *mebasseret* in v. 9? I will offer six indications which, taken together, convince me that the referent is a single woman.

First, v. 9 heavily focuses on the feminine nature of the person addressed with 5 feminine verb forms and 2 feminine suffixes. Is this mere grammatical coherence with a neutral collective *mebasseret*, a matter restricted to gender without any reference to sex, as one might expect from a person writing in Latin, or in modern French? Does it not invite a suspicion that a more concretely feminine person is envisioned?

Second, can that collective be asked to climb a hill? Does language which identifies "Zion" with "herald" lead naturally to an image of mount Zion, or the city of Jerusalem, climbing a hill? One may doubt that this author, who writes so subtly and with such clear imagery, could have meant this.

Third, it is not easy to believe that a collective Jerusalem, which looms so large in prophetic literature and prophetic imagery, and is so ambiguous, and so sinful, here punished double for her sins, can be imagined as suddenly sent out to proclaim comfort to the cities of Judah, without any time provided or account given of awakening and conversion. In 40,2 the mysterious voice asks unidentified members of the heavenly court to speak tenderly to Jerusalem. In the feeling and imagination of this poet, can the Jerusalem of v. 2, receiving tender comfort, be imagined now in v. 6 as a unified free spirit – free to take or refuse orders, to answer back to God, and to lead others[14]?

Fourth, on the hypothesis that vv. 9-11 is a continuation of the vocation narrative form, (a hypothesis which has some intrinsic probability and is supported by many commentators) did the poet imagine mount Zion, or its collective inhabitants, participating in the dialogue between God and the heavenly court? Surely here, as in 1 Kings 22,21 and Isa 6,8 a single individual must be envisaged for this role. Even on general literary grounds, the collective Jerusalem is too ambiguous a figure to be imagined as entering into this dialogue with an intervention so personal and so bitter in tone as we read in vv. 6-7. More to the point, is this vocation narrative a metaphor for a new vocation of the city of Jerusalem, or does it record a personal experience of a writer? All the other examples of vocation narrative are of individual persons. This narrative could be a personal experience – such experiences are common among mystics[15]. The narrative does follow existing literary models, but that does not imply fiction. All of our historical or biographical writing follows narrative models which can be identified by literary analysis, even though writers often may not advert to them. If the vocation narrative is taken as memory of personal experience, then the speaker is certainly an individual, and she has characterized herself as a woman. If it is not a memory, surely it is at least stylized as a memory, and as such asserts the reality of a woman in this role.

Fifth, though it is true the inhabitants of Zion can be indicated by a feminine noun, as in *bat yerushalaim,* or *yoshebet yerushalaim*, it must be asked whether the designation *mebasseret* is equally fitted to indicate,

14. Contrast Isa 16,3-4 where "the daughter of Jerusalem" has a salvific role vis-à-vis the daughter of Moab. Here the imagery is continuous and fully imaginable – the role of Moab and of Jerusalem are consistent from 15,1 to 16,4. Or contrast the command to Jerusalem in 51,17-23, where Jerusalem must gradually turn things around. Similarly 52,1-2.

15. Apart from the classical accounts of mystic experience in the writings of, for example, Ignatius Loyola and Theresa of Avila, one might consider the growing literature of the thousands of people in the last few years who have experienced "near-death experiences", or "out-of-body experiences", to be found in pocket books in every bookstore. Ignatius was almost continuously conscious of the Heavenly court, and of the individual Persons and persons, and of himself as present to them.

not an individual, but a collectivity. The word indicates one who is a herald, and that image has its own limits. These are very different from the multiplicity suggested by "daughter" or "dweller". A feminine collectivity in 54,1 is imagined as singing, and as stretching her tents, etc. And in 51,16 God addresses Jerusalem, and in the following verse God issues a command to Jerusalem with a feminine imperative singular verb form commanding her to get back on her feet. And in 52,1.2 and 9, with other feminine imperatives, Jerusalem is told to awake, to rise up, and to sing for joy. Everywhere Jerusalem/Zion, in the sense of its inhabitants, is the receiver of news good and bad. Never is she commanded to play the role of a prophet to others. I would argue that all of those activities fit easily into the image of a collectivity which would carry them out in myriad separate ways. The activity of herald is not of this sort – it is in fact hard to invoke an image in which a collectivity proclaims a message to another collectivity. Dt 27,14 has something close to it on Mount Garizim, but the actual speakers are named individuals, and the situation is a formal liturgy.

Moreover, the *mebasser* image occurs again (in masculine form) in Second Isaiah, in 41,27 and in 52,7, and he is not Zion or Jerusalem, but rather he is explicitly bringing good news about God to Zion and to Jerusalem. He is not a collective, but an individual person. He is equally unidentified. Is this the same person as in 40,9? It appears to be the person who authors Isa 40–55, and one would naturally suppose it is the same person as in 40,9, if only because this same unusual term is used. Then why masculine? I would argue that the question has to be reversed, why feminine in 40,9. The masculine almost never needs to be explained in biblical Hebrew[16], and certainly it is a neutral designation which would be used when the herald is being considered in any way as a typical figure in a general context. In 41,27 and 52,7, the historical person in masculine grammatical form is one of a series of messengers (prophets, sentinels) adduced as part of a general argument about God. But in 40,6 and 9, the focus for an instant is, not on God, but on the precise historical reality of the prophet. That is why the form is feminine.

Sixth, surely Jerusalem is one of the cities of Judah, not a messenger to the cities of Judah. Why is the prophetess sent as herald, not only to Jerusalem, but also to "the cities of Judah"? The answer is clear, this vocation is presented as corresponding to the vocation of First Isaiah, and that vocation was to a mission which would last specifically "until cities lie waste without inhabitant and houses without people" (Isa 6,11)[17].

16. Cf. P. JOÜON – T. MURAOKA, *A Grammar of Biblical Hebrew*, Rome, 1991, §89 a.
17. Cf. HOLTER, *Zur Funktion der Städte Judas* (n. 13).

I conclude that the more natural understanding of 40,9 is that *mebas-seret*, like *yoshebet* in 12,6, or *bat* in many texts, is not in apposition with, but rather governs Jerusalem/Zion in a construct structure. It does not denote the "inhabitant(s)" of the city, but rather simply a "herald" to the city[18]. And the most natural translation is the following, "Climb a high mountain, you herald to Zion; lift up your voice powerfully, you herald to Jerusalem; lift if up and fear not; say to the cities of Judah – 'Look, here is your God'". These commands are addressed to a woman, the same woman who answered in v. 6, and probably who wrote all the beautiful prose and poetry of chapters 40–55, particularly all the feminine imagery about home and children and birth, which is so distinctive of Second Isaiah. This should not be surprising, since Josiah consulted a woman prophetess in 2 Kings 22 and that seemed strange to no one. She is not called a *nabi'*, as was First Isaiah (and Huldah), because her role is not that of a public personage addressing divine messages to the king and warnings to the people. Rather she is a writer. And she writes interpretations of the prophetic messages which are recognized as such. She is a compiler, editor and commentator on "*the prophet*" Isaiah. She thrives in an era of "late prophecy" characterized by a belief that prophecy was fixed in the past, and not to be practised any more[19]. She has the unique title of *mebasser(et)*, whose message includes a reversal of the bad news of old, but confirms "the prophet" while interpreting him. The author/editor of the book Isaiah knew this as a historical fact, thought it was a significant fact needing to be noted, and therefore chose to point it out at the turning point in chapter 40, and to allow its hermeneutical implications to be felt as early as chapter 12.

5. *Conclusion*

This argument stands or falls on cumulative probabilities, and legitimate circular argumentation, through the whole series of points. The structure of the presentation in this essay begins with, and appears to place special demands upon, the translation "She saying" in 40,6. But that is only one point. Its place in this paper is due to the order of discovery, and to nothing more. If one rejects it, (and it is a point which needs thorough study by those competent in technical grammar), and if one then reverts to "And I said", the remaining arguments may still be persuasive. If so, and if one accepts the conclusion, then one might go around the circle of argument once again, and perhaps revisit this point and re-revert to "She saying"!

18. The translators of the Septuagint and of the Vulgate also read it this way.
19. Cf. PETERSEN, *Late Isrealite Prophecy* (n. 11). His thesis is thoroughly persuasive.

If this argument is accepted, it invites a rereading of the whole book of Isaiah for signs of this feminine voice. Chapter 12, for example, is usually read as a conclusion to the opening testimony of the historical Isaiah. Its opening verse, praising God for wrath followed by salvation, encapsulates the structural meaning of the whole book of Isaiah, and is in fact a formula expressive of the structure of each of the prophetic books and of the prophetic collection as a whole. Its concluding verse commands this same praise a second time, in less analyzed form, "the holy one of Israel is in our midst" (i.e. as wrath + comfort). It is heard through the hearing of women, as argued above in the Introduction. Thus chapter 12 may be understood as an edited hymnic unit which evokes the whole message and hermeneutic of the interpreted Isaiah. And the whole book of Isaiah is presented to the Jews and to the Church as a prophet's sealed testimony and torah made public and expounded by a woman.

Concordia University   Sean McEVENUE
7141 Sherbrooke Street West
Montreal, Quebec H4B 1R6
Canada

HISTORY AND ESCHATOLOGY IN DEUTERO-ISAIAH

Deutero-Isaiah borrowed the basic structure of his view of history and eschatology from the Enthronement Psalms. This is the thesis that I will defend in this contribution in honour of my teacher and friend Wim Beuken. In preparation, challenged on this by studies that have thematized Deutero-Isaiah's eschatology, I will attempt to describe the main lines of Deutero-Isaiah's drama by an explicit use of this technical term, which Beuken's commentary deliberately avoids (I)[1]. After a discussion of the dependence between Isa 40–55 and the texts of the psalms in question I will finally arrive at my actual thesis: history and eschatology in Deutero-Isaiah exist in a certain mutual tension – a tension that, as I see it, can be better understood against the background of the two types of Enthronement Psalms in their different perspectives (II).

I

Deutero-Isaiah is usually given an important place in surveys on the eschatology of the Old Testament[2]. In addition, the term eschatology can be found in casual remarks in commentaries and monographs that are devoted to his work. Once in a while an article appears that deals exclusively with the subject of the eschatology of Deutero-Isaiah[3]. If one reads through this literature, it becomes apparent that there are divergent opinions on the eschatological nature of Deutero-Isaiah's message[4].

This difference in opinion is caused by two things. In the first place, Old Testament scholars vary in their definition of the concept of eschatology. In the second place, there are differences in the interpretation of central terms and conceptions in Isa 40–55. I am thinking particularly of

---

1. W.A.M. BEUKEN, *Jesaja* (POT), Nijkerk, 1979 (II^A) and 1983 (II^B). His restraint in using this term can be related to his fear 'de verkondiging van de profeet zo te systematiseren, dat er een soort algemene waarheid uit resulteert' (of systematizing the preaching of the prophet to such an extent that it results in some kind of general truth: cf. II^A, p. 13).

2. See, e.g., J. SCHREINER, *Eschatologie im Alten Testament*, in M. SCHMAUS *et al.* (eds.), *Handbuch der Dogmengeschichte* IV, Freiburg, 1986, pp. 1-31, esp. pp. 14-15.

3. A. SCHOORS, *L'eschatologie dans les prophéties du Deutéro-Isaie*, in *RechBib* 8 (1967) 170-128.

4. Cf. A. RICHTER, *Hauptlinien der Deuterojesaja-Forschung 1964-1979*, in C. WESTERMANN (ed.), *Sprache und Struktur der Prophetie Deuterojesajas*, Stuttgart, 1981, pp. 89-123, esp. pp. 114ff.

the semantic relationship between Deutero-Isaiah's terms for the 'former', the 'latter', the 'coming' and the 'new', and of the referential connections seen between these terms and the whole of the Deutero-Isaiah's conceptual world. Here exegesis has gone in different directions and this has had, also given the definition of eschatology that one supports, considerable consequences for the evaluation of the eschatological character of Deutero-Isaiah's message.

In an earlier study I attempted to rechart the meaning and reference of the terms for the former, the latter, the coming and the new in Isa 41–48[5]. It is true that this semantic field is not the only subject that deserves attention in connection with the question of Deutero-Isaiah's eschatology (think, for example, of an image such as the vanishing of the heavens and the perishing of the earth in Isa 51,6, which has little to do with the opposition former/new), but it allows us to catch sight of the most important viewpoint. In this first section I will attempt from this line of approach to create some order in the discussion on Deutero-Isaiah's eschatology by taking up a number of questions and dilemmas that continually arise in the discussion. The dilemmas include the following: the expectation of a definitive salvation or eschatology, continuity or discontinuity, historical or suprahistorical intervention. Questions to be discussed are: are the seeds of the idea of two aeons already present in Isa 40–55, in what sense can one call this eschatology 'actualized', and does it offer salvation conditionally or unconditionally? The issue is not so much whether Deutero-Isaiah's message can be called eschatological (I assume as much) as what happens to the concept of eschatology if one defines it on the basis of Deutero-Isaiah's vision.

1. *Expectation of Definitive Salvation or Eschatology*

Among those who, in classifying the Old Testament expectation of salvation, seem prepared to accept a not too strict definition of eschatology, there are also those who nevertheless are not willing to use the term for Deutero-Isaiah's message. One of the factors involved in this judgment is that no essential distinction is made between Deutero-Isaiah's concepts of latter, coming and new. Schoors can be viewed as an outstanding example of this. "Si les 'choses nouvelles' font songer à une réalité peu ordinaire, elle ne consiste cependant que dans le fait que Yahvé réalisera le salut par la main d'un païen, Cyrus. Ces textes n'ont rien d'eschatologique"[6].

5. H. LEENE, *De vroegere en de nieuwe dingen bij Deuterojesaja*, Amsterdam, 1987.
6. SCHOORS, *L'eschatologie* (n. 3), p. 115 ("If the 'new things' are considered within a

Indeed, in agreement with Schoors I would rather not call Deutero-Isaiah's statements about *Cyrus* 'eschatological'. But this only gives half an answer to the question of Deutero-Isaiah's eschatological character. On the basis of my research, I must maintain that Cyrus' appearance does not fall under the category of new things; this event is presented as the end of the former and also partially as the coming, but it definitely does not belong to the new.

The question remains as to whether it is useful to employ the term 'eschatological' for Deutero-Isaiah's expectations of the new. We will have to examine below the sense in which this specific expectation can be called eschatological or, in other words, what it means for the concept of eschatology if we allow this to be coloured by Deutero-Isaiah's expectations of the new things.

Is it possible to check the uncontrolled use of the term 'eschatological' by reserving it, as is repeatedly argued, for expectations of a *definitive* act of God? I believe that this specification does not help because divine acts are always definitive about something. By definition one could say, divine action is definitive action. This difficulty becomes clear in Deutero-Isaiah's view of Cyrus. One must certainly call the sending of Cyrus to Babel, as Deutero-Isaiah sees it, a definitive action on the part of Yhwh – also without feeling obligated to use the term 'eschatological' in *this* connection. The appearance of Cyrus as the 'outcome' of the 'former' decides the question of whether Yhwh can be called צדיק over against the gods (cf. 41,26; 43,9; 45,21), but it does not decide the question of how the worldwide salvific *acknowledgement* of this righteous God will be realised. With reference to this acknowledgement it is only the new that is decisive. The concept of definitive action does not in itself create a clear distinction between 'eschatological' and 'non-eschatological' conceptions.

We must therefore search for a better way to sharpen the definition of eschatology. I believe that such a definition, certainly where Deutero-Isaiah is concerned but possibly elsewhere as well, is not very useful as long as the concept *goal* is not included as an essential element. Thus the expectation of that action of Yhwh that decides the achieving of the goal that he has set for Israel and for humanity is eschatological. Eschatology presumes that God has a goal for people and the world. Representations

reality that is not very ordinary, it consists, nevertheless, only in the fact that Yahweh will achieve his salvation by the hand of a pagan, Cyrus. These texts contain nothing of an eschatological nature"). Cf. ID., *I Am God Your Saviour: A Form-Critical Study of the Main Genres in Is. XL–LV* (SVT, 24), Leiden, 1973, pp. 304-305. D. MICHEL, *Deuterojesaja*, in *TRE* VIII, 510-530, would also like to avoid the term eschatology for Deutero-Isaiah (p. 519).

of that definitive future action of God that enables him to achieve this goal are eschatological. Conversely then, statements about the future are not eschatological if (a) the question of the goal of God's actions does not yet play a role and (b) these statements deal simply with the achieving of *a* goal and not *the* ultimate goal.

Of course, such a definition must take into account considerable differences in eschatological ideas between Old Testament passages, differences that amount to differences in the further description and explication of the goal (among others, its explicit universality) and of the radicality of the changes that are considered necessary for its achievement. But whether or not they lead to the final goal in any way seems to me to be the essential part of the definition.

With respect to the Old Testament Vriezen argued for a broad definition of eschatology, in which the definitive nature of Yhwh's expected intervention appears to play the main restrictive role. In the prophetic message is it possible to discover "any elements in which a definitive, decisive expectation regarding the future of the world is expressed"[7]? But the fact that Vriezen makes such a close connection between the Old Testament eschatology and the election of Israel (I will return to this point) makes it clear that in his view of eschatology the goal-directedness of Yhwh's actions is at least just as important.

Eschatology is not concerned with the question of 'what the future may bring', however radical, but with the question of whether Yhwh will succeed in achieving his goal. It involves the question of whether Yhwh will be able to break through the barriers that apparently stand in the way of this realization and to eliminate them for good.

Thus eschatology is in the first place an answer to a problem and only secondarily a complex of images as to what we can expect. Here I can partly agree with Schunck's formulation. According to him, the eschaton is joined with the notion, essential to faith in Yhwh, that Israel's God wants to lead his people "zu einem unverrückbar feststehenden Ziel"[8]. This goal is that Yhwh be regarded as the only God. "Die Anerkennung Jahwes und die Befolgung seines Willens konstituieren das Eschaton, – unabhängig von Zeitfaktoren"[9]. The latter, independence from tempo-

---

7. T.C. VRIEZEN, *Prophecy and Eschatology*, in *SVT* 1 (1953) 199-229 [= *Prophetie und Eschatologie*, in H.D. PREUSS (ed.), *Eschatologie im Alten Testament*, Darmstadt, 1978, pp. 88-128], p. 203.

8. K.-D. SCHUNCK, *Die Eschatologie der Propheten des alten Testaments und ihre Wandlung in exilisch-nachexilischer Zeit*, in PREUSS (ed.), *Eschatologie* (n. 7), pp. 462-480 [= *SVT* 26, Leiden, 1974, pp. 116-132], p. 467 ("to an immovable, certain goal").

9. *Ibid.*, p. 473 ("The acknowledgement of Yhwh and obedience to his will constitute the eschaton – independent of temporal factors").

ral factors, can cause some difficulty, although Schunck does raise an important point. Nevertheless, I believe it is better to hold that the term eschatology is also related to concrete images – images in which temporal categories always play a role. According to this eschatological imagination the achieving of the goal lies in the (near or not too near) future. The fact that it is sometimes asserted that this future is already a reality now does not change anything: the assertion is then understood as a *paradoxical* statement. I will return to these temporal aspects. But the goal is indeed the most important: without a quest for the goal there is no eschatology.

In terms of Deutero-Isaiah Yhwh's goal is: worldwide acknowledgement as the Creator God (cf. 41,20; 42,10ff.), praise by the people that he has formed (cf. 43,21; 49,3), his glorification in Israel (cf. 44,23), the festive revelation of his kingship (cf. 42,10-13; 52,7-10). According to Deutero-Isaiah, it is this goal that Yhwh will achieve due to the new that is proclaimed. The outcome of the former (Cyrus) is decisive for the question of whether Yhwh, in comparison to the 'gods', may truly be called the only God; but the new is decisive for the question as to whether Yhwh, for the salvation of the people, may in fact be acknowledged by them to be God.

2. *Continuity and Discontinuity*

In definitions of that which is to be understood as eschatology in the Old Testament, emphasis is often placed on the breach, the discontinuity. Thus, for example, Lindblom says: "Wenn die Propheten von einer Zukunft reden, die nicht nur eine Fortsetzung der in dieser Welt waltenden Verhältnisse bedeutet, sondern etwas Neues und ganz anderes mit sich bringt, da haben wir das Recht, den Terminus Eschatologie zu verwenden"[10]. According to Lindblom, who had denied the eschatological nature of Isa 40–55 in an earlier publication on the basis of a stricter definition, there can be no doubt that Deutero-Isaiah's message can be called eschatological in this sense.

In contrast, Schoors stressed that Deutero-Isaiah places the emphasis more on the continuity of salvation history than on a radical change in the historical situation. The message of the prophet is not: "Behold, I make all things new. Behold, I realize a definitive renewal". In Schoors'

---

10. J. LINDBLOM, *Gibt es eine Eschatologie bei den alttestamentlichen Propheten?*, in PREUSS (ed.), *Eschatologie* (n. 7), pp. 31-72 [= *Studia Theologica* 6 (1952) 79-114], esp. p. 42 ("If the prophets speak of a future, which does not only refer to a continuation of the dominant circumstances of this world but to something new and entirely different, then we are justified in using the term eschatology").

view it is appropriate to paraphrase this message: "Yahweh will not abandon you. He has made you his people now and forever, and he will remain faithful to the special covenant that binds him to you". And that is why Schoors holds that the term eschatology is incorrect in connection with this prophet[11].

Schoors' comment on the emphasis on Yhwh's faithfulness to Israel must be endorsed. This is a basic motif of Deutero-Isaiah's message, but I do not see this as a convincing argument against its full eschatological value. According to Deutero-Isaiah it is precisely the fact that Yhwh achieves his goal with Israel and thus with humanity that has not yet been demonstrated. It is in this that the new is actually new. Whoever defines eschatology in terms of the goal to be achieved by Yhwh – a goal to which he remains faithful in spite of all opposition – need not see any tension between salvation history and eschatology.

It is Vriezen in particular who indicated the right direction here in his phrasing. For him the core of eschatological expectations of the Old Testament lay in the trust that God is faithful to Israel, in spite of empirical evidence to the contrary. "That is why the prophets (and not Deutero-Isaiah alone) distinguish between two Israel-types: Israel as the empirical people that perishes, and Israel as the people of God, which exists and remains, visible only to the eye of faith"[12]. "Only if we bear in mind the double meaning of the name Israel can we follow the prophets, especially Deutero-Isaiah"[13].

Deutero-Isaiah does indeed speak repeatedly of Israel's election (41,8f.; 42,1; 43,10; 44,1f.; 45,4; 48,10; 49,7). Even more striking is the fact that this work expresses the unity of salvation history and eschatology in its confession of Yhwh as creator, designer and completer of Israel (בורא, יוצר, עושה). The second dramatic episode of Deutero-Isaiah's book (42,18–44,23) is completely dominated by this confession (cf. 43,1; 44,2). It is this episode, which in 43,18-19 expresses the contrast former/new most sharply ("Remember not the former things ... behold, I am doing a new thing..."), that *simultaneously* expresses the deep unity of salvation history. That which Yhwh will realize by means of the new is nothing else than the fulfilment of his creational goal with Israel (cf. 43,7.21; 44,21). Thus discontinuity (former/new) is embedded in continuity. Israel's answer does not automatically lie in the extension of history up to and including Cyrus; even after this historical proof of God's sovereignty it is not obvious that the answer is coming – but it

---

11. SCHOORS, *L'eschatologie* (n. 3), p. 127.
12. VRIEZEN, *Prophecy* (n. 7), p. 205.
13. *Ibid.*, p. 222.

does fall within the lines of what Yhwh intended with this people from the very beginning.

Many exegetes believed they had to recognize this continuity of salvation history in a certain weakening of Deutero-Isaiah's opposition of former/new itself. I would rather hold that the opposition former/new as such is intended to express a real opposition and is therefore not an indication of a correspondence or analogy (as the opposition former/*latter* is)[14]. In my opinion then the term 'new Exodus' is hardly adequate in this connection – particularly because it stresses the analogy former/new so much more strongly than Deutero-Isaiah himself apparently does and, moreover, it is too much prompted by our canonical view of the Exodus as depicted by the Pentateuch. Nevertheless, this real opposition of former/new is enclosed by continuity in Deutero-Isaiah's literary composition – confer 42,18–44,23 in particular. The balanced terminology of creation, used in connection with the existence of Jacob-Israel, is the most important means of expressing this.

3. *Historical or Suprahistorical*

For this dilemma we can once again start with a quotation from Vriezen on Deutero-Isaiah: "From various terms and images used by the prophet it appears that for him salvation he expected and probably still saw enacted in part, far transcended what may be called a historical event"[15]. What happens here, Vriezen comments in a discussion with Lindblom, "takes place within the historical framework of the world, but it is something that definitely changes this world..."[16].

What is a historical event? What is history? Here, whatever definition one chooses, terminological clarity is needed. The Old Testament itself does not have a term for 'history' any more than it does for 'eschatology'. It has been commented that 'God's work' in Proto-Isaiah begins to approach such an inclusive concept[17]. I myself would like to propose this as a definition: in the Old Testament history is the movement of peoples and kingdoms, seen in connection with its influence on the national and political existence of Israel, to which the decisive political and national events in Israel itself also belong. According to the Old Testa-

---

14. The following oppositions are to be distinguished in Isa 40–48:
   former ↔ latter
   former [incl. latter] ↔ coming
   former [incl. latter, having come] ↔ new
15. Vriezen, *Prophecy* (n. 7), p. 217.
16. *Ibid.*, p. 218.
17. Cf. K. Elliger, *Der Begriff »Geschichte« bei Deuterojesaja*, in *Kleine Schriften zum Alten Testament* (TB, 32), München, 1966, pp. 199-210, esp. p. 204.

ment view Yhwh is the sole ruler of history. If one accepts this definition, then in Deutero-Isaiah the coming, just as the former and the latter,
does belong to history and does concern historical events, but the new
does not.

As we saw, Deutero-Isaiah's interest in history is determined by the
following point of view: it gives the decisive answer concerning Yhwh's
being God (41,1-5; 41,21-29; 43,9-13; 44,6-8). History reveals God's
righhteousness (45,20-21). It does not do this by means of Yhwh's isolated acts but by means of the correspondence of beginning and end, tradition and contemporary experience. The creation order itself is implied
in this orderliness of history (45,18ff.). Thus in spite of its chaotic aspect, history promises the habitableness of the earth for every human
being. It is history that can demonstrate that Yhwh "did not create the
earth a chaos". Obviously, Deutero-Isaiah does not give an objective or
impartial image of that which occurs on the world stage. For him historical reality is always what is at stake in a legal action. It demands a decision, a choice, it demands a clear insight.

The new things, however, do not belong to this history. It seems fair
to me to put it this way. One must ensure that the new does not cancel
history or make it irrelevant, because it is this history that the new
wishes to endorse as proof of Yhwh being the only God. What is essential in the new is this endorsement. But although history reveals God's
righteousness, in itself it does not appear to be able to make Israel reflect
this in his own justice (see Isa 46 and 48,3-6a in particular). Yhwh
achieves this through the new.

In this sense it is correct to say, with Vriezen, that, according to
Deutero-Isaiah, the new will still take place within the framework of history. In any case, the new is not the end of history, but it provides an
adequate answer to history.

The question as to whether or not the new in Deutero-Isaiah belongs
to historical reality can also be applied to another definition of history.
In modern opinion, a historical event is characterized by the movement
which it in turn sets off. A historical event is not only caused but is also
itself a cause with consequences, and it is these consequences that make
an event a *historical* event.

What is remarkable in Deutero-Isaiah's imaging of the new is that the
events therein no longer borrow their significance from their consequences. The way through the desert just barely borrows its meaning
from the fact that it leads to Jerusalem. This way points directly towards
Yhwh. The way through the desert in itself means the praise of Yhwh
(see 43,19ff. in particular). Thus in Deutero-Isaiah's metaphorical lan-

guage the way can represent the whole, both in time (the arrival in Zion is sometimes understood by it) and in space (along the sides of the way the whole of creation blooms). It is true that a certain narrative chronology is not completely lacking in Deutero-Isaiah's anticipation of the new – an indication that Deutero-Isaiah nonetheless sees this happening, in one way or another, within the framework of history. Yet I believe it is better not to say that the new will change the world, or will result in the changing of the world. A stronger formulation seems in order here: the new *is* the changing of the world.

A thorough comparison of Deutero-Isaiah's presentation of the new things with the presentation of the new man in Ezekiel 36 and with the presentation of the new covenant in Jeremiah 31 does not lie within the scope of this article. In these texts, however, both the renewal of the person as well as the closing of the new covenant are clearly 'historically' situated, namely, *after* the return of Israel to the land. These internal changes are necessary to assure Israel of a long stay in the country in the future; one could almost say that they are necessary to allow history to continue in its old way. The new man is built into history, so to speak. In Deutero-Isaiah, however, the return itself is (the image for) the new – and for the rest hardly anything more is asked. That which is called new in Ezekiel and Jeremiah is not as clearly as in Deutero-Isaiah a response, an answer to the whole of history, and therefore it does not have those cosmic dimensions.

The most essential point is that in Deutero-Isaiah history and eschatology do not merge. History establishes (sometimes, almost) that Yhwh is right; eschatology promises that ultimately Yhwh will also be declared to be right.

4. *Unity of Time or Two Aeons*

According to Schreiner the return of the exiles and the return of the Lord to Zion marks the beginning of a new era, "eine Heilszeit, die nie mehr enden soll (Is 54,7-10). Das ist noch nicht der kommende, von dieser Weltzeit getrennte Aion der Apokalyptik, aber vielleicht eine erste Anregung zu dieser Sicht"[18]. In this connection he points to the expectation of the new heaven and the new earth in Isa 65,17, a text that belongs to Trito-Isaiah and thus actually no longer falls within the framework of this article.

---

18. SCHREINER, *Eschatologie* (n. 2), p. 7 ("a time of salvation that will never end (Isa 54,7-10). It is not yet the coming age of the Apocalyptic, separated from the time of this world, but perhaps a first stimulation to this view").

In the meantime the quotation leads us to a following series of questions with respect to Deutero-Isaiah's eschatology. First of all, does new refer to an event or to a situation? It is difficult to state this in a few words. "Behold, I am doing a new thing" becomes concretized as "I point out a way in the desert" (43,19). The latter in its turn appears to be a metonym for "I cause you to return". The entire complex of images that Deutero-Isaiah uses for the new can be summarized as follows: the way (of Yhwh) through the desert, returning home to Zion. The reader is presented with actions rather than a situation. Returning is first of all an act of God: "with their own eyes they see how Yhwh returns to Zion" (52,8; cf. 40,10). It is at the same time a human act of faith and of obedience, a divine invitation that is accepted wholeheartedly.

The metaphor of Isa 54 is the strongest in causing one to think of the promise of a lasting *situation* of salvation: a city with foundations. An earlier, completely different image of the new is the establishment of the משפט on earth by the Servant of Yhwh (42,4) – a salvific order in which one apparently takes part by listening to the תורה of the Servant, and thus again, through an act of obedience (cf. 42,4; 51,4). Even when static images are used for the new it involves the actions that are understood to belong to it. In Deutero-Isaiah 'new' is representative more of an action than of a situation. In any case 'new' does not refer to any definite period.

Here one should take into account the dramatic nature of Deutero-Isaiah's text that is so rightly stressed by Beuken; Isa 40–55 carries us with it in the chronology of a drama. But it is not possible – and this is important for this section of the discussion – to point to one specific moment where the earlier ends and the new begins.

It is easiest to illustrate this on the basis on Isa 48. In this chapter the drama comes to a temporary end. With the fall of Babylon (Isa 47) the former has come, but history continues; in all history's obvious power of proof an anticipation of the future is still needed. The optimistic way in which Deutero-Isaiah's drama takes its leave from Cyrus is remarkable: "he will prosper in his way" (48,15). The political events continue, even though we will hear nothing more about the Persian ruler and all our attention will be drawn by matters of another order from now on.

History does not stop in Isa 48. On the other hand, with respect to the new things, they are created in Isa 48, appearing at the moment of Israel's purification; but as נצרות (48,6) they were already present in some mysterious way *before* this dramatic moment. After all, Yhwh had kept his Servant, who speaks for the first time in 48,16, hidden for a long time (cf. נצר, 42,6). I will discuss the close relationship between this Servant and the new below.

Thus in Deutero-Isaiah's drama, in no way is there a marked boundary between former and new as if two periods were involved. The 'eschaton' was apparently also present before Isa 48, just as world history also continues after Isa 48.

Many feel that the doctrine of the two aeons is the most essential feature of apocalyptic. Others believe that all of eschatology requires a more or less elaborate idea of two aeons and that apocalypse has only to do with the seriousness of the breach between the two and with the question of whether the coming aeon will also belong to history. But previous to this is the question just discussed as to whether in Deutero-Isaiah's eyes a new period begins at all with the new. To put it mildly, this is not stressed in Deutero-Isaiah's book.

Does Deutero-Isaiah's idea nevertheless contain certain starting points for the later apocalyptic development? In order to be able to answer this question we must once again concentrate on Deutero-Isaiah's evaluation of history. One might imagine that apocalypse begins where history is no longer regarded as being able to make God's actions directly visible. Apocalypse is then linked with a secularization of the world. Because this age is far removed from the liberating reality of God (von Rad: "soteriologische Entleerung"), a future age must arise. This notion is alien to Deutero-Isaiah. According to him, it is history that yields the obvious proof that Yhwh is the only God. The fact that there "is no righteous and liberating God" beyond Yhwh (45,21) must be grasped from the recent world events (viewed in light of Israel's tradition), although this proof alone, this proof in itself, is not yet able to elicit the adequate response from Israel.

At the very most, in the shortcoming of history in this last crucial matter, so astutely realized by Deutero-Isaiah, lies perhaps a starting point for an apocalyptic understanding of some texts in his book by later readers. In this connection the shift of the meaning of the 'former things' between Deutero- and Trito-Isaiah is remarkable. Where Deutero-Isaiah still speaks very positively about the former (Israel's fundamental salvation history as is now confirmed in Cyrus on a global scale), in Trito-Isaiah this word appears to be reinterpreted into a reference to the evil time that will pass (61,4; 65,16f.)[19].

In Deutero-Isaiah's own drama we find nothing of such a *Vorher-Nachher* of subsequent aeons[20]. The close relationship of the new with

19. Cf. J.T.A.G.M. van Ruiten, *Een begin zonder einde. De doorwerking van Jesaja 65:17 in de intertestamentaire literatuur en het Nieuwe Testament*, Amsterdam, 1990, pp. 38ff.

20. When Deutero-Isaiah speaks about the vanishing of the heavens and the perishing of the earth, he does not refer to the political reality in which Cyrus operates but to the world in its enmity for Yhwh's Servant, Isa 51,6; cf. 50,9.

the 'having come' of the former things, just as an answer is related to a (actually confirmed) word, here argues strongly against the schematic of two aeons. In Deutero-Isaiah the 'eschaton' does not cancel history, as is the case in apocalypticism.

5. *Realized Eschatology*

Before I go into the most important issue of the realized eschatology in Deutero-Isaiah, an interim summary of the previous steps would be useful.

a. The term 'eschatology' seems less adequate in connection with the things to come (Cyrus) than in connection with the new things. The use of the term 'eschatology' for the expectation of the new is justified by the fact that, according to Deutero-Isaiah, Yhwh will achieve his goal only in the new.

b. The new means a breach in the sense that something similar has never yet been demonstrated. But at the same time former and new are enclosed by continuity. It is in the new that Yhwh holds on to his creational intentions with Israel and through it finally brings his people to completion.

c. The new does not itself belong to history (in a plausible definition of this concept), but it does provide an adequate answer to that which Yhwh has shown through history. In this way the new is very closely related to history and it therefore seems to be able to occur only against the historical decor.

d. One cannot speak of two aeons in Deutero-Isaiah. In particular, the apocalyptic idea that history would not be capable of making God's liberating actions visible is completely alien to Is 40–55.

In connection with Deutero-Isaiah's expectation of salvation it is widely spoken of as 'realized eschatology', 'present eschatology', 'actualized eschatology' and 'actualizing eschatology'[21]. The last term is better than the first three for those who would rather relate eschatology to the expectation than to the object that is expected. But I will not go into more detail on this point now. Vriezen, for example, calls Deutero-Isaiah's message actualizing eschatological, describing his intention in using this term as follows: "the kingdom of God is not only seen coming in *visions* but it is *experienced* as coming"[22].

If one asks how, in literary terms, this impression of an actualizing eschatology arises, in my view it must be said that it arises through the

21. Cf. PREUSS (ed.), *Eschatologie* (n. 7), p. 13.
22. VRIEZEN, *Prophecy* (n. 7), p. 227.

completely dramatic character of Deutero-Isaiah's text. This dramatic character has two effects in particular. In the first place it ensures that the text causes us to witness Cyrus' campaign in phases. In a series of 'trial scenes' the drama makes the reader a contemporary of this critical juncture, i.e., a historical course that should demonstrate clearly that Yhwh is the only God.

In the second place, however, the text also involves the reader with the new, and it does so in a special way. The images of Deutero-Isaiah's announcement of salvation do indeed continually speak of this new as something future; but this future reality is already now present in the performative words that Yhwh speaks: the oracle of salvation to the servant Jacob-Israel.

As a consequence of these performative words we see this Servant undergoing a series of changes during the dramatic progress of Isa 40–48 (cf. 41,15; 44,22; 48,10). The performativity of the word of salvation is so real for Deutero-Isaiah that this word takes shape more and more in the Servant who is addressed by it (42,1; 48,16; etc.). This is, very briefly, my attempt to answer the crucial question of the integration of the figure of the עבד יהוה in the whole of Deutero-Isaiah's theological design.

I therefore believe that Deutero-Isaiah's conception of the new may be called eschatological in the sense that it concerns a future in which Yhwh will attain his goal: the human answer to history. Without the new, history can only lead to the unmasking and shaming of humans. But this future answer is not exclusively prospective. In a certain sense it is already anticipated in the dramatic character of the servant Jacob-Israel changed by Yhwh's word.

This Servant thus graphically embodies Yhwh's covenant with the people (42,6; cf. 49,8) and he gives his torah to the nations at a certain moment in the drama (49,1; cf. 42,4). This is anything but prospective eschatology; it happens in and through this text. And in this sense one can, in my view, indeed speak of an 'actualizing' eschatology in Deutero-Isaiah. To the summarizing statements above I will thus add the following:

e. The eschatology of Deutero-Isaiah is actualizing because it actually brings near and makes present God's salvific future in the figure of the Servant.

6. The Conditional or Unconditional Offer of Salvation

Finally, in this survey I would like to look at the dilemma introduced by Fohrer into the discussion on the eschatology of Deutero-Isaiah: that

of conditional and unconditional salvation. According to Fohrer, the offer of salvation is conditional in classical prophecy. It appeals to the decision of the hearer. In Deutero-Isaiah, however, the punishing judgement is past and the salvific future is absolutely fixed[23].

Fohrer constructs an eschatological drama from elements of Isa 40–55
without taking into account the dramatic character of the text itself. The
mere fact that Deutero-Isaiah does not offer a futuristic report of that
which will successively happen but a drama that causes the reader (anew
with every reading) to undergo the decisive changes already points to
the fact that the reader himself is ascribed an important role in the action. The speaking Servant, who as the Israel changed by the performative word of Yhwh (Isa 49,3) gives access to the new, retains his appeal-
ing character for the individual hearer and reader.

In connection with the promise of salvation in Deutero-Isaiah H.P.
Müller states: "vom Dialog zwischen Gott und seinem Volk hängt es ab,
ob zukünftige Wirklichkeit eröffnet oder verschlossen, gegeben oder
verweigert wird"[24]. This could (unintentionally) be a good description of
the significance of the Servant as a covenant for the people, for no one
less than this Servant embodies the dialogue which Müller has in mind.
The question of whether the future is opened or remains closed depends
on the question of whether the Servant is accepted in this mediating role.
Only by listening to the voice of the Servant does the hearer or reader of
this dramatic text personally participate in the new. Illustrative of this is
the difference between 44,22 and 55,7. The 'return to me' in 44,22 is
directed toward the servant Jacob-Israel as a dramatic character and
there as a creative imperative signifies his unconditional and inevitable
return to Yhwh. But that which, in the course of the drama, is realized in
the Servant becomes yet again in 55,7 an exhortation for the individual
hearer to change, in the footsteps of the Servant, his life: "Let the
wicked forsake his way … let him return to the Lord … for he will
freely pardon". I do not see a real contradiction between these passages.

The difficulty of Fohrer's view is made clear particularly where he
speaks of a collective or corporative participation in salvation[25]. I cannot
go extensively into the question of universalism but I do not believe that

---

23. G. FOHRER, *Die Struktur der alttestamentlichen Eschatologie*, in PREUSS (ed.),
Eschatologie (n. 7), pp. 147-180 [= *TLZ* 85 (1960) 401-420]. For a summary of his view
of Deutero-Isaiah's eschatology, see ID., *Das Buch Jesaja* (ZBK, 3), Zürich, ²1966, p. 7.

24. H.P. MÜLLER, *Mythos und Transzendenz*, in PREUSS (ed.), *Eschatologie* (n. 7), pp.
415-443 [= *EvT* 32 (1972) 97-118], esp. pp. 431-432 ("whether the future reality is
opened or closed, is given or refused, depends on the dialogue between God and his
people").

25. FOHRER, *Struktur* (n. 23), p. 170.

according to Deutero-Isaiah whole peoples would turn to Yhwh en masse. All the ends of the earth do indeed view themselves as invited to salvation, but every inhabitant of the earth must decide personally, in the presence of history, whether he or she wants to belong to the seed of Israel (45,22ff.; cf. 44,5). On the other hand, whoever may count him- or herself as part of Israel's historical remnant, Jews by birth (46,3), is far from righteousness and only belongs to the seed of the Servant by listening (48,17ff.; cf. 50,10). The core of the whole problem of the *Ebed* lies in the fact that in Deutero-Isaiah 'Israel' slowly but surely changes from a historical to an eschatological entity. In Deutero-Isaiah the Servant ultimately has little to do with an empirical people (I am using Vriezen's terminology here). Inversely proportional to Deutero-Isaiah's universalism, one could say, is the increasing concentration of salvation in this one dramatic figure of the Servant as the Israel created by Yhwh himself (49,3) – the suffering Servant who will justify the many sharing in his knowledge (53,11) and who thus becomes the prototype of the post-exilic pious[26]. *In their knowledge and experience the eschaton is present*[27].

It is difficult to accommodate Deutero-Isaiah's eschatological conception within the dilemma of either/or or before/after. At most it can be established that every chronological idea of an eschaton, as intended by Deutero-Isaiah, cannot be anything but deficient as an *idea*. The new has already begun, but it will also have to begin in every hearer personally.

I will conclude this description of Deutero-Isaiah's concept of dramatic theology by saying that the reader may find a recapitulative approach such as the above too 'holistic'. When interpretation becomes too smooth, it evokes the idea that it is an exegetical construction. In agreement with Beuken, however, I believe that Deutero-Isaiah's book itself challenges one again and again to such an attempt at synthetic understanding and that this is why the theological shape of possible diachronical layers in the text, if one believes that such layers can be isolated, will always have to be weighted against the theology of the

---

26. Cf. J.C. BASTIAENS, *Interpretaties van Jesaja 53. Een intertextueel onderzoek naar de lijdende Knecht in Jes 53 (MT/LXX) en in Lk 22:14-38, Hand 3:12-26, Hand 4:23-31 en Hand 8:26-40*, Tilburg, 1993, pp. 100ff.

27. Cf. R. BULTMANN, *History and Eschatology*, Edinburgh, 1957, p. 21: "If it depends on the obedience of men whether the goal of history can be attained, then how can the divine promise be granted? This problem cannot be answered, because the future state of welfare in the Old Testament is thought of as welfare within this world". One can say: Deutero-Isaiah's answer to this problem is the suffering Servant and his seed. Therefore I do not agree with Müller that no prophet could disappoint so deeply as Deutero-Isaiah because he overlooked the openness of the future: cf. *Mythos* (n. 24), p. 433, n. 38. A statement like that is not verifiable: Deutero-Isaiah's successors (see Trito-Isaiah) may have thought about *history* less optimistically than he did but firmly adhered to his *eschatology*.

whole[28]. In line with Beuken, I would strongly argue for the continuation of the use of the name 'Deutero-Isaiah' for *this* theology and not for the theology of one or another hypothetical basic text.

Again, one could attempt to understand certain tensions in this whole better against the background of the various traditions from which Deutero-Isaiah draws (now I mean by this name the collective of authors that is probably responsible for Isa 40–55). The second part of this contribution will be devoted to the tradition historical place of Deutero-Isaiah's eschatology.

II

With regard to Yhwh's plan for history and Cyrus' role in it, Deutero-Isaiah stands in the tradition of Isaiah and Jeremiah. They too see the coming disaster connected with political events. The difference between the Assyrian king in Isaiah, Nebuchadnezzar in Jeremiah and Cyrus in Deutero-Isaiah is that the latter no longer means disaster for Israel but for the peoples, or rather for the gods of the peoples.

The judgement in Deutero-Isaiah is not so much that which occurs by military means on the battlefield but consists of the shaming of Yhwh's opponents in court, in the trial that Yhwh carries out with them concerning history. While it is possible to call the older prophetic announcement of judgement eschatological insofar as Yhwh in and through this judgement is considered to achieve his goal (for example in Proto-Isaiah and Zephaniah, through a 'remnant' of Israel in which he will be glorified), in Deutero-Isaiah the concept of the remnant plays only a modest role and there are no eschatological ideas directly connected to it (46,3; cf. 45,20). In general one can say that the connection between the execution of Yhwh's judgement via history on the one hand and the realization of Yhwh's ultimate intentions on the other is more problematic in Deutero-Isaiah than in his prophetic predecessors.

Thus differences between Deutero-Isaiah and older prophecy on this point are: (a) Cyrus signifies liberation for Israel and not disaster as was the case with the kings of Assyria or Babylon, and (b) just *because of this* the connection between history and eschaton in Deutero-Isaiah seems to have become less obvious.

The eschaton enters the world of Isaiah 40–55 via the dramatic figure of the Servant. Some of the changes that the servant Jacob-Israel under-

---

28. Cf. H. LEENE, *Auf der Suche nach einem redaktionskritischen Modell für Jesaja 40–55*, in *TLZ* 121 (1996) 803-818. E.g., one cannot save Deutero-Isaiah's unconditionality by assuming a separate '*qarob*-layer' (Hermisson).

goes in the drama (the wiping out of sins: 44,22; refining: 48,10; the gift of the Spirit: 48,16; cf. 42,1) cause one to think of the changes that are proclaimed for every individual Israelite in Ezekiel 36 and which must lead to a 'new person' there. Just what exactly the literary relationship is here cannot be explored in this contribution. This also holds for the promise of the new covenant in Jeremiah 30–31. My current impression is that this new covenant involves a younger conception, and that Jeremiah's Book of Comfort presupposes both Ezekiel and Deutero-Isaiah and unites elements from them in itself[29]. I believe that one seeks in vain for a salient analogy in the writings of Isaiah, Jeremiah and Ezekiel where the basic structure of the whole of Deutero-Isaiah's view of history and eschatology is concerned. For this an entirely different group of texts is to be considered – the Yhwh *malak* psalms. These psalms break up into two types, namely, that of the so-called theme psalm (Pss 93, 97, 99) and that of the imperative hymns (Pss 47, 95, 96, 98). I would like first to reconsider the issue of priority in the light of the many points of contact between Isaiah 40–55 and these psalms. The points of contact concern both Ps 93 (from the first group) and Pss 96 and 98 (from the second group). Ps 93 is generally viewed as pre-exilic, and Pss 96 and 98 stem from the Persian period. Of the last two, Ps 98 is the oldest[30]; Ps 96 not only assumes Ps 98 is known but also takes up elements from the pre-exilic Pss 93 and (particularly) 29. Recent research has demonstrated that there is no reason to avoid painstakingly the term 'ascension of the throne' in the exegesis of these psalms[31]. Ps 93 places the action of Yhwh becoming King in primeval time. Ps 98 allows it to coincide with Israel's liberation from exile and with the worldwide acknowledgement and praise of Yhwh, which the song itself invites. Ps 96 seeks a certain *Ausgleich* between these ideas of a primeval and imminent royal crowning by, within the framework of the very same 'eschatological' call as in Ps 98, also quoting the phrase from Ps 93 about the unshakeable earth. But we will first look at the details.

In the rendition of Pss 98 and 96 given below the *possible* points of contact with Isaiah 40–55 are underlined. The places concerned are given in the right margin. If the point of contact involves a word (phrase) or clause that also appears in the other psalm, this is indicated

29. Cf. H. LEENE, *Unripe Fruit and Dull Teeth (Jer 31,29; Ex 18,2)*, in E. TALSTRA *et al.* (eds.), *Narrative and Comment*. FS W. Schneider, Amsterdam, 1995, pp. 82-98, esp. p. 95.

30. I share this view of the diachronical relationship of Pss 96 and 98 with T. BOOIJ, *Psalmen* III (POT), Nijkerk, 1994, p. 154.

31. Cf. B. JANOWSKI, *Das Königtum Gottes in den Psalmen. Bemerkungen zu einem neuen Gesamtentwurf*, in *ZTK* 86 (1989) 389-454.

by *double* underlining. The underlining involves only for a small part striking linguistic analogies in a strict sense of the word[32]. In the commentary following each psalm the points of contact are discussed and weighed.

Psalm 98

1 A psalm.

Sing to Yhwh a new song,	Isa 42,10
for he has done marvellous things.	
His right hand has got him liberation,	
his own holy arm.	Isa 52,10

2 Yhwh has made known his liberation,	
before the eyes of the nations revealed his righteousness.	Isa 52,10; 53,1
3 He has remembered his steadfast love and faithfullness	
to the house of Israel.	
All the ends of the earth have seen	
the liberation of our God.	Isa 45,22; 52,10

4 Make a joyful noise to Yhwh, all the earth,	
break forth and rejoice and sing.	Isa 44,23; 49,13; 52,9
5 Sing for Yhwh with the lyre,	
with the lyre and the sound of melody.	Isa 51,3
6 With trumpets and the sound of the horn	
make a joyful noise before the King, Yhwh.	Isa 44,23; 52,7

7 Let the sea roar and all that fills it,	
the world and those who dwell in it.	Isa 42,10
8 Let the rivers clap their hands,	
let the mountains rejoice together.	Isa 55,12; 44,23; 49,13

9 before Yhwh, for he has come	
to judge the earth.	
He will judge the world with righteousness	
and the peoples with equity.	Isa 51,5

Ps 98,1 שירו ליהוה שיר חדש. Also literally in Isa 42,10[33] – זרוע קדשו. Isa 52,10 is the only other place in the Old Testament where the connec-

---

32. For a methodological discussion, see A.L.H.M. VAN WIERINGEN, *Analogies in Isaiah* (Applicatio, 10), Amsterdam, 1993, pp. 1-29; cf. H. LEENE, *Psalm 98 and Deutero-Isaiah: Linguistic Analogies and Literary Affinity*, in R.-F. POSWICK (ed.), *Actes du quatrième Colloque International Bible et Informatique*, Paris, 1995, pp. 313-340.

33. The other occurrences of the clause are Ps 96,1 and 149,1; cf. Ps 33,3 and 144,9. In Ps 40,4 שיר חדש occurs without the *verbum* שיר.

tion appears. זרוע and ימין rarely appear in parallel or coordination: Ps 44,4; 89,14 (in addition to יד); Isa 62,8; cf. 48,13f.

Ps 98,3 וראו כל אפסי, cf. Isa 52,10 ראו כל אפסי ארץ את ישועת אלהנו ארץ את ישואת אלהינו. See also Isa 45,22 והושעו כל אפסי ארץ. That the ends of the earth see something or are liberated is not stated anywhere else in the Old Testament.

Ps 98,4 רנו[34] ... הריעו ... פצחו ... הריעו, cf. Isa 44,23 רנה ... פצחו ... פצחו ורננו. The combination of the *three* roots only appears in Ps 98,4 and Isa 44,23. פצח also appears in Isa 14,7, in addition to Deutero-Isaiah (44,23; 49,13; 52,9; 54,1; 55,12) and Ps 98,4, always next to the root רנן. As a matter of fact, Ps 98,4a looks even more like Ps 66,1 and 100,1 הריעו לאלהים (ליהוה) כל הארץ.

Ps 98,5 וקול זמרו, literally in Isa 51,3; for the rest nowhere else in the Old Testament.

Ps 98,7 הים ומלאו, literally in Isa 42,10; for the rest only in Ps 96,11 (1 Chron 16,32).

Ps 98,8 ימחאו כף, literally in Isa 55,12. The one time it is said of the rivers, the other time of all the trees of the field. מחא כף does not appear elsewhere in the Old Testament; מחא יד appears in Ezek 25,6 (not metaphorically). Another expression for 'clapping hands' is תקע כף, which is used in Ps 47,2 in a similar connection; see also 2 Kings 11,12 הכה כף, also related to the crowning of the king.

Ps 98,9 ישפט ... עמים, cf. Isa 51,5 וזרעי עמים ישפטו. As the object of שפט, עמים only appears in Ps 67,5 כי תשפט עמים מישור and Ps 96,13[35].

In addition, in the translation given above there are also a few common words marked that do not occur within the same syntactic pattern or the same word combination but that are found in areas of the striking similarities and therefore could increase the impression of relatedness. Ps 98,1f. ישועתו, הושיעה, cf. Isa 52,10 ישועה. Ps 98,2 לעיני הגוים, cf. Isa 52,10 לעיני כל הגוים; without כל the expression is common, see Lev 26,45; Ezek 5,8; 20,9.14.22.41; 22,16; 28,25; 38,23; 39,27; with כל in 2 Chron 32,23. Ps 98,2 גלה; in the area of זרוע (cf. 98,1) this *verbum* (in Niphal) occurs only in Isa 53,1. Van der Ploeg draws attention to this point of contact[36]; one could also think of the parallelism of גלה Niphal and ראה in 40,5[37]. Ps 98,6 הריעו, cf. Isa 44,23. Ps 98,6 המלך יהוה, cf. Isa 52,7 מלך אלהיך. Ps 98,7 ישבי, cf. Isa 42,10 וישביהם. Ps 98,8 הרים ירננו, cf. 44,23, 49,13.

34. Isa 49,13 רנו ... יפצחו ... רנה; 52,9 פצחו רננו.
35. דין עמים Isa 3,13; Ps 96,10; Job 36,31.
36. J.P.M. VAN DER PLOEG, *Psalmen* II (BOT), Roermond, 1974, p. 158.
37. Cf. J. JEREMIAS, *Das Königtum Gottes in den Psalmen: Israels Begegnung mit dem kanaanäischen Mythos in den Jahwe-König-Psalmen* (FRLANT, 141), Göttingen, 1987, p. 136.

Psalm 96

1	<u>Sing to Yhwh a new song</u>,	Isa 42,10
	sing to Yhwh, all the earth.	
2	Sing to Yhwh, bless his name,	
	<u>announce his liberation</u> from day to day.	Isa 40,7; 41,27; 52,7.10
3	Declare <u>his glory</u> among the nations,	Isa 42,12
	his marvellous works among all the peoples.	

4 For great is Yhwh, and greatly to be praised,
   he is to be feared above all gods.
5 For all the gods of the peoples are idols,
   but Yhwh made the heavens.
6 Honour and majesty are before him,
   strength and beauty are in his sanctuary.

7	Ascribe to Yhwh, o families of the peoples,	
	ascribe to Yhwh <u>glory</u> and strength.	Isa 42,12
8	Ascribe to Yhwh the <u>glory</u> due his name,	Isa 42,12
	bring an offering and come into his courts.	
9	Worship Yhwh in (his) holy splendor,	
	tremble before him, all the earth.	
10	Say among the nations: <u>Yhwh is king</u>,	Isa 52,7
	yea, the world <u>is established</u>, <u>it shall not be moved</u>;	Isa 40,20
	he will judge the peoples with equity.	

11	Let the <u>heavens</u> be glad and let <u>the earth sing for joy</u>,	Isa 49,13
	let <u>the sea</u> roar <u>and all that fills it</u>.	Isa 42,10
12	Let the field exult and everything in it,	
	let <u>all the trees of the wood rejoice</u>	Isa 44,23; 55,12
13	for Yhwh, for he has come,	
	he has come to judge the earth.	
	He will <u>judge</u> the world with righteousness,	
	and the <u>peoples</u> in his faithfullness.	Isa 51,5

Ps 96,1 שירו ליהוה שיר חדש. Also literally in Isa 42,10[38].

Ps 96,10 (1 Chron 16,31) יהוה מלך, cf. Isa 52,7 מלך אלהיך[39]. – (1 Chron 16,30) אף תכון תבל בל תמוט, cf. Isa 40,20 להכין פסל לא ימוט. For the collocation of כון and מוט, see Ps 38,17f.; 93,1; 112,6f.; 140,11f. Ps 93,1 is the only other place that suggests that the תבל could be moved. Isa 40,20 apparently aims at a contrast between the foundation of an un-faltering idol and the foundation of the earth by Yhwh, Isa 40,21f.

38. Not mentioned: Ps 96,8 (I Chron 16,29) הבו ליהוה כבוד שמו שאו מנחה, cf. Isa 43,23 וכבדתני לא העבדתיך במנחה. The root כבד and the word מנחה occur so often that one could not say that there is literary dependence.
39. The other places with Yhwh/God as the subject of מלך are: Ex 15,18; 1 Sam 8,7; Isa 24,23; Ezek 20,33; Mic 4,7; Ps 47,9; 93,1; 97,1; 99,1; 146,10.

Ps 96,11 (1 Chron 16,31) ישמחו השמים ותגל הארץ, cf. Isa 49,13 רנו שמים וגילי ארץ. The only other text that has גיל with ארץ as subject is Ps 97,1. – (1 Chron 16,32) הים ומלאו, literally in Isa 42,10, otherwise only in Ps 98,7[40].

Ps 96,12 (cf. 1 Chron 16,33) אז ירננו כל עצי יער, cf. Isa 44,23 פצחו הרים רנה יער וכל עץ בו. Also see Isa 55,12. To my knowledge, the image of the rejoicing trees does not occur anywhere else in the Old Testament.

Ps 96,13 עמים ... ישפט, cf. Isa 51,5 ישפטו עמים וזרעי. As the object of שפט, עמים only occurs yet in Ps 67,5 כי תשפט עמים מישור and Ps 98,9[41].

Separate words that could perhaps increase the impression of relatedness are: Ps 96,2 (1 Chron 16,23) בשר, cf. Isa 40,7.7; 41,27; 52,7.7. Ps 96,3.7.8 (1 Chron 16,24.28.29) כבוד, see, among others, Isa 42,12 but also Ps 29. Ps 96,2 (1 Chron 16,23) ישועה, see in particular Isa 52,7,10.

It goes without saying that the differences between Deutero-Isaiah and both psalms are as relevant as the similarities in the answer to the issue of dependence. Words in Ps 98 that do not occur in Isa 40–55 are: מזמור (v. 1; the root is present in Isa 51,3), אמונה (v. 3), כנור (v. 5.5), חצצרות (v. 6), שופר (v. 6), רעם (v. 7), תבל (vv. 7.9) and the root פלא (v. 1). The use of זכר in Ps 98,3 is not typical of Deutero-Isaiah. זכר with Yhwh as subject occurs in Deutero-Isaiah only in Isa 43,25, namely with respect to Yhwh no longer remembering Israel's sins. Within the context of Isa 40–55 בית ישראל acquires a somewhat reproving tone (46,3; cf. בית יעקב 46,3; 48,1). It is preferably the *servant* Jacob-Israel rather than the *house* that is called the object of Yhwh's salvific act. These facts make clear that one would be going too far in attributing the same author to the psalm and (parts of) Isa 40–55.

Ps 96 also contains many words that do not occur in Isa 40–55: אלילים (v. 5), הוד (v. 6), מקדש (v. 6), משפחה (v. 7), הבו (vv. 7.8), חצר (v. 8), הדרה (v. 9; cf. Ps 29,2), תבל (vv. 10.13), רעם (v. 11), עלץ (v. 12), שדי (v. 12), אמונה (v. 13) and the root פלא (v. 3). More striking are the sayings that appear to contradict Deutero-Isaiah's diction and/or theology. He does not use ברך to praise Yhwh (Ps 96,2). Rather than שמים עשה (Ps 96,5), Deutero-Isaiah would have used ברא שמים (cf. Isa 42,5; 45,18), שמים נטה (cf. Isa 40,22; 42,5; 51,13) or טפח שמים (cf. Isa 48,13). He denies that there is any other god than Yhwh (cf. 41,23; 44,6;

---

40. In contrast, ארץ ומלאה occurs 8 times: Deut 33,16; Isa 34,1; Jer 8,16; 47,2; Ezek 19,7; 30,12; Mic 1,2; Ps 24,1. Does this have to do with the fact that the last phrase has priority and that הים ומלאו arose in the area of the word ארץ? Cf. especially Ps 24,1 and 98,7: the 'resounding' of the world in this last verse is odd.

41. שפט בין עמים Mic 4,3; דין עמים Isa 3,13; Ps 96,10; Job 36,31.

45,5.14.21), and one can thus say that his monotheism goes beyond that of Ps 96,4f[42].

If we take stock of the above data we could say that, as long as we omit the common features between both psalms, the relatedness with Isa 40–55 concerns Ps 98 most of all. Yet one cannot say that the relation between Ps 96 and Isa 40–55 runs through Ps 98 exclusively – think of the rejoicing of the earth and of the trees in Ps 96,11f. We find the most striking similarity between Isa 40–55 and Ps 96 in Isa 40,20 (cf. Ps 96,10: "The Lord reigns. The world is firmly established, it cannot be moved"). Ps 96,10 is probably, however, a quotation from Ps 93,1, and Isa 40,20ff. rather reminds one of this psalm *directly*. Conversely, the word 'glory' in Ps 96 causes one to think sooner of Ps 29 than of Deutero-Isaiah.

Is Ps 98 dependent on Isa 40–55? Consideration of the points of contact has caused me to doubt the correctness of this view, which is most current among exegetes[43].

Thus, for the understanding of the term שיר חדש in Ps 98,1 and Ps 96,1 one need not rely on the very pregnant use of the root חדש in Deutero-Isaiah. חדש in the psalm has no specific Deutero-Isaiac connotations. The term probably stems from the individual lamentation and song of thanksgiving (see, for example, Ps 40); its use in Pss 96 and 98 clearly carries traces of it[44]. Thus the term has retained a more original colour there than in Isa 42,10-13.

The most striking analogies between Ps 98 and Deutero-Isaiah are to be found in Ps 98,1-3 and Isa 52,10. At first glance one could argue that the priority lies in the prophetic text. In Isa 52,10 cd וראו כל אפסי ארץ

---

42. Ps 96,5 is considered by several commentators to be a later addition, although is was already taken up into 1 Chron 16,25; cf. J. JEREMIAS, *Königtum* (n. 37), p. 122, n. 1. However v. 4b does not sound Deutero-Isaiac without v. 5 either.

43. For example, F. DELITZSCH, *Biblischer Kommentar über die Psalmen*, Leipzig, ⁵1894, *a.l.*: "Anfang und Schluß sind aus Ps. 96. Dazwischen ist fast alles aus Jes. II" ("The beginning and the close are from Ps 96. Almost everything in between is from Isa II (= Isa 40–66)"). The latter is, in any case, exaggerated; see above. According to Jeremias, for both psalms the question of priority may in all likelihood be settled in favour of Deutero-Isaiah: cf. JEREMIAS, *Königtum* (n. 37), p. 127. With regard to Ps 98 in particular there can be no doubt in his mind, because the points of contact here are to be found in typically Deutero-Isaiac phrases (p. 133). Jeremias cites H.L. Ginsberg as an opponent of this view: see *Eretz Israel* 9 (1969) 45-50, esp. pp. 47-48. Ginsberg himself appeals to S. Mowinckel (*Psalmenstudien* II, Kristiana, 1923) and Y. Kaufmann (האמונה הישראלית תולדות II, 721-725). J.P.M. VAN DER PLOEG, *Psalmen* II, p. 148, names A. Maillot – A. Lelièvre as those who regard Deutero-Isaiah as dependent on Psalm 96. See also J. BECKER, *Messiaserwartung im Alten Testament* (SBS, 83), Stuttgart, 1977, p. 46; F. MATHEUS, *Singt dem Herrn ein neues Lied: Die Hymnen Deuterojesajas* (SBS, 141), Stuttgart 1990, p. 49.

44. Cf. JEREMIAS, *Königtum* (n. 37), p. 126.

את ישׁועת אלהינו forms a fine chiastic parallelism with ab את חשׂף יהוה
זרוע קדשׁו לעיני כל הגוים; in comparison to this Ps 98,3cd appears less anchored in the literary context. It is therefore certainly a possibility that
Ps 98,1-3 freely adapted Isa 52,10. But there is a complication in that not
everyone is convinced of the originality of Ps 98,2 in its current form:
the verse interrupts the very regular 3+2 metre of the psalm with its
3+2+2. For this reason Bardtke (BHS) suggests that לעיני הגוים could
have been added later on the basis of Isa 52,10[45]. Kraus asks whether an
entire colon could have been left out of Ps 98,2[46].

Apart from this, it remains remarkable that, given the supposed influence of Isa 52, characteristic theological terms of Deutero-Isaiah such as
גאל and נחם (cf. 52,9) find no echo in the psalm.

If there is a relation of dependence between Isa 45,22 and Ps 98,3,
then the priority lies more with the psalm verse, which is theologically
less far-reaching, than the other way around. 'Being saved' goes beyond
the ends of the earth 'seeing the salvation'. That the peoples take part in
Israel's salvation as spectators fits in with the tradition of the song of
thanksgiving and therefore is not in itself typically Deutero-Isaianic: the
onlookers see what has happened to the supplicant (see, for example, Ps
40,4)[47]. It is not very likely that the 'sound of melody' of Ps 98,5 stems
from Isa 51,3, but rather, Deutero-Isaiah would be in a song tradition
here as well[48].

Ps 98,7 and Ps 96,11 (1 Chron 16,32) הים ומלאו do not seem to be
dependent on Isa 42,10 יורדי הים ומלאו. This last connection is odd. It
can only be understood if one sees that Isa 42,10-13 as a whole is intent
on emphasizing that it is the *human* singers who are invited to sing the
new song. This is the only passage in Isa 40ff. in which attention is paid
not only to the desert but also to the desert *inhabitants* in their settlements. The relation of dependence is then turned around: the attention in
Deutero-Isaiah consciously shifts from the sea of the psalm to the sea-
men. In 42,10-13 Deutero-Isaiah is determined to make the circle of
singers as wide as possible and to carry the song beyond the edges of the
earth, as it were – with the result that the new song becomes a seaman's
song.

It is generally supposed that the clapping of hands has to do with the
crowning of the king. If this is so (see also 2 Kings 11,12!), then one
must say that the phrase in Ps 98,8 has a more original connection than

45. See also *ibid.*, pp. 132-133.
46. H.-J. KRAUS, *Psalmen* II (BKAT), Neukirchen-Vluyn, [5]1978, p. 846.
47. *Pace* JEREMIAS, *Königtum* (n. 37), p. 134.
48. *Pace* DELITZSCH, *Psalmen* (n. 43), *a.l.*

in Isa 55,12. In the direct surroundings of Isa 55,12 the kingship of Yhwh is otherwise not emphasized[49].

All things considered, one must say that the priority in the relation of dependence, which is in itself strong, lies rather in Ps 98 than in Isa 40–55 or even in a possible Deutero-Isaiac basic text inasfar as the texts in question were a part of it.

As far as Ps 96 is concerned the results are the same. One could think of בשר in Ps 96,2: this word presupposes the image of the joyful messenger in Deutero-Isaiah[50], which in the psalm is then blurred into a daily spreading of the message. But upon closer examination this is highly unlikely. In Deutero-Isaiah there is talk of a messenger to Zion (41,27; 52,7) and of a message that Zion itself must pass on to the towns of Judah (40,9). In Ps 96,2 one must think of many (cf. Ps 68,12) who must bring the message of Israel's liberation to the peoples, just as an individual Israelite, who is liberated by Yhwh, announces this in a large community. In this connection, one should compare Ps 40,10 and also notice the other points of contact between Ps 96 and Ps 40: שיר חדש in v. 4, נפלאות in v. 6, אמונתך ותשועתך in v. 11, יגדל יהוה in v. 17.

In addition to this detailed look at both psalms, there is yet another important point of view that deserves to be considered in the answer to the question of dependence. The correspondences with the psalms in Isa 40–55 are localized in a limited number of texts spread throughout this corpus, mainly in the so-called 'eschatological hymns' or in other closing climactic passages (42,10-13; 44,23; 45,22-25; 49,13; 52,7-10; 55,12-13). There appears to be an exception in Isa 51,5, cf. Ps 96,13. However, the theme of Yhwh as שפט is so emphatically present in the psalm literature (see, for example, Ps 75 and 82) that Ps 96 certainly need not rely on Deutero-Isaiah in this case. For that matter, the term שפטי הארץ can be found in Isa 40,23, a passage for which, according to many exegetes, Deutero-Isaiah is dependent on existent hymnic statements about Yhwh's kingship. In the other cases one realizes that modern form critical insight is necessary in order to associate such closing hymnic texts with one another and to isolate them from their present literary environment. It is difficult to imagine that a psalmist who was inspired by Deutero-Isaiah proceded so selectively. The opposite is more likely: the composers of Isaiah 40–55 borrowed from an existent hymnic tradition for certain pivotal points of their dramatic composition, or even from these very songs passed on to us in Pss 98 and 96.

49. Or is it Israel's own kingship that is meant? Cf. Isa 55,3.
50. Cf. *Ibid.*, *a.l.*

In this way it can also be understood better how these psalms could express Yhwh's act in such relatively plain words. This act of liberation is undoubtedly Israel's return from exile, but the images that Deutero-Isaiah uses for this (the levelling of mountains, a way in the desert, the watering of the drought and profuse plant growth) are missing entirely in the psalms. General terms of thanksgiving express the act of liberation. In the priority of Isa 40–55 or, possibly, its basic text this would be difficult to explain.

Given these observations one cannot avoid the impression that prejudice has played a role in the current answer to the question of priority. This prejudice then concerned two points in particular, namely, (a) the dating of Deutero-Isaiah's prophecies before the fall of Babylon in 539 B.C. and (b) the rejection of a pre-exilic idea of Yhwh's ascension to the throne, so that the influence from Deutero-Isaiah's eschatology would form an almost necessary explanation for the appearance of these ideas in the two psalms.

With regard to the first point, the early dating of Deutero-Isaiah's prophecies, it can be said that this objection is no longer valid of certain more recent redaction critical hypotheses. Thus Van Oorschot attributes the passages concerned in Isa 40–55 to editorial layers that did not arise until about 520/521 and about 500 B.C.[51]. In such a model the psalms could *look back* to the liberation and nevertheless *precede* this editions. But I do not believe that Isa 40–55 could exist before 515 B.C., even in its oldest contours. There is no Deutero-Isaiac *Grundschrift* to reconstruct that is not already determined in its structure by the semantic field of former/latter/coming/new, and it is this semantic field *that answers a post-exilic problem*: Yhwh has proved in Cyrus that he is God by the correspondence of former and latter, but in order to make Israel react to it something new is needed. Thus Isa 40–55 probably originated after 515 B.C. – the established priority of Pss 98 and 96 is at most an extra argument.

The argument that Deutero-Isaiah would be needed to explain, if not to justify, the representation of Yhwh's eschatological ascension to the throne in Pss 98 and 96 is sharply articulated in Kraus[52]. But there is little to be said against the presupposition that Yhwh's ascension to the throne was experienced and celebrated in Jerusalem's cult already long before the exile. Then Deutero-Isaiah is not the necessary religious-historical key but rather Pss 98 and 96 form the connection between that celebration and Deutero-Isaiah's eschatology.

51. J. VAN OORSCHOT, *Von Babel zum Zion: Eine literarkritische und redaktionsgeschichtliche Untersuchung* (BZAW, 206), Berlin - New York, 1993, pp. 166, 242.
52. Cf. KRAUS, *Psalmen* (n. 46), I, p. 103; II, pp. 834-844, 846-847.

Now that we have answered the question of priority we can finally return to the basic structure of Deutero-Isaiah's view of history and the eschaton and reconsider this structure in the light of the Yhwh *malak* psalms in both of their forms. The influence of (a statement such as) Ps 93,1f. can be clearly seen in Isa 40,20-22 (see also Ps 96,10). The influence of (statements such as those in) Ps 96 and 98 can be found in Isa 42,10-13 and 52,7-10 in particular.

What function does a statement such as that of the theme psalm 93 receive within Deutero-Isaiah's dramatic theological design? That Yhwh is King means, according to Isa 40,21-23, that he is Creator. That Yhwh as the Creator-King has firmly established the foundations of the earth allows one to draw the conclusion that Yhwh causes the rulers of the earth to be idle. The field in which Yhwh *proves* that he is Creator is the field of history. Thus Isa 40 already indicates the framework within which Cyrus in Isa 40–44 must be understood. The use of the title of King for Yhwh in connection with Cyrus' appearance (41,21; 43,14; 44,6) is directly related to this. This title brings us into the atmosphere of Ps 93 and of a kingship from time immemorial that is now gloriously confirmed in the judicial proceedings with the gods. But in Isa 45 especially it appears that the creation order itself is implied in the fact that Cyrus is the fulfilment of earlier predictions.

In a completely different place in Deutero-Isaiah's design we detect the influence of two songs of a more recent date, the imperative hymns 96 and 98: they determine to a strong degree Deutero-Isaiah's presentation of the new. Isa 42,10-13 forms the hymnic answer to Yhwh's proclamation that he will cause something new to sprout. Isa 44,23 also presents the reaction to a statement about the new – Israel's reversal. Isa 52,7-10 is related to 42,10-13 not only in terms of tradition history, but also as a reflection of Yhwh's kingly *entrance* into Zion, which dramatically follows on 42,13 as a reflection of his *departure* as triumphant warrior. Isa 42,10-13 and 52,7-10 form the two main pillars in the dramatic basic structure of Deutero-Isaiah's entire book. In the context both passages are closely related to statements about the Servant of the Lord.

In my study on the earlier and new things I have argued that the contrast former/new in Deutero-Isaiah has no precedents terminologically[53]. I must amend this to state that Deutero-Isaiah's school in the Yhwh *malak* psalms encountered two kinds of statements about Yhwh's kingship, of which the one kind referred to something old (cf. Ps 93,2 מעולם מעז,) and the other to something new (cf. Ps 96,1; 98,1 שיר חדש). To put

53. LEENE, *Vroegere* (n. 5), p. 22.

it differently, these psalms already confront us with a certain tension between the idea that Yhwh's kingship goes back to primeval time (and *thus* can be proved in contemporary world experience)[54] and the idea that Yhwh's becoming king is only completed in eventual acknowledgement and praise. In this manner these psalms generated the stimulus to the theological reflection to which Isa 40–55 attests in such an impressive way. The tension between the present evidence of Yhwh's kingship on the one hand and the resistance to its definitive revelation on the other, for which Deutero-Isaiah offers us a dramatic 'solution', is already prepared within the collection of Enthronement Psalms with its two types. Here we find, in my opinion, by far the main and most striking background for Deutero-Isaiah's view of history and the eschaton in their mutual relationship.

Polanenstraat 17   Henk LEENE
NL-1165 GX Halfweg

54. The peculiarity of Ps 93 lies in "Vermittlung von urzeitlichem Geschehen und Erfahrungswirklichkeit" ("the mediation of primeval event and reality of experience"): cf. E. OTTO, *Mythos und Geschichte im Alten Testament. Zur Diskussion einer neuen Arbeit von Jörg Jeremias*, in *BN* 42 (1988) 93-102, esp. p. 100.

LAWSUIT, DEBATE AND WISDOM DISCOURSE
IN SECOND ISAIAH

1. INTRODUCTION

Ever since Old Testament form criticism coined the term and genre 'prophetic lawsuit', its structure, origin and nature in Second Isaiah and elsewhere have been a matter of dispute. Reviews of the history of research are generally available[1]. Not only the terminology causes confusion, as may be inferred from discussions of the Hebrew verb *rîb*, the connotations of the terms 'lawsuit' and 'Gerichtsrede'[2], but also ideas about origin and development of the genre in the history of prophetism. In addition, the polemic genres in Second Isaiah[3] are often distinguished from lawsuits in older prophecy and dealt with separately[4]. A. Schoors even spoke about the Second Isaianic *rîb* against the nations as a genre *sui generis*, because more specifically than the usual prophetic lawsuit it dealt with the *Anspruchstreit* in defence of YHWH's claims[5]. Further distinction between the genres lawsuit and disputation/contention in Second Isaiah, each with its own characteristics and setting added even

1. For discussions about the prophetic lawsuit, its structure and original setting, see J. LIMBURG, *The Lawsuit of God in the Eighth Century Prophets* (Dissertation Union Theology Seminary Richmond), Virginia, 1969; A. SCHOORS, *I Am God Your Saviour: A Form-Critical Study of the Main Genres in Is. XL–LV* (SVT, 24), Leiden, 1973, pp. 176-189; K. NIELSEN, *Yahweh as Prosecutor and Judge: An Investigation of the Prophetic Lawsuit (Rib-Pattern)* (JSOT SS, 9), Sheffield, 1978, pp. 5-26; M. DE ROCHE, *Yahweh's Rîb against Israel: A Reassessment of the So-called "Prophetic Lawsuit" in the Preexilic Prophets*, in *JBL* 102 (1983) 563-574; D.R. DANIELS, *Is There a "Prophetic Lawsuit" Genre?*, in *ZAW* 99 (1987) 339-360.
2. About the root *rîb* itself, I.L. SEELIGMANN, *Zur Terminologie für das Gerichtsverfahren im Wortschatz des biblischen Hebräisch*, in *Hebräische Wortforschung*. FS W. Baumgartner (SVT, 16), Leiden, 1967, pp. 257-257; J. LIMBURG, *The Root* ריב *and the Prophetic Lawsuit Speeches*, in *JBL* 88 (1969) 291-304; DE ROCHE, *Yahweh's Rîb* (n. 1), pp. 563-566; DANIELS, *Is There a "Prophetic Lawsuit" Genre?* (n. 1), p. 340; G. LIEDKE, *rîb Streiten*, in *THAT* II, col. 771-777; H. RINGGREN, in *TWAT* VII, col. 496-501.
3. For this term SCHOORS, *I Am God Your Saviour* (n. 1), p. 176; H.D. PREUSS, *Deuterojesaja. Eine Einführung in seine Botschaft*, Neukirchen-Vluyn, 1976, p. 21.
4. Especially because of the lawsuits against the nations and gods 41,1-7; 21-29; 43,8-13, 44,6-8; see E. VON WALDOW, *Der traditiongeschichtliche Hintergrund der prophetischen Gerichtsreden* (BZAW, 85), Berlin, 1963, pp. 42-53; SCHOORS, *I Am God Your Saviour* (n. 1), pp. 239-244; NIELSEN, *Yahweh as Prosecutor* (n. 2), pp. 62-73; DE ROCHE, *Yahweh's Rîb* (n. 1), p. 571 deals with them separately because of their trilateral nature.
5. SCHOORS, *I Am God Your Saviour* (n. 1), p. 239; NIELSEN, *Yahweh as Prosecutor* (n. 1), p. 66.

more to this confusion. However, this form-critical distinction introduced and worked out by Begrich and gradually refined by other scholars[6], obscured the lack of conspicuous difference in style of reasoning
between discourse texts that use legal language and texts that do not in
Second Isaiah. In my thesis, I mounted a case for abandoning this secondary and highly arbitrary form-critical distinction[7]. I hope, it will
please Wim Beuken that after so many years I return to our first love,
Second Isaiah. In this contribution to his *liber amicorum*, I will try to
gather up the *quaestio* of the contention where I left it since.

2. PROPHETIC LAWSUIT, CULTIC LAWSUIT, COVENANT LAWSUIT

Beside prophetic *rîb* or prophetic lawsuit, the form-critical terms
'cultic lawsuit' and 'covenant lawsuit' have been used. They stand together for three different origins that have been suggested. The term
'cultic lawsuit' intends to indicate that the origin of this prophetic genre
was sought and found in the cult of ancient Israel[8]. One of the duties of
cult-prophets beside intercessions and prediction would have been to
raise YHWH's accusation and judgment against Israel when YHWH's
covenant had been violated. The prophetic lawsuit was supposed to have
its roots in this ritual of the cultic lawsuit. In his dissertation on Second
Isaiah von Waldow distinguished between prophetic lawsuits of a cultic
type (Isa 41,1-5; 41,21-29; 43,8-13; 44,6-8) and one of a 'profani-
sierter'(secularized) type (Isa 45,22-28; 50,1-3). Both were spoken in
cultic gatherings of the exiled Judaeans in Babylon[9]. Characteristic for

---

6. See following SCHOORS, *I Am God Your Saviour* (n. 1), R.F. MELUGIN, *The Formation of Isaiah 40–55* (BZAW, 141), Berlin, 1976, once more J. VAN OORSCHOT, *Von Babel
zum Zion. Eine literarkritische und redaktionsgeschichtliche Untersuchung* (BZAW,
206), Berlin - New York, 1993, pp. 24ff., 29ff.

7. In addition, I indicated that genre and style of ancient Near Eastern literary dia-
logues and contentions might throw more light upon the reflectional discourse in Second
Isaiah, M. DIJKSTRA, *Gods voorstelling. Predikatieve expressie van zelfopenbaring in
Oudoosterse teksen en Deuterojesaja* (Dissertationes Neerlandicae. Series Theologica, 2),
Kampen, 1980, pp. 174-180, 376-380.

8. E. WÜRTHWEIN, *Der Ursprung der prophetischen Gerichtsrede*, in *ZTK* 49 (1952)
1-16; F. HESSE, *Wurzelt die prophetische Gerichtsrede im israelitischen Kult?*, in *ZAW*
65 (1953) 45-53; SCHOORS, *I Am God Your Saviour* (n. 1), p. 189. The term 'cultic lawsuit' has the disadvantage that it seems to refer to a religious or cultic court, cf. e.g. Ezek
44,23-24; 2 Chr 19,8-11; perhaps also Hos 4,3. See J.R. LUNDBLOM, *Contentious Priests
and Contentious People in Hosea IV 1-10*, in *VT* 36 (1986) 53-57.

9. E. VON WALDOW, *Anlaß und Hintergrund der Verkündigung des Deuterojesajas*
(Diss. Bonn), 1953, pp. 37-39; later he modified this view under the influence of H.J.
BOECKER, *Redeformen des Rechtslebens im Alten Testament*, 2. erweiterte Auflage
(WMANT, 14), Neukirchen-Vluyn, 1970, see E. VON WALDOW, *Der traditionsgeschicht-*

both of them was the identity of judge and plaintiff, who should not be confused in secular legal practice. The third term stands for a third line of thought, which explains prophetic *rîb* against the backgrond of international law. Form and ceremonies in the realm of proposing, concluding and breaking treaties of ancient Near Eastern diplomacy, would have provided the model for prophetic lawsuits. Also in this context, the identity of judge and plaintiff would be an explicable motive. According to this view, a suzerain could charge a vassal with breach of treaty and then bring judgment against him as YHWH did to Israel after breaking the covenant[10].

A more detailed discussion of these origins and analogies may be dispensed with here[11]. Let it suffice that as yet no conclusive unequivocal evidence exists linking the *rîb* texts with either the form of treaties and the content of the Sinai Covenant. Even the appeal to Heavens and Earth cannot unequivocally be understood as evidence for such a treaty or covenant background. In general, it may be assumed that legal speech forms in treaties have their origins in ancient Near Eastern legal forms and practice too. Since international treaties in structure and intention often follow the basic forms of sworn statements in private contracts, court decisions and so on, it is hardly conceivable that international treaty law as such served as a literary intermediary for the prophetic *rîb* genre. More plausibly legal speech forms and practice found their way separately into international diplomacy, into prophetic discourse and wisdom literature.

A rather broad consensus exists that the *Redeformen des Rechtslebens* in prophetic lawsuits have to be sought primarily in the adoption and adaptation of legal speech forms from ancient Israelite jurisdiction. The term 'lawsuit' is less adequate for such a prophetic genre using such legal language, because a real court case or lawsuit supposes at the least a complex of legal procedures (summons to the court, legal charges, requisitoir, defence and so on). Westermann warned against a too detailed analysis of prophetic lawsuits "... weil es sich um eine stark *abstrahierende* Stilisierung, nicht um eine Nachahmung der Rechtsakte

liche Hintergrund (n. 4), pp. 12-25; see SCHOORS, *I Am God Your Saviour* (n. 1), pp. 185-186; NIELSEN, *Yahweh as Prosecutor* (n. 1), pp. 19-21.

10. H.B. HUFFMON, *The Covenant Lawsuit in the Prophets*, in *JBL* 78 (1959) 285-295; J. HARVEY, *Le "Rîb-pattern" réquisitoire prophétique sur la rupture de l'alliance*, in *Bib* 43 (1962) 172-196; ID., *Le plaidoyer prophétique contre Israël après la rupture de l'alliance. Étude d'une formule littéraire de l'Ancien Testament* (StB, 22), Bruges - Paris, 1967.

11. See the criticism of R.E. CLEMENTS, *Prophecy and Tradition*, Atlanta, GA, 1975, pp. 19-23; D.J. MCCARTHY, *Der Gottesbund im Alten Testament* (SBS, 13), Stuttgart, 1967, pp. 60-61; NIELSEN, *Yahweh as Prosecutor* (n. 1), pp. 54-55; DE ROCHE, *Yahweh's Rîb* (n. 1), pp. 573-574; DANIELS, *Is There a "Prophetic Lawsuit" Genre?* (n. 1), pp. 355-358.

handelt"[12]. The impression often created by such texts that the roles of judge, witness, plaintiff and so on are not carefully kept apart, is presumably more the result of literary abstraction than a development in covenant theology. That YHWH usually acts as a plaintiff and sometimes may utter the verdict too is also explicable within the framework of two contending parties arguing their cases[13]. In secular legal practice it was certainly not felt appropiate that a plaintiff or prosecutor acted as a judge, even if such a situation may have occurred occasionally[14].

When looking for the origins of the lawsuit in Second Isaiah, certain elements of circular reasoning are not always apparent during debates. For instance, speaking of the original setting of the prophetic lawsuit, one has to be aware that the majority of texts on which reconstructions of the administration of justice and its distinctive speech forms are based, stem from prophecy and wisdom[15]. Apart from prophecy and wisdom, the Old Testament does not contain many narrative texts that clarify legal practice and language[16]. The preliminary observation that the style of reasoning and argument in secular legal administration was imitated also in other realms of ancient Near Eastern settings and sources of literature (international diplomacy, incantation literature, school debates and so on) supports the assumption that this may have happened in prophetic literature too. As in other types of literature, the discourse of arguing and giving evidence was adopted from its original *Sitz im Leben* in a secondary literary setting, i.e. *Sitz in der Rede/ Literatur*[17]. The general setting of greater parts of Second Isaiah's discourse may indeed be found in the speech forms of legal administration. Despite this conclusion, I have continued to look for a more specific literary setting which Second Isaiah used and adapted for his message.

12. C. WESTERMANN, *Forschung am Alten Testament. Gesammelte Studien* (TB, 24), München, 1964, p. 135.
13. DE ROCHE, *Yahweh's Rîb* (n. 1), pp. 569-572; H. RINGGREN, in *TWAT* VII, col. 501.
14. BOECKER, *Redeformen* (n. 1), pp. 86-89; SCHOORS, *I Am God Your Saviour* (n. 1), pp. 241-242. The case of 1 Sam 22,11-16 is not really conclusive. The incident is described as a case of Saul's high-handedness of which his servants disapprove (a mock trial!), see DE ROCHE, *Yahweh's Rîb* (n. 1), pp. 572-574.
15. For this kind of legal language, metaphors and style in the context of wisdom discourse of wisdom dialogue, see Job 9,2-3.14-16.27-29; 11,10; 13,3; 16,19-21; 19,6-7; 24-25; 23,2-7, also the speeches of Elihu in Job 32,12; 33,5.13.31-33; 35,1-4 etc.
16. Josh 7; Judg 6,29-31; 20,1-11; 1 Sam 22,6-19; 1 Kings 21; Ruth 4; Jer 26.
17. G. FOHRER, *Exegese des Alten Testaments* (UTB, 267), Heidelberg, 1973, pp. 85, 95-97; O.H. STECK, *Exegese des Alten Testaments. Leitfaden der Methodik. Ein Arbeitsbuch für Proseminare, Seminare und Vorlesungen*, Neukirchen-Vluyn, [12]1989, pp. 116-117.

3. SECOND ISAIAH AND ANCIENT NEAR EASTERN WISDOM DISCOURSE

Where does this specific discourse of persuasion have its origin? In anticipation of a rhetorical analysis of Isa 40,12-31 (see below, 4), I take a closer look at the literary practice of wisdom as found in ancient Egyptian and Mesopotamian 'philosophy', those genres that the ancient Near East developed for reflection on human behaviour, divine dispensation and world order[18]. Despite a cautionary remark that Mesopotamian literature would not yield readily to modern theories of rhetorical criticism, William W. Hallo suggested that some potential insights are to be gained by a rhetorical approach to the literature which had its place in the formal curriculum of the scribal schools. After all, it is defendable that 'the birth of rhetoric' took place in Mesopotamia along with the related notion of Sumerian humanitas: *nam-lú-ulu$_6$*[19]. Forms of this primal Mesopotamian humanism or 'philosophy' about human etiquette, man's destiny and the operation of the world are not only the myths[20], but also the distinctive wisdom genres, especially the genres of discursive dialogue and soliloquy[21].

It is neither my intent to survey here ancient Near Eastern wisdom literature in general, nor the development of literary soliloquies and dialogues in particular. Recent studies and surveys are available and in this essay I would like to reap the fruits for my view on the literary form and origin of Second Isaiah's way of reflectional discourse. The use of the

18. W.G. LAMBERT, *Babylonian Wisdom Literature*, Oxford, 1960, pp. 1-20.

19. W.W. HALLO, *Origins: The Ancient Near Eastern Background of Some Modern Western Institutions* (Studies in the History and Culture of the Ancient Near East, 7), Leiden - New York - Köln, 1996, pp. 169-184, esp. 174-175, 183-184.

20. Concerning myth as 'primitive' speculative philosophy, see G.S. KIRK, *Myth: its Meaning and Functions in Ancient and Other Cultures*, Cambridge, 1970, p. 252; J.P. ALLEN, *Genesis in Egypt: The Philosophy of Ancient Egyptian Creation Accounts* (YES, 2), New Haven, 1988; H. Graf REVENTLOW, *Hauptprobleme der alttestamentliche Theologie im 20. Jahrhundert* (EdF, 173), Darmstadt, 1982, pp. 171-172, the last seeing mythical thinking as a form of "menschliche Weltbewältigung".

21. Cf. DIJKSTRA, *Gods voorstelling* (n. 7), pp. 174-180; D.O. EDZARD, *Literatur*, in *RLA* VII, pp. 43-44; B. ALSTER, *Sumerian Literary Dialogues and Debates and their Place in Ancient Near Eastern Literature*, in E. KECK et al. (eds.), *Living Waters*. FS F. Lokkegaard, Copenhagen, 1990, pp. 1-16; M.E. VOGELZANG, *Some Questions about the Akkadian Disputes*, in G.J. REININK – H.L.J. VAN STIPHOUT (eds.), *Dispute Poems and Dialogues in the Ancient and Medieval Near East: Forms and Types of Literary Debates in Semitic and Related Literatures* (OLA, 42), Leuven, 1991, pp. 47-58; K. VAN DER TOORN, *The Ancient Near Eastern Literary Dialogue as a Vehicle of Critical Reflection*, in *ibid.*, pp. 59-76; S. DENNING-BOLLE, *Wisdom in Akkadian Literature, Expression, Instruction, Dialogue* (Mededelingen en Verhandelingen Ex Oriente Lux, 27) Leiden, 1992, pp. 85-176. On monologues, see DIJKSTRA, *Godsvoorstelling* (n. 7), pp. 41-42; D.O. EDZARD, *Selbstgespräch und Monolog in der akkadischen Literatur*, in T. ABUSCH et al. (eds.), *Lingering over Words*. FS W.L. Moran (HSS, 37), Atlanta, GA, 1990, pp. 149-162.

term 'Dialogue' as a genre designation goes back to classical antiquity[22], but the art of persuasion is certainly older, even if cuneiform literature did not provide us with a work or canon of rhetorical prescriptions as in the case of classical literature. Still, I consider these practical works of wisdom to be a better source for the study of the art of persuasion in Second Isaiah than classical or modern rhetorical theories[23]. We do not know what name was given to this form of wisdom literature in the ancient Near East itself. Even the word 'Wisdom' might be a misnomer as applied to this kind of Mesopotamian literature, and 'humanities' be the better term[24], but scholars agree that a conventional form of reflective prose originated from discussions as early as in the 2nd Millennium BC[25], whether in verbal exchanges of everyday life or in the schools, though its *floruit* belonged to the 1st Millennium BC. Dialogue and debates form part of many a genre from the ancient Near East, ranging from epic poems (Gilgamesh and Enkidu, Gilgamesh and Ishtar) to the Sumerian 'tensions' (contentions[26]) and models of legal debate from the Edubba literature. A compound of real or rhetorical questions and answers, affirmations, accusations and refutations permeates the style of all kinds of debates, including school debates, literary styled court procedures and even diplomatic letters[27]. Such legal debates and juridical speech left a strong imprint on more fictional literature as particularly might be noted in the Sumerian disputations. The impact of legal language and procedure may be less in the later Akkadian offshoots[28] and in literary dialogues, but the idea of vindication still prevails. They continue to betray affinities with legal contention and school disputations. The proprium of literary dialogues in the more restricted sense, is that

22. Cf. A. HERMAN – G. BARDY, *Dialog*, in *RAC* III, col. 928-955; VAN DER TOORN, *The Ancient Near Eastern Literary Dialogue* (n. 21), pp. 59-60; DENNING-BOLLE, *Wisdom* (n. 21), pp. 69-84.

23. Y. GITAY, *Prophecy and Persuasion: A Study of Isaiah 40–48* (Forum Theologiae Linguisticae, 14), Bonn, 1981, pp. 34-45.

24. LAMBERT, *Babylonian Wisdom Literature* (n. 18), p. 1; but see DENNING-BOLLE, *Wisdom* (n. 21), p. 29; HALLO, *Origins* (n. 19), pp. 184-185.

25. See the Ugaritic "juste souffrant" (*RS* 25.460 = *Ugaritica* V, 265-273) as a predecessor of *Ludlul bēl nēmeqi*, W. VON SODEN, in *UF* 1 (1969) 191-193; ID., in *TUAT* III/1, pp. 140-143. Old Babylonian "a man and his god", an early dialogue (*pace* Lambert), perhaps akin to a Sumerian prototype (cf. S.N. KRAMER, ³*ANET*, pp. 589-591; W. VON SODEN, in *TUAT* III/1, pp. 135-140; DENNING-BOLLE, *Wisdom* (n. 21), pp. 158-165.

26. See the surveys in DIJKSTRA, *Gods voorstelling* (n. 7), pp. 174-177; J. BOTTÉRO, *La «tenson» et la réflexion sur les choses en Mésopotamie*, in REININK – VAN STIPHOUT (eds.), *Dispute Poems and Dialogues* (n. 21), pp. 7-22. On the Akkadian disputations, see VOGELZANG, in *ibid.*, pp. 46-57; DENNING-BOLLE, *Wisdom* (n. 21), pp. 85-135; HALLO, *Origins* (n. 19), pp. 175f.; excerpts in *TUAT* III/1, pp. 180-187.

27. See, for instance, R. HESS, *Rhetorical forms in EA 162*, in *UF* 22 (1990) 137-138.

28. On this matter, see VOGELZANG, in REININK – VAN STIPHOUT (eds.), *Dispute Poems and Dialogues* (n. 21), pp. 56-57.

they do not cover a spectrum of subjects, but concentrate on a *quaestio*, a single issue[29]. They enclose a literary genre developed for critical reflection on traditional wisdom topics. Usually, they hold to a basic dialogue between two or more speakers.

The wisdom soliloquy goes a step further in just using a dialectic style of reasoning. The form of the external dialogue is abandoned for an internal or inner dialogue, as for instance in the Egyptian poem of "The Man who was tired of Life" (or "A Dispute between a man and his Ba'"), perhaps also the Babylonian "Theodicy", in which dialogue in the sense of a real duologue or conversation is no longer transparent. What counts in these discussions is the deliberate attempt to contrast opposite views in order to test traditional tenets. Such is true also in parts of Ecclesiastes where the Preacher talks to himself and puts his own achievements to the test, struggling in vain for understanding. Finally, still another literary genre of reflective nature is perhaps developed and therefore to be distinguished from the dialogue: the soliloquy that is essentially dialogical in structure and nature, a dramatic composition that discusses an issue in a continuous discourse with – or even without – an audience representing two or more contrasting views. As indicated above, Westermann rightly noted the inadequacy of such designations as disputation and *Gerichtsrede*, because in Second Isaiah they are not debates that contain opposite views, or where different voices state their case[30]. They are very one-sided in a sense, being in reality soliloquies, even when the speaker addresses and quotes his audience. Actually, some speeches in Second Isaiah come close to the kind of reflectional literature that we meet in such inner dialogues as *ludlul bēl nēmeqi*, the epilogue of Job (Job 29–31), the speeches of Elihu (Job 32–37) and the divine speeches in the Book of Job (Job 38–41). Each from their own perspective they articulate questions and strive after answers that seek to arrive at a new theological perspective.

4. "WHO HAS EVER MEASURED THE WATERS IN THE HOLLOW OF HIS HAND?" (ISA 40,12-31)

Usually the poem Isa 40,12-31 is classified as a disputation. Despite the efforts to define the disputation as an indepedent genre[31], doubts

---

29. VAN DER TOORN, in REININK – VAN STIPHOUT (eds.), *Dispute Poems and Dialogues* (n. 21), pp. 61-65.

30. WESTERMANN, *Forschung am Alten Testament* (n. 12), p. 125; W.A.M. BEUKEN, *Jesaja IIa* (POT), Nijkerk, 1979, p. 35.

31. For this discussion, see VON WALDOW, *Der traditiongeschichtliche Hintergrund* (n. 4), pp. 47-50; H.J. HERMISSON, *Diskussionsworte bei Deuterojesaja. Zur theolo-*

were expressed time and again whether one should speak of a genre[32]. As we indicated before, the differences between lawsuit and dispute are arbitrary, if they exist at all. The disputation speech may be considered a form or style of persuasion developed by wisdom teachers, which either in an instructional or a reflectional style seeks to convince the listeners. In my opinion, this poem[33] is a fine specimen of wisdom discourse[34]. It has been said before that the opening verses belong to a wisdom type of disputation[35]. but I think that the influence of wisdom discourse extends far beyond the first series of rhetorical questions and statements. The whole poem is deeply influenced by wisdom vocabulary and its lines of reasoning.

The questions introduced by *mî*, which are typical of wisdom rhetoric, invite an implied audience to respond to the question who assisted YHWH when he made the Heavens and the Earth, not to answer it. Who assisted him as his counsellor? There is some irony in these questions.

gischen Argumentation des Propheten, in *EvT* 31 (1971) 665-680; MELUGIN, *Formation* (n. 6), pp. 28-44; SCHOORS, *I Am God Your Saviour* (n. 1), pp. 188-189; PREUSS, *Deuterojesaja* (n. 3), pp. 21-22; B.D. NAIDOFF, *The Rhetoric of Encouragement in Isaiah 40 12-31: A Form-Critical Study*, in *ZAW* 83 (1981) 62-63; L. RUPPERT, *Die Disputationsworte bei Deuterojesaja in neuem religionsgeschichtlicher Sicht*, in R. LIWAK – S. WAGNER (eds.), *Prophetie und Geschichtlicher Wahrheit*. FS S. Herrmann, Stuttgart - Bern - Köln, 1991, pp. 317-325.

32. MELUGIN, *Formation* (n. 6), p. 31; see also Westermann's criticism, in *Forschung am Alten Testament* (n. 12), p. 125: "Es genügt hier von der Redeform der Disputation zu reden"; he preferred the term *Bestreitung* (refutation), because only one of the parties is heard. See, moreover, HERMISSON, *Diskussionsworte bei Deuterojesaja* (n. 31), pp. 665-669; D. MICHEL, *Deuterojesaja*, in *TRE* III, p. 512; VAN OORSCHOT, *Von Babel zum Zion* (n. 6), p. 24.

33. The unity of this text is defended by BEUKEN, *Jesaja II^A* (n. 30), pp. 35-38; WESTERMANN, *Forschung am Alten Testament* (n. 12), pp. 127-132; *Interpreter's Bible* V, pp. 434-446; MELUGIN, *Formation* (n. 6), pp. 90-93, PREUSS, *Deuterojesaja* (n. 3), pp. 50-51; R.J. CLIFFORD, *The Function of Idol Passages in Second Isaiah*, in *CBQ* 42 (1980) 450-464, esp. p. 457; GITAY, *Prophecy and Persuasion* (n. 23), pp. 81-97; NAIDOFF, *The Rhetoric of Encouragement* (n. 31), pp. 62-76, but some assume that the text was composed from four independent sections, originally independent disputations in form and content (*e.g.*, Melugin, Naidoff and see also VAN OORSCHOT, *Vom Babel zum Zion*, pp. 93-94); Westermann, Muilenburg, Beuken and Gitay think of an original literary unit. A different view on the integrity of Isaiah 40 is found in J.C. DE MOOR, *The Integrity of Isaiah 40*, in M. DIETRICH – O. LORETZ (eds.), *Mesopotamica – Ugaritica – Biblica*. FS K. Bergerhof (AOAT, 232), Kevelaer - Neukirchen-Vluyn, 1993, pp. 181-215.

34. Connections between Second Isaiah and wisdom literature are more often suggested, than systematically discussed; see VON WALDOW, *Der traditionsgeschichtliche Hintergrund* (n. 4), pp. 47-53; S. TERRIEN, *Quelques remarques sur l'affinité de Job avec le Deutero-Isaïe*, in *Volume du Congrès. Genève 1965* (SVT, 15), Leiden, 1966, pp. 295-210; B. GROSSE, *La création en Proverbes 8,12-31 et Isaïe 40,12-24*, in *NRT* 115 (1993) 186-193.

35. VON WALDOW, *Der traditionsgeschichtliche Hintergrund* (n. 4), pp. 47-50, MELUGIN, *Formation* (n. 6), pp. 31-35; VAN OORSCHOT, *Von Babel zum Zion* (n. 6), p. 24.

From the start there might be some confusion over the antecedent of these *mî* questions. Is it YHWH or someone else using his hand as a measuring instrument[36]? But rhetorical questions do not ask for information; they are meant to produce effect[37]. In the rhetorical development of this first sentences it becomes clear that the question states an issue: Who is able to teach God how to act in world and history? The questions infer that mortal man is nothing compared with El Yahweh. The nearest parallel to such an opening offers Job 38,2-4:

> Who is the one who darkens my counsel
> with words without knowledge!
> Brace yourself like a man;
> I will question you, and let him instruct me
> Where were you when I laid earth's foundation
> explain to me, if you gained insight.
> Who marked off its dimensions you surely know
> or who stretched a measuring line across it...

In the Book of Job YHWH addresses Job directly, but it is quite easy to transform it into the usual indirect style of the wisdom discourse found in our text. Likewise, for instance, Proverbs 30,4 and similar rhetorical questions found in Elihu's discourse (Job 34,13; 36,23). "Die Rede als ganze ist ein Streitgespräch des Weisen, das sich außer an den Gesprächsgegner an den umsitzenden Kreis der Genossen wendet und ihm das Problem zur gemeinsamen Prüfung und Beurteilung vorlegt"[38]. Compare the question: "Who appointed him over the earth? Who put him in charge of the whole world?"(Job 36,23)[39]. There are many similarities in form and content between the speeches of Elihu and Isa 40,12-31[40]. These questions share the same issue in their contexts: the impossi-

---

36. This ambiguity is often understood as a dilemma: cf. BEUKEN, *Jesaja II^A* (n. 30), p. 40; J.L. KOOLE, *Jesaja II/1* (COT), Kampen, 1985, pp. 52-53. However, it is an overt question probably deliberately phrased as such. It reminds me of a school-teacher who once asked her class on Mothers' Day: "Who is always looking after you?" She, of course wanted to start the class talk about 'mother', but all the childern answered in unison: God!

37. GITAY, *Prophecy and Persuasion* (n. 23), pp. 88-89.

38. G. FOHRER, *Das Buch Hiob* (KAT, 16) Gütersloh, 1963, p. 466. The secondary origin of Elihu's discourse in the Book of Job is generally accepted. It deals with the *quaestio* thrown up in Job speeches, but it is not really part of the debate despite the setting. The author couched his refutation in a personal criticism of Job and his friends (*ibid.*, pp. 40-41, 445). Though in reality a long soliloquy, its style is dialogic throughout. Alternately, it addresses Job and his friends, but an even broader audience sometimes is implied (Job 34,1-4; 35,34).

39. The parallel with Isa 40,12-13 is clear. Job 36,23 reminds with *drkw* of Second Isaiah's *b'rh mšpṭ* and *drk tbwntw* (Isa 40,14). For similar questions, see Baruch 3,15.29ff., Sir 1,2-3.6-7; 18,4-5; 43,31.

40. Job 35,5 and Isa 40,26; 36,5 (*kbyr*//*kbyr kḥ*); 36,26 (*šqy'*), 37,23 (*šgy' kḥ*); 34,18f. and 40,23.

bility for any mortal or divine being to perceive the world and to grapple
with the purpose of life and with human destiny. Has there ever been a
human being, a primeval man who could act as a kind of divine
councellor[41]? Similar questions and statements are also posed in ancient
Mesopotamian wisdom literature:

> Who knows the will of the gods in heaven?
> Who understands the plans of Anzanunzu?
> Where have mortals learnt the way of god?
> (*Ludlul bēl nēmeqi* II, 36-38)
> Der Herr durchschaut das Reden der Götter im Herzen,
> was immer ... [...], seinen ... [...] kennt man nicht.
> Marduk durchschaut das Reden der Götter im Herzen.
> Kein Gott erfahrt seinen Ratschluß.
> (*Ludlul bēl nēmeqi* I, 29-32)[42]

The reflective nature of these words are clear from their context. The
writer is a devotee of Marduk and the real issue is why Marduk allows
his servant to suffer. He confirms that the world is made and ruled by
Marduk, from whom justice is expected by him and any of his servants,
but his ways are inscrutable even for the other gods, let alone men. The
author sets out to solve this personal mystery of his life, but raises his
problem to a general level in this maxime about the remoteness and in-
scrutability of the gods. Second Isaiah follows a similar line of reasoning. Starting from this premise of the inscrutable Creator God, he aims at
finding an answer to the complaints, the suffering of Israel, helping them
once more in history to deny the claims of rival gods.

Though I am aware that there is still a broad gap between the resigned
speech of such wisdom rhetoric and the impassioned prophetic oration
inspired by firm belief, the oratory style shows similar lines of reasoning
and flexibility in persuasion. Second Isaiah's oratory skills are not so
much marked by a rigid pattern of thought as by continuous appeals –
rational, emotional and ethical – to the understanding of the audience.
The discourse is replete with wisdom vocabulary, for instance, counsel,
insight, knowledge and teach, but also strength, power, indefatigable,
everlasting. Questions and arguments guide the listener to deeper insight
in the nature and works of the supreme El YHWH[43]. The *mî* questions

41. Cf. R.H. WHYBRAY, *The Heavenly Counsellor in Isaiah XL 13-14: A Study of the
Sources of the Theology of Deutero-Isaiah*, Cambridge, 1971. Allusions in Gen 5,22-24;
Job 15,7-8; 38,4.21; Ps 8,6; Jer 23,18-22 suggest knowledge of a kind of primal man
with almost divine status in Israelite tradition.

42. LAMBERT, *Babylonian Wisdom Literature* (n. 18), p. 41 and VON SODEN, in *TUAT*
III/1, pp. 116, 122 respectively.

43. G. VON RAD, *Weisheit in Israel*, Neukirchen-Vluyn, 1970, p. 34: "Auch das ist der
Stil der katechetischen Lehrfrage, die sich offenbar an Hymnenthemen anschließt". See

are rhetorical, meant to convince like the *hēn* statements[44]. In wisdom discourse, series of rhetorical questions often alternate with affirmative speech (Job 33,12-13; 34,12-13; 36,5.22-21.29-30; 40,36–41,3). Rhetorical questions, affirmative statements with the help of imperatives, cohortatives, *'al*+iussive/imperfect forms, noun clauses and descriptive imperfects make up the elements of a persuasive type of discourse. Compare the following string: "Do not long for the night..., beware of turning to evil..., Look! God is exalted in his power..., Who has prescribed his ways for him..., Remember..., Look! God is great beyond understanding..., who can understand how he spreads out the clouds...?" (Job 36,20-29). This line of persuasion leads to the *quaestio*: "To whom, then, will you compare El?". Though the divine name YHWH has been used in passing (Isa 40,13), it is significant that the ancient divine name El is used in this crucial question for the nations just mentioned. The name and appellative El was shared from days afar between Israel and the surrounding nations. Its frequent reappearance is further evidence that not only Israel, but also the nations belong to the backcloth of Second Isaiah's discourse.

Many scholars have difficulties with 40,18-20[45], finding in v. 40,21f the original continuation of the dispute. But 40,18-20 is by style and contents a genuine part of the kind of persuasive discourse, used by Second Isaiah. In such a discourse the parable as a device of persuasion has its natural place. Other prophets too knew how to use this device in their instructional and persuasive orations (Amos 3,3-8, Isa 5,1-4; 26,23-29)[46]. The transition from "To whom, then, will you compare El" to "what image/likeness..." is subtle, but deliberate. The first question is still in the realm of praise, but the second is modifying the question into a introductory phrase for a parable. In this way, the latter turns a sentence of hymnic exaltation[47] into an issue of reflection, as often happens

---

further *THAT* I, col. 307 and VON WALDOW, *Der traditionsgeschichtliche Hintergrund* (n. 4), p. 49.

44. The *hēn* statements are not an answer or a conclusion (von Waldow, Schoors, Melugin, Whybray *et al.*), see K. ELLIGER, *Deutero-Jesaja* I (BKAT, XI/1), Neukirchen-Vluyn, 1978, p. 45; GITAY, *Prophecy and Persuasion* (n. 23), pp. 88-91.

45. See lately VAN OORSCHOT, *Von Babel zum Zion* (n. 6), pp. 312-318 once more using the classical literary-critical instrumentarium in ascribing Isa 40,18-20 to a "Götzenbilderschicht", the last layer in a unlikely complicated and tedious redactional history of Isaiah 40–55.

46. C. WESTERMANN, *Vergleiche und Gleichnisse im Alten und Neuen Testament* (Calwer Theologische Monographien, 14), Stuttgart, 1984, p. 134; M. DIJKSTRA, *Gelijkenissen in Amos*, in *NTT* 48 (1994) 177-190, esp. pp. 179-180.

47. The sentence "To whom will you compare God" (also Isa 40,25; 46,5) has its closest parallels in hymnic praise, which expresses in Israel and the ancient Near East the incomparability of God: see C.J. LABUSCHAGNE, *The Incomparability of Yahweh in the*

in an instructional wisdom discourse: *l^emah haddābār domèh* "To what shall I compare this case..."[48]. The word 'image' or 'replica' (*d^emût*) is deliberately chosen to introduce the description of the manufacture of the *pèsèl*. The semantic range of the word *d^emût* refers to outward appearance, as well as to essence and quality. It allows for such a transition between a concrete meaning: replica and the abstract connotation *Vergleich* (comparison)[49]. Simultaneously, comparison with making an image includes elements of metaphorically used 'creational' vocabulary. The parable is deliberately couched in a nominative form[50], describing the process of how to manufacture an idol (also 45,6-7[51])[52]. It happens in an ironically versed interrogative style, provoking the audience to respond to the implied allegation that God is a thing.

Would they agree to such a monstrous statement? The parable implies that El is fashionable as "the idol that a craftsman casts, a goldsmith overlays with gold, soldering it with silver joints[53]. The thing that is fashioned from a levy..."[54]. Would the supreme God be subject to the

Old Testament (Pretoria Oriental Series, 5), Leiden, 1966. The formula of incomparability is often combined with epithets and participle predicates (*ibid.*, pp. 21-22, 28ff., 65: *e.g.*, Exod 15,11; Deut 33,26, 1 Kings 8,23; Pss 18,32ff.; 35,10; 77,14-15; 86,8ff.; 89,7ff.; 113,4-9; Isa 46,9f.; Jer 10,6, Micah 7,18; Dan 4:32, Job 36,22 etc.). For examples of ancient Near Eastern parallels, see *ibid.*, pp. 33-45; DIJKSTRA, *Gods voorstelling* (n. 7), pp. 98-129; RUPPERT, *Die Disputationsworte bei Deuterojesaja* (n. 31), pp. 317-325.

48. J. JEREMIAS, *Die Gleichnisse Jesu*, Göttingen, [8]1970, pp. 99-100.

49. H.D. PREUSS, in *TWAT* II, col. 266-277, esp. col. 275-276; KOOLE, *Jesaja II/1* (n. 36), p. 61.

50. On types of parables, see JEREMIAS, *Gleichnisse* (n. 48), pp. 99-102; DIJKSTRA, *Gelijkenissen* (n. 46), pp. 186-189.

51. Comparison of our text with 46,5f is instructive. The character of the parable is there even more indirectly formulated. The nominal subject is not the idol itself, but the people who offer silver and gold to have their own El made.

52. The majority of nominative parables have the form of a scene, describing an event of everyday life e.g. the farmer (Isa 28,23ff.), the watchman (Ezek 33,1ff.). Sometimes the parable is couched in interrogative style, e.g. Isa 28,23ff.; Amos 3,3ff.; see further Mk 4,26-29; Mt 13,30-34; Mt 7,25-27 = Lk 6,46; Mt 13,44; 13,45-46; 13,47-48; 18,12-14; 20,1-16; 21,28-32; Lk 10,30ff.; 12,16ff.; 14,28-33; 15,4-7.8-10; 15,12-32; 17,7-10; 18,1-8; 17,9-14.

53. See M.C.A. KORPEL, *Soldering in Isaiah 40:19-20 and 1 Kings 6:21*, in *UF* 23 (1991) 219-222.

54. *hamsukkan t^erûmāh* 'the thing that is fashioned from a levy' (see also the contribution of K. van Leeuwen in the present volume pp. 273-287). The participle is dependent on *happesel*. For this construction, see G. PFEIFER, *Das nachgestellte erläuternde Partizip – eine Stileigentümlichkeit des Amosbuches*, in *ZAH* 6 (1993) 235-238. We take *t^erûmāh* in its usual sense 'contribution, levy' and not as a postament: cf. J.P. FOKKELMAN, *ŚDY TRWMT in II Sam. 1 21a*, in *ZAW* 91 (1979) 290-292; KOOLE, *Jesaja II/1* (n. 36), p. 65; KORPEL, *Soldering* (n. 53), p. 222. See also Old-Babylonian *tarimtu* 'gift'. In a similar context, see *t^erûmat kèsèp ûn^eḥošèt* (Exod 35,21.24). Many proposals have been suggested for this old crux. For recent surveys, see BEUKEN, *Jesaja II^A* (n. 30), p. 46; KOOLE, *Jesaja II/1* (n. 36), p. 65; H.G.M. WILLIAMSON, *Isaiah 40,20 – A Case of*

craft of an artist, caught in an image made by an expert and placed on a pedestal by its worshippers? There is much irony in the detailed description, in particular in the metaphors for 'creation'. Though there are no immediate associations between YHWH who spread out the earth (Isa 42,5; 44,24; Ps 136,6) and who firmly established it, so that it cannot be moved (Isa 45,18; Pss 93,2; 104,5), and the manufacture of idols, the listeners could certainly get the point. The prophet seems to provoke his audience asking them to admit that his and their supreme deity El is identical to one of their handmade images. Worshippers from the nations, and certainly many of the learned priests, would object that a deity is represented in his image[55], but also that such a likeness does not imply a static, permanent and material identity. They would not really appreciate the prophets reproach that they exchanged the glory of the immortal God for images (Rom 1,13), but Second Isaiah does not discuss beliefs about God's material presence and visibility. He is polemicizing in order to induce the listener to his firm belief in the true nature of the inscrutable God, as he is praised in the hymns of Israel.

The parable introduced by a question, stating once more the issue of Gods (in)comparability, is an integral part of this discourse and marks it even more as a piece of theological persuasion. The transition between v. 21 and 22 is not smooth, but this is apparently due to the inclusion of a hymnic fragment into a wisdom discourse. Though using a persuasive type of discourse, Second Isaiah still hints at the sources of his faith and

---

Not Seeing the Wood for the Trees, in *Bib* 67 (1986) 1-19; M. HUTTER, *Jes 40,20 – kulturgeschichtliche Notizen zu einer Crux*, in *BN* 36 (1987) 31-36; A. FITZGERALD, *The Technology of Isaiah 40:19-20+41:6-7*, in *CBQ* 51 (1989) 426-446, esp. 441ff.; KORPEL, *Soldering* (n. 53), p. 222. I follow T.N.D. METTINGER, *The Elimination of a Crux? A Syntactic and Semantic Study of Isaiah xl 18-20*, in *Studies on Prophecy: A Collection of Twelve Papers* (SVT, 26), Leiden, 1974, pp. 77-83, maintaining the MT, though interpreting the text grammatically in a rather different way. I read the passive participle, derived from SKN II "to shape, fashion" (Gray, Schoors, Mettinger), attested in several derivatives in Ugarit (KTU 1.4 I.43 etc), assuming that the word *t^erûmāh* is the second accusative or accusative of material (GK §117hh) of the transitive verb. Elsewhere I will explain the background of this concise remark: the habit of making sacred objects with levies (Exod 32,2ff.; 35,22; Judg 8,22-27).

55. Egyptian and Mesopotamian reflective tradition tended to make a careful distinction between the image of the deity and his 'real presence'. On the mystical presence, or "Einwohnung", see E. HORNUNG, *Der Eine und die Vielen. Ägyptische Gottesvorstellungen*, Darmstadt, 1973, pp. 124ff.; S. MORENZ, *Ägyptische Religion* (Die Religionen der Menschheit, 8), Stuttgart, ²1977, pp. 158ff., esp. 161-162; K.H. BERNHARDT, *Gott und Bild. Ein Beitrag zur Begründung und Deutung des Bilderverbotes im Alten Testament* (Theologische Arbeiten, 2), Berlin, 1956, pp. 68ff.; PREUSS, *Verspottung fremder Religionen im Alten Testament* (BWANT, 92), Stuttgart, 1971, pp. 46-47; J. RENGER, *Kultbild*, in *RLA* VI, pp. 307ff; J. HEMPEL, *Das Bild in Bibel und Gottesdienst* (Sammlung gemeinverstandlicher Vorträge aus dem Gebiet der Theologie und Religionsgeschichte, 212), Tübingen, 1957, pp. 30-31; C.H. RATSCHOW, *Bilder und Bildverehrung*, in *RGG* I, col. 1268-1270.

theology: the hymns of Israel. In a wisdom discourse, topics of hymnic praise may become subject to reflection and serve the line of thought. For a question such as "Have not you understood the foundations of the earth?"[56], one could once more refer to the words of Elihu (Job 36,29[57]; 37,15-16). However, these questions were often meant to deny human understanding of the works of creation. In the Babylonian Theodicy too the Friend of the Sufferer adduces the works of the gods as evidence to teach the remoteness of the divine mind (*Theodicy*, XXIV)[58].

Second Isaiah's question goes one step further when he implicitly acknowledges that understanding the earth's foundations may lead to knowledge of God. The question here is not about the beginnings of Gods revelation, but it explores the feasibility of a natural theology: the world as source for human reflection about the divine[59]. It marks our discourse once more as a developing piece of reflectional wisdom. The message of the prophet appeals for *fides quaerit intellectum*, a faith rooted in observation and understanding of the world. In similar vein, we find the exhortation to lift the eyes and observe the Heavens in v. 26. Not to worship them but to view them as a source of knowledge created by YHWH, to serve as signs to mark seasons, days and years (Gen 1,14). The difference from Babylonian astral science and worship seems subtle, but it is of fundamental significance. In vv. 22-24, the point at issue is repeated, but in stylistic variation from the mouth of the Holy One himself (v. 25). The prophet still speaks to the nations and uses common language to denote God. As in West Semitic, *qādôš* alternates with El in v. 18 (also Job 6,10). The whole section is perhaps directed against astral worship, but focuses also on YHWH's praise as Creator and Redeemer of Israel. As such it anticipates the hymn that closes this discourse in Isa 42,10ff.

Sometimes Isa 40,27-31 is thought to be the only real dispute[60], because the view of the other party is cited. But even such a quotation does not turn a discourse into a real dialogue. It is of greater significance that

56. BEUKEN, *Jesaja II^A* (n. 30), p. 46; KOOLE, *Jesaja II/1* (n. 36), pp. 66-67 *et al.* opt for *môs^edôt hā'āreṣ* as an object. It is a subtle form of progressive parallellism (Beuken). The foundations are perhaps subject of the pu^cal NGD.

57. Reading *mî* instead of *'im* with the majority of commentaries.

58. LAMBERT, *Babylonian Wisdom Literature* (n. 18), p. 87; VON SODEN, in *TUAT* III/1, pp. 155-156.

59. A.S. HERBERT, *The Book of the Prophet Isaiah 40–66* (The Cambridge Bible Commentary), Cambridge, 1975, p. 27; VON RAD, *Weisheit* (n. 43), pp. 211-212. If Heaven and Earth can proclaim the glory of God (Ps 19), they may also be sources of understanding.

60. WESTERMANN, *Forschung am Alten Testament* (n. 12), p. 128; MELUGIN, *Formation* (n. 6), p. 35-36; SCHOORS, *I Am God Your Saviour* (n. 1), pp. 256ff.

the words of Israel's complaint are couched in legal terms[61]. However this does not make our text a lawsuit either. Once more it shows how futile the distinction between dispute and lawsuit remains, seeing that alleged disputes use legal language and style, whereas speeches in lawsuits are often couched in disputational phrases and speech forms.

5. A DISCOURSE ANALYSIS OF ISA 40,12–42,13

If Isa 40,12-31 indeed be a specimen of theological wisdom discourse, it would be difficult to accept that the prophet suddenly abandons his *quaestio*, when introducing YHWH's speech in 41,1ff. After his introductory discourse with mankind, Israel and the nations included, Second Isaiah does not start a new debate, but continues in the style of an 'inner dialogue' that invites the nations to respond to YHWH's claims over and against their own. I define here the 'inner dialogue' as a reflectional or persuasive discourse in which an implied author[62] not only addresses the involved parties, but also let them speak, 'hearing' them address one another. The internal speaker of the discourse becomes also the external narrator, who gradually introduces the contending parties (Isa 40,25, 27, 41,1ff. etc.). The parties alluded to remain participants in the whole discourse, either silent, or silenced, but as such they continue to participate in the 'dialogue'. This remains primarily a discourse of human reflection – even where God is introduced speaking –, using rhetorical means to persuade and to change the audience's attitude[63]. Rhetorical criticism in general and discourse analysis in particular have made clear that when studying devices of writing, the composition and promulgation of ancient scripts and their intended effect upon their audience, scripts and means of grammatical cohesion and characteristic verbal syntax[64], leading to semantic coher-

61. See the same collocation of *mišpāṭ* etc. in Job 19,7-8.
62. W.J.M. BRONZWAER, *Implied Author, Extradiegetic Narrator and Public Reader: Gérard Genette's Narratological Model and the Reading Version of Great Expectations*, in *Neophilologus* 62 (1978) 1-18; M. BAL, *De Theorie van vertellen en verhalen. Inleiding in de narratologie*, Muiderberg, ⁵1990, pp. 25-29.
63. Here I agree with GITAY, *Prophecy and Persuasion* (n. 23), pp. 2 and 229, but I believe also that such a rhetorical analysis will gain more from form-criticism and discourse analysis of the ancient Near Eastern rhetoric curriculum than from studying the art of persuasion according to classical rhetoric theory and practice, see also HALLO, *Origins* (n. 19), pp. 170-173.
64. From the vast literature on rhetorical criticism and discourse analysis in relation to Hebrew verb and syntax, we refer to W. SCHNEIDER, *Grammatik des biblischen Hebräisch. Ein Lehrbuch*, München, ¹⁰1980, pp. 182ff., 222ff.; P.J. MACDONALD, *Dis-*

ence, may help the hearer to make proper inferences from one proposition to the next. It should be borne in mind that the prophet's statement made in view of the nations and Israel early in his discourse, triggers a sequence of inferences for the whole discourse. If we become aware of coherency and a sense of logicalness and persuasion in the speeches following the opening discourse in Isa 40,12-31, it becomes also evident that they possess cohesion through a consistent set of characteristic strategies (or macrostructures), supported by a network of cohesive devices in grammar and style. We may conclude then that elements of different genres were composed into a higher unity of expository and persuative discourse.

Muilenburg, Beuken and others saw 41,1–42,4/13 as a single poem or composition[65], but as indicated above strings of semantic markers and fixed expressions have turned a sequence of apparently distinct speech-units into a cohesive discourse comprising at least Isa 40,12–42,13. The fact that the prophet introduces the *quaestio* to both the nations and Israel first and then introduces YHWH into a dialogue in which Israel and the nations participate, seems to imply the junction of different discoursive speeches into a higher entity of speech. On 41,1–42,4 Muilenburg remarks that the literary character of the poem is determined throughout by its setting in the court of law, its formal construction and its prevailing dramatic style[66]. But as said above, the literary setting is not a court of law, but a wisdom discourse whose rhetorical devices also include legal expressions as means of persuasion.

In Isa 41,1ff, YHWH starts to speak, apparently unintroduced after the prophet's prologue. But such an appearance is deceptive, for

course Analysis and Biblical Interpretation, in W.R. BODINE (ed.), *Linguistics and Biblical Hebrew*, Winona Lake, IN, 1992, pp. 153-175; R.E. LONGACRE, *Discourse Perspective on the Hebrew Verb*, in *ibid.*, pp. 177-189; D.A. DAWSON, *Text-Linguistics and Biblical Hebrew* (JSOT SS, 177), Sheffield, 1994, pp. 122-153; Th.B. DOZEMAN – B. FIORE, *Rhetorical Criticism*, in *Anchor Bible Dictionary* V, col. 712-719; D.F. WATSON – A.J. HAUSER, *Rhetorical Criticism of the Bible: A Comprehensive Bibliography with Notes on History and Method* (Biblical Interpretation Series, 4), Leiden - New York - Köln, 1993; J.C. EXUM – D.J.A. CLINES (eds.), *The New Literary Criticism and the Hebrew Bible* (JSOT SS, 143), Sheffield, 1993.

65. *Interpreter's Bible* V, pp. 447ff.; MELUGIN, *Formation* (n. 6), pp. 90ff.; BEUKEN, *Jesaja II*[A] (n. 30), pp. 35-38; CLIFFORD, *The Function of Idol Passages* (n. 33), pp. 452ff.; GITAY, *Prophecy and Persuasion* (n. 23), pp. 231-233 distinguishes three rhetorical units 40,12-31; 41,1-29; 42,1-13; see, however, W.A.M. BEUKEN, *Mišpāṭ: The First Servant Song and its Context*, in *VT* 22 (1972) 1-30; DIJKSTRA, *Gods voorstelling* (n. 7), pp. 380-385 on the coherence of the first Servant Song and Isaiah 40–41.

66. *Interpreter's Bible* V, p. 447.

YHWH's presence and ability to speak for himself is already indicated in 40,25. It is not his direct speech that comes as a surprise, but his words that take the named audience by surprise. Firstly, YHWH asks the islands to continue to listen quietly to him. In wisdom discourse, this Hiph^{c}il of ḤRŠ begs the challenged party, which is eager to respond, to wait and to listen till the speaker has finished (Job 13,13; 33,31-33)[67]. Job 33,31-33 is an interesting parallel, because Elihu's speech is also an 'inner dialogue', exactly as in our text, showing that the style of dialogue is imitated. Secondly, the peoples from afar are asked to renew their strength, or perhaps better: to take courage[68]. This should be taken in a positive sense[69]. It is a rhetorical device to encourage the listeners and to open their mind for another set of arguments.

Whether imitation of a court case is implied, as has often been suggested, remains to be seen. Actually YHWH suggests to an outside party, presumably Israel: "Let them (the peoples) come forward, and afterwards speak out. Let us together draw near for a judgment...". This may include both YHWH and his people, or both parties contending. These introductory sentences do not necessarily form the preliminaries to engage in a lawsuit. M. de Roche has mounted a considerable case for abandoning the term lawsuit in a number of alleged prophetic lawsuits[70], because when two parties are arguing their cases amongst themselves, they try to solve disagreement, but such an argument is not a trial as such. This does not mean that Second Isaiah never drew upon images and forms from legal procedures, but they do not immediately turn a discourse into a court case, or imply a legal setting. This kind of legal language is used also in wisdom dialogue and dispute[71]. Isa 41,1-4 continues the discourse started in 40,12ff. and introduces in a surprising turn of speech YHWH, who claims the amazing rise to power of king Cyrus as his work[72].

---

67. GITAY, *Prophecy and Persuasion* (n. 23), p. 118, n. 34.

68. I read imperative *haḥlîpû ko^{a}ḥ*, because of the parallellism, though the iussive parallel to v. 1bA is not impossible. MT may be the result of contextual harmonization, see for a similar formula Job 38,3; 40,7.

69. KOOLE, *Jesaja II/1* (n. 36), p. 87.

70. DE ROCHE, *Yahweh's Rîb* (n. 1), pp. 570-571; DANIELS, *Is There a "Prophetic Lawsuit Genre?* (n. 1), p. 340.

71. Cf. n. 15; see, for instance, *mišpāṭ* 'justice, case' as referring to the issue of disagreement between Job and God (Job 19,7; 23,4; 35,2 etc.).

72. The ancient view that Abraham is meant still has supporters; see references in KOOLE, *Jesaja II/1* (n. 36), pp. 87f.; G.H. JONES, *Abraham and Cyrus: Type and Antitype*, in *VT* 22 (1972) 304ff.

Vv. 5-7 are much disputed for integrity and content[73]. Most commentaries agree that YHWH still continues to speak to somebody about the islands. Because of the new turn of speech in v. 8: "But you, Israel my servant", I suppose that Israel was included in YHWH's speech in v. 1bB and is also spoken to in vv. 5-7. Presumably, these verses describe the islands' behaviour before YHWH's called them to listen. That is: their response to the military and political success of Cyrus[74]. Their fears were a poor counsellor for them. They drew near, came and started to encourage one another, saying each one to his ally: "Be strong!" (Deut 31,6.23; Josh 1,6 etc)[75]. As a kind of flash back (nachholende Erzählung) these verses describe not so much idol manufacture, but rather the futile preparations for war to encounter the impending threat of Cyrus[76]. Whether they refuse to be encouraged by YHWH's words remains an open question, but it is clear that YHWH continues to encourage his own people.

The reassurance of Israel couched in the well known form of the oracle of salvation or encouragement[77] does not need much discussion here. As in the opening discourse (40,12-31) after addressing Israel and the

73. ELLIGER, *Deutero-Jesaja* (n. 44), pp. 114-115,127ff.; R.P. MERENDINO, *Der Erste und die Letzte. Eine Untersuchung von Jes 40–48* (SVT, 31), Leiden, 1981, pp. 90ff.; lately replacement after 40,19f. was once more defended by FITZGERALD, *The Technology* (n. 54), pp. 431ff.; VAN OORSCHOT, *Von Babel zum Zion* (n. 6), p. 3144. However, I subscribe to the integrity of the text; see MUILENBURG, *Interpreter's Bible* V, pp. 451-452; MELUGIN, *Formation* (n. 6), p. 95; CLIFFORD, *The Function of Idol Passages* (n. 33), pp. 452ff.; KOOLE, *Jesaja II/1* (n. 36), pp. 84-85, 94ff.

74. So, for instance MUILENBURG, *Interpreter's Bible* V, pp. 451-452; R. NORTH, *The Second Isaiah*, Oxford, 1964, pp. 95-96; GITAY, *Prophecy and Persuasion* (n. 23), p. 117, n. 24; KOOLE, *Jesaja II/1* (n. 36), pp. 84-85.

75. Whether despite the futility of the divine images (Isa 40,18-20), the matter once more is referred to a new divine statue remains to be seen. V.7 may refer to weapon-manufacture and preparation for war, cf. *paṭṭîš* Jer 23,29; 50,23 (the hammer of the whole earth = Babel!); *dèbèq* as an element of an armour, or a mail-shirt, 1 Kings 22,34, see S. SMITH, *Isaiah Chapters XL–LV: Literary Criticism and History* (Schweich Lectures 1940), London, 1944, pp. 159-160.

76. KOOLE, *Jesaja II/1* (n. 36), pp. 94ff. supposes that the final words of v. 5 are a quotation from the mouth of the islands, referring to the approach of the enemies, i.e. Cyrus' armies, whereas v. 6 may refer to mutual support of allies. This would comply with the use of perfect and consecutive imperfect at the beginning and end of v. 5. See older translations such as KJV, RSV, NBG. If the description of 41,2-3 contains some veiled references to Cyrus' *Blitzkrieg* in 547 BCE, 41,5-7 might contain references to Croesus' efforts to form an alliance with the Greek cities, and the preparation of lavish gifts for the oracles of Delphi winning the favour of the Delphian Apollo, in order to learn the outcome of his confrontation with Cyrus, see HERODOTUS, I.51ff., 79.

77. WESTERMANN, *Forschung am Alten Testament* (n. 12), pp. 117ff.; SCHOORS, *I Am God Your Saviour* (n. 1), pp. 32ff; MELUGIN, *Formation* (n. 6), pp. 13ff.; J.M. VINCENT, *Studien zur literarischen Eigenart und zur geistigen Heimat von Jesaja, Kapitel 40–55* (BET, 5), Frankfurt a.M., 1977, pp. 125-136; for criticism on this distinction between oracle and proclamation of salvation, see DIJKSTRA, *Gods voorstelling* (n. 7), pp. 365-376.

nations together, YHWH turns to Israel[78] with a multitude of consoling words. Isa 41,8ff. is parallel to and at the same time continuation of 40,27-31. Isa 41,14-16 is a separate oracle clearly marked as such by a renewed address[79], but the *n'm YHWH* formula indicates that the divine discourse is still continued by the prophet, who finishes this time with the promise that Israel will rejoice in the Lord[80]. As part of the discourse, the oracles of encouragement are evoked by doubts about God's goodwill expressed in Israel's complaint that its cause is disregarded by his God (Isa 40,27). A similar situation may be found in *Ludlul bēl nēmeqi*, in which the sufferer's disappointed trust in Marduk is restored by favourable oracles given in several dreams[81].

I cannot deal here with all the syntactic, semantic ramifications and rhetorical devices that make out the coherent strategy and macrostructure of Second Isaiah's persuasive discourse at this point. The analysis of 42,17-20, which turns rather unexpectedly to a new image: desert travellers desperate for water, requires for more detailed analysis[82]. Scholars agree that they are individuals from Israel, but the outside party filing the complaint is more difficult to identify. So much seems clear that someone brings the debate back to reality after the high expectations of 41,8-16. Are the silenced islands finally speaking out, giving YHWH a piece of their mind? Perhaps the answer lies in the next part of the discourse. In Isa 41,21–42,9 the silent participants are the rival gods. Together with their worshippers, they are challenged to contend with YHWH and his people, perhaps in response to 42,17-20. In particular,

78. Note the reverse order Israel//Jacob different from 40,27 and 41,14 (also 41,1 LXX). For the significance of the inversion, see J.T. WALSH, *Summons to Judgement: a Close Reading of Isaiah xli 1-20*, in *VT* 43 (1993) 362-363.

79. Double oracles are more often found in Second Isaiah: 43,1-4+5-7; 44,1-5+6-11; 44,22-28+45,1-8; 45,9-13+14-16; 49,7+8-12; see P.B. HARNER, *The Salvation Oracle in Second Isaiah*, in *JBL* 88 (1969) 423 ff., esp. p. 426; DIJKSTRA, *Gods voorstelling* (n. 7), p. 322, n. 13. The female forms are due to the metaphors used *tl^ct//rmt* 'worm//grub': cf. DIJKSTRA, *Gods voorstelling* (n. 7), pp. 322-325; BEUKEN, *Jesaja II*[A] (n. 30), p. 80; KOOLE, *Jesaja II/1* (n. 36), p. 112.

80. The prophet as the implied speaker of our text refers to the Halleluja, the song of thanksgiving that Israel will sing after the victory over Israel's adversaries. They are not identical to the nations far off as one of the contending parties (41,1.5; 42,1.4.6), because this would not fit well with Second Isaiah's message. To take them as metaphors of physical hindrances and religious difficulties alone (KOOLE, *Jesaja II/1*, p. 115) falls somewhat short of the metaphor used of 'threshing the mountains'. More likely the powers that be are meant (v. 11; BEUKEN, *Jesaja II*[A], p. 84).

81. LAMBERT, *Babylonian Wisdom Literature* (n. 18), pp. 48ff., 345; VON SODEN, in *TUAT* III/1, p. 127. The most interesting one is the third in which a girl appears: "'Fear not', she said... 'Be delivered from your wretched state, you whoever have seen the vision in the night time'".

82. See lately WALSH, *Summons to Judgement* (n. 78), pp. 367ff.

the words *ûmē'ēllèh wᵉ'ēn yôᶜēṣ wᵉ'èš'ālēm wᵉyāšîbû dābār* "Amongst these (gods), there is no counsellor, no-one to give answer when I ask them", completes once more the general backcloth of contention, creating the backstage for presentation of the servant of the LORD in Isa 42,1ff. The gods finally disappear from the discourse, but the nations addressed in 41,1 remain present, even if they were asked to keep silent so that the gods could speak for themselves. In the perception of speaker and listeners they are still present, Israel included, when YHWH's devastating verdict is passed in 41,29. The presentation and installation of the Servant (42,1-7) is also intended for the nations and the islands far off.

The epilogue of YHWH (42,8-9) concludes the discourse with a personal statement of YHWH. V. 9 recalls clearly 41,22.26 and v. 8 the uselessness of the gods and their images, as in 41,29, as well as further back in 40,19-20; 41,6-7. In particular, the emphasis on the self-presentation as *'ᵃni YHWH hû' šᵉmî* "I am YHWH, that is my name" (42,8) finally superseding after the ancient divine name *hā'ēl YHWH*[83] the initially used El (40,18) seems to imply that the audience with which the discourse started is still supposed to be present. This agrees with the second plural pronoun in Isa 42,9 and the imperatives of the following hymn, which Second Isaiah used consistently to address the nations including Israel. Also the imperatives of the final hymn (42,10-13) are addressed to the world at large: *miqṣeh ha'āreṣ* "from the one end of the earth to the other", including Israel dispersed to all corners of the earth (Isa 43,5-6).

6. SUMMARY

Discourse analysis leads to the conclusion that Isa 40,12–42,13 is a rhetorical unity. Moreover I have established that this first discourse is addressed to mankind including Israel. Alternately mankind, the nations, Israel and even the gods participate. In this discourse the central issue is whether or not YHWH is willing to deliver Israel from slavery, and not so much his creational power. This divine power is not really challenged, let alone a point of issue, either in the ancient Near East, or in Israel. In this respect, Second Isaiah's discourse, like the discourses in

---

83. M. DIJKSTRA, *Yahweh-El or El Yahweh?*, in M. AUGUSTIN – K.-D. SCHUNCK (eds.), *»Dort ziehen Schiffe dahin...«: Collected Communications to the XIVth Congress of the International Organization for the Study of the Old Testament, Paris 1992* (BEATAJ, 28), Frankfurt a.M., 1996, pp. 43-52.

the Book of Job, fits into the patterns of ancient near Eastern Wisdom, but at the same time exceeds them, becoming trancedent in their outlook for exiled Israel. Though the composition usually excels in rhetorical consistency as for theme and style, transitions in the direction of speech are not always transparent, that is grammatically and semantically marked. In particular, the ironical objection of Isa 41,17 appears at first sight to come out of the blue, but can be construed as a sceptical reaction of YHWH's rivals, in a way confirming Israel's doubt about YHWH's will to save his people.

The use of legal style and refutation in this discourse aims at the sound judgment of the listeners. In other words, the text does not describe or even imitate legal procedures, let alone a lawsuit, either prophetic or cultic, but suggests at most a sphere of legal contention within the framework of a persuasive discourse. Legal language and metaphor are by nature well suited to serve such a discourse. They are not the record or the documents of a court case. Presumably, there was not any implied liturgical setting. In their final form these texts do not seem to serve a purpose other than to be a discourse couched in a persuasive and forensic style. A splendid piece of prophetic oratory in which Second Isaiah by all rhetorical means seeks to confirm his audience in its belief of Gods trancendence over nature, making a case for Israel's impending redemption and its election as YHWH's servant for the world.

Burgemeester Van Trichtlaan 26   Meindert DIJKSTRA
NL-3648 VH Wilnis

AN OLD CRUX
הַמְסֻכָּן תְּרוּמָה IN ISAIAH 40,20

In his commentary on Second Isaiah our now retiring colleague Beuken writes that it is "impossible to derive *hamm^{e}sukkān* from the stem *skn*, 'to be useful'". After having enumerated some of the problems and the answers that have been given till now, he concludes: "The discussion does not seem to be finished yet"[1]. It is to that discussion that this article will give a modest contribution.

In the context of Isaiah 40, v. 20 obviously constitutes the continuation of v. 19. Both verses deal with the fabrication of idols, though it is questionable whether in the verses 19 and 20 two different kinds of idols (a metal and a wooden one) are concerned or only one idol, a metal one (v. 19), with a wooden pedestal (v. 20).

About the question whether the two verses have constituted an original part of the message of the prophecy of Isaiah 40, the opinions are very different. According to a great part of scholars the verses 19 and 20 are to be considered as a secondary expatiation added to the preceding verse (18) that speaks of the incomparability of God[2]. The author who inserted here the passage about the idol(s) would have been inspired particularly by the term ערך דמות *'ārak d^{e}mūt*, (v. 18); he would have understood that term in the concrete sense of "to set up an image"[3], just like Aquila, Targum and Vulgate did. Some exegetes suppose that the verses speaking of the idol(s) originally constituted a separate unity to which Isa 41,7 or 41,6-7 would have belonged as well. Elliger speaks of a fragment from a "Spottlied auf die Götzenfabrikanten"[4]. As a consequence, the supporters of this vision transposed the verses 41,(6-)7 – where the craftsmen encourage

1. W.A.M. Beuken, *Jesaja* II^A (POT), Nijkerk, ^{2}1986, p. 46.

2. K. Budde, in A. Bertholet (ed.), *Die Heilige Schrift des Alten Testaments*, Tübingen, 1922-1923; P. Volz, *Jesaja* II (KAT), Leipzig, 1932; J. Steinmann, *Le livre de la consolation d'Israël* (LD, 28), Paris, 1960; G. Fohrer, *Das Buch Jesaja* III (ZBK), Zürich, 1964 (counts v. 18 also to the addition); C. Westermann, *Das Buch Jesaja: Kap. 40–66* (ATD, 19), Göttingen, 1966; J.L. Mc Kenzie, *Second Isaiah* (AB, 20), Garden City, NY, 1968; A.S. Herbert, *The Book of the Prophet Isaiah* (CBC), Cambridge, 1975; R.P. Merendino, *Der Erste und der Letzte. Eine Untersuchung von Jes. 40–48* (SVT, 31), Leiden, 1981, pp. 87ff.

3. K. Elliger, *Jesaja* II (BKAT, XI/1), Neukirchen, 1978, pp. 65ff., 73f.; Beuken, *Jesaja* II^A (n. 1), p. 45.

4. Elliger, *Jesaja* II (n. 3), p. 115, and see also pp. 66, 69.

each other in the realization of the image – to chapter 40, either between the verses 19 and 20 or after v. 20. The first way has already
been chosen by Condamin[5]. The second way has been followed by
NEB:

> 18 What likeness will you find for God
>   or what form to resemble his?
> 19 Is it an image which a craftsman sets up,
>   and a goldsmith covers with plate
>   and fits with studs of silver as a costly gift?
> 20 Or is it mulberry-wood that will not rot which a man chooses,
>   seeking out a skilful craftsman for it,
>   to mount an image that will not fall?
> 6[a] Each workman helps to others,
>   each man encourages his fellow.
> 7[a] The craftsman urges on the goldsmith,
>   the gilder urges the man who beats the anvil,
>   he declares the soldering to be sound;
>   he fastens the image with nails
>   so that it wil not fall down[6].

If 41,(6-)7 is placed after v. 20, the woodworker of v. 20 finds himself
somewhat strange and lost in between the metalworkers. If 41,(6-)7 is
inserted between v. 19 and v. 20, the metalworking is paid dispropor-
tionately attention to as well[7] (though in 44,9-20 the opposite is found!).
North rightly contests the moving of 41,(6-)7: "To bring in all the ludi-
crous details of xli. 6f. here would be to reduce the austere majesty of xl.
12-26 to something like farce"[8].

If the verses represent nevertheless an originally independent song on
the idols, it would be possible indeed to suppose that the prophet has
quoted parts of that song in different places of his prophecy.

The question whether the words under consideration are authentic and
whether they have always constituted part of Isaiah's prophecy in this

---

5. Vv. 6-7: A. CONDAMIN, *Le livre d'Isaïe* (EB), Paris, 1905; cf. B. DUHM, *Das Buch
Jesaja* (HKAT), Göttingen, 1914; F. FELDMANN, *Das Buch Isaias*, Münster, 1925; E.J.
KISSANE, *The Book of Isaiah* II, Dublin, 1943; A. PENNA, *Isaia* (La Sacra Bibbia), Torino,
1964; E. OSTY – J. TRINQUET, in *La Sainte Bible* (École Biblique de Jérusalem), Paris,
1973. Only v. 7: H. OORT, *Het Oude Testament* II, Leiden, 1901, p. 470; H.T. OBBINK –
A.M. BROUWER, *De Bijbel*, Leiden, [7]1949, p. 509.

6. Cf. FOHRER, *Jesaja* III (n. 2), (only v. 7); vv. 6-7: VOLZ, *Jesaja* II (n. 2), A.S.
HERBERT, *Isaiah* (n. 2), p. 25, thinks it possible that the passage 40,19-20 and 41,6-7 is
connected with 44,9-11, where in vv. 9-10 "the same word for image occurs". A.
SCHOORS, *Jesaja* (BOT, 9), Roermond, 1972, p. 252, inserts 41,6-7 after 40,19-20, but
takes the verses for authentical.

7. ELLIGER, *Jesaja* II (n. 3), p. 79.

8. C.R. NORTH, *The Second Isaiah*, Oxford, 1964, p. 86.

place[9], are, comparatively speaking, of a small importance[10]. The author who used the words of verses 19f. in the present context – either the prophet or a later editor – must have heard a significant meaning in the words in this place. The beginning of v. 19 may have been meant or heard as an answer on the question of v. 18: "To whom will you liken God?". The answer probably starts in that case with a new question: "May be to an image that…?".

The ה before פסל *pèsèl* is probably with LXX (μη) and Vulgata (*num*) to be considered as a particle of interrogation[11], though the possibility of an "Artikel zur Determinierung von Gattungsbegriffen" (Ges-K, §126 1) should not be excluded (cf. Elliger: "so ein Gottesbild"; Duhm: "so ein Schnitzbild"; Koole: "zo'n beeld"). In any case the ה as a particle of interrogation is not impossible: the gemination of the following פ does not constitute a deciding objection (cf. Lev 10,19; BL, §80g). The image spoken of in v. 19a is called פסל *pèsèl*. The noun פסל *pèsèl*, derived from the stem פסל, "to cut stone", originally indicated an image of stone, afterwards a carven, wooden image (beside מסכה *massēkā*, "a cast image"), but in Judg 17,3f. it is already a metal image.

V. 19 has brought about a lot of discussion, particularly about the last three words: ורתקות כסף צורף *ūr⁽ᵉ⁾tuqôt kèsèf ṣōrēf*. Does the word רתקות *r⁽ᵉ⁾tuqôt* mean a silver chain (cf. already Targum), that the goldsmith forges in order to adorn the image or to fasten it[12] or to provide it with a fence[13]? Or is to be thought of silver plates used for the further adornment of the gold covered image[14] (cf. Vulgata: *laminis argenteis figuravit argentarius*)? It is however worth while to consider Korpel's suggestion in *Ugarit-Forschungen* 23. First she draws attention to the

9. Defended by NORTH, *Second Isaiah* (n. 8), pp. 85-86; H. FREY, *Das Buch der Weltpolitik Gottes: Jes. 40–55*, Stuttgart, 1937, cf. M.C.A. KORPEL, *Soldering in Isaiah 40:19-20 and 1 Kings 6:21*, in *UF* 23 (1991) 219-222, spec. p. 219: "The structural analysis of the text … shows a remarkable symmetry in the chapter's three canto's". J.C. DE MOOR, *The Integrity of Isaiah 40*, in M. DIETRICH – O. LORETZ (eds.), *Mesopotamica – Ugaritica – Biblica*. FS K. Bergerhof, Neukirchen-Vluyn, 1993, pp. 181-216, spec. p. 207: "Obviously the elimination of v. 16 and/or v. 19-20 … leads to a destruction of this beautiful symmetry".
10. Cf. BEUKEN, *Jesaja II*[A] (n. 1), p. 45.
11. Buber, NEB, TOB, Groot Nieuws Bijbel; J. REIDER, *Etymological Studies in Biblical Hebrew,* in *VT* 2 (1952), p. 118; NORTH, *Second Isaiah* (n. 8), p. 85; P.E. BONNARD, *Le Second Isaï* (EB), Paris, 1972, p. 93; KORPEL, *Soldering* (n. 9), p. 219.
12. Leidse Vertaling (H. Oort), NEB ('studs of silver'); P. TRUDINGER, *"To whom then will you liken God?": Isaiah XL 18-20*, in *VT* 17 (1967) 220-225, spec. p. 224; HERBERT, *Isaiah* (n. 2), *ad locum*; S. SMITH, *Isaiah XL-LV*, London, 1944: "metal alloy poured into the sockets to keep the idol standing firmly upright, to avoid 'tottering'".
13. NORTH, *Second Isaiah* (n. 8), p. 86; cf. WESTERMANN, *Jesaja 40–66* (n. 2), *ad locum*.
14. T.N.D. METTINGER, *The Elimination of a Crux? A Syntactic and Semantic Study of Isaiah xl 18-20*, in *Studies on Prophecy* (SVT, 26), Leiden, 1974, pp. 77-83; cf. J.L. KOOLE, *Jesaja II/1*, Kampen, 1985, p. 63.

meaning of the Hebrew verb רתק, "to connect, chain" (cf. Nahum 3,10; (1QH 8,35); Eccles 12,6 *ketib*) and to cognate words in other Semitic languages, where the basic meaning of רתק is "to patch, to sew"; particularly one of the meanings of the verb *rtq* in Arabic, "to solder"[15], is interesting. Moreover, considering the fact "that in the ancient Near East a smith often used silver to join sheets of gold by soldering" (because of the lower melting point of silver)[16], she comes to the conclusion that רתקת *r*e*tuqōt* should be interpreted as "welds, soldering seams"[17]. In her translation of v. 19 she assumes in v. 19b a double duty of the *b* of v. 19a":

> and the goldsmith plates it with gold,
> and with *rtqwt* of a goldsmith's silver[18].

Preferable to this translation of v. 19b is in my view: "and he forges silver welds".

The principal problem is presented by v. 20 and particularly by the first words המסכן תרומה *ham*e*sukkān* t*e*rūmā*. If we do not delete the words for convenience' sake[19] or leave them aside as untranslatable because vv. 19b and 20a would only contain "die notdürftig zurechtgesetzten Trümmer eines ehedem umfangreicheren Textes" (Elliger)[20], v. 20a procures us several difficulties.

First of all we have to answer the question whether v. 20 speaks of the fabrication of a second (now wooden) image after the cast (probably metal) image of v. 19. The older translations (Dutch Statenvertaling, King James, Diodati, Segond, cf. already Kimchi) and also most of the translations and commentaries of the 19th and 20th centuries[21] think in-

---

15. KORPEL, *Soldering* (n. 9), p. 221, quoting A. BIBERSTEIN DE KAZIMIRSKI, *Dictionnaire arabe-français* I, Paris, 1860, p. 817.

16. KORPEL, *Soldering* (n. 9), p. 221, quoting A. LUCAS, *Ancient Egyptian Materials and Industries*. Revised edition of J.R. HARRIS (Histories and Mysteries of Man), London, 1989 (= 1962), pp. 216-217, 252.

17. KORPEL, *Soldering* (n. 9), pp. 221-222.

18. *Ibid.*, p. 219.

19. NORTH, *Second Isaiah* (n. 8), p. 85.

20. ELLIGER, *Jesaja* II (n. 3), p. 62.

21. Dutch Leidse Vertaling (H. Oort), Spanish *Versión moderna*, Italian *Versione riveduta*, Neue Zürcher Bibel, NBG, Buber, Osty–Trinquet, Bible de Jérusalem, TOB; A. DILLMANN, *Der Prophet Jesaja* (KEHAT), Leipzig, ⁵1890; BUDDE (n. 2); FELDMANN, *Isaias* (n. 5); J. RIDDERBOS, *De profeet Jesaja* (Korte verklaring der H. Schrift), Kampen, 1926; C.C. TORREY *The second Isaiah*, New York, 1928; FREY, *Das Buch der Weltpolitik Gottes* (n. 9); J. FISCHER, *Das Buch Isaias* II (*Kap. 40–66*) (Die Heilige Schrift des Alten Testaments), Bonn, 1939; KISSANE, *Isaiah* II (n. 5); L. DENNEFELD, *Les grands prophètes* (La Sainte Bible, VII), eds. L. PIROT – A. CLAMER, Paris, 1952; WESTERMANN, *Jesaja 40–66* (n. 2); BONNARD, *Le second Isaïe* (n. 11), p. 93: "Celui qui est démuni pour son ex-voto".

deed of a second image and relate the term מסכן *mᵉsukkān* to the word מסכנות *miskēnut*, "poverty" (Deut 8,9), and מסכן *miskēn*, "poor" (Eccles 4,13; 9,15f.; Sir 4,3; 30,14), a word that via Arabic has arrived in the Romance languages: Spanish *mezquino*, "poor, miserable", Italian *meschino*, "poor, needy, miserable", French *mesquin*, "parsimonious, miserable". In that line many translations render the beginning of v. 20 like the King James version does: "He that is so impoverished that he hath no oblation", or relate the notion "poor" to the offering: "Colui che fa povera offerta" (Diodati), "Wer nur ärmlich geben kann" (Neue Zürcher Bibel).

The poorer offering than the one from v. 19 would find expression in the material used for the given image: wood instead of metal. Dillmann interpreted this way of thinking as follows: "Ärmere, deren Mittel zu einem Metallbild nicht reichen, lassen es von Holz machen"[22]. This exegesis is based on the rendering of Hebrew המסכן תרומה *hamᵉsukkān tᵉrūmā* into: "He that is too poor for a (votive) offering". Such a translation is however hardly possible and does not find any support in the ancient versions. Moreover, it is not very likely that the man who is too poor for giving a metal image, would be able to recruit a skilful craftsman (v. 20b' חרש חכם יבקש לו *ḥārāš ḥākām yᵉbaqqēš lō*) for the fabrication of a wooden image[23].

Another group of scholars interpretes מסכן *mᵉsukkān* as a kind of tree[24] or as a kind of (hard)wood, either mulberry-wood[25] or ebony[26]. The supporters of this interpretation refer to the Akkadian term *mesukkannu* probably designating a certain species of trees, some of which produce the ebony[27]. It is very likely that Jerome already explained the word in this way as he writes: "amsuchan quod genus ligni est im-

22. DILLMANN, *Jesaja* (n. 21), p. 372.
23. Cf. DUHM, *Jesaja* (n. 5), p. 210; ELLIGER, *Jesaja* II (n. 3), p. 61.
24. MC KENZIE, *Second Isaiah* (n. 2), p. 20: מסכן תרומה *mᵉsukkān tᵉrūmā*: "a tree of consecration = a tree fit for consecration"; cf. H.G.M. WILLIAMSON, *Is. 40,20 – A Case of Not Seeing the Wood for the Trees*, in *Bib* 67 (1986) 1-20; M. HUTTER, *Jes. 40,20 – kulturgeschichtliche Notizen zu einer Crux*, in *BN* 36 (1987) 31-36.
25. Bible de la Pléiade II (1959), American Catholic Holy Bible (1961), NEB, HERBERT, *Isaiah* (n. 2), p. 23.
26. E. LIPIŃSKI, skn *et* sgn *dans le sémitique occidental du nord*, in *UF* 5 (1973) 191-207, spec. p. 206; cf. BEUKEN, *Jesaja* IIᴬ (n. 1), p. 46.
27. Cf. W. VON SODEN, in *Akkadisches Handwörterbuch* II, Wiesbaden, 1967, p. 678a: "Makan-Baum, Dalbergia Sissoo". For a hard and durable kind of wood has also been chosen by New American Bible; E. KÖNIG, *Das Buch Jesaja*, Gütersloh, 1926; I.W. SLOTKI, *Isaiah* (Socino Books of the Bible), Bournemouth, 1949; G.R. DRIVER, *L'Ancien Testament et l'Orient*, in *Orientalia et Biblica Lovaniensia* 1 (1957), p. 129; A.R. MILLARD, *Is. 40, 20, toward a Solution*, in *TynB* 14 (1964), pp. 12-13; KOOLE, *Jesaja* II/1 (n. 14), p. 65; cf. Groot Nieuws Bijbel: "Een beeld van duurzaam hout".

putribile". Some of the translators that opt for this interpretation transpose the following word תרומה *t^erūmā* to the end of v. 19, where they would characterize the "golden" image of v. 19 "as a costly gift" (NEB, Herbert). Most scholars, however, maintain תרומה *t^erūmā* in v. 20 and conceive it – like many of the adherents of the first mentioned exegesis of the verse – in the sense of "a votive offering"[28]. In this way Beuken translated v. 20a: "Als wijgeschenk kiest hij ebbehout, hout dat niet verrot" ("As a votive offering he chooses ebony, wood that will not rot"). The words עץ לא ירקב *'ēs lō' yirqab*, "wood that does/will not rot" are considered here as an apposition or as a (later added) elucidating gloss upon the less known word מסכן *m^esukkān*.

Against this explanation shoud not only be objected the strange fact that the apposition or gloss is separated then from the word מסכן *m^esukkān*, which it is supposed to elucidate, but also and especially the fact that in this way of interpretation v. 20 is not a logical continuation of v. 19. The question who is the person that chooses the wood and seeks out the skilful craftsman, remains unanswered. Is it the same person that unmentioned gave the order to make the image of v. 19, or is v. 20 speaking of another one? Here too arises the question whether the two verses deal with two different images, v. 19 with a metal, v. 20 with a wooden image, may be cut out of a tree? In this case the verses show a strange anticlimax: first a metal image richly adorned with gold and silver and then a simple wooden one without any precious metal. Is only one image dealt with, then the sequence is even more surprising: in that case one might expect that the fabrication of the wooden core (v.20) would have been mentioned before the covering with gold (v. 19).

A third way of interpretion explains מסכן תרומה *m^esukkān t^erūmā* as "he who prepares an image". LXX apparently thought already into this direction. That appears from the translation: ὁμοίωμα κατασκεύασεν αυτόν. LXX uses here the same word ὁμοίωμα as in the question of v. 18: τίνι ὁμοιώματι ὁμοιώσατε αυτόν, where LXX probably understood the word ὁμοιώμα in the concrete sense of "a statue". The translation of v. 20 in LXX led some scholars to emendation of the Hebrew text. So Duhm changed the text into המכן תמונה *hamm^ekōnēn t^emūnā* "der, der ein Bildnis aufstellt"[29]. With regard to the emendation of תרומה *t^erūmā*, Driver drew the attention to the fact that a change of the

---

28. Cf. Bible de la Pléiade: "bois de mûrier du prélèvement".
29. At first, DUHM, *Jesaja* (n. 5), pp. 210-211, suggested מסכן תמונה *m^esakkēn t^emūnā*, "der mit dem Messer ein Bildnis schnitzt" (סכן *skn* pi'el as a denominative from *sakkīn*, 'knife'. CONDAMIN, *Le livre d'Isaïe* (n. 5), *ad locum*, emendated the text into: למשכן *lmškn*, (or למכון *lmkwn*) תמונה *tmwnh*, "pour faire un support à l'image".

consonants is superfluous, arguing that תרמה *t^erāmā* or *t^erīmā* (as he reads instead of *t^erūmā*) can have the meaning of "some kind of dedicatory offering of great value, possibly an effigy of some divine or semidivine being"[30].

As for the word מסכן *m^esukkān* scholars especially referred to Ugaritic texts in order to defend a translation similar to that of the Septuagint. So, in 1957, J. Gray referred to a couple of texts one of them occurring in a supplication of Baal directed to El and asking for a son for Dn'el: *nṣb skn 'el 'ebh.*

Gray translated these words as follows: "One who may set up the "stele" of his ancestral God"[31]. A second text is an inscription on a stele dedicated to Dagon in Ras Shamra; here the word *skn* must be – according to Gray – somthing which one has "set up" (*dš'lyt*)[32]. In virtue of the Ugaritic noun *skn*, rendered as "stele", Gray suggests for the verbal form of Isa 40,20a the meaning "to set up", changing moreover MT in *ham^esakkēn t^emūnā*, "he who would set up an image". As an other possibility he suggests *hamiskān y^erōmēm*, "would one set up an image?"[33]. Aistleitner joins Gray in rendering the noun *skn* in the quoted texts as "Denkmal, Figur, Statue" or in other cases as "Zustand (beste Form)"[34]. Schoors meant to support Gray's interpretation by calling special attention – besides the noun *skn*, "stele" – to denominative verbal forms with the root *skn* showing a similar meaning: he mentions UT 51:I.42-43: *ṣ' il dqt k'amr sknt khwt ym'an*, which he translated – substantially according to Aistleitner – into: "El's bowl, chased with the shape of a lamb, *formed* in the likeness of an animal of yman"[35]. And as another example of this verbal form he points to UT 51:I.21: *šskn m' mgn rbt (atrt ym)*, rendered by Aistleitner as: "*lasse herstellen* Geschenke für die Herrin..."[36].

---

30. G.R. DRIVER, in *JTS* 36 (1935), p. 397.

31. J. GRAY, *The Legacy of Canaan*, Leiden, 1957, pp. 75ff., referring to C.H. GORDON, in *Ugaritic Handbook*, 2 Aqht I.27; II.16 (= KTU 1.17:I.27; II.16).

32. GRAY, *The Legacy* (n. 31), p. 192, referring to GORDON *Ugaritic Handbook* (n. 31), 69.1 (= KTU 6.13).

33. GRAY, *The Legacy* (n. 31), p. 192.

34. J. AISTLEITNER, *Wörterbuch der ugaritischen Sprache*, Berlin, 1963, nos. 1908-1909. M.J. MULDER, *Versuch zur Deutung von* sokènèt *in 1 Kön. I 2,4*, in *VT* 22 (1972) 43-54, spec. p. 47, mentions also PRU II.21.8 = UT 1021,8: *wb. 'ly skn.yd'.rgmh*, cf. our note 41.

35. A. SCHOORS, *Two Notes on Isaiah XL–LV*, in *VT* 21 (1971) 501-505, spec. p. 502; AISTLEITNER, *Wörterbuch* (n. 34), nr. 1908; cf. our note 74. Cf. J.C DE MOOR, *The Seasonal Pattern in the Ugaritic Myth of Ba'lu*, Neukirchen, 1971, p. 50: "its shape as in the region of Ym'an".

36. Cf. J. AISTLEITNER, *Die mythologischen und kultischen Texte aus Ras Schamra*, Budapest, ²1964, p. 37; SCHOORS, *Two Notes* (n. 35), pp. 501f.; MULDER, *Versuch zur Deutung* (n. 34), p. 48.

This kind of texts and their interpretations induced several scholars to change המסכן *hamᵉsukkān* in Isa 40,20a into a pi'el form, like Gray already did, to read *ham(m)ᵉsakkēn tᵉrūmā* and to translate "He who makes a votive image"[37] or "Der die Weihegabe herstellen läßt"[38]. Mettinger maintained the pu'al form of MT and rendered *mᵉsukkān* as "a thing formed, an image"[39].

Lipiński, however, contested the opinion that *skn(t)* would mean a stele. According to him the above mentioned texts from 2 Aqht do not speak of the erection of a stele at all. The son desired for Dn'el would rather be spoken of as "un surgeon, intendant du dieu de son père"[40]. And the text UT 69,1 (= KTU 6.13) *skn. d š'lyt ṭryl.ldgn.pgr* was translated by Lipiński in this way: "*Substitut* que Saryelli a voué à Dagan en forme de stèle"[41]. In Lipiński's opinion the word *skn* would not mean stele, but something like "intendant" or "substitute"[42].

Other scholars too expressed their doubt on the assumed meaning "stele" for *skn*[43]. For the interpretation of Isa 40,20a some exegetes preferred to call special attention to the meaning "manager, intendant, governor" for the root *skn* in Ugaritic and other ancient Near Eastern texts[44]. As early as in the Amarna letters *sakanu* is found a couple of times[45], particularly in the expression *liskin šarru*, "may the king take (good) care of (his country)"[46]. Examination of these texts led Mulder to the conclusion: "Ein *sukinu* ist also jemand dem Verantwortung auferlegt ist, z.B. seitens des Königs einer Provinz gegenüber. ... Vielleicht trifft die Übersetzung 'Verwalter' oder auch 'Vertreter' noch am besten zu"[47]. In the Old Testament the root סכן *skn* occurs in a similar meaning,

---

37. A. SCHOORS, *Jesaja* (BOT, 9), Roermond, 1972, p. 251: "De maker van een votiefbeeld". The Dutch Willibrord translation: "Wie een votiefbeeld wil maken".

38. FOHRER, *Jesaja* (n. 2), p. 26.

39. METTINGER, *The Elimination of a Crux?* (n. 14), pp. 77-83.

40. LIPIŃSKI, skn et sgn (n. 26), p. 197.

41. *Ibid.*, pp. 200-201. In *Ugaritic Textbook* 1021,8, quoted at the end of our note 34, Lipiński (p. 199) rejects the meaning 'stele' for *skn* as well. He translates the text (from a private letter, addressed to the king): "Et quand *l'intendant* montera (au palais), il connaîtra son avis".

42. *Ibid.*, pp. 199ff.

43. R. DUSSAUD, *Deux stèles de Ras Shamra portant une dédicace au Dieu Dagon*, in *Syria* 16 (1935), p. 177, suggested for *skn* the translation "offrande (?)" and for *pgr* "sacrifice" (UT 69.I = KTU 6.13), cf. however our note 63.

44. E.g. MULDER, *Versuch zur Deutung* (n. 34), p. 46; cf. LIPIŃSKI, skn et sgn (n. 26), pp. 195-199.

45. MULDER, *Versuch zur Deutung* (n. 34), p. 45, refers to EA 285,26; 286,34. 35(?).38; 287,13.17.40; 288,48; 290,29.

46. Cf. C. RABIN, *Etymological miscellanea*, in *Scripta Hierosolymitana* 8 (1961), p. 395.

47. MULDER, *Versuch zur Deutung* (n. 34), p. 45.

so in 1 Kings 1,2.4 the the part. fem. qal סכנת *sōkènèt* for Abishag, the young girl that had to "take care" of King David in his old days, and in Isa 22,15 the part. masc. qal הסכן *hassōkēn* as a title for Shebna. Shebna's function, indicated by *hassōkēn*, is explained in the following words as אשר על הבית *ašèr 'al-habbayit*, "which is over the house", that is the man who is responsible for the king's household[48]. In Ps 139,3 the psalmist professes in front of YHWH: כל דרכי הסכנת *kol dᵉrākay hiskantā*. This phrase with a verb form from סכן *sākan* hif'il, finds its parallel in the words ארחי ורבעי זריתה *'orḥī wᵉrib'ī zērītā*, "you have traced (זרע *zārā* pi'el, "to measure out") my path and my resting place" and must mean in this context: "you take care of", "you watch over (cf. LXX προεῖδες, van προ-οράω) all my ways"[49]. In Num 22,30 Lipiński translated the second question of Balaam's ass (with סכן *sākan* hi'fil) in a similar way: "Ai-je jamais fait le surveillant (ou: "l'intendant") en agissant avec toi?" (cf. LXX ὑπεροράσει). Finally, in Eliphaz's exhortation to Job (Job 22,21) סכן *sākan* hif'il must mean something like "to pay attention to" in the phrase: "Pay attention to Him (God) and so you will live in peace."

Some scholars start from this kind of meaning of *sākan* in Ugaritic and biblical texts for interpreting מסכן *mᵉsukkān* in Isa 40,20. Though סכן *sākan* pi'el or pu'al does not occur in biblical Hebrew, it is thinkable that these conjugations express an intensivation of the meaning of qal and hif'il. So Reider[50] wrote in 1952: סכן *skn* is "to keep, to guard, to care for ... the Pi'el is used instead of the Kal ... to emphasize the intensive and iterative action, which is peculiar to a steady occupation or practice". In this line Isa 40,20a would speak of an intensive and repeated care (or: supervision) of a תרומה *tᵉrūmā*. Generally, authors change the form מסכן *mᵉsukkān* into a pi'el and read *mᵉsakkēn*[51], but in my opinion the change is not necessary. Starting for our text from סכן *skn* in the meaning "take care of", and taking into account that the pi'el can also contain a causative aspect[52], the passive aspect of the pu'al might be met by the notion: "to be charged with the care of...". The term המסכן *ham(m)ᵉsukkān* then would mean "the man that is charged with the care of a (the) *tᵉrūmā*".

48. Cf. *Ibid.*, p. 51: "Vorsteher des königlichen Hofstaates".

49. LIPIŃSKI, skn *et* sgn (n. 26), p. 194: "toutes mes démarches, tu les surveilles".

50. J. REIDER, *Etymological Studies in Biblical Hebrew*, in *VT* 2 (1952) 113-130, spec. pp. 117-118.

51. *Ibid.*, p. 117; ELLIGER, *Jesaja* II (n. 3), p. 61; MULDER, *Versuch zur Deutung* (n. 34), p. 50; TRUDINGER, *"To whom then will you liken God?"* (n. 12), pp. 224-225; cf. our note 65.

52. GK, §52g, Joüon, §52d.

In the meantime Lipiński's objections against the meaning stele for סכן *skn* have proved to be wrong. The signification stele for *skn* appears to be firmly attested in the Ugaritic texts, as has been agreed by divers expert scholars[53]. The word has to be connected with the Amorite word *sikkanum* which is found in Mari, Emar and Munbaqah[54]. The words *skn* and *sikkanum* are probably to be derived from a root *sakānum*, "to dwell"[55] (cf. Arabic *sakana*, "to rest, to dwell") and to be connected with the Akkadian verb *šakānum*, "to place"[56]. The connection between *skn*, "stele", and the root *sakanum*, "to dwell"[57], may be explained from the fact that a stele probably played a prominent part in the cult of the dead[58], where the dead ancestors/fathers were thought to be present in the family cult of their descendants and where their deities and spirits were supposed to be dwelling in the standing stone[59]. So the translation of *skn* as given before by Gray and Schoors appears to be substantially correct. In KTU 1.17:I.27 De Moor[60] translates *nṣb.skn.'il'ibh* however as follows: "someone to set up the stelae of his father gods". So he reads a plural "stelae" instead of the singular and "father gods" (the deified ancestors)[61] instead of the usual translation "the god of the fa-

---

53. E.g. M. DIJKSTRA – J.C. DE MOOR, *Problematical Passages in the Legend of Aqhâtu*, in *UF* 7 (1975), p. 175; J.C. DE MOOR, *El the Creator*, in G. RENDSBURG *et al.* (eds.), *The Bible World*. FS C.H. Gordon, New York, 1980, pp. 184-185, n. 66; ID., *The Ancestral Cult in KTU 1.17 I 26-28*, in *UF* 17 (1986) 407-409; G. DEL OLMO LETE, *Mitos y leyendas de Canaan*, Madrid, 1981, p. 595; J. TROPPER, *Nekromantie. Totenbefragung im Alten Orient und im Alten Testament*, Neukirchen, 1989, pp. 129ff.; M. DIETRICH – O. LORETZ, *Mantik in Ugarit*, Münster, 1990, pp. 69-75; cf. M. DIETRICH – O. LORETZ – J. SAMMARTIN, *Zur ugaritischen Lexikographie XII*, in *UF* 6 (1974), p. 43: "Sichere Belege für *škn* 'stele' sind in UT 69,1; CTA 17 I 27.45, II 16 gegeben".

54. J.-M. DURAND, *Le nom des bétyles à Ebla et en Syrie*, in J.-M. DURAND – J.R. KUPPER (eds.), *Miscellania babyloniaca*. FS M. Birot, Paris, 1985, pp. 79-84; D. ARNAUD, *Emar VI.3. Textes sumériens et accadiens*, Paris, 1986, 125:35-41; DIETRICH – LORETZ, *Mantik* (n. 53), pp. 68-69; cf. J.C. DE MOOR, *Standing Stones and Ancester Worship*, in *UF* 27 (1995) 1-20, spec. pp. 9-10.

55. Cf. B. LAFONT, in *Archives epistolaires de Mari I/2* (ARM, 26), Paris, 1988, pp. 492-493.

56. *The Assyrian Dictionary of the Oriental Institute of the University of Chicago* 17/1, 116ff.

57. TRUDINGER, *"To whom then will you liken God?"* (n. 12), p. 224, assumes that from the meaning "to dwell with" סכן *skn* developed to the meaning "to be familiar or well acquainted with". For the verb סכן *škn* pi'el she wonders: "Could not the Pi'el (sic!) participle המסכן *hamᵉsakkēn* mean 'he who really knows' that is the 'connoisseur' of idols, the man who is prosperous enough to be able to afford the very best".

58. Cf. M. DIETRICH – O. LORETZ – W. MAYER, *Sikkanum 'Betyle'*, in *UF* 25 (1989) 135-137.

59. Cf. LAFONT, *Archives I/2* (n. 55), pp. 492-493.

60. See DE MOOR, *The Ancestral Cult* (n. 53), pp. 407-409; ID., *Standing Stones* (n. 54), p. 7.

61. Cf. DE MOOR, *El the Creator* (n. 53), pp. 184-185: "the god (or: El) who is the

ther"[62]. The main thing for our aim is the fact that the rendering stele (stelae) for *skn* has been confirmed here. The same conclusion applies – in spite of Lipiński's translation – for UT 69.1 (= KTU 6.13), where the words *skn.dš'lyt tryl.ldgn.pgr* should be rendered "Stele that raised Tharyelli for Dagan, a *pgr*"[63].

As for the Ugaritic verbal form *skn*, the meaning "to shape, to construct" appears to be certain as well[64]. So for the interpretation of מסכן *mᵉsukkān* in Isa 40,20 there seem to be two possibilities. Starting from the meaning "to take care of" one might consider the מסכן *mᵉsukkān* – as we saw before – as the man who was charged with the care of a (the) תרומה *tᵉrūmā*. Starting from the meaning "to shape, to construct" the מסכן *mskn*[65] may have been as well the man who had to shape or construct a (the) תרומה *tᵉrūmā*. Here too the passive aspect of the pu'al form might be met by rendering מסכן *mᵉsukkān* as "the man who was charged with the construction of a (the) תרומה *tᵉrūmā*".

The word תרומה *tᵉrūmā* is generally understood in the sense of a "(votive) offering"[66]. It is however doubtful whether תרומה *tᵉrūmā* in this case has to do anything with an offering at all. Taking the line that the verb רום *rūm* means "to rise, to be high", the original meaning of תרומה *tᵉrūmā*, even in a cultic context, might rather be "a levying of obligation", "an imposed contribution" than a voluntary offering for a cultic purpose, though in some cases in the present text the contributor himself is allowed to determine what and how much he is disposed to contribute (Exod 25,2ff.; 35,5ff..21ff.)[67]. In Deut 12,6.11.17 תרומה *tᵉrūmā* is clearly differentiated from נדבה *nᵉdābā* (the only text where it is different, is found in Ezra 8,25.28).

---

father"; ID., *The rise of Yahwism: The Rise of Israelite Monotheism* (BETL, 91), Leuven, 1990, pp. 232-233.

62. E.g. K. VAN DER TOORN, *Ilib and the 'God of the Father'*, in *UF* 25 (1993) 379-387.

63. The word *pgr* means in all Northwest Semitic languages 'corpse' (HAL, 861a). Is the stele identified here with the corpse of an ancestor? Cf. DE MOOR, *Standing Stones* (n. 54), pp. 5-6. Cf. also K. SPRONK, *Beatific Afterlife in Ancient Israel and in the Ancient Near East*, Neukirchen-Vluyn, 1986, pp. 150, 250, who for Lev 26,30 and Ezek 43,7 also maintains the meaning 'corpses'.

64. Cf. KORPEL, *Soldering* (n. 9), p. 222; J.C DE MOOR, *An Anthology of Religious Texts from Ugarit*, Leiden, 1987, p. 46; ID., *The Integrity of Isaiah 40* (n. 9), p. 189.

65. KORPEL, *Soldering* (n. 9), p. 222; she reads, like many scholars before her (cf. *supra*, n. 33, 37, 38, 51), pi'el המסכן *hammᵉsakkēn*, but she gives the term a new interpretation: "the one who shapes the pedestal"; cf. DE MOOR, *The Integrity* (n. 9), p. 189.

66. FOHRER, *Jesaja* III (n. 2), p. 26: "Weihegabe"; W. VON SODEN, *Mirjam-Maria »Gottesgeschenk«*, in *UF* 2 (1970) 269-272, spec. p. 271, thinks that *tᵉrūmā* originally meant 'Geschenk'. REIDER, *Etymological Studies* (n. 50), p. 117, renders Isa 40,20a: "the keeper (guardian or caretaker) of 'sacred contributions'".

67. Cf. ELLIGER, *Jesaja* II (n. 3), pp. 61, 77-78.

Fokkelman has rightly argued that תרומה *t^erūmā* must have had originally a much larger field of meanings than the mere cultic one. So in 2 Sam 1,21a there is still a non cultic meaning to be assumed: שׂדי תרומת *ś^edê t^erūmōt* can hardly signify anything else than "fields situated high (in the mountains)"[68] (cf. NEB: "the uplands"). We hold the view that in our text too תרומה *t^erūmā* must be related with the notions "high" and "to rise", "to raise" as connected with the Hebrew root רום *rūm*. Depending on the interpretation that is chosen for המסכן *ham(m)^esukkān*, the word תרומה *t^erūmā* may have the sense of "raising" an image on a pedestal, or the "pedestal" itself[69], upon which the image is raised.

In any case, in our opinion the term תרומה *t^erūmā* in v. 20 does not mean a second (wooden) image after the cast one of v. 19[70]. So in v. 20 there is neither question of a second image that is inferior (given by a poor person) nor of an image that is superior[71] to the image spoken of in vv. 19f. If however vv. 19f are concerned with one single image, then only v. 19 can speak about the image itself. If v. 20 too would speak of the image of v. 19, the act of choosing the wood (v. 20a") could only refer to the – then to be assumed – hardwood core of the image. It would however be strange that the very first act of choosing the wood is mentioned then after the description of the following acts, the construction of the image and its decoration with gold[72]. It is more likely that v. 20 describes the final work that has to be done in order to complete the making of the image: after casting and decorating the image it has to be set up upon a pedestal. For every new action in the process the text mentions the artisan who is an expert on accomplishing that specific act: the חרשׁ *ḥārāš* who casts the image (in Canaan generally made of bronze[73]), the צרף *ṣōrēf*, "the melter" who covers the image with gold and solders the plates of gold with silver, and then the מסכן *m^esukkān* who has to set up the image on a pedestal, looking for another workman, again חרשׁ

---

68. J.P. FOKKELMAN, śdy trwmt *in 2 Sam 1,21a*, in *ZAW* 91 (1979) 290-292.

69. KORPEL, *Soldering* (n. 9), p. 222; DE MOOR, *The Integrity of Isaiah 40* (n. 9), p. 189; cf. NORTH, *Second Isaiah* (n. 8), p. 86: "a platform or base for the image"; cf. ELLIGER, *Jesaja* II (n. 3), p. 79.

70. Against KISSANE, *Isaiah* II (n. 5); E.A. LESLIE, *Isaiah*, New York - Nashville, 1963, p. 142; FOHRER, *Jesaja* (n. 2); WESTERMANN, *Jesaja 40–66* (n. 2); PENNA, *Isaia* (n. 5).

71. TRUDINGER, *"To whom then will you liken God?"* (n. 12), p. 225, because: "the statue carved out of the trunk of a hardwood tree … a tree whose roots are still firmly in the ground, is much better founded, much less liable to be moved or shaken".

72. *Ibid.*, p. 221.

73. P. COLLINI, *Studi sul lessico della metallurgia nell'ebraico biblico e nelle lingue siro-palestinesi del II e I milleno a.C.*, in *SeL* 4 (1987) 10-12; O. NEGBI, *Canaanite Gods in Metal: An Archaeological Study of Ancient Syro-Palestinian Figurines*, Tel Aviv, 1976. In Babel the images generally were cut out of wood and then covered with gold.

ḥārāš, who has to set tight (להכין *leḥakīn*) the image[74]. Setting up an image on a pedestal is a specific and responsible work, specially if it is a question of a large image, like that of Nebuchadnezzar in Daniel 3. It is, however, not easy to determine what was exactly the task of the מסכן *mesukkān*. Starting from the root סכן *skn* in the meaning "to take care of", the מסכן *mesukkān* is to be seen as "the man who is charged with the care (supervision) of raising the image upon a pedestal"; starting from the verb סכן *skn* in the meaning "to shape, to construct", the first two words of v. 20 must indicate "the man who is charged with the construction of the pedestal"[75]. In any case the מסכן *mesukkān* has to choose for the pedestal a piece of hardwood that will not rot and to seek out a skilful craftsman whose job it is to set tight (להכין *leḥakīn*) the image on the pedestal so that it can not fall or be moved[76].

Apparently it is not accidental that the construction of the image and pedestal is described in terms that remind of the work of creation of Israel's God[77]. The verb רקע *rāqaʿ* piʿel (v. 19a"), the "hammering out" of the plates of gold for the cover of the image, recalls the רקיע *rāqīaʿ*, the "firmament", that God hammered out as a plate overarching the earth (Gen 1,7) and the verb רקע *rāqaʿ* qal used for God the Creator who hammered out (the floor of) the earth (Isa 42,5; 44,24; cf. Ps 136,6) and who has beaten out (רקע *rāqaʿ* hifʿil) the firmament, hard as a mirror of cast metal (Job 37,18). The verb כון *kūn* hifʿil in the last half stich of v. 20 reminds of God who by his power and wisdom has fixed/set tight the mountains (Ps 65,7) and the earth (Jer 10,12; 51,15; cf. polel in Isa 45,18). If the parallels between the construction of an idol and God's work of creation are read against the background of the question asked in v. 18: "To whom will you liken God?", the purpose of the parallels becomes evident. So far as appearances go, the creating work of the artist may resemble the creating work of God[78], the results of their work show how much the work of God is incomparable: the dead and dumb

74. Cf. for the process M. WEIPPERT, *Metall und Metallverarbeitung*, in K. GALLING (ed.), *Biblisches Reallexikon*, Tübingen, ²1977, pp. 220-224, spec. p. 223; KORPEL, *Soldering*, p. 222, points to the Ugaritic parallel (KTU 1.4:I) of the process: a "divine craftsman (*ḥrš*) pours silver and gold, overlays various pieces of furniture with silver, gold and electrum, among them a socle (*kt*), and finally fashions a bowl that is shaped (*sknt*) like one from the Yamʾanu country". Cf. DE MOOR, *Anthology* (n. 64), p. 46, and our n. 35 with the text belonging to it.

75. Cf. ELLIGER, *Jesaja* II (n. 3), p. 80: "den mit der Leitung oder auch mit einer bestimmter Teilarbeit 'Betrauten'".

76. CONDAMIN, *Le livre d'Isaïe* (n. 5): "il s'agit de la fixer solidement dans une niche ou sur un piedestal", cf. NORTH, *Second Isaiah* (n. 8), pp. 85-86; SMITH, *Isaiah XL–LV* (n. 12), pp. 171ff.; KOOLE, *Jesaja* II/1 (n. 14), p. 64.

77. Cf. KORPEL, *Soldering* (n. 9), pp. 220-221.

78. NORTH, *Second Isaiah* (n. 8), p. 86.

idol of the artist vanishes into nothingness beside the majestic and living creation of Israel's God, the only One who is really *El* (v. 18) and who alone is able to prove his being God[79].

In the same line is the emphasis that is laid in the last words of v. 20 on the fact that the image is fixed in such a way that it may not "totter" or "fall down" (מוט *mūṭ* nif'al) like once did the statue of the Philistine God Dagon (1 Sam 5,3ff.). It is nothing else than a poor attempt to make the image resemble the God of Israel, the immovable "Rock"[80] (Deut 32,4.15.18.30f.37; 1 Sam 2,2; 2 Sam 22,9.32.47; 23,3; Ps 18,3.32.47; 28,1; 62,3.7f.; etc.; Isa 17,10; 26,4; 30,29; 44,8; 51,1), whose throne is firm from of old (Ps 93,2; cf. 103,19). Whereas the makers of the idol had to protect their idol from tottering or falling down, YHWH is the only God, אל *'ēl*, who protects his people (Ps 16,8; 62,3.7), his king (Ps 21,8) and his city (Ps 46,6), indeed the whole earth (Ps 93,1) from being shaken or moved[81] (cf. God's "covenant of peace", ברית שלומי *bᵉrīt šᵉlōmī*, that "shall not be shaken", מוט *mūṭ* qal, Isa 54,10). A similar conclusion can be drawn from the use of the verb בחר *bḥr*[82]. Here again the incomparability is stressed of the God who "elects" (בחר *bḥr*) his people in order to strenghten and support it with his victorious right hand (Isa 41,8-10; cf. 45,4) in respect of an idol, for which men have to "elect" (בחר *bḥr*) a piece of wood that can not rot away for making a solid pedestal in order to keep the idol upright.

So, the verses 19 and 20 are, at least in the present text of Isaiah 40, a striking answer on the question of v. 18: "To whom will you liken God or what likeness will you apply to Him?".

A problem till now in v. 20 is the article (?) ה *ha* before מסכן *mᵉsukkān*. Because dageš forte after the article ה *ha* is usually missing in the consonants מ *m*, נ *n*, and ל *l* with šᵉwa mobile, particularly in מ *mᵉ* as a participial prefix, there is formally no indication whether ה *ha* is to be considered as a (definite) article or as an interrogative particle. If ה *ha* is intended as an article, the construction המסכן תרומה *hamᵉsukkān tᵉrūmā* is however unusual. Intended as expressing a genitival relation, the phrase would rather read מסכן (ה)תומה *mᵉsukkan (hat)tᵉrūmā*, the first word being in statu constructo with the nomen rectum (ה)תרומה *(hat) tᵉrūmā*[83]. Another possibility is however, to take המסכן *hamᵉsukkān* for a

79. Cf. BEUKEN, *Jesaja* II^A (n. 1), p. 45.
80. Cf. C.J. LABUSCHAGNE, *The Incomparability of Yahweh in the Old Testament*, Leiden, 1966, p. 76.
81. Cf. TRUDINGER, *"To whom then will you liken God?"* (n. 12), pp. 224-225.
82. Cf. KOOLE, *Jesaja* II/1 (n. 14), p. 63.
83. GK, §20m with note 2; Joüon, §35c2.

participle (status absolutus) with תרומה *t^erūmā* as the object in accusative[84].

Apart from this issue we are inclined to opt for the interpretation of v. 20a as a question and to interpret ה *ha* as an interrogative particle, just like the ה *ha* that introduces v. 19. The verses 19 and 20 may give two answers to the questions of v. 18, both in the form of a new question. To the question: "To whom will you liken God?", v. 19 replies: "To an image made and decorated by a craftsman?" and v. 20 replies with the question: "To a man who, by his electing and creating work, brings about a solid pedestal for keeping the image upright and firmly fixed?". In that way both verses stress the incomparability of Israel's God[85]. The God of Israel, the Creator of heaven and earth, can not possibly be compared with an image that, instead of creating other beings, has to be created by men; nor can the God who protects his people and the earth from being shaken or moved, be compared with a man who is only able to protect an idol from tottering or falling down.

Anna van Burenlaan 6   Kees VAN LEEUWEN
NL-3851 RV Ermelo

---

84. GK, §116f, k; Joüon, §121 l, o.
85. Cf. LABUSCHAGNE, *The Incomparability* (n. 80), pp. 108-111.

ISAIAH 42,10-12
"SING TO THE LORD A NEW SONG..."

I. INTRODUCTORY

10 Sing to the Lord a new song, his praise from the end of the earth!
Let the sea roar and all that fills it, the coastlands and their inhabitants.
11 Let the desert and its towns lift up their voice, the villages that Kedar inhabits;
let the inhabitants of Sela sing for joy, let them shout from the top of the mountains.
12 Let them give glory to the Lord, and declare his praise in the coastlands.

13 The Lord goes forth like a soldier, like a warrior he stirs up his fury;
he cries out, he shouts aloud, he shows himself mighty against his foes. (NRSV)

By far the majority of exegetes regard Isa 42,10-13 as an integral whole and therefore link v. 13 with the preceding vv. 10-12[1]. However, many exegetes regard vv. 10-17 as the larger unit[2] so that vv. 10-13 would then form a subdivision of it. On the internal organisation, structure and unity of vv. 10-17, however, there is no agreement[3]. S.

1. Cf. for instance T.K. CHEYNE, *The Book of Isaiah*, London, 1870, p. 153; K. MARTI, *Das Buch Jesaja* (KHC, X), Tübingen, 1900, p. 290; G.E. WRIGHT, *Isaiah*, London, 1965, p. 106; B. DUHM, *Das Buch Jesaja*, Göttingen, ⁵1968, pp. 314-316; A. SCHOORS, *Jesaja* (BOT), Roermond, 1972, pp. 267-268; R.N. WHYBRAY, *Isaiah 40–66* (NCB), London, 1975, pp. 76-78; J. SCULLION, *Isaiah 40–66* (OTM, 12), Wilmington, DE, 1982, pp. 44-45; J.L. KOOLE, *Jesaja II. Deel 1* (COT), Kampen, 1985, pp. 166-174. Although also J. MUILENBURG, *The Book of Isaiah Chapters 40–66* (The Interpreter's Bible, 5), New York, 1956, pp. 467-474, too regards vv. 10-13 as a separate strophe, he nevertheless sees it as part of a larger poem, namely vv. 5-17.
2. Cf. for instance H. GRESSMANN, *Die literarische Analyse Deuterojesajas*, in ZAW 34 (1914) 254-297, p. 294; J.L. MCKENZIE, *Second Isaiah* (TB, 20), Garden City, NY, 1968, pp. 42-47; A.S. HERBERT, *The Book of the Prophet Isaiah: Chapters 40–66*, Cambridge, 1975, pp. 43-46; R.P. MERENDINO, *Der Erste und der Letzte. Eine Untersuchung von Jes 40–48* (SVT, 31), Leiden, 1981, pp. 256-274; K.P. DARR, *Like Warrior, Like Woman: Destruction and Deliverance in Isaiah 42:10-17*, in CBQ 49 (1987) 560-571. E. KÖNIG, *Das Buch Jesaja*, Gütersloh, 1926, pp. 373-376, also discusses vv. 10-17, but he sees this as part of a large whole, namely vv. 10-25.
3. Thus vv. 10-12 is sometimes seen as a smaller unit of vv. 10-17, cf. for example P. VOLZ, *Jesaja II übersetz und erklärt* (KAT, 9), Leipzig, 1932, pp. 29-30; C.R. NORTH, *Isaiah 40–55*, London, 1952, pp. 65-67; H. FREY, *Das Buch der Weltpolitik Gottes. Kapitel 40–55 des Buches Jesaja* (Die Botschaft des Alten Testaments, 18), Stuttgart, ⁴1954, pp. 72-73; G. FOHRER, *Das Buch Jesaja, 3. Band Kapitel: 40–66* (ZBK), Zürich - Stuttgart, 1964, pp. 53-54; P.E. DION, *The Structure of Isaiah 42.10-17 as Approached through Versification and Distribution of Poetic Devices*, in JSOT 49 (1991) 113-124, p. 119; J.M. VINCENT, *Studien zur literarischen Eigenart und zur geistigen Heimat von Jesaja, Kap. 40–55* (BET, 5), Frankfurt a.M. - Bern - Las Vegas, 1977, p. 49, also regards vv. 10-12 as a smaller unit.

Mowinckel[4], for example, regards vv. 10-17 as a coherent unit based on the similarities that he finds between these verses and the enthronement psalms and based on his hypothesis that all the texts could be traced back to a common cultic *Sitz*, namely the enthronement festival.

The demarcation and unity of vv. 10-13 is usually based mainly on form-critical grounds[5]. W.A.M. Beuken[6] complies with this by speaking of Isa 42,10-13 as a "Loflied op Gods sterke daden" and even begins a completely new section in his commentary at v. 10. However, it is C. Westermann[7] in particular, in agreement with Gunkel[8], who makes 42,10-13 an independent *Gattung* by labelling it as one of the "eschatologischen Loblieder". Westermann speaks of 42,10-13 as a "neuer Psalmentyp" that Deutero-Isaiah created on the basis of the special circumstances of his announcement[9].

Although Crüsemann also regards 42,10-13 as a unit and typifies it form-critically as an "imperativische Hymnus"[10], he says that it is actually not a real hymn, but rather a prophetic announcement ("prophetische Verkündigung")[11]. Beuken also avoids the term "eschatologischen Loblieder" because he feels it could lead to misunderstanding. According to Beuken, vv. 10-13 should be form-critically viewed together as a unit, despite the fact that the content could give cause for

---

4. S. MOWINCKEL, *Die Komposition des deuterojesajanischen Buches*, in ZAW 49 (1931) 87-112, p. 96 (n. 2). For Mowinckel, it is unbelievable that L. KÖHLER, *Deuterojesaja (Jesaja 40–55) stilkritisch untersucht*, Gießen, 1923, p. 107 could separate vv. 14-17 from vv. 10-13: "Was Köhler veranlaßt hat, vv. 14-17 von vv. 10-13 zu trennen, ist mir unbegreiflich" (*ibid.*, p. 96, n. 2). Cf. also S. MOWINCKEL, *Psalmenstudien II. Das Thronbesteigungsfest Jahwäs und der Ursprung der Eschatologie*, Amsterdam, 1961, pp. 49-50, 195, 214, 241. VINCENT, *Studien* (n. 3), pp. 54, 61 and E. NIELSEN, *Deuterojesaja. Erwägungen zur Formkritik, Traditions- und Redaktiongeschichte*, in VT 20 (1970) 190-205, p. 203, concur with Mowinckel's view that vv. 10-17 has a common cultic *Sitz im Leben*.

5. GRESSMANN, *Die literarische Analyse* (n. 2), p. 295, for example refers to it as a hymn; M. HALLER, *Das Judentum. Geschichtsschreibung, Prophetie und Gesetzgebung nach dem Exil* (Die Schriften des Alten Testaments, II/3), Göttingen, ²1925, p. 34, speaks of a "prophetischer Hymnus".

6. *Jesaja deel II^A* (POT), Nijkerk, 1979, p. 134.

7. Cf. C. WESTERMANN, *Das Loben Gottes in den Psalmen*, Göttingen, ²1961, pp. 108-110; ID., *Sprache und Struktur der Prophetie Deuterojesajas* (Calwer Theologischen Monographien, 11), Stuttgart, 1981, pp. 74-80.

8. H. GUNKEL – J. BEGRICH, *Einleitung in die Psalmen. Die Gattungen der religiösen Lyrik Israels*, Göttingen, 1933, pp. 329, 344, speaks of "eschatologischen Hymnen". Cf. also J. BEGRICH, *Studien zu Deuterojesaja* (TB, 20), München, 1963, p. 54.

9. C. WESTERMANN, *Das Buch Jesaja, Kap. 40–66* (ATD, 19), Göttingen, 1966, p. 85.

10. F. CRÜSEMANN, *Studien zur Formgeschichte von Hymnus und Danklied in Israel* (WMANT, 32), Neukirchen-Vluyn, pp. 69-70.

11. *Ibid.*, p. 48.

viewing vv. 8-12 and vv. 13-17 as smaller units[12]. J. Morgenstern[13] sees 42,10-13 as a psalmodic fragment that was not originally part of the text, but has simply been included here for doxological purposes. K. Elliger[14] concludes that "Es ist formgeschichtlich also ein Unding, 13 von 10-12 zu trennen". Koole[15] maintains that v. 13 reflects the true reason and content of the song of praise (vv. 10-12) and Spykerboer[16] writes that without v. 13 the preceding hymn would have no real theme.

From this brief review it would appear that the demarcation of vv. 10-13 is based mainly on form-critical arguments. However, it would also appear that there is no agreement on the exact form-critical elements that would comprise 42,10-13.

The question is actually whether form-critical arguments and a hypothetical *Sitz im Leben* may be used as the main grounds for demarcating a text – in this case Isa 42,10-13. My hypothesis is that form-critical – and thus extratextual – criteria have been enforced on 42,10-13 so that the internal textual evidence consequently has not come fully into its own. Form-critical arguments – that the "beschreibende Lob" must follow the call to praise and that v. 13 must therefore be linked to the preceding vv. 10-12 – do not allow any latitude for the unique nature of this section of text.

The view that I wish to propose here is: (i) that vv. 10-12 form an integral strophe; (ii) that vv. 10-12 have a closer connection with the preceding verses than with v. 13 and the following verses; and (iii) that although v. 13 as such also forms a complete strophe, it should rather be linked with v. 14 and subsequent verses.

In this paper no attention is paid to the question of whether Isa 42 underwent an editorial growth process or how this process might have taken place. Neither is this an attempt to reconstruct that process. Instead I have focused on the text in its final form.

II. ISAIAH 42,10-12

Consequently, a form-critical perspective has not been used here in examining 42,10-12, but instead, an attempt has been made to allow the independent and unique nature of the text itself to emerge.

12. BEUKEN, *Jesaja* (n. 6), p. 316 (n. 1, 2).
13. J. MORGENSTERN, *The Message of Deutero-Isaiah in its Sequential Unfolding*, in *HUCA* 30 (1959), p. 50.
14. K. ELLIGER, *Deuterojesaja. 1. Teilband. Jesaja 40,1–45,7* (BKAT, XI/1), Neukirchen-Vluyn, 1978, p. 243.
15. KOOLE, *Jesaja* II (n. 1), p. 167.
16. H.C. SPYKERBOER, *The Structure and Composition of Deutero-Isaiah with Special Reference to the Polemics against Idolatry*, Meppel, 1976, p. 94.

The following arguments could be put forward in support of the idea that vv. 10-12 form an integral strophe: The introductory words שִׁירוּ לַיהוָה ("sing to the Lord...") with which v. 10 begins, are a well-known introductory formula. Another notable characteristic of vv. 10-12 is that this forms an inclusio since the words לַיהוָה ("to the Lord") and תְּהִלָּתוֹ ("his praise") appear in both v. 10 and v. 12[17]. This section is also syntactically uniform in the sense that following the imperative (שִׁירוּ, "Sing") there are no less than five jussives (יִשְׂאוּ, "let them lift up", v. 11a; יָרֹנּוּ, "let them sing", v. 11b; יִצְוָחוּ, "let them shout", v. 11b; יָשִׂימוּ, "let them give", v. 12; יַגִּידוּ, "let them declare", v. 12). In content too the jussives share common ground since they are all concerned with proclaiming the praise of Yahweh. Further coherence is created in vv. 10-12 by no less than three occurrences of the stem ישׁב in these verses (יֹשְׁבֵיהֶם, "their inhabitants", v. 10b; תֵּשֵׁב, "inhabits", v. 11; יֹשְׁבֵי סֶלַע, "inhabitants of Sela", v. 11b). Another significant repetition is the word אִיִּים ("coastlands") which occurs in both v. 10b and v. 12.

A glance at v. 13 gives further confirmation that vv. 10-12 form an integral whole: In v. 13 a distinct change of subject may be detected. In contrast to the preceding third person plural jussives of vv. 10-12, in v. 13 we find the third person singular, יֵצֵא ("He goes forth..."), with Yahweh as subject. Watts[18] justifiably claims that v. 13 marks a new beginning by placing the name Yahweh emphatically at the start of the sentence construction. Verse 13 is a proclamation that thematically belongs to the subsequent section[19]. The terminology of v. 13 is also a complete departure from what preceded it. Here Yahweh is compared to a warrior, and military terminology from the Holy War tradition is used to describe him. One could also speak of a theophany description[20] in v. 13. Smart[21] goes on to say that the inclusion of v. 13 with vv. 10-12 is

---

17. Those who regard v. 12 as a gloss or as superfluous, therefore overlook the inclusio and its function: cf. eg. DUHM, *Jesaja* (n. 1), p. 318; MARTI, *Jesaja* (n. 1), p. 290.

18. J.D.W. WATTS, *Isaiah 34–66* (WBC, 25), Waco, TX, 1987, p. 129. Watts is therefore one of the few exegetes who allocates v. 12 to the preceding section. He regards Isa 41,21–42,12 as one long section. However, his view that the book of Isaiah has a "dramatic structure" consisting of "acts", "scenes" and "role development and reversal" is not convincing.

19. P.A.H. DE BOER, *Second-Isaiah's Message* (OTS, 11), Leiden, 1956, p. 46 also regards v. 13 as a "heading".

20. For a comprehensive discussion of the theophany description cf. J. JEREMIAS, *Theophanie. Die Geschichte einer alttestamentliche Gattung* (WMANT, 10), Neukirchen-Vluyn, 1965, esp. pp. 7ff.; WESTERMANN, *Das Buch Jesaja* (n. 9), p. 86, however, refers to v. 13 as an epiphany.

21. J.D. SMART, *History and Theology in Second Isaiah: A Commentary on Isaiah 35; 40–66*, London, 1967, p. 89; cf. also J. SKINNER, *The Book of the Prophet Isaiah: Chapters XL–LXVI*, Cambridge, 1917, p. 34.

very unlikely since in v. 13 the accent is on the wrath of Yahweh against his enemies while vv. 10-12 concern the world's praise of Yahweh.

To conclude, it should also be noted that v. 13 forms such an integral unit that one could even speak of a strophe. Like vv. 10-12, v. 13 also forms an inclusio in that it both begins and closes with the stem גבר (כגבור, "like a soldier"; יתגבר, "he shows himself mighty"). The fact that v. 13 forms a unit on its own is further confirmed by the fact that in v. 14 we encounter another oracle and Yahweh is introduced in the first person singular (החשיתי, "I have held my peace"). Like vv. 10-12, v. 13 is thus a separate strophe. Vincent[22] is therefore correct when he says "Inhaltlich und rhythmisch ist V. 13 unabhängig und bildet auch eine 'kleine Einheit'".

When one takes a closer look at the individual lines of vv. 10-12, the following emerges: In v. 10a there is alliteration in the large number of s-sounds. This is probably intended to emphasise the comprehensive na- ture of the praise. There is a verb missing in the second verse segment (תהלתו מקצה הארץ, "... his praise from the end of the earth") so that one could speak of an ellipsis here. This half of the verse gives a clearer explanation of what is meant by שיר חדש[23], "a new song". In this con- text "new song" does not merely mean that new words must be used, but implies that Yahweh must be praised for something completely new. חדש should therefore be understood qualitatively[24]. All the wording in the rest of the section ("those who go down to the sea"; "the coastlands and their inhabitants"; "the desert..."; "the villages..."; "the inhabit- ants of Sela..."; "from the tops of the mountains", v. 11; "in the coastlands", v. 12) gives a more detailed account of what is meant by "... his praise from the end of the earth". The emphasis is that everyone, the whole earth, should praise Yahweh. The ellipsis that began in v. 10a, is continued in 10b[25]. The imperative שירו is understood in v. 10b so that both halves of the verse indicate who should sing the new song in hon- our of Yahweh. The two halves of the verse therefore also stand in paral- lel making it unnecessary to introduce a text-critical change here as many exegetes have been inclined to do[26]. Merendino[27] is justified in

---

22. VINCENT, *Studien* (n. 3), p. 49.

23. However, I do not intend to discuss the other instances where the expression שיר חדש also occurs (cf e.g. Pss 33,3; 96,1; 98,1; 149,1).

24. KOOLE, *Jesaja* (n. 1), p. 169.

25. In view of the double ellipsis, Vincent's view, *Studien* (n. 3), p. 42, that an en- jambment between v. 10a en 10b is highly improbable, does not hold water.

26. Many exegetes change the text, particularly on grounds of Pss 96,11 and 98,7, to read: ירעם הים ומלאו ("Let the sea roar and all that fills it"), cf. for instance DUHM, *Jesaja* (n. 1), p. 318; HALLER, *Das Judentum* (n. 5), p. 33; MARTI, *Jesaja* (n. 1), p. 290;

keeping to the Masoretic text and remarks that מְלֹאוֹ ("what fills it") is personified here and has special reference to all the living beings in the sea and, in conjunction with the expression "those who go down to the sea", indicates the totality of everything concerned with the sea. Clearly, 10b is syntactically dependent on 10a and is therefore inextricably linked to it.

In the first half of v. 11a, we find the first of a series of jussives (יִשְׂאוּ, "let them lift up"). We also encounter a double ellipsis: firstly, the word קוֹל ("voice") is understood after יִשְׂאוּ and secondly the verb יִשְׂאוּ is understood in the second half of the verse. The two halves of 11a are in semantic parallel in the sense that they are geographic indicators of those who should lift up their voices:

> ... the desert and its towns
> the villages that Kedar inhabits

It is also clear that v. 11a is closely linked to what precedes it. Apart from this jussive being a continuation of the imperative, as far as sentence construction is concerned, the beginning of v. 10b shows a remarkable similarity to v. 11a:

הים ומלאו
מדבר ועריו

The second half of v. 11a again recalls the second half of 10b by reintroducing the stem יָשַׁב.

The jussives are continued in v. 11b ("let them sing"; "let them shout") so that this line is linked as closely as possible with the preceding v. 11a. In addition there is an anadiplotic relationship between v. 11a

MUILENBURG, *Isaiah* (n. 1), p. 473; WESTERMANN, *Jesaja* (n. 9), p. 84; FOHRER, *Jesaja* (n. 3), p. 53; CRÜSEMANN, *Studien* (n. 10), p. 69 n. 2; SMART, *History* (n. 21), p. 88; MCKENZIE, *Second Isaiah* (n. 2), p. 42; BEUKEN, *Jesaja* (n. 6), p. 134; VINCENT, *Studien* (n. 3), p. 40. Cf. also L.C. ALLEN, *Notes and Studies*, in *JTS* 22 (1971), pp. 146-147 for a comprehensive discussion and further examples of text-critical changes. VOLZ, *Jesaja* (n. 3), p. 29, changes the text to יאדררהו ים ("Ihn feire das Meer", i.e. "the sea glorifies him") and WATTS, *Isaiah* (n. 18), p. 113, also supports this view. J. SCHILDENBERGER, *Parallelstellen als Ursache von Textveränderungen*, in *Biblica* 40 (1959) 188-198, p. 197 suggests יודוהו ("es sollen ihn preisen..."). The literal translation that is therefore proposed here is: "Those who go down to the sea (= seafarers) and what fills it".

27. MERENDINO, *Der Erste und die Letzte* (n. 2), p. 257; KOOLE, *Jesaja II* (n. 1), pp. 169-170, also appeals for the maintenance of the Masoretic text and as motivation, refers to the parallel between the "seafarers" and the people of the desert in v. 11. DION, *Structure* (n. 3), pp. 117-118 indicates that a change is unnecessary since there is nothing wrong with the grammar or plain meaning of the MT. Cf. also C. VON ORELLI, *Der Prophet Jesaja* (Kurzgefaßter Kommentar Alten und Neuen Testament, IV/1), München, ³1904, p. 156.

and v. 11b because the stem ישב that occurs at the end of v. 11a recurs at the beginning of v. 11b. The function of this would therefore be to imply that everyone should sing a song for Yahweh.

V. 11b as such has a chiastic structure:

ירנו סלע ישבי מראש הרים יצוחו
 a   b   b   a

Y. Gitay[28] is justified in saying that the function of this chiasmus is that it calls attention to the numerous people who praised God and that the two verbs which open and close this line and the associated assonance (ירנו, יצוחו; cf also v. 12 where the same figuration of style occurs) emphasise the joyful celebration before God. In v. 11b as in v. 10a, the preposition מן is used to indicate the extent of the praise and the place from which it must be proclaimed (cf. מקצה הארץ, v. 10a, "from the end of the earth"; מראש הרים, v. 11b, "from the tops of the mountains"). In view of this, the place names "Kedar" (v. 11a) and "Sela" (v. 11b) should probably not be seen as exact geographical indicators, but as *pars pro toto*[29] for the earth as a whole and as the extreme boundaries of the author's world.

It has already been indicated that v. 12 forms an inclusio with v. 10 so that vv. 10-12 form an integral strophe in themselves. When one takes a closer look at v. 12, it appears that v. 12 also has a chiastic structure:

ישימו ליהוה כבוד ותהלתו באיים יגידו
 a   b   b   a

As in the previous verse, the function of the chiasmus is to underline the overwhelming praise that Yahweh deserves. As in the previous line (v. 11b) in v. 12 too there is a marked assonance, brought about by the u-sounds of the third-person plural verb forms. All four verbs emphasise the joy with which Yahweh should be praised. It should also be noted that because of the chiasmus, the כבוד ("glory") and ותהלתו ("his praise") of Yahweh are clearly linked together.

From this review it can be concluded that, for syntactic, semantic and stylistic reasons, vv. 10-12 form a demarcated strophe. In these verses, the accent falls on the all-embracing and overwhelming praise that should be sung to Yahweh in the form of a new song.

---

28. Y. GITAY, *Prophecy and Persuasion: A Study of Isaiah 40–48* (Forum Theologiae Linguisticae, 14), Bonn, 1981, p. 132.
29. Cf. VINCENT, *Studien* (n. 3), p. 51.

III. THE RELATION OF ISAIAH 42,10-12 TO THE
PRECEDING AND SUBSEQUENT SECTIONS

The next issue is whether vv. 10-12 should be associated primarily with v. 13 and the subsequent section or with the preceding section. The answer to this question does have some effect on the way in which the entire section is interpreted, for instance, what should comprise the content of the new song (cf. v. 10). It has already been indicated that for form-critical reasons, many exegetes have linked vv. 10-12 with v. 13 and the verses that follow it. I should like to suggest that there is sufficient reason to believe that vv. 10-12 should be associated with the preceding rather than the subsequent section[30].

Deliberate word usage in particular creates a clear link between vv. 10-12 and the preceding verses. The first example that must be mentioned is the keyword חדש ("new", v. 10a) which refers back to חדשות ("new things", v. 9a). This last verse is part of a firm directive from Yahweh (an oracle) and concerns the "new things" to be accomplished through his servant. Spykerboer[31] justifiably notes that v. 10 is not only formally joined to v. 9 by way of the catchword "new", but it follows and continues 42,9. The proclamation of the new things leads to the call to sing a new song.

The word תהלה which, as already indicated, fulfils a prominent function in vv. 10-12 (cf. "his praise", v. 10 and v. 12), is also encountered in the preceding section. In point of fact, the word כבוד that occurs in one line together with תהלה in vv. 10-12 (cf. the discussion in v. 12), also occurs in v. 8 in the same line as תהלה. In the context of vv. 10-12, these words are concerned with the "praise" and the "glory" that must be brought to Yahweh. In contrast to this the words in v. 8 are used in a polemic fashion to indicate that Yahweh will not share his "praise" and "glory" with idols.

It has already been shown that the verb stem ישב has a prominent position in vv. 10-12. The stem also occurs in v. 7. However, it should also be mentioned that, just as in v. 11b, the stem (ישבי סלע, "inhabitants of Sela") also occurs in a status constructus form (ישבי חשך, "inhabitants of darkness") in v. 7. Here too the words are used to emphasise a contrast. In vv. 10-12 they are used to describe those who praise Yahweh, while in v. 7 they apply to those who are in distress.

Another word usage worth mentioning is that of the verb stem נגד. In v. 12 it is used in a jussive form (יגידו, "let them declare") to describe

---

30. L.G. RIGNELL, *A Study of Isaiah Ch. 40–55* (Lunds Universitets Årsskrift, N.F. 52/5), Lund, 1956, p. 31, is one of few who speaks of vv. 5-12 as a unit. He therefore does not regard v. 13 as part of what precedes it.

31. SPYKERBOER, *Structure* (n. 16), p. 94.

the "praise" with Yahweh as object, and in v. 9a it is used in the participium form (מגיד) with Yahweh himself as subject ("new things I now declare").

This review confirms the close connections between vv. 10-12 and particularly with the preceding vv. 5-9. Lindblom[32] is therefore justified in remarking that the content of vv. 10-12, which follow immediately after the oracle, is a very appropriate sequel to the declaration about the sublime task entrusted to Israel.

The recurrence of the word הארץ, ("the earth", v. 10a) also forges a link with what precedes it (cf. v. 5a and v. 4b). From this it would appear that vv. 10-12 not only refer to the oracle (vv. 5-9) but also to the song of the servant (vv. 1-4). While הארץ in vv. 10-12 is concerned with the extent of the praise and in v. 5 with the tradition of creation, in vv. 1-4 it is related to the establishment of משפט ("justice") on earth. However, there is yet another connection between vv. 10-12 and vv. 1-4. I have already referred to the occurrence of the word איים ("coastlands") in vv. 10-12. This word actually occurred earlier in v. 4b where it is mentioned in the same breath as הארץ. There is also a structural similarity[33] to be seen between v. 4b and v. 12:

ולתרתו איים ייחילו
ותהלתו באיים יגידו

The verb stem נשא that is used in v. 11a to describe the way the cities praise Yahweh (ישאו, "let them lift up"), is used to refer to the servant in v. 2 where it is said "he will not lift up his voice" (ולא ישא). The verb שׂים is used in v. 12 concerning the "glory" that must be given to Yahweh (ישימו, "let them give…") and in v. 4 concerning the "justice" that must be established by the servant (ישׂים, "he has established…").

All these repetitions – even though the words may not necessarily have the same meaning in every case – confirm that there is also a deliberate link between vv. 10-12 and vv. 1-4.

The oracle section (vv. 5-9) is also related to the preceding servant song (vv. 1-4) by way of word repetition. The *hiphil* form of the verb יצא is used in both vv. 1-4 (יוצי, v. 1b and v. 3b) and vv. 5-9 (להוציא, v. 7) to describe the actions of the servant. The recurrence of the word רוח also forges a connection between these two sections (cf. v. 1b and v. 5). In both cases this word is used in terms of the powerful presence of

---

32. J. LINDBLOM, *The Servant Songs in Deutero-Isaiah, A New Attempt to Solve an Old Problem* (Lunds Universitets Årsskrift, N.F. 47/5), Lund, 1951, p. 24.

33. Cf. GITAY, *Prophecy* (n. 28), p. 122.

Yahweh. The *hiphil* form of the verb שׁמע is found in both sections. In one case it is used of the servant who does not raise his voice (לֹא־יַשְׁמִיעַ, v. 2) and in the other of Yahweh who does in fact announce the "new things" (אַשְׁמִיעַ, v. 9, "I let you hear…").

This review confirms that there are various links between vv. 1-4 and 5-9, based on obvious word repetition. We have already seen that vv. 10-12 have strong links with vv. 5-9 in particular and also with vv. 1-4. Therefore the logical conclusion is that the three strophes (vv. 1-4, vv. 5-9 and vv. 10-12) are fully interrelated. At any rate we could say that vv. 10-12 are primarily related upwards rather than downwards. The "new song" therefore, is not primarily concerned with the war terminology and the comparison of Yahweh to a warrior (cf. v. 13), but in fact with the work of the servant, with the presence and work of Yahweh and particularly with his act of creation as described in vv. 5-9. Van der Meer[34] is correct when he says that the focus on the creative power of Yahweh in vv. 5-9 culminates in the call to sing a song of praise to Yahweh and concludes with that "new song" in vv. 10-12. In other words, the section that precedes vv. 10-12 should be seen as motivation for the song of praise. Verse 13 is therefore not intended as a motivation for vv. 10-12 – the call to praise, since this motivation has already been provided in the verses that precede vv. 10-12. Verse 13 was rather designed to effect the transition to the following passage[35].

It has already been indicated that vv. 10-12 should be linked upwards rather than downwards[36] and that v. 13 introduces something new. However, this does not imply that v. 13 stands completely apart from the preceding context. This verse is indeed part of the text as it now presents itself. One could even say that by way of word usage a link is forged between v. 13 and the preceding section of Isa 42[37]. What does in fact clearly emerge here is that v. 13 should not be seen as motivation for vv. 10-12 but instead, is linked downwards with what follows as will be shown.

Form-critical arguments are also used to indicate that v. 13 should be seen as motivation for the preceding calls to praise[38]. But form-critical

34. W. VAN DER MEER, *Schepper en Schepsel in Jes. 42:5*, in H.H. GROSHEIDE – J.C. DE MOOR – C.J. DEN HEYER – S.E. SCHEEPSTRA – W. VAN DER MEER – E. DE VRIES (eds.), *De Knecht. Studies rondom Deutero-Jesaja aangeboden aan Prof. Dr. J.L. Koole*, Kampen, 1978, pp. 118-126, esp. p. 126.

35. C.T. TORREY, *The Second Isaiah*, New York, 1928, p. 329.

36. Although SCHOORS, *Jesaja II* (n. 1), p. 267 speaks of vv. 10-13, he believes that the reviser intended it as a conclusion to the preceding vv. 1-9.

37. The verb stem יצא which plays a prominent role in vv. 1-9 in particular (cf. vv. 1b, 3b and 7), recurs again in v. 13.

38. Cf. for instance F. DELITZSCH, *Das Buch Jesaja* (BCAT, III/1), Leipzig, 1889, p. 437 who even in the previous century saw v. 13 as a call to praise.

arguments are not convincing here either: Westermann, for example, does not keep to his own form-critical principles as far as vv. 10-13 are concerned. As already indicated, Westermann divides vv. 10-13 into a specific *Gattung*, namely the "eschatologischen Loblieder"[39]. Westermann says that one of the characteristics of the "eschatologischen Loblieder" is that the song of praise is based on a perfectum form that does not refer to something that has already happened, but rather to something in the future[40]. The truth is, however, that the verbs of v. 13 are not in the perfectum form, but they are imperfecta (יצא, "he goes forth"; יעיר, "he stirs up"; יריע, "he cries out"; יצריח, "he shouts aloud"; יתגבר, "he shows himself mighty"). Although according to Westermann's own definition, the section 42,10-13 does not meet the criteria of the "eschatologischen Loblieder", nevertheless he still divides vv. 10-13 into this *Gattung*[41]. Crüsemann[42] also admits that vv. 10-13 show deviations in terms of this *Gattung*: The customary motivating כי – and consequently the grammatical link with the previous verses – is not found in v. 13.

To recap: Form-critical arguments may not be used as the sole grounds for regarding v. 13 to be part of vv. 10-12. Even if one should employ form-critical arguments, vv. 10-13 would still not fulfil all the requirements. Although the author or final editor of Deutero-Isaiah was probably influenced by the traditional literary genres, he was still at liberty to adapt the genres for his own purposes[43]. Stereotyped genres, or form-critical arguments, should therefore not be used as the only or decisive criterion in demarcating pericopes.

I have already attempted to show that v. 13 introduces a new beginning, and even forms a separate strophe. Nevertheless there is a close connection between v. 13 and v. 14 – at any rate, closer than that between v. 13 and vv. 10-12. It is no accident that the conspicuous comparisons, both of which relate to Yahweh, occur directly after each other in vv. 13 and 14 (כגבור, "like a soldier"; כאיש מלחמות, "like a warrior", v. 13; כיולדה, "like a woman in labour", v. 14). Although the two comparisons function to provide a contrast – the strong soldier versus the woman in labour – they do not contradict each other[44]. The *tertium*

---

39. Cf. *supra* n. 7 and 9.
40. *Sprache und Struktur* (nn. 7), p. 74.
41. *Ibid.*
42. CRÜSEMANN, *Studien* (n. 10), p. 70.
43. Cf. R.F. MELUGIN, *Deutero-Isaiah and Form Criticism*, in *VT* 21 (1971) 326-337, p. 337.
44. Cf. GITAY, *Prophecy* (n. 28), p. 124 who comments: "In regard to the relationship between vv 13 and 14, the picture drawn in v 13 contradicts the one of v 14".

comparationis in both comparisons is the omnipotence of Yahweh and his active presence[45] in the crisis of the exile. This aspect of Yahweh's imposing presence and his powerful impact on the environment is also expressed in v. 15. Another similarity between v. 13 and v. 14 is that in both cases theophanic language is used[46]. Darr[47] points out the auditory character of both comparisons (the warrior "cries out", "shouts aloud", v. 13; and the "woman in labour" "cries out", "gasps" and "pants", v. 14).

Some exegetes also produce form-critical considerations to prove that v. 14 has no connection with the preceding v. 13. Westermann[48], for instance, separates vv. 14-17 from what precedes it by saying that it belongs to the "Heilsankündigung" *Gattung* and that it also contains certain elements of the "Volksklage". Elliger[49], actually agrees with this by saying that no example exists for the transition from a hymn (v. 13) to a long "Jahwerede" (vv. 14-17). Elliger[50] maintains that even as far as the content is concerned v. 14 has nothing in common with the preceding v. 13 and Beuken[51] even begins a completely new section in his commentary at v. 14.

Nevertheless, I believe that I have already produced sufficiently convincing arguments that there is a close link between v. 13 and v. 14 and that form-critical arguments alone are not enough to vindicate a clear division between v. 13 and v. 14.

IV. Conclusion

Consequently, the following remarks can be made in conclusion: The call to praise in vv. 10-12 should be regarded as an independent strophe. Verse 13 is not primarily linked to vv. 10-12 and therefore should not be regarded as motivation for vv. 10-12. Verses 10-12 should rather be linked to the preceding vv. 1-9. Verses 1-9 which deal with the actions of the עבד, Yahweh's act of creation, Yahweh's loving behaviour toward those in distress, the restoration of משפט and Israel's new task,

---

45. M.I. GRUBER, *The Motherhood of God in Second Isaiah*, in *RB* 90 (1983) 351-359, p. 355 also makes the pertinent remark that in "natural childbirth the woman's role is active rather than passive".

46. MUILENBURG, *Isaiah* (n. 1), p. 472.

47. DARR, *Like Warrior* (n. 1), p. 567.

48. WESTERMANN, *Jesaja* (n. 1), p. 87; cf. also SCHOORS, *Jesaja* (n. 1), p. 268-269.

49. ELLIGER, *Deuterojesaja* (n. 14), p. 243.

50. *Ibid.* SPYKERBOER, *Structure* (n. 16), p. 95 counters Elliger by indicating that in v. 14 the accent is not on a woman in travail, but as in v. 13 on the action of Yahweh.

51. BEUKEN, *Jesaja* (n. 1), p. 145.

should therefore be seen as motivation for vv. 10-12. The "new song" of vv. 10-12 must be sung about the matters in vv. 1-9. In this case the motivation stands at the beginning of the call to praise. Although v. 13 as such forms a strophe, it is still more closely linked to the section that follows it.

Most exegetes, as well as W.A.M. Beuken[52] to whom this *Festschrift* and this article are dedicated with great respect, are deluded into linking v. 13 primarily with vv. 10-12 by *formgeschichtliche* arguments. Consequently, the individuality and unique nature of this section of text cannot come into its own.

Faculty of Theology   Willem S. PRINSLOO
University of Pretoria
Pretoria 0002
South Africa

---

52. Cf. also my positive review of Beuken's *Jesaja deel II,* in *Bib* 63 (1982) 126-129.

THE CYRUS ORACLE (ISAIAH 44,24–45,7)
FROM THE PERSPECTIVES OF SYNTAX, VERSIFICATION
AND STRUCTURE

In this article I intend to describe forms and structures in the famous Cyrus oracle in Isa 44,24–45,7, and then try to determine how a proper understanding of these phenomena could lead to a more exact representation of the poem's message, and of the course of poetic communication. My main concern is with the question of how versification is supported by a remarkable syntax, and how it contributes to strophe composition. This puts versification in an intermediate position, which means that both its relation with language, especially syntax, and the interface with strophe and stanza composition should be investigated. That done, we will be able to give a well-founded indication of the poem's focal point and of the spearhead of the poetic communication.

What occurs along the linear axis as the first decision by the poet is straight away a fact of form, in harmony with and motivated by the creation and contours of larger textual units. The messenger formula at the beginning is not restricted to the customary three words, "thus saith X", with the subject usually indicated by a proper name. The double apposition to the subject *yhwh* expands the formula to fill an entire line (the first verse, Isa 44,24ab)[1]. In this way, the *inquit* covers an entire bicolon. Following this introduction by the poet the speaking voice shifts and we get the first verse from the deity. This is a triadic line, proudly opened by the long form of the first person singular (the three syllables of אנכי), of which each colon contains a verbal predicate. These are three *qal* participles constituting an asyndetic series.

The difference in level between introductory voice and the subsequent speaker is usually dramatic. Deutero-Isaiah, however, adopts a technique which drastically reduces this sort of gap. He provides a certain continuity between 24ab and the tricolon 24cde, and a gradual transition, by also choosing *qal* participles for the appositions in his own opening line. The first of these, גאל, immediately qualifies Yahweh as the deity who made Israel the chosen people by delivering them from Egypt. Thus the

---

1. In this article, the abbreviations v. and vv. refer to the Masoretic verses in the usual numbering; the word "verse" is used in a strictly literary sense to indicate the full poetic line, i.e. a bicolon or tricolon. The letters a, b, c, d, e, f refer to cola; 1f for instance means the sixth colon (= the third B-colon) of Isa 45,1.

opening colon, however formulaic, manages straight away to establish
the close and intimate bond between God and people and to raise favourable expectations in the audience. One expectation leads into the
present: God, "the redeemer", may deliver us again, freeing us from the
hands of the current superpower. The second *qal* participle constitutes a
smooth transition to, and a complement of, the three participles used by
God himself in his tricolon. It refers to the creation of man – more
exactly, of "you", i.e. the Judaean listener to whom Deutero-Isaiah
addresses himself – whilst the series of *qal* participles mentions the creation of the cosmos as the work of God.

These five participles together form a series which is firm enough to
determine the first strophe. At the same time, they are the counterparts to
another string of participles, another five chosen from the *qal* register.
These are found in 45,7, each of them is a predicate of God, they all refer again to his power as Creator, and again presuppose the first person
as a subject[2]. This repetition completes a circle. The poem is framed by
an extensive use of inclusio – a form of closure which can hardly be sur-
passed. This figure is even more conspicuous since the body of the poem
is entirely made up of bicola, whereas the tricola have been selected by
the creator to occupy the borders: the first verse (one tricolon) and the
last strophe (three tricola) spoken by God[3].

On his own verse 24ab the poet has bestowed a modest form of
parallelismus membrorum by dividing the word-pair "your Redeemer ...
who forms you in[4] the womb" across the two halves. It is, however, the
coherence of the opening strophe, and even more the circular framing of
his poem as a whole, which inspired and determined his first choice of
the *qal* participles. Systematically adopting one specific morphological

2. The "I" is virtually present in Isa 45,7; for a correct understanding and translation,
it should be taken from v. 6c. Notice that, moving towards the end of the poem, "I" always occurs in its short form: אני in Isa 45,3c (i.e. the first colon of the sixth strophe) and
three times more in the final strophe Isa 45,5-7.

3. This pattern of 16 bicola (leaving aside the introductory v. 24ab) framed by four
tricola presupposes a text-critical decision taken by Beuken and many other commentators: v. 26d (reading ולעֵרי יהודה תבנינה) should be deleted, as it is redundant and especially because it intrudes between "her ruins" in 26e and the antecedent of the suffix -*ha*
in v. 26c, the name "Jerusalem". In this article, a new argument in favour of this decision
is provided by a word count leading to the predicative spearheads of both halves – about
which more later.

4. The preposition *min* can mean "in", without referring to any separative moment in
terms of time or space; see for instance Gen 11,2a where people journey "*in* the East
(מקדם)", or Gen 3,24 (the cherubs live *at* the East of the Garden) and Jonah 4,5. For the
notion "*in* the womb" cf. Isa 44,2 and 49,5 (unlike 49,1 which indicates a *terminus a quo*,
and the well-known collocation יצא מבטן). See also the information *sub* 1c and 4c in
BDB, under the entry מן, pp. 578b and 581b.

register is a decision of style which now proves to have been attuned to the textual units of at least three higher levels.

The syntax of God's first statements (24cde) determines the first half of the oracle. Six of the seven subsequent verses assume as their subject the personal pronoun of the first person singular. To put it differently: God's very first word, *'anoki*, is virtually present and functional in vv. 25-28a. Consequently, a correct rendering of the syntax of God's opening sentence is of crucial importance. Many translations and commentaries start off with "I am the LORD, who... " etc., but this is wrong. The tetragrammaton is not the predicate of a nominal sentence. God does *not* proclaim his identity here by revealing his name to the exiles through his prophet; they have known that for a long time. What we really have here is a verbal sentence in which *yhwh* is only an apposition; what is being predicated is his activity as Creator. The proper name is no more than an apposition to the subject "I"[5]. The *seghol* in the participles in 24cd shows that these actually have a verbal function, governing objects[6]. Hence, the correct translation would be:

> It is I, the LORD, who make everything,
>> Who alone stretch out the heavens
>>> And unaided spread out the earth.

This rendering also aptly foreshadows the construction of the clauses in the second strophe, where all verses end in a finite verb form in the 3rd person[7].

---

5. Thus correctly W.A.M. BEUKEN, *Jesaja* II^A, II^B, III^AB (POT), Nijkerk, 1979-1989, in his commentary, p. 228, in agreement with only few exegetes: C. WESTERMANN, *Das Buch Jesaja, Kap. 40–66* (ATD, 19), ³1976, pp. 124, 126; P.-É. BONNARD, *Le second Isaïe*, Paris, 1972, p. 163; and the translators of JPS2 and the *Bible de Jérusalem*. The wrong option (*yhwh* as nominal predicate) can be found in KJ, NBE, NEB, KBS³; BUBER and ROSENZWEIG in their *Verdeutschung*; C.R. NORTH, *The Second Isaiah*, Oxford, 1964, p. 45; NBG; JOÜON-MURAOKA, *Grammar*, §138e.

6. The trio "everything // heaven // earth" is the verbally governed object to the actions "he makes // stretches out / pounds". If, however, the participle form עשה has a *sereh* as in Ps 121,2b, we have nominal governing and the form is a part of a construct state combination with "heaven and earth". The Isaiah text denotes an action, the verse from the Psalms refers to a quality of God which syntactically is an apposition.

7. The translation "it is I" enables us to avoid a conflict between the first and third persons. Take for instance v. 25ab, which now reads, with the virtual subject in brackets: "[It is I] who annul the omens of diviners, and make fools of the augurs; who turn sages back and make nonsense of their knowledge." The words I have taken from the JPS translation, which unfortunately renders the participles in v. 24cde with a past tense. This is unlikely to be correct, as the long string of participles following v. 25 simply refer to a present which transcends temporal limitations.

The influence of the third person of the imperfect forms which close off six verses has anyway not been limited to the B-cola containing them. Close observation shows that God, in his long first-person speech, also uses a third-person morpheme in the A-colon of

Now that the proper name has proved to be "only" an apposition, if it is placed between brackets we notice that the remaining words of the poetic line 24cde all have their counterparts. The three participles are always followed by an object (another trio: everything, heaven, earth), and the rhyme on the long -*i* makes us realize that *'anoki*, *l^ebaddi* and *me'itti* also make up a series. This technique results in a *parallelismus membrorum* which thanks to its triple basis has maximum impact. The words on -*i* are mutually explanatory. In this way, the poet himself gives us a clue which helps us when we have to consider the *k^etib* and *q^ere* for the last word[8]. The pronoun "I" becomes "I alone" and then *me'itti*, which literally means "from with me", and in this context: "of my own accord", i.e. "on my own initiative", "on my own". So, I follow the Masoretes in their *q^ere*.

It is no coincidence that the parallelism of 24cde consists of three triads, that the words with the internal rhyme -*i* all consist of three syllables, and that scansion of the verse results in 3 + 3 + 3 stresses[9]. The poet is applying the ternary principle, i.e. presenting things in threesomes[10]. This is visible not only at the level of sound, syllables, words, and metre, but also in the form of larger textual units. Two more forms of the ternary principle can also be mentioned: all strophes in the second half (45,1-7) consist of three full poetic lines. When we return to the first half we see that there the strophes make up an ascending series of 2 + 3 + 4 verses (v. 24 / 25-26ab / 26cd-28cd). This means that the first strophe is one verse short, and the last one has one verse extra. The deficit in the one strophe nicely balances the surplus in the other, so that these strophes, too, conform to the standard and fully respect the exact average of three verses per strophe. Finally, it is clear that the last strophe in the poem, 45,5-7, forms the climax of the ternary construction with its three times three cola. These numbers are a heuristic signal: is the final strophe the

v. 26a, and speaks of "*his* servant" instead of "my servant". This would argue in favour of changing our translation to: "I am the one who makes... breaks... turns back... confirms the word of his servant... says..." etc.

8. Strictly speaking, the *k^etib* reads *my 'ty*, which may be vocalized as *mi 'itti*, "who is with me?": an independent nominal sentence. Such an element, however, is ruled out by the completely parallel structure of the three clauses 24cde. The *q^ere* should be followed.

9. After reducing two auxiliary vowels in order to obtain a pre-Masoretic number of syllables, my tentative scansion of v. 24cde is as follows:

$$o\ o\ ó\ o\ o\ ó\ /\ o\ ó\ o\ o\ o\ ó\ /\ o\ ó\ o\ o\ o\ ó$$

10. A magnificent and multifaceted application of the ternary principle in narrative prose is Gen 38; see my article *Genesis 37 and 38 at the Interface of Structural Analysis and Hermeneutics*, in L. DE REGT – J. DE WAARD – J.P. FOKKELMAN (eds.), *Literary Structure and Rhetorical Strategies in the Hebrew Bible*, Assen, 1996, pp. 152-187.

climax of the whole in more respects than the strictly quantitative?
The starting point of almost all predication there is formed by a triple
אני יהוה, with on the reverse side a triple use of the nominal negation
אין which alliterates with *'ani*. In strophe I, the simple notion "I
alone" still only hides what the speaker thinks of other gods, their
power and their existence. The reverse side, however, of his uniqueness is worked out in great detail in the final strophe. A long string
of variants tells us that God is unequalled.

This proud denial of the existence and influence of other gods creates an acute opposition between one (the true God) and many (the
idols), which we now recognize in strophe 2. The three objects in the
plural represent the heathen world and its religious mumbo-jumbo, v.
25. The objects in 26ab are singular: the word of God's servant and
the counsel of his messengers. These singulars become reality as a result of God's actions; this effectiveness is in stark contrast to the
oracular sayings and specious divination of the Mesopotamic context
in which the exiles live. Verse 25 describes demolition at the cost of
the heathens, verse 26ab deals with construction in favour of Israel.
The link with God's first verse on his creative power is made by a phonetic chiasm. Most of *l^ebaddi* and the consonants aleph + taw of *me'itti*
return in the phrase "the omens of the oracle priests": *'otot baddim*.
The sound repetition marks the contrast between the validity and
uniqueness of God's work, and the pretence of pluriform but powerless
paganism.

A poet is always able to exploit any grammatical category and raise it
to the function of a stylistic or structural category. This is clearly manifest in the first stanza. A clever combination of morphology and
anaphora defines the size of the second and third strophes. For the first
positions in verses 25-26b the poet systematically selects *hiphil* participles – another trio – and at the beginning of the verses in 26c-28d he returns to the *qal*, consistently employing the root אמר three times as a
participle. Moreover, the poet makes a structural use of the article: the
three verses in the second strophe do not have it, the three subsequent
verses do add the article to the *qal* form *'omer*[11]. These stylistic facts
inescapably guide the correct division into strophes[12]. It is appropriate at
this point to give the Hebrew text in the desired layout. These three strophes I will call stanza I.

---

11. A similar structural device, either inserting or leaving out the article in anaphoric
position, is also found in vv. 5-7 and 8-10 in Job 9, and there also supports the correct
demarcation of strophes. The toggling between *qal/hiphil* has a comparable function.
12. Here I differ from the division Beuken gives on p. 228 of his commentary.

24ab	כה אמר יהוה גאלך	ויצרך מבטן
cde	אנכי יהוה עשה כל	נטה שמים לבדי רקע הארץ מאתי
25ab	מפר אתות בדים	וקסמים יהולל
cd	משיב חכמים אחור	ודעתם ישכל
26ab	מקים דבר עבדו	ועצת מלאכיו ישלים
cd	האמר לירושלם תושב (..)	וחרבותיה אקומם
27ab	האמר לצולה חרבי	ונהרתיך אוביש
28ab	האמר לכורש רעי	וכל חפצי ישלים
cd	ולאמר לירושלם תבנה	והיכל תוסד

The syntax of the second and third strophes is rigorous. Each verse opens with a predicative participle and ends with an imperfect singular. Between these verb forms there are always objects[13]. Thus, the verse structure is consistently chiastic; spread over the bicola we always see the P + O // O + P pattern. The finite forms which close all verses except the last are always factitive or causative and all have the mighty God of Israel as their subject. All B-cola start with the conjunction w^e.

The destructive actions in v. 25 are moreover held together by the rhyme in y^eholel and $y^esakkel$, which also draws our attention to the synonymy of their meanings. The verse containing the positive actions (26ab) is marked by the inner rhyme of *meqim* and *yashlim*. These enclosing forms enter into a chiastic relation with the name of Jerusalem and the imperfect $^{a}qomem$ in v. 26ce[14]. A striking figure, since this crosswise construction moves beyond the strophe boundary. Paradoxically, the clear demarcation of the strophe sharpens our eye for the continuity in the stanza, which exceeds the boundary between the strophes. Here I am no longer referring to the underlying syntactic continuity of the omnipresent P + O / O + P pattern governed by *'anoki*, but to the progressive continuity of the strophes already demarcated.

The chiasm also invites us to look for a relation between strophes 2 and 3 at the levels of meaning and content. Of course we find it, thanks to the semantic line from "the word of his servant" to the triple "saying" which constitutes the anaphora of strophe 3. This relation suggests that the content of "the word of his servant//the counsel of his messengers" may very well be identical to what God says in the third strophe.

13. A direct object occurs nine times; in the four A-cola of the third strophe an indirect object follows the participle (in 27a//28a the address of "saying", in 26c and 28c the subject referred to, sc. "of Jerusalem"); 28d is exceptional in that the noun "temple" has been promoted to subject as a result of the passive construction.

14. This crosswise phenomenon does not prove but indicates that 26d should be deleted.

The commands God issues there have meticulously been included as embedded discourse in the verbal envelopes. They refer to the rebuilding of the ruins of Judah's capital, and the elimination of obstacles like the rivers of the deep. After analysing v. 28, however, we find ourselves on firmer ground with regard to the word and the servant.

Who is his servant, anyway? In a linear reading which has not yet reached v. 28 we can try and extract the answer from strophe 2. The "servant" forms a word-pair with "his messengers", and within the strophe structure (two verses about demolition, one verse about construction) these messengers are the obvious counterparts to the diviners and sorcerers who are part of the environment. Identifying the "messengers" with the prophets is an attractive interpretation. Would the servant then be one of them? Maybe the poet himself? That's going one step too far for me. I notice that "his servant" is situated in the fifth A-colon from the beginning, and that the fifth A-colon from the end also has "my servant". I would like to remind the reader that the epithet "my servant" or "the servant of the Lord" is used sparingly in the Hebrew Bible, and until now has only been granted to Moses, Joshua and David; it is an honorary title.

Who could this servant possibly be? We cannot formulate an answer until we have further explored the connections between the second and third strophes. There is the fact that the diagonal line from *yashlim* to *yᵉrushalayim* (connecting 26b with 26c) is copied at the end of the third strophe, in its surplus verse. Add to this the fact that the rebuilding and inhabitation of the city are mentioned not only in 26ce, at the beginning of the strophe, but also at the end in 28cd. Who is it who pronounces the two remarkable *niphal* forms *tibbaneh* and *tiwwased* in favour of city and temple? In 28b we hear that the Persian Cyrus fulfills all God's purposes. The vertical parallelism created in this way between the B-cola (both in third position within their strophes) already suggests that Cyrus belongs in the messengers' camp, or in any case to the party of God. However, the parallelism goes further. The honorary title "my servant" in v. 26a (even though there it has the third-person suffix) is the counterpart of an honorary title bestowed by God himself in v. 28a, when he personally addresses Cyrus as "my shepherd"! Can we now say that in the second instance the "servant" of 26a refers to the Persian autocrat? I will postpone the decision for a while, but will point out that the question of who is speaking in the final verse 28cd (i.e. the subject of the infinitive *le'mor*) is beginning to press.

The anaphora from the root *'mr* governing the third strophe is even more elaborate as it is always followed by the preposition *lᵉ*. Its meaning shifts: "with respect to" or "in favour of" is used in vv. 26c, 28a, and 28c, whereas it means "to" in v. 27a[15]. It is accompanied by two pairs of predicates in third-degree direct discourse. The outer pair says of the city: "let it be rebuilt/inhabited", the inner pair says to the deep and Cyrus, respectively: "be dry" and "[he is] my shepherd". Whilst v. 26c has practically the same content as 28c, the envelope made up of 28cd together with 26ce tells us about the city that one of "her ruins" is the temple of which the (re)foundation is announced in 28d. The negative elements "ruins" and "streams" are on the same vertical line. Their feminine plural forms, with the polarity dry/wet, in both verses follow a singular (the city and the deep), whilst in v. 28 only singular forms are mentioned. A sound play connects 26e diagonally with 27a, *horboteha... horabi*. At right angles to this one there is another diagonal: all consonants of *tušab* recur in v. 27b.

The emphasis on the vocal and oral, on speech and voice is prominent from 26a onwards (*dbr*). In this way, the very first sentence of the poem loses its formulaic, threadbare character to give way to a Chinese boxes effect. The poet quotes his Lord who introduces himself, speaking to proclaim his power, and within that framework also quotes himself. I have indicated this by progressive indentation:

> Thus says the LORD...:
>> "It is I who confirms the word of his servant..."
> ... who says in favour of Jerusalem:
>> "Let it be inhabited!"
> ... who says to the deep:
>> "Be dry!"
> ... who says of Cyrus:
>> "[He is] my shepherd!"

The opening verse 24ab, being spoken by the prophet, is first-degree direct discourse and introduces God's first-person speech; taken from v. 24c the whole of the first stanza is embedded speech, which means second-degree; within this speech, there are again embedded speeches of the third degree: the two commands, each consisting of three words, relating to Jerusalem, in 26ce and 28cd, and inside these the 3 + 4 words making up the speeches to/about the deep (command in 27a, announcement or intention in 27b) plus the announcement about Cyrus. These words are certainly not an order to him; they represent an appointment

---

15. NB. The passive forms closing off 26c // 28c are third-person feminine, not second-person, so that "Jerusalem" is being spoken about. In 28d the preposition is virtually present and changes its meaning again to "to": since *hekal* is masculine, *tiwwased* is this time an imperfect in the second person! These small but tricky shifts are rendered correctly in the JPS-translation.

(in 28a) and an expression of trust (in 28b). This already reveals much of the special position accorded to Cyrus by the poet and by the speaker quoted by him, God. From a linear point of view the poet is the first to speak; God follows as the next speaker. From a thematic and chrono-logical point of view, however, God is the first to speak and the poet fol-lows, as God's mouthpiece.

The contents of the third strophe are extremely varied – so much the better that its contours are determined by an envelope. Verses 26ce and 28cd, referring to the city mentioned by name and its buildings (ruins/temple), make up a frame, which, in the first instance, warrants the inte-gration of the final verse into its strophe and into the first stanza. But now a paradoxical effect occurs, which places the final line 28cd in a separate position.

The reader may first experience the quality of v.28cd as a surplus or an excess by recognizing the relation between 26ab and 28ab. The con-siderable similarity of these verses, each making up the third line within its strophe, leads to the expectation that the third strophe is finished with the line about Cyrus, the more so when we remember the standard of three lines per strophe. But here we have verse 28cd sticking out rather noticeably – could this poetic line be of special importance? This suspi-cion is borne out by a whole range of phenomena which further expose the peculiar position of the verse; this surplus is full of surprises.

I will start with a simple word count. If we leave the five words of the final line aside for a moment, the three remaining verses in the third strophe contain exactly the same number of words as do the first and second strophes:

strophes:	# 1	# 2	# 3
number of words:	16	16	16 + 5

These figures already suggest that v.28cd is something extra and special.

Reading through the third strophe, one is immediately struck by the *ha'omer* trio, the compelling anaphora introducing each verse. This lends rather a shock effect to the entrance to the fourth verse: we see the same root, but there are two deviations. The verb is now in the infinitive, and the conjunction w^e has squeezed itself in front. The very last word of strophe and stanza is also a striking deviation: after six glaringly transi-tive verb forms with God as a powerful subject, either in the first or in the third person, we now have a passive form in the second person refer-ring to a material object. What does all this mean?

The conjunction with which 28cd opens principally has two functions. I interpret this w^e as a *waw explicativum*. As a carrier of its own specific meaning it may be translated by "namely". Its second function relates to the fact that the conjunction, having been squeezed in, derails the strict regularity of the anaphoric series. The purpose of this is to prevent a misunderstanding on the reader's part: without the conjunction, we might fall into the trap of assigning to *le'mor* its "normal" formulaic function which we know so well from narrative prose, and which we usually render either by a colon or the phrase "as follows" or a similar cliché.

The insertion of the waw explicativum draws our attention to the fact that this time, *le'mor* is no hackneyed phrase and should be restored to its full function as an infinitive. Immediately, however, we are faced with the question of who is in fact speaking. The most obvious answer in these cases is the answer which takes full account of the grammar: the person who uses *tibbaneh* // *tiwwased* to refer to the city and the temple is the subject of the sentence core governing the infinitive phrase, i.e. the subject of the immediately preceding predicate *yashlim* in v. 28b: Cyrus!

This infinitive is modal instead of final. Cyrus "will fulfill My purposes, namely by saying of Jerusalem: "Let it be rebuilt." The preposition l^e does double duty and changes its meaning in the B-colon[16]. To quote the JPS translation[17]:

> He shall fulfill all My purposes!
> He shall say of Jerusalem, "She shall be rebuilt",
> And to the Temple: "You shall be founded again".

We draw the consequence from the envelope structure: the word of Cyrus is congruent with the word of God in favour of Judah and the exiles. A considerable honour for this conqueror after his meteoric ascent! The rebuilding of the city is a result of the destiny God has bestowed on Cyrus by calling him "my shepherd".

The very last colon contains another surprise by referring to the heart of the city: no more anonymous ruins, but the temple itself. The capital will be rehabilitated; this can only be fully achieved if the sphere of the

---

16. The shift from about to to is not really a problem; it is more limited than the shift in the meaning of $l^ema'an$ from 45,3-4. In v.3c this word is a conjunction, but in v. 4a "only" a preposition!

17. The correct reading of the infinitive and its subject was already given in GK, §114p anyway: "all' mein Begehren wird er vollenden, und zwar indem er (Koresch) zu Jerus. spricht etc.". The rendering of the JPS ignores the waw explicativum; understandable, but not entirely correct, if we take into account the shock effects intended by the deviations observed in 28cd. Moreover, the infinitive has been translated with a finite form. From a strictly grammatical point of view this is permitted, cf. JOÜON – MURAOKA, §124q or the strophe following: the infinitives in Isa 45,1c//e are equivalent to the imperfect forms which conclude the cola in v. 1d//f. For the variation participle /infinitive see the anaphoric series of Ps 113,6-9.

sacred is also included, and the worship of the true God is allowed to take place again. Permission for this comes from the Persian whose word is congruent with that of the God of Israel. There is a certain symmetry here which becomes clearer when we compare v. 26b to v. 28b again. In the same way as God fulfills the word of this servant, his shepherd Cyrus, who may even be called his servant, will fulfill all God's purposes.

This is an effective reciprocity, or even a magnificent synergism – but only thanks to God's initiative, as stanza II will disclose. The passive verb forms in the concluding verse of the first stanza in fact prevent us from calling Cyrus the true master builder. Using a passive implies keeping one's options open as to the agent of the action, or wanting to keep hidden from view the part played by that particular person.

The second stanza: Isa 45,1-7

לכורש אשר החזקתי בימינו	כה אמר יהוה למשיחו	1ab
ומתני מלכים אפתח	לרד לפניו גוים	cd
ושערים לא יסגרו	לפתח לפניו דלתים	ef
והדורים אושר	אני לפניך אלך	2ab
ובריחי ברזל אגדע	דלתות נחושה אשבר	cd
ומטמני מסתרים	ונתתי לך אוצרות חשך	3ab
הקורא בשמך אלהי ישראל	למען תדע כי אני יהוה	cd
וישראל בחיר	למען עבדי יעקב	4ab
אכנך ולא ידעתני	ואקרא לך בשמך	cd
אזרך ולא ידעתני	זולתי אין אלהים	אני יהוה ואין עוד	5abc
אני יהוה ואין עוד	וממערבה כי אפס בלעדי	למען ידעו ממזרח שמש	6abc
אני יהוה עשה כל אל	עשה שלום ובורא רע	יוצר אור ובורא חשך	7abc

The new messenger formula in 45,1a need not lead us into thinking that a new oracle starts here. The large amount of attention paid to Cyrus is a continuation from vv. 26 and 28. On the contrary, there are far more important arguments to view vv. 1-7 as an integral part of the poem as a whole; these may be found in the formal decisions made by the poet. In the first place, we see here the same technique as regards the messenger formula as in 44,24, only tripled. There, the messenger formula was extended to one verse, a bicolon, but here it is stretched so far as to cover three verses: the entire complex of the six cola or three bicola which make up 45,1 has become one long drawn-out *inquit*. The extended messenger formula now fills an entire strophe. This aspect alone is already responsible for the demarcation of the fourth strophe of the poem.

The discursive level of the fourth strophe is also of essential importance. Do we have first or second-degree discourse here? The poet is not
addressing a "you" at this point, as he was in 44,24. He tells us that God
is addressing Cyrus. We now have to distinguish the grammatical persons in this passage. Cyrus is still a third person singular, as in v. 28[18].
God himself, however, appears as a first person throughout the entire
strophe[19]. As a consequence, this strophe is still second-degree discourse, following on or on the same level as the bulk of the first stanza
(after the introductory v. 24ab). The final boundary of the strophe is a
supporting phenomenon: the transition to third-degree direct discourse
in vv. 2-7. Starting from v. 2a, God directly addresses Cyrus in the second person, so that strophes 5-7 (= 45,2-7) contain his actual words. In
44,28 God was still speaking *about* Cyrus, from 45,2 onwards he is
speaking *to* him. At last, we reach the oracle proper.

Extending a messenger formula to a three-line strophe is exceptional,
but at the same time characteristic of Deutero-Isaiah's impressive command of language and broad rhetoric. As it happens, this strophe is also
one vast period. Viewed in isolation, each of the cola 1d or 1f is an independent clause. However, if they are included in the prosodic system of
the strophe they turn out not to be[20]. These cola are the counterparts of
the infinitive clauses 1c and 1e, and in retrospect reveal the subject of
the forms לרד and לפתח: the same person who immediately preceded 1c
as the subject of the finite form החזקתי: "I", i.e. God.

A linear perusal of v.1 shows the sentence core (predicate plus subject
of the messenger formula, which constitutes the main clause) in front,
followed by two forms for the indirect object; attached to this is an ad-
jectival clause of three words ("whose right hand I have grasped")
which in turn is illustrated in the four clauses of v. 1cdef: twice through
modal infinitives which are in first position and denote transitive actions
(subdue, open), twice through imperfect forms which conclude the
verses and are also transitive verbs. The syntax of 1cdef, like the quartet
of cola in 2abcd, still follows the P + O // O + P framework which dominated strophes 2 and 3. The infinitives may be called anaphoric, not only

18. There are four morphemes for Cyrus in the third person: the suffixes responsible
for the rhyme of v.1a and 1b, and the suffix of *lpnyw* in v. 1c // 1e.

19. Notice that the first person is absent in v. 1a. It could not have been used there
anyway, because of the formulaic character of the clause as the stock messenger formula.
Morphemes for God in the first person are explicitly present in v. 1b and d, and implicitly
in 1c and 1e (as subjects of the infinitives). The identity of the agent hiding underneath
the passive in v. 1f. should now no longer be a mystery.

20. The infinitive may easily be continued by finite forms: JOÜON – MURAOKA,
§124q.

because they are both introduced by the preposition l^e (here in a modal sense, "by..."), but also because they are followed by a repeated l^efanaw (which itself forms the transition to the $l^efaneka$ which opens the oracle proper in v. 2a).

The complement l^efanaw is an extension of $limšiḥo$. In this way, Cyrus becomes the beneficiary of God's words and actions in each of the three A-cola. The division of the first verse into two cola is a delicate matter. We know we have put the caesura in the right position when we observe rhyme, alliteration and assonance in the first and final words:

KO	'amaR	yhwh	limšiḥo
l^eKOREŠ	^{ʾa}ŠER	heḥ^{e}zaqti	bimino

There is a balanced division of 4 + 4 words, and the same vowel on the edges of the cola: head and tail of each colon contain the long -o. The deity is in third position: first as a proper name, then as subject. The conclusions of the cola contain largely similar vowels, on the basis of the same nominal formation *$qatīl$: l^e/b^e attached to m^esih/y^emin. The name "Cyrus" does not appear until the B-colon, but, being an apposition, presupposes enjambment. His office has been stated earlier, straight away in the A-colon – a significant order. Cyrus's personal identity is less important than his office, which moreover is not his own creation, but has as origin and reference the name-giving deity: Cyrus receives an honorary title[21] which should shock the Judaeans even more than the word "shepherd", as it is so specifically Israelite and Yahwist: he has become "the Lord's anointed".

Like its predecessor, the strophe ends on a passive verb form. This "closing" (sgr) is a cornerstone not only through its position, but also semantically. Both horizontally and vertically, it is the antonym of the verb "to open" ($ptḥ$), whose $piel$ in the sense of "ungird" completes verse 1cd, and whose qal starts verse 1ef immediately after that. In this way, a tight figure of contiguity ($ptḥ/ptḥ$) welds the second and third verses together. The arrangement of singular (Cyrus in 1ab) versus plurals (his opponents in a quartet of cola, 1cdef) mirrors what happened in vv. 25 and 26ab: the wrong sort of clergy (in the plural) is being ridiculed, and the servant authorized.

The strophe has a kind of physical directness, to the detriment of the kings (their loins are ungirded, they are taken prisoner) and a certain

---

21. Bestowing honorary titles is an activity which is explicitly named or lexicalized later on in the poem (v. 4d) by means of the verb *kny ($piel$). Hence, each of the designations "shepherd", "servant", and "anointed" is, as the Arabs would say, a $kunyah$ granted to Cyrus.

physical proximity in favour of the victorious king; at least, this is suggested by "his hand" and "his face" (God is busy on his account, in
front of his eyes, *lpnyw*). Cyrus will gain victory over peoples and kings.
His spectacular military and political successes, however, are no more
than illustrations of a subclause about the powerful hand of God, and
result from God's decision to grant him an exclusive title, only known to
a small nation. Cyrus may feel himself to be king of kings, but the true
significance of the title remains hidden, and will be revealed in the sixth
strophe. The doors and gates he rushes into in v. 1ef have not been
opened by him, and Cyrus does not know yet that their opening may
offer a view of another form of riches than the strictly material.

The verses in 45,1 constitute the fourth of seven strophes and consequently occupy the middle of the poem. They have been preceded by
nine verses full of participles governed by the voluminous אנכי. The nine
verses still to come certainly do not leave the divine "I": the slim form
אני serves as anaphora and articulates them into three strophes[22]. Strophes 1-3 were spoken to Israel, strophes 5-7 are addressed to Cyrus personally. They move on a different discursive level from that of v. 1. As
they constitute the content announced by v. 1ab, they are third-degree
direct discourse. This happens to be the exact level at which the last nine
words of stanza I were found, and these were, not coincidentally, the
words of God referring for the first time explicitly to Cyrus, his obedience, and his assignment. In this way, strophes 5-7 (i.e. vv. 2-7) together
make up the actual oracle to Cyrus.

The order of the fifth strophe, vv. 2-3ab, is primarily chronological.
The beginning (with *hlk lpny*) refers to a military campaign (v. 2a).
Next, the strophe takes us on a tour of various obstacles (2bcd) which
are eliminated effortlessly (2bcd), and finally in v. 3ab arrives at the aim
of the campaign, the hidden treasures Cyrus is to receive. This objective
is marked by the selection of a verb tense which does not occur anywhere else in the poem, the perfect consecutive (ונתתי). This is the only
verb in the verse, and it is in a leading position; for the first time, there
is no verb in a B-colon[23].

It is not Cyrus who does the dirty work on the campaign, but God
himself. The pronoun which refers to him is situated at the very beginning of v. 2. Why is this "I" there at all? Isn't it redundant, since the

---

22. The form *'ani* is literally in the first position in vv. 2a and 5a. In the sixth strophe
it also occurs in the first A-colon, this time as the content of knowledge, in an object
clause.

23. I am leaving aside the introductory verse 24ab for the moment. After strophe 5
two more B-cola without predicate follow, and that straight away, in v. 3d and v. 4b. In
v. 5b and v. 6b we get nominal predicates.

verb אלך already constitutes a finite verb form? This sort of redundancy is only apparent; it invites the reader to ponder a possible stylistic function. Let us read colon 2a again. The relation between God and Cyrus is close: they are next to each other, practically eye to eye; this contiguity of the forms for "I ... you" pointedly precedes the verbal predicate. To tidy up, the poet chooses the *pi'el* register, which is close to his heart[24]. This results in a strongly assonant chain, *'ᵃwaššer – 'ᵃšabber – 'ᵃgadde'*, against which walls, doors, and bolts do not stand a chance[25]. These plurals, which had already been part of a construct state combination in v. 2cd, are replaced by the nouns of v. 3ab, another set, this time of *sᵉmikut* twosomes. The three words for "opening" and "closing" at the end of the previous strophe now acquire counterparts in the three words for "hiding" which occupy the final positions in strophe 5. The last root, *str*, does not differ much phonetically from the *sgr* which closed off strophe 4 and reveals a semantic connection[26]. It now becomes clear why v.1ef mentioned doors and gates: they belong in the series of obstacles. The only question that remains is what exactly is meant by the "treasures of darkness". Could "darkness" have been used figuratively, or are we talking only about gold and silver? The two plural nouns completing the strophe as B-colon strike us as pleonastic, given the roots *ṭmn* and *str*. What sort of squared obscurity is this?

The poet loses no time in providing us with a remarkable answer. In his next strophe he squares the aspect of purpose and resolution, and the resulting hierarchy of meanings. We are immediately confronted with an anaphora in the shape of a repeated *lᵉma'an*, which occurs first as a conjunction, next as a preposition, and whose meaning has everything to do with aims and purposes.

Are we, however, justified in separating the final clause "that you may know" from v. 3ab by means of a strophe boundary? This would deviate from what the Masoretes considered to be a unit, by including a quartet of cola in v. 3. Is it necessary to accept the following syntactic construction: a final clause (v. 3c) plus apposition (3d), another double complement (4a/b), only then followed by the main clause v. 4c, which

24. This poem forms part of the Book of Consolation, as we may call Isa 40–55. The key word for "consoling" is a *pi'el* which impressively opens the collection and is supported in the overture (40,1-11) by a string of other *pi'el* forms. See my article about this in *OTS* 21 (1981). See also in our poem the end of v. 1cd and the beginning of v. 4d and v. 5c.

25. The assonant chain also helps us in determining the correct reading of the kᵉtib *'wšr*, which is not a *hiphil* but a *pi'el*, *'ᵃwaššer* or possibly *'ᵃyaššer*. I am following Beuken (cf. his commentary, pp. 235 and 323) in the view that *durim*, taking into account the Akkadian cognate, means "ring-walls".

26. In Job 3,10 *sgr* and *str* form a word-pair, and as predicates dominate the bicolon.

is doubled in 4d? Many translations and commentaries adopt a different course.

Yet, this demarcation of the sixth strophe is correct, as proved by its powerful structure[27]. We notice how it is framed by the opposition of knowing God (in the present) versus not having known God (in the past), with Cyrus as the subject of the same verb. The diagonal formed by this inclusio is intersected by the repetition of the motif of "calling you by name", in 3d and 4c. These observations result in a chiasm which dominates and defines the strophe as an envelope. Perhaps we should say, however, that verses 3cd and 4cd follow an ABC-C'B'A' pattern. At a point somewhere between knowing and calling there is also a phonetic link which gives us the idea to draw a line from the proper name *yhwh* to the verb "bestowing an honorary title": all consonants of *'ᵃkannᵉka* recur in the object clause *ki 'ᵃni yhwh*.

The last words are extremely important, for two reasons: the nominal clause soon reappears three times as a main clause which to a large extent determines the aspect of the final strophe, and v. 3c is the moment when God reveals himself to the Persian. In contrast to the combination in v. 24c, אני יהוה is this time indeed predicative[27]. The actual self-revelation occurs here and in the next strophe. This delicate moment is also marked by the sudden frequency of proper names. The quartet of cola responsible for the long deferment of the sentence core 4c ends on a proper name four times: in the A-cola we get *yahweh //ya'qob*, both imperfect forms originally; in the B-cola we twice get the name of Israel, which also has an imperfect as one of its components. Only two persons are being referred to, who are immediately qualified further. In v. 3d Cyrus is told that Yahweh is "the God of Israel". Verse 4ab is even more striking. It forms the pivot of the strophe, is completely nominal and has a closed structure because of the chiastic arrangement of "my servant – Jacob // Israel – my chosen". Hence, the entire strophe is in fact dominated by a concentric pattern[28]. In the following diagram, words are denoted by lower-case letters, phrases by capitals[29]:

---

27. The problem may be formulated in terms of syntax: can a sentence core of the *wyqtl* type be preceded by a subclause or a complement? This is permitted, see for instance Gen 22,4a, 1 Sam 4,20a, and Isa 6,1a; see also GK, §111, especially note 1 referring to our passage.

28. Notice that the *qal* participle which follows in v. 3d is an unmistakable apposition: the article renders it attributive. Contrast this with the *qal* participles of v. 24cde.

29. In the diagram which now follows, the phrase "the God of Israel", indicated by a capital D, is the only phrase without a counterpart.

```
A B      /      C D
e f      /      f' e'
C'       /      B'A'
```

The syntax also confirms the three-verse structure of the strophe, since the entire complex, in imitation of the astonishing agility of strophe 4, is again one sentence[30].

The centre is valuable. Two honorary titles, illustrating the meaning of *knh*, lovingly surround the name of the people. Since God has chosen Israel (*beḥiri*), no *berihe barzel* can stop him in the campaign which will bring deliverance[31]. The bolts, too, are in the B-colon of a pivotal line. God's *šBR* clears them away, v. 2c. Contrary to "his servant" in v. 44,26a, "my servant" here is accompanied by an unmistakable identification. Two different counts starting at the borders and moving inwards point to the weight of this honorary title. The words for "servant" occur in the fifth A-colons from the beginning and from the end of the poem. This may be considered a coincidence, but for the fact that this couple is linked to another balance of honorary titles. A word count, i.e. of much smaller units, leads us to the extremely careful positioning which balances "my shepherd", as a term of Cyrus's election, with "my servant" for Israel: the words *ro'i* in 44,28a and *'abdi* in 45,4a both occupy the 45th positions from the beginning and end[32].

This sort of precision is not there for nothing, and its application at exactly this point has excellent reasons. The careful positioning of the honorary titles both serves and refers to the balance between the two stanzas. In the first half of the poem Israel is told how exceptional Cyrus is, in the other half Cyrus is told how exceptional this small bunch of exiles on the rivers of Babylon are. This is the focal point of the rhetoric which has been developed in the course of the two stanzas:

	introduc-tory voice	speaker	level of discourse	address	message
stanza I	prophet	God	2nd degree	Israel	Cyrus is my shepherd
stanza II	God himself	God	3rd degree	Cyrus	Israel is my servant

30. This statement should be taken prosodically; strictly speaking, it is no longer valid after the late *knh*. The verbs in v. 4d each provide us with an independent clause (consisting of 1 word plus 2 words, respectively), if 4d is viewed on its own and purely linguistically; however as a counterpart to "calling" (v. 4c), *'knk* forms part of one vast tension arc encompassing the entire strophe.

31. The word for "chosen" is not coincidentally derived from the same nominal formation pattern as the honorary title Cyrus receives in 45,1a, the "anointed".

The messages are clearly complementary. Both sides, the conqueror and the small group of exiles, are being informed about the true or essential quality of the other party. The balance between the two parts creates an image of splendid reciprocity[33].

God's choosing of Israel is so remarkable as to completely determine the Persian autocrat's destiny. Both Cyrus's assignment and his essence are indicated by the double "I am calling you by name". The balance and reciprocity of the stanzas should not let us lose sight of the fact that at the same time we are confronted here with a complicated multi-stage structure representing a hierarchy of ends and means. Cyrus is not appointed because of his attractive personality. He does not become conqueror as a purpose in itself. Even the knowledge of God he acquires by God's revealing himself personally to him is not a goal in itself, because the first *l^ema'an* is followed by and overruled by the second. Thus the heart of the sixth strophe, the pre-eminently revelational strophe, indicates that means and ends are eventually subordinate to God's love for and care of his chosen people. This hierarchy implies a radical reversal of priorities for the person addressed – I do not mean the historical Cyrus here, but rather the object of the song, the character in the universe evoked by the lyric. At the same time, the surprising rearrangement of means and ends offers to the poet's Judaean audience the explanation of God's radical and startling gesture of calling a Persian his Anointed.

The last strophe shows a balance of positive and negative: the deity says three times "I am Yahweh", and this never occurs on its own. His being in the right is always supported by its reverse indicated by the nominal negation אין, another trio. This reverse side is inextricably linked to the identification "I am Yahweh", since the point of this strophe is God's uniqueness, dormant in v. 24de but here being thoroughly worked out in a fully ternary textual unit. The balance may be extended even further: there are five participle predicates celebrating God again as the almighty Creator, all of which have been reserved for the concluding verse 7. In addition, there are five negative sentences in all, four of which eradicate the existence of the gods[34].

The "I am the LORD" which in strophe 6 is revealed to Cyrus for the first time is expanded in strophe 7. The interdependence between both

---

32. This word count presupposes the deletion of v. 26d as not original, but at the same time justifies this deletion.

33. A third count reinforces the previous two. As stated before, "my shepherd" and "my servant" each occur in the eighth A-colon of their respective stanzas. Moreover, they are both flanked by a proper name.

34. The double עוד אין alternates with זולת and אפס בלעדי. In v. 5a there is one verb accompanied by the negation לא.

units is extremely powerful, and is based on the polarity "knowing" vs. "not knowing":

in order to + know + that I am Yahweh	(v. 3c)
"you did not know me"	(v. 4d)
--	
"you did not know me"	(v. 5c)
in order to + know + that I am Yahweh	(v. 6a.c)

We recognize a chiasm whose diagonals again cross a strophe boundary (dotted line) – a technique we have seen before when moving from strophe 2 to strophe 3. In the heart of the concluding strophe, Cyrus becomes a representative of the pagan world; he need not keep the enlightenment to himself. The inhabitants of his realm, widely spread as effectively indicated by the merism "from East to West" which moreover causes a remarkable enjambment in v. 6a/b, will also share in the revelation. This higher purpose is more important than the fact that Cyrus, as the victor, will be girded by God (v. 5c); the hierarchy of purposes has not been forgotten in these formidable hymnal final chords[35]. Here also comes a new "so that", introducing a long, final and in itself compound sentence (v. 6ab), and reminding us of the ternary principle.

The fact that this third l^{e}ma'an is again linked to "knowing" brings me to a survey of the four strophes making up the second stanza. Strophes 4-5 may aptly be classified under "action", strophes 6-7 reveal that the meaning of these many actions on God's part can be found in revelation, and hence may be fitted under the heading of "knowledge".

The arrangement of the six cola in vv. 5-6 is concentric. In the centre we have knowing/not knowing God (5c + 6a), around this the competition is being eliminated, and the outer ring consists of v. 5a and v. 6c which are completely identical. The negative "there is none else" is replaced in the last line. Verse 7 forms the climax of the strophe; it doubles the tempo set by the predicates in 7ab and in the very last colon introduces the all-encompassing term "all these things" which clearly refers back to God's very first colon, 44,24c, and thus closes the circle perfectly. This forces us to re-analyse the syntax. In the clause אני יהוה עשׂה כל אלה the proper name is again no more than an apposition (unlike 5a // 6c!), and the form עשׂה (with its seghol) is another participle predicatively used which verbally governs its object! "I the LORD do all these things" (thus correctly JPS).

---

35. As pointed out earlier, this "girding" is the exact opposite of "ungirding the loins of kings" (who are the captives of the great conqueror). Both verbs are in the pi'el.

In v. 7a and 7b the objects form pairs of opposites. The pair light/ darkness explains the pair happiness/evil. The word *šalom* here replaces the word "good", which again is no coincidence. It is the capstone of the double word-play linking God and Cyrus in their *yašlim* in favour of Jerusalem[36]. The participles form a series ab/ cb /c, because the verbs "create" and "make" are both used twice. The colon which contains only one participle, the very last one, offers the synthesis which transcends the polarities in v. 7ab by employing just one all-inclusive term as object. God is the Lord of polarities, in roughly the same way as in the Song of Hannah[37]. Hence, there are two cola in which poles are distinguished, whereas the colon containing the holy name offers a synthesizing discourse. This mirrors God's first verse, in which the synthesis was mentioned first in 24c and the differentiation came in 24de, by means of the merism of "heaven" and "earth".

The first word in the final verse contributes to the outer frame of the poem, since this *yoṣer* also occurred in 24b. Its object here is the darkness, in exactly the same (fourth) position as in v. 3a. The sounds of *yoṣer* not only (literally) set the tone in v. 7 with its *'or* and two occurrences of *bore'*, plus another four o-sounds, but also form the echo of the word accompanying the darkness in v. 3a: *'oṣᵉrot*, treasures. If we view the contrast between light and darkness as part of a long list of polarities, the attractive option emerges of interpreting the treasures Cyrus will find figuratively, and assigning them a spiritual meaning: the light that shines on him is the light of the revelation, in addition to the light which, as the sun, reaches from East to West in v. 6. The biggest treasure for Cyrus is getting to know the true God.

The poem is truly laced with polarities:

earth	–	heaven
diviners	–	servant, messengers
folly	–	wisdom
waters	–	drought
ruins	–	rebuilding
king Cyrus wins	–	kings who lose
open	–	close
break open	–	hide
call you	–	my chosen
not knowing	–	getting to know
West	–	East

36. This is why we should stick to the MT instead of following the Qumran variant in the large Is^a scroll, which has *ṭob* here!

37. See *Vow and Desire* = Vol. IV of NAPS, Assen, 1993, Chapter 1 of which offers an extensive analysis of this poem and its polarities.

none else	–	I alone
darkness	–	light
evil	–	happiness

It is improbable that any one of the pairs given here is ethically or emotionally neutral. The reader may easily regroup them into a positive versus a negative series, and it is unlikely that light and darkness are only physical categories in this sort of creative language. Light goes with happiness, darkness with ignorance and danger.

The various repetitive devices which round off the poem in one vast and powerful inclusio together form the iconic signal that has been applied by the poet, out of a profound inner need, to express in this way the all-inclusiveness of God's creating the universe and writing history.

Willinklaan 14   Jan P. FOKKELMAN
NL-2341 LW Oegstgeest

STRUCTURE AND REDACTION
ISAIAH 60,1–63,6[1]

In his masterful commentary to the Book of Trito-Isaiah, Wim Beuken has treated Isaiah 60,1–63,6 as a redactional unit[2]. Being very much aware of the intertextual links which are so important to the understanding of the Book as a whole, Beuken does not deny the obvious links with other chapters, especially ch. 59[3]. But he does not view these links as decisive evidence against his division of the text. With his characteristic open-mindedness, however, he recognizes the lack of unanimity among recent scholarship with regard to the redactional history of these chapters[4] which in turn must be attributed to the lack of irrefutable evidence which might convince all.

Far from being able to say the last word in these complicated matters, I want to draw attention to the possibility of making a more consistent use of the analysis of poetic structure in order to trace redactional processes. Starting point for this investigation was Isa 61,10–62,9 which has been written in colometric form in 1QIs[a] and is marked in its margin as a compositional unit[5]. I asked myself: If the Qumran scribe apparently saw this song as a unit, why are all modern interpreters convinced that a new unit starts at 62,1? None of the ancient manuscripts has a $p^e tu\d{h}ah$ or $s^e tumah$ between Isa 61,11 and 62,1[6]. The present division of the Hebrew text into two separate chap-

---

1. Thanks are due to Marjo Korpel (Utrecht) who suggested the subject to me and was kind enough to comment on several drafts of this article.

2. W.A.M. BEUKEN, *Jesaja, deel III A* (POT), Nijkerk, 1989, pp. 157-158.

3. See also W.A.M. BEUKEN, *Servant and Herald of Good Tidings: Isaiah 61 as an Interpretation of Isaiah 40–55*, in J. VERMEYLEN (ed.), *The Book of Isaiah / Le livre d'Isaïe. Les oracles et leurs relectures. Unité et complexité de l'ouvrage* (BETL, 81), Leuven, 1989, pp. 411-442.

4. See his learned recapitulations of previous scholarship in *Jesaja, deel III A* (n. 2), pp.159, 195-6, 224-5, 246-7. See furthermore S. SEKINE, *Die Tritojesajanische Sammlung (Jes 56–66) redaktionsgeschichtlich untersucht* (BZAW, 175), Berlin, 1989, pp. 68-104, 140-150; O.H. STECK, *Studien zu Tritojesaja* (BZAW, 203), Berlin, 1991, esp. pp. 119-166; J.L. KOOLE, *Jesaja III vertaald en verklaard* (COT), Kampen, 1995, pp. 223-225, 260-263, 289-291, 313-315.

5. This was noted first by H. BARDTKE, *Die Parascheneinteilung der Jesajarolle I von Qumran*, in H. KUSCH (ed.), *Festschrift Franz Dornseiff zum 65. Geburtstag*, Leipzig, 1953, p. 72, who did not, however, draw any consequences from his observation.

6. Cf. J.M. OESCH, *Petucha und Setuma. Untersuchungen zu einer überlieferten Gliederung im hebräischen Text des Alten Testaments* (OBO, 27), Freiburg, 1979, p. T 28*.

ters must be attributed to Stephen Langton's divison of the Vulgate
text into chapters which was taken over for the first time in a Hebrew
Bible in the second Bomberg edition of 1521. The division between
ch. 61 and ch. 62 is not supported by any ancient witness. Therefore it
seems worthwhile to study the structure of the song in 61,10–62,9 in
somewhat greater detail and to investigate what its relationship with
the surrounding text may be.

I. THE SONG IN ISA 61,10–62,9

1. *Colometric Division*

First of all it is necessary to compare the colometric division
adopted by the Qumran scribe with that of the Masoretic Text as represented by the Codex Leningradensis (Petropolitanus) B19[A] (CL). To
this end I put the two side by side in columns, numbering the cola of
1QIs[a] for easy reference and providing CL with the number of the dividing accents according to their numbering in the *Tabula Accentuum*
accompanying BHS.

	1QIs[a]		CL
	Petuḥah		Setumah
1	שוש אשיש ביהוה	[7]	שוש אשיש ביהוה
2	תגל נפשי באלוהי	[5]	תגל נפשי באלהי
3	כיא הלבישני בגדי ישע	[5]	כי הלבישני בגדי־ישע
4	מעיל צדקה יעטני	[2]	מעיל צדקה יעטני
5	כחתן ככוהן פאר	[5]	כחתן יכהן פאר
6	וככלה תעדה כליהא	[1]	וככלה תעדה כליה
7	כיא כארץ תוציא צמחה	[5]	כי כארץ תוציא צמחה
8	וכגנה זרועיה תצמיח	[2]	וכגנה זרועיה תצמיח
9	כן יהוה אלוהים יצמיח צדקה		כן אדני יהוה יצמיח צדקה
		[5]	ותהלה
10	ותהלה נגד כל הגואים	[1]	נגד כל־הגוים
11	למען ציון ולוא אחרוש	[5]	למען ציון לא אחשה
12	ולמען ירושלם לוא אשקוט	[2]	ולמען ירושלם לא אשקוט
13	עד יצא כנוגה צדקה	[5]	עד־יצא כנגה צדקה
14	וישועתה כלפיד תבער	[1]	וישועתה כלפיד יבער

continued on next page

1QIsª		CL	
15	וראו גואים צדקכי	[5]	וראו גוים צדקך
16	וכול מלכים כבודך	[2]	וכל־מלכים כבודך
17	וקראו לך שם חדש	[5]	וקרא לך שם חדש
18	אשר פי יהוה יקובנו	[1]	אשר פי יהוה יקבנו
19	והיית עטרת תפארת ביד יהוה	[2]	והיית עטרת תפארת ביד־יהוה
20	וצנוף מלוכה בכף אלוהיכי	[1]	וצנוף מלוכה בכף־אלוהיך
21	ולוא יאמר לכי עוד עזובה	[7]	לא־יאמר לך עוד עזובה
22	ולארצך לוא יאמר עוד שממה	[5]	ולארצך לא־יאמר עוד שממה
23	כיא לכי יקראו חפצי בהא	[5]	כי לך יקרא חפצי־בה
24	ולארצך בעולה	[2]	ולארצך בעולה
25	כיא חפץ יהוה בכי	[5]	כי־חפץ יהוה בך
26	וארצך תבעל	[1]	וארצך תבעל
27	כיא כבעול בחו[ו]ר בתולה	[5]	כי־יבעל בחור בתולה
28	יבעלוכי בניך	[2]	יבעלוך בניך
29	ומשוש חתן על כלה	[5]	ומשוש חתן על־כלה
30	ישיש עליך אלוהיך	[1]	ישיש עליך אלהיך
31	על חומותיך ירושלם	[7]	על־חומתיך ירושלם
32	הפקדתי שומרים כול היום כול הלילה	[5]	הפקדתי שמרים
			כל־היום וכל־הלילה תמיד
		[2]	לא יחשו
33	לוא יחשו המזכירים את יהוה	[5]	המזכירים את־יהוה
34	אל דמי לכמה	[1]	אל־דמי לכם
35	ואל תתנו דמי לו	[2]	ואל־תתנו דמי לו
36	עד יכין ועד יכונן		עד־יכונן ועד־ישים את־ירושלם
		[1]	תהלה בארץ
37	ועד ישים את ירושלם תהלה בארץ		
	Setumah?		
38	נשבע יהוה בימינו ובזרוע עוזו	[2]	נשבע יהוה בימינו ובזרוע עזו
39	אם אתן עוד דגנך מאכל לאיביך		אם־אתן את־דגנך עוד מאכל לאיביך
		[5]	
40	אם ישתו בני נכר תירושך	[5]	ואם־ישתו בני־נכר תירושך
41	אשר יגעתי בוה	[1]	אשר יגעת בו
42	כיא אם מאספיהו יאכולוהו	[5]	כי מאספיו יאכלהו
43	ויהללו את שם יהוה	[2]	והללו את־יהוה
44	ומקבצו ישתוהו בחצרות קדשי	[1]	ומקבציו ישתהו בחצרות קדשי
45	אמר אלהיך		
	Petuḥah		Setumah

The first observation to be made on the basis of this comparison is that there is an astounding degree of agreement between 1QIs[a] and CL which is more than a thousand years younger. Of the 45 cola indicated by the Qumran scribe only 6 are divided differently in CL (9-10, 32-33, 36-37). As with other such comparisons we have made at Kampen, the only conclusion can be that the reliability of the major dividing accents found in medieval Masoretic manuscripts is much higher than many scholars seem to realize[7]. The smallest Masoretic accent delimiting a colon is 7 (*R*[e]*ḇi*[a]') in this relatively small portion of text. Although this observation agrees more or less with the findings of others[8], it should not induce us to draw hasty conclusions. The major dividing accents do offer us a reliable basis for colometric analysis, but a problem one encounters is that even much smaller dividers may sometimes mark the end of a colon, for example accent No. 12 (*T*[e]*ḇir*) in Isa 60,11aA, 12aA, 21bA and hence possibly also in 62,6b. Further study of the manuscripts may reveal that such cases rest on erroneous tradition.

The differences between the two manuscripts are mostly of an orthographic nature and these instances need not concern us here. The variant reading ככהן in line 5 is clearly inferior to MT because the parallel colon also uses the asyndetic imperfect. Also inferior is the ולא אחרוש in line 11. MT is supported by the parallel colon. The feminine תבער for MT יבער in line 14, וקראו in line 17 and יקראו in line 23 are grammatical variants. The different order of words in line 39 and the extra אם in line 42 do not result in a different colometry.

In the lines 9-10 1QIs[a] has the correct division, as recognized by BHK[3], BHS and many authors. The Masoretes were probably led astray by the ellipsis (gapping) of the verb in the second colon. In lines 32-33 1QIs[a] follows the syntax. Both cola might be read with 4 stresses (see the *Maqqefs* in CL) and therefore this division might be acceptable. However, MT is definitely preferable because in 1QIs[a] אל דמי לכמה (line 34) is left dangling in the air. The Qumran scribe did not recognize the vocative המזכרים. In lines 36-37 both 1QIs[a] and CL have abnormally long, though slightly different cola. Apparently both had difficulty in establishing a satisfactory breaking-point in the on-running sentence. Enjambement (or so-called 'synthetical parallelism') often caused this kind of problem in the tradition of Hebrew poetry. I shall return to this matter below. Also the extra colon line 45 will be evaluated later on when we are going to study the verse structure.

---

7. Cf. P. SANDERS, *The Provenance of Deuteronomy 32* (OTS, 37), Leiden, 1996, pp. 102-132.
8. E.g., *ibid.*, pp. 111-119.

With regard to rhythmical structure it may be observed that the number of stressed syllables varies between 2 and 5 which lends support to our earlier conclusion that no rigid metre may be assumed in Hebrew poetry[9]. The Masoretes sometimes equalize the number of stresses in using the *maqqef* (e.g. line 3), but omit to do this in other cases (e.g. line 7), or add the *maqqef* where it disturbs the equilibrium (e.g. lines 16, 31, see also lines 19-22). Apparently they too did not strive after complete rhythmical harmony.

2. *Delimitation of Verses*

In the further analysis of the poetic structure we shall use the method developed at Kampen[10]. Usually the verses are delimited in accordance with the dividing accents of the Masoretic tradition, as indicated above. As soon as a weaker major dividing accent is encountered, as indicated by a *higher* (sometimes *equal*) number according to the *Tabula Accentuum*, we start a new verse. Although we do not attach great value to the rhythmical symmetry of verses I will add the number of major stresses for further study in the future. The very fact that sometimes differences in colometric division can be found in the manuscripts entitles us to evaluate the Masoretic accents critically. Here internal parallelism binding the constituent parts of the verse together is our most important criterion. As with all parallelism, the argument gains in force if a word pair can be demonstrated to exist in other poetic texts and may therefore be regarded as a standard pair.

3	(7)	שׂושׂ אשׂישׂ ביהוה	61,10aA
3	(5)	תגל נפשׂי באלהי	61,10aB

61,10aA   *Verily I rejoice in Yhwh,*
61,10aB   *my soul shall exult in my God;*

Internal parallelism: אלהים ‖ יהוה ;ב ‖ ב[11]; גיל ‖ שׂושׂ.

---

9. Cf. J.C. DE MOOR, *The Art of Versification in Ugarit and Israel*, in Y. AVISHUR – J. BLAU (eds.), *Studies in Bible and the Ancient Near East*. FS S.E. Loewenstamm, Jerusalem, 1978, pp. 119-139.

10. For some recent expositions of this method see J.C. DE MOOR – W.G.E. WATSON (eds.), *Verse in Ancient Near Eastern Prose* (AOAT, 42), Neukirchen-Vluyn, 1993; J. KIM, *The Structure of the Samson Cycle*, Kampen, 1993; SANDERS, *The Provenance* (n. 7), pp. 101-102; M.C.A. KORPEL, *Metaphors in Isaiah LV*, in *VT* 46 (1996) 43-55; ID., *The Female Servant of the Lord in Isaiah 54*, in B. BECKING – M. DIJKSTRA (eds.), *On Reading Prophetic Texts: Gender-Specific and Related Studies in Memory of Fokkelien van Dijk-Hemmes*, Leiden, 1996, pp. 153-67.

11. Cf. Isa 35,1; 65,18,19; 66,10; Ps 35,9.

61,10bA   כי הלבישני בגדי־ישע   (5)   3
61,10bB   מעיל צדקה יעטני   (2)   3

61,10bA   *for he has clothed me with garments of liberation,*
61,10bB   *with a mantle of righteousness he has covered me,*

Internal parallelism: ישע[12] ǁ ; מעיל ǁ בגד ; ־ני ǁ ־ני; יעט (unique) ǁ לבש ǁ
צדקה[13].

61,10cA   כחתן יכהן פאר   (5)   3
61,10cB   וככלה תעדה כליה   (1)   3

61,10cA   *as a bridegroom decks himself with a priestly ribbon,*
61,10cB   *and as a bride adorns herself with her finery.*

Internal parallelism: כ ǁ כ ; חתן ǁ כלה[14]; כהן ǁ עדה (unique); פאר ǁ כלי[15].

61,11aA   כי כארץ תוציא צמחהה   (5)   4
61,11aB   וכגנה זרועיה תצמח   (2)   3

61,11aA   *For as the earth brings forth its shoots,*
61,11aB   *and as a garden makes sprout what is sown in it,*

Internal parallelism: כ ǁ כ ; ארץ ǁ גנה[16]; יצא hiph. ǁ צמח hiph.[17]; ־ה ǁ ־ה.

61,11bA   כן אדני יהוה יצמיח צדקה   (10?)   5
61,11bB   ותהלה נגד כל־הגוים   (1)   3

61,11bA   *so the Lord Yhwh will make sprout righteousness,*
61,11bB   *and praise before all nations.*

Internal parallelism: The *Pašṭa* of CL is unacceptable, as perceived by
almost all scholars. See above. The pair תהלה ǁ צדקה is well-estab-
lished[18].

62,1aA   למען ציון לא אחשה   (5)   4
62,1aB   ולמען ירושלם לא אשקוט   (2)   4

62,1aA   *For Zion's sake I will not keep silent,*
62,1aB   *and for Jerusalem's sake I will not fall silent,*

Internal parallelism: שקט ǁ חשה ; לא ǁ לא ; ירושלם[19] ǁ ציון; למען ǁ למען
(unique).

---

12. Cf. Isa 59,17; Ezek 26,16.
13. Cf. Isa 45,8; 62,1; etc., with Y. AVISHUR, *Stylistic Studies of Word-Pairs in Biblical and Ancient Semitic Literatures* (AOAT, 210), Neukirchen-Vluyn, 1984, pp. 87-88,
226, 266, 283, 288, 293.
14. Cf. Isa 62,5; Jer 7,34; 16,9; 25,10; 33,11; Joel 2,16.
15. Compare כלי תפארת, Ezek 16,17. 39; 23,26.
16. Cf. Gen 13,10; Ezek 36,35.
17. Cf. Ps 104,14.
18. Cf. Isa 45,25; Ps 35,28; 48, 11; 119,164.
19. Cf. Isa 2,3; 31,9; 37,22; 40,9; 41,27, etc.

| 62,1bA | עד־יצא כנגה צדקה | (5) | 3 |
| 62,1bB | וישועתה כלפיד יבער | (1) | 3 |

62,1bA   *until her righteousness comes forth as brightness,*
62,1bB   *and her liberation burns as a torch.*

Internal parallelism: צדקה ǁ (unique); נגה ǁ לפיד[20]; כ ǁ כ; בער ǁ יצא[21]ישועה.

| 62,2aA | וראו גוים צדקך | (5) | 3 |
| 62,2aB | וכל־מלכים כבודך | (2) | 2 |

62,2aA   *And nations will see your righteousness,*
62,2aB   *and all kings your glory.*

Internal parallelism: גוי ǁ מלך[22]; כבוד ǁ צדק[ה][23]; ־ך ǁ ־ך.

| 62,2bA | וקרא לך שם חדש | (5) | 4 |
| 62,2bB | אשר פי יהוה יקבנו | (1) | 4 |

62,2bA   *And you will be called by a new name,*
62,2bB   *which the mouth of Yhwh will pronounce.*

Internal parallelism: נקב ǁ קרא (unique).

| 62,3aA | והיית עטרת תפארת ביד־יהוה | (2) | 4 |
| 62,3aB | וצנוף מלוכה בכף־אלהיך | (1) | 3 |

62,3aA   *And you will be a crown of beauty in the hand of Yhwh,*
62,3aB   *and a royal diadem in the hand of your God.*

Internal parallelism: עטרת ǁ צנוף[24]; תפארת ǁ מלוכה (unique); ב ǁ ב; יד ǁ כף[25]; יהוה ǁ אלהים (see 61,10a).

| 62,4aA | לא־יאמר לך עוד עזובה | (7) | 4 |
| 62,4aB | ולארצך לא־יאמר עוד שממה | (5) | 4 |

62,4aA   *And you shall no more be called 'Abandoned One',*
62,4aB   *and your land shall no more be termed 'Desolate'.*

Internal parallelism: עזובה ǁ שממה[26]; עוד ǁ עוד; אמר ǁ אמר; לא ǁ לא.

| 62,4bA | כי לך יקרא חפצי־בה | (5) | 4 |
| 62,4bB | ולארצך בעולה | (2) | 2 |

20. Cf. Jer 4,4; 21,12.
21. See above, note 13.
22. Cf. Isa 52,15; 60,3.16; Jer 27,7; Ps 72,11; 102,16; 135,10.
23. Cf. Isa 58,8; Ps 97,6; Prov 8,18; 21,21.
24. Cf. Ezek 21,31 (tr. 21,26).
25. Cf. Jer 15,21; Ps 18,1; AVISHUR, *Stylistic Studies* (n. 13), pp. 184, 257, 295, 302, 501, 640, 701.
26. Cf. Zeph 2,4.

62,4bA   *For you will be addressed as 'My delight is in her',*
62,4bB   *and your land as 'Married one'.*

Internal parallelism: ל ‖ ל; ־ך ‖ ־ך; חפץ ‖ בעל (unique in this and the next verse)[27].

3	(5)	כי־חפץ יהוה בך	62,4cA
2	(1)	וארצך תבעל	62,4cB

62,4cA   *For the delight of Yhwh will be in you,*
62,4cB   *and your land will be married.*

Internal parallelism: בעל ‖ חפץ; ־ך ‖ ־ך.

3	(5)	כי־יבעל בחור בתולה	62,5aA
2	(2)	יבעלך* בנ[ו]יך*	62,5aB

62,5aA   *For as a young man marries a maiden,*
62,5aB   *so your Builder* will marry you*[28],*

Internal parallelism: בעל ‖ בעל; in putting בחור and בנה in parallelism, the poet is obviously hinting at the verbs בנה ‖ בחר used in connection with Zion in 1 Ki 8,16.44.48.

3	(5)	ומשוש חתן על־כלה	62,5bA
3	(1)	ישיש עליך אלהיך	62,5bB

62,5bA   *and as the bridegroom rejoices over the bride,*
62,5bB   *your God will rejoice over you.*

Internal parallelism: על ‖ על; שוש ‖ משוש[29].

2	(7)	על־חומתיך ירושלם	62,6aA
2	(5)	הפקדתי שמרים	62,6aB

62,6aA   *On your walls, o Jerusalem,*
62,6aB   *I appoint watchmen;*

---

27. In Deut 21,13-14 there is an implicit relation between the two.

28. Although much speaks in favour of maintaining MT – see BEUKEN, *Jesaja, deel III A* (n. 2), pp. 229-230; KOOLE, *Jesaja III* (n. 4), pp. 298-299; D. BARTHÉLEMY, *Critique textuelle de l'Ancien Testament*, t. 2, Fribourg, 1986, pp. 428-429 – its text stands under the suspicion of having wanted to avoid the rather strong metaphorical language which is, however, supported by the parallelism between 62,5a and 62,5b (see also 61,10). For God as the Builder of Zion see especially Ps 147,2, with M.C.A. KORPEL, *A Rift in the Clouds. Ugaritic and Hebrew Descriptions of the Divine*, Münster, 1990, pp. 386-389. In Isa 62,7 the verb כן Polel is used which is also a verb describing God's building of Zion, cf. *ibid.*, p. 388. Of course, the poet is making clever use of the metaphorical meaning of בנה in the sense of building a family.

29. Cf. Isa 65,18 (external parallel); 66,10 (collocation).

Internal parallelism: שמר ‖ חומה[30].

2	(12?)	כל־היום וכל־הלילה	62,6bA
3	(2)	תמיד לא יחשו	62,6bB

62,6bA   *All the day and all the night*
62,6bB   *they shall never be silent.*

Internal parallelism: The standard pairs תמיד[31] ‖ כל היום and ‖ כל הלילה תמיד[32] clearly support the decision to regard accent No. 12 (*Tᵉḇir*) as a major divider here, even though it was perhaps not intended as such by the Masoretes.

2	(5)	המזכרים את־יהוה	62,6cA
2	(1)	אל־דמי לכם	62,6cB

62,6cA   *O you who invoke Yhwh,*
62,6cB   *there be no silence for you!*

Internal parallelism: דמי ‖ זכר Hiphil (antithetical; unique).

3	(2?)	ואל־תתנו דמי לו	62,7aA
3	(12?)	עד־יכונן ועד־ישים את־ירושלם	62,7aB
2	(1)	תהלה בארץ	62,7aC

62,7aA   *And do not grant him silence*
62,7aB   *until he establishes and makes Jerusalem*
62,7aC   *a praise in the land.*

Internal parallelism: Again the seeming lack of parallelism confuses both the Qumran scribe and the Masoretes. Even though they have the same extremely unbalanced colometry, and therefore deserve serious consideration, we believe they did not recognize that the on-running sentence is a tricolon, as indicated by the pairs כון ‖ נתן[33], תהלה ‖ דמי (antithetical)[34] and ארץ ‖ ירושלם[35]. Apparently the verse seeks to provide an answer to Lam 2,15.

5	(2)	נשבע יהוה בימינו ובזרוע עזו	62,8aA

62,8aA   *Yhwh has sworn by his right hand and his strong arm*

Internal parallelism: none (unicolon). Even though the rather long colon (five stresses) and the standard pair זרוע ‖ ימין[36] render it attractive to

---

30. Cf. Jer 51,12; collocation in Cant 5,7.
31. Cf. Jer 52,13; Ps 72,15; Prov 15,15.
32. Cf. Isa 21,8; 60,11.
33. Cf. Ps 78,20; 2 Chron 17,5.
34. Cf. Jer 48,2.
35. Cf. Jer 4,5.
36. Cf. Ps 89,14; 98,1.

deviate from the identical division found in 1QIs[a] and CL, the exactly matching number of stresses in the next colon argues against such a decision.

5	(5)	ואם־אתן את־דגנך עוד מאכל לאיביך	62,8bA
3	(5)	ואם־ישתו בני־נכר תירושך	62,8bB
3	(1)	אשר יגעת בו	62,8bC

62,8bA   *"I will not again make your grain food for your enemies,*
62,8bB   *and foreigners will not drink your must*
62,8bC   *for which you have laboured.*

Internal parallelism: אם ‖ אם; מאכל ‖ תירוש (unique); נכר ‖ איב (unique); ־ך ‖ ־ך.

3	(5)	כי מאספיו יאכלהו	62,9aA
2	(2)	והללו את־יהוה	62,9aB

62,9aA   *For those who garner it shall eat it,*
62,9aB   *and shall praise Yhwh,*

Internal parallelism: הלל ‖ אכל[37].

4	(1)	ומקבציו ישתהו בחצרות קדשי	62,9bA
2	(0)	[אמר אלהיך]	(62,9bB)

62,9bA   *and those who gather it shall drink it in the courts of my sanctuary,*

(62,9bB)   *(says your God)".*

Internal parallelism: None in MT, but see below. It is possible to connect v. 9bA with the preceding bicolon. However, the strong parallelism need not be internal, it can just as well be external, connecting the two verses to form one strophe. Moreover, 1QIs[a] has an extra colon which makes our verse a bicolon. Since this bicolon creates the external pairs אמר ‖ הלל[38] and אלהים ‖ יהוה, 1QIs[a] counsels against taking v. 9bA as the final colon of a tricolon. In MT it is a verse-line in its own right (a unicolon), but the bicolon of 1QIs[a] is preferable because it constitutes the more difficult reading as God is speaking of himself in the third person in 62,9aB and because it ignores the introduction of the direct speech in v. 8aA.

3. *Delimitation of Strophes*

Just as the delimitation of verses is governed by two opposing forces – dividing accents and binding parallelism – so the delimitation of stro-

---

37. Cf. Joel 2,26; Ps 78,63; see also Ps 22,27.
38. Cf. Judg 16,24; Jer 31,29; Ps 106,48.

phes makes use of the dividing forces of distinctive markers of separation[39] and the binding force of *external* parallelism (parallelism between consecutive verses). And just as the length of cola and verses may vary according to the mood of the poet or singer, so the length of strophes is not always the same. In the majority of cases the strophic division coincides with the Masoretic division into verses by means of the *sof pasuq*, but as with their dividing accents a critical evaluation of their choices remains necessary. At Kampen we have established all this with the help of texts which have preserved the strophic division in the form of an acrostic or by horizontal lines drawn on a tablet or scroll[40]. Therefore it is admissable to use the same devices to recover the strophic division in cases where no ancient witnesses for it have been discovered thus far.

STROPHE 61,10a
Sep. ↑: Setumah <Petuḥah>; paronomasia; jussive; repetitive ב.
Sep. ↓: None.
Ext. ‖: Absent. I regard v. 10a as an independent strophe of one verse-line because v. 10b and 10c are much more strongly connected by their external parallelism.

STROPHE 61,10b-c
Sep. ↑: כי; repetitive נ־י; chiastic swapping (indirect object).
Sep. ↓: Repetitive כ; swapping (prepositional adjunct).
Ext. ‖: Attire, esp. בגד ‖ כלי[41].

STROPHE 61,11
Sep. ↑: כי; repetitive כ; swapping (prepositional adjunct; object).
Sep. ↓: כן; swapping (subject).
Ext. ‖: צמח ‖ צמח.

STROPHE 62,1
Sep. ↑: למען (repetitive); repetitive לא; swapping (prepositional adjunct).
Sep. ↓: Chiastic swapping (prep. adj.); repetitive כ.

---

39. Like *pᵉtuḥah* and *sᵉtumah*, emphatic particles and syntactic constructions (repetition, chiasmus or swapping), certain expressions found at the beginning or end of strophes.

40. See esp. M.C.A. KORPEL – J.C. DE MOOR, *Fundamentals of Ugaritic and Hebrew Poetry*, in W. VAN DER MEER – J.C. DE MOOR (eds.), *The Structural Analysis of Biblical and Canaanite Poetry* (JSOT SS, 74), Sheffield, 1988, pp. 1-61; J.C. DE MOOR, *Narrative Poetry in Canaan*, in *UF* 20 (1988) 149-171; J.C. DE MOOR – W.G.E. WATSON, *General Introduction*, in DE MOOR – WATSON (eds.), *Verse in Ancient Near Eastern Prose* (n. 10), pp. ix-xviii; E. VAN STAALDUINE-SULMAN, *The Aramaic Song of the Lamb*, in *ibid.*, pp. 265-292.

41. Cf. Ezek 16,39.

STROPHE 62,2
Sep. ↑: Repetitive ו and ך־.
Sep. ↓: Swapping (subject).
Ext. ‖: Suffixes ך־; כבוד ‖ שם[42];

STROPHE 62,3-4a
Sep. ↑: Repetitive ב.
Sep. ↓: Repetitive לא; אמר; repetitive ל; repetitive עוד; swapping (prep. adj.).
Ext. ‖: The Masoretes connected v. 4a with v. 4b-c, thus creating a strophe of three verse-lines with strong contra-indicative markers of separation in the middle (כי; repetitive ל). Probably they did not recognize the antithetical parallelism between the bridal attire (which in the ancient world made her a 'queen'[43]) and the terms עזובה and שממה.

STROPHE 62,4b-c
Sep. ↑: כי; repetitive ל; swapping (prep. adj.).
Sep. ↓: כי; repetitive ך־; swapping (subject).
Ext. ‖: בעל ‖ בעל; ארץ ‖ ארץ; חפץ ‖ חפץ; כי ‖ כי.

STROPHE 62,5
Sep. ↑: כי; repetitive בעל.
Sep. ↓: <Setumah>; <Petuḥah>; repetitive ל; swapping (adverbial adjunct).
Ext. ‖: Marriage imagery; כלה ‖ בתולה[44].

STROPHE 62,6a-b
Sep. ↑: <Setumah>; <Petuḥah>; swapping (prep. adj.); vocative.
Sep. ↓: Swapping (adverbial adjunct).
Ext. ‖: שמר ‖ חשה לא[45].

The Masoretes took v. 6c with the preceding two verse-lines as a consequence of their erroneous division of v. 6b (see above). The strong external parallelism between v. 6c and v. 7 argues against separating these verses from each other.

STROPHE 62,6c-7
Sep. ↑: Vocative; command in the form of a noun phrase.
Sep. ↓: <Setumah> in BR?; tricolon; jussive.
Ext. ‖: דמי ‖ דמי; אל ‖ אל; את ‖ את; תהלה[46]; זכר ‖ תהלה.

---

42. Cf. Isa 59,19; AVISHUR, *Stylistic Studies* (n. 13), pp. 179, 249; KIM, *Samson Cycle* (n. 10), p. 206.

43. R. PATAI, *Sex and Family in the Bible and the Middle East*, Garden City, 1959, pp. 65f. See also Ezek 16,12; Cant 1,4.12-14; 3,6-11.

44. Cf. Jer. 2,32.

45. The watchmen were supposed to call out continuously what they saw. Cf. 2 Ki 9,17-20; Isa 21,6.11-12; 52,8; Jer 31,6.

46. Compare 1 Chron 16,4.

STROPHE 62,8

Sep. ↑: <Setumah> in BR?.

Sep. ↓: Tricolon; repetitive אם.

Ext. ‖: שבע followed by an oath introduced by אם. Antithetical parallelism between YHWH's strong arm and Zion's enemies.

STROPHE 62,9

Sep. ↑: כי; swapping (subject).

Sep. ↓: Setumah <Petuhah>; swapping (subject); אמר.

Ext. ‖: אלהים ‖ יהוה ; [49]אמר ‖ הלל ; [48]שתה ‖ אכל ; [47]קבץ ‖ אסף.

4. *Delimitation of Canticles*

The next higher unit in North-West Semitic poetry is the canticle or stanza. It too is often indicated in the ancient tablets and manuscripts themselves, sometimes by horizontal lines, sometimes by spaces, as in the Hebrew tradition by the pre-Masoretic *petuhot* and *setumot*. Our study of these larger units comprising one or (usually) more strophes has learnt us that their beginning and end is often also marked by a change of subject. Again these separating mechanisms are balanced by a binding force. The strophes of a canticle are mostly connected by external parallelism.

CANTICLE 61,10

Sep. ↑: Setumah <Petuhah>; change of subject.

Sep. ↓: Change of subject.

Ext. ‖: Roots שוש ‖ ישע[50]; שוש ‖ חתן[51].

CANTICLE 61,11–62,1

Sep. ↑: Change of subject.

Sep. ↓: Change of subject.

Ext. ‖: יצא ‖ יצא (inclusion); צדקה ‖ צדקה (responsion); wordplay between כנגה (11aB) and כנגה (1bA).

CANTICLE 62,2–4a

Sep. ↑: Change of subject.

Sep. ↓: Change of subject.

47. Cf. W.G.E. WATSON, *The Hebrew Word-pair* קבץ ‖ אסף, in *ZAW* 96 (1984) 426-434; AVISHUR, *Stylistic Studies* (n. 13), pp. 637, 642.

48. Very frequent, both in Ugaritic and Hebrew.

49. Cf. KIM, *Samson Cycle* (n. 10), p. 357.

50. Cf. Zeph 3,17 (external) as well as the collocation in Isa 12,3; Ps 35,9; 40,17; 51,14; 70,3.

51. Cf. Isa 62,5; Jer 7,34; 16,9; 25,10; 33,11.

Ext. ‖: מלך ‖ מלוכה (responsion); כבוד ‖ תפארת (responsion)[52]; קרא ‖
אמר (responsion)[53]; יהוה ‖ יהוה (concatenation).

CANTICLE 62,4b-5
Sep. ↑: Contrasting names, indicating a new beginning which is set forth in v. 5.
Sep. ↓: Change of subject.
Ext. ‖: כלה ‖ בעולה (inclusion); בעל ‖ בעל (concatenation); יהוה ‖
אלהים.

CANTICLE 62,6–7
Sep. ↑: Change of subject.
Sep. ↓: Change of subject; <Setumah?>.
Ext. ‖: ירושלם ‖ ירושלם (inclusion); אל ‖ לא (concatenation); דמי ‖ חשה
(unique; responsion).

CANTICLE 62, 8–9
Sep. ↑: <Setumah?>.
Sep. ↓: Setumah <Petuḥah>; closing phrase changing the subject.
Ext. ‖: Imagery of the harvest; אמר ‖ שבע (inclusion)[54]; יהוה ‖ יהוה
(responsion) ‖ אלהים (inclusion); אכל ‖ מאכל (concatenation); שתה ‖
שתה (responsion).

5. Delimitation of Subcantos

The canticles of the song must apparently be grouped into three subcantos, A (61,10-62,1), B (62,2-5) and C (62,6-9). The first is bracketed by the antithetical pair גיל (61,10aB), שקט/חשה (62, 1a) as well as שוש (61,10aA) ‖ ישועה[55] (62,1bB; responsion/inclusion). Several other external parallelisms keep this subcanto together: יהוה (61,10aA) ‖ יהוה (61,11bB, inclusion); ישע (61,10bA) ‖ ישועה (61,1bB, inclusion); צדקה (61,10bB) ‖ צדקה (61,11bA, inclusion) ‖ צדקה (62,1bA, responsion); פאר (61,10cA) ‖ נגה (62,1bA, responsion)[56].

In all strophes of the second subcanto (B) Zion is addressed in the second person and in all strophes the name of God occurs: יהוה (62,2bB) ‖ יהוה (62,3aA) ‖ אלהיך (62,3aB) ‖ יהוה (62,4cA) ‖ אלהיך (62,5bB). The two canticles of this subcanto are concatenated by the re-naming of

---

52. Cf. Isa 4,2; see also the collocation in Exod 28,2.40.
53. See KIM, Samson Cycle (n. 10), pp. 294, 347, 360.
54. Cf. Amos 8,14.
55. See n. 50.
56. Compare the external parallelism between נגה and תפארת in Isa 60,19.

Zion. Her "new name" (62,2bA) will be חפצי־בה[57] (62,4b) instead of
שממה || עזובה (62,4a). Apparently שם has to be understood in the sense of
'epithet', a usage also known in Akkadian[58]. Furthermore the following
links may be noted: קרא (62,2bA) || אמר[59] (62,4a) || קרא (62,4bA, inclu-
sion/concatenation); ארצך (62,4aA) || ארצך (62,4bB.4cB, concatenation/
responsion); שמם (62,4aB) || בנה (62,5aB, inclusion)[60].

The third subcanto is bracketed by ירושלם (62,6aA) || ירושלם (62,7aB)
|| חצרות קדשי (62,9bA, inclusion/responsion)[61]. Other connecting links
are: שמר (62,6aB) || אויב (62,8bA, antithetical responsion)[62]; יהוה
(62,6cA) || יהוה (62,9aB, responsion); תהלה (62,7aC) || הלל (62,9aB, in-
clusion); נתן (62,7aA) || נתן (62,8bA, responsion).

6. Macrostructure

We are now able to write out the structure of the song in full.

A.i.1

3	(7)	שוש אשיש ביהוה	61,10aA
3	(5)	תגל נפשי באלהי	61,10aB

61,10aA   *Verily I rejoice in Yhwh,*
61,10aB   *my soul shall exult in my God;*

A.i.2

3	(5)	כי הלבישני בגדי־ישע	61,10bA
3	(2)	מעיל צדקה יעטני	61,10bB
3	(5)	כחתן יכהן פאר	61,10cA
3	(1)	וככלה תעדה כליה	61,10cB

61,10bA   *for he has clothed me with garments of liberation,*
61,10bB   *with a mantle of righteousness he has covered me,*
61,10cA   *as a bridegroom decks himself with a priestly ribbon,*
61,10cB   *and as a bride adorns herself with her finery.*

A.ii.1

4	(5)	כי כארץ תוציא צמחהה	61,11aA
3	(2)	וכגנה זרועיה תצמח	61,11aB

57. Cf. M. Noth, *Die israelitischen Personennamen im Rahmen der gemeinsemiti-
schen Namengebung*, Stuttgart, 1928, pp. 32, 223.

58. *CAD* (Š) 3, p. 285a.

59. See n. 53.

60. Compare the antithetical use of the roots שמם and בנה in Isa 61,4; Ezek 36,36;
Zeph 1,13. See also Amos 9,14.

61. Cf. Ps 116,19.

62. Cf. Ps 41,3; 71,10.

5	(10?)	כן אדני יהוה יצמיח צדקה	61,11bA
3	(1)	ותהלה נגד כל־הגוים	61,11bB

61,11aA   *For as the earth brings forth its shoots,*
61,11aB   *and as a garden makes sprout what is sown in it,*
61,11bA   *so the Lord Yhwh will make sprout righteousness,*
61,11bB   *and praise before all nations.*

A.ii.2

4	(5)	למען ציון לא אחשה	62,1aA
4	(2)	ולמען ירושלם לא אשקוט	62,1aB
3	(5)	עד־יצא כנגה צדקה	62,1bA
3	(1)	וישועתה כלפיד יבער	62,1bB

62,1aA   *For Zion's sake I will not keep silent,*
62,1aB   *and for Jerusalem's sake I will not fall silent,*
62,1bA   *until her righteousness comes forth as brightness,*
62,1bB   *and her liberation burns as a torch.*

B.i.1

3	(5)	וראו גוים צדקך	62,2aA
2	(2)	וכל־מלכים כבודך	62,2aB
4	(5)	וקרא לך שם חדש	62,2bA
4	(1)	אשר פי יהוה יקבנו	62,2bB

62,2aA   *And nations will see your righteousness,*
62,2aB   *and all kings your glory.*
62,2bA   *And you will be called by a new name,*
62,2bB   *which the mouth of Yhwh will pronounce.*

B.i.2

4	(2)	והיית עטרת תפארת ביד־יהוה	62,3aA
3	(1)	וצנוף מלוכה בכף־אלהיך	62,3aB
4	(7)	לא־יאמר לך עוד עזובה	62,4aA
4	(5)	ולארצך לא־יאמר עוד שממה	62,4aB

62,3aA   *And you will be a crown of beauty in the hand of Yhwh,*
62,3aB   *and a royal diadem in the hand of your God.*
62,4aA   *And you shall no more be called 'Abandoned One',*
62,4aB   *and your land shall no more be termed 'Desolate'.*

B.ii.1

4	(5)	כי לך יקרא חפצי־בה	62,4bA
2	(2)	ולארצך בעולה	62,4bB

3	(5)	כי־חפץ יהוה בך	62,4cA
2	(1)	וארצך תבעל	62,4cB

62,4bA   *For you will be addressed as 'My delight is in her',*
62,4bB   *and your land as 'Married one'.*
62,4cA   *For the delight of Yhwh will be in you,*
62,4cB   *and your land will be married.*

B.ii.2

3	(5)	כי־יבעל בחור בתולה	62,5aA
2	(2)	יבעלך* בנ[י]ך*	62,5aB
3	(5)	ומשוש חתן על־כלה	62,5bA
3	(1)	ישיש עליך אלהיך	62,5bB

62,5aA   *For as a young man marries a maiden,*
62,5aB   *so your Builder* will marry you*,*
62,5bA   *and as the bridegroom rejoices over the bride,*
62,5bB   *your God will rejoice over you.*

<Setumah/Petuḥah> _____

C.i.1

2	(7)	על־חומתיך ירושלם	62,6aA
2	(5)	הפקדתי שמרים	62,6aB
2	(12?)	כל־היום וכל־הלילה	62,6bA
3	(2)	תמיד לא יחשו	62,6bB

62,6aA   *On your walls, o Jerusalem,*
62,6aB   *I appoint watchmen;*
62,6bA   *All the day and all the night*
62,6bB   *they shall never be silent.*

C.i.2

2	(5)	המזכרים את־יהוה	62,6cA
2	(1)	אל־דמי לכם	62,6cB
3	(2?)	ואל־תתנו דמי לו	62,7aA
3	(12?)	עד־יכונן ועד־ישים את־ירושלם	62,7aB
2	(1)	תהלה בארץ	62,7aC

62,6cA   *O you who invoke Yhwh,*
62,6cB   *there be no silence for you!*
62,7aA   *And do not grant him silence*
62,7aB   *until he establishes and makes Jerusalem*
62,7aC   *a praise in the land.*

<Setumah?> . . . .

C.ii.1

5	(2)	נשבע יהוה בימינו ובזרוע עזו	62,8aA
5	(5)	ואם־אתן את־דגנך עוד מאכל לאיביך	62,8bA
3	(5)	ואם־ישתו בני־נכר תירושך	62,8bB
3	(1)	אשר יגעת בו	62,8bC

62,8aA   *Yhwh has sworn by his right hand and his strong arm*
62,8bA   *"I will not again make your grain food for your enemies,*
62,8bB   *and foreigners will not drink your must*
62,8bC   *for which you have laboured.*

C.ii.2

3	(5)	כי מאספיו יאכלהו	62,9aA
2	(2)	והללו את־יהוה	62,9aB
4	(1)	ומקבציו ישתהו בחצרות קדשי	62,9bA
2	(0)	[אמר אלהיך]	(62,9bB)

62,9aA   *For those who garner it shall eat it,*
62,9aB   *and shall praise Yhwh,*
62,9bA   *and those who gather it shall drink it in the courts of my*
          sanctuary,

(62,9bB)   *(says your God)".*

SETUMAH <PETUḥAH> _____

The structure we have found appears to be highly regular: three subcantos consisting of two canticles each, and all canticles in turn counting two strophes (pattern: 2 + 2 | 2 + 2 ‖ 2 + 2 | 2 + 2 ‖ 2 + 2 | 2 + 2). This alone enhances the possibility that the Qumran scribe was right in considering Isa 61,10–62,9 a complete song. This canto is bracketed by the name of God (61,10a ‖ 62,9bB). Moreover, גיל/שׂושׂ (61,10a), שׂושׂ (62,5b) and הלל (62,9aB) form responses connecting the first strophe (A.i.1) with the last strophes of both subcanto B (ii.2) and C (ii.2). The circumstance that 61,10 and 62,3-5 describe the restoration of Zion in terms of marriage has always been troubling those who followed Langton in separating the two passages. The תהלה of 61,11bB which is balanced by צדקה in 61,11bA clearly corresponds to צדק before the nations (62,2aA) and her תהלה in 62,7aC. All this argues strongly against separating 61,10-11 from 62,1-9.

II. THE CONTEXT OF THE SONG: ISAIAH 60–62

Of course scholars have long noted the intertextual links discussed in the previous section. For these and other reasons most interpreters are of the opinion that Isa 60–62 – some verses excepted – form a compositional unit. It is striking indeed that these chapters describe the restoration of Zion in terms which are identical or at least very similar. A few examples may suffice to illustrate this point. It is time for rejoicing (60,15; 61,3.7.10; 62,5), mourning must come to an end (60,20; 61,2-3). Zion is no longer an abandoned woman (60,15; 62,4; 62,12), but a radiant bride (60,1-3.17.19.21; 61,10-11; 62,1-2)[63]. The תחת- and עוד- phrases (60,15.17; 61,3,7 and 60,18-20; 62,4.8 respectively) underline the definitive nature of this change. YHWH will liberate his people (root ישע, 60,17; 61,10; 62,1.11). Foreigners will no longer be Zion's oppressors, they themselves (60,10; 61,5; 62,8; cf. 61,9; 62,2) and their kings (60,3.10-12.16; 62,2) will be subservient to Israel. They will hand over their riches (60,5-6.11.17; 61,6). Zion's children will return (60,4.9; 62,5) and their rebuilt capital will be a beauty (תפארת, 60,7.9.13.19-21; 61,3.10; 62,3) and object of praise (60,6, 18; 61,3; 62,7.9), YHWH's own cherished plantation (60,21; 61,3). Righteousness will cover Zion like a splendid cloak (60,17; 61,3.10.11; 62,1.2; note the use of עטה in 61,3; 62,10). Such close parallels render it fully understandable that previous scholarship has tried to keep intact as much of the chapters 60–62 as was reasonable possible. Yet there are some problems which must be addressed now and again I shall try to show how analysis of the poetic structure may help to solve them.

1. *The Immediate Context of Isa 61,10–62,9*

It is obvious that 62,8-9 and 61,5-6 contradict each other. Whereas the former passage states that the Israelites themselves will labour for their own bread and wine, and will enjoy these products thoroughly without any interference of enemies, the latter passage seems to *correct* this picture in stating that the Israelites themselves, being priests, will be exempted from such slavish labour. Foreigners will do it for them. In my opinion this indicates that 61,1-9 can hardly be ascribed to the author of our song. On the contrary, it seems that these verses constitute a later expansion of the song. Making use of several motives taken from Deutero-Isaiah this poet elaborates themes from the song 61,10–62,9. Probably he derived the priesthood of the Israelites from 61,10[64] which he interpreted in the light of 62,5 where he already must have read

---

63. The wording of 60,1 indicates that here too the radiating faces of bride and groom are meant. See J.C. DE MOOR, *An Anthology of Religious Texts from Ugarit*, Leiden, 1987, p. 145, n. 32.
64. And Ex 19,6 of course.

"your sons" instead of "your builder". Probably he himself was responsible for this change, because in 61,4 he elucidates that in reality it will not be God who will rebuild Zion, as 62,5 had stated originally, but the liberated exiles (61,1-3).

The impression that we are dealing with a different hand here is confirmed by an analysis of the poetic structure. The passage immediately preceding Isa 61,10–62,9 has an entirely different structure. Without repeating the whole tedious process of analysis, I confine myself to presenting the results: canticles of 3 + 3 + 3 strophes (61,1aA-1bC; 1cA-2aC; 3aA-3bB[65] I 4aA-4bB; 5aA-5bB; 6aA-6bB I 7aA-7bB; 8aA-8bB; 9aA-9bB). Remarkably enough also the passage following our song (62,10-12) has this structure: a canticle of 3 strophes (62,10aA-10bC; 11aA-11bB; 12aA-12bB). Here too we encounter Deutero-Isaianic motifs interwoven with further explanations of the preceding song. In my opinion Isa 61,1-9 and 62,10-12 stem from the same hand. This is not only suggested by their identical structure, but also by the correspondence between 61,8 באמת פעלתם ונתתי I 62,11 ופעלתו לפניו (cf. Isa 40,10). The description of the Israelites as priests in 61,6 tallies with the עם־ הקדש of 62,12. So it seems that this later poet expanded the song 61,10–62,9 with an embracing structure which betrays his own style in using a different structural model.

It is possible, though not entirely certain, that Isa 63,1-6 was added by the same poet. Here too one might discern two canticles of 3 strophes each: 63,1aA-1bB; 1cA-2aB; 3aA-3bB I 3cA-4aB; 5aA-5bB; 6aA-6aC. In that case the person expanding the song 61,10–62,9 has added exactly three canticles before it (61,1-9) and after it (62,10-63,6). The concepts of righteousness and liberation recur (63,1c) and it is in line with 61,2 to round up the whole poem with the utter destruction of the disobedient foreign nations in 63,1-6. Doubtlessly Isa 59,16-18 offered the poet a model to elaborate. If Isa 63,1-6 is indeed from the same hand as 61,1-9 and 62,10-12, it lends support to Wim Beuken's decision to take 63,1-6 with the preceding chapters[66].

2. Isaiah 60 – A Further Expansion

As we have seen, many scholars are of the opinion that Isa 60–62 must be regarded as interrelated chapters forming a more or less complete whole. In my opinion, however, chapter 60 presupposes the chap-

---

65. Taking ציון לבעלי לשׁום as a gloss, with BEUKEN, *Jesaja, deel III A* (n. 2), pp. 198-199.

66. *Ibid.*, pp. 157-158, 246-247.

ters 61–62 in their expanded form. It borrows extensively from the terminology of both. Yet it can hardly be attributed to the same author because its poetical structure differs significantly from both the original song 61,10–62,9 and the expansions 61,1-9 and 62,10–63,6. If we disregard the prose gloss 60,12[67] the following structure emerges: 3 + 2 l 2 + 2 l 2 + 2 l 2 + 2 l 3 + 2 (60,1aA-3aB; 4aA-5bB l 60,6aA-7bB; 8aA-9cB l 60,10aA-11bB; 13aA-14bB l 60,15aA-16bB; 17aA-17cB l 60,18aA-20bB; 21aA-22bB). One of the reasons for further expansion may have been the wish to clarify a contradictory point in the first expansion. Whereas 61,5-6 had removed doubt as to who would have to toil on the Israelite fields – foreigners – it stated at the same time that the Israelites themselves would have to rebuild their cities (61,4). Somebody discovered that this was not in complete harmony with the nationalistic tradition about the conquest of Canaan, "And I gave to you a land which you did not work in, and cities which you did not build, and you dwell in them, vineyards and olive groves which you did not plant, from which you are eating" (Josh 24,13)[68]. The Canaanites remaining in the land had no option but to do forced labour for the Israelites[69]. So Zion's bright future would only be a really complete restoration if again *all* slavish labour were done not by the Israelites themselves but by their former enemies. This was in full accordance with a promise of the first Isaiah (Isa 31,8). It was for this reason that the author of the second expansion to Isa 61,1–63,6 stipulated pointedly, "Foreigners shall build up your walls" (Isa 60,10).

CONCLUSION

In this study I wanted to demonstrate the importance of careful analysis of poetic structure for a reconstruction of the redaction history of texts. First I drew attention to the colometric division of the text in 1QIs[a] 61,10–62,9. Apparently the Qumran scribe saw this pericope as a compositional unit. Analysis of its poetic structure revealed an amazingly regular composition. This fact renders the modern distribution of the poem over two chapters dubious. Such a division is not supported by any ancient witness. Usually the chapters Isa 60–62 or, as Wim Beuken has proposed, Isa 60–63,6, are seen as the more or less well-preserved

---

67. *Ibid.*, p. 173.
68. See also Deut 6,10-11. Cf. W.T. KOOPMANS, *Joshua 24 as Poetic Narrative*, Sheffield, 1990, pp. 333-335, 441-442.
69. Deut. 20,11; Josh 16,10; 17,13; Judg 1,28.30.33.35; 1 Ki 9,15-21.

kernel of the work of Trito-Isaiah. Analysis of this wider context of the song 61,10–62,9 indicated that Beuken's delimitation is supported by structural arguments. However, it was argued on the basis of content as well as structure that the song 61,10–62,9 was expanded in two distinct redactional phases. First, somebody surrounded it by two evenly built units, 61,1-9 and 62,10–63,6. One of the reasons for this expansion was the wish to eliminate the idea that in Zion's bright future the Israelites themselves would have to till their land (62,8 "for which you have laboured" ⇔ 61,5-6 "foreigners shall be your plowmen and vinedressers"). A second redactor added chapter 60 which again betrays its different origin by a structure differing from both the original song and its first expansion. Whereas the latter stated that the Israelites themselves would have to rebuild their ruined cities (61,4), the second expansion forces foreigners to do this (60,10), thus bringing the hope for restoration into full harmony with the nationalistic theology of the conquest of Canaan.

Ulco de Vriesweg 29
NL-8084 AR 't Harde

Johannes C. DE MOOR

INTERTEXTUALITY AND WIRKUNGSGESCHICHTE

DER NEUE HIMMEL UND DIE NEUE ERDE
BEOBACHTUNGEN ZUR REZEPTION VON
GEN 1–3 IN JES 65,16B–25

In zahlreichen Studien und in einem wegweisenden Kommentar hat Wim Beuken das Verstehen von Jes 56–66 wesentlich gefördert. Seine neuen Einsichten sind durch einen offenen Blick auf diese elf Kapitel gewonnen, der sich von Einengungen durch vorgefaßte Entstehungshypothesen freihält. So kommen in Tritojesaja kontextuell geschaffene Aussageprofile zum Vorschein, die mit Sinn für theologische Ausdruckslinien im Ablauf literarischer Zusammenhänge auch über die Grenzen von Jes 56–66 hinaus zu entdecken sind; nicht zuletzt am Thema des Gottesknechts hat Beuken gezeigt, wie Tritojesaja mit Deuterojesaja auf der literarischen Ebene sachlich verbunden ist. Dem Schreibenden ist es eine besondere Freude, den Jubilar zu ehren und ihm zu danken für die Freundlichkeit vielfältigen Gedankenaustausches im gemeinsamen Bemühen um den in Jes 56–66 gegebenen Schlußabschnitt des Jesajabuches. Als Zeichen unseres Dankes wenden wir uns deshalb einmal mehr Tritojesaja zu. Aber für diesmal nur einem kleinen, aber gewichtigen Einzelproblem, der textgenetischen Frage nämlich, ob sich die in *Jes 65,16b-25* entworfene Heilswende neben anderen Texten innerhalb und außerhalb des Jesajabuches auch an den *Anfangskapiteln der Genesis* orientiert. Wir betrachten dafür zunächst das Textstück Jes 65,16b-25 bezüglich Integrität und Anlage in sich (I), achten dann auf die offenkundige Rezeption von Jes 43,16-21, die für unsere Fragestellung besonders bedacht werden muß (II), und erörtern schließlich ausführlicher das Verhältnis zu Gen 1–3 (III). Ein letzter Abschnitt (IV) skizziert Folgerungen zur Einordnung des Ergebnisses.

I

Untersucht man dem Vorbild Beukens[1] gemäß Jes 65,16b-25 im *gegebenen literarischen Rahmen*, dann trifft man auf ein Textstück, das in seinem engeren und weiteren Kontext überlegt situiert ist. Es gehört

---

1. W.A.M. BEUKEN, *Jesaja deel III^B* (POT), Nijkerk, 1989, pp. 57-96. 157-160; ID., *Isaiah Chapters LXV–LXVI: Trito-Isaiah and the Closure of the Book of Isaiah*, in J.A. EMERTON (ed.), *Congress Volume Leuven 1989* (SVT, 43), Leiden - New York - Köln, 1991, pp. 204-221.

zur dritten (65,13-25) von fünf Gottesreden, die das voranstehende Gebet 63,7–64,11 beantworten und ausweislich der in der Forschung vielfach vermerkten Rückbezugnahmen auf den Anfang zugleich den Schluß des Jesajabuches bilden wollen.

Es handelt sich in der vorliegenden Gestalt um ein *literarisch einheitliches* Textstück. Der parallele Aufbau der fünf Reden[2] zeigt, daß (1) auch v. 25 dem ursprünglichen Textbestand der dritten Rede zuzurechnen ist[3] und (2) in diesem Vers Jes 11,6-9 aufgegriffen wird und nicht umgekehrt[4]. Obwohl sie sich in Metrik und Nominalstil abhebt, ist auch die Schlangenaussage v. 25aγ integraler Bestandteil des Textes[5]. Sie steht in der abfolgeparallelen Rezeption von Jes 11,6-9 (11,6aα / 65,25aα; 11,7b / 65,25aß; 11,9a / 65,25b) sachentsprechend genau an der Stelle von Jes 11,8[6] und wird von einer Aufnahme von Jes 11,9 gefolgt. Daß Jes 65 bei der Rezeption von Jes 11 ursprünglich ausgerechnet Jes 11,8 übersprungen haben sollte, ist angesichts der Sachakzente von Jes 65 ausgeschlossen: Schlangen sind in Jes 11,8 die dereinst aufgehobene Gefährdung für kleine Kinder (Säuglinge, Entwöhnte), Jes 65 betont für den Heilszustand aber nicht zuletzt, daß das Sterben von Kindern nicht mehr sein wird (v. 20a.23a)[7]. Natürlich fällt auf, daß v.

2. 65,1-7.8-12.13-25; 66,1-4.5-24, siehe O.H. STECK, *Studien zu Tritojesaja* (BZAW, 203), Berlin - New York, 1991, pp. 217-228, 248-262. Eine abweichende Gliederung gibt BEUKEN, *Jesaja* (n. 1), pp. 57-62, 97-99, 114-116, 127f.

3. Cf. STECK, *Tritojesaja* (n. 2), pp. 223f, 225f, 253f, 260f; ID., »... *ein kleiner Knabe kann sie leiten«. Beobachtungen zum Tierfrieden in Jesaja 11,6-8 und 65,25*, in H.J. HAUSMANN – H.-J. ZOBEL (eds.), *Alttestamentlicher Glaube und Biblische Theologie*. FS H.D. PREUß, Stuttgart - Berlin - Köln, 1992, pp. 104-113, 108f; ferner J.T.A.G.M. VAN RUITEN, *Een begin zonder einde. De doorwerking van Jesaja 65:17 in de intertestamentaire literatuur en het Nieuwe Testament,* Sliedrecht, 1990, pp. 41-45; ID., *The Role of Syntax in the Versification of Is 65:13-25,* in E. TALSTRA – A.L.H.M. VAN WIERINGEN (eds.), *A Prophet on the Screen: Computerized Description and Literary Interpretation of Isaianic Texts* (Applicatio, 9), Amsterdam, 1992, pp. 118-147; jetzt W. LAU, *Schriftgelehrte Prophetie in Jes 56–66* (BZAW, 225), Berlin - New York, 1994, pp. 134-141 (für Jes 65,16b-25); P.A. SMITH, *Rhetoric and Redaction in Trito-Isaiah: The Structure, Growth and Authorship of Isaiah 56–66* (SVT, 72) Leiden - New York - Köln, 1995, pp. 128-152; anders K. KOENEN, *Ethik und Eschatologie im Tritojesajabuch. Eine literarkritische und redaktionsgeschichtliche Studie* (WMANT, 62), Neukirchen-Vluyn, 1990, pp. 172f.

4. Cf. STECK, *Knabe* (n. 3); J.T.A.G.M. VAN RUITEN, *The Intertextual Relationship between Isaiah 65,25 and Isaiah 11,6-9,* in F. GARCÍA MARTÍNEZ u.a. (eds.), *The Scriptures and the Scrolls*. FS A.S. van der Woude (SVT, 49), Leiden - New York - Köln, 1992, pp. 31-42; cf. auch BEUKEN, *Jesaja* (n. 1), pp. 91-93.

5. Anders häufig die ältere Forschung, auch BEUKEN, *Jesaja* (n. 1), p. 91; KOENEN, *Ethik* (n. 3), pp. 172f; LAU, *Prophetie* (n. 3), p. 140; siehe jedoch STECK, *Knabe* (n. 3), p. 109; VAN RUITEN, *Role* (n. 3); ID., *Relationship* (n. 4), pp. 39-41.

6. Cf. STECK, *Knabe* (n. 3), p. 109; VAN RUITEN, *Relationship* (n. 4), pp. 39f.

7. Jes 65,20.23 orientiert sich entsprechend Ex 23,24 / Jes 65,11 womöglich an Ex 23,26, hat aber nicht Fehlgeburt und Unfruchtbarkeit im Blick, sondern den frühen Tod geborener Kinder.

25aγ nicht die Formulierung von Jes 11,8 aufnimmt. Aber man sollte nicht besserwissen, was der Text hätte tun müssen[8]; der Befund könnte vielmehr mit der Frage zu tun haben, die wir hier untersuchen.

Die masoretische Textfassung von 65,16b-25 fordert im ganzen keine textändernden Eingriffe. Lediglich in v. 18a sind die imptt. pl. schwerlich ursprünglich, da die dritte Gottesrede sonst durchgängig die Frevler und nicht die Frommen anredet; für den ursprünglichen Text kommen stattdessen Imperfekte oder Substantive in Betracht[9].

Der Gesamtaufbau der dritten Rede im Rahmen der Anlage von Jes 65f muß uns hier nicht noch einmal beschäftigen, wohl aber der *Mikroaufbau des Teilstücks v. 16b-25* innerhalb von Jes 65,13-25. Nach der Einleitung v. 13aα[1] bieten v. 13aα[2].13aß.13b und in dreigliedriger Schlußverbreiterung (Knechte v. 14a – Frevler v. 14b-15a – Knechte v. 15b-16a) v. 14-16a vier Antithesen, die das Ergehen von Frommen und Frevlern gegenüberstellen. V. 16b blickt im Textablauf zurück und voraus. Die Aussage gibt einerseits für das Ergehen der Frommen in den Antithesen eine abschließende Begründung, die die Wende gegenüber dem Bisherigen hervorhebt. Andererseits aber ist diese Begründung mit ihrem Wendeaspekt (cf. הראשנות v. 16b.17b) die Aussage, die in v. 17-25 für das Ergehen der Frommen nun bezüglich des nahen Künftigen weiter ausgeführt wird[10], wie die sich entfaltenden Begründungen (v. 17-23) zeigen. Beachtet man in v. 17-25 Syndesen und Asyndesen, dann ergibt sich für diese Entfaltungen künftigen Frommenergehens folgende Feingliederung[11]. *V. 17-18a* (Ringschluß »ich schaffe jetzt«) begründen das Ende der früheren Nöte mit der künftigen Neuschöpfung von Himmel und Erde, die gegenüber v. 17b / v. 16b neu Freude zur Folge hat. *V. 18b-19* begründen diese Freude als entsprechende Schöpfungstat an Jerusalem und deren Volk (61,7.10, cf. Zef 3,14) mit der Folge, daß sich Jahwe an beiden freut (62,5, cf. Zef 3,17) und sich dort Weinen und

---

8. Zu KOENEN, *Ethik* (n. 3), pp. 172f n. 82.

9. Siehe zur Diskussion *ibid.*, pp. 171f n. 75; VAN RUITEN, *Begin* (n. 3), pp. 46, 119f; zur Entscheidung und zum Grund der von MT bezeugten Änderung cf. STECK, *Studien* (n. 2), pp. 218, 253.

10. Zur Kontextfunktion von v. 16b cf. zur Diskussion KOENEN, *Ethik* (n. 3), pp. 170f und besonders BEUKEN, *Jesaja* (n. 3), pp. 59f, 62, 79f; STECK, *Studien* (n. 2), pp. 218f, 228, 253; VAN RUITEN, *Role* (n. 3), pp. 121f, 136f, 144f.

11. Dafür müssen Textsignale und Entsprechungen zur Anlage aller Gottesreden in Jes 65f beachtet werden, cf. STECK, *Studien* (n. 2), pp. 217-228. Andere Gliederungsvorschläge zu Jes 65,16b-25 z.B. bei E. SEHMSDORF, *Studien zur Redaktionsgeschichte von Jesaja 56–66*, in ZAW 84 (1972) 517-562, 562-576, 518-520; KOENEN, *Ethik* (n. 3), pp. 170-183; BEUKEN, *Jesaja* (n. 1), pp. 59-62; VAN RUITEN, *Begin* (n. 3), pp. 41-50; ID., *The Influence and Development of Is 65,17 in 1 En 91,16*, in J. VERMEYLEN (ed.), *The Book of Isaiah. Le livre d' Isaïe. Les oracles et leurs relectures* (BETL, 81), Leuven, 1989, pp. 161-166, 161f.

Klagegeschrei nicht mehr finden. Diese Folge (v. 19 im Kontrast zu den
Frevlern v. 14b) wird in *v. 20-23* in drei לֹא(+וְ) und כִּי(+וְ)-Satzfolgen
weiter entfaltet im Sinne nunmehr gegebener Langlebigkeit der
Frommen, die dem Gottesvolk den Erfolg eigener Arbeit ermöglicht und
es so als »Gesegnete Jahwes« ausweist. In diesem Sinne sprechen (1)
v. 20a + v. 20b.21 von dieser Langlebigkeit mit der Folge, Hausbau und
Weinpflanzung nun sicher genießen zu können, (2) v. 22a + v. 22b
davon, daß man solchen Genuß wegen solcher Lebenserwartung statt
anderer folglich selbst haben kann, und (3) v. 23a + b davon, daß Arbeit
und Lebensweitergabe infolge der Segnung Jahwes also nicht vergeblich
sein werden. Die Entfaltungen führen ihrerseits den Kontrast in den
Antithesen v. 13-16a für die Frommen aus, womit sich die rück- und
vorweisende Funktion von v. 16b bestätigt. Wie fügen sich die beiden
Schlußverse in die Aussagenfolge v. 16b-25? Direkte Weiterführung
von v. 23 sind sie nicht[12]; auch in der sprachlichen Gestaltung setzen sie
sich von den לֹא(+וְ) und כִּי(+וְ)-Satzfolgen v. 20-23 durch וְהָיָה ab.
V. 24f ist nach den Weiterentfaltungen v. 20-23 vielmehr sachliche
Weiterführung von v. 19[13], wie die Wiederaufnahme von Jahwe als
Subjekt und die inhaltliche Beziehung v. 24 / v. 19 (שָׁמַע) zeigen. Daß
das Ende der dritten Rede so gestaltet ist, hängt mit überlegten
Entsprechungen in den Abschlüssen der fünf Gottesreden von Jes 65f
überhaupt zusammen[14]: Die Jes 65f rahmenden Reden schließen mit
dem Ergehen der Frevler (65,7b; 66,24), die Reden dazwischen hingegen sämtlich mit dem Doppelaspekt verweigerter / eröffneter Jahwe-
kommunikation (cf. 65,24 auf der Linie 65,12aβγ; 66,4αγδ; siehe auch
65, 6bα[1]; 66,23 und im vorangehenden Buchkontext 58,9; 50,2 und
30,19[15]), wie sie der Ausgangsthematik 65,1-2a entspricht, und Tun /
Nicht-Tun des Bösen (cf. v. 25b mit 65,12b; 66,4b), wie es der
Ausgangsthematik 65,2b-7 entspricht. V.24.25b halten für den Heilszustand der Frommen abschließend den Kontrast zu dem Verhalten fest,
das für die Frevler in 65,12; 66,4 entsprechend 65,1-7 zu resümieren ist;
dem kultischen Mißbrauch von Tieren durch die Frevler in 65,1-7; 66,1-
4.17 steht hier das neue Mensch-Tier-Verhältnis für die Frommen im
Heil v. 25a (cf. 65,10 und bezüglich der Frevler 66,24) gegenüber.

---

12. Cf. auch VAN RUITEN, *Role* (n. 3), pp. 122f, 130, 132, 139, 145-147.
13. Cf. STECK, *Studien* (n. 2), pp. 218, 253f; VAN RUITEN, *Role* (n. 3), pp. 146f.
14. Cf. STECK, *Studien* (n. 2), pp. 223f; ID., *Knabe* (n. 3), p. 108.
15. Zur Rezeption von Jes 30,18-26.27-33 in Jes 63,7–66,24 cf. STECK, *Studien* (n. 2),
pp. 241, 257-260; ID., *Der sich selbst aktualisierende »Jesaja« in Jes 56,9–59,21*, in
T.W. ZWICKEL (ed.), *Biblische Welten. FS M. Metzger* (OBO, 123), Fribourg - Göttingen,
1993, pp. 215-230, 225 n. 30. Ist Jes 65,16b-25 auch eine überbietende Relecture von Jes
30,18-26 (cf. 30,19/65,19b.24; 30,23-25/65,21-23.25; 30,26 [60,19f]/65,17)?

V. 24f mit der Rezeption vom Jes 11,6-9 bilden so einschließlich v. 25a einen sachlichen Zusammenhang und fügen sich samt 65,13-23 in die Gesamtgestaltung der Gottesreden von Jes 65f. Gottes vorlaufende Gebetserhörung bezieht sich dabei auf die in v. 20-23 noch nicht genannten, mit der Zusage v. 25a beseitigten Gefährdungen für Herden (65,10!) und die Kinder der Frommen durch Wolf, Löwe und Schlange, und das Schlußresümee v. 25b für Fromme und Tierwelt in der Heilszeit bekräftigt im Buchzusammenhang 11,9a und exponiert wie bereits diese Aussage den Kontrast zu Jes 1,4.3[16]: Nicht nur die Frevler mit ihrem aktuellen Verhalten, auch der Abfallstatus des ganzen Gottesvolkes (im Kontrast zum Verhalten der Tiere), den das Jesajabuch von seinem Anfangskapitel an wahrnimmt, wird in der Heilswende, wie sie Jes 65f faßt, im Untergang der Frevler und im Gottesvolk der Frommen definitiv überwunden sein (66,24, cf. 59,20). Was die sachliche Abfolge der Aussagen v. 17-25 in dieser so strukturierten Anlage angeht, sind wir gegen Lau[17] und Aejmelaeus[18], die solchen Fragen aus dem Wege gehen, nach wie vor der Meinung, daß auch sie sich an der Abfolge entsprechender Aussagen des voranstehenden Gebets orientieren[19]. Daraus ergeben sich die strukturellen Einschnitte in 65,17-18a (63,19b-64,3), 65,18b-19 (64,4), 65,20-23 (64,5-7) und 65,24-25 (64,8-9)[20], auf die wir bereits durch interne Textbeobachtungen zur sprachlichen Strukturierung von 65,16b-25 gestoßen waren.

Schon auf Grund der Anlage der Aussagenfolge 65,13-25 und der Beziehungen zum voraufgehenden literarischen Kontext muß man sich jedes Verständnis, das die Erschaffung eines neuen Himmels und einer neuen Erde umdeutet[21] und nicht zum Nennwert nimmt, verbieten; auch die Wiederaufnahme von 65,17 in 66,22 setzt ein solch reales Verständnis voraus. Der Nahkontext zeigt, daß mit v. 17a eine umfassende Rahmenbedingung für Jerusalem und ihr Volk im Heil geschaffen wird[22]. Warum sie nötig ist, obwohl dabei gemäß Jes 65f Jerusalem,

---

16. Cf. STECK, *Knabe* (n. 3), p. 106.

17. *Prophetie* (n. 3), passim in der textgenetischen Analyse von Jes 65f.

18. A. AEJMELAEUS, *Der Prophet als Klageliedsänger. Zur Funktion des Psalms Jes 63,7–64,11 in Tritojesaja*, in ZAW 107 (1995) 31-50, p. 46.

19. Cf. STECK, *Studien* (n. 2), besonders pp. 221-225.

20. *Ibid.*, pp. 224f.

21. Siehe jüngst die ratlosen Behauptungen bei KOENEN, *Ethik* (n. 3), pp. 168-178, besonders 171f n. 76 (»poetische[r] Überschwang«); LAU, *Prophetie* (n. 3), p. 136 (»emphatische Redeweise«) und SMITH, *Rhetoric* (n. 3), p. 147 (»a hyperbolic expression«); gründlich erörtert die Frage VAN RUITEN, *Begin* (n. 3), pp. 51-60, freilich ohne klares Ergebnis.

22. Cf. BEUKEN, *Jesaja* (n. 1), p. 94; STECK, *Studien* (n. 2), p. 254. Eine Modifikation der Alternative Beukens wird sich aus dem vorliegenden Beitrag ergeben.

Heilsland, Heilsvolk der Frommen, ferne Gebiete der Erde mit Menschen und Diaspora (66,19-21) diesen Wechsel von der ersten in die Neuschöpfung von Himmel und Erde überdauern, wird noch zu fragen sein.

II

Jes 65,16b-25 ist auch abgesehen von der Gesamtplanung Jes 65f und der Orientierung an Jes 63,7–64,11 *nicht* einfach *frei formuliert*. Wie längst gesehen und von Beuken in seinem Kommentar hervorgehoben, werden hier auch Aussagen aus Jes 56–63,6, aber ebenso aus Jes 40–55 aufgegriffen und Aussagelinien von dort jetzt abschließend gebündelt[23]. Das Anliegen unserer Arbeiten war es zu zeigen, daß auch Jes 1–39 in diesen literarischen Horizont einbezogen werden muß. Aber das Textstück hat noch weit mehr Spendegut aus damals literarisch maßgeblichen Schriften im Blick.

Auffallend sind vor allem Entsprechungen zu Texten aus den anderen Prophetenbüchern, die wie Jes 65f mit dem Problem der Redekommunikation zwischen Jahwe und Volk zu tun haben; in diesem Sinne konvergiert Jes 65 nicht zuletzt in v.16b-25 mit der Heilsthematik von Sach 8 (cf. besonders 8,4f.6.8.10-13.17.19.20-23) nach Sach 7 (cf. besonders 7,2.3-5.8-10.13 und überhaupt die Abfolge Jes 56–65,7 / Sach 7 und Jes 65,8–66,24 / Sach 8) und vor allem mit Passagen in dem Jes nachfolgenden Jeremiabuch[24], die sich im literarischen Kontext im Sinne jener Redekommunikation darstellen[25].

23. Cf. Steck, *Studien* (n. 2), pp. 41, 254f und die Hinweise dort 264; ferner Id., *Gottesknecht und Zion. Gesammelte Aufsätze zu Deuterojesaja* (FAT, 4), Tübingen, 1992, pp. 170-172.

24. Siehe dazu z.B. Sehmsdorf, *Studien* (n. 11), p. 527f (zu 65,19b); Koenen, *Ethik* (n. 3), pp. 227f; Steck, *Studien* (n. 2), pp. 250, 251, 260. Für den Zusammenhang von 65,17-19 ist auch eine Rezeption von Ps 48 nun bezüglich der Heilsvollendung zu erwägen, die im voraus die definitive Aufhebung von Jer 6 ankündigen will.

25. Cf. zum Einfluß von Jer 14ff Steck, *Studien* (n. 2), p. 225; ebenso muß man eine Orientierung an Gebet und Gottesantworten Jer 32f in Betracht ziehen. Umgekehrt könnte es in dem jungen MT-Überschuß *Jer 33,14-26* eine jüngste Überarbeitung geben, die mit den Bestandesgarantien für die levitischen Priester (33,18.21.22bß) sowie mit 33,25b–26 ihrerseits auf Jes 65f reagiert, um gegenüber dem Erwartungsbild dort die in Jer 33 exponierten Heilsaspekte (für eine Heilsphase davor? – so ausdrücklich 4Esr 7,26ff) zu wahren. Jedenfalls fällt auf, daß 33,25b in Aufnahme von Jer 31,35-37, aber abweichend von Jer 31,37 und anders als 31,35aßy, die asyndetisch angeschlossenen »Ordnungen des Himmels und der Erde« (cf. Hi 38,33ff!), wie sie bestehen, hervorhebt und mit dem Bestand des Gesamtvolkes verbindet. Schafft diese Textebene damit Heilsfreiraum gegenüber Jes 66,22 (cf. 65,17), mit den levitischen Priestern gegenüber Jes 66,21, mit der Betonung ganz Israels (cf. auch Mal 3,22-24) gegenüber den Einschränkungen des Heilsvolkes in Jes 65f (und Sach 11f) und mit der Betonung der Davididenerwartung als Heilsperspektive nach 587, weswegen Jer 33,14-26 ins Jeremiabuch eingeschrieben wird, gegenüber dem Fehlen dieser Perspektive im Schluß des Jesajabuches? Cf. zu Jer 33,14-

Sicher orientiert sich Jes 65 an einer Fassung der Tora, die die Segen-
und Fluchkataloge Lev 26 und Dtn 28,30 enthält; daß Textaussagen von
dort zumal für v. 16-25 herangezogen wurden, ist seit langem gesehen[26].
Man muß in diesem Rahmen aber auch bedenken, daß trotz abwei-
chender, weil aus anderen Quellen gespeister Formulierungen erstaun-
liche sachliche Konvergenzen mit Dtn 31 und insbesondere mit Dtn 32[27]
bestehen. Für das theologiegeschichtliche Vorgepräge von Jes 65f ist
besonders Ps 37 zu beachten.

Raumgründe verbieten es, diesen Bezugnahmen und der Art der
Verarbeitung mit textgenetischen Fragestellungen näher nachzugehen.
Wir beschränken uns auf den für 65,17 wichtigsten Spendetext: *Jes
43,16-21*[28]. Warum wählt Jes 65 gerade diesen Text? Spielt im Zuge der

---

26 z.B. W. GROSS, *Israels Hoffnung auf die Erneuerung des Staates*, in J. SCHREINER (ed.),
Unterwegs zur Kirche. Alttestamentliche Konzeptionen (QD, 110), Freiburg - Basel -
Wien, 1987, pp. 87-122, dort 106-112; Y. GOLDMAN, *Prophétie et royauté au retour de
l'exil* (OBO, 118), Fribourg - Göttingen, 1992, pp. 9-64, 218-237; K. SCHMID, *Buchgestalten des Jeremiabuchs*, theol. Dissertation, Zürich, 1996 (Masch.), pp. 53-65, 321-
324.

26. Siehe dazu z.B. SEHMSDORF, *Studien* (n. 11), pp. 525-528; STECK, *Studien* (n. 2),
p. 254; SMITH, *Rhetoric* (n. 3), p. 151, cf. 143. Der Ansatz für diese Rezeption ist die
Qualifikation der Frommen als »Gesegnete Jahwes« (65,23) in Aufnahme von
61,9(;44,3). Wie sich die Heilsformulierungen in Jes 65,16b-25 durch Aufhebung
pentateuchischer Fluchaussagen, durch Überhöhung von Aussagen für die Zeit vor der
Heilswende und durch Weiterführung in Jes, insbesondere in Jes 60–62, voranstehender
Heilsaussagen bilden, läßt sich am Beispiel *Jes 65,21* zeigen. Die Aussage greift nicht
Am 5,11 (gegen T. PODELLA, *Notzeitmythologem und Nichtigkeitsfluch*, in B. JANOWSKI
u.a. [eds.], *Religionsgeschichtliche Beziehungen zwischen Kleinasien, Nordsyrien und
dem Alten Testament* [OBO, 129], Fribourg - Göttingen, 1993, pp. 427-454, 433f) und
wohl auch nicht Am 9,14 auf, sondern ausweislich der Formulierung Dtn 28,30 mit Blick
auf Jer 29,5.28 (pl.-Formulierung) aus der Zeit vor der Heilswende und in v. 21bß
angesichts des Wortlauts eindeutig Jes 37,30 (par. 2 Kön 19,29) aus demselben
Jesajabuch! Der letztgenannte Rückgriff ist besonders bezeichnend, weil er zeigt, daß Jes
65f die Aussagen Jes 37,30-32 in ihrem Kontext als das Rettungsparadigma für das wahre
Gottesvolk in Jerusalem und Juda versteht, das der Heilsvollendung von Jes 65f
schließlich teilhaftig werden wird und auf das die Heilsaussagen in dem an die Jesa-
jaerzählungen des Buches anschließenden Textkomplex Jes 40–66 zielen; cf. in diesem
Zusammenhang auch die von BEUKEN, *Jesaja, deel III^B* (n. 1), pp. 148f aufgewiesene
Verbindung Jes 66,24/36,3;37,26 und siehe zur vorausweisenden Funktion von Jes 36–39
in der Schlußformation des Jesajabuches O.H. STECK, *Die Prophetenbücher und ihr
theologisches Zeugnis*, Tübingen, 1996, Teil I, Abschnitt II 6c.

27. Cf. besonders Dtn 32,4.16.20-22.24f.36(!). Die Konvergenzen erhöhen sich noch,
wenn man sich die literarische Entstehung von Jes 65f als Fortschreibung eines Jesajabuches vorstellen darf, dessen Endgerichtsaussagen Dtn 32,34-43 auffallend nahestehen.
In Jes 58,14abα, das unseres Erachtens auf dieselbe literarische Ebene wie Jes 65f gehört
(siehe dazu STECK, *Studien*, pp. 40, 178, 195), ist eindeutig Dtn 32,13 aufgegriffen.

28. Cf. zur Rezeption jüngst BEUKEN, *Jesaja* (n. 1), pp. 81f; VAN RUITEN, *Begin* (n.
3), pp. 54-59; KOENEN, *Ethik* (n. 1), pp. 171f; zum ursprünglichen Sinn von 43,16-21 cf.
R.G. KRATZ, *Kyros im Deuterojesaja-Buch. Redaktionsgeschichtliche Untersuchungen zu
Entstehung und Theologie von Jes 40–55* (FAT, 1), Tübingen, 1991, pp. 68-72.

Formulierung der Gebetsantwort Jes 65f eine Rolle, daß Jes 42, wie BEUKEN gezeigt hat[29], aber auch Jes 43 schon für Jes 63,7–64,11 maßgeblich herangezogen werden, so daß sich die Applikation dieser Textgrundlage hier nun fortsetzt[30]? Bedenkt man, daß 65,17 v. 16b kontrastiert, liegt noch näher, daß die Heranziehung über den Begriff צרות in v. 16b erfolgt ist. Er wurde im Gebet 63,9 für die Not im Zusammenhang des Exodusgeschehens vorgefunden[31], wozu ja auch זעק / צעק vor der Rettung, Hunger, Durst, vorzeitiger Tod in der Wüste (cf. 65, 13f. 19b. 20ff) gehören, die wegen der Vergehen Israels nicht definitiv von Jahwe beseitigt wurden (63,10-13.15ff), sondern bis in aktuelle Notlagen[32] fortwirken. In diesem Sinne sind – kontextuell am nächstliegenden – offenbar die צרות 65,16b verstanden, und über sie gelangt man zu den Aussagen vom neuen, nun definitiv notwendenden Exodus Jes 43,16-21. Man rezipiert die ראשׁנות dort (43,18), die in 65,16 den Plural צרות (cf. auch Dtn 31,17.21) nach sich ziehen, freilich nicht als die erste Exodusrettung (43,16f), sondern als die bislang anhaltenden Nöte seit der Exoduszeit, und die Heimkehrwende dort (43,19-21) versteht man von der Heilswende, die gemäß Jes 65f den Frommen entsprechend jetzt auch daheim unmittelbar bevorsteht. Jes 65 extrahiert gemäß solch rezeptionell-neulesender Aneignung aus Jes 43 also nicht nur Einzelformulierungen (43,18a. 19aα¹; auch das Erwählungsvolk 65,22 stammt aus 43,20); diese werden in rezeptivem Sinn vielmehr mitsamt ihrem Kontext bedacht. Wie oft in Rezeptionsvorgängen der Prophetenüberlieferung spenden vorgegebene Aspekte der Heimkehr auch hier Züge der Heilsvollendung am Ziel und werden entsprechend für die Situation des – in Jes 65f im Zuge vollzogener innerer Scheidung enger gefaßten – Heilsvolkes im Heilsland fortgeführt. So entsprechen im vorliegenden Fall dem Weg in der Wüste (43,19bα) dort dann Jerusalem (65,18b-19) und das Haus (65,21f), den Strömen in der Wüste (43,19bß?.20b) dort dann das Essen (und Trinken, cf. 65,13aß) der Frommen (65,21f), der Ehrung durch die Tiere (43,20a) in Jes 65 dann die Aussicht v. 25, und dem Lobpreis des Volkes 43,21b entspricht jetzt das Ziel 66,23 auf der oben erwähnten Linie 65,1-2a.12aßγ.24; 66,4aγδ, die der Jesaja des Buches im Nahkontext 63,7aα eröffnet hat. Daß Jes

---

29. Cf. die Hinweise in STECK, *Studien* (n. 2), pp. 240f.

30. Stehen als jeweilige Folgetexte Jes 43,22-28 und Jes 66,1-4 (cf. 56,7) sowie Jes 44,1-5(8) und Jes 66,5-24 in textgenetischer Entsprechung?

31. Angesichts des Nahkontextes sind die Exodusnöte dort jedenfalls eingeschlossen. Cf. zur Stelle I. FISCHER, *Wo ist Jahwe? Das Volksklagelied Jes 63,7–64,11 als Ausdruck des Ringens um eine gebrochene Beziehung* (SBB, 19), Stuttgart, 1989, pp. 131-141; BEUKEN, *Jesaja* (n. 1), pp. 12f, 80.

32. Cf. FISCHER, *Wo ist Jahwe?* (n. 31); BEUKEN, *Jesaja* (n. 1).

65,17a.18b statt עשׂה nun ברא schreibt, könnte auf den ersten Blick mit dem Einfluß von Jes 41,(17-)20b sowie insbesondere 48,7[33] erklärt werden, doch läßt sich aus solchen Bezügen kein hinreichender Grund für die Ersetzung von עשׂה durch ברא finden, zumal 66,22 wieder עשׂה steht. Auf jeden Fall geht Jes 65 aber mit der Beziehung von 43,19a auf Himmel und Erde (v. 17a) und Jerusalem (v. 18b) eigene Wege. Die Berücksichtigung von Aussagen aus Jes 40–55 allein kann nicht dazu geführt haben. Die חדשׁ-Aussagen dort (siehe noch 41,15; 42,9.10; 48,6) weisen nirgends auf Himmel und Erde, und die Himmel und Erde-Aussagen bilden keinen Ansatz, der direkt zu der Formulierung 65,17 führte; vielmehr sind die Erschaffung von Himmel und Erde in Jes 40–55 das Verläßliche, von dem für Jahwes Heilswende ausgegangen werden kann. Hinzu kommt, daß man außer Jes 45,18a, wo längst nicht in der 65,17 eigenen Formulierungsdichte ברא für den Himmel und dann auch für die Erde gebraucht wird, in Jes 40–55 zwar ברא für den Himmel, für die Erde dort aber andere Verben antrifft (42,5; 45,18a). Eine Kontexteinwirkung dieser Aussagen aus Jes 40–55 auf 65,17-25 ist auch sonst nicht erkennbar. Ist die Formulierung 65,17a von einer anderen Orientierung geprägt?

III

Daß Jes 65 die Paradieserzählung in der *Genesis* kennt, ist wegen der integralen Aussage zur Schlange in 65,25aγ offenkundig; sie greift, wie schon oft gesehen[34], aus dem Fluch über die Schlange den Text Gen 3,14 auf. Schon deshalb ist die Frage berechtigt, ob sich die Formulierung von 65,17 nicht an Gen 1,1 orientiert. Die Frage muß, obwohl in der aktuellen Tritojesaja-Diskussion kaum je gestellt, geschweige denn genauer erörtert, bejaht werden. Eine Reihe von Indizien führt zu diesem Urteil. Wie wir noch sehen werden[35], wäre eine Rezeption von Aussagen der biblischen Urgeschichte in prophetischem Textgut keineswegs singulär; Rückgriffe auf Gen und speziell auf Gen 1–9 finden sich auch sonst im wachsenden Prophetencorpus. Hinzu kommen Formulierungsindizien. Wertet man die statistischen Erhebungen von

33. Zur Rezeption von Jes 48 cf. weiter 48,1 / 65,9.15f sowie 48,6f / 65,17f; cf. ferner im einzelnen KRATZ, *Kyros* (n. 28), p. 120 n. 461.

34. Cf. jüngst z.B. BEUKEN, *Jesaja* (n. 1), p. 91 (lies 3,14); KOENEN, *Ethik* (n. 3), pp. 172f; LAU, *Prophetie* (n. 3), p. 140; zum Verständnis siehe STECK, *Knabe* (n. 3), p. 109 mit SEHMSDORF *Studien* (n. 11), p. 523; da die Schlange in 65,25b eingeschlossen ist, ist die partielle, an אכל in 65,25a anschließende Aufnahme von Gen 3,14(.19) keine Fluchaussage mehr, sondern eine göttliche Nahrungszuweisung!

35. Siehe unten n. 46.

Van Ruiten[36] näher aus, gibt es im AT außer Gen 1,1 keine Aussage, in der ברא mit göttlichem Subjekt unmittelbar danach von syndetisch verbundenen Objekten שמים und ארץ gefolgt begegnet[37]! Auch die Akzentuierung der Aussage 65,17 in zeitlicher (fut. instans) und qualitativer (חדש) Hinsicht legt nahe, daß eine Vorgabe wie die Gen 1,1 formulierte das Gegenüber bildet, von dem sich Jes 65,17 abheben will. Hinzu kommt, daß sich Gen 1,1 und 65,16b.17b unbeschadet Jes 43,18a auch in בראשית / הראשנות treffen. Es ist also schon von der Formulierung her gesehen das bei weitem Wahrscheinlichste, daß sich Jes 65,17 an Gen 1,1 orientiert. Nimmt Jes 65,17-25 auf Gen 1,1 und 3,14 Bezug, dann offenbar auf die literarische Kompositgestalt der Genesis (oder bereits des Pentateuch) aus priesterschriftlichen und nichtpriesterschriftlichen Textebenen; das Textstück kennt somit den Textbestand Gen 1–3. Wenn wir dem Rezeptionsvorgang näher nachfragen, bestätigt sich diese Folgerung; man braucht gar nicht auf die auffallenden Gemeinsamkeiten von Jes 65 mit Urzeit-Paradies-Mythen abzuheben[38], die im Rückblick auf 51,3 (Verbindung mit Jerusalem!) eine Rezeption von Gen 2,8-15 anzeigen könnten[39].

Wie wurde Gen 1,1 aus der Sicht von Jes 65 gelesen? Offenbar nicht als abgesetzte Überschrift zum biblischen Schöpfungsbericht, sondern als grundlegende Handlungsaussage göttlichen Schöpferwirkens über eine erste Erschaffung von Himmel und Erde[40], der hier nun eine neue, immer bestehende (66,22) folgen soll.

36. *Begin* (n. 3), pp. 81-89.

37. Cf. *ibid.*, p. 88 die Aufstellung für ברא, gefolgt von שמים und ארץ mit den weiteren formal wortstatistisch ermittelten Belegen Gen 1,20-22.26-28; 6,6-7; Dtn 4,32; Jes 42,5; 45,7-8.12.18; Ps 89,12-13; 102,19-20. Diese scheinbare Belegmenge schrumpft unter sachlichem Vergleichsaspekt auf Jes 42,5; 45,12.18 zusammen; ein thematisch wichtiger Text wie Ps 102,26-28 kommt bei solch sinnfrei statistischer Suche freilich überhaupt nicht in den Blick. Daß die in Jes 65,17a gebrauchte Formulierung an Gen 1,1 erinnert, vermerkt R.N. WHYBRAY, *Isaiah 40–66* (NCB), London, 1975, p. 276.

38. Cf. die Hinweise bei STECK, *Knabe* (n. 3), p. 113 mit n. 67-69.

39. Cf. Jub 4,26, s. unten.

40. Zu erwägen ist, ob nicht schon Jes 65,17 die Vorlage so liest, wie es in Jub 2,2-3 entgegentritt: Der erste Schöpfungstag umfaßt Gen 1,1-5! Dann gehörte in den ersten Schöpfungstag mit Himmel und Erde auch das Wasser hinsichtlich Regen und Tau (Jes 65,21-23 und cf. die Engelgarantien bezüglich Gen 8,21f in Jub 2,2!), das Licht (statt Sonne und Mond, siehe unten zur Rezeption von Jes 60,19) und womöglich auch die lebensspendende רוח (Jes 65,20.22b.23), wenn man רוחות בריותו (4Q216, V, 9) auch dahingehend verstehen darf. Zum hebräischen Text von Jub 2,2-3 cf. jetzt *Qumran Cave 4 VIII. Parabiblical Texts,* Part 1 (DJD, XIII), Oxford, 1994, pp. 13-16 (J.C. VANDERKAM / J.T. MILIK), zur Rezeption von Gen 1 in Jub eingehend O.H. STECK, *Der Schöpfungsbericht der Priesterschrift* (FRLANT, 115), Göttingen ²1981, pp. 291-318, zu Jub 2,2-3 besonders pp. 294, 303f, 306 n. 57; J.C. VANDERKAM, *Genesis 1 in Jubilees 2*, in *DSD* 1 (1994) 300-321, besonders pp. 306-310.

Warum aber arbeitet unser Textstück einen solchen Neubeginn göttlichen Schöpfungswirkens bezüglich Himmel und Erde heraus? Sind in dem hier vorgewiesenen Heilszustand nicht allein noch Fromme da, deren Wohlverhalten nun einfach die Segensaussichten von Lev 26,3-13 und Dtn 28,1-14 im Rahmen der bestehenden Schöpfung wieder eintreten lassen könnte? Für Jes 65f ist diese Applikation schon deshalb verwehrt, weil das Israel der Gegenwart nicht mehr vor der Alternative von Lev 26 und Dtn 28 steht, sondern gleichsam im Ende dieser Aussagenfolge inmitten der Auswirkung der Flüche und der Exilsstrafe gemäß Lev 26,14-45 und Dtn 28,15-68. Vor allem aber sieht, wie sogleich näher auszuführen ist, Jes 65f im Rahmen des Buches Himmel und Erde in der gegenwärtigen Situation vor dem nahen Heil in einer Defizienz, die der göttlichen Überwindung im Heil bedarf und zu der radikalen Sicht einer Neuschöpfung von Himmel und Erde treibt.

Schon das Bedenken der gegenwärtigen und künftigen Lebensverhältnisse der Frommen macht das Ungenügen der bestehenden Schöpfungsgrößen Himmel und Erde *als solcher* für das Leben im Heil bewußt. Mit einem *neuen* Himmel und einer *neuen* Erde als göttlich neugeschaffener Rahmenbedingung des in Jes 65f verheißenen Heilszustandes werden nämlich die Lev 26 und Dtn 28 in Fluchfolgen zugespitzten, stetigen Erfahrungsdefizienzen der bestehenden Schöpfung verbunden und überwunden: Ein neuer, immer Regen spendender Himmel und eine neue, nie mehr eisenharte Erde (Lev 26,3ff; Dtn 28,12 [cf. Jes 55,10] gegenüber Lev 26,19; Dtn 28,23 als Widerspruch zu Gen 1,11f; 8,22f!) sind die Voraussetzung für eine uneingeschränkte Nahrungsaufnahme, wie sie Jes 65,21 vorstellt, und eine neue Erde womöglich auch die Voraussetzung, um nun Tiere in der Art von 65,25 hervorzubringen (cf. Gen 1,24). – Das theologische Interesse an der Aufhebung von Erfahrungsdefizienzen der ersten Schöpfung im künftigen Heilszustand zeigt sich in Jes 65 auch an Verbindungen zu den Fluchaussagen in Gen 3. Den Fluch über die Schlange Gen 3,14f hat 65,25 direkt aufgegriffen und nun in eine neue Nahrungszuweisung (cf. Gen 1,29f) ohne erkennbaren Fluchcharakter verwandelt: Das Brot (cf. Gen 3,19aα) der Schlange wird entgegen dem, was man empirisch im Bereich der ersten Schöpfung seit jeher erlebt, nun wirklich עפר sein und damit die heilsbezeichnende Ungefährlichkeit der Schlangen gewährleisten[41]. Die Formulierungen in 65,20-23 orientieren sich insbesondere an Lev 26 und Dtn 28[42]; in der Sache bestehen aber darüber hinaus auffallende

---

41. Cf. die Hinweise n. 34.

42. Zu weiteren Textorientierungen, insbesondere zu den von Beuken herausgearbeiteten an den עבד יהוה-Texten, cf. die Hinweise n. 23, 24.

Verbindungen zu Gen 3,16.17-19, die schwerlich Zufall sind, sondern Aufhebungen von dort verfügten Daseinszügen für Mann und Frau in der Heilszeit bedeuten: Dem Zusammenhang von mühseliger Arbeit auf der verfluchten אדמה bis zum Tode (Gen 3,17b-19) steht hier das in Langlebigkeit auf einer neuen Erde erfahrene Gelingen der Arbeit an Haus und Weingarten gegenüber (65,20-22.23aα, cf. 62,8f), und die Kinder, die nun schmerzfrei (cf. Jes 66,7 sachlich mit Gen 3,16) geboren werden (65,23aß / Gen 3,16 ילד q.), bleiben jetzt alle am Leben (65,20.23bß). In alledem handelt es sich um die Heilssituation der Gesegneten Jahwes (65,23), womit Gen 1,28 für den neuen Rahmen der Heilszeit aufgenommen ist. Ob Jes 65 bei der Langlebigkeit auch an eine Verbindung zu Gen 5, beim Weinberg auch an Gen 5,29 (cf. 66,13); 9,20 gedacht hat?

Wenn man Jes 65 nach Jes 60 liest oder nach unserem Vorschlag zum Werden des Jesajabuches sogar von Anfang an in diesem literarischen Zusammenhang lesen muß, enthält die Rezeption von Gen 1,1 durch 65,17 noch mehr als im unmittelbaren Kontext ausgedrückt ist. Auch die Thematik Finsternis-Licht aus Gen 1,2.3-5.14-18 gerät auf der genetischen Ebene von Jes 65 in den Blick und erscheint in Aussagen wie Jes 60,2a (Gen 1,2); 60,19 (Gen 1,3-5); 60,19f (Gen 1,14-18) jetzt überboten durch Züge der neuen, schon dort (cf. die Abfolge Jes 60–62) wie hier in 65,17-20 auf Jerusalem und ihr Volk gerichteten neuen Schöpfung, und die in Jes 61,7.10 genannten Freudenaussagen bezüglich Volk und Jerusalem werden in Jes 65 als von Jahwe geschaffene Freude (65,18b–19a) über solch neue Schöpfung (65,18a) verstanden.

Die Aussagen in Jes 65f selbst und die Art der Rezeption von Gen 1–3 zeigen, daß der Text die Neuschöpfung von Himmel und Erde nicht als Neubeginn nach einem Zwischenzustand von totalem Chaos und Leere, von noch-nicht-Existenz der Schöpfung (Gen 1,2) oder von siebentägigem Schweigen (4Esr 7,30) sieht. Es gibt, wie wir sahen, in dieser Sicht definitiver Heilswende Kontinuierliches – die Frommen, ferne Menschen, die Tiere, das Land (65,9f), Jerusalem, das auch gemäß 65,18f nicht von neu auf errichtet, sondern zu neuer Qualität umgeschaffen wird –, aber hinsichtlich der qualitativen Rahmenbedingungen werden Himmel und Erde gegenüber den durchgängig ambivalenten Erfahrungen mit Himmel und Erde der ersten Schöpfung neu geschaffen zugunsten von Mensch und Tier im Zustand vollendeten Heils.

Wie wird das zugehen? Woran denkt Jes 65 beim Ende von Himmel und Erde der ersten Schöpfung? Mit dieser Frage kommen wir zu einem

letzten und von uns schon mehrfach herausgestellten[43] Aspekt, der eine
Entstehung der Aussage 65,17 anscheinend vor allem nötig gemacht hat.
Wenn Jes 65f von vornherein ein Text ist, der das Jesajabuch zu Ende
schreibt, dann ist hier berücksichtigt, daß das große, in 66,6.14.15f.18
letztmals angekündigte und 66,24 in seinem Endeffekt konstatierte
Feuerweltgericht in Aussagen des voranstehenden Jesajabuches so
gezeichnet ist, daß dabei auch Himmel und Erde (der ersten Schöpfung)
gemäß gestaffelten Aussagen im Buchablauf vergehen werden, dabei
aber, wie die Kontexte zeigen, nicht zuletzt Jerusalem und die an ihm
Orientierten bewahrt bleiben, wie 65,17 mit Rückbezug auf 63,19b;
64,9f (Himmel-Jerusalem) und 66,5-24 mit Rückbezug auf 64,3-6.7.14
vor dem Textablaufhintergrund der vorangehenden Buchaussagen vom
Weltgericht in Himmel und Erde umfassender Reichweite (13,[10.]13;
24,4[text. em.]-6; 34,2-4; 51,6) zeigen[44]. Selbst eine Wiedererrichtung
von Himmel und Erde nach deren Zerstörung ist im Buch wahrscheinlich schon vor 65,17 in Aussicht genommen (51,16)[45]. Demnach
ist die Formulierung von 65,17a auch davon bestimmt, daß in diesem
Weltgericht das Ende des Schöpfungsvorgangs von Gen 1,1 gesehen
wird. Das Ende der Ära der ersten Schöpfung ist hier in bestimmten
Aspekten de facto in Blick genommen! Das auch kanongeschichtlich
bemerkenswerte Verfahren, für Weltgerichtsaussagen Genesis- (bzw.
Tora-)Texte zu bedenken, ist im Werden von Jes keineswegs singulär;
schon die Jesaja-Apokalypse reflektiert die dafür notwendige Aufhebung der Sintflut-Noah-Garantien für den Weltbereich und auch dort
schon sind Jerusalem und Gottesvolk davon ausgenommen (Jes 26,20f;
cf. 54,9f)[46].

43. Cf. O.H. STECK, *Bereitete Heimkehr. Jesaja 35 als redaktionelle Brücke zwischen
dem Ersten und dem Zweiten Jesaja* (SBS, 121), Stuttgart, 1985, p. 75; ID., *Studien* (n. 2),
pp. 12, 222, 227, 254.

44. Zu Jes 13.24.34 cf. STECK, *Heimkehr* (n. 43); ID., *Studien* (n. 2), (Register) und
jüngst B.M. ZAPFF, *Schriftgelehrte Prophetie – Jes 13 und die Komposition des
Jesajabuches. Ein Beitrag zur Erforschung der Redaktionsgeschichte des Jesajabuches*
(FzB, 74), Würzburg, 1995. Zu der in der älteren Forschung für Jes 65,17 immer wieder
herangezogenen Aussage Jes 51,6 cf. STECK, *Gottesknecht* (n. 23), pp. 60-72, 73-91; ID.,
Studien (n. 2), p. 240, anders VAN RUITEN, *Begin* (n. 3), pp. 52f. Auch eine rezeptionelle
Beziehung zu Jer 4,23-26 nach 4,19-22 muß man mit B. DUHM, *Das Buch Jesaja* (HK,
III/1), Göttingen, ⁴1922, p. 479, in Betracht ziehen.

45. Siehe dazu STECK, *Gottesknecht* (n. 23), pp. 71, 168f, 170f; ID., *Studien* (n. 2), pp.
19, 29, 32, 192, 193f, und schon F. DELITZSCH, *Jesaja*, Leipzig, ³1879, p. 665.

46. Siehe dazu bei STECK, *Gottesknecht* (n. 23), pp. 90, 107, und jetzt C.R. SEITZ,
Isaiah 1–39 (Interpretation), Louisville, 1993, pp. 179-184. Zur Rezeption von Gen 1.8
und Gen 6–9 im Wachstum von Jer siehe SCHMID, *Buchgestalten* (n. 25), pp. 173f, 304,
307; zur Rezeption von Gen 1 in Jer 4,23-26 siehe jetzt A. BORGES DE SOUSA, *Jer 4,23-26
als P-orientierter Abschnitt*, in ZAW 105 (1993) 419-428.

Macht man die literarischen Orientierungen von Jes 65,17a ausdrücklich, dann trägt die hier angekündigte Neuschöpfung von Himmel und Erde also eine dreifache Akzentuierung. (1) Das Geschehen ist, im Buchkontext gesehen, im Zuge der definitiven Heilswende göttliche Restitution der weltumfassenden Größen »Himmel« und »Erde«, die in dem zuvor stattfindenden universalen Weltgericht, wie es das Jesajabuch erwartet, vergehen; der richtend-rettende Gott ersetzt gleichsam in diesem Endgeschehen Himmel und Erde der ersten Schöpfung ohne Zwischenzustand durch deren Neuschöpfung in lebenswesentlichen Qualitäten für die Frommen aus Gottesvolk und Völkern, so daß kontinuierliche Größen bleiben können. (2) Das Geschehen ist, hinsichtlich der in der Forschung zu unserem Text vielfach problematisierten Relation Himmel-Erde-Jerusalem-Jahwevolk, im Buchkontext (Jes 1; 24-27; 33-35; 51,1–16; 63,9–64,11) und im Nahkontext (Jes 65,17.18.19-25) gesehen, Aufhebung der Diastase zwischen dem in den Endereignissen weltweiten Vergehen von Himmel und Erde und der Bewahrung Jerusalems und des Gottesvolkes. (3) Das Geschehen ist, im Nahkontext und dessen Rezeption von pentateuchischen Fluchaussagen gesehen, die notwendige Neuerrichtung von Himmel und Erde als qualitativer Lebensbedingung entsprechend Gen 1 und in Aufhebung von Lev 26,19 (»euren (!) Himmel«, »eure (!) Erde«); Dtn 28,23f[47].

Sind wir mit unseren Beobachtungen zur Textgenese von Jes 65,16b-25 auf der richtigen Spur, dann ist festzustellen, daß sich auch dieses Textstück in seinem Bestreben, die unmittelbar bevorstehende Heilswelt der Jahwefrommen vorzuführen, der Orientierung an weiten literarischen Horizonten verdankt. Im Sinne der Textgenese übermittelt der Jesaja des Buches in Jes 65f literarisch und sachlich die letzte seiner Jahwebotschaften. Jahwe führt dem Propheten – so ist die Meinung – darin Aussagen zu Ziel und Ende, die seine Botschaften schon im gesamten voranstehenden Buch durchziehen. Er knüpft dafür, auf das voranstehende Gebet eingehend, insbesondere an die »Jesaja« schon früher gegebene Botschaft Jes 43,16-21 an und gibt ihr für die Weiterführung in unserem Textstück eine Schlüsselrolle. Und zwar aus zwei Gründen. Erstens, weil die jetzt ergehende Botschaft als weitere, jetzt zielhafte Explikation der dort gegebenen Ankündigung »siehe, ich mache Neues« (43,19) aufgefaßt ist. Und zweitens, weil dem Propheten als Antwort auf die Sicht des Gebets 63,7–64,11 kundwerden soll, wie die Heimkehr der Gottesvolkes (Jes 43) in umfassender Wende der Nöte

---

47. Zum Vorstellungshintergrund dieser beiden Texte cf. jetzt U. STEYMANS, *Deuteronomium 28 und die adê zur Thronfolgeregelung Assarhaddons. Segen und Fluch im Alten Orient und in Israel* (OBO, 145), Fribourg - Göttingen, 1995, besonders pp. 284-291.

seit dem Exodus (Jes *63f) im definitiven Heilszustand im Lande ihre Entsprechung haben wird.

Jahwe gleicht sich in seinem Handeln und in seinen Botschaften. Diese Voraussetzung leitet auch die literarischen Außenbeziehungen der Textgenese. In diese Sicht gehört nämlich, daß die Jahwebotschaften in den Prophetenbüchern zu entsprechendem Handeln Jahwes zusammengesehen werden müssen und so eine höhere Sacheinheit darstellen. Im Dienste dessen ist es textgenetisch bezeichnend, daß ablösend, weiterführend, ja überbietend an entsprechende Gottesbefragungen, Gebete und nachfolgende Gottesantworten angeknüpft wird, wie sie sich in Jer 14ff.32f und in Sach 7f finden. Daß der Prophet dabei zu hören bekommt, was auch in Entsprechung zu den Kundgaben Jahwes an Mose in Dtn 31f steht, gehört gleichfalls in die höhere Sacheinheit maßgeblicher Überlieferungen, die die Textgenese hier bestimmt. Und es ist Ausdruck der unmittelbaren Gottesgewißheit, die den für Jes 65f verantwortlichen Tradenten in ihrem Schriftstudium eigen war, daß in dieser schriftgebundenen Vergewisserung des künftigen Heils Jahwe im Dienst dessen nicht nur die in Lev, Dtn einstmals angekündigte, seit langem eingetretene Fluchsituation, sondern auch seine erste, in Gen kundgegebene Schöpfung mit ihren seit jeher erlebten Ambivalenzen und Erfahrungsdefizienzen definitiv begrenzt und überschreitet.

Für unsere Sicht des Wachstums der Prophetenbücher ist dies alles ein Hinweis mehr, daß diese Aussagen in das Spätstadium im Werden des Jesajabuches gehören. Befindet man sich damit in der frühhellenistischen Zeit Israels, dann scheint auch klar, daß sich die Orientierung nicht nur auf Einzeltexte aus Gen bis Dtn richtet, sondern mit Bezugnahme auf Gen 1ff und die Schlußkapitel des Dtn auf Anfang und Ende der Tora, deren Geltung hier im prophetischen Traditionsbereich durch eschatologische Perspektiven einer neuen Schöpfung zugunsten Jerusalems und der Frommen aus Israel und den Völkern überboten wird.

IV

Man fragt sich, warum der Tritojesajadiskussion die Frage einer Rezeption von Gen 1–3 durch Jes 65 so wenig Beachtung wert ist und alles daran gesetzt wird, den Nennwert von 65,17 mit textfernen Manipulationen herabzumindern[48]. Die Antwort ist naheliegend: Weil ein Vorverständnis von Tritojesaja und der scheinbar frühen Zeit dieser Texte, die die Kompilation Gen 1–3 noch gar nicht gekannt haben

---

48. Cf. n. 21.

können, die Untersuchung von vornherein steuert. Daß man dabei einen
biblischen Text und den vorausgesetzten prophetischen Autor auch gern
noch von »Apokalyptik«, wie man sie als Klischeebild zu kennen meint,
freihalten will, tut ein Übriges.

Nicht zuletzt die frühe Rezeption[49] von Jes 65,17 und 66,22 lehrt es
anders. Uns scheinen Jes 65f und solche Rezeptionstexte zeitlich alle
viel näher beieinanderzuliegen und in weiterführender oder kritischer
Aufnahme der Schlußkapitel von Jes den enormen Einfluß des Jesajabuches als »Stimmführer»[50] am Anfang einer maßgeblichen Propheten-
büchergruppe gerade in seiner sachlichen und positionellen Endper-
spektive Jes 65f zu zeigen. Wie man gegenüber der radikalen Endsicht
von Jes 65f herkömmlichen, im Prophetencorpus gegebenen Heilserwartungen gleichwohl Raum verschafft hat, könnte, wie erwähnt, in
einer letzten Akzentuierung in dem MT-Sonderguttext Jer 33,14-26 zu
greifen sein. Wie man sich Jes 65 zugunsten der immer noch weitergel-
tenden Lebensordnung von Gen 1ff entwunden hat, läßt sich den
wichtigen Überlegungen von Krüger[51] zu Hintergrund und Front von
Qoh 1,9-11 entnehmen. Wie man in solcher Kontroverse Jes 66,22 im
Blick auf Jahwe und seine Zeit(ordnung) rezipiert hat, ist in Ps 102,26-
28 zu erkennen[52]; die Aussage hat über den Mosepsalm 90[53], an dem
sich Ps 102 wohl orientiert[54], auch Gen 1ff im Auge. Neben den

49. Cf. dazu Van Ruiten, *Begin* (n. 3), pp. 67-81, 112-207; U. Mell, *Neue
Schöpfung. Eine traditionsgeschichtliche und exegetische Studie zu einem soterio-
logischen Grundsatz paulinischer Theologie* (BZNW, 56), Berlin - New York, 1989,
pp. 69-257.
   50. Cf. dazu Steck, *Studien* (n. 2), p. 34; Id., *Gottesknecht* (n. 23), pp. 168-172, 205.
Cf. die Hochschätzung des Propheten des Jesajabuches auch in rabbinischen Quellen, s.
dazu *RAC* XVII, Lfg. 132/133, Stuttgart, 1995, Art. *Jesaja* (P. Jay), pp. 779-781. Cf. in
diesem Zusammenhang auch die Rezeption der Prophetenbücher(reihe) in *Offb* mit der
aufallenden Zusammenschau der Bücher Jes und Ez. Der Frage der Relecture des
Textabfolge (!) des Jesaja*buches* (insbesondere Jes 6–66) in der Textabfolge von Offb
(insbesondere Offb 4–22) wäre auf der Basis der sicheren Textbezugnahmen unter
Anwendung von weitergehenden Einsichten aus dem Relecturevorgang im Wachsen der
Prophetenbücher näher nachzugehen; vgl. die Untersuchung des Materials mit wichtigen
ersten Folgerungen durch J. Fekkes III, *Isaiah and the Prophetic Traditions in the Book
of Revelation* (JSNT SS, 93), Sheffield, 1994, besonders pp. 106-290.
   51. T. Krüger, *Dekonstruktion und Rekonstruktion prophetischer Eschatologie im
Qoheletbuch,* in A.A. Diesel (ed.), *Jedes Ding hat seine Zeit... Studien zur israelischen
und altorientalischen Weisheit.* FS D. Michel (BZAW, 241), Berlin, 1996, pp. 107-129.
   52. Cf. O.H. Steck, *Zu Eigenart und Herkunft von Ps 102,* in *ZAW* 102 (1990) 357-
372, 368f; ferner F. Sedlmeier, *Zusammengesetzte Nominalsätze und ihre Leistung für
Ps CII,* in *VT* 45 (1995) 239–250, 245f; G. Brunert, *Ps 102 im Kontext des Vierten
Psalmbuchs,* Münster i.W., 1994.
   53. Cf. dazu die Erwägung bei T. Krüger, *Psalm 90 und die »Vergänglichkeit des
Menschen»,* in *Bib* 75 (1994) 191-219, pp. 211f.
   54. Cf. Steck, *Zu Eigenart* (n. 52), pp. 364-369.

vielfältigen Rezeptionen von Jes 65f schon in Sach 14 + Mal[55], ferner z.B. in 11QPs[a] Zion[56], im äthHen[57], in Bar[58] zeigen die spätisraelitischen Aussagen von der neuen Schöpfung[59] mehrfach, daß Jes 65,17 und Gen 1ff ins Verhältnis zueinander gesetzt wurden, cf. z.B. LXX Jes 65,22 / Gen 2,9 und ebenso im Jesajatargum[60]; Jub 1,29[61]; 4,26 (Eden / Berg Zion!); 5,12 (Sintflut) und die bei Mell und Van Ruiten näher besprochenen Belege insbesondere aus äthHen, Qumran und der tannaitischen Überlieferung. Bezieht man auch Jes 65f selbst in diese spätisraelitische Gedankenwelt ein, ergeben sich für die theologie-geschichtliche Traditionsbildung und deren Genesis- / Tora-Rezeption ganz neue, noch nicht erfaßte Perspektiven.

Wassbergerstr. 56   Odil Hannes STECK
CH-8127 Forch

---

55. Cf. O.H. STECK, *Der Abschluß der Prophetie im Alten Testament. Ein Versuch zur Frage der Vorgeschichte des Kanons* (BThSt, 17), Neukirchen-Vluyn, 1991, pp. 42-60, 67-69, 113-126.

56. Text in J.A. SANDERS, *The Psalms Scroll of Qumrân Cave 11 (11QPs^a)* (DJD, IV), Oxford, 1965, pp. 85-89; cf. mit Jes 60.62.66.

57. Cf. den Hinweis in STECK, *Heimkehr* (n. 43), p. 78; ID., *Studien* (n. 2), pp. 36, 39, 41, 44; G.W.E. NICKELSBURG, *Resurrection, Immortality, and Eternal Life in Intertestamental Judaism*, (HTS, 26) Cambridge, MA - London, 1972 (zur Rezeption von Jes 56–66 in spätisraelitischen Texten), zu äthHen ID., *Jewish Literature Between the Bible and the Mishnah: A Historical and Literary Introduction*, London, 1981, p. 49; ID., *Enoch, First Book of*, in *ABD* 2, pp. 508-516, 509, und besonders M.-T. WACKER, *Weltordnung und Gericht. Studien zu 1 Henoch 22* (FzB, 45), Würzburg, 1982, pp. 250-253; MELL, *Schöpfung* (n. 49), pp. 119-126; VAN RUITEN, *Influence* (n. 11); ID., *Begin* (n. 3), pp. 122-125.

58. Cf. O.H. STECK, *Das apokryphe Baruchbuch. Studien zu Rezeption und Konzentration »kanonischer« Überlieferung* (FRLANT, 160), Göttingen, 1993, pp. 204-239.

59. Cf. dazu P. BILLERBECK, *Kommentar zum Neuen Testament aus Talmud und Midrasch*, Bd. 3, München, 1926 (Neudruck 1954), pp. 840-847; K. BERGER, *Das Buch der Jubiläen* (JSHRZ, I/3), Gütersloh, 1981, pp. 320f, und besonders MELL (cf. n. 49). Speziell zur Rezeption von Jes 65,17ff. in Offb 21 siehe J.T.A.G.M. VAN RUITEN, *The Intertextual Relationship between Isaiah 65,17-20 and Revelation 21,1–5b*, in *EstBib* 51 (1993) 473-510; FEKKES, *Isaiah* (n. 50), pp. 227-230, 255-260 (Offb 21,4b-5: Jes 65,19b-20a.16 in Verbindung mit Jes 43,18f!).

60. Cf. dazu J.B. SCHALLER, *Gen 1.2 im antiken Judentum*, theol. Dissertation Göttingen, 1961 (Masch.), pp. 51f.

61. Cf. MELL, *Schöpfung* (n. 49), pp. 152-158; VAN RUITEN, *Begin* (n. 3), pp. 69-81, 95f; O.H. STECK, *Die getöteten »Zeugen« und die verfolgten »Tora-Sucher« in Jub 1,12. Ein Beitrag zur Zeugnis-Terminologie des Jubiläenbuches II*, in *ZAW* 108 (1996) 70-86, pp. 76ff.

EZEKIEL SALUTES ISAIAH
EZEKIEL 20,32-44

As a young scholar I met Willem Beuken the day that I had been newly admitted to the meetings of the "Oudtestamentische Werkgezelschap". During the meal break he took me aside for a discussion on the twentieth chapter of Ezekiel, the topic of my doctoral dissertation[1]. I was immediately on my guard and perhaps a little defensive. After the publication of my thesis I felt that I had seen enough of Ezekiel, for the time being at least, and I had tried to banish him from my mind. Nevertheless, subconsciously I still considered the book of Ezekiel, and especially its 20th chapter, to be my own private hunting ground. Although six years older than I, the intruder appeared very young for his age. My reaction during our brief discussion must have been slightly patronizing and not very cordial, especially when he started questioning me about the second half of Ez 20. I had confined myself in my dissertation to the study of the first half of the chapter, having postponed any in-depth analysis of the second part to the indefinite future. I was even more annoyed when I discovered that my interlocutor had recently published an article of his own on Ez 20, focusing on its second part and its ties with the first[2].

Some time later I read the article in question with growing appreciation. It was written in Dutch and published in an excellent albeit underrated periodical. Although its methodological approach proved to be ahead of its time, the contribution went completely unnoticed in scholarly circles. Beuken never continued his explorations into Ezekiel preferring to move on to Deutero- and Trito-Isaiah. It may perhaps not be fortuitous that the one Ezekiel chapter he chose to examine in-depth shows remarkable connections with Deutero- and Trito-Isaiah. On the occasion of his retirement, therefore, and in honour of his outstanding achievements, it may be appropriate to return to Beuken's innovative views on Ezekiel and to reconsider this prophet's salute to Isaiah. At the same time, it may allow me to answer some of the questions brought to the fore at our first meeting, and perhaps, to advance some new ones.

1. J. LUST, *Traditie, redactie en kerygma bij Ezechiël. Een analyse van Ez 20*, Brussels, 1969.
2. W. BEUKEN, *Ez 20: Thematiek en literaire vormgeving in onderling verband*, in *Bijdragen* 33 (1972) 39-64.

Beuken's remarks on the topic can be summarized as follows. Ez 20 comprises two pericopes: (1) the elder's request and God's refusal to be consulted, clothed in a denunciation of Israel's history (1-31); (2) a communal lament that Israel may be assimilated into the heathen cults, countered by an announcement of salvation which holds out the prospect of true worship on the holy mountain (32-44). Both parts of the chapter constitute independent prophecies. Their literary genres and their *Sitz-im-Leben* are different. Each of them has a refined inward unity, built up by structure and topic. As for vv. 27-29, it is argued that they offer a midrash-like interpretation of the preceding verses in which Israel is depicted as having gone from the desert straight into exile. Although the two major parts of the chapter were originally independent, in the final text they are closely interconnected and constitute a unified artistic literary composition. The condemnation based on Israel's history and the announcement of its salutary future have come to be considered as a thematic unity.

Of course our summary cannot do justice to the treasure chest of the philological, stylistic, structural, and intertextual observations presented in the article. It may, however, allow the reader to sense some of its renewing characteristics. Long before it had become fashionable in continental exegesis, the author made use of a synchronic approach, focusing on the stylistic features of the final text. In contrast to many more recent protagonists of the various synchronic methods, Beuken succeeded in combining his sound rhetorical observations on the final text with equally well balanced diachronic views on the historical growth of the passage.

In the following contribution I will focus primarily on the second part of Ez 20. On the basis of an initial reading, I will offer a general presentation of the passage together with some text critical observations, comparing the Hebrew text with the Greek. In a subsequent reading I will focus on the interpretation of the passage, engaging, asit were, in a dialogue with W. Beuken[3].

---

3. In this discussion we will also take into account the observations of the leading commentaries such as G.A. COOKE (ICC), Edinburgh, 1936; W. ZIMMERLI (BKAT, 13), 2 vols., Neukirchen, 1969; = (Hermeneia), Philadelphia, 1979, 1983; H.F. FUHS, (Echter), 2 vols., Würzburg, 1984, 1988; M. GREENBERG, *Ezekiel 1–20* (AB), Garden City, NY, 1983; B. MAARSINGH (POT), 3 vols., Nijkerk, 1985, 1988, 1991; W.H. BROWNLEE, *Ezekiel 1–19* (WBC), Waco, TX, 1986; L.C. ALLEN, *Ezekiel 20–48* (WBC), Waco, TX, 1990; *Ezekiel 1–19* (WBC), Waco, TX, 1994; K.-F. POHLMANN, *Der Prophet Hesekiel* (ATD, 22/1), Göttingen, 1996 (esp. p. 31); and of the articles and studies on Ez 20 published after Beuken composed his paper, such as D. BALTZER, *Ezechiel und Deuterojesaja* (BZAW, 121), Berlin, 1971; P. WEIMAR – E. ZENGER, *Exodus. Geschichten und Geschichte der Befreiung Israels* (SBS, 75), Stuttgart, 1975, pp. 146-154; R. LIWAK,

1. FIRST READING OF 20,32-44

The pattern of a quotation followed by a refutation lies at the basis of this "disputation speech". In the first part of Ezekiel, similar disputations can be found in 11,1-13.14-21; 12,21-25.26-28; 18,1-32. Exceptionally, the present composition is not introduced by a word-event formula.

The quotation in 20,32 is often interpreted as a defiant expression of the people's desire to be like the nations. The essence of the refutation seems to be given in v. 33: "I will reign over you", although it is not immediately clear how this constitutes a response to the people's envisaged service of the idols. The three following sections, each of which ends with the "recognition formula", elaborate the basic refutation (vv. 34-38; 39-42; 43-44). The first illustrates the Lord's ruling: in a new exodus He will gather his people and judge them. The second describes the entry into the promised land. The third concerns the people's recognition of their guilt.

In order to facilitate a comparison with MT, the following translation renders the LXX according to the edition of Ziegler[4]. *Italics* draw attention to differences with MT, or to interpretative translations. The brackets signal "pluses" in MT.

32. *nor shall this come up in your mind*[5]. (32) And it shall not be as you say: "We shall become like the nations, like the tribes of the countries, and worship wood and stone".
33. *Therefore*[6] as I live, says the Lord [ ], surely with a mighty hand and an outstretched arm, and with wrath poured out, I will be king over you.
34. I will bring you out from the peoples and *take you out* of the countries where you are scattered, with a mighty hand and an outstretched arm, and with wrath poured out;
35. and I will bring you into the wilderness of the peoples, and there I will enter into judgement with you face to face.

Ueberlieferungsgeschichtliche Probleme des Ezechielbuches, Bochum, 1976; A. GRAFFY, *A Prophet Confronts His People* (AnBib, 104), Rome, 1984; J. PONS, *Le vocabulaire d'Éz 20*, in J. LUST (ed.), *Ezekiel and His Book* (BETL, 74), Leuven, 1986, pp. 214-233; T. KRÜGER, *Geschichtskonzepte im Ezechielbuch* (BZAW, 180), Berlin, 1989; F. SEDLMEIER, *Studien zu Komposition und Theologie von Ezechiel 20* (SBB, 21), Stuttgart, 1990; S. OHNESORGE, *Jahwe gestaltet sein Volk neu* (FzB, 64), Würzburg, 1991; K.-F. POHLMANN, *Ezechielstudien* (BZAW, 202), Berlin, 1992; D. BARTHÉLEMY, *Critique textuelle de l'Ancien Testament* (OBO, 50/3), Fribourg - Göttingen, 1992, esp. pp. 156-160.
    4. Göttingen, ²1968.
    5. LXX and MT seem to split vv. 31 and 32 in different ways. LXX appends the first phrase of MT v. 32 to the end of v. 31.
    6. LXX connects v. 33 strongly with 32 through the opening διὰ τοῦτο in v. 32.

36. As I entered into judgement with your fathers in the wilderness of the land of Egypt, so I will enter into judgement with you, says the Lord [ ].

37. I will make you pass under the rod, and I will let you go in *by number*[7].

38. I will *choose out*[8] *from you the ungodly* and the rebels, *for* I will bring them out of the land where they sojourn, but *they* shall not enter the land of Israel. Then you will know that I am the Lord.

39. As for you, O house of Israel, thus says the Lord [ ]: *Get rid of*[9] *your habits*, every one of you, and hereafter, if you [ ] listen to me, you shall no more profane my holy name with your gifts and your *practices*.

40. For on my holy mountain, the mountain height of Israel, says the Lord [ ], there all the house of Israel shall serve me *to the end*[10] [ ][11]; *and* there I will accept [ ], and there I will *look upon* your *first-offerings and the firstlings of your wave-offerings*[12], with all your sacred things.

41. As a pleasing odor I will accept you, when I bring you out from the peoples, and *take* you out of the countries where you have been scattered; and I will manifest my holiness among you in the sight of the nations.

42. And you shall know that I am the Lord, when I bring you into the land of Israel, [ ] the country *to* which I lifted up my hand to give it to your fathers.

---

7. The end of v. 37 in Hebrew is problematic: במסרת הברית. For a good survey of the problems and its solutions, see BARTHÉLEMY, *Critique textuelle* (n. 3), pp. 156-158. Aquila's literal translation renders the expression by: εν δεσμοις της διαθηκης "in the bonds of the covenant", similarly Theodotion has δια κλοιου της διαθηκης. Symmachus reads εν τη παραδοσει της διαθηκης which seems to interpret the term משרת as "tradition" or *masorah*. The Septuagint εν αριθμω appears to have read במספר "in number" for MT במסרת. It has no equivalent for the term ברית. The word in question may be a corrupt dittography of the first word in v. 38: וברותי. The Septuagint translator may not yet have found it in his *Vorlage*. The expression read by the Septuagint (to bring in by number) can also be found in 1 Chron 9,28. With GREENBERG (*Ezechiel* [n. 3], pp. 372-373) Barthélemy refuses to accept the reading of LXX as the original one. It is supposed to be inappropriate in our context, 1 Chron 9,28 being said to show that the expression means "to take the account of items as they come in" in order to check that they are all present. According to Greenberg, this is the opposite of the "selection" or "weeding out" which the context in Ezekiel calls for. While we can certainly agree that the first part of the verse implies a selection, the second part does not have to repeat exactly the same idea. It may express a further continuation of the argumentation, saying that, once selected, the exact number will be brought in. Compare this with v. 40 where it is said that this will be "all Israel, all of it".

8. The verb ברר (ברותי v. 38) has a positive meaning "to select, to choose", or a negative meaning "to purge out, to reject". In v. 38 the context presupposes the negative connotation. The Greek verb opts in favour of the positive meaning.

9. In v. 39 LXX εξαρατε ("eradicate") may be based on the reading השליכו ("throw away") for MT לכו. In a similar context, the expression השליכו can be found in v.7. This explanation, however, leaves the verb עבדו unexplained. It is perhaps more likely that the translator read עברו for MT עבדו, and that he read לכו עברו as one expression.

10. For the Greek εις τελος in v. 40, a rendition of כלה, compare 11,15.

11. The Greek has no equivalent for בארץ in this verse.

12. For Greek τας απαρχας των αφορισμων υμων, equivalent of משאתכם, compare v. 31. Επισκεπαζω ("to look upon") is used here as a translation of דרש. The term usually renders פקד.

43. And there you shall remember your ways and [ ][13] doings with which you have polluted yourselves; and you shall *beat your faces* for all the evils [ ][14].

44. And you shall know that I am the Lord, when I deal *so* with you, that my name *may not be profaned* according to your evil ways, nor according to your corrupt doings, [ ][15], says the Lord [ ].

2. A CLOSER READING OF EZ 20,32

What does the quotation mean, and in whose mouth is it put? Is it in the same vein as 1 Sam 8,20: "let us become like all the nations" (והיינו גם אנחנו ככל הגוים), in which the people are clamouring for a king? If so, this would explain the Lord's reaction, stating strongly that He will be their king: Ez 20,33. Alternatively, is the tone of the quotation rather similar to that in Ez 33,10 and 37,11 in which the Jews express their utter despair? In that case, its wordings should perhaps be compared with 25,8 where Moab insults Judah by describing her as being "like all the nations"? Following Zimmerli's lead, Beuken, Baltzer, Graffy, and Allen[16], favour the second possibility. According to them, the quoted people despondently accept that they have become like the nations: their God has abandoned them. The large majority of commentators, however, definitely prefer the first option[17]. In their view the quotation expresses the arrogant wish of the people. On the question at hand, we side with the majority. Our reasons can best be explained in dialogue with Beuken since he offers the most explicit argumentation in favour of the alternative option. We will also admit Graffy to the dialogue since he adds a new element into the discussion.

a. Beuken suggests that the verb form נהיה, introducing the quotation here and in Neh 2,17, supports a complaint in the future. It is to be compared with היינו and ונהי, two verb forms that look back on calamities in the past. Against this suggestion it should be noted that the rare occur-

13. The Greek has no equivalent for the first כל.
14. The Greek has no equivalent for the concluding "that you have committed" (אשר עשיתם).
15. The Greek has no equivalent for בית ישראל.
16. BEUKEN, *Ez. 20* (n. 2), pp. 49-52; BALTZER, *Ezechiel und Deuterojesaja* (n. 3), pp. 4-5; WEIMAR – ZENGER, *Exodus* (n. 3), p. 152; GRAFFY, *A Prophet Confronts His People* (n. 3), p. 66; ALLEN, *Ezechiel* (n. 3), pp. 11-12, and perhaps also POHLMANN, *Ezechielstudien* (n. 3), p. 63 who does not discuss the verse but briefly suggests that it reflects the implications of the condemnation of Israel in the foregoing section.
17. Among the more recent studies see, e.g., GREENBERG, *Ezechiel* (n. 3), p. 371; PONS, *Vocabulaire* (n. 3), p. 227; SEDLMEIER, *Studien* (n. 3), pp. 317-319; OHNESORGE, *Jahwe* (n. 3), p. 154.

rences of נהיה at the beginning of a main clause, do not voice a complaint concerning the future. In such a context the verb form appears to be a cohortative, expressing a wish, or an agreement, concerning the future. This is particularly clear in Gen 44,9 where the sons of Jacob say to Joseph: we *agree* to become your servants, and in 1 Sam 14,40 where David says to the people: (for the casting of the lots) you shall be at one side, I and my son *agree* to be at the other side. Beuken does not mention these cases, probably because they do not fit his purpose. Neh 2,17, the passage adduced by Beuken in support of his thesis, appears to express a wish, not a complaint: we *wish* to suffer disgrace no longer. Following after a cohortative, the sentence can also be understood as a subordinate clause: "Come, let us build the wall of Jerusalem, that we may no longer suffer disgrace" (RSV). A similar subordinate sentence can be found in Gen 38,23, although with the particle פן preceding the verb נהיה: "Let her keep the things as her own, *lest* we be laughed at".

Beuken tries to find further support for his view in several passages in which the perfect form היינו or the imperfect with a *waw conversivum* ונהי are used. It is true that these verb forms often refer to a complaint about a situation in the past. It does not follow, however, that the imperfect form נהיה refers to complaints concerning the future. The imperfect נהיה should rather be compared with והיינו, the perfect preceded by a *waw conversivum*. All of the passages in question unambiguously express agreement or longing, and not a complaint[18]. The most relevant case is to be found in 1 Sam 8,20: "we wish to have a king over us that we also me be like all the nations".

b. Beuken's main reason for interpreting the quotation as a complaint is the Lord's positive reaction. The oracle of salvation granted in v. 40 would make no sense in an answer to a nation disobeying its own God, and desiring to become like the other nations.

Such reasoning might have been difficult to contradict if the Lord's answer had been a straightforward oracle of salvation. It is, however, much more complex. The basic refutation in v. 33 sounds threatening. The Lord will reign over his people with "wrath poured out". How will this happen? The first part of the explanation is to be found in the oracle of judgement in vv. 24-38. It distinguishes two groups within the nation. The rebels will be purged out and shall not enter the land (v. 38). The second part addresses the remaining group who will be brought into the land promised to their fathers (v. 42). This leads us to the conclusion that the oracle makes perfect sense as an answer to the rebellious claim

18. Gen 34,16; 47,25; Jos 2,20; 1 Sam 8,20; 17,9.

of a part of the people who wish to become like the nations. Beuken pays little attention to the threatening mood of the basic refutation and to the first part of its explanation. He rushes forward to the second part, in order to find a positive answer to the quotation in v. 32.

A comparison with the disputation in 11,14-21 confirms our view. The passage shows many similarities with 20,32-44. It clearly distinguishes between two groups within Israel. The group being quoted are arrogantly boasting that the land is given to them. They are identified as the ones who stayed in Jerusalem during the first period of the exile. The remaining group consists of those who were deported to Babylon. The oracle responding to the quotation announces salvation, not for those who uttered the arrogant claim, but for the exiled members of the nation. For the inhabitants of Jerusalem the oracle sounds threatening. Their land will be purged from all its abominations (v. 18).

c. Beuken seems to overlook the threatening oracle in vv. 34-38 because, in his view, the complaint of the exiled people "we will have to serve wood and stone" is clearly answered in v. 40 in the Lord's promise that "they shall serve me on my holy mountain". The expression "to serve wood and stone" is rather common in Deuteronomy and is a reference to idolatry. In Dt 4,28; 28,36.64 the service of wood and stone is one of the curses to be inflicted on Israel if it fails to follow God's laws. In contrast to Deuteronomy, however, where the expression employs the verb עבד, the phrase in Ezekiel uses the verb שרת. Like Trito-Isaiah, Ezekiel further employs this verb exclusively in his descriptions of the true cult of the Lord in the final days (40-48)[19]. According to Beuken, this adds a bitter connotation to the complaint of the people. Their fear of an imposed pagan cult sharply contrasts with the promises of an ideal cult of the Lord at the end of the days.

One should not forget, however, that the promised future service of the Lord in 20,40 is described with the verb עבד (and not שרת). If a direct contrast had been intended between the service of idols in the exile (v.32) and the true service of the Lord in the final days (v. 40) one might have expected to find the verb שרת in both passages.

Together with Zimmerli, Beuken notes that, with the exception of Ez 20,32, the verb שרת occurs in Ezekiel exclusively in the editorial additions of chapters 40-48. It is slightly puzzling that for Zimmerli and Beuken, this observation does not raise questions concerning the authentic Ezekelian character of Ez 20,32 and of the oracles that follow upon it. At the present, however, such questions must remain beyond our con-

19. Is. 56,6; 60,7.10; Ez 40,46; 42,14; 43,19; 44,11.12.15.17.19.27; 42,4.5; 46,24.

cern. It may be more important at this point to search for a more satisfactory explanation of the unexpected use of שרת in 20,32. Sedlmeier
may have found the right track. His detailed analysis of the meaning of
the verb in its respective contexts demonstrates that it always refers to
service with a "public" character[20]. In Ez 20,32, it expresses the arrogant and stubborn will of the nation to publicly serve the gods of the
gentiles, and, as such, no longer have to be the YHWH-people in the eyes
of the whole world. If this interpretation of the verb שרת and its use in
20,32 are correct, the continued reading of the quotation as a complaint
is seriously undermined.

d. In support of his own views, Beuken cites Zimmerli, without much
comment. In a rather weak argumentation, the latter suggests that the quotation in 20,32 should not be compared with 1 Sam 8,20, but rather with
the complaints quoted in Ez 33,10 and 37,11. Sedlmeier rightly notices the
arbitrary character of Zimmerli's choice which underrates the parallel with
1 Sam 8 in favour of two Ezekiel passages[21]. The allusions to 1 Sam 8 offer a fine example of intertextuality. The reader of Ez 20,32-33 is expected
to have the Samuel passage in mind in order to grasp the Lord's royal
claims as an answer to the people's wish to serve other gods. In Samuel's
days the Israelites, wanting to be like the nations, expressed their wish to
be ruled by a king (1 Sam 8,5). The Lord understands this desire as an
unfaithfulness towards him and his kingship over them (8,7). He adds that
this unfaithfulness was already apparent from the outset: from the day He
brought them up out of Egypt until this day they forsook Him and served
other gods (8,8). This passage in Samuel makes the connection between
the themes of Israel's service of other gods and the Lord's kingship over
Israel explicit and thus explains how the Lord's oracle in Ez 20,33 answers the quotation of the people in 20,32.

It should be added that Zimmerli's two parallels found in Ezekiel
are taken from the final part of the book. The quotation in Ez 20 belongs to the first part, and thus should be compared, first of all, with
the remaining quotations in these chapters. We already observed the
interesting similarities with Ez 11,14-22 and concluded that the passage in question supports our interpretation of the quotation in 20,32.

e. The parallel with 11,14-22 leads us to an important question: Who
voices the claim? It is obvious that the people in Jerusalem are quoted in

---

20. SEDLMEIER, *Studien* (n. 3), pp. 322-340. The suggestion made by ENGELKEN in
TWAT VIII, 502, that שרת in Ez 20,32 refers to the primitive cult of the patriarchs, seems
to be totally unwarranted.
21. SEDLMEIER, *Studien* (n. 3), p. 318.

11,15, but in 20,32 the situation seems to be different. According to Graffy the utterance is clearly attributed to the exiles. He adds, furthermore, that all the quotations in the disputes with the exiles (12,27; 33,10; 37,11) express despair and hopelessness, whereas those attributed to the people left in Jerusalem have a confident, arrogant tone: 11,3,15; 12,22; 18,2; 33,24[22].

Seen in its present context, the quotation in 20,32 seems indeed to be put in the mouth of the exiles who are seated before Ezekiel (20,1) with the purpose of consulting the Lord. One should not forget, however, that originally, the dispute in 20,32ff was probably construed as an independent unit. The identification of the opponents of the prophet should be sought within that unit. We will see that, according to v. 38, they were the inhabitants of Judah. It is not impossible that the final text agrees with that identification. In the final composition, Ezekiel's interlocutors are identified as a group of elders from Israel who came to the prophet to inquire of the Lord (v. 1). Since the introduction to the book situates Ezekiel among the exiles, it is usually taken for granted that these elders belong to the prophet's fellow exiles. One cannot exclude the possibility, however, that they may have been visitors comming from Israel[23]. It is certainly true that, when these elders come and sit before the prophet in chs. 8 and 14, he entertains them concerning the situation in Jerusalem. In ch. 8 this is facilitated by a visionary experience which transports the prophet into his own country. In ch. 14, where the elders come to make an inquiry in exactly the same fashion as in ch.20, the prophet addresses them as representatives of the people sojourning in Israel (v. 7, compare 20,38), and not as members of the exilic community.

Finally, Graffy's contention that the quotations in 12,27; 33,10; 37,11 voice complaints of the exiles, may be in need of some correction. It is by no means sure that 12,27 is a complaint[24], nor that it belongs to a dispute with the exiles; 33,10 belongs to a context similar to that of 18,2, and probably addresses those left behind in Jerusalem; according to Pohlmann[25] 37,11.12a.14 is the original core of 37,11-14, and is also a description of a dispute with the people in Judah; 37,12b-13 is an insert.

22. GRAFFY, A Prophet Confronts His People (n. 3), pp. 66-67.
23. Compare with the fugitive(s) who come to announce the fall of Jerusalem to the prophet: 14,22-23; 24,27; 33,21-22.
24. See J. LUST, Le messianisme et la Septante d'Ézéchiel, in Tsafon 1 (1990) 3-14, esp. pp. 9-11.
25. Der Prophet Hezekiel (n. 3), p. 117.

3. THE BASIC REFUTATION AND THE FIRST PART OF ITS EXPLANATION: 20,33 AND 34-38

In the foregoing section we already had to deal with some aspects of the basic refutation and of the immediately following explanatory oracle. Further observations remain to be added. The basic statement of the refutation is introduced by the oath formula: חי אני, as in Ez 18,3 and 33,11. The essence of the refutation lies in the words "I will reign (אמלך) over you". Although an allusion to Ex 15,18 is not excluded, we already noted that this statement definitely recalls 1 Sam 8. The link with the book of Samuel is enforced by the observation that this is the only place in Ezekiel where the Lord is said to act as a king.

The verb is accompanied by three explanatory phrases: "with strong hand", "with outstretched arm", and "with wrath poured out". The first two almost always refer to the Lord's activity in the first exodus (see, e.g., the "Creed" in Dt 26,8). The final phrase is more typical of Ezekiel (שפך חמה 7,8; 9,8; 14,19; 20,8.13.21…) adding a threatening connotation to the Lord's reign. According to Greenberg, Ezekiel intentionally uses traditional expressions with a shocking twist. Adding a third phrase of his own coinage, he asserts that the Lord's power that was unleashed against Egypt in the first exodus will now be turned against rebellious Israel.

The following judgement scene (vv. 34-38) lists a series of *perfecta consecutiva* describing the consequences of the Lord's reign. He will lead his people into the desert once again and purify them in a new exodus period. Ezekiel shares the theme of a second exodus with Deutero-Isaiah[26]. While the theme of exodus in Isaiah primarily means liberation, however, in Ezekiel it stands for judgement and trial.

The series of *perfecta consecutiva* opens with the "gathering and return" verbs. They are usually applied to the Lord's intervention implying a gathering of the dispersed and their entry into the promised land. We will encounter and discuss this stereotype in vv. 41-42. Here, however, the application is remarkably different. The gathering leads to an entry into the "desert of the nations". Note the repetition of the three solemn qualifying phrases: "with strong hand, with outstretched arm, and with wrath poured out". If the repetition is intended, it must imply a special emphasis. If not, it may be a repetitive resumption following an editorial insert intended to apply the oracle to a new public: that of the diaspora in postexilic times.

---

26. See BALTZER, *Ezechiel und Deuterojesaja* (n. 3), pp. 1-26 and Isa 52,1.11-12; 43,16-19.

The "desert of the nations" (v. 35) is not a geographical notion. It constitutes the typological antithesis of the "desert of Egypt" explicitly connected with the first exodus (v. 36). The "face to face" (v. 35) encounter in this desert between God and his people recalls the Sinai or Horeb event where the Lord spoke with them "face to face" (Dt 5,4).

The expression in v. 37 "to pass under the staff" is an allusion to the counting of animals for the tithe (Lev 27,32). It does not signify mere counting, however, but selection[27]. In its application to the judgement of the people in the desert it implies that only the selected ones will be allowed to enter into the Promised Land. The parallel phrase in v. 37 is slightly cryptic: והביאתי אתכם במסרת הברית and is a *hapax* in the Bible. The best parallel can perhaps be found in the Qumranic literature. In 1QS 6,14 it is said that the instructor may bring in (ויביאהו) a new member into the covenant (בברית) if he suits the discipline (מוסר)[28]. Similarly, the biblical expression in Ezekiel appears to imply that only those who passed under the rod, i.e., those who have been selected, will be allowed into the covenant and its discipline. The unvocalised masoretic text allows of this interpretation. The vocalised text seems to refer to "bonds" or to "tradition", and is known for its connections with the "masorah" and the "masoretes"[29]. In any event, the parallels to the Hebrew biblical text all seem to belong to the post-biblical literature. The Septuagint reading "and I will bring you in by number" may be a witness to an earlier form of the text which read במספר instead of במסרת. A comparison with 1 Chron 9,28 explains its implications. The full number of those who passed under the rod, all of them (compare v. 40), will be allowed to enter the promised land[30].

The summarizing statement in v. 38 confirms that the rebels will be purged out and will not be allowed to enter. This negative statement concludes the first part of the answer to the quotation and may be the original answer.

"The land in which they reside as aliens" (ארץ מגוריהם v. 38) is an allusion to Canaan before the entry into it as into the land of the promise. The identification is made explicit in Ex 6,4, a text which recalls Gen 17,8; 28,4; 36,7; 37,1; 47,9[31]. If in Ez 20,38 the reference is also to Canaan, then the rebels are situated there and not in Babylon. Nowhere does the expression appear to refer to the exile.

27. See the detailed description in *mishnah Bekhorot* 9,7.
28. Compare 1QS[a] 1,6 and see our textcritical observations.
29. GREENBERG, *Ezechiel* (n. 3), pp. 372-373; compare W. BACHER, *A Contribution to the History of the Term "Masorah"*, in *JQR* 3 (1891) 785-790.
30. See the text critical note.
31. See J. LUST, *Exodus 6,2-8 and Ezekiel*, in M. VERVENNE (ed.), *Studies in the Book of Exodus* (BETL, 126), Leuven, 1996, pp. 209-224, esp. p. 214.

4. The Entry into the Promised Land, and the Recognition of Guilt: 20,39-42 and 43-44

The first verse of the second section (v.39) presents a number of problems appearing to suggest that the Lord encourages the service of the idols. According to Beuken this is irony. In his commentary, published more than 10 years later, Greenberg comes to the same conclusion, without being aware of the proposals of his predecessor. The Greek version reads the text in a different way: "Get rid of his habits, each one of you". It continues in a positive mood: "and thereafter, if you listen to me, then you shall no longer profane...". Here again, according to Greenberg, MT is to be understood as ironical. He may be right. The Greek text seems to imply a simplification of a difficult Hebrew text.

Who is addressee? The "you" at the beginning of the sentence seems to refer to the "house of Israel" without any restrictions. The next verse emphasizes that the "whole" house of Israel "all of it" will serve the Lord on his holy mountain. No reference seems to be made to the selection procedure described in the foregoing passage. It should not be overlooked, however, that the expression כל בית ישראל כלה in 20,40 was coined by the editor of the book of Ezekiel and exclusively used to indicate the house of Israel in its ideal proportions. In 11,15 it refers to those living in "dispersion" (v. 16). They are clearly distinguished from those who live in Jerusalem and who preposterously claim to be the real Israel. A similar contrast occurs in chapter 36 where the present inhabitants of Israel are called "Edomites" (v. 5). They boast that the land is given to them, but they are contrasted with the real owners, the whole Israel, all of it (כל ישראל כלה) who will soon come to their land (v. 8). A similar distinction may also be implied in chapter 20,32-44. If this is true, then those rebel Israelites who want to serve wood and stone must be the present inhabitants of Israel. With all the dispersed Israelites they will be brought into the desert and be judged. They will be purged out of the nation. Then the remainder, the real Israel, their full number (v. 37), will be brought into the land.

The terminology expressing the notion that Israel will serve the Lord on his holy mountain is somewhat unusual. In fact, it constitutes the only instance in Ezekiel in which the place of the temple is called "my holy mountain (הר קדשי)". The expression is typical of some late strands in Isaiah: 11,9; 56,7; 57,13; 65,11.25; 66,20[32]. Like the theme of the new exodus, the motif of the service of the Lord on his holy mountain differs in its connotations between Isaiah and Ezekiel. In Isaiah all the nations

---

32. See also Ps 2,6; Jl 2,1; 4,17; Ob 16; Zeph 3,17.

are invited to the worship of the Lord on his mountain (Is 56,6-7; 66,20). In Ezekiel, however, the service (יעבדני) of the Lord is exclusively reserved to the ideal house of Israel. The use of the verb עבד in this eschatological cultic context is exceptional. We already noted that in the final part of Ezekiel and in Trito-Isaiah, the verb שרת is employed. One reason why the verb עבד is preferred in Ez 20,40 may be that a comparison with 1 Sam 8 is intended, as was the case in 20,32. In the Samuel passage, the Lord accuses his people of having served (עבד) other gods, from the day they left Egypt[33].

The third person plural verbs are slightly anomalous in a context where the public is addressed in the second person plural. The end of v. 40 as well as vv. 41-42 return to second person plural. Similar switches occur frequently in other passages in Ezekiel, as well as elsewhere in the Bible. A comparison should especially be made with the dispute in Ez 11,14-21 where the second person plural references to dispersed Israel in v. 17 interrupt a series of third person plural references to the same group. This phenomenon is often taken to be a symptom of a later editorial intervention. Such an intervention is difficult to prove, however, when other indications are lacking.

In v.40 the emphasis is on the triple שם, stressing that it is "there", on that mountain, that Israel will worship. In the present context, "there" contrasts with "the nations" among whom the people were dispersed (vv. 34), and with the "desert of the nations" where they were judged (35-36). In the final composition, it contrasts perhaps even more with "every high hill" (v. 28) in Israel where, according to a late editor, the people used to make their sacrifices[34]. The use of the word ראשית in v. 40, with its overtone of firstling offerings, recalls the contrasting horror of the offerings of the firstborn in vv.26 and 31.

Verses 41-42 describe the entry into the promised land with Ezekiel's stereotypical terminology: יצא, קבץ, בוא[35]. In the book of Ezekiel the announcement of this event is usually expressed in three sentences of which the first two are parallels. As a model we take Ez 34,13:

I will bring them out (הוצאתם) from the peoples (עמים)
and gather them (קבצתים) from the countries (ארצות)
and will bring them (הביאתם) into their own land (אדמתם).

33. The term משאות (gifts, lifted up) is also a hapax in Ezekiel.
34. See GREENBERG, *Ezechiel* (n. 3), p. 379.
35. See F. HOSSFELD, *Untersuchungen zu Komposition und Theologie des Ezechielbuches* (FzB, 20), Würzburg, 1977, pp. 309-314; J. LUST, *"Gathering and Return" in Jeremiah and Ezekiel*, in P.-M. BOGAERT (ed.), *Le Livre de Jérémie* (BETL, 54), Leuven, 1981, pp. 119-142.

Other attestations of the theme, using a similar formulation, can be found in Ez 36,24; 37,21. In all these texts a similar triad of verbs occurs. The second and third are most constant: קבץ and הביא. The first is more variable, largely depending on the context. The subject of the three verbs is always the Lord and the object is his people. A relative clause often describes the countries from which the Israelites are to be gathered as the nations in which they have been "scattered" or "dispersed" (פוץ)[36]. Other passages in Ezekiel use part of the stereotypical formulas, or employ them in a slightly altered form: 28,25; 29,13-14; 37,12; 39,27. Among these, 29,13-14 is especially noteworthy. It applies the theme to the Egyptians. Also, it displays variants which are remarkably similar to the terminology used by Jeremiah in 29,14 and elsewhere. The most typical variant is the replacement of the *hiphil* הביא by the *hiphil* of שוב "to bring back, to return". This leads us to some intriguing observations. Whereas Jeremiah announces a "return" into the Promised Land, the Book of Ezekiel does not mention a "return". It prophesies, rather, that the Lord will gather his dispersed people and bring them from the "diaspora" into the Promised Land. This corresponds with one of the basic themes of the book: according to Ezekiel Israel was dispersed into the desert of the nations (Ez 20,23.35) before it reached the Promised Land. The entry into the land is still to come. Moreover, the repeated reference to the "gathering" of the "dispersed" seems to postulate a diaspora situation rather than an exilic one. The liberation from exile is not normally described as a gathering of the dispersed. The expressions in question most likely betray a post-exilic situation in the Persian and Greek periods[37].

The phrase "raise up my hand" (נשא ידי) in v. 42 recalls the first part of the chapter where the same phrase occurs as a refrain in vv.5-6.15.23. Modern translations usually interpret this expression as an oath formula. LXX presents a different interpretation. In vv. 5 and 6 it has ἀντελαβόμην τῇ χειρί ("I helped with my hand"). The translator obviously understood the phrase as a reference to the Lord's active intervention. In the other occurrences it has a more literal rendition, using the verb ἐξαίρω ("to lift up"). Even then, the context in v. 42 makes it clear that the translator did not think of an oath: the Lord is said to have lifted up his hand *towards* the land (εἰς την γην) to give it to the fathers. This

36. In Ez 11,17 the notion of the bringing into the land (*hiphil* of בוא) is replaced by that of the giving (נתן) of the land, as an answer to the claim voiced in v.15 (cf. Ex 6,8b).

37. See LUST, "*Gathering and Return*" (n. 35), pp. 140-142; C. LEVIN, *Die Verheißung des neuen Bundes* (FRLANT, 137), Göttingen, 1985, pp. 168-169, 188-189, 196, 202-203; POHLMANN, *Ezechielstudien* (n. 3), pp. 62-63; *Der Prophet Hesekiel* (n. 3), p. 31.

does not seem to imply a gesture of an oath, but rather an active intervention[38].

The final stage of the refutation (vv. 43-44) concerns the people's recognition of their own wickedness and stresses that the Lord has delt with them not according to their deeds but for the sake of his name. The recurrence in v. 44 of the phrase "act for the sake of my name", prominent in vv. 1-31, serves to strengthen the link between the two parts of the chapter. The sequence of remembering, loathing, and knowing is also found in the late editorial section in Ez 36,31-32.

5. CONNECTIONS WITH THE FIRST PART OF THE CHAPTER, AND CONCLUSIONS

In the final composition, the disputation speech (32-44), with its hopeful prospect, contrasts with Ezekiel's portrayal of Israel's shameful past in the first part of the chapter (1-31). The lack of introductory formulas[39] at the beginning of the second section clearly indicates that the editor conceived the two parts of the chapter as belonging together. In his article, Beuken convincingly demonstrates that several expressions recurring in both parts, as well as contrasting themes, strengthen the connections between the two units. More emphasis should perhaps be laid on the direct link between the end of the historical survey[40] in v. 23 where it is said that the Lord lifts up his hand towards his people in the wilderness "to scatter them among the nations and to disperse them through the countries", and the beginning of the salvation oracle in v. 34 where the Lord announces that He will "bring (them) out from the peoples and gather (them) out of the countries where (they) are scattered" to bring them to the wilderness of the peoples. Taking up the wordings of the final part of the historical survey, the editor of the chapter directly connects the announced new wilderness period with the dispersion after the first. The entry into the Promised Land has not yet been realised. It will come about after a judgement in the desert, which will purge out the rebels (v. 38). Then, finally, the Lord will bring his people into the land that he already wanted to give to their fathers (v. 42).

38. See J. LUST, *The Raised Hand of the Lord in Deut 32:40 according to MT, 4QDeut^q, and LXX*, in *Textus* 18 (1995) 33-45; *Exodus 6,2-8 and Ezekiel* (n. 31), pp. 218-224.

39. It is well known that in Ezekiel the respective units are introduced by formulas such as the word-event formula "the word of the Lord came to me".

40. With ZIMMERLI, *Ezechiel* (n. 3), pp. 450-451, BEUKEN, *Ez 20* (n. 2), pp. 42-44, and many others, we assume that vv. 27-29 are a late insert; see also LUST, *Traditie, redactie en kerygma bij Ezechiël* (n. 1), pp. 102-103.

Beuken's interpretation of the quotation in 20,32 has proved to be difficult to accept. In an argumentation based on a series of observations which cannot be repeated here, the present contribution has demonstrated that Ezekiel's opponents were voicing an arrogant claim, and not an exasperated complaint. Furthermore, a closer reading of the context has led us to the growing conviction that, at least in the dispute as an originally independent unit and perhaps also in the final text, those who voiced the said arrogant claim must have been inhabitants of Jerusalem.

The promise of the gathering of the dispersed raised questions concerning the situation of the final editor. Our suggestion is that a distinction should be made between the circumstances in which he lived and those of Ezekiel. The editor was most likely operating in a diaspora situation. When, in a literary fiction, he let Ezekiel address the problems of his diaspora public, he was obliged to do so within the framework of the traditional localisation of Ezekiel. While he used Ezekiel's style and vocabulary, several traces, nevertheless, reveal his own co-ordinates.

Some of my views are different from those of W. Beuken vintage 1972. His interpretation of Ez 20 may have developed since then. It cannot be denied, however, that his stylistic and intertextual analysis of 1972 remains exemplary.

van 't Sestichstraat 34   Johan LUST
B-3000 Leuven

"THE SERVANT OF THE LORD":
A PARTICULAR GROUP OF JEWS IN EGYPT
ACCORDING TO THE OLD GREEK OF ISAIAH
Some Comments on lxx Isa 49,1-6 and Related Passages

I

In his commentary on Isaiah 40–55[1] Wim Beuken has made a very stimulating and important contribution to the discussion about the passages that deal with the Songs of "the Servant of the Lord", by interpreting these passages within the whole of the Hebrew (Masoretic) text of Deutero-Isaiah. This contribution to the volume in honour of our jubilee will not go into this exegetical discussion, but it will deal with aspects of the interpretation of the Servant of the Lord as reflected in the first and oldest translation of the Book of Isaiah, the Old Greek of Isaiah (hereafter: LXX Isa[iah]). In an excursus on the history of interpretation regarding the passages about the Servant, Beuken introduces LXX Isaiah as "de eerste interpretator van de Knecht, uiteraard in de context van Jes. 40–55 zelf"[2]. In line with other scholars he further states that in LXX Isaiah the Servant of the Lord is seen as "Israel" in the first and second 'song', but as an individual, presumably the prophet himself, in the third and fourth 'song'[3]. Leaving aside for the moment the interpretation of the third and fourth 'song' in LXX Isaiah we concentrate on the idea of the Servant as "Israel" in the first and second 'song' in LXX Isaiah.

It is a well-known observation that, different from MT (cf. 1QIsa-a), in LXX Isa 42,1a the Servant of the Lord is presented explicitly as "Jacob" and "Israel". Both versions read in translation as follows:

(MT) Behold my servant, whom I uphold, my chosen, in whom my soul delights

(LXX) Jacob is my servant, I will help him; Israel is my chosen, my soul has accepted him.

The Greek text is easily understood as an interpretation of the verse in the light of other passages where "Jacob" and "Israel" are called the

---

1. W.A.M. Beuken, *Jesaja IIA* (POT), Nijkerk, 1979; *Jesaja IIB* (POT), Nijkerk, 1983.
2. *Jesaja IIB*, p. 307.
3. *Ibid.*, p. 307. See also H. Haag, *Der Gottesknecht bei Deuterojesaja* (EdF, 233), Darmstadt, 1985, p. 47.

servant of God (cf. Isa 44,1.21; 45,4), but one wonders to whom this designation might refer: to the people of Israel as a whole, or to a part of the people. Beuken suggests that the Greek speaking Jewish community in the diaspora is behind a passage like LXX Isa 42,1. P. Grelot, commenting on LXX Isa 49,5f., speaks of the Jews in Egypt ("les Juifs d'Égypte")[4].

In this article several passages from LXX Isaiah will be discussed in order to try to give a more specific answer to the question to whom the designation 'Israel' (and 'Jacob') as name of the Servant of the Lord might refer according to LXX Isaiah. Since LXX Isa 49,1-6 is a most important passage in this regard, we will deal first with this one. Secondly, starting from a particular aspect of this passage we will discuss some other texts of LXX Isaiah (outside LXX Isa 40–55, or 40–66!) which are likely to be seen as related passages.

Before doing so, a few remarks on method may be in order.

It is generally agreed upon that the many and often remarkable differences between MT and LXX Isaiah do not go back to a Hebrew Vorlage which was in close agreement with LXX Isaiah. This is very unlikely indeed in the light of the fact that the Qumran texts of Isaiah do support MT at most of the places where LXX do not agree with MT. In order to reach a better understanding of LXX Isaiah the best thing therefore is to take this Greek version seriously in its own right by means of a *contextual* approach. The aim of this method is to find out whether there are clear indications of coherence, on the level of text and of content, within a given passage (immediate context) and between passages within the whole of LXX Isaiah (context of the book as a whole). All this is of course to be done in comparison with MT and the Qumran texts of Isaiah (1QIsa-a, 1QIsa-b; hereafter: 1Qa, 1Qb) as far as available.

II

Isa 49,1-6:

Vs 1 (MT-LXX):

שִׁמְעוּ אִיִּים אֵלַי   ἀκούσατέ μου νῆσοι
וְהַקְשִׁיבוּ לְאֻמִּים מֵרָחוֹק   καὶ προσέχετε ἔθνη· διὰ χρόνου πολλοῦ
                                      στήσεται λέγει

---

4. BEUKEN, *Jesaja* (n. 1), p. 307. P. GRELOT, *Les Poèmes du Serviteur* (LD, 103), Paris, 1981, p. 92. Another view is expressed by J.C. BASTIAENS, *Interpretaties van Jesaja 53*, Tilburg, 1993, p. 124 (the obedient part of the people).

יְהוָה מִבֶּטֶן קְרָאָנִי   κύριος, ἐκ κοιλίας
מִמְּעֵי אִמִּי הִזְכִּיר שְׁמִי: μητρός μου ἐκάλεσε τὸ ὄνομά μου

MT has a text with two clauses (cf. 1Qa, 1Qb), but LXX offers a text
with three, the clause "after a long time it shall come to pass, says the
Lord" being the extra one. The last word of vs 1a (מרחוק) has not been
taken in the local sense (so MT), but as referring to time, and syntactically speaking this word has not been read as part of the second colon.
The Greek στήσεται λέγει constitutes a plus over against MT (cf. 1Qa,
1Qb), whereas κύριος reflects Hebrew יהוה which, different from MT
(cf. 1Qa, 1Qb), has been separated from the words that follow.

The new clause, "after a long time it shall come to pass, says the
Lord", has to do with the motif of the (ancient) counsel (βουλή) of God
in LXX Isaiah[5]. See in particular LXX Isa 25,1:

Κύριε ὁ θεός μου, δοξάσω σε, ὑμνήσω τὸ ὄνομά σου, ὅτι
ἐποίησας θαυμαστὰ πράγματα, βουλὴν ἀρχαίαν ἀληθινήν·
γένοιτο, κύριε,

O Lord God, I will glorify you, I will sing to your name, for you
have done wonderful things, an ancient (and) faithful counsel.
So be it, o Lord.

This throws light on the use of στήσεται in our text, because this verb is
found in LXX Isa 46,10 in connexion with the 'counsel' of God: πᾶσά
μου ἡ βουλὴ στήσεται (MT עצתי תקום). In the context of 49,1-6 the
new clause expresses the idea that the coming of the Servant has been
planned long ago.

The last part of the verse has been rendered in LXX in a way typical
of LXX Isaiah: two words/expressions considered as parallel to each
other (ממעי אמי//מבטן and הזכיר שמי//קראני) are translated only by one
word or expression[6].

Vs 2 (MT-LXX):

וַיָּשֶׂם פִּי כְּחֶרֶב חַדָּה   καὶ ἔθηκε τὸ στόμα μου
                                    ὡσεὶ μάχαιραν ὀξεῖαν
בְּצֵל יָדוֹ הֶחְבִּיאָנִי   καὶ ὑπὸ τὴν σκέπην τῆς χειρὸς αὐτοῦ
                                    ἔκρυψέ με

5. On this motif see in particular I.L. SEELIGMANN, *The Septuagint Version of Isaiah*
(MVEOL, 9), Leiden, 1948, p. 110.
6. See J. ZIEGLER, *Untersuchungen zur Septuaginta des Buches Isaias* (AA, XII/3),
Münster, 1934, pp. 46-56.

וַיְשִׂימֵ֫נִי֙ לְחֵ֣ץ בָּר֔וּר   ἔθηκέ με ὡς βέλος ἐκλεκτὸν
בְּאַשְׁפָּת֖וֹ הִסְתִּירָֽנִי׃   καὶ ἐν τῇ φαρέτρᾳ αὐτοῦ ἐσκέπασέ με

Both versions of this verse are closely corresponding to each other. As to MT לחץ – LXX ὡς βέλος: compare 1Qa כחץ (but with supralinear correction to לחץ [1Qb: lacuna]). The reading כחץ of 1Qa may be due to harmonization to כחרב in vs 2a; the same principle may apply to the Greek text: cf. ὡσεὶ μάχαιραν in vs 2a.

The use of ἐκλεκτός (MT ברור, = 1Qa, 1Qb) reminds one of a text like LXX Isa 42,1: Ισραηλ ὁ ἐκλεκτός μου (MT בחירי). There is no need, however, to suppose that the parent text of LXX Isa 49,2 read בחיר instead of ברור, because the Hebrew ברור can have the meaning of 'select', 'chosen'; see e.g. 1 Chron 7,40; 9,22.

Vs 3 (MT-LXX):

וַיֹּ֣אמֶר לִ֔י עַבְדִּי־אָ֑תָּה   καὶ εἰπέ μοι Δοῦλός μου εἶ σύ,
יִשְׂרָאֵ֕ל אֲשֶׁר־בְּךָ֖ אֶתְפָּאָֽר׃   Ισραηλ, καὶ ἐν σοὶ δοξασθήσομαι

Also here LXX corresponds closely to MT. Both contain the name "Israel" as the name, to be taken in a symbolical sense, of the Servant. We need not deal here with the question of the genuineness of the reading "Israel". It is important to note that the most ancient witnesses (1Qa, 1Qb, and LXX) attest this reading.

The Hebrew עבד is rendered here as δοῦλος. This rendering is also found in vs 5 (see also vs 7), whereas in vs 6 the equivalent παῖς is used. In LXX Isaiah the latter one is employed much more frequently than the one of our verse. There is no indication to assume that in our pericope (plus vs 7) both equivalents are to be understood as conveying a different connotation. Both seem to carry the meaning of "servant" in the pericope under discussion.

Vs 4 (MT-LXX):

וַאֲנִ֤י אָמַ֙רְתִּי֙ לְרִ֣יק יָגַ֔עְתִּי   καὶ ἐγὼ εἶπα Κενῶς ἐκοπίασα
לְתֹ֥הוּ וְהֶ֖בֶל כֹּחִ֣י כִלֵּ֑יתִי   καὶ εἰς μάταιον καὶ εἰς οὐθὲν ἔδωκα
                                        τὴν ἰσχύν μου
אָכֵן֙ מִשְׁפָּטִ֣י אֶת־יְהוָ֔ה   διὰ τοῦτο ἡ κρίσις μου παρὰ κυρίῳ
וּפְעֻלָּתִ֖י אֶת־אֱלֹהָֽי׃   καὶ ὁ πόνος μου ἐναντίον τοῦ θεοῦ μου

Again, LXX does not offer here remarkable differences in comparsion with MT. There is, however, an interesting difference in nuance between

MT אָכֵן (=1Qa; 1Qb: אך) and LXX διὰ τοῦτο. Hebrew אָכֵן expresses a strong contrast ('assuredly'), but the situation in LXX is a bit different. The Greek reads in translation, "Therefore is my judgment with the Lord, and my labour/travail before my God". This text seems to express the idea that, though the servant has given his strength in vain, he knows that his judgment is with the Lord, *because* (cf. "therefore") the Lord had said, "in you I will be glorified" (vs 3b). So the Greek διὰ τοῦτο makes sense if understood in the light of vs 3b.

The Hebrew פעלה has the meaning of 'recompense' (cf. 40,10). The equivalent in Greek (πόνος) is used only here in LXX (Isaiah and the rest). The Hebrew פעלה occurs also in 40,10; 61,8; 62,11, and 65,7. LXX has τὸ ἔργον in 40,11 and in the parallel passage of 62,11 (about God who will come to Sion; 'the work' in both verses in LXX refers contextually to the 'flock' [40,8], and to the 'holy people' [62,11] that will be brought to Sion by God). The same equivalent, be it in the plural, is found in 65,7, whereas in 61,8 the Greek offers the rendering μόχθος ('labour').

The Greek πόνος is found at some (8) places in LXX Isaiah. Two are of particular interest, because they are part of another passage about the Servant of the Lord: 53,4 (καὶ ἡμεῖς ἐλογισάμεθα αὐτὸν εἶναι ἐν πόνῳ [MT נגוע), and 53,10 (καὶ βούλεται κύριος ἀφελεῖν ἀπὸ τοῦ πόνου τῆς ψυχῆς αὐτοῦ [MT עמל). In both places it conveys a meaning ('travail, trouble') similar to that of 49,4. The use of the same Greek word in these texts may point to a particular relationship between 49,4 and 53,4.10.

Vs 5 (MT-LXX):

אָמַר יְהֹוָה וְעַתָּה	καὶ νῦν οὕτως λέγει κύριος
יֹצְרִי מִבֶּטֶן לְעֶבֶד לוֹ	ὁ πλάσας με ἐκ κοιλίας δοῦλον ἑαυτῷ
לְשׁוֹבֵב יַעֲקֹב אֵלָיו	τοῦ συναγαγεῖν τὸν Ιακωβ
וְיִשְׂרָאֵל לֹא יֵאָסֵף	καὶ Ισραηλ πρὸς αὐτόν· συναχθήσομαι
וְאֶכָּבֵד בְּעֵינֵי יְהֹוָה	καὶ δοξασθήσομαι ἐναντίον κυρίου
וֵאלֹהַי הָיָה עֻזִּי׃	καὶ ὁ θεός μου ἔσται μου ἰσχύς

The Greek reads in translation as follows: "And now, thus says the Lord who formed me from the womb to be his own servant to gather Jacob and Israel to him; – I shall be gathered and glorified before the Lord, and my God shall be my strength".

At the beginning of the verse LXX has a plus: οὕτως. MT = 1Qa, but 1Qb (+ כה) agrees with LXX.

The rendering τοῦ συναγαγεῖν clearly reflects an interpretation of the Hebrew לְשׁוֹבֵב (MT = 1Qa, 1Qb) in the sense of "gathering" of the people of Israel from the dispersion (see also the next verse). The Greek πρὸς αὐτόν ("to him") testifies not only to אֵלָיו, but also, very likely, to לוֹ as the parallel reading. (MT has a well-known Ketib/Qere here: Ketib לֹא, and Qere לוֹ. The reading לוֹ, reflected by LXX, is also attested by 1Qa [1Qb: lacuna]; 4Qd has the reading לֹא. Thus, both readings are attested at an early stage.)

As for the verbal form יֵאָסֵף (MT = 1Qa; [1Qb: lacuna]) LXX presents a different text, both as to number (1 sing.; MT 3 sing.) and as to syntax. In MT (cf. 1Qa) the verbal form belongs to the preceding words, but in LXX the word συναχθήσομαι is clearly part of the clause made up together with the words that follow: "I shall be gathered and I shall be glorified before the Lord".

The interesting thing is that according to this phrase the servant is supposed to be someone who will be "gathered" too. The same verb in Greek is used here as in the preceding phrase (συνάγω) where it is said that the Servant has been formed in order to "gather" the people of Israel. Here we have a clear indication that the Servant "Israel" (vs 3) who is called to gather the people of Jacob/Israel, is seen as a group, because it makes sense of a group, not of an individual, to say, that one shall "be gathered". With other words, the Servant is to be understood collectively, be it not in the sense of the people of Israel as a whole[7], but of a group within the people. They will be "gathered", i.e. brought together like a flock and brought back to the place where they came from, and then be "glorified" (δοξασθήσομαι; compare vs 3 where the same is said of God). The Servant as a group is supposed to be outside the land of Israel.

Vs 6 (MT-LXX):

וַיֹּאמֶר נָקֵל	καὶ εἶπέ μοι Μέγα σοί ἐστι
מִהְיוֹתְךָ לִי עֶבֶד	τοῦ κληθῆναί σε παῖδά μου
לְהָקִים אֶת־שִׁבְטֵי יַעֲקֹב	τοῦ στῆσαι τὰς φυλὰς Ιακωβ
וּנְצִירֵי יִשְׂרָאֵל לְהָשִׁיב	καὶ τὴν διασπορὰν τοῦ Ισραηλ ἐπιστρέψαι
וּנְתַתִּיךָ לְאוֹר גּוֹיִם	ἰδοὺ τέθεικά σε εἰς φῶς ἐθνῶν
לִהְיוֹת יְשׁוּעָתִי	τοῦ εἶναί σε εἰς σωτηρίαν
עַד־קְצֵה הָאָרֶץ׃	ἕως ἐσχάτου τῆς γῆς

---

7. For this exegesis see ORIGEN, *Contra Celsum*, I, 55.

LXX: "And he said to me, It is a great thing for you to be called my servant, to establish the tribes of Jacob, and to recover the dispersion of Israel; behold, I have made you for a light to the nations, that you should be for salvation to the end of the earth".

The main differences between MT and LXX concern the two aspects of the task of the servant. In MT, so it seems, the task to restore the people of Israel is (too) little (a) matter (MT נָקֵל, = 1Qa; 1Qb: הנקל); therefore, God has made the servant a light to the nations. In LXX things are different:

"It is a great thing for you
to be called my servant,
to establish the tribes of Jacob, [...]".

The emphasis of this part of the verse is not only on the restoration of the people (as is the case in MT: "to be[8] a servant in order to re-establish the tribes of Jacob [...]"), but first of all on the notion of being *called* my servant as an element in its own right. The expression, "It is a great thing...", is best understood in the light of the verse in LXX as a whole, particularly the second part of it, because the Greek ἰδοὺ (τέθεικά σε ...) seems to introduce an explanation of why it is a great thing "to be called my servant". The last phrase of this part is most revealing:

"([...] for a light to the nations,)
that *you* should be for salvation to the end of the earth".

Whereas MT (=1Qa, 1Qb [partly legible]) reads "my salvation", the salvation of God, "may reach to the end of the earth", LXX has it that "you", *the servant*, may be for salvation to the end of the earth. One is reminded here of LXX Isa 42,1-4: the servant Jacob shall bring forth judgment to the nations (vs 1.4; cf. MT), and "in his law[9] the nations shall trust" (vs 4: καὶ ἐπὶ τῷ νόμῳ αὐτοῦ ἔθνη ἐλπιοῦσιν; cf. MT).

Thus, LXX vs 6 does not present one of the two aspects of work of the Servant as something which is a little matter (or, too little a matter). On the contrary, in being a light and salvation to the nations it is a great thing to be the servant of the Lord. The task "to establish the tribes of Jacob and to recover the dispersion of Israel" is not regarded as something minor, but as part of the work of the servant. Just as in vs 5 vs 6a is about the gathering of the people of Israel from the exile. For the Greek διασπορά, 'the dispersion', or 'the dispersed', see also LXX Dan

---

8. MT: מהיותך, = 1Qa, 1Qb [partly].

9. So according to the conjecture of Ziegler (νομῳ); the manuscript tradition, however, has the reading ὀνοματι, but this may be the result of a Christian reworking of the text (compare Mt 12,21).

12,2, and II Macc 1,27. The reading of MT Ketib, נצירי, is also attested by 1Qa, 1Qb; for the Qere נצורי, see also Jerome, Comm.: *nesure*, 'the preserved'.

Our discussion of the Greek of Isa 49,1-6 in comparison with MT (+ 1Qa, 1Qb) has brought to light some aspects of meaning and content which are not, or with less emphasis to be found in MT. Though the gathering of Israel by the Servant is common to both texts, LXX is more univocal as to the aspect of the dispersion of the people of Israel (cf. συνάγω in vs 5, and διασπορά in vs 6). As to the full task of the Servant LXX vs 6 emphasizes more than in MT the role of the Servant as being someone "for salvation to the end of the earth".

There is one aspect in LXX vs 5 which is not present in MT (cf. 1Qa): the Servant "Israel" (vs 3) shall "be gathered (and then glorified)". It points to the view of the Servant as a particular group, and it is in view of this aspect that we will discuss in the next section other passages of LXX Isaiah which seem to refer to the same group as in 49,5. The interesting thing is that these passages are not part of Isa 40–55, or 40–66, but of Isa 1–39.

III

Chapters 10, 11, and 19 of LXX Isaiah offer passages which, unlike in MT (cf. 1Qa), are clearly related to each other: 10,24; 11,16, and 19,18f.24f. They share a great interest in a group of Jews in Egypt.

Isa 10,24 (MT-LXX):

לָכֵן כֹּה־אָמַר	διὰ τοῦτο τάδε λέγει
אֲדֹנָי יהוה צְבָאוֹת	κύριος σαβαωθ
אַל־תִּירָא עַמִּי	Μὴ φοβοῦ ὁ λαός μου
יֹשֵׁב צִיּוֹן	οἱ κατοικοῦντες ἐν Σιων
מֵאַשּׁוּר בַּשֵּׁבֶט יַכֶּכָּה	ἀπὸ Ασσυρίων· ὅτι ἐν ῥάβδῳ πατάξει σε
וּמַטֵּהוּ יִשָּׂא־עָלֶיךָ	πληγὴν γὰρ ἐγὼ ἐπάγω ἐπὶ σε
בְּדֶרֶךְ מִצְרָיִם:	τοῦ ἰδεῖν ὁδὸν Αἰγύπτου

According to LXX "my people who dwell in Sion" should not be afraid of Assyrians. They will smite them with a rod, for God (with emphasis [ἐγώ!]) brings a stroke on his people "to see the way to Egypt". In MT (cf. 1Qa) the Assyrians are the subject of the last part of the text ("and they will lift up their staff against you as the Egyptians did"), but in LXX God is the subject.

It is not necessary, nor probable to presuppose a parent text different from MT-1Qa, for the Hebrew seems to have been read this way: "Assyrians will lift their staff against you on the way to Egypt", and this might have been reformulated for some reason or another as it stands. One can imagine that "his/their staff" (the staff of Assyria) has been taken, in the light of 10,5, in the sense of the rod of God's anger. The phrase "to see the way to Egypt" is also found in Deut 28,68, i.e. in a context where the curse of going into exile is the subject matter.

The Greek text evokes the picture of some disaster which will meet God's people "who dwell in Sion" (for the expression οἱ κατοικοῦντες ἐν Σιων, see also LXX Isa 12,6): they have to go to Egypt because of Assyrians.

Isa 19,24-25 (MT-LXX[10]):

בַּיּוֹם הַהוּא	τῇ ἡμέρᾳ ἐκείνῃ
יִהְיֶה יִשְׂרָאֵל שְׁלִישִׁיָּה	ἔσται Ισραηλ τρίτος
לְמִצְרַיִם וּלְאַשּׁוּר	ἐν τοῖς Ασσυρίοις καὶ ἐν τοῖς Αἰγυπτίοις
בְּרָכָה בְּקֶרֶב הָאָרֶץ:	εὐλογημένος ἐν τῇ γῇ,
אֲשֶׁר בֵּרֲכוֹ יְהוָה צְבָאוֹת	ἣν εὐλόγησε κύριος σαβαωθ
לֵאמֹר	λέγων
בָּרוּךְ עַמִּי מִצְרַיִם	εὐλογημένος ὁ λαός μου ὁ ἐν Αἰγύπτῳ
וּמַעֲשֵׂה יָדַי אַשּׁוּר	καὶ ὁ ἐν Ασσυρίοις
וְנַחֲלָתִי יִשְׂרָאֵל:	καὶ ὁ κληρονομία μου Ισραηλ

The differences between MT (cf. 1Qa, 1Qb [partly]) and LXX, particularly the ones in vs 25, are interesting and well-known. According to LXX "Israel" shall be "third" among the Assyrians and the Egyptians, and "blessed on earth". And the earth was blessed by God in saying:

"Blessed be my people in Egypt and among Assyrians,
and my inheritance Israel".

Quite different from the Hebrew text as attested by MT and 1Qa the Greek is about "my people in Egypt" (not: "among Egyptians", as in vs 24). But what about the phrase, "and among Assyrians"? Contextually

---

10. For a more detailed discussion of the verses from LXX Isa 19,16-25 see A. VAN DER KOOIJ, *The Old Greek of Isaiah 19:16-25: Translation and Interpretation*, in C.E. COX (ed.), *VI Congress of the International Organization for Septuagint and Cognate Studies, Jerusalem 1986* (SBL SCS, 23), Atlanta, GA, 1987, pp. 127-166.

speaking it seems that "among Assyrians" (without article) in vs 25 is related to "Assyrians" of LXX vs 23 (καὶ εἰσελεύσονται Ασσύριοι εἰς Αἴγυπτον), that is to say, Assyrians who will enter, in the military sense of the word, the land of Egypt. Cf. LXX vs 23 (ending): "the Egyptians shall serve the Assyrians" (καὶ δουλεύσουσιν οἱ Αἰγύπτιοι τοῖς Ασσυρίοις). It means that "my people in Egypt and among Assyrians (in Egypt)" is referring to a group of Jews in Egypt only. The last part, "my inheritance Israel", is best understood as parallel expression to "my people".

The idea of Jews in Egypt is in line with the rest of LXX Isa. 19,16-25, especially vs 18f.:

Isa 19,18-19 (MT-LXX):

בַּיּוֹם הַהוּא יִהְיוּ	τῇ ἡμέρᾳ ἐκείνῃ ἔσονται
חָמֵשׁ עָרִים בְּאֶרֶץ מִצְרַיִם	πέντε πόλεις ἐν Αἰγύπτῳ
מְדַבְּרוֹת שְׂפַת כְּנַעַן	λαλοῦσαι τῇ γλώσσῃ τῇ Χανανίτιδι
וְנִשְׁבָּעוֹת לַיהוָה צְבָאוֹת	καὶ ὀμνύουσαι τῷ ὀνόματι κυρίου
עִיר הַהֶרֶס יֵאָמֵר לְאֶחָת:	Πόλις ασεδεκ κληθήσεται ἡ μία πόλις
בַּיּוֹם הַהוּא	τῇ ἡμέρᾳ ἐκείνῃ
יִהְיֶה מִזְבֵּחַ לַיהוָה	ἔσται θυσιαστήριον τῷ κυρίῳ
בְּתוֹךְ אֶרֶץ מִצְרַיִם	ἐν χώρᾳ Αἰγυπτίων
וּמַצֵּבָה אֵצֶל־גְּבוּלָהּ	καὶ στήλη πρὸς τὸ ὅριον αὐτῆς
לַיהוָה:	τῷ κυρίῳ

As I have argued elsewhere[11] LXX is about five cities in Egypt in which *Jews* shall live. One of these cities shall be called "City of *asedek*" i.e. the righeousness. Since this name is known from Isa 1,26 (MT-LXX) as the name of Jerusalem, the one city seems to have a status similar to that of Jerusalem[12]. There will also be an altar (a legitimate one because of the equivalent θυσιαστήριον instead of βωμός which denotes an illegitimate one), presumably in the one city.

Our last passage is Isa 11,16 (MT-LXX):

וְהָיְתָה מְסִלָּה	καὶ ἔσται δίοδος
לִשְׁאָר עַמּוֹ אֲשֶׁר יִשָּׁאֵר	τῷ καταλειφθέντι μου λαῷ
מֵאַשּׁוּר	ἐν Αἰγύπτῳ

---

11. *Ibid.*, pp. 135-138.
12. As to the aspect of the transliteration ἀσεδεκ as illustration of the Canaanite language, see *ibid.*, p. 137.

כַּאֲשֶׁר הָיְתָה לְיִשְׂרָאֵל   καὶ ἔσται τῷ Ισραηλ

בְּיוֹם עֲלֹתוֹ   ὡς ἡ ἡμέρα ὅτε ἐξῆλθεν

מֵאֶרֶץ מִצְרָיִם: ἐκ γῆς Αἰγύπτου

The differences in the first part of the verse concern "*my* people" (MT=1Qa: "his people") and "in Egypt" (MT=1Qa: "in Assyria"). As to vs 16b the difference is of a syntactical nature: in MT (cf. 1Qa) this part of the verse starts with "as" ("as there was to Israel [...]"), but in LXX the comparison with the past is made in the clause following "Israel": "and it shall be to Israel *as* the day when he came forth out of the land of Egypt".

It is to be noted that the Hebrew text of Isa 11,11-16 (MT-1Qa) is characterized by a close agreement in wording between vs 11 an vs 16:

vs 11:   אֶת־שְׁאָר עַמּוֹ אֲשֶׁר יִשָּׁאֵר מֵאַשּׁוּר וּמִמִּצְרַיִם

וּמִפַּתְרוֹס וּמִכּוּשׁ וּמֵעֵילָם וּמִשִּׁנְעָר וּמֵחֲמָת וּמֵאִיֵּי הַיָּם:

vs 16:   לִשְׁאָר עַמּוֹ אֲשֶׁר יִשָּׁאֵר מֵאַשּׁוּר

The only difference is that the countries enumerated in vs 11 after "Assyria" are not mentioned again in vs 16. The phrase which occurs in both texts concerns "the remnant of his people which is left from Assyria". This inclusio in the pericope of vs 11-16 which marks the composition of the Hebrew text, points to an emphasis on the exiles of Israel in Assyria[13].

The situation in LXX vs 11-16 is different:

vs 11: τὸ καταλειφθὲν ὑπόλοιπον τοῦ λαοῦ, ὃ ἄν καταλειφθῇ ἀπὸ τῶν Ασσυρίων καὶ ἀπὸ Αἰγύπτου καὶ Βαβυλωνίας καὶ Αἰθιοπίας καὶ ἀπὸ Αἰλαμιτῶν καὶ ἀπὸ ἡλίου ἀνατολῶν καὶ ἐξ Αραβίας

vs 16: τῷ καταλειφθέντι μου λαῷ ἐν Αἰγύπτῳ

The text of LXX as it stands distinguishes between "the remnant of the people that is left from the Assyrians and from Egypt etc." and "my people that is left in Egypt". The last one is surely the same group as "my people in Egypt" of 19,25; cf. also 10,24 where "my people (who dwell in Sion)" has to go to Egypt. Thus, LXX vs 11 is about the dispersion of Israel all over the world, whereas vs 16 refers to a particular

---

13. For a recent discussion of Isa 11,11-16 see now H.G.M. WILLIAMSON, *The Book Called Isaiah,* Oxford, 1994, pp. 125ff.

group of Jews in Egypt. It is further to be noted that LXX vs 16b is formulated in such a way (see above) that "Israel" is parallel to "my people":

"And there shall be a passage to *my people* that is left in Egypt,
and it shall be to *Israel* [...]".

Summarizing our observations on the LXX passages mentioned above
it will be clear that they have in common the motif of "my people in
Egypt". These texts clearly testify to an interest in a particular group of
Jews in Egypt. They seem to offer a rather complete picture:
LXX Isa 10,24 is about their going to Egypt;
LXX Isa 19,18f.24f. is about their stay in Egypt and their expected
high position;
LXX Isa 11,16 is about their return.
The fact that in 10,24 this group is called "my people who dwell in
Zion" suggests that their return will be to Sion. In 11,16 and 19,25 this
group is called "Israel".

IV

It is now to be asked whether these texts about "my people in Egypt"
are related to the passage about the Servant of the Lord in LXX Isa 49,1-
6. Some elements do point, in my view, to a specific relationship. The
passages of LXX Isa 11,11-16 and LXX Isa 49,5-6 have something in
common which is not attested in MT (cf. 1Qa): namely the distinction
between two groups which are in exile, (a) the people of Israel, and (b) a
particular group of Jews. This is a clear indication that the Servant who
is supposed to be in exile and who "shall be gathered" (49,5) is to be
equated, within the whole of LXX Isaiah, with "my people in Egypt" in
11,16. Another element which favours this assumption is the name of
"Israel": it is the name of the Servant in 49,3, and it is the name of "my
people in Egypt" in 11,16 and 19,25.
The above raises the question whether there are other passages in
LXX Isaiah which might refer to the same group, called "my people" or
"Israel". I think there are, but it would lead us too far to discuss more
texts from LXX Isaiah in this article. As to the text quoted in the intro-
duction of this article, LXX Isa 42,1, it might well be that the names of
"Israel" and "Jacob" are not to be understood as referring to the people
of Israel, but, just as in 49,3.5, to the Servant as a particular group of the
Jewish people.

The texts discussed in this article reveal an important aspect of the way in which the translator produced his Greek version of the book of Isaiah, viz. by interpreting passages in the light of other ones which he considered to be related to each other. It is therefore worthwhile to study specific readings and passages in the Old Greek of Isaiah, first of all, within the whole of LXX Isaiah. Because of the coherence between the Greek passages mentioned above it is not probable, nor necessary to suppose a different Hebrew text in one of the passages to account for the differences between LXX and MT, the more so since 1Qa (and 1Qb as far as available) is in agreement with MT.

The above passages about "my people in Egypt" in LXX Isaiah raise the intriguing question of whether these passages do refer to a particular group of Jews in Egypt at the time when LXX Isaiah was written (middle second century B.C.). This is likely indeed, for as has been argued by scholars LXX Isaiah shows traces of an actualizing interpretation, a type of interpretation which is fully in line with the assumption at that time, namely that the ancient prophecies are to be read and interpreted as referring to the present or the near future (cf. for instance the *pesharim* of Qumran).

Through Josephus we know of a particular group of Jews in Egypt in the second century B.C. that had fled from Jerusalem at the time of the crisis in the sixties of that century: the priest Onias (IV), member of the high-priestly family of the Oniads, and his followers. They got the permission from the Ptolemaic king to build a temple in Leontopolis, in the nome of Heliopolis. In his request to build a temple at that place Onias begs the king

> to build a temple to the Most High God in the likeness of that at Jerusalem
> [...]. For this indeed is what the prophet Isaiah foretold, 'There shall be an
> altar in Egypt to the Lord God' (Ant. xiii, 67f.).

As I have argued elsewhere[14] this claim of Onias fits very well the text of LXX Isa 19,18f.: first, it is actually the text of LXX Isa 19,19 that is cited here, and secondly, the reading "City of *asedek*", the city of righteousness, being the name of Jerusalem in Isa 1,26 (see above), suggests clearly that one of the cities in Egypt where the Jews will live is seen as having a status similar to that of Jerusalem.

The text of LXX Isa 10,24 makes also perfect sense if understood as referring to the flight of Onias and his followers to Egypt. The phrase

14. A. VAN DER KOOIJ, *Die alten Textzeugen des Jesajabuches* (OBO, 35), Freiburg - Göttingen, 1981, pp. 54-55.

"my people who dwell in Zion" seems to convey the meaning of the priests and Levites who 'dwell' on Sion, the temple mount. This element would fit in too, because it is likely that the group of Onias, the priest, did consist primarily of priests and Levites.

Just as with other groups of the time (Samaritans, the community of Qumran), the group of Onias tried to legitimize their claims on the basis of passages in "the books of the ancestors"[15], in their case the book of Isaiah. In the light of the available evidence it seems likely that "my people in Egypt" in LXX Isaiah refers to the (priestly) group of Onias, a group that understood themselves as the Servant of the Lord[16].

Oranje Nassaulaan 21A   Arie VAN DER KOOIJ
NL-2361 LA Warmond

---

15. For this expression see Prologue Wisdom Ben Sira, 10.
16. For a parallel of the Servant as identified with a particular group see Dan. 11,33 and 12,3 ("the wise"). See e.g. H.L. GINSBERG, *The Oldest Interpretation of the Suffering Servant*, in *VT* 3 (1953), pp. 402-403; J.J. COLLINS, *Daniel: A Commentary on the Book of Daniel*, Minneapolis, 1993, pp. 385, 393.

"HIS MASTER'S VOICE"?
THE SUPPOSED INFLUENCE OF THE BOOK OF ISAIAH
IN THE BOOK OF HABAKKUK

This contribution, which is dedicated warmly to my highly esteemed teacher, Wim Beuken, deals with the relationship of another teacher, the prophet Isaiah, and someone who, according to some exegetes, was a pupil of his. I do not refer to the anonymous prophet(s) of chapters 40–66 of the Book of Isaiah, but to the prophet Habakkuk. However, the master had turned sixty-five a long time before; he was probably already dead[1], when the pupil was born[2], and a relationship could begin. Therefore, I restrict myself to the relationship of the *book* of Isaiah and the *book* of Habakkuk. In this contribution I will consider some of the similarities between both collections with regard to theme and vocabulary, which have been put forward in other studies, especially in a study of Walter Dietrich[3]. The question is whether these similarities point to the conclusion that Habakkuk is dependent on Isaiah or not. I will examine

---

1. Isaiah lived in the 8th century B.C. According to most exegetes the prophecies of Isa 1–39 are no unity, but rather reflect a complex literary entity. Some prophecies are traced back to the prophet himself, others to a redaction in the 7th century B.C. or even to a post-exilic redaction. Cf. B. Duhm, *Das Buch Jesaia* (HKAT, III/1), Göttingen, [4]1922; O. Kaiser, *Das Buch des Propheten Jesaja* I (ATD, 17), Göttingen, [5]1981 and II (ATD, 18), Göttingen, 1973; H. Barth, *Die Jesaja-Worte in der Josiazeit. Israel und Assur als Thema einer produktiven Neuinterpretation der Jesajaüberlieferung* (WMANT, 48), Neukirchen-Vluyn, 1977; O. Eissfeldt, *Einleitung in das Alte Testament*, Tübingen, [3]1964, pp. 407-444; T.C. Vriezen – A.S. van der Woude, *Literatuur van Oud-Israël*, Katwijk aan Zee, [8]1984, pp. 221-226; B. Childs, *Introduction to the Old Testament as Scripture*, London, 1979, pp. 310-338.
2. Habakkuk acted at the end of the 7th century B.C. See: P. Humbert, *Problèmes du livre d'Habacuc*, Neuchâtel, 1944; P. Jöcken, *Das Buch Habakuk. Darstellung der Geschichte seiner kritischen Erforschung mit einer eigenen Beurteilung* (BBB, 48), Köln - Bonn, 1977; cf. Eissfeldt, *Einleitung* (n. 1), pp. 526-557; Vriezen – Van der Woude, *Literatuur* (n. 1), pp. 253-255; Childs, *Introduction* (n. 1), pp. 447-456. According to some, the prophecies of Habakkuk underwent a thorough reworking at the end of the Babylonian exil: see J. Jeremias, *Kultprophetie und Gerichtsverkündigung in der späten Königszeit Israels* (WMANT, 35), Neukirchen-Vluyn, 1970, pp. 55-110; E. Otto, *Die Stellung der Wehe-Worte in der Verkündigung des Propheten Habakuk*, in *ZAW* 89 (1977) 73-107.
3. W. Dietrich, *Habakuk – ein Jesajaschüler*, in H.M. Niemann – M. Augustin – W.H. Schmidt (eds.), *Nachdenken über Israel, Bible und Theologie*. FS K.-D. Schunck (BEATAJ, 37), Frankfurt a.M., 1994, pp. 197-215. Some attention to the relationship between Habakkuk and Isaiah has also been paid by J. G. Janzen, *Habakkuk 2:2-4 in the Light of Recent Philological Advances*, in *HTR* 73 (1980) 53-78, esp. pp. 72-78 and by B. Peckham, *The Vision of Habakkuk*, in *CBQ* 48 (1986) 617-636, esp. pp. 629-634.

398 J.T.A.G.M. VAN RUITEN

the relationship of both books from the perspective of the pupil. The
book of Habakkuk therefore functions as point of departure.

1. THE FIRST COMPLAINT AGAINST INJUSTICE (HABAKKUK 1,2-4)

Habakkuk complains to God about the evil which is happening before
his eyes (Hab 1,2-4). How is it possible that God allows this injustice,
that He does not hear (ולא תשמע), and that He does not save (ולא תושיע)?
Dietrich has put forward that the prophet Isaiah also let his hearers know
that God will not hear (Isa 1,15: אינני שמע)[4]. The relationship between
Hab 1,2 and Isa 1,15 is strengthened, according to Dietrich, by the occurrence of תורה, משפט, and ריב in both Hab 1,2-4 and Isa 1,10-17[5].

However, when one compares both texts (Hab 1,2-4 and Isa 1,10-17)
more closely, one discovers that the similarities between both texts are
small. The similarity between Hab 1,2 ("and thou wilt not hear": ולא
תשמע), and Isa 1,15: "I will not hear": אינני שמע) does exist. In both texts
the verb שמע is preceded by a negation. However, the intent of the statement is quite different in both texts. Habakkuk asks why God does not
save, and why He allows evil, whereas in Isaiah the intent is that God
does not hear the prayer as long as the hearers will not give up the social
injustice they commit (Isa 1,10-17). In addition, Hab 1,2 has much more
in common with other texts in the Old Testament. I only refer to the occurrence of the collocations of the words "to cry" or "to cry for help"
(שוע or זעק) and "to hear" with negation (לא שמע) or "to save" with negation (לא ישע)[6]. Also the occurrence of תורה, משפט, and ריב in both
Hab 1,2-4 and Isa 1,10-17 is not a compelling argument for the dependency of Hab 1,2-4 on Isa 1,10-17. The words occur in many other places
in the Old Testament. Finally, many elements of Isa 1,10-17 are not
taken up by Habakkuk, whereas Dietrich does not take in consideration
other collocations of words in Habakkuk 1,2-4[7]. This allows only one

4. *Habakuk* (n. 3), p. 198.
5. See Hab 1,3-4; Isa 1,10.16.17.
6. The verb שוע in combination with "not hearing" or "not answering" occurs in Ps
88,14; Job 19,7; 24,12; 30,20; Lam 3,8. The verb זעק/צ in combination with "not hearing" or "not answering" occurs in Lam 3,8; Job 19,7; compare also Pss 77,2.8ff; 88,2;
142,2.6; Job 35,12. The "not hearing" of a complaint belongs to judgements which the
prophets announce the disobedient people: 1 Sam 8,18; Jer 11,11-12; Micah 3,4; with
other verbs: Jer 7,16; 14,12; cf. also Jer 20,8. The verb זעק/צ occurs in parallelism with
the root שוע in Exod 2,23; 1 Sam 5,12; Hab 1,2; Job 19,7; 35,9; Lam 3,8; and with the
root ישע in Deut 22,27; 2 Kings 6,27; Hab 1,2; cf. Judg 3,9.15; Isa 19,20; Neh 9,27;
Compare *THAT* II, col. 568-575; *TWAT* II, col. 628-639 (esp. 631-633).
7. The collocation of שד and חמס occurs also in Isa 60,18; Jer 6,7; 20,8; Ezek 45,9
and Amos 3,10. The collocation of ריב and מדון occurs also in Jer 15,10; the collocation

conclusion: the similarity between Habakkuk and Isaiah on this point is too small to speak about a verifiable relationship, let alone dependency.

In addition, Dietrich is of the opinion that Hab 1,2-4 functions as a bridge between the early and the later Isaianic tradition[8]. Habakkuk offers Third Isaiah material to formulate his message. Dietrich has three arguments in favour of this opinion. Firstly, the word חמס does not occur in First Isaiah, but it does indeed occur in Third Isaiah (Isa 59,6; 60,18; cf. Isa 53,9). Secondly, the combination of the words זעק and שמע (cf. Hab 1,2) occurs also in Isa 30,19, which is, in the opinion of Dietrich, a late text. The promise of Isa 30,19 is an answer to the complaint of Hab 1,2-4. Finally, according to Dietrich, the collocation of the words עמל and און occurs outside Hab 1,3 only in Isa 10,1 and Isa 59,4. Having pointed to the similarities between Habakkuk and Third Isaiah, Dietrich exclaims triumphantly: "Habakuk, ein Mitglied der Jesaja-Schule!".

The arguments which Dietrich puts forward to prove his hypothesis that Habakkuk functions as bridge between First and Third Isaiah are, in my opinion, not strong. The word חמס occurs not only in Hab 1,2-3 and Third Isaiah, but also in many more places in the Old Testament. It descends from a social and legal context. On the one hand it is used in a context of wealth obtained by oppression (Amos 3,10; 6,3; Micah 6,12; Zeph 1,9; Pss 72,14; 73,6; 74,19ff; 140,2.5.12; Prov 3,31; 4,17; 10,6; 16,29), on the other in a context of different forms of violation of justice (Exod 23,1; 19,16; Deut 22,24; Jer 6,7; 20,8; Ezek 7,23; Hab 1,2; Pss 7,17; 25,19; 27,12; 35,11; 55,10; 58,3; Job 19,7)[9]. The word חמס is so often used that the occurrence in Habakkuk and Third Isaiah does not point to a compelling connection between both collections. Furthermore, the combination of the words צ/זעק and שמע occurs also outside Hab 1,2 and Isa 30,19. The word צ/זעק is used in many cases in the meaning of complaining against God. It concerns a complaint of the people or of an individual, especially a mediator. God hears the complaints for which in many cases the verb שמע (e.g. Exod 3,7; 22,22.26; Num 20,16; Deut 26,7; Ps 34,18; Neh 9,27.28; 2 Chron 20,9) or ענה (1 Sam 7,19; Isa 30,19) is used[10]. Finally, the observation that the collocation of the

---

of יצא and משפט occurs also in Isa 42,1 (יצא *hiph'il*; object); משפט as subject of יצא in Hos 6,5; Pss 17,2; 37,6; משפט with another verb, but with a comparable meaning in Num 27,5; Isa 51,4; Jer 48,21; 51,9-10; Zeph 3,15; Ps 94,15; Job 27,2; 34,5. Compare also the collocation of the words יצא and תורה which occurs in Micah 4,2 (= Isa 2,3).

8. *Habakuk* (n. 3), p. 198.

9. Cf. also Isa 59,4; 60,18; Ezek 7,11; 8,17; 12,19; 45,9; Mal 2,16]. See *TWAT* II, col. 1056ff; W.A.M. Beuken, *Jesaja* II[A] (POT), Nijkerk, 1989, p. 132. Cf. also Dietrich, *Habakuk* (n. 3), p. 209, n. 7.

10. See *THAT* II, col. 574.

words עמל and און occurs outside Hab 1,3 only in Isa 10,1 and Isa 59,4 is inaccurate. Both words occur in one sentence or in parallelism also in Pss 7,15; 10,7; 55,11; 90,10; Job 4,8; 15,35.

2. THE ANSWER OF GOD (HAB 1,5-11)

In the book of Habakkuk God answers the complaint of the prophet with the sending of a people from afar, viz. the Chaldeans (Hab 1,6), to punish his own people (Hab 1,5-11)[11]. This answer of God is connected with the first complaint of the prophet through the repetition of some phrases. I point to the "proceeding of justice from themselves" (Hab 1,7; cf. 1,4), to the "coming for violence" (Hab 1,9; cf. 1,2-3). See also the collocation of "to see" and "to look upon" in Hab 1,3.5. Dietrich points to several resemblances between this passage and the book of Isaiah[12]. Firstly, he points to the similarity between Hab 1,5-11 and Isa 10,1-3. Both texts have the same pattern of thought. Those who are responsible for legislation in Judah increase wealth illegally. However, they do not know how to save themselves ultimately: "What will you do on the day of punishment, in the storm which will come from afar?" (Isa 10,3). The reaction of God against the injustice in his own country is the sending of the Assyrians. (cf. Isa 10,5-19). Secondly, Dietrich points to the similarity of the description of the Babylonian army in Habakkuk (Hab 1,7-10) and the description of the Assyrian army in Isaiah (Isa 5,26-29). In both passages, the hostile forces are described as unstoppable and irresistible. Thirdly, the introduction of the oracle (Hab 1,5) is a combination of three allusions to the book of Isaiah (Isa 5,12; 29,9; 7,9). Finally, Dietrich connects Hab 1,11a with Isa 28,15.18 because of the use of עבר in both texts, and Hab 1,11b with Isa 10,10-11 because of the use of כח in both texts. I will discuss these proposals one by one.

First, the similarity between Hab 1,5-11 and Isa 10,1-3 as far as the theme is concerned is evident. God reacts against injustice in the land with the sending of a foreign nation from afar. In the book of Isaiah it is connected with an oracle of judgement (Isa 5,25-30; 10,3) which follows an utterance of woe (Isa 10,1-2); in the book of Habakkuk the oracle of judgement follows a complaint of the prophet. Although the thematic similarity between both books is clear, it does not seem to be a *unique* similarity. It occurs also elsewhere, see e.g. Amos 6,14; Isa 5,25-30; Jer 5,15; Jer

---

11. For this and other interpretations of the answer of God, see: JÖCKEN, *Das Buch Habakuk* (n. 2).
    12. *Habakuk* (n. 3), pp. 198-201.

1,14.15; 4,6; 6,1.22; 10,22; 13,20; 25,9 etc. Besides, the description of injustice in both passages (Hab 1,2-4; Isa 10,1-2) is quite different. Finally, the similarity between Isa 10,3 and Hab 1,5-11 as far as the lexemes are concerned is restricted to the collocation of the words מרחוק en בוא. The grammatical-syntactical connection between these words is different (Isa 10,3 "the storm which *will come from afar*"; Hab 1,8, "their horsemen *come from afar*"), while the collocation occurs in many other places in the Old Testament (see below). The conclusion is that it is improbable that Isa 10,3 functions as the specific background of Hab 1,5-11.

Second, there seem to be more agreements between Hab 1,5-11 and Isa 5,25-30, than between Habakkuk and Isa 10,1-3. God reacts against injustice in the land with the sending of a foreign nation from afar. In Isa 5,26-29 it is connected with an oracle of judgement which follows a series of utterances of woe (Isa 5,8-24). Especially, the verbal similarities between Isa 5,26.28 and Hab 1,6.8 are striking. We point to the words בוא; מהרה; קל; מרחוק; גוי which occur in both texts:

Isa 5,26	Hab 1,6.8
He will raise a signal for **a nation** (לגוים), <u>afar off</u> (מרחוק), and whistle for it from the ends of the earth; and lo, HASTILY (מהרה), *swiftly* (קל) it comes (יבוא)! .... 28... their horses' hoofs seem like flint...	6 For lo, I am rousing the Chaldeans, that bitter and HASTY **nation** (... הגוי והנמהר), who march through the breadth of the earth, to seize habitations not their own.... 8 Their horses are *swifter* (וקלו) than leopards... their horsemen come <u>from afar</u> (יבאו מרחוק)

Although there are several similarities between both texts, there are also many differences. I point to the formulation of the activity of God (in Isaiah: "He will raise a signal" and "He will whistle"; in Habakkuk: "I am rousing"), to the mentioning of negative characteristics of the foreign nation, like "bitter" (Hab 1,6), their gluttonous character (Hab 1,6-7.9-10), and the implicit jugdement on the Chaldeans (Hab 1,6-7.11). The description of the Assyrian army in Isa 5,26-29 does not focus on this gluttonous character at all, it describes the strength of the army in rather a positive way. Besides, the similarities between both texts are not unique in the Old Testament. As mentioned before, the reaction of God against injustice in the land with the sending of a foreign nation from afar occurs in many other texts in the Old Testament. The collocation of the words בוא and רחק occurs also in Deut 28,49; 29,21; Josh 9,6.9; 1 Kings 8,41; 2 Kings 20,14 (= Isa 39,3); Isa 5,26; 10,3;

30,27; 43,6 (*hiph'il*); 46,11; 49,12; 60,4.9 (hiph'il); Jer 4,16; 5,15; Zech 6,15; 2 Chron 6,32[13]. The prophetic announcement of judgement foretells on the one hand a catastrophe coming from afar (Deut 28,49; Isa 5,26; 10,3; Jer 4,16; 5,15; Hab 1,8; cf. Isa 30,27), on the other hand the removing of Israel far away (Isa 6,12; Jer 8,19; 27,10; Joel 4,6; cf. Ez 11,16). In the oracles against the foreign nations this foretelling is a judgement on the enemies (Isa 13,5; Joel 2,20). The oracles of salvation speak on the one hand of the fact that Israel is brought from a far country (Isa 46,11), on the other hand it is YHWH who carries back his people from a far country (Isa 43,6 [בוא *hiph'il*]; 49,12; 60,4.9 [*hiph'il*]; Jer 30,10; 46,27). Furthermore, the salvation is brought to countries far away (Jer 31,10; cf. Isa 49,1; 66,19)[14].

Third, according to Dietrich the introduction of the oracle (Hab 1,5) is a combination of three allusions to the book of Isaiah (Isa 5,12; 29,9; 7,9). As far as the first allusion is concerned, one can point to the phrases "Look upon (ראו) the nations and see (והביטו) ... For I am doing a work (פעל פעל) in your days" (Hab 1,5) which have some similarities with Isa 5,12 ("But they do not regard (לא יביטו) the deeds (פעל) of the Lord, or see (לא ראו) the work of his hands"). Although it is not impossible that the order to look upon the nations and to see what YHWH is doing refers to the despair of Isaiah that the people are not regarding the work of YHWH[15]. it must be said that the collocation of the words ראה and נבט occurs quite often in the Old Testament[16]. The combination of ראה or נבט with the mentioning of a work of God also occurs more often in the Old Testament[17]. Finally, the root תמה occurs in most cases with a visual observation[18].

The second allusion in Hab 1,5 to the book of Isaiah concerns the phrase "Wonder and be astounded" (והתמהו תמהו). The imperatives in Hab 1,5 are both from the root תמה, "be astounded". The root occurs only in a few places in the Old Testament (Gen 43,33; Deut 28,28; Isa 13,8; 29,9; Jer 4,9; Hab 1,5; Zech 12,4; Ps 48,6; Job 26,11; Qoh 5,7). In most cases it concerns the human reaction to a visual observation of

13. For the collocation of גוי and רחוק see Deut 28,49; Isa 5,26; 66,19; Joel 4,8; Micah 4,3.

14. Cf. *THAT* II, col. 769-771; *TWAT* VII, col. 490-496.

15. Cf. PECKHAM, *The Vision* (n. 3), p. 630.

16. *TWAT* V, col. 137-140, esp. col. 137); *TWAT* VII, col. 225-266, esp. col. 231.

17. The collocation of ראה and פעל (Hab 1,5; Pss 90,16; 95,9), and of ראה and מעשה (Ex 34,10; Deut 3,24; 11,7; Judg 2,7; Isa 29,23; Pss 8,4; 107,24; Qoh 7,13) referring to a work of YHWH also occurs elsewhere the Old Testament. The collocation of נבט with פעל or מעשה does not occur outside Isa 5,12 (with מעשה) and Hab 1,5 (פעל).

18. See Gen 43,33; Deut 28,28; Isa 13,8; 29,9; Hab 1,5; Zech 12,4; Ps 48,6; Qoh 5,7.

something that has been caused by God. Only in the case of Hab 1,5 is the root repeated. According to Dietrich the repetition of this root occurs also in Isa 29,9 ("Stupefy yourselves and be in a stupor": התמהמהו ותמהו). However, it must be said that in MT Isa 29,9 it is not the case of a repetition of one and the same root. The first imperative התמהמהו is from the root מהה "to linger, to tarry" (*hithpalpel*), whereas the second imperative ותמהו is derived from the root תמה, "be astounded" (*qal*). If the first imperative was derived from the root תמה, then the form should have been והתתמהו. The editor of BHS in fact does recommend changing the form of MT with reference to Hab 1,5. However, the ancient versions (LXX, Vg, Targ, Syr) presuppose two different roots for the two imperatives in Isa 29,9. Moreover, from a text-critical point of view there is no reason to change the MT. In fact MT Isa 29,9 does not contain an inaccurate tradition, but a word-play: two different roots provide two verbal forms which are very close to each other. Of course, there is affinity of sound between Hab 1,5 and Isa 29,9, but I think the repetition in Hab 1,5 is due much more to the stylistic pecularities of the book of Habakkuk than to the influence of Isa 29,9[19]. Nor does the context of Isa 29,9 give us arguments to suppose that Hab 1,5 refers to that text.

The third allusion concerns the phrase "that you would not believe if told" (לא תאמינו כי יספר) which is supposed to refer to Isa 7,9 ("If you will not believe, surely you shall not be established": אם לא תאמינו כי לא תאמנו). The similarity between both texts concerns the verb אמן (in both texts: *hiph'il* 2nd pl masc) with negation. However, the verb אמן is used often with a negation[20]. If Habakkuk here referred to Isa 7,9 it would have been curious that he does not take over the repetition of the verb אמן, although it would fit very well in the stylistic pecularities of Habakkuk.

Finally, Dietrich connects Hab 1,11a with Isa 28,15.18 because of the use of עבר in both texts, and Hab 1,11b with Isa 10,10-13 because of the use of כח in both texts. It must be said that in both cases the similarities between Isaiah and Habakkuk are very small. The verb עבר occurs 548 times in the Old Testament with different connotations. The collocation of עבר and חלף occurs only in Isa 8,8 and Hab 1,11, but Dietrich does not refer to this Isaianic text. The verbal agreement between Hab 1,11b

---

19. I refer here to the repetition of words in Hab 1,4 (משפט + יצא), 5 (פעל), 6 (לא לו), 8 (פרשיו) and 9 (בצע).

20. See: Gen 45,26; Exod 4,1.8.9; Num 14,11; 20,12; Deut 9,23; 28,66; Judg 11,20; 1 Kings 10,7; 2 Kings 17,14; Isa 7,9; Jer 12,6; 40,14; Micah 7,5; Hab 1,5; Pss 78,8.22.32.37; 106,24; Job 4,18; 9,16; 15,15.22.31; 24,22; 29,24; 39,24; Prov 26,25; Lam 4,12; 2 Chron 9,6; 32,15. Often it concerns the human reaction of something that has been caused by God.

and Isa 10,10-13 consists only in the word כה. This word occurs 124 times in the Old Testament. It must be admitted that in both cases it is part of a warning against trusting in their own strength. But this idea also occurs more often in the Old Testament. Neither a big army nor great strength could help men, if God will not help him (Deut 8,17; 1 Sam 2,9; Zech 4,6; Ps 33,16; Dan 8,22.24).

3. THE SECOND COMPLAINT (HAB 1,12-17)

After the first complaint of the prophet (Hab 1,2-4) and the first answer of God (Hab 1,5-11) the prophet complains again (Hab 1,12-17). The Babylonians who are brought by God as an answer to the first complaint are frightening. The remedy is worse than the disease[21]. Dietrich points to the influence of several Isaianic texts on Hab 1,12-17[22]. As far as Hab 1,12-13 is concerned he points to the word-pair משפט and יכח (Hab 1,12b), which occurs twice in Isa 11,3-4, to the collocation of שים and משפט (Hab 1,12b), which occurs also in Isa 28,17 ("I will make justice the line"), and to the words צור and יסד, which in the opinion of Dietrich alludes to Isa 28,16, because of the use of יסד in combination with אבן, As far as Hab 1,14 is concerned, Dietrich points to the occurrence of משל (Hab 2,14), which is used in Isaiah to characterize the political leaders in Jerusalem. I will go into these proposals one by one.

Firstly, the word-pair משפט and יכח occurs outside Hab 1,12b and Isa 11,3-4 also in Isa 2,4 (= Micah 4,3); Ezek 5,15; Job 22,4; 23,4. Besides, the word יכח occurs often with expressions which are connected with משפט, e.g. יכח with ריב in Hos 4,4; Micah 6,2; Job 13,6; 40,2. Secondly, as far as the collocation of שים and משפט is concerned it must be said that the construction and meaning Hab 1,12b is different from Isa 28,17. The specific construction of שים ל in Hab 1,12b occurs in a more

---

21. The passage Hab 1,12-17 can be divided into two parts: v. 12-14 and v. 15-17. In the first part, v. 12-14, the speaker addresses himself to YHWH (2nd pl masc). The use of the direct address does not occur in v. 15-17, whereas the 1st sg is used only in Hab 2,12. In the second part, v. 15-17, the use of 3rd sg masc prevails, it describes the ungodly of Hab 2,13. The separation of the two parts is not absolute, while in v. 13-14 the theme of the fish is already mentioned (v. 14: "the fish of the sea"; "the crawling things"); moreover the use of the verb בלע, "to swallow", in v. 13 can be used in connection with fishing (e.g. Jona 1,3; Jer 51,34). Some exegetes point to the genesis of Hab 1,12-17. The first verses (Hab 1,12-13), which have many words in common with Hab 1,2-4, are concerned with a new complaint against the internal political leaders, whereas Hab 1,14-17 betrays an exilic redaction which condemns the Babylonians, which had been called to summon Judah. See JEREMIAS, *Kultprophetie* (n. 2), pp. 78-81; E. OTTO, *Die Theologie des Buches Habakuk*, in *VT* 35 (1985) 274-295, esp. p. 280.

22. *Habakuk* (n. 3), pp. 201-202, 204-205.

or less comparable meaning in Gen 45,8.9; Judg 1,28; 8,33; 11,11; 1 Kings 10,9; Ezek 14,8; Ps 18,44; 1 Chron 26,10. Closest to Hab 1,12 seems the construction in 1 Kings 10,9[23]. In this text the king is ordained to execute justice and righteousness. As far as the words צור and יסד are concerned it should be mentioned that in Hab 1,12 צור is used as epithet of YHWH. This occurs quite often in the Old Testament[24]. In Isa 28,16 the parallel word אבן is used, but in that phrase אבן is not used as epithet of God. In my opinion both passages don not have enough elements in common to speak about the influence of Isaiah on Habakkuk at this point. Thirdly, Dietrich connects Hab 1,14 with Isaiah because of the use of משל, which is used in Isaiah to characterize the political leaders in Jerusalem (Isa 3,4; 28,14; cf. 39,2; 40,10; 51,5). However, the root משל[I] is used 102 times in the Old Testament[25]. It can mean "dominate" in a non-political sense[26], and in a political sense[27]. Besides, also YHWH occurs as subject of משל[28]. The construction in Hab 1,14 is close to Prov 6,7 where is said of an ant that it has no chief, officer or ruler (משל). More probable is that Hab 1,14 contains an ironical allusion to Gen 1,26.

4. THE SECOND ANSWER OF GOD (HAB 2,1-5)

In Hab 2,1-5 YHWH gives his second and decisive answer. Hab 2,1-3 first deals with some preliminary matters. The prophet is ordered to write the vision upon tablets (v. 2), because the fulfillment of the vision is a long time coming (v. 3), whereas Hab 2,4-5 contains the actual answer of God[29]. It might be that also Hab 2,6-20 are part of the answer of

23. Cf. HUMBERT, *Problèmes* (n. 2), pp. 121-122.

24. Deut 32,4.15.18.30.31-37; 1 Sam 2,2; 2 Sam 22,3.32.47; 23,3; Isa 17,10; 26,4; 30,29; 44,8; Hab 1,12; Ps 18,3.32.47; 19,15; 28,1; 31,1; 62,3.7.8; 71,3; 73,26; 78,35; 89,27; 92,16; 94,22; 95,1; 144,1. Cf. HUMBERT, *Problèmes* (n. 2), pp. 122-123.

25. See *THAT* I, col. 930-933; *TWAT* V, col. 73-77.

26. In these cases משל is mostly constructed with ב: Gen 3,16; 37,8; Ex 21,8; Deut 15,6; Jo 2,17; Ps 8,7; 19,14; 105,21; 106,41; Prov 12,24; 16,32; 17,2; 19,10; 22,7; Lam 5,8.

27. Gen 45,8.26; Josh 12,2.5; Judges 8,22-23; 9,2; 14,4; 15,11; 2 Sam 23,3; 1 Kings 5,1; Isa 3,4.12; 14,5; 16,1; 19,4; 49,7; Jer 22,30; 30,21; 51,46; Ezek 19,11; Zech 6,13; Job 25,2; Prov 23,1; 29,2.12.26; Qoh 9,17; 10,4; Dan 11,3-5.39.43; Neh 9,27; 2 Chron 7,18; 9,26; 23,20.

28. Isa 40,10; 63,19; Ps 22,29; 59,14; 66,7; 89,10; 103,19; 1 Chron 29,12; 2 Chron 20,6; cf. Micah 5,1.

29. See, e.g., E. SELLIN, *Das Zwölfprophetenbuch*, Leipzig, 1922, pp. 349-351; F. HORST, *Die Zwölf Kleinen Propheten* (HAT, 14), Tübingen, 1954, pp. 178-180; W. RUDOLPH, *Micha – Nahum – Habakuk – Zephanja* (KAT, XIII-3), Gütersloh, 1975, p. 216. According to others the answer is restricted to v. 4: see, e.g., A. VAN HOONACKER, *Les Douze Petits Prophètes*, Paris, 1908, pp. 477-478; D. DEDEN, *De kleine Profeten*

God, but through their form they should be separated from Hab 2,4-5, and they can be considered as a commentary on the revelation.

Dietrich points to the similarity between Hab 2,2-3 and three passages of Isaiah: 8,1-4; 8,16-17; 30,8-11. He stresses that the similarity does not concern especially one of these passages. Habakkuk refers to all three passages. The verbal similarities, however, between the text of Habakkuk and the texts of Isaiah are little. They are limited to כתב (Isa 8,1), חכה (Isa 8,17) and כתב על לוח (Isa 30,8). Moreover, these words occur in many other passages of the Old Testament.

5. THE WOE-ORACLES (HAB 2,6-20)

The five woe-oracles (Hab 2,6b-8.9-11.12-14.15-17.18-19) can be seen as the commentary on the revelation of God which the prophet receives (Hab 2,4-5). The revelation itself is the answer to the second complaint of the prophet (Hab 1,12-17). The woe-utterances are put in the mouth of the people conquered by Babylon (Hab 2,6a). They describe the criminal (cf. Hab 1,4b.13b; 2,4-5) in the light of the injustice he commits.

This reversal of hope from the coming of a superpower as punishment for the excessive wealth of the leaders in Jerusalem to its sentence is an important thematic similarity between the books of Habakkuk and Isaiah[30]. I refer to Isa 10,5-19 and to the oracles against the nations (Isa 13–23; 30; 34). However, this theme is not unique to Isaiah and Habakkuk, but it occurs also in other prophetic books of the Old Testament, e.g. Jer 46–51; Ezek 25–35; Nahum 1–3.

As far as the form is concerned, the series of woe-oracles consists of five strophes which are built up in a similar way. Each strophe consists of three or four lines, to which the first and fourth woe-oracle add an identical refrain (v. 8cd; 17cd)[31]. Each strophe begins with הוי, followed by a colon in which the verb has the form of a participle and which introduces the description of the addressee. The next colon which is parallel to this colon has in most cases also a verb in the form of a participle[32]. The strophe always ends with a line introduced by כי[33]. The

(BOT), Roermond, 1953, p. 263; A.S. VAN DER WOUDE, *Habakuk. Zefanja* (POT), Nijkerk, 1978, pp. 31-32, 36-38.

　　30. Cf. also DIETRICH, *Habakuk* (n. 3), p. 204.

　　31. JEREMIAS, *Kultprophetie* (n. 2), pp. 61-62; W. JANZEN, *Mourning Cry and Woe Oracle* (BZAW, 125), Berlin, 1972, p. 65; J. VERMEYLEN, *Du prophète Isaïe à l'apocalyptique. Isaïe I–XXXV miroir d'un demi-millénaire d'expérience religieuse en Israël* II, Paris, 1978, p. 643.

　　32. In Hab 2,12 the participle is continued by a *perfectum consecutivum* (cf. GK §112n; P. JOÜON, *Grammaire de l'hébreu biblique*, Rome, 1947, §119r) and in Hab 2,15 by an *infinitivus absolutus* (cf. GK §113hz).

middle lines are alternately varied. In the first and third woe-oracle the middle line is a tricolon introduced by ולוא. In the second and fourth oracle the middle line is introduced by ל, which indicates the purpose of the deeds of the addressee. As far as the genre is concerned, the use of an accusation and an oracle of judgement belongs to the core of the woe-oracles. The characteristic features of this are the omission of a messenger-formula and the omission of a clear (formal) mark to indicate the transition of accusation to judgement.

In the final form the woe-oracles are directed to Babylon. According to Jeremias and Otto the text is the product of a redaction history. At first the prophet directed the woe-oracles to the leaders in Judah[34]. After the destruction of Jerusalem the exilic redaction of the text re-interpreted the words of the prophet and directed them to Babylon. Dietrich accepts the stratification of the woe-oracles. In his attempt to demonstrate the influence of Isaiah on Habakkuk he first deals with the original form of the woe-oracles. He points to the similarity between the original form with the woe-oracles in Isa 5,8-24. They both aim at the social abuse in Judah. The woe-oracles of Isaiah once functioned as model for Habakkuk. Then, Dietrich points to the similarities of the individual woe-oracles with Isaianic texts, from which he deduces the influence of Isaiah on Habakkuk. With regard to Hab 2,6b-7 he points to *hiph'il*-form of the root כבד which occurs regularly in the book of Isaiah to charactarize the influential people in the country (e.g. Isa 5,13; 22,18; cf. 10,3), and with regard to Hab 2,9.11 to the use of מרום in Isa 22,16. In addition, he observes a relationship between Hab 2,12 and Isa 1,21.26 on the basis of the use of פריה and עיר. Finally, Hab 2,15-16 uses the words שתה and שכר of Isa 5,11.22, and interprets them in a symbolic way. As far as the exilic re-interpretation is concerned Dietrich refers to the use of שלל in Isa 10,6-7 (cf. Isa 8,4) which influenced Hab 2,8, and to the many similarities between Hab 2,13 and Second Isaiah on the basis of the use of the terms יעף and יגע. From this he deduces an Isaianic redaction of the woe-oracles of Habakkuk[35]. He is confirmed in his view by the fact that also Hab 2,18-19 betrays many similarities with Second Isaiah. Finally, he points to the influence of Isa 11,9 and Isa 6,3 in Hab 2,14.

33. This means that as far as the fifth woe-oracle is concerned Hab 2,19 was originally put before Hab 2,18: cf. JEREMIAS, *Kultprophetie* (n. 2), p. 64.

34. According to Jeremias the following verses are originally directed to the internal leaders of Judah: Hab 2,6b-7.9 and 11.12.15-16.19. He makes the assumption that the prophet made use of texts of the wisdom literature. Cf. *Kultprophetie* (n. 2), pp. 57-75. According to Otto the original text is made up of the following verses: Hab 2,6b-7.9-10.12-11.15-16. Cf. *Die Stellung der Wehe-Worte* (n. 2).

35. DIETRICH, *Habakuk* (n. 3), p. 207: "Wir sind bisher mit der Annahme einer einzigen, exilischen Bearbeitungsschicht ausgekommen, die wie schon Habakuk, der Jesajaschule nahesteht, allerdings viel näher dem Zweiten als dem Ersten Jesaja".

It is striking that Dietrich in many cases accepts the agreement of just one word to prove the influence of Isaiah on Habakkuk, whereas these words occur also quite often in other places in the Old Testament. Firstly, the *hiph'il*-form of the root כבד (Hab 2,6b-7) occurs 17 times[36]. The use of כבד (*hiph'il*) with על in 1 Kings 12,10.14; Isa 47,6; 2 Chron 10,10.14 is closer to Hab 2,6b than the use of כבד (*hiph'il*) in Isa 5,13 and 22,18. Secondly, the word מרום not only occurs in Hab 2,9 and in Isa 22,16, but also in 51 other places in the Old Testament. The frequent use of this term in poetic and prophetic literature makes the dependency of Hab 2,9 on Isa 22,16, as Dietrich suggests, not convincing. Thirdly, with regard to the collocation of the words פריה and עיר we can point not only to Hab 2,12 and Isa 1,26, but also to Num 21,28 (?); Deut 2,36; 3,4; Isa 22;2; 25,2; 32,13-14; Jer 44,25. The phrases in Hab 2,12 are much closer to Micah 3,10, Jer 22,13 and Prov 24,13. Fourthly, the word שׁתה occurs in 39 passages (19 times as verb, 20 times as noun), whereas the word שׁכר occurs in 211 passages. The words occur as collocation outside Isa 5,11.22 and Hab 2,16 in other places in the Old Testament (e.g. 2 Sam 11,13; Jer 51,7.39; Cant 5,1). Fifth, as far as the exilic re-interpretation is concerned the verb שׁלל is used in 16 passages in the Old Testament, the noun even 72 times. The frequent use of the terms יעף and יגע in Second and Third Isaiah is striking indeed, but the words are used also elsewhere in the Old Testament[37]. The two words are linked together oudside Hab 2,13, also in Isa 40,28.30.31; Jer 51,58. The text of Hab 2,13 is nearly identical with Jer 51,58.

6. HABAKKUK 2,14 AND ISAIAH 11,9

At the end of this contribution I would like to explore the supposed influence of Isa 11,9 on Hab 2,14 a little further[38]. The similarities between Hab 2,14 and Isa 11,9 are evident as can be seen in the following scheme[39]:

36. Only once with the object עבטיט (Hab 2,6b).
37. The word יעף occurs in Josh 24,13; 2 Sam 23,10; Isa 40,28.30.31; 43,22; 47,12.15; 49,4; 57,10; 62,8; 65,23; Jer 45,3; 51,58; Hab 2,13; Pss 6,7; 69,4; Prov 23,4; Job 9,29; Lam 5,5; the verb יגע (qal) occurs in Judg 4,21; 1 Sam 14,28.31; 2 Sam 21,15; Isa 40,28.30.31; 44,12; Jer 2,24; 51,58.64; Hab 2,13.
38. DIETRICH, *Habakuk* (n. 3), p. 207.
39. On the one hand many commentators on the book of Habakkuk have pointed to the similarity between Hab 2,14 and Isa 11,9, and most commentators have concluded that Hab 2,14 is a gloss taken from Isa 11,9. See: K. MARTI, *Dodekapropheton* (KHAT, 13), Tübingen, 1904, p. 345; W. NOWACK, *Die kleinen Propheten* (HAT, III/4), Göttingen, ²1903, p. 286; SELLIN, *Zwölfprophetenbuch* (n. 29), pp. 354-355; HUMBERT, *Problèmes* (n. 2), p. 53; HORST, *Die Zwölf Kleinen Propheten* (n. 29), p. 178; K. ELLIGER,

Isaiah 11,9   *Habakkuk 2,14*

9a לא ירעו ולא ישחיתו
b בכל הר קדשי
c כי מלאה הארץ   14a כי תמלא הארץ
d דעה את יהוה   b לדעת את כבוד יהוה
e כמים לים מכסים   c כמים יכסו על ים

9a They shall not hurt or destroy
b in all my holy mountain;
c for the earth shall be full   14a For the earth shall be full
d of the knowledge of YHWH   b with the knowledge of the glory
                                                                   of YHWH,
e as the waters cover (the bottom   c as the waters cover (the bottom
   of) the sea   of) the sea.

The similarities between Hab 2,14a-c and Isa 11,9c-e are obvious.
Both texts have nine words and roots in common (את; ידע; הארץ; מלא; כי;
יהוה; כמים; כסה; ים)[40]. Only a few words occur only in one text and not
in the other. I refer to כבוד (Hab 2,14b), to ל (Isa 11,9e), and to על (Hab
2,14c). Moreover, the comparison of the fullness of the earth with the
knowledge of (the glory of) YHWH with the covering over the sea with
the waters occurs only in Isa 11,9 and Hab 2,14. Although the collocations of מלא and הארץ, and of ידע and יהוה occur in many other places in
the Old Testament, the phrase that "the earth shall be full with the
knowledge of YHWH" occurs only in Isa 11,9 and Hab 2,14. The collocations of מים and כסה[41], and of ים and כסה[42] occur also elsewhere in the
Old Testament. However, the collocation of מים; כסה and ים occurs only
in Isa 11,9 and Hab 2,14 in one sentence.
    Although the similarities between both texts are obvious, there are
many differences as far as grammar and syntax are concerned. I point to
the form of the root מלא (מלאה in Isa 11,9c and תמלא in Hab 2,14a), to
the form of ידע (דעה in Isa 11,9d and דעת plus ל in Hab 2,14b), to the
form of כסה (מכסים in Isa 11,9e and יכסו in Hab 2,14c), to the preposition before ים (ל in Isa 11,9e and על in Hab 2,14c), and to the sequence
of the words כסה and ים. Despite the overwhelming agreements between

Das Buch der zwölf kleinen Propheten (ATD, 25), Göttingen, 1950, pp. 46-47; JEREMIAS,
Kultprophetie (n. 2), p. 63. On the other hand, many commentators on the book of Isaiah
consider Isa 11,9 as a later addition, taken from Hab 2,14. See: K. MARTI, *Das Buch
Jesaja*, Tübingen, 1900, pp. 112-113; DUHM, *Jesaja* (n. 1); VERMEYLEN, *Du prophète
Isaïe* I (n. 31), pp. 275-279; KAISER, *Jesaja* (n. 1), pp. 239-248.
    40. When one also includes כ and ה as independent words, then both texts even have
eleven words in common.
    41. See Ezek 26,19; Job 22,11; 38,34; cf. also Gen 7,19.20; 8,2; Exod 14,28; Jer
46,8; Ps 104,6.
    42. Exod 15,10; Josh 24,7; Ps 78,53; Job 36,30; cf. also Exod 14,28; Jer 51,42.

both texts, the differences between them make it unlikely that one text is directly dependent on the other. Perhaps it is safer to say that both texts are dependent on another (unknown) text or tradition.

The knowledge of YHWH implies a religious-ethical situation. Those who know his name, who adhere to YHWH, will be saved by YHWH. Only those who give up idolatry and iniquity are able to know YHWH. Those who do not know YHWH are sinning against him. The are forgetting him and they are unfaithful. God desires "steadfast love and not sacrifice, *the knowledge of God*, rather than burnt offerings" (Hos 6,6). Therefore "my people go into exile for *want of knowledge*" (Isa 5,13). According to Hos 4,1-2 the lack of the knowledge of God means "swearing, lying, killing, stealing, and committing adultery; they break all bounds and murder follows murder". In the time of salvation YHWH will give his people righteouness, justice, love, faithfulness, and *knowledge of YHWH* (cf. Hos 2,21). Everybody will participate in the knowledge, because "the earth shall be full of the knowledge of YHWH" (Isa 11,9). This knowledge is the condition for the righteous rule (Isa 11,3-5) and the harmony in the animal world (Isa 11,6-9). Also the messiah is equipped with the spirit of knowledge (Isa 11,2)[43].

In Hab 2,14 the notion of the knowledge of YHWH that shall fill the earth (Isa 11,9) is combined with the knowledge of YHWH's *glory* (כבוד) that will fill the earth. Most often the glory of YHWH fills the tabernacle or the temple[44]. The texts which speak of the presence of YHWH outside the temple speak most often of *something of* YHWH that fills the land or the earth, e.g., the knowledge, the praise, the faithfulness[45]. The eschatological perspective of Hab 2,14 shows that injustice and exploitation will no longer exist, but that the earth will be filled with *the knowledge of the glory* of YHWH. The glory of YHWH fills the earth as universal salvation, as can be seen also in Num 14,21 (cf. Isa 6,3). Behind it functions the concept of the submission of all people to the dominion of God, witness the prophecy of the day of YHWH in Isaiah 2, in which all people submit themselves to YHWH as far as it follows his glory and his majesty[46]. I think it is possible that texts about the future salvation of the people in Zion and especially about the future salvation of all the people who will go to Jerusalem function as background for the formulation in Isa 11,9 and Hab 2,14[47].

43. *TWAT* III, col. 479-512.
44. See, e.g., Exod 40,34.35; 1 Kings 8,11; Ezek 10,4; 43,5; 44,4; Hag 2,7; 2 Chron 5,14; 7,1.2.
45. *TWAT* IV, col. 876-886, esp. col. 878-879.
46. *TWAT* IV, col. 23-40, esp. col. 36-38.
47. See e.g. Isa 40,5; 60,1-3; 66,18. Cf. JEREMIAS, *Kultprophetie* (n. 2), p. 63; *TWAT* IV, col. 36-37.

7. Conclusion

It was the purpose of this contribution to consider some of the similarities between the books of Isaiah and Habakkuk with regard to theme and vocabulary, especially those which have been put forward by Dietrich. The conclusion is that it is very difficult to confirm the view that Habakkuk is dependent on Isaiah. One can point to some general parallels between both collections, e.g. Gods reaction against injustice in the land with the sending of a foreign nation from afar, and the punishment of the foreign nation at a later moment. However, these agreements are too general and too little specific. The common use of words is in most cases too small to conclude the dependency. Whether Habakkuk was a pupil, or not, his use of words is in many cases quite different. To answer the question in the title of this contribution: Habakkuk does not speak in "his master's voice"!

In my opinion Dietrich has used a methodology which is too general and too informal. It is insufficient to point to one or two similar words, and hence to conclude the dependency of one text on the other. If there is no explicit indicator that points from one text to another, I think a text should have at least two words in common with another text. These collocations of two or more words should be connected in a comparable synctactical way. Moreover, I think that this collocation of words should point to a unique agreement between two texts. Finally, common themes and the literary context help to the settlement of the dependency of one text of another. The examples of dependency of Habakkuk on Isaiah could not meet these conditions.

Middelhorsterweg 37   J.T.A.G.M. van Ruiten
NL-9751 TB Haren (Groningen)

WISDOM OF SOLOMON 3,1–4,19
AND THE BOOK OF ISAIAH

Old Testament scholars do fully agree that the Book of Isaiah is rather frequently used by the author of the Book of Wisdom. At least three quotations from the Book of Isaiah are solid proof that the author of the Book of Wisdom knew and used the *Greek* Isaiah.

Wisd 2,12   ἐνεδρεύσωμεν τὸν δίκαιον, ὅτι δύσχρηστος ἡμῖν ἐστιν
Isa 3,10   δήσωμεν τὸν δίκαιον, ὅτι δύσχρηστος ἡμῖν ἐστιν

Wisd 15,10   σποδὸς ἡ καρδία αὐτοῦ
Isa 44,20   γνῶστε ὅτι σποδὸς ἡ καρδία αὐτῶν

Wisd 5,18   ἐνδύσεται θώρακα δικαιοσύνην καὶ περιθήσεται
Isa 59,17   καὶ ἐνεδύσατο δικαιοσύνην ὡς θώρακα καὶ περιέθετο

Especially the first example is documentary evidence that the author of the Book of Wisdom had at his disposal a Greek Isaiah text which can be identified as the Septuagint type. First, because the Hebrew text of Isa 3,10 (אמרו צדיק כי־טוב) is at variance with the Septuagint. And second, since δύσχρηστος is to be found within the Septuagint in these two passages only.

Scholars who have made up inventories of passages from the Book of Isaiah which have been adopted by the author of the Book of Wisdom[1], rarely if ever point to the question whether or not a kind of *coherence* could be detected between the quotations and adaptions from Isaiah used in the Book of Wisdom. As far as the present author is aware of, only J. Suggs has ever made such an attempt: "Wisdom's treatment of the suffering and vindication of the 'child of God' shows itself on close examination to be a homily based chiefly on Isa 52_{13}– 53, with some help from earlier and later passages in the canonical book. This is true of all of Wisd 2_{10}–5, except for a gap that extends from 3_{15} to 4_{13} in which direct dependance upon Isaiah is doubtful"[2]. It

---

1. J. FICHTNER, *Der AT-Text der Sapientia Salomonis*, in *ZAW* 57 (1939) 155-192; P.W. SKEHAN, *Isaias and the Teaching of the Book of Wisdom*, in *CBQ* 2 (1940) 289-299; J. SUGGS, *Wisdom of Solomon 2₁₀-5: A Homily Based on the Fourth Servant Song*, in *JBL* 76 (1957) 26-33; A.G. WRIGHT, *The Literary Genre Midrash*, Staten Island, NY, 1967, pp. 125-127; C. LARCHER, *Études sur le livre de la Sagesse* (EB), Paris, 1969, pp. 86-103; G.W.E. NICKELSBURG, *Resurrection, Immortality and Eternal Life in Intertestamental Judaism* (HTS, 26) Cambridge, MA, 1972, pp. 61-66.
2. SUGGS, p. 29. This view is firmly repeated some pages later: "The apparent lack of Isaianic material from Wisd 3_{15} to 4_{13}..." (p. 31).

may be wondered why Suggs is so determined in bringing forward Wisd 3,15–4,13 as a passage in which should only be found doubtful connections with the Book of Isaiah.

This contribution therefore will investigate the literary unit of Wisd 3,1–4,19 in its relation to the Book of Isaiah. The 'gap' as described by Suggs forms an integral part of this larger section within the Book of Wisdom. As far as possible special attention will be paid to the *coherence* of quotations from and allusions to the Greek Isaiah in this part of the Book of Wisdom.

Wisd 3,1–4,19 is to be considered the *centre* of the first part of the Book of Wisdom (1,1–6,21)[3] which has been composed as a concentrical symmetry:

A)	1,1-15	Exhortation to Justice which brings immortality[4]
B)	1,16-2,24	Speech of the wicked
X)	3,1-4,19	Problems of reward and retribution
B')	4,20-5,23	Vindication of the just and Final Judgement
A')	6,1-21	Exhortation to Wisdom which is easily found

The section under consideration ('X')[5] has been made up of three paragraphs (3,1-12; 3,13–4,6; 4,7-19) which can be coined as 'paradoxes'[6]. From Wisd 3,1 onwards the author in three rounds sets out the differences which in his view do exist between the destiny of the just and the punishment of the wicked. And there is no doubt of it that his full sympathy is with the just who fears God and suffers for that[7].

These three 'paradoxes' unfold a similar structure. A section which describes the life of the just is followed by a section in which the wicked is characterized:

3. P.W. SKEHAN, *The Text and Structure of the Book of Wisdom*, in *Traditio* 3 (1945) 1-12; J.M. REESE, *Plan and Structure in the Book of Wisdom*, in *CBQ* 27 (1965) 391-399; A.G. WRIGHT, *The Structure of the Book of Wisdom*, in *Bib* 48 (1967) 165-184; ID., *Numerical Patterns in the Book of Wisdom*, in *CBQ* 29 (1967) 524-538; P. BIZETTI, *Il libro della Sapienza. Struttura e genere letterario* (SupRivBib, 11) Brescia, 1984, pp. 49-67; U. OFFERHAUS, *Komposition und Intention der Sapientia Salomonis*, Bonn, 1981; A. SCHMITT, *Zur dramatischen Form von Weisheit 1,1–6,21*, in *BZ* 37 (1993) 236-258.

4. These characteristics have been adopted from D. WINSTON, *The Wisdom of Solomon* (AB, 43) New York, ³1982, p. xiv.

5. We do not need to go into Schmitt's view that Wisd 3,1–4,19 could have the same function as the Greek στάσιμον μέλος ('pause song') which was sung between the scenes of a drama; SCHMITT, *Zur dramatischen Form* (n. 3), p. 256.

6. A. SCHMITT, *Weisheit* (Neue Echter Bibel, 23/23) Würzburg, 1989, p. 26.

7. L. RUPPERT, *Der leidende Gerechte. Eine motivgeschichtliche Untersuchung zum Alten Testament und zwischentestamentlichen Judentum* (FzB, 5), Würzburg, 1972, esp. pp. 70-105.

First paradox

Wisd 3,1-9	The just will be rewarded with immortality	(21 lines)[8]
3,10-12	The godless will be punished	(8 lines)

Second paradox

Wisd 3,13-15	Blessed be the childless woman and the eunuch	(9 lines)
3,16-19	The destiny of children of adultery	(7 lines)
4,1-2	Better to be childless with virtue	(7 lines)
4,3-6	than godless with progeny	(11 lines)

Third paradox

Wisd 4,7-15	The just who dies early is in God's hand	(16 or 18 lines)[9]
4,16-19	The godless will be dead for ever	(12 lines)

First, it strikes the eye that in the first and third paradox the lines dealing with the *just* are relatively *lengthy* as compared with the short statements about the godless. The reason for this would be that in Wisd 1,16–2,24 the author has given much room to the ample deliberations of the wicked. As a contrast to them, now in 3,1–4,19 the just has been brought into prominence.

Second, it can hardly be coincidence that the *middle paradox* has a different structure, as it has not only been made up of *two* antithetical sets (the just / the godless), but has also a very specific point of reference: childless and just opposite to quiverful and godless. According to traditional biblical thought the categories should have been framed otherwise: just and quiverful / childless and goddless.

The factual structure of the second paradox (Wisd 3,13–4,6) – being the centre of the three paradoxes which in their turn form the centre of the first part of the Book of Wisdom (1,1–6,21) – draws the reader's attention. At the very beginning of the second paradox there are two catch-words (στεῖρα [3,13], εὐνοῦχος [3,14]) which make it very plausible that the author of the Book of Wisdom is referring here to a couple of passages in the book of Isaiah. With their help the specific message of the first paragraph (3,13-15) of the second paradox is elucidated as being a *biblical* tradition which is at variance with earlier and more 'classical' biblical texts in which childlessness is considered a fundamental disgrace.

---

8. WRIGHT, *The Structure* (n. 3), consistently talks about 'verses' which is not quite correct.

9. Wisd 4,15 has been bracketed in Ziegler's textcritical edition, since it is considered a gloss from Wisd. 3,9; J. ZIEGLER, *Sapientia Salomonis* (Septuaginta... Gottingensis XII/1), Göttingen, ²1980, p. 107; "Wohl frühe Glosse"; SCHMITT, *Weisheit* (n. 6), p. 32. One should not preclude, however, the possibility to consider Wisd 4,15 a deliberate *inverted quotation*. This stylistic literary phenomenon has been described in detail by P.C. BEENTJES, *Discovering a New Path of Intertextuality: Inverted Quotations and Their Dynamics*, in L.J. DE REGT – J. DE WAARD – J.P. FOKKELMAN (eds.), *Literary Structure and Rhetorical Strategies in the Hebrew Bible*, Assen, 1996, pp. 31-50.

Although at first glance one might wonder if it is possible at all to consider Wisd 3,13 (ὅτι μακαρία στεῖρα ἡ ἀμίαντος) a deliberate allusion to Isa 54,1 (εὐφράνθητι, στεῖρα ἡ οὐ τίκτουσα), an important additional argument one should bear in mind is that the Isaian text under discussion, viz. Isa 54,1, within the Book of Isaiah immediately follows on the Fourth Servant Song (Isa 52,13–53,12) [10], which adoption within the Book of Wisdom is not only abundantely documented, but is also precisely the passage which plays such a prominent role just before (1,16–2,24) and just after (5,1-23) the section of paradoxes[11].

It is hard to avoid the impression that the author of the Book of Wisdom has created a kind of cursory reading of the Book of Isaiah, since the description of the eunuch in Wisd 3,14-15, who is introduced as a second example of the just, has clearly been influenced by Isa 56,1-5 to which several points of contact can be listed.

Wisd 3,14a καὶ[12] ὁ εὐνοῦχος ὁ μὴ ἐργασάμενος ἐν χειρὶ ἀνόμημα
Isa 56,2   μακάριος ἀνὴρ ὁ ... διατηρῶν τὰς χεῖρας αὐτοῦ μὴ
       ποιεῖν ἀδίκημα

Wisd 3,14c δοθήσεται γὰρ αὐτῷ ... χάρις ἐκλεκτὴ καὶ κλῆρος ἐν
       ναῷ κυρίου

Isa 56,5   δώσω αὐτοῖς ἐν τῷ οἴκῳ μου ... τόπον ὀνομαστὸν κρείτ-
       τω υἱῶν καὶ θυγατέρων, ὄνομα αἰώνιον δώσω αὐτοῖς καί
       οὐκ ἐκλείψει

Instead of living on by sons and daughters, which within the Old Testament is considered the traditional way of being remembered (cfr. Sir 44,8-9.13-14), the eunuch will receive "something better than sons and daughters": a memorial and an everlasting name in God's own house and within His walls.

The author of the Book of Wisdom not only with the help of the words 'children / childless', but also by using the thematic notion of 'bearing fruit' in a metaphorical way has closely intertwined the motifs of the childless woman and the eunuch into a new text, in which some

10. I feel my view strengthened by my teacher's conviction that the appeal to rejoice (Isa 54,1) builds on the recognition of the Servant ("... bouwt deze oproep tot vreugde voort op de erkenning van de Knecht"); W.A.M. BEUKEN, *Jesaja* IIB (POT), Nijkerk, 1983, p. 247. Cf. J.L. KOOLE, *Jesaja* II (COT), Kampen, 1990, p. 275: "Maar ons hfdst. [= Isa 54, PCB] volgt niet voor niets op de aankondiging van de Knecht des HEREN...".

11. A very fine analysis of Isaiah 54 is offered by W.A.M. BEUKEN, *Isaiah LIV: The Multiple Identity of the Person Addressed*, in A.S. VAN DER WOUDE (ed.), *Language and Meaning: Studies in Hebrew Language and Biblical Exegesis* (OTS, 19), Leiden, 1974, pp. 29-70.

12. In consequence of the parallel construction of Wisd 3,13 and 3,14, the word μακάριος is presupposed here.

obvious allusions to two Isaian passages, viz. Isa 54,1 and Isa 56,1-5 can be detected[13].

It is, however, not only the middle section (3,13–4,6) of Wisd 3,1–4,19 in which passages from the Book of Isaiah have been adopted and thoroughly reworked. In the two paradoxes surrounding this middle section another structural pattern seems to turn up. For both at the *opening* of the first and third paradox, i.e. where the vindication of the *just* is explicitly described, a number of adoptions and allusions from Deutero-Isaiah have been incorporated into the Book of Wisdom. And, strikingly enough, it will appear that there is even one Isaian text which can be found in both paradoxes.

The purpose of the second paradox (3,13–4,6) was to convince the reader that the traditional conception in which childlessness is to be explained as a curse from God needed a fresh re-examination. In both the preceding (3,1-12) and the subsequent (4,7-19) paradox another traditional dogma is criticized, viz. that God is rewarding the just with a long life and is punishing the godless with a premature death. Political events in the second century BCE, however, have definitely demolished this traditional conception. Biblical texts like Jer 12,1 and the Book of Job as a whole to a certain degree had already brought to light that this old dogma was at variance with reality. But especially during the reign of Antiochus IV Epiphanes (175-164 BCE) many pious Jews died as a result of suppression and persecution. Precisely those who with their lifes fought to perserve the Torah and to secure respect for Israel's God fell victim to Seleucide rule. Their lifes were suddenly hewn down and their strong faith to God could not be rewarded with a long life, as they were prematurely killed on the battle-field. The just died in their struggle for preserving the Jewish faith, whereas the godless who were in league with the Hellenistic tyrants kept alive. This crucial problem is dealt with in the first and third paradox, and it should not surprise that such a central biblical concept is attended by biblical quotations and allusions in order to lay authority upon the new ideas brought to the fore by the autor of the Book of Wisdom.

Having ascertained above that the author of the Book of Wisdom at the opening of the second paradox (3,13-15) has incorporated allusions to Isa 54,1 and Isa 56,2-5, it can hardly be a surprise that in the opening lines of the third paradox – in which a fresh view relating to the destiny of the just is introduced – he harks back to Isa 57,1-2.

13. Would it be far-fetched to hold the possibility that Isaiah 55 has been skipped over by the author of the Book of Wisdom, as some themes from the opening lines of this prophetic text (thurst, water, bread) are dealt with in a special literary way, viz. the *synkriseis* of 11,1-14 and 16,1-4, in the third part of the Book of Wisdom (11,1–19,22)?

First, one should notice that both contexts are very similar. The second paradox came to an end with a statement on "children engendered in unlawful union" (Wisd 4,6), which in fact picks up a theme from Wisd 3,16: "The children of adultery...; they have sprung from a union forbidden by the law..." (REB). It is precisely such an audience which is addressed in Isa 57,3-4: "You children of a soothsayer, you spawn of an adulterer and a harlot ... children of sin" (REB).

Second, both Isa 57,1-2 and Wisd 4,7ff. are dealing with the death of the just. I do fully agree with Beuken that, in spite of some notions (אסף, שלום, משכב, and נוח), the Hebrew text of Isa 57,1-2 should not too soon be attributed a reference to a beatific afterlife. The prophetic text in fact brings forward that the ethical and religious behaviour during one's life on earth will produce dissimilarity in death. Opposite to the rest which falls to those who walked in God's ways, the prophet describes the uncontrollable bustle which the godless will undergo[14]. That one should be carefull not to assume too soon that in the Hebrew text of Isa 57,1-2 the beatific afterlife is at stake is clearly demonstrated by the Greek translation of Isa 57,2: ἔσται ἐν εἰρήνη ἡ ταφὴ αὐτοῦ... It is precisely the noun ταφὴ which has no equivalent in the Hebrew parent text. It should be considered, however, a clear indication of what the Greek translator(s) had in mind with regard to the semantics of אסף and נוח: to be gathered to his fathers, to rest in a grave. 'Peace' and 'grave' are metaphors for death and grave.

It is very interesting to have a closer look in what way the author of the Book of Wisdom is processing this Isaiah passage into his own argumentation. His special focus appears to be the verb αἴρομαι which in Isa 57,1 (LXX) has been used twice. Within the Wisdom context it is explained in a very special way, which is clearly demonstrated by Wisd 4,10:

εὐάρεστος θεῷ γενόμενος ἠγαπήθη καὶ ζῶν μεταξὺ ἁμαρτωλῶν μετετέθη,

being an unequivocal reference to Gen 5,24 (LXX):

καὶ εὐηρέστησεν Ενωχ τῷ θεῷ καὶ οὐχ ηὑρίσκετο, ὅτι μετέθηκεν αὐτοῦ ὁ θεός[15].

It is certainly not the aim of the third paradox of the Wisdom text to lay all emphasis on Henoch. Its specific function is that a very well known

---

14. W.A.M. BEUKEN, *Jesaja* IIIA (POT), Nijkerk, 1989, pp. 55-56.
15. Cf. Sir 44,16 (Gr.): Ενωχ εὐηρέστησεν κυρίῳ καὶ μετετέθη ὑπόδειγμα μετανοίας ταῖς γενεαῖς.

Old Testament text should support and accelerate a new trend of thinking, which is introduced in the lines preceding (4,7-9) and following (4,12-15) this reference to Henoch.

Whereas commentators at Wisd 4,7ff. unanimously refer to Isa 57,1-2[16] which is in fact rather general, as far as the present author is aware of, none of them commenting upon Wisd 4,7a (Δίκαιος δὲ ἐὰν φθάσῃ τελευτῆσαι, ἐν ἀναπαύσει ἔσται) points to Isa 57,20 (LXX):

οἱ δὲ ἄδικοι οὕτως κλυδωνισθήσονται καὶ ἀναπαύσασθαι οὐ δυνήσονται[17],

which in an antithetical way chimes in with the Wisdom text.

The influence of Isaiah 57 within the Book of Wisdom has not yet come to an end. For we should bear in mind that Wisd 4,7a, being the opening line of the third paradox, reminds of a phrase to be found in the first paradox, viz. Wisd 3,3b: οἱ δέ εἰσιν ἐν εἰρήνῃ. This phrase could be a clear allusion, in an antithetical way too, to Isa 57,21: אין שלום אמר אלהי לרשעים[18]. As the Greek text of this Isaian line, however, is at variance (οὐκ ἔστιν χαίρειν τοῖς ἀσεβέσιν, εἶπεν κύριος ὁ θεός) a direct adoption cannot be established with absolute certainty. The fact, however, that both the Hebrew and the Greek text of Isa 57,19 has already laid emphasis on the notion of 'peace' could be adduced as evidence in favour of the relationship as mentioned above.

Whether the connection between Wisd 3,3 and Isa 57,19-20 is accepted or not, scholars do anyway assume that Wisd 3,3b is an obvious reminiscence of Isa 57,2a (LXX): ἔσται ἐν εἰρήνῃ ἡ ταφὴ αὐτοῦ. That being the case, one should be aware, however, of at least one major alteration in the target text. Whereas in Isa 57,2 (LXX) it is the *grave* of the just which will be in peace, in Wisd 3,3b it is the *just themselves* who are in peace[19].

16. Already C.L.W. GRIMM, *Das Buch der Weisheit* (Kurzgefasstes Exegetisches Handbuch zu den Apokryphen des Alten Testament, 6) Leipzig, 1860, p. 101: "Dem Schrifsteller scheint bei vs. 7.10-12.14f. die Stelle Jes. 57,1-2 vorgeschwebt zu haben". It is rather puzzling, therefore, why Isa 57,1-2 is *not* mentioned in the detailed analysis by A. SCHMITT, *Der frühe Tod des Gerechten nach Weish 4,7-19*, in E. HAAG – F.-L. HOSSFELD (eds.), *Freude an der Weisung des Herrn*. FS H. Groß (SBB, 13), Stuttgart, 1986, pp. 325-347.

17. Within Isaiah 40–66 the verb ἀναπαύειν is only to be found in Isaiah 57, viz. 57,15 and 57,20! The noun ἀνάπαυσις occurs only in Isa 65,10.

18. Cfr. Isa 48,22 which is almost identical.

19. Only in Wisd 3,1f., and 5,15 δίκαιος has been used in the plural. Descriptions relating to the godless are nearly almost in the plural; only in 1,9; 5,14 (ἀσεβής) and 3,19 (ἄδικος) a singular has been used.

As L. Ruppert has convincingly demonstrated, the Book of Isaiah in Greek has a special predilection for the 'passio iusti' as a motive[20]. The author of the Book of Wisdom has adopted this motive into his composition, first and foremost with the help of numerous quotations and allusions to the Fourth Servant Song, which has deeply influenced the content and structure of Wisd 2,10–5,23. In the middle of this Wisdom composition, however, there is an apparent lack of references to this Fourth Servant Song. A closer examination of Wisd 3,1–4,19 makes it plausible that here at least a number of echo's are found from Isaianic material that comes on the heels of the Fourth Servant Song, viz. Isaiah 54, 56, and 57. It is beyond doubt that in the first part of the Book of Wisdom (1,1–6,21) we come across a special kind of 'structural use of Scripture'[21], viz. a cursory reading of the Fourth Servant Song and its subsequent chapters (Isaiah 52,13–57,21).

Preludelaantje 6   Pancratius C. BEENTJES
NL-3438 TT Nieuwegein

---

20. RUPPERT, *Der leidende Gerechte* (n. 7), p. 62. The marked Greek text of Isa 3,10, which has literally been quoted in Wisd 2,12, belongs to this stream!

21. This notion has amply been described by D. PATTE, *Early Jewish Hermeneutic in Palestine* (SBL DS, 22) Missoula, 1975, esp. pp. 184-199; 263-277. See also P.C. BEENTJES, *Jesus Sirach en Tenach*, Nieuwegein, 1981, pp. 51-55.

THE LANGUAGE OF SUFFERING IN JOB 16–19 AND IN THE SUFFERING SERVANT PASSAGES IN DEUTERO-ISAIAH

In this paper I shall discuss four chapters of the book of Job which have a typical feature in common – each of these chapters is in some way linked to texts dealing with the Suffering Servant in Deutero-Isaiah. Job's speeches in chapters 16, 17 and 19 contain lexical units and syntagmatical patterns that are reminiscent of the texts about the Suffering Servant, in chapter 18 it is the description of the wicked by Bildad that evokes passages about the Isaianic Servant. Some of these correspondences have been noted before[1]; what I shall attempt to do here is to give a more comprehensive overview of these relationships and to indicate how they depend on each other and share a common 'language of suffering' with the 'songs' of the Suffering Servant, especially with Isaiah 52,13–53,12 (henceforth Isaiah 53).

I. THE DESCRIPTION OF THE INNOCENT SUFFERER IN JOB 16, 17 AND 19

1. *Job 16,7-17*

These verses contain a lament of Job, directed against his God, whom he has challenged to trial (cf. 13,18-22). He feels that he has been cast out: God has given him up to the ungodly, the wicked (16,10-11), and at the same time he is powerless in the hands of God himself (16,7-9; 16,12-14). The lament is composed in such way that the confrontation with the wicked is encompassed by Job's struggle with God (x, y, x'). Who are these wicked people, however? It is clear that they should not be identified with Job's friends. From an historical point of view it might be possible to identify them – as some scholars

---

1. In the 1870's there was a vivid debate about the relationship between Job and the Suffering Servant of Deutero-Isaiah: cf. L.C.F.W. SEINECKE, *Der Evangelium des Alten Testaments. Erklärung der Weissagung Jesaias, C. XL–LXVI*, Leipzig, 1870; S. HOEKSTRA, *Job, 'de knecht van Jehovah'* עבד יהוה, in *ThT* 5 (1871) 1-56; A. KUENEN, *Critische bijdragen tot de geschiedenis van de Israëlitischen godsdienst. VIII. Job en de lijdende knecht van Jahveh*, in *ThT* 7 (1873) 492-542, especially pp. 541ff. This discussion centered round the question of a possible 'identification' of Job and the Isaianic Servant. See also S. TERRIEN, *Quelques remarques sur les affinités de Job avec Deutero-Esaie*, in *Volume du Congrès: Geneva 1965* (SVT, 15), Leiden, 1967, pp. 295-310; J.E. HARTLEY, *The Book of Job* (NICOT), Grand Rapids, MI, 1988, pp. 11-15.

do[2] – as Jewish (?) people who remained behind at the time of the Babylonian exile, taking possession of the land of the exiles and coming into conflict with them when they returned to rebuild the country and the temple. The text *in its actual form*, however, does not specify who these wicked people are. Whoever they are and whatever their motives may be, they oppose both God and Job. It is, perhaps, only to be expected that they oppose God and the righteous, but what is their reason for turning against Job as well? Clearly, they do not think of him as being righteous. How can someone who has lost almost all of his family and all of his possessions be called righteous? The traditional concept of divine retribution prohibits them from doing so. Job's three 'friends' try to persuade him to turn away (שׁוב, cf. 22,23) from what they see as his pride and haughtiness. Nevertheless, there are others who have known Job, the people of his clan (19,13-20; 30,1-15), and it is they who have become wicked, they oppose Job and do not only think of him as an unjust and ungodly person, but even treat him as such. Job, once an honoured and beloved patriarch, has become a true sinner, who dares to contradict the venerable traditional beliefs and even challenges God to trial. The text suggests that Job is isolated by members of his own people, not by strangers, not by people who are in some way remote to him[3]. His old friends and all those who once came to ask his advice – the advice of a 'wise man' (29,7-10.11-17) – have become his opponents and even his persecutors: "They have gaped at me with their mouths; they have struck me insolently on the cheek; they mass themselves together against me" (16,10)[4]. To Job even those who would in all likelihood think of themselves as devout people have become 'wicked' by their actions. These 'wicked' people in turn view Job as an apostate, out of grace with God. How can these harsh and contradictory views be reconciled?

At the end of his lament, Job forcefully proclaims his innocence: "though there is no violence in my hands, and my prayer is pure" (16,17). The word 'violence' characterizes the conduct of the wicked who are his enemies, and even God seems to act wickedly (16,9.12-14). In contrast, Job adopts a 'non-violent' attitude, not only in his actions (cf. 'in my hands') but also in his speech ('and my prayer is pure'; cf. 6,30).

2. Cf. J. VERMEYLEN, *Le méchant dans les discours des amis de Job*, in W.A.M. BEUKEN (ed.), *The Book of Job* (BETL, 114), Leuven, 1994, pp. 101-127.
3. It has to be stressed that the text in its actual form – its final edition – does not intend to suggest that these opponents of Job have a different background. They are not (or no longer) to be identified with the adversaries of the returning exiles; they are members of the same community as Job.
4. Quotations are taking from the New Revised Standard Version, unless we felt obliged to deviate from this translation.

Job 16,7-17 and Isaiah 50,4-9 & 53,7-10a

There are two words in Job 16,10 connecting it with Isaiah 50,6a: the verb נכה (to strike) and the noun לחי (cheek). We can therefore speak of a fairly strong connection[5]. Isaiah 50,6a reads, "I gave my back to those who *struck* me, and my *cheeks* to those who pulled out the beard". This verse is part of the third 'song' of the Suffering Servant. Although the Servant is threatened by enemies belonging to his own people, he daily puts his trust in God, who prepares him to be a prophet and teacher in the community. The texts of Job and Isaiah have several elements in common – threats of enemies belonging to one's own people, insolent treatment, certainty of innocence (with forensic connotations) and trust in God, who in the end will restore the sufferer to his rights (cf. Job 16,19-21).

In the exegetical literature Job 16,17a ("though there is no violence in my hands") is seen as a reminiscence of Isaiah 53,9[6]. A comparison between the Hebrew text clearly shows these verses to be related: על לא־ חמס בכפי (Job) and על לא־חמס עשה (Isaiah). Unfortunately, reminiscences or quotations from other biblical texts are all too often treated as isolated phenomena[7]. This is a consequence of the fact that many scholars use a rather restricted definition of reminiscences or quotations. In the text discussed here we see that two stichs within the same sequence (Job 16,7-17) are closely related to two songs of the Suffering Servant (16,10 + 16,17a). It is reasonable to assume that the author of the book of Job knew the texts he was alluding to or quoting, not as independent texts, but as fragments of a much greater unit of sense[8]. Once these two stichs are rec-

---

5. Compare what J.T.A.G.M. VAN RUITEN says about reminiscences which are not explicit quotations: "[…] In most cases the reference is implied. We have therefore formulated *minimum conditions* which a text has to satisfy in order to be considered as having been influenced. These conditions concern *the vocabulary* that texts have *in common*: at least two words of a text must be in common with Is 65:17. Added to this, the words must be *comparably syntactically connected*, while moreover this combination of two, or more, words must be *unique* in the OT", in *Een begin zonder einde. De doorwerking van Jesaja 65:17 in de intertestamentaire literatuur en het Nieuwe Testament*, Amsterdam, 1990, p. 245. Although my approach is not comparable with Van Ruiten's method (i.e. *Wirkungsgeschichte*), the stress on the combination of lexical and syntactical criteria is a common feature.

6. Cf. R. GORDIS, *The Book of Job: Commentary, New Translation, Special Studies* (Moreshet Studies, 2), New York, 1978, p. 178: "16:17. Stich *a* is almost surely a reminiscence of Isa. 53:9".

7. A new approach of defining 'quotations' and 'reminiscences' can be found in intertextual studies, which have gained ground during the last twenty years. See also J.C. BASTIAENS, *Interpretaties van Jesaja 53. Een intertextueel onderzoek naar de lijdende Knecht in Jes 53 (MT/LXX) en in Lk 22:14-38, Hand 3:12-26, Hand 4:23-31 en Hand 8:26-40* (doctoral dissertation), Tilburg, 1993.

8. We can find many parallels between the book of Job and other Old Testament

ognized as 'signs' which on a symbolic level[9] point to the Suffering Servant of Deutero-Isaiah, it is not difficult to catch the semantic parallels between the second part of Job 16,17 and the second part of Isaiah 53,9:
"and my prayer is pure" (ותפלתי זכה) on the one hand and "there was no
deceit in his mouth" (ולא מרמה בפיו) on the other. Even the formulaic expressions 'to be given up to [the ungodly]' and 'to be cast into the hand of
[the wicked]' remind us at once of the semantically reversed parallels in
Isaiah 53,5 ("But he was wounded for our transgressions, crushed for our
iniquities"). If we are right in supposing that the final editing of the book
of Job occurred after the completion of the prophecies of Deutero-Isaiah,
we have here a fine example of the way in which texts of the book of Job
communicate with other known texts of Old Testament literature[10]. In my
concluding paragraph I shall discuss the meaning of the relationship with
the Deutero-Isaiah texts and its consequences for interpretation.

Job 16,19-21 and Isaiah 49,4 & 50,7-9

In chapters 16–17 we find Job arguing with his three friends, but even
more with his God and with himself, in an effort to understand the
meaning of his present terrifying and agonizing condition. The language
of the discourse he utters is not bound by the logical principles of a report. Job is suffering, and in his suffering he uses the language and the
paradigmatic patterns of one who suffers. This explains why Job in one
and the same speech can both strongly oppose God and immediately afterwards express his trust in the same God. This switch in language,
which is typical of other laments as well[11], is found in the transition
from 16,7-17 to 16,18-22. Since God represents not only justice but
mercy as well, and since Job cannot find a single human being to maintain his rights, it is to God he appeals. In spite of his argument with God
he invokes his God as 'a witness in heaven'.

---

books, especially the book of Proverbs, the Psalms, Lamentations and Isaiah. HARTLEY,
Job (n. 1), p. 13, remarks: "These numerous parallels suggest that the author of Job was
very familiar with Israel's literature, particularly the hymns and Wisdom literature".
  9. I.e. the level of connotations and references to other 'texts'. The first 'text-level' –
the text in its material form – is open for every reader and any kind of textual analysis;
the level of connotations and references to other 'texts' requires an informed reader, who
must give sense to the signs the text offers him.
  10. For this dating of the book of Job, cf. A. DE WILDE, *Das Buch Hiob* (OTS, 22),
Leiden, 1981, especially pp. 52-58 ('Datierung'). De Wilde concludes that Job must be
dated about 400 B.C.: "Eine Datierung um 400 vertreten auch Kuenen, Budde, Driver-
Gray, Dhorme, Bleeker, Hölscher, Fohrer, Epping-Nelis, Irwin, Horst, Rowley e.a." (p. 58).
A similar opinion is represented by J.L. CRENSHAW, *Job, Book of*, in D.N. FREEDMAN
(ed.), *The Anchor Bible Dictionary* III, New York, 1992, pp. 858-868, esp. pp. 863-864.
  11. For this phenomenon, compare Ps 6, 22 and 28.

To a certain extent, a semantic and structural parallel of Job 16,19 can be found in Isaiah 49,4: "But I said: I have labored in vain, I have spent my strength for nothing and vanity; yet surely (אכן) my cause is with the Lord, and my reward with my God". Compare this with the Job text: "Even now, in fact (גם עתה הנה), my witness is in heaven, and he that vouches for me is on high". An additional parallel can be found in Isaiah 50,7-9, "The Lord God helps me; therefore I have not been disgraced; therefore I have set my face like a flint, and I know that I shall not be put to shame; he who vindicates me is near. Who will contend with me? Let us stand up together. Who are my adversaries? Let them confront me. It is the Lord God who helps me; who will declare me guilty?" Just like the Servant, Job is sure that the only help he can expect must come from God. No one but God can 'judge' his case (16,21). His friends have failed in what they should have done – pray to God on his behalf and intercede for him. The difficult reading מליצי רעי (16,20) most probably means: "My intercessors, my (so-called) friends [...]"[12]. The only result of the friends' speeches seems to be that they feed Job's resistance and drive him into the arms of his God. Although Job's relationship with God is utterly different from that of the Servant, he becomes increasingly certain that the God he is arguing with must also be the God who will prove his innocence and who will restore his rights, as he did with the Servant (16,19a: "Even now, in fact, my witness is in heaven"). The interrelated parallels with the Isaiah texts have to be seen against the background of the quotation in 16,17.

2. *Job 17,1-16*

Job 16–17 is a textual unit. Chapter 17 continues with a lament, and again we see different and even contradictory sentiments alternating with each other. Of special interest here is 17,1-9, where we find Job complaining to God about his friends and about all those who have dissociated themselves from him. Job has become a 'byword' (משל, probably to be vocalized as a noun), men are spitting in his face, his limbs are nothing more than a shadow and all are appalled at this (שמם על *qal* – verse 8). Job accuses his friends of having held on to their own opinions of divine retribution – the destiny of the righteous (צדיק) and the wicked (חנף – mostly רשעים) – without making any attempt to put themselves in *his* position.

12. GORDIS, *Job* (n. 6), p. 179: "The meter of MT may be defended as containing an anacrusis, with the first two nouns being in the vocative and, therefore, outside the rhythm pattern. The verse may then be rendered: 'Oh, my intercessors, my friends! It is to God that my eye weeps'. The bitter irony is obvious".

Job 17,1-9 and Isaiah 50,6 & 52,13-14

Once the relationship between Job 16,10 and Isaiah 50,6aα is recognized, it is not difficult to discover a parallel relationship between Job 17,6b and Isaiah 50,6b (17,6b: "and I am one before whom people spit"). Although the words are not the same, the *image* of 'spitting in the face' clearly is. And even the wording of the verse (ותפת לפנים אהיה) evokes, as Gordis has noted[13], a passage of the Suffering Servant, namely Isaiah 53,3 (וכמסתר פנים ממנו) – same construction). Thus the whole of 17,6 evokes the humiliation the Suffering Servant had to undergo. In the same way Job is humiliated by his people and isolated by those who once honoured him.

A second reminiscence of the Servant is evoked by the description of Job's physical suffering (17,7), followed by the comment in 17,8a that "the upright are appalled at this" (ישמו ישרים על־זאת). The verb שמם (*qal*) + the preposition על (to be appalled at) is found in Isaiah 52,14: כאשר שממו עליך רבים, "Just as there were many who were *appalled at* him […] so he […]", followed by a parenthesis, "so marred was his appearance, beyond human semblance, and his form beyond that of mortals". It is not just the corresponding *words* that create the relationship between these texts, but also the similar context in which these words function, i.e. the semantic use of these words in relation to their position in the sentence and the textual unit. Only the reader who knows the two texts quite well can detect these relationships and can thus give supplementary meaning to the sense of the textual unit. Such a reader will find it interesting to see that not only does 17,8 evoke Isaiah 52,14 – and thus the lot of the Suffering Servant – but 17,4 evokes the preceding verse in Isaiah as well (52,13). In Job 17,4 we read: כי־לבם צפנת משכל על־כן לא תרמם, "Since you have closed their minds to understanding, you shall not exalt [them]". The noun שכל ('understanding') is related to the corresponding verb, which we find in Isaiah 52,13: הנה ישכיל עבדי ("See, my Servant will gain insight"), and the verb רום is found in the same verse of Isaiah: ירום ונשא וגבה מאד ("He shall be exalted and lifted up, and shall be very high"). In his lament, Job accuses God of having closed the 'heart' of his friends to understanding – they are unable to gain any insight in Job's struggle. As a result, they will not be exalted by God (cf. NRSV: "therefore you will not let them triumph"). This lack of understanding goes together with contempt for Job, the presumed sinner,

13. *Ibid.*, pp. 182-183: "Stich b is to be rendered 'I have become spittled in the face', a breviloquence for 'I have become one in whose face men spit'. For the construction, cf. Isa. 53,3: 'As one from whom there is a hiding of face' = 'one from whom men hide their faces'".

and with a feeling of horror for his suffering, which is apparently well-deserved. Job complains about his friends' conviction that they are 'righteous', knowing very well that they cannot be. What then is the meaning produced by the evocation of the lot of the Suffering Servant in the words רום שֹכל, (verse 4) and שמם על (verse 8), together with the reminiscence to Isaiah 50,6 in 17,6? It is a hermeneutic principle that in cases like these the various elements producing a meaningful relationship between this text and that dealing with the Suffering Servant should be taken together; isolated elements cannot produce such a meaningful relationship, but a combination of elements and the way they are connected and function on a syntactic level can provide additional insights to help with the interpretation of the text. In Job 17,3-10 we find several links with the texts dealing with the Suffering Servant, both on a semantic and a syntactic level. Signifying elements may stand in a parallel, opposite or contradictory relationship, and this helps us determine how the relationship is to be interpreted. In Job 17,3-10 we can discern the dynamic of the paradox, which is common to both Job's situation in relation to his friends and to the situation of the Suffering Servant in relationship to his converted persecutors. The main similarity is in the paradox of truth – Job's friends think of themselves as devout and reasonable people who belong to the צדיקים, whereas Job's opinion of them is just the reverse – they lack insight (17,4.10), they are horrified by the one who suffers, whom they hold in contempt (17,6.8), and they are in fact not righteous and not wise at all (17,8-10). A somewhat similar paradox is found in the fourth song of the Suffering Servant – the Servant was held in contempt by his persecutors, who had no insight in God's plan and the Servant's place in it, but who thought they were right to include the Servant among the wicked (רשעים – cf. Isaiah 53,9aα). Thus the lexical and syntactic similarities between Job 17,3-9 and Isaiah 50,6 and 52,13–53,12 connect these texts and produce in the mind of the reader a new field of meaningful relationships.

3. *Job 19,1-29*

In chapter 19 Job accuses his friends of not giving him any comfort but 'crushing' (דכא) him with their words (19,1; cf. Isaiah 53,5aα: מדכא מעונתינו and 53,10aα: ויהוה חפץ דכאו). Their humiliating words have a wrong effect on Job – he turns away from them, although he still hopes for their compassion (19,21a). In 19,7-20 Job complains about God's treatment of him and about the social alienation caused by this treatment. He is crying for justice, but there is none (19,7: ואין משפט); instead, God has taken away Job's glory (כבוד) and treats him as if he were some kind of fortified city, and not just a 'tent' (19,12). In 19,13-20 Job describes his social isolation – he is betrayed not only by the members of his clan, but even by his own family and by his old friends. His terrible loneliness is reflected in his disgusting physical appearance: "My bones cling to my skin and to my flesh" (19,20a).

Job, however, cannot simply bow his head and die; he cannot abandon his hope that God is also his 'redeemer' (גאל)[14] who must feel obliged to save him from a humiliating death. Job is sure, therefore, that he will see God in his present life and that God will vindicate him (19,21-27). The same God who has struck Job with his hand (19,21) will come and rise up to rescue him.

Job 19,7-27 and Isaiah 49,7; 52,14aα-b; 53,2-3; 53,4b; 53,11aα

In this chapter, too, we find several lexical correspondences between the Job text and the songs of the Suffering Servant. We should not restrict ourselves, however, to these lexical correspondences as such, but we should also take into account their syntagmatic use and the semantic frame in which they function. The lexical elements in the texts have a certain formal relationship which underlines the basic themes they have in common.

In 19,7-20 Job describes his desperate situation – he longs for justice, but what he finds is injustice. God has stripped him of his glory (כבוד) and has taken away the crown of his head, i.e. the sign of his honourable position as a kind of elder statesman (19,9)[15]. A similar fate befell the Suffering Servant of Deutero-Isaiah; he, the prophet of YHWH and a leader of the community, was deprived of his honour and despised. The verbs בזה ('despise'; 53,3) and חשב ('hold in account'; 53,3) reflect this fundamental lack of human dignity. Job finds himself in a similar situation. He is not only humiliated in the eyes of his clan and his friends, but even the members of his own household want to dissociate themselves from him. In Job 19,19 the verb תעב (*piel*, abhor) is used; men with whom Job could talk confidently now 'abhor' him. Compare this use of the verb with Isaiah 49,7, where God speaks to his Servant, to the one

---

14. גאל in this 'theological' sense is a key-word in Deutero-Isaiah (41,14; 43,14; 44,6; 44,24; 47,4; 48,17; 49,7; 49,26; 54,5), where God is the redeemer from the Babylonian exile. Nevertheless, God can also be a redeemer of individuals, as 'the avenger of wrong' (Gordis); cf. Ps 119,54; Prov 23,11.

15. HARTLEY, *Job* (n. 1), pp. 285-286: "When God stripped him of his honour and removed the crown from his head, he deposed Job from his high position as elder statesman".

"deeply despised, *abhorred* by the nations" (תעב *niphal*). Job's experience shows that social isolation and physical distress go together (19,20), and the same holds good for the Servant, whose repulsive appearance causes him to be expelled from the community (Isaiah 53,2-3).

Now that we are aware of the existence of weak semantic correspondences between Job 19,19-20 and Isaiah 49,7 and 53,2-3 it is interesting to observe that a far more intensive link with the Suffering Servant of Deutero-Isaiah is created in Job 19,21, the next verse. This stronger link does not only arise because of lexical similarity, but also because of a clear parallel in dramatic development. When Job has spoken of his social isolation and his physical distress, he turns to his friends and asks them desperately to have mercy on him, "for the hand of God has struck me" (כי יד־אלוה נגעה בי). Similarly, when the narrator in Isaiah 53,1-11aαβ has spoken of the appearance of the Servant and his being neglected by everyone, he affirms: "Surely he has borne our infirmities and carried our diseases; yet we accounted him *stricken* (נגוע), struck down by God (מכה אלהים) and afflicted. But he was wounded for our transgressions, crushed for our iniquities" (מדכא מעונתינו - 53,4-5a). It is not only the lexical correspondence (נגע) that is of interest here, but also the similar reasoning: prosperity or poverty, social standing or loneliness can never be isolated from God's actions towards humankind (compare יד־אלוה in Job with זרוע יהוה in Isaiah 53,1). Suffering in all its aspects leads to God, though in different ways and with different evaluations. Although Job struggles with God and God's justice, however, he knows nevertheless that this very same God must also rehabilitate him. This intuition is never completely lost, thus explaining the sudden shifts in Job's reasoning, so very typical for the whole book of Job – in spite of everything that has happened, Job is certain that 'his Redeemer lives' (19,25: גאלי חי) and that, in the end, out of his 'flesh' he will 'see God' (מבשרי אחזה אלוה). Similarly, the narrator in Isaiah 53,1-11aαβ states that the Servant, after the suffering he has had to endure, will finally 'see' (53:11: מעמל נפשו יראה), i.e. he will gain insight because of his being exalted by God[16].

To summarize: the lexical correspondences between Job 19,7-27 and the texts concerning the Suffering Servant in Deutero-Isaiah help the reader to recognize some deeper correspondences between these texts, which are not only based on lexical parallels, but also on syntactic units and a comparable development of the theme of suffering related to God's justice. These correspondences create a network of interrelated

---

16. 1QIs^ab (and LXX) read 'will see *light*' (אור) – and 'light' certainly refers here to 'insight' in the plan of God (cf. Is 52,13a: הנה ישכיל עבדי).

words and symbols, and provide the reader with a meaningful background against which these texts can be interpreted. Job's suffering and
his quest for divine justice on the one hand, and the fate of the Suffering
Servant, his position in the community and his loyalty to God on the
other hand, can be better understood when the reader interrelates these
texts and interprets them against their common background. This is not
to deny the differences between these texts; on the contrary, by interre-
lating and contrasting those aspects that the texts have in common, readers will gain a far better understanding of the differences and will
achieve a more comprehensive interpretation.

II. Job 18

1. *The inevitable suffering of the wicked*

In Job 18 Bildad delivers his second speech. This is the only text discussed in this paper which is not spoken by Job. Following a complaint
against Job (18,2-4), Bildad sketches the fate of the wicked: their ruin is
irreversible when their 'light' fades away (18,5-6), their own plans trip
them up (18,7-10) and at the end disease and Sheol await them (18,11-
16). Their deaths are dishonourable: once the wicked have disappeared
from the earth, there is no memory left of them (18,17-19). Bildad concludes his speech by insisting that 'west and east' are appalled at the fate
of the wicked, the fate of all those 'who do not know God' (18,20-21).
Bildad seems to hope that his warning will stop Job from blaming his
God, whom Job holds responsible for the injustice that has befallen him.

2. *Job 18,5-21 and Isaiah 52,14a, 53,4a and 53,8*

A further investigation of the description of the 'wicked' (רְשָׁעִים,
18,5) in this chapter reveals several points of similarity with Isaiah 53.
Disease consumes the skin of the wicked (18,13); a fatal disease such as
leprosy is a fitting symbol of their inescapable fate. The same fate had
befallen the Suffering Servant, whose disgusting appearance was 'beyond that of mortals', but who in fact bore the diseases of his people
(53,4a). Was not Job himself afflicted by a skin disease, so that everyone
tried to escape from his presence (cf. Job 2,7-8; 19,17,20)? These are
mere thematic parallels, but together with other parallels to be discussed
below they are of some value.

In Old Testament anthropology there is no sharp distinction between
life and death as in 'western' anthropologies. A man who is smitten by a
severe disease and isolated from the community already lives in the

realm of death. Related to this view of life and death, the theme of posterity is very common. Without posterity there is no life and no future; there
is no blessing on a house without children. This basic experience of life
and death finds further expression in the notion of 'remembrance' – if no
one remembers the name of the wicked, their posterity is of no use. The
wicked are distinguished by the fact that they are not remembered: "their
memory perishes from the earth, and they have no name in the street [...]
They have no offspring or descendant among their people, and no survivor
where they used to live" (Job 18,17.19). The same theme of posterity
plays an important part in the evaluation of the fate of the Suffering Servant in Isaiah 53. The Servant is taken away from the earth and seems to
share the destiny of the wicked in that he has no descendants, so that no-
body will reflect on the significance of his life: "by an oppressive judgement he was taken away; of his generation (דור), who would think about
it?" (53,8a). Within the context of Deutero-Isaiah, those who confess their
sins and learn to see the true significance of the life of the Servant become
his 'posterity', and they will be called 'servants' (עבדים – for the first time
in Isaiah 54,17!); these servants and the task they have to fulfill play a
major role in the third part of Isaiah (56–66)[17].

Against this background two other similarities between Job 18 and Isaiah
53 can be noted. Whereas in Job 18,18 the wicked are driven 'from light
into darkness', in Isaiah 53,11 it is said that the Servant, who had gone
through darkness (Isaiah 50,10) will see 'light'. Added to this, at the end of
chapter 18 of the book of Job we find a typical lexical correspondence[18]
with the fourth song of the Suffering Servant: in Job 18,20 it is said that
"they of the west are *appalled* (שׁמם *niphal* + על) at the fate [of the
wicked]" and that "horror seizes those of the east"; compare this with
Isaiah 52,14-15a, "Just as there were many who were *appalled* (על+שׁמם) at
him [– so marred was his appearance...], so he shall startle many nations".

What can we learn form this? The description which Bildad gives of the
wicked is marked by the same language as is used by the narrator in Isaiah 53,
who could very well have described his view of the Servant by using Bildad's
words, as in fact he does, but differently: he describes how he *saw* the Servant
in relationship to the way he sees him now. Thus the two texts shed light on
each other. Job 18 can provide the reader of Isaiah 53 with background information concerning the attitude of the narrator towards the Servant, who was
thought of as being one of the wicked (cf. רשעים in Isaiah 53,9a).

---

17. Cf. W.A.M. BEUKEN, *The Main Theme of Trito-Isaiah – 'The Servants of YHWH'*,
in *JSOT* 47 (1990) 67-87.
18. 'Lexical correspondence', i.e. the same verb with the same preposition in a comparable context of meaning.

CONCLUSION

Readers of the book of Job will discover in chapter 16 two reminiscences to the Suffering Servant of Isaiah (16,10 refers to Isaiah 50,6 and
16,17 refers to Isaiah 53,9). These clear reminiscences function as a sign
or marker: what is said here and in the following chapters can be interpreted against the background of the life of the Suffering Servant in
Isaiah. Once a link with these texts in Isaiah has been established, a
frame of reference emerges which helps to interpret the words and images depicting the suffering of Job and the fate of the wicked. In each of
the chapters discussed here (Job 16–19)[19] correspondences will be found
with texts dealing with the Suffering Servant in Isaiah 49 and 50, and
especially in Isaiah 53. The reverse also holds true, however: readers
who have studied chapters 16 to 19 of the book of Job will have a valuable background for the interpretation of the suffering the Servant en-
dures. It will be clear that the nature, the cause and the purpose of the
suffering of the Servant differ from Job's suffering, but it will also be
clear that both texts make use of the same language, of similar or corresponding words and symbols. These correspondences do not lead to a
kind of identification of Job and the Servant, but they show that both the
Servant (or those speaking of him) and Job, different as they may be,
share a common language, which is the language of suffering. Readers
who can understand the relationship between these texts will gain a
deeper insight in the startling questions which in any generation will rise
anew, questions concerning human conduct, human suffering and the
justice of God.

It gives me great pleasure to dedicate this paper to Professor W.
Beuken, my former teacher at the University of Amsterdam. I remember
with gratitude his enthusiasm and keen interest in the work of his students. In this same spirit he supervised my PhD research dealing with
interpretations of Isaiah 53 in Luke-Acts. I am very grateful to him and
pray that God will bless him with many fruitful years to come[*].

Boomgaardstraat 64   Jean Charles BASTIAENS
B-2600 Antwerpen

19. There are many other references to Deutero-Isaiah to be found in the book of Job
(cf. HARTLEY, *Job*, pp. 12-15), but in chapters 16–19 we have a concentration of references to the songs of the Suffering Servant, especially to Isaiah 50,4-9 and Isaiah 53.

* I would like to thank Dr. M. de Winter for improving the English translation of this
paper.

CONSOLATION AND COMPOSITION
IN A RABBINIC HOMILY ON ISAIAH 40
PESIQTA' DE RAV KAHANA' 16

"Isaiah is full of consolation", says the Babylonian Talmud, tractate Baba Batra 14b. This point fits well in the argument of the talmudic sages, but only tells half the truth. The medieval commentator Abraham Ibn Ezra, often depicted as the first critical Bible scholar, recognises that chapter 40 is a caesura in the book of Isaiah, which is thus divided between words of rebuke and words of consolation[1]. That the rabbis of the talmudic period, however, considered Isaiah as <u>the</u> book of consolation, however, is apparent in one of the collections of rabbinic homiletic midrashim on prophetic books. The reference here is to the ten homilies called the "Three of Rebuke and the Seven of Consolation", preserved in the rabbinic collection of sermons for special shabbats and festivals, *Pesiqta' de Rav Kahana'*, chapters (*pisqa'ot*) 13-22[2]. The key-verses in the "Seven of Consolation" are all taken from the second part of the book of Isaiah, whereas for the "Three of Rebuke", passages especially from Jeremiah and Lamentations are included[3].

The cycle of ten sermons of rebuke and consolation was composed for the ten weeks surrounding *Tisha'h be-'Av*, the day of remembrance for the destruction of the first and the second temples in Jerusalem. One would assume that they would be connected to Haftarot (readings from the Prophets), to be read on the three shabbaths before and the seven after the Ninth of 'Av. However, none of the classical rabbinic sources (Mishnah, Tosefta', Talmudim) mentions these ten fixed haftarot for

---

1. *The Commentary of Ibn Ezra on Isaiah*, Vol. I, ed. M. FRIEDLÄNDER, London, 1873, pp. 169-170. Ibn Ezra (1089-1164), explicitly states that the prophesies in the second part of the book of Isaiah, beginning with Isa 40, deal with the Babylonian exile. A full citation is given in n. 6, *infra*.

2. *Pesiqta' de Rav Kahana'*, ed. B. MANDELBAUM, New York, 1962. For questions regarding the date (which is much disputed, ranging from the 3th to the 7th centuries CE) and the author, I refer to the introduction of the above-mentioned edition, or G. STEMBERGER, *Introduction in Talmud and Midrash*, Edinburgh, 1996, pp. 291-296. See also L.M. BARTH, *The "Three of Rebuke and Seven of Consolation": Sermons in the Pesiqta' de Rav Kahana'*, in *JJS* 33 (1982) 503-515.

3. BARTH, *Sermons* (n. 2), p. 515. That the rabbis considered Isaiah as the prophet of consolation, as opposed to Jeremiah, the prophet of calamity, is, among others, also apparent in *Avot de Rabbi Natan*, 40.

these particular shabbats[4]. On the contrary, later sources and liturgical practices presuppose a fixed ten-sermon cycle. Lewis M. Barth's hypothesis that subsequent liturgical use of these haftarot goes back to their use in the *Pesiqta'* is therefore very plausible[5]. This means that the selection of the haftarot coincided with the compilation of the sermons transmitted in *Pesiqta' de Rav Kahana'*.

It is not the purpose of this paper to deal at length with historical questions surrounding the *Pesiqta'* or the cycle of ten sermons. Rather, I will study one sermon in detail: pisqa' 16 on Isaiah 40, the watershed chapter between rebuke and consolation, both in the book of Isaiah and in the cycle of ten sermons in the *Pesiqta'*. The first words of the pseudepigraphic author, denoted as Deutero-Isaiah, are paradigmatic for the subject at hand: נחמו נחמו אמי, "Comfort, O comfort my people". When the words of the Deutero-Isaiah are to be read in the context of the Babylonian exile and the destruction of the first temple, in the context of the *Pesiqta'*, the objective of the consolation should be extended to all the dramatic events in Jewish history: the fall of the two temples, the advent of the diaspora, and the other catastrophes remembered on *Tisha'h be-'Av*[6].

I will study the homily from a form-analytical perspective, defining its forms and functions, dealing with the bigger forms that are characteristic of a rabbinic homily and the smaller forms that are present in this

---

4. On the connection between haftarot and midrashic homilies, see M. BREGMAN, *The Triennial Haftarot and the Perorations of the Midrashic Homilies*, in *JJS* 32 (1981) 74-84. On the so-called "Haftarah homilies", see B. KERN, *Tröstet, tröstet mein Volk! Zwei rabbinische Homilien zu Jesaja 40,1 (PesR 30 und PesR 29/30)* (Frankfurter Judaistische Studien, 7), Frankfurt am Main, 1986, pp. 69-73. On the question whether there were already fixed Torah readings in the early rabbinic period, see J. HEINEMANN, *The Triennial Lectionary Cycle*, in *JJS* 19 (1968) 41-48, who answers this question negatively. Heinemann, however, is concerned with regular weekly Torah lections, and not with holidays.

5. BARTH, *Sermons* (n. 2), pp. 506-509.

6. Of course, one cannot assume that the rabbinic compiler(s) of the *Pesiqta'* made any distinction between the authors of the first and the second part of Isaiah. However, since *Tisha'h be-'Av* became the day of remembrance for all these catastrophes, Isaiah 40 was read as a "hint to" or "illustration of" (זכר) future events (not a prediction: see C.R. SEITZ, *How is the Prophet Isaiah Present in the Latter Half of the Book?*, in *JBL* 115 (1996) 219-240, pp. 223-224). See also Ibn Ezra on Isa 40: "These first comforting promises, with which the second part of the book of Isaiah begins, refer, as R. Moses Hakkohen believes, to the restoration of the temple by Zerrubbabel; according to my opinion to the coming redemption from our present exile; prophesies concerning the Babylonian exile are introduced only as an illustration (זכר) showing how Cyrus, who allowed the captive Jews to return to Jerusalem, …". The text is defective at this point: FRIEDLÄNDER (ed.), *Ibn Ezra* (n. 1), p. 170, n. 3 completes with "… was appointed for the mission by the Almighty long before".

particular one[7]. The plain study of the form, though chronologically the first, is only one aspect of the form-analysis; the question of the function of these forms with regard to the generation of meaning and message in the co-text (literary context) of the sermon is the second one. A central part of the latter is to trace the function of the individual comments *qua midrash*; that is, to establish how these comments are comments on the specific text of Isaiah 40. *Pesiqta' de Rav Kahana'* is indeed a homiletic midrash; and, even though this is often overlooked, a homiletic midrash is more than just a homily; it is a homily based on the specific exegetical operations of the rabbinic midrash[8]. Midrash, that is commentary on well defined Scriptural verses, is the generating factor of meaning, the vehicle of the message of the homily. Of course, one should not end with the question *how* the midrash works; this should lead to a better understanding of *what* the midrash says about the text. This is the way in which the relation between the next two paragraphs should be conceived: first the formal side is considered, and then the contents.

7. This study stands in a tradition of research initiated by the late German judaic scholar Arnold Goldberg, professor in the *Seminar für Judaistik* in Frankfurt am Main. In general, the form-analytical method developed in his school lays at the basis of this study. See A. GOLDBERG, *Form-Analysis of Midrashic Literature as a Method of Description*, in *JJS* 36 (1985) 159-174. Especially, the subject of rabbinic homilies was treated extensively in the doctoral dissertation of one of Goldberg's students, D. LENHARD, *Die rabbinische Homilie. Ein formalanalytischer Index*, Frankfurt am Main, 1994 (not yet published). Even more related to our subject, the same group of scholars developed a *Pesiqta' Rabbati* – project, leading to, among others, publications on the sermons about Isaiah 40 in this other homiletic collection (PR 29/30 and 30), which is related to the *Pesiqta' de Rav Kahana'* in several ways. See e.g. A. GOLDBERG, *Ich komme und wohne in deiner Mitte. Eine rabbinische Homilie zu Sacharja 2,14 (PesR 35)* (Frankfurter Judaistische Studien, 3), Frankfurt am Main, 1977; ID., *Die Peroratio (Chatima) als Kompositionsform der Rabbinischen Homilie*, in *FJB* 6 (1978) 1-22; ID., *Versuch über die hermeneutische Präsupposition und Struktur der Peticha*, in *FJB* 8 (1980) 1-60; B.A.A. KERN, *Die Pesiqta' Rabbati 29/30 Nahamu und die Pesiqta' de Rav Kahana' 16 Nahamu – ein Gegenüberstellung zweier Textzeugen aus Parma*, in *FJB* 11 (1983) 91-112; ID., *Tröstet* (n. 4). A separate form-analytical study on the treatment of Isaiah 40 in *Pesiqta' de Rav Kahana'* is, to the best of my knowledge, not realised in this group (KERN, *Die Pesiqta' Rabbati 29/30*, is purely text-critical comparison), but could make a contribution, or a new start, to the form-analytical project which, unluckily, seems to have ended with the death of Goldberg in 1991.

8. A. GOLDBERG, *Die funktionale Form Midrasch*, in *FJB* 10 (1982) 1-45; ID., *Midraschsatz. Vorschläge für die descriptive Terminologie der Formanalyse rabbinischer Texte*, in *FJB* 17 (1989) 47-56; L. TEUGELS, *Midrasj in de bijbel of midrasj op de bijbel? Een exemplarische studie van het huwelijk van Rebekka en Isaak (Gn 24) in de bijbel en de rabbijnse midrasj.* Unpublished doctoral dissertation, Leuven, 1994; ID., *Midrasj in, en, op de bijbel? Kritische kanttekeningen bij het onkritische gebruik van een term*, in *NTT* 49 (1995) 273-290.

The Homily and Its Forms

A rabbinic homily, the form to which all the pisqa'ot of *Pesiqta' de Rav Kahana'* comply, consists in its ideal-typical form of three parts: 1. the petichah, sometimes called "proem"; 2. the "body" or exposition of the pericope-text; and 3. the chatimah, the conclusion, also called "peroration"[9].

To start with the second part: the body is, rather typically, in most homilies much shorter than the petichah. It consists of exegetical expositions on the verses of the pericope in question, in our case Isaiah 40. As in most rabbinic homilies, only the first verse of the chapter is explicitly dealt with. This verse is called the (first) pericope-verse. The restriction to the first verse, is, however, only formal. Often the rest of the pericope is, at least mentally, included. The same holds for the petichah-verse and the chatimah-verse and is a general characteristic of rabbinic midrash. This is what makes midrash an exemplary intertextual genre, that is to say: the connection laid between several verses is in fact a connection between textual units[10].

The petichah, whose form and whose function especially is much discussed[11], is a very characteristic part of the homiletic midrash, later also applied in exegetical midrashim. A petichah consist of three parts: a petichah-verse, taken from a different biblical book as the verse under consideration in the midrash (the pericope-verse), often from the *Ketuvim*, is (1) cited and (2) explained. The explanation concentrates first on the petichah-verse independently, but gradually the interpreta-

---

9. Cf. GOLDBERG, *Chatimah* (n. 7), pp. 17-18; KERN, *Tröstet* (n. 4), pp. 57-68; LENHARD, *Die rabbinische Homilie* (n. 7). These three components are the minimum. In the so-called *Yelamdenu* or *Tanchuma* midrashim, the petichah is preceded by the *Yelamdenu*-introduction. Sometimes an additional part that has been called *semikhah* by GOLDBERG, *Die Semikha. Eine Kompositionsform in der Rabbinischen Homilie*, in *FJB* 14 (1986) 1-70, is situated between the petichah and the body.

10. D. BOYARIN, *Intertextuality and the Reading of Midrash*, Bloomington, 1990. Though Goldberg does not use the term "intertextuality", this is exactly what he means when he says: "Die Beziehung zwischen Perikopenvers und Hatimavers ist daher sehr oft eine Beziehung zwischen zwei biblischen Texteinheiten" (GOLDBERG, *Chatimah*, p. 10).

11. J. HEINEMANN, *The Poem in the Aggadic Midrashim: A Form-Critical Study*, in ID. – D. NOY (eds.), *Studies in Aggada and Folk-Literature* (ScrHie, 22), Jerusalem, 1971, pp. 100-122, argues that a petichah is an independent small homily, functioning as the introduction to the reading of the weekly parashah in the synagogue. Others before Heinemann (Zunz, Theodor, Maybaum, Bacher, Mann) defined the petichah as an introduction to a larger homily. In reaction to Heinemann, Peter Schäfer argues that the petichah must be considered as a homily on its own, the word petichah meaning "explanation", and not "introduction". Cf. P. SCHÄFER, *Die Peticha – ein Proömium?*, in *Kairos* 12 (1970) 216-219. More recently, Arnold Goldberg, among others, has argued that the petichah is mainly a literary phenomenon. Cf. GOLDBERG, *Petichah* (n. 7).

tion works towards some link with the pericope-verse. Finally (3), the pericope-verse is cited.

The last part of the homily, the chatimah, always has a positive, consoling tone[12]. Like the petichah, it has a threefold structure. The key-verse, the chatimah-verse, is cited at the end of the homily and is almost invariably a verse from the Prophets (3). It is preceded by a short word of consolation and promise, often with an eschatological tone (2). These two elements form the characteristic part of the chatimah. The transition from the body of the homily to the consoling word is effected by an additional exposition of a verse of the pericope, usually the second one. This verse is cited at the beginning of the chatimah form (1). In homilies dealing with texts from the Torah, the distinction between the pericope-verse (Torah) and the chatimah-verse (Prophets) is clear. However, in our particular homily, the chatimah-verse is the same as the pericope-verse: Isaiah 40,1. The other verse, with which the chatimah starts, is Isaiah 40,2. This construction is made possible by two coinciding factors: the fact that the pericope in question is already a prophetic text, and the fact that this prophetic text, Isaiah 40,1, already has a consoling content. The result is that pisqa' 16 is consoling from beginning to end[13].

The three constituting forms each fulfil a specific function in the co-text of the homily: The petichah introduces the homily in an enigmatic way. The connection between the apparently unrelated petichah-verse and the pericope-verse is gradually made clear; and, when the connection is clear, it ends with the citation of the pericope-verse. Hereby the second part, the body, is introduced. The function of the body is the exposition of the verses of the pericope under consideration. The chatimah connects the exposition of the pericope-verses with the final word of consolation[14].

In the next paragraph, I will study parts of the midrashic homily from an exegetical point of view. The focus will be on how the first words of Isaiah 40 are expounded and explained in the different midrashic units, crossing the borders between the three compositional forms of the homily. In each of these three larger forms, midrash-sentences are present as the basic small forms, the building-stones of the exposition. The basic

12. E. STEIN, *Die homiletische Peroratio im Midrasch*, in *HUCA* 8-9 (1931-32) 353-371; BREGMAN, *The Triennial Haftarot* (n. 4); GOLDBERG, *Chatimah* (n. 7).

13. On the specific question of the chatimah in homilies dealing with the Prophets (*Pesiqta' de Rav Kahana; Pesiqta Rabbati*) see BREGMAN, *The Triennial Haftarot* (n. 4), pp. 80-84; BARTH, *Sermons* (n. 2), p. 515.

14. Since the chatimah does not have a fixed introductory formula, one only realises that it is a chatimah when one reaches the end. As a rule, a chatimah starts of as just another explanation of the pericope-verse. This is also part of its function.

structure of the midrash-sentence is "lemma + comment"; that is, an explicitly-cited part of Scripture is provided with a comment on one or more of its specific aspects[15]. Sometimes, smaller identifiable forms are used in the exposition of the petichah, the body, or the chatimah. They play a role in the exposition of the pericope-text and therefore their function can be compared to that of the midrash-sentence. An example of such form is the mashal, in our text abundantly present in the body of the homily. The hierarchy of the forms in the *Pesiqta'* can be schematically represented as follows.

> the work: Pesiqta' de Rav Kahana'
>> the Three of Rebuke and the Seven of Consolation
>>> the distinct homilies (pisqa'ot)
>>>> petichah
>>>> body
>>>> chatima
>>>>> mashal
>>>>> midrash-sentence

The Hermeneutics and Contents of the Midrash[16]

"Comfort ye, comfort ye My people, says your God. Speak to the heart of Jerusalem" (Isa 40,1-2). These words, that are found at the turning point in the composition of the book of Isaiah, are given different explanations in the tradition of interpretations. Since it is not clear who the addressees are, the different ancient translations have filled in this gap in their own way: the priests (LXX), the prophets (Tg), the people (Vg)[17]. In our homily, not only the subject but also the object of the comforting are exposed to different interpretations, as well as the question why double language (Comfort, comfort) is used here. When viewed separately, the distinct explanations present themselves as wholly independent, even atomistic remarks on one or more words of

---

15. The lemma is the specific part of Scripture on which the exposition focuses. This part can be smaller or larger than one verse. The difference is particularly important in the body of the homily, since here the exegesis focuses on particular parts or words of the pericope-text. Apart from this distinction, "lemma" and "verse" are used as synonyms in this study. GOLDBERG, *Die funktionale Form* (n. 8); ID., *Midraschsatz* (n. 8); P.S. ALEXANDER, *Midrash*, in R.J. COGGINS – J.L. HOULDEN (eds.), *A Dictionary of Biblical Interpretation*, London, 1990, pp. 452-459.

16. The translation of *Pesiqta'* in this article is generally taken from W.G. BRAUDE – I.J. KAPSTEIN, *Pesiqta' de-Rav Kahana'*, Philadelphia, 1975, pp. 287-301. In cases where this translation is very free or enlarged, I substituted it for a more literal rendering. Translations of biblical verses not occurring in the *Pesiqta'* are based on the *New Revised Standard Version*, Oxford, 1989 but also adapted when required by the rabbinic commentary.

17. W. BEUKEN, *Jesaja* II^A (POT), Nijkerk, 1979, p. 15.

the initial verses of Isaiah 40. When considered together, however, the interpretations reflect the rich scale of meanings which the text evokes. In this paragraph, I will investigate the interpretations in the different midrashic units, the exegetical operations or reasonings that lie behind them, the characteristic literary forms of rabbinic midrash that can be recognised in them, the functions they fulfil in the larger whole of the homily and their contribution to its general message. Because of the limits posed on this article, I have made a selection of some units with a view to presenting a variety of hermeneutical operations and forms.

Unit 1 starts with the citation of the petichah-verse Job 4,17: "Shall mortal man act more justly than God? Shall a man outshine his maker?". This verse is immediately applied to Boaz, a well-known righteous person, who comforted Ruth with the words "It had been told and told me" (הגד הגד לי) (Ruth 2,11). A double link to Isa 40,1 is implied: the comforting, and the double expression (נחמו נחמו). The reason for the double expression about Ruth is expounded at length. For example, it is said that Ruth's good conduct both in the house and in the field had been told to Boaz. The exposition ends up, via an *a minori ad maius* (*qal-va-chomer*) argument, with a multiple link to Isaiah 40,1-2: "Now does it not follow (קל וחומר) that if Boaz, speaking kind words, comforting words, to the heart of Ruth, succeeded in comforting her, how much more (על אחת כמה וכמה), when the Holy One comes to comfort Jerusalem, and says 'Comfort ye, comfort ye, My people, says your God', He will succeed in comforting her?". The focus of the interpretation is on the repeated נחמו, "Comfort ye", but also on the fact that "says your God" is stated explicitly, as a contrast with the human being Boaz, identified with the mortal man mentioned in the petichah-verse. Moreover the words "to comfort" and "heart" (Isa 40,2) are found in the immediate co-text of Ruth 2,11: "May I continue to find favor in your sight, my lord, for you have comforted me and spoken to the heart of your servant" (2,13). The latter is a good example of the intertextual reading of the midrash. Two texts, two co-texts, and not just two verses are brought together in the midrash, thereby accentuating otherwise unstressed aspects of meaning of the pericope-text. God's comforting is compared to the comforting of a human and thus presented in conceivable terms. A possible explanation for the repetition is given: God's comforting has many facets, just as the many things that were "told and told" about Ruth to Boaz. And when God asks to speak "to the heart" of Jerusalem, this can be compared to the comforting words Boaz spoke to Ruth. The hermeneutical formula *qal-va-chomer* moreover, indicates that God's comforting still surpasses human comforting, thus answering the question posed at the beginning by the cited petichah-verse: "Shall a man outshine his maker?"[18].

The repeated "Comfort ye, comfort ye" is also the key-problem in unit 4. Petichah-verse Ps 45,8: "Thou hast loved righteousness, and hated wickedness, therefore God, thy God, hath anointed thee with the oil of gladness above thy fellows" is, among others and as the last in the series, applied to Isaiah. The hermeneutical move made here is called "petirah"[19]. With the characteristic introduction-formula "Rabbi xx applied the text to (פתר ב...)", the verse is construed as dealing with Isaiah. Examples are given of how Isaiah "has loved righteousness" and how God has "anointed him above his fellows". The latter is explained to mean that Isaiah received a double portion of the divine power; because God anointed him Himself, with his own spirit, which is visible in the fact that Isaiah prophesied in double terms: "Awake, awake" (Isa 51,9), "Rejoicing, I will rejoice" (Isa 51,17) and "Comfort ye, comfort ye" (Isa 40,1). The force and the strength of the repetition are expressed in this interpretation, emphasizing that God and Isaiah together are the authors of the phrase "Comfort ye, comfort ye, says your God". A fact which is usually taken for granted, i.e. that Isaiah is divinely inspired and speaks not his own, but God's words, is stressed in this interpretational unit.

In unit 6, the petichah-verse: "All thy lovers have forgotten thee, they seek thee not; for I have wounded thee with the wound of an enemy" (Jer 30,14), is "read differently" and applied to Job. For this purpose the letters of מכת אויב "the wound of an enemy", are reversed to read מכת איוב "the wound of Job". This, to modern readers, highly illegitimate exegesis is, however, not a-contextual. Just as Job received a "double wound" but was comforted with a double recompense (Job 42,10), so Israel who is terribly wounded by the exile, will receive a double recompense of comfort. This is implied by the double "Comfort ye, comfort ye" of Isa 40,1. Since the addressees of the prophesies of Isaiah and Jeremiah are easily interchangeable, the double expression can be transferred from Isaiah to Jeremiah without problem. Israel will be cured, just as Job was cured. Such is also related Jer 30,17. The fact that the co-text of the story of Job is also taken into account is, furthermore, proved by Job 42,11: "they showed sympathy and comforted him for all the evil

18. A comparable midrash is found in unit 5. Song 8,1: "O, that Thou wert like a brother to me", is there applied to Joseph. The intertext, this time explicitly cited, is "And he comforted them by speaking to their hearts" (Gen 50,21). At the end, by means of a *qal-va-chomer*, a link is established with Isa 40,1-2.

19. Expositions based on a petirah mainly appear, though not exclusively and also not always, in petichot. See GOLDBERG, *Petichah* (n. 7).

that the Lord had brought upon him". To the rabbis, therefore, this is not an illegitimate but an intertextual interpretation which furthermore conveys the possibility of elucidating the pericope-verse (Isa) by expounding the petichah-verse (Jer).

Unit 7 goes on with Job, who experienced God's chastening and restoring powers in his own body and life, and thus became a prototype and a sign of hope for Israel in difficult times. Unit 8 also has a petichah-verse taken from the book of Job (as had unit 1). This seems to point to a thematic connection laid between Job and the suffering Jerusalem. In any case this demonstrates that there is a certain continuation between the different petichot in our pisqa'. Even though they constitute formal units of their own, their meanings overflow the formal boundaries. As such, unit 6 serves as an intertext for units 7 and 8 and vice versa. The information we already have about Job as the prototype of the suffering Jerusalem, must be kept in mind while reading the next units of the pisqa'. The petichah-verse of unit 7 causes some difficulties because of the unsure reading of the Hebrew: "Surely He stretcheth not out his hand against a ruinous heap, when anyone has suffered disaster, He (offers) him consolation" (Job 30,24). The interpretation runs as follows: God never leaves a people in disaster but comforts it by citing the disasters that came to another people, and vice versa. In the case of the exiles mentioned in the Bible, ten tribes were first sent into exile and then the tribes of Judah and Benjamin, so that each could comfort the other[20]. This is, according to this interpretation, the meaning of the repeated "Comfort ye, comfort ye": comfort each other.

In units 8 the word עַמִּי "my people" is read as עִמִּי, "with Me". Without entering the details of the interpretation, the point scored here is that the prophet and God comfort Jerusalem together. As in unit 4, the co-operation between God and Isaiah is stressed. In the continuation of the unit, the co-operation and the extent of the consolation is elaborated even further, both in space and time: "Comfort her, ye who are in the regions above, comfort her ye who are in the regions below. Ye who are alive comfort her, ye who are dead comfort her. Comfort her in this world, comfort her in the world-to-come". Unit 8 closes with a link to the former unit: "Comfort her for the Ten Tribes, comfort her for the Tribes of Judah and Benjamin. It is all these I mean by 'Comfort ye, comfort ye with Me'". With this location of Jerusalem at the centre of the universe, the petichot of the homily come to their conclusion.

20. Here it is again seen that the compilers of the homily, even though they do not claim openly that Isa 40 is written in the context of the Babylonian exile, still see it as a prophecy dealing with this event. See n. 6.

Units 9 and 10 constitute the main body of the homily. In unit 9, Isa 40,1 is expounded at length by means of no less than four meshalim (parables) that serve their role in the exposition in their characteristic narrative way: by means of a fictive story about a situation on earth, a point is made about God's dealing with people[21]. In a mashal not a word, a lemma, is focused upon (as in the midrash-sentence) but, rather, a topic or theme present in the verse and its co-text. This theme is not revealed at the start, but gradually, by way of comparison. The details of the mashal proper are modelled after the situation that is to be illustrated: the relation between God and his people, put forward in the nimshal. The comparable power-relations explain the efficacy and the popularity of the king-mashal. In each of the four meshalim, a different aspect of the relationship between God and Israel after the destruction of the temple has become the main focus of attention. The description is so general that both the first and the second temples are brought to mind. The three first meshalim are triplet-meshalim. They are short and simple, and variants of each other: A king has a palace, a vineyard or a flock of sheep which are destroyed in one way or another. Who has to be comforted, the king or the palace, the vineyard or the sheep? Of course the king. Therefore, Isa 40,1 is cited at the end as "Comfort Me, comfort Me, My people". Three aspects of the relation between God and Israel after the destruction are indicated. The temple is God's palace; the land of Israel, that has been called God's vineyard, is partially destroyed; and the people, God's flock (Isa 40,11), is decimated. Because of this triple loss, God is mourning and therefore has to be comforted. These meshalim evoke many aspects of God's relation with Israel, of which I will mention only one, because it contradicts in a sense the lesson we learned from Job in units 6 to 8. When it is said in Job 42,11 that Job was "comforted for all the evil that the Lord had brought upon him", only a one-sided view of God's relation with human beings is emphasized. The meshalim reveal that God suffers to the same extent when his temple or his people are destroyed. When I said that the meshalim contradict the former interpretation in a sense, I do not mean that they are mutually exclusive. Anywise, this is not the case for the editor of this homily, because he did not conceive it as a scrap-book, but as a consistent whole. Daniel Boyarin would call this

---

21. A. GOLDBERG, *Das schriftauslegende Gleichnis im Midrasch*, in *FJB* 9 (1981) 1-90; D. STERN, *Parables in Midrash*, Cambridge, 1991. On the meshalim in *Pesiqta' de Rav Kahana'*, see C. THOMA – S. LAUER, *Die Gleichnisse der Rabbinen. Erster Teil. Pesiqta' deRav Kahana'* (Judaica et Christiana, 10), Bern, 1986, esp. pp. 233-239.

the double voice of the Torah, personified or hypostasized in two subsequent interpretations in a single coherent homily[22].

The fourth mashal, though redactionally connected with the third one[23], establishes a different point. It focuses on the fact that, in Isa 40,1, Israel is called God's people: "my people". This is not always the case in the Bible. This mashal, which is more elaborate than the first three, deserves to be cited in full.

mashal	*nimshal*
In the name of R. Levi, R. Berechia told a parable: A king had a vineyard which he proceeded to turn over to a tenant. When the vineyard produced good wine, the king used to say: "How good is the wine of my vineyard!" When it produced bad wine, the king used to say: "How bad is my tenants wine!" Whereupon the tenant said: "My lord king, when the vineyard produces good wine you say, 'How good is the wine of my vineyard!' And when it produces bad wine you say, 'How bad is my tenants wine!' Yet good or bad, the wine is yours".	Likewise, in the beginning, the Holy One said to Moses: "Come now therefore and I will send thee unto Pharaoh, that though mayest bring forth My people, the children of Israel, out of Egypt" (Ex 3,10), but after Israel did that unspeakable deed of theirs, what did he say? "Go, get thee down; for thy people have dealt corruptly" (Ex 32,7). Whereupon Moses replied: Master of the universe, when the children of Israel sin, they are called mine; but when they are free from sin, they are called Thine. Yet sinful or sinless, they are Thine: "They are Thine people and Thine inheritance" (Deut 9,29). "Destroy not Thy people, and Thine inheritance" (Deut 6,29). "Lord, why doth Thy wrath wax hot against Thy people" (Ex 32,11).

This mashal can be called an "indirectly antithetical parable"[24], in that the comparison between the human and the divine is not conceived as an analogy but rather as an opposition. The point which is scored is that God is *not* like a human lord; He loves Israel in their good and bad moments. It might seem that this point has already been made with respect to the human lord at the end of the mashal proper, and that not an opposition but rather an equality is meant. However, the reader/hearer knows that, in earthly relationships, the harsh attitude of the owner of

22. BOYARIN, *Intertextuality* (n. 10), p. 78.
23. They are introduced together as "R. Berechia said two things". The third mashal is given in his own name, the fourth in the name of R. Levi. The question of the authenticity of the attributions of interpretations to named sages is beyond the scope of this paper. By stating "as R. xx says" or the like, I do not make any historical claim, but just take the attribution of the *Pesiqta'* for granted.
24. THOMA – LAUER, *Die Gleichnisse* (n. 21), p. 239.

the vineyard more often than not prevails. Therefore, the remark of the tenant anticipates the nimshal: it might seem that God is like an earthly ruler because some passages in the Bible seem to suggest this, but this is not the full perspective because, in the end, God repents of his anger against Israel and accepts them once more as his people. As is generally the case, the mashal does not "fit" entirely. This is precisely what generates part of its message. Notwithstanding the comparison, a chasm is revealed between the human and the divine; the revelation of this chasm is one of the functions of the mashal.

In this mashal, an additional comparison can be found, namely between the events associated with the Exodus and those associated with the exiles. The message generated by the comparison is this: just as in the past, in the paradigmatic period of the Exodus, God repented of his anger against Israel, so also now, God will accept Israel, disregarding the mistakes which they have made. This point is especially clear in a kind of appendix at the end of the mashal: "Why wouldst Thou destroy Thy people? And Moses would not stop speaking endearingly of them – so said R. Simon – until God once again called them 'My people': 'And the Lord repented of the evil which He said He would do unto His people' (Ex 32,14)". In some manuscripts, a citation of the pericope-verse is added: "This is meant by 'Comfort ye, comfort ye My people'". The pericope-verse is expected at the end of a mashal and even when it is not cited explicitly, it needs to be included mentally; because here the link between Moses/the Exodus on the one side, and (Deutero-)Isaiah/the two destructions/the two exiles on the other side, is made explicit by means of a midrash which connects the verses by playing on two words occurring in both. The first word, explicitly pointed at by R. Simon's is "my people". The second one has to be discovered in the Hebrew text: what is translated as "repented of" is the nif'al of exactly the same verb used in Isa 40,1: וינחם. In the co-text of the book of Isaiah, this promise of divine repentance is replete with associations. As the introduction to the consoling second part of the book of Isaiah, it contrasts sharply with the preceding part which contained many rebukes and negative prophesies. The theme of the vineyard calls especially to mind the song of the vineyard in Isaiah 5, the message of which is diametrically opposed to that of the mashal. In the co-text of the *Pesiqta'*, this message of consolation contrasts with the former three "homilies of rebuke". Again, the situation of both destructions and both exiles cannot be disentangled. What is said about the first destruction can be applied directly to the second one and its aftermaths, which the readers/hearer of the homilies in the *Pesiqta'* still believe to witness, every generation in its own way. In the fourth mashal, an additional, hidden, aspect of the phrase נחמו נחמו is thus revealed: the aspect of divine repentance involved in his summons to console his people. This aspect is revealed in the nif'al of the verbal form which is used here.

The perspective of God's continuing comforting, beyond the generation of the destruction, is also the explicit message of the tenth unit. Here, the second half of Isa 40,1 is lemmatized. The phrase translated as "says you God" has the Hebrew verbal form יאמר. In mishnaic and later Hebrew, this form denotes as a rule a future tense. This shift in the use of Hebrew verb forms (and other aspects of the language) opened up possibilities for new interpretations which the midrash generously exploits. Here, the occasion is grasped to explain that God did not just speak in the past, to one specific generation, but that he will keep on speaking to, and comforting, every generation. On this hopeful note, the body of the sermon ends, making way for the chatimah.

It has already been established that the contrast between the chatimah, which as a rule is hopeful and comforting, and the body of the homily, is not as sharp in this sermon as is usually the case. In unit 11, the chatimah begins as an exposition of the second pericope-verse: Isa 40,2. Thus far, it is not clear to the unwarned reader/hearer that this is no longer part of the body of the sermon. In a way, it can even be conceived as such. A smooth transition at the end, however, leads us straight into the main part of the chatimah: the final consoling message which culminates in the citation of the chatimah-verse, which is, quite surprisingly, the pericope-verse with which we are already so familiar! This strong literary composition deserves to be, at least partially, cited.

> "Speak ye to the heart of Jerusalem" (Isa 40,2). The children of Israel sinned with the head, they were smitten in the head, yet they will be comforted at the head. They sinned with the head: "Let us make a head, and let us return into Egypt" (Num 14,4); and they were smitten in the head: "The whole head is sick" (Isa 1,5); yet they will be comforted at the head: "Their king is passed before them, and the Lord at the head of them" (Micah 2,13) (...[25]) They sinned with the heart, they were punished at the heart, yet they will be comforted by the heart. They sinned with the heart: "Yea, they made their hearts as an adamant stone" (Zech 7,12). They were punished at the heart: "And the whole heart faint" (Isa 1,5). Yet they will be comforted by the heart: "Speak ye to the heart of Jerusalem" (Isa 40,2) (...[26]) They sinned in double measure, they will be smitten in double measure, and will be comforted in double measure. They sinned in double meas-

----

25. The texts goes on in the same way with the eye, the ear, the nose and other part of the human body.

26. The text goes on with even more parts of the human body and other aspects of Israel's sin, punishment and consolation.

ure: "Jerusalem sinned a sin" (Lam 1,8). They will be smitten in double
measure: "She hath received of the Lord's hand double for all her sins"
(Isa 40,2). And they will be comforted in double measure: "Comfort ye,
comfort ye My people" (Isa 40,1).

With the enumeration of what might seem to be just another trio
("they sinned such and such, they were smitten by such and such, they
will be comforted by such and such"), the exposition of the second
pericope-verse very naturally flows over into the consoling kernel of the
chatimah, with, at the climax, the citation of the first pericope-verse,
alias the chatimah-verse. Exegetically, the point scored in this exposition
is, once again, the solution to the problem of the double "Comfort ye".
Formally and functionally, the sermon is brought to its final conclusion
in the form of a perfect circle, starting and ending with the same verse.
However, its content has been filled with new meanings during the
course of the homily, leading from the question, in the first petichah,
whether God will succeed in comforting its people, to the assurance that
this will be the case, and in a double measure at that.

Chatimah

One last question that no doubt came up at some point in the minds of
those less familiar with rabbinic interpretations, still needs to be dealt
with. Is the fantasy of the rabbis not too unbridled? Did they not make
up all this? Or, do they not read into the text what they want to find in
it? Perhaps it can be comforting to know that the rabbis asked the same
question with regard to Isaiah. "R. Simon said: Israel said to Isaiah, Our
teacher Isaiah, perhaps all the things you say you make up out of your
own head? Isaiah replied, Scripture does not say, 'Your God said', but
'Your God will keep on saying'"[27]. So that everybody can make his own
judgement and give his interpretation, each according to the ways of his
time. A comforting idea for those active in a discipline were it is hard to
finds subjects still unexplored*.

Universiteit Utrecht   Lieve TEUGELS
Faculteit der Godgeleerdheid
POB 80105
NL-3508 TC Utrecht

27. *Pesiqta' de Rav Kahana'* 16,10.

* With many thanks to professor Wim Beuken who not only taught me to appreciate
the beauty of the book of Isaiah but also fed my interest in rabbinic studies by the constant references to Jewish interpretations in his exegetical classes in Leuven.

QUOTATIONS FROM ISAIAH
AND MATTHEW'S CHRISTOLOGY
(MT 1,23 AND 4,15-16)

In this contribution I will study two quotations from Isaiah, which within the New Testament only occur in Matthew. The first quotation is taken from Isa 7,14 and can be found in Mt 1,23, the second is taken from Isa 8,23b-9,1 and is quoted in Mt 4,15-16. Both quotations belong to the category of the so-called formula quotations to which a great number of studies have already been dedicated[1]. My interest in the citation of Old Testament texts in the New Testament was awakened by Prof. Dr. W.A.M. Beuken. At the beginning of the 1980s we gave joint lectures on the subject at the Catholic Theological University of Amsterdam[2]. Ever since, this type of research has never failed to fascinate me.

Our joint projects introduced me to two points of departure which have proven to be particularly constructive. The first is that in a study about traces of the Old Testament in the New, the Hebrew text and the version of the Septuagint (LXX) deserve equal attention. The second point of departure is that quotations can be considered as a sign that indicates a fundamental interconnection of at least two texts: a quotation continues to refer to the textual unit from which it derives, while simultaneously it is interwoven into a new literary context. Combining these two points of departure, new light is shed on quotations. They form the backbone of intertextual chains, within which often subtle semantic transformations develop, which partly result from the transition from one language (Hebrew) to the other (Greek).

In this article I will illustrate this method on the basis of two quotations from Isaiah[3]. In both cases I will first try to specify the origin of

---

1. See especially: K. STENDAHL, *The School of St. Matthew and Its Use of the Old Testament* (Acta Seminarii Neotestamentici Upsaliensis, 20), Lund, ²1967; R.H. GUNDRY, *The Use of the Old Testament in St. Matthew's Gospel* (NovTSup, 18), Leiden, 1967; W. ROTHFUCHS, *Die Erfüllungszitate des Matthäus-Evangeliums. Eine biblisch-theologische Untersuchung* (BWANT, 88), Stuttgart - Berlin - Köln - Mainz, 1969.

2. The results of one of those lecture series was published in: W. BEUKEN *et al.*, *Brood uit de hemel. Lijnen van Exodus 16 naar Johannes 6 tegen de achtergrond van de rabbijnse literatuur*, Kampen, 1985.

3. In 1991 I co-authored an article with S.J. Noorda on two other formula quotations in Matthew that were taken from Isaiah: *Christelijke schriftgeleerdheid. De vervullingscitaten in Mt 8,17 en 12,17-21*, in T. BAARDA – H.J. DE JONGE – M. MENKEN (eds.), *Jodendom en vroeg-christendom: continuïteit en discontinuïteit*, Kampen, 1991, pp. 81-101.

the quotation. Next I will focus on the level of semantics and will search for an answer to the following questions. What meaning do the quoted words and sentences have within the textual unit from which they were taken? Which semantic transformations result from the translation of the Hebrew original into Greek (the LXX)? What meaning do these citations acquire through their insertion into Matthew's stories about Jesus and which special accents do they introduce into his christology?

I. MATTHEW'S INTERPRETATION OF ISAIAH 7,14

1. *The Origin of the Citation*

The formulation of the citation from Isa 7,14 in Mt 1,23 is almost exactly the same as the Septuagint. There is only one marked difference: in the LXX καλέσεις is mentioned whereas here Matthew uses the third person plural (καλέσουσιν). This difference can be explained from the context. Two verses earlier the angel has told Joseph that he must give Mary's child the name Jesus (1,21: καλέσεις). In order to avoid unnecessary misinterpretation Matthew is forced to avoid the use of καλέσεις in his quotation of Isa 7,14.

The version from the LXX differs from the Hebrew text on a number of points. These differences are interesting because they explain why Matthew preferred the formulation from the LXX to that of the Hebrew text. To illustrate the comparison I quote the three versions parallel to each other:

Hebrew text Isa 7,14: הנה העלמה הרה וילדת בן וקראת שמו עמנו אל
LXX Isa 7,14: ἰδοὺ ἡ παρθένος ἐν γαστρὶ ἕξει καὶ τέξεται υἱόν,
 καὶ καλέσεις τὸ ὄνομα αὐτοῦ Ἐμμανουήλ
Mt 1,23: ἰδοὺ ἡ παρθένος ἐν γαστρὶ ἕξει καὶ τέξεται υἱόν,
 καὶ καλέσουσιν τὸ ὄνομα αὐτοῦ Ἐμμανουήλ.

The Hebrew text successively contains an adjective (הרה), a participle (ילדת) and a finite verb (קראת). Within this sentence structure the emphasis is on the special name the woman will give her child. The adjective and the participle describe the situation of the woman in question: at the moment the statement is made, she is already pregnant and in fact on the point of giving birth. In the LXX the sentence is constructed differently. There, three coordinate verbs are used, all of them in the future tense (ἕξει καὶ τέξεται... καὶ καλέσεις). Here too, the sentence refers to the near future; this is clear from the words which follow the prophet's statement. The formulation of the LXX is particularly suitable for the purpose with which Matthew cites Isa 7,14. In his view this verse heralds events which are to take place centuries later: the statement made in the past is fulfilled with the birth of Jesus.

Another phenomenon which requires our attention is that העלמה ("the young woman") has been replaced by ἡ παρθένος in the LXX. There are three reasons why the selection of this word is not at all obvious: a) except for in Isa 7,14, ἡ παρθένος as a translation of העלמה only occurs in Gen 24,43, where it refers to Rebekah[4]; b) elsewhere in the LXX ἡ παρθένος is usually the translation of בתולה ("virgin"); c) a more common rendering of עלמה would have been νεᾶνις[5]. In Mt 1,23 we encounter the same term as the one opted for in the LXX. This confirms that this citation was taken from the LXX and not from the Hebrew text. In this case too, the formulation of the LXX fits admirably into the context into which Matthew incorporates the citation, for the statement in Isaiah is to emphasise that Mary's pregnancy was not caused by a man, but is the result of a mysterious union between her and the Holy Spirit.

In the Hebrew text it is the woman herself who names the child Immanuel, at least when the masoretic vocalisation is taken as a point of departure (קָרָאת: 3 fem. sg.). Another vocalisation is possible (קָרָאתָ: 2 masc. sg.). The fact that the Hebrew corpus of consonants permits various interpretations is also perceptible in the multiform nature of the Greek versions of the text. The form καλέσεις in LXX[BA] and in Aquila, Symmachus and Theodotion presupposes a Hebrew text with the above-mentioned alternative vocalisation, while καλέσει in LXX[א] corresponds with the masoretic vocalisation[6]. In this situation it is not very surprising that Matthew again makes a selection of his own (καλέσουσιν), in contrast to the various possibilities which we find in the manuscripts of the LXX[7].

That the adjective הרה is translated as ἐν γαστρὶ ἔχειν is not exceptional: elsewhere in the LXX this adjective is rendered in the same way[8]. However, it is interesting that the LXX usually opts for ἐν γαστρὶ

---

4. In the Hebrew text of Gen 24 she is described in vv. 14.55 as a young girl (נער), in v. 16 as a virgin (בתולה) and in v. 43 as a young woman (עלמה). The LXX uses παρθένος to represent all these terms.

5. See in the LXX Exod 2,8; Ps 67,25; Cant 1,3; 6,7. It is also notable that Aquila, Symmachus and Theodotion in their representation of Isa 7,14 opt for νεᾶνις.

6. In addition there is the reading of καλέσετε in LXX[QL], which adapts the subject of the verb to correspond to the previously used second person plural (δώσει... ὑμῖν), assuming that the child is given its name by a plural subject.

7. A vague parallel to the καλέσουσιν in Mt 1,23 can be found in 1 QS[a]: וקרא שמו עמנו אל. According to GUNDRY, The Use (n. 1), p. 90, the verb form used in 1 QS[a] can be read as a pual perf. ("he shall be called") or as a qal perf. ('they will call him'). Some manuscripts (D pc bo[mss]; Or Eus) adapt Mt 1,23 to conform to the LXX and read καλέσεις.

8. See Gen 16,11; 38,24f; Exod 21,22; Judg 13,5.7; 2 Sam 11,5; 2 Kings 15,16; Amos 1,13.

λαμβάνειν when the Hebrew text does not have the adjective הרה but the corresponding verb. Clearer even than the Hebrew root words, the Greek terms express a subtle difference in meaning: ἐν γαστρὶ ἔχειν indicates that a woman is expecting a baby, whereas ἐν γαστρὶ λαμβάνειν emphasises the conception as being the beginning of the pregnancy. In the Hebrew text as well as in the LXX version of Isa 7,14 the moment of conception is not in the speaker's perspective[9]. He focuses the attention on the condition of the expectant mother without speaking of the role of the father. In Mt 1,23, the fact that the role of the father remains undiscussed is seized upon as an argument in favour of the assertion that Jesus has no biological father.

The question as to the origin of the citation from Isa 7,14 can also be answered in another way. Mt 1,23 contains a second citation, likewise taken from Isaiah (Isa 8,8; cf. also 8,10): μεθ᾽ ἡμῶν ὁ θεός. This second citation is added because the first contains an element that requires further explanation: Ἐμμανουήλ. The meaning of that term is not immediately clear to Greek readers since the word is merely a transcription from the Hebrew עמנו אל. This same transcription can be found in the LXX version of Isa 7,14. In the Hebrew text of Isa 8,8.10 again עמנו אל is used, but here the LXX does not opt for a transcription but chooses to present a translation in Greek (μεθ᾽ ἡμῶν ὁ θεός), which is reproduced by Matthew. This further confirms that in 1,23 Matthew goes back to the LXX.

2. Isaiah 7,14 in its Original Context

A citation sparks off interaction between two texts. It is woven into a new literary framework, but since it stems from another text, it continues to refer to its original context. For a better understanding of that interaction, I will first discuss the meaning of Isa 7,14 in its original context to be able to assess the significance this statement has acquired through its integration into the first chapter of Matthew.

Isa 7,14 is embedded in a long textual unit (Isa 7,1–8,20), which refers to a turbulent period in the history of the southern kingdom, known as the Syro-Ephraimite war (735-732 BC) and also described in 2 Kings 16,1-20 and 2 Chron 28,1-8. During that war, Ahaz is king of Judah. The northern kingdom (Israel) and Aram (Syria) have united under the pressure of the Assyrian urge for expansion and are trying by military means to force the southern kingdom into participating in their coalition. The

9. LXX[BLC] has λή(μ)ψεται instead of ἕξει (LXX[אAQ]); Aquila, Symmachus and Theodotion have ἐν γαστρὶ (om. Symm.) συλλαμβάνει.

enemy's armed forces are already at the gates of Jerusalem. This political-military fact evokes mixed reactions in Jerusalem. From Isa 7,17 we gather that there are three parties: king Ahaz, the other members of the house of David, and the people. The people have confidence in a coalition with Aram and Israel (cf. Isa 8,6); the members of the royal family, however, fear that this coalition will weaken their position, since Aram and Israel want a political blood relative on the throne of Judah who is not of the house of David. Therefore they entertain the idea of calling in Assyria. The text suggests that Ahaz himself has not yet made a clear choice between the two alternatives. He is busy inspecting the water systems, which are of vital importance in case of a siege. This indicates that he has no intention of teaming up with Aram and Israel. According to 2 Kings 16,1-20 and 2 Chron 18,1-8 he reportedly took political steps to secure Assyrian support, but this information is lacking in Isaiah.

Within Isa 7,1-8,20 two subunits can be distinguished: 7,1-25 and 8,1-20[10]. An argument in favour of this is the fact that Isaiah presents his theological view of the political crisis before a mixed audience. In 7,1-25 Ahaz functions as Isaiah's direct discussion partner; Isaiah also aims his words beyond Ahaz at the other members of the royal family ("the house of David"). This can be inferred from the alternate use of the second person singular (7,11) and the second person plural (7,9.13ff)[11]. In 8,1-20 the prophet no longer addresses the king and the house of David but focuses on the people. He denounces the fact that the people have refused "the waters of Shiloah that flow gently"; he dissociates himself from their political preference and warns them of retaliations from the Assyrians.

Let us now concentrate on the structure and line of thought of Isa 7,1-25, the direct context of Isa 7,14. This subunit opens with an introduction (vv. 1-2) which briefly describes the critical situation in and around Jerusalem. The rest of the text is in direct speech, introduced by brief narrative sentences (vv. 3.10.12.13), which together paint a rather complex picture of the communicative situation. In vv. 3 and 10 God is mentioned as the speaker. In v. 3 he addresses the prophet, and in v. 10 Ahaz; however, the formulation of this latter verse ("YHWH spoke again to Ahaz") suggests that the message which the prophet is to convey to Ahaz (v. 4: "say to him") is simultaneously being listened to by the king. In fact in vv. 4-9 the dialogue between Isaiah and Ahaz is al-

---

10. Cf. the arrangement in Y. GITAY, *Isaiah and His Audience: The Structure and Meaning of Isaiah 1-12* (SSN, 30), Assen, 1991, pp. 129-135, 147-151.

11. See *ibid.*, p. 139: "Isaiah moves from one subject to another: Ahaz, the royal house, and vice versa".

ready in full swing. The mission which God has ordered the prophet to carry out fades into the execution of that mission without the transition being clearly marked. All this implies that the prophet merely functions as God's instrument and that the words of Isaiah come from God himself.

By God's order the prophet tells Ahaz that he need not fear the two kings who have laid siege to Jerusalem. "These two smouldering stumps of firebrands" will soon disappear from the political stage. Ahaz will hold out as long as he trusts in God. God is even prepared to give a sign in order to convince the king of this hopeful perspective. Ahaz replies that he does not want to accept this offer of a sign. Who the next words (vv. 13-17) are aimed at cannot be inferred from the narrative statement with which they are introduced ("he said": there is no addressee). The designation "house of David" and the use of the plural in vv. 13.14a indicate that the prophet now aims his words beyond Ahaz, at the other members of the royal family[12]; vv. 16-17, however, revert to the singular and the focus switches back to Ahaz. The members of the royal family are reproached, not only for provoking the people, but also God. Their attitude is contrasted with that of Ahaz, who after all does not want to put God to the test. To the members of the royal family God gives a sign of his own accord. This sign differs from the sign that Ahaz was pledged since he could ask for one that was outside the usual pattern of things, whereas the sign that is given to the house of David consists of a series of events which occur within everyday reality. The description of the sign begins in v. 14 but continues into the next few verses. The sign embodies a number of consecutive events which together show that within the next few years there will be a positive change in the situation of the southern kingdom which is presently so sorely beset. The separate elements of this description are not equally clear. The name of the woman who is pregnant and who is soon to have a baby is not mentioned. The article ("the young woman") suggests that the prophet speaks about someone who is known to the listeners. In view of the addressees we may assume that a lady of the royal household is meant. The emphasis is not on the pregnancy or birth but on the events which are to follow. The mother will call her child Immanuel. With this name she gives voice to her belief that the favourable transformation of Judah's fate is effected by God himself. Verses 15 and 16 further qualify this change. When

12. See D.E. GARLAND, *Reading Matthew: A Literary and Theological Commentary on the First Gospel* (Reading New Testament Series), New York, 1993, p. 23: "... the prophet does not address King Ahaz by name but says: 'Hear then, O house of David!'".

the child is weaned, it must choose its own food. It is then old enough to distinguish between good and evil, that is, between what is edible and what is not[13]. His food will consist of butter and honey. This is evidence not of scarcity but of abundance. Verse 16 adds a further explanation. That in his early youth the child will know nothing but prosperity, is connected with the fact that Israel and Aram will by then have vanished from the political arena. Verse 17 announces the dawning of "such days as have not come since the day that Ephraim departed from Judah". Does this mean that the glorious times of David and Solomon which preceded the division between the northern and the southern kingdom, will be revived? His listeners have barely grasped this interpretation or Isaiah cuts it off. He does this by introducing another tyrant at the close of v. 17: the king of Assur. In effect a period of even greater tribulation will arrive. Aram and Israel will indeed have faded from the scene, but their downfall is attended by the rise of an even more formidable enemy.

Verses 18-25 with their repetitive refrain of "on that day" (vv. 18.20.21.23) take up the subject of the days to come according to v. 17. Isaiah intimates that the king of Assyria, who will overrun Aram and Syria, also poses a serious threat to Judah. Ironically it is exactly this superpower which the royal family considers to be a strong ally. The prophet is of a totally different opinion: according to him a pro-Assyrian policy will lead to a total catastrophe. In v. 22 again butter and honey are mentioned. These words now refer to the food of the small number of people who will survive the coming disaster. The sentences in question betray a mixture of hope and fear. Still, even here butter and honey are a symbol of abundance. It is true that the imminent catastrophe will be so great that only few will survive that dark period, but on the other hand a young cow and two sheep will produce sufficient food to sustain the survivors.

3. The Meaning of Isaiah 7,14 in Mt 1,18-25

In what way is the citation from Isa 7,14 integrated into Mt 1,18-25? What function does it have within this passage and how does the meaning of the words from Isaiah in their new context relate to their original meaning?

Mt 1,18-25 is ingeniously composed. It opens with the angel's mission to Joseph (A: vv. 18-21) and ends with a report which shows that

---

13. That לדעתו does not have a final but a temporal meaning is communicated by v. 16 where a temporal clause introduced by בטרם is used.

Joseph carries out the angel's instructions to the letter (A': vv. 24-25)[14]. These two segments enfold vv. 22-23 (B) in which we find the two citations from Isaiah, preceded by an introductory formula.

The citation from Isa 7,14 is splendidly integrated into the whole. This is demonstrated by the numerous connections between the citation and the surrounding verses[15]:

Mt 1,23 (Isa 7,14)	Mt 1,18-21.24v
Ἰδοὺ ἡ παρθένος ἐν γαστρὶ ἕξει	ἐν γαστρὶ ἔχουσα (v. 18)
καὶ τέξεται υἱόν,	τέξεται δὲ υἱόν (v. 21) and ἔτεκεν υἱόν (v. 25)
καὶ καλέσουσιν τὸ ὄνομα αὐτοῦ	καὶ καλέσεις τὸ ὄνομα αὐτοῦ
Ἐμμανουήλ	Ἰησοῦν (v. 21) and καὶ ἐκάλεσεν τὸ ὄνομα αὐτοῦ Ἰησοῦν (v. 25).

These connections leave no doubt that the citation relates to the entire narrative which surrounds it, not only to the verses which precede it[16]. This is confirmed by the words τοῦτο δὲ ὅλον from the introductory formula. The links between the citation and the verses surrounding it are so strong that one wonders whether perhaps the story from Mt 1,18-25 was not constructed partly on the basis of Isa 7,14. The story revolves around three crucial moments (pregnancy, birth and name giving) which are discussed in Isa 7,14. All these critical moments are covered by the γένεσις of Jesus (v. 18).

Mt 1,18-25 in turn is closely linked up with Mt 1,1-17, where likewise an answer is sought to the question of Jesus' origin or ancestry (γένεσις: 1,1.18). In the genealogy with which Matthew opens his gospel, Jesus' ancestry is traced back to David and Abraham; however, in v. 16 the regular succession of the various generations is interrupted by the announcement that Joseph is indeed Mary's husband but not Jesus' biological father. In 1,18-25 the evangelist elaborates further on this intriguing pronouncement and offers more information into the origin of Jesus, expressed by two non-human authorities: by the angel and by God himself. The words of the angel (vv. 20-21) are addressed to

14. See R. PESCH, Eine alttestamentliche Ausführungsformel im Matthäus-Evangelium, in BZ 10 (1966) 220-245, and 11 (1967) 79-95. A similar composition can be found in Mt 21,1-9: there the formula quotation (vv. 4-5) occupies a central place between Jesus' instructions to two disciples (vv. 1-3) and the discharge of that order (vv. 6-9).

15. This arrangement is taken from D. HAGNER, Matthew 1–13 (WBC, 33A), Dallas, 1993, p. 15, who in this context makes the following remark: "Matthew deliberately constructs his narrative around the quotation in midrashic fashion so that the wording of the quotation is reflected in the angelic revelation and in the fact of fulfilment..." (16).

16. In contrast with ROTHFUCHS, Erfüllungszitate (n. 1), p. 57: "Die Anführung von Js 7,14 bezieht sich auf das Vorhergehende (v 20f) und setzt v 24f keineswegs voraus, obwohl diese Verse selbstverständlich mitgemeint sind".

Joseph. The words of God (τὸ ῥηθὲν ὑπὸ κυρίου: v. 22) can be found in the quotation from Isa 7,14 and function exclusively within the communication between the evangelist and his readers.

Thus the text distinguishes between two communicative levels. The angel tells Joseph not to be afraid to take Mary into his home, since the child that was conceived in her owes its existence to the Holy Spirit. He must acknowledge Mary's child as his own and give the child a meaningful name: Jesus. Through Joseph, himself a "son of David", Jesus can be considered as a legitimate descendant of David (cf. 1,1.17). Joseph is convinced by the angel and in vv. 24-25 he does exactly as he has been told. In vv. 22-23 the narrator informs his readers that the story he is telling is the fulfilling of the Scripture. Consequently the readers are given more information than Joseph. They not only learn what the angel tells Joseph, but through the quotation from Isa 7,14 they are also provided with additional arguments on the basis of which they must acknowledge the correctness of Joseph's attitude.

This additional information concerns two elements. The first is that the possible suspicion that Mary's pregnancy was caused by sexual intercourse with another man is entirely unfounded. That Joseph considered casting her off might suggest that he was inclined to believe that his wife's pregnancy could be explained as the result of adultery or rape. The readers are handed an extra key to interpret her special position: she is the virgin (ἡ παρθένος) who is mentioned in the LXX version of Isa 7,14. The second element is the name Immanuel. This name does not correspond to the name that Joseph is to give the child. The difference is enhanced by the fact that in the citation (contrary to the LXX!) καλέσουσιν is mentioned whereas the angel in v. 21 tells Joseph: "you are to name him Jesus" (καλέσεις). The plural form καλέσουσιν might indicate that God is the subject of the action described here[17], but in view of the communicative function of vv. 22-23 it is more obvious to consider the plural form as an invitation to Matthew's readers[18]: they must see Jesus as a sign of God's presence in their midst.

4. Semantic Transformations

In what way does the meaning which Isa 7,14 acquires through its integration into Mt 1,18-25 relate to the original meaning of this verse? There is some continuity in that the words from Isa 7,14, both in their

17. Cf. W. GRUNDMANN, *Das Evangelium nach Matthäus* (THKNT, I), Berlin, 1968, p. 70.

18. Cf. U. LUZ, *Das Evangelium nach Matthäus, 1. Teilband: Mt 1–7* (EKKNT, I/1), Zürich - Neukirchen-Vluyn, 1985, p. 100.

original and in their new context, are attributed to God. In Isa 7,1-25
the prophet functions as the voice of God (see especially 7,3.10). The
words in 7,14 which he aims at the house of David, are God's own
words. The additional information which Matthew imparts to his readers, is explicitly asserted to come from God. The fact that God himself
is the source of the statement from Isa 7,14 has a rhetorical function: a
person has to come up with very strong arguments to be able to ignore
this statement, for it would mean going against the highest imaginable
authority.

Another aspect indicating continuity is that Isa 7,14 deals with the
birth of a child that will be a living symbol of God's presence among
his people. We discover this in Matthew: Jesus' disciples give him
the name of Emmanuel because in him they see the embodiment of
God's proximity to his people. It is also interesting to note that Matthew is familiar with the original literary context of Isa 7,14. The fact
that the evangelist connects distant verses (Isa 7,14 en 8,8.10) indicates this. The original context has left more traces in Matthew: the
mention in Isa 7,1 of the father (Jotham) and grandfather (Uzziah) of
king Ahaz corresponds to the register in Mt 1,9 (Uzziah – Jotham –
Ahaz)[19]; further on, in Isa 7,2.13 the house of David is mentioned,
while in Mt 1 both Jesus (1,1) and Joseph (1,20) are called "son of
David".

Matthew's rendering of Isa 7,14 is also characterized by semantic
transformations, indicating discontinuity. In Isa 7,1-25 the announcement concerns the imminent birth of a child who will grow up in a
period in which the people of Judah will be liberated by the hand of
God from the political pressure which is weighing them down. In Mt
1,18-25 the child from Isa 7,14 is identified with Jesus, a figure who
is not to appear until centuries later. His birth too is placed in the
perspective of an approaching liberation; in this case, however, liberation of the people from their sins is meant. The political trouble is
translated into moral guilt. Furthermore, Jesus is to play an active
role in the liberation process. It is he who has come to save his people
from their sins and he achieves this by giving his life as a ransom for
many (20,28).

A second semantic transformation is realised through the substitution
of העלמה by ἡ παρθένος. The LXX hereby forms the bridge between

---

19. The usual reference to 1 Chron 3,12ff is less accurate where Mt 1,9 is concerned.
The names from Mt 1,9 (Ὀζίας, Ἰωαθάμ and Ἀχάζ) correspond with Isa 7,1 and differ
from 1 Chron 3,12ff where Uzziah, both in the Hebrew text and in the LXX, is called
Azariah (as עזריה and Ἀζαριά respectively).

the Hebrew text and the first gospel. The Hebrew text mentions a pregnant woman. In opting for the term ἡ παρθένος the LXX emphasises the fact that at the moment Isaiah addresses the house of David, the woman is still single and has not yet had sexual intercourse with a man. Her pregnancy and confinement are events which are to take place in the near future (note the use of the future tense!). The fact that ἐν γαστρὶ ἕξει is chosen to describe her pregnancy, an expression which leaves the role of the man unmentioned, cannot be used for the idea that she will become pregnant without having begun a relationship with a man. The term ἡ παρθένος however does imply that the child to be born will be her first-born. In Mt 1,23 the term used in the LXX is repeated. But even when two texts contain the same word, it may mean one thing in one text and something completely different in the other. This rule applies here. The term παρθένος, which in the LXX applies to a woman who is as yet unmarried, undergoes a semantic transformation in Matthew, for there the word pertains to Mary, a woman who is already betrothed. Her husband plays an important role in the story; in fact the entire story is narrated from his point of view. From the moment at which Mary is betrothed, she is juridically considered to be Joseph's wife (1,20.24) and Joseph is considered to be her lawful husband (1,16.19). Shortly after she has been given in marriage, it turns out that she is pregnant. This discovery is made before she has left her parental home and has moved in with Joseph. The fact that Joseph wants to break off his relationship with his wife is evidence that he does not consider himself to be the biological father of her child. The obvious question of whether perhaps someone else qualifies for that role, is not answered by the angel, nor by the words from Isaiah, which are attributed to God. These two non-human speakers focus the attention on something completely different: on Jesus' heavenly origin. Their statements are of a theological nature. The angel announces that Jesus is a special child, whose life will from the very beginning be marked by God's Spirit and will thus be able to save his people from their sins. The quotation from Isa 7,14 defines the special position of Jesus' mother by means of the term παρθένος from the LXX. Through its use in this particular story this term acquires the specific meaning 'virgin' which the word itself does not necessarily carry, and thus serves to strengthen the idea that Jesus' origin is an unfathomable mystery.

II. MATTHEW'S INTERPRETATION OF ISAIAH 8,23B-9,1

1. *The Quotation from Isaiah 8,23b-9,1 in Matthew 4,15-16*

In Mt 4,15-16 we find a lengthy citation from Isa 8,23b-9,1:

Γῆ Ζαβουλὼν καὶ γῆ Νεφθαλίμ,
ὁδὸν θαλάσσης, πέραν τοῦ Ἰορδάνου,
Γαλιλαία τῶν ἐθνῶν,
ὁ λαὸς ὁ καθήμενος ἐν σκότει
φῶς εἶδεν μέγα,
καὶ τοῖς καθημένοις ἐν χώρᾳ καὶ σκιᾷ θανάτου
φῶς ἀνέτειλεν αὐτοῖς.

The origin of this citation cannot be determined unequivocally. The wording partly links up with the LXX and partly with the Hebrew text. Moreover, the formulation in the LXX differing on a number of points from the Hebrew text is a complicating factor. The numerous discrepancies are related to the fact that Isa 8,23b–9,1 in the Hebrew text is in the third person, whereas the second person is used in the LXX. In this respect Mt 4,15-16 corresponds to the Hebrew text.

In Matthew, Isa 8,23b is strongly condensed. Only five geographical names have been retained. First the land of Zebulun and the land of Naphtali are mentioned; subsequently further details about their position are given: by or in the direction of the sea[20] and beyond Jordan; and finally the two regions together are referred to as the "Galilee of the gentiles". This enumeration corresponds to the geographical names in the narrative sentences which precede the quotation (4,12f: Galilee – by the sea (the lake) – the district of Zebulun and Naphtali)[21]. In Matthew both Zebulun and Naphtali are referred to as γῆ. This corresponds with the

20. The expression ὁδὸν θαλάσσης can be interpreted in two ways. It can apply to the trade route which led from Damascus to the Mediterranean ("on the road to the sea"; in that case θαλάσσης is a genitive of direction, cf. Mt 10,5: εἰς ὁδὸν ἐθνῶν). However, this interpretation offers no explanation for the accusative ὁδὸν in the middle of a series of nominatives. The second solution is to understand ὁδὸν by analogy with the Hebrew דֶּרֶךְ (cf. 1 Kings 8,48) as a preposition (see ὁδὸν in the LXX, e.g. Deut 1,19; 11,30): the two regions are opposite the sea or by the sea (see F. BLASS – A. DEBRUNNER, *Grammatik des neutestamentlichen Griechisch*, bearbeitet von F. REHKOPF, Göttingen, 1979, 15. Auflage, par. 161.1; W. BAUER, *Griechisch-Deutsches Wörterbuch zu den Schriften des Neuen Testaments und der frühchristlichen Literatur*, herausgegeben von K. ALAND und B. ALAND, Berlin - New York, 1988, 6. völlig neu bearbeitete Auflage, column 1123). The sea then refers to the Sea of Galilee, not to the Mediterranean. I prefer the second option, which also fits best in the context: ὁδὸν corresponds with the preposition πέραν, and ὁδὸν θαλάσσης with παραθαλασσίος in 4,13.

21. G. THOMPSON, *Called-Proved-Obedient: A Study in the Baptism and Temptation Narratives of Matthew and Luke*, in *JTS* 11 (1960) 1-11, points out that the place indications in Mt 4,12-13 and 4,15 have been ordered chiastically.

Hebrew text (twice ארצה) and deviates from the LXX (χώρα – γῆ). There is a minor correspondence with the LXX in the spelling of Naphtali (Νεφθαλίμ with a final μ versus נפתלי). In the use of דרך הים Matthew links up with the choice in the LXX: in both cases we find the hardly elegant Greek expression ὁδὸν θαλάσσης. As does the LXX, Matthew refers to Γαλιλαία, a proper name instead of the less definite גליל ("district").

In Mt 4,16 the parallelism is expressed by the twofold use of the participle form of κάθημαι (the Hebrew text and the LXX have two different verbs here) and by the two aorists εἶδεν and ἀνέτειλεν. The use of this last mentioned grammatical category corresponds to the Hebrew text (twice a qal form) rather than with the LXX, where we encounter first an imperative (ἴδετε) and then a future tense (λάμψει). The selection of the aorists is extremely functional. In this way Matthew emphasises that the future event of which the LXX version speaks, has become reality with Jesus' ministry. Also remarkable is the prominent, initial position of φῶς in Mt 4,16a, contrary to both the Hebrew text and the LXX; this phenomenon too contributes to the parallelism between 4,16a and 4,16b. As regards the hendiadys ἐν χώρᾳ καὶ σκιᾷ θανάτου ("in the dark land of death") the versions of Matthew and of the LXX are similar, while at this point both differ from the Hebrew text. The final word of the quotation (αὐτοῖς) is rather redundant after the dative used previously, and it diverges from the prepositional expression in the Hebrew text (עליהם) and the LXX (ἐφ' ὑμᾶς).

This sums up the principal similarities and differences. The data which have been collected do not permit a clear conclusion as to the origin of the quotation. The author of the first gospel allows himself great freedom in his rendering of the words from Isaiah. It is interesting that Matthew is not the first to do so. Also the LXX offers a free translation of the Hebrew text. This diversity can be explained by the obscurity of the Hebrew text, a phenomenon which is partly to blame for the fact that the text of Isa 8,23b–9,1 has long circulated in various versions. It is possible that for his presentation of Isa 8,23b–9,1 Matthew goes back to a text, the origin of which we can no longer exactly trace. However, this explanation is strongly hypothetical. A more obvious explanation is that Matthew was familiar with the Hebrew as well as with the Greek version and that he revised the quotation thoroughly with a view to fitting it into his story about Jesus[22].

22. See W.D. DAVIES – D.C. ALLISON, *A Critical and Exegetical Commentary on the Gospel According to Saint Matthew, Volume I* (ICC), Edinburgh, 1988, p. 380: "What we probably have before us is an independent rendering of the Hebrew with influence from the LXX".

2. *Matthew's Interpretation of Isaiah 8,23b–9,1*

In the previous section we saw that there are considerable differences between the Hebrew text and the LXX version of Isa 8,23b–9,1 and that Matthew has strongly condensed this text. The omitted parts may have affected Matthew's interpretation of the verse from Isaiah. In order to examine the accuracy of this assertion, it is essential that we first form an idea of the original meaning of Isa 8,23b–9,1.

Isa 8,23b in particular is far from clear in the Hebrew text. There we find the following statement:

כעת הראשׁון הקל ארצה זבלון וארצה נפתלי
והאחרון הכביד דרך הים עבר הירדן גליל הגוים

This sentence consists of two parallel segments: הראשׁון corresponds to האחרון, and the hifil הקל with the hifil הכביד[23]. The first pair of concepts could be a time adjunct ("in the past" – "in the future"), but they could also be conceived as ordinals ("the first [aggressor]" – "the last"). The two verbs are ambiguous as well: the hifil form of קלל means "to belittle", the hifil form of כבד here means either "to oppress" or "to glorify"[24].

Combining these possibilities we can develop two different interpretations. The first is that 8,23b describes the escalating disaster overtaking the northern kingdom (Israel): the first Assyrian invasion (under Tiglath-pileser III in 733-32) is soon followed by a second, even more disastrous than the first (under Shalmaneser V in 722). The verse links up remarkably well with Isaiah's theological analysis of the political situation in the period of the Syro-Ephraimite war (7,1–8,20). The fall of the northern kingdom marks the beginning of a period of peace for Judah, that is to say, for the nation that now wanders in darkness and that will soon see a great light (9,1). The text contains a sharp contrast between the situation of Israel (8,23b) and the situation of Judah (9,1). Verses 9,5-6 illustrate that this hoped-for turning point coincides with the birth of a new scion at the royal palace; when he ascends the throne of David, the southern kingdom will enter a long period of peace.

The second interpretation likewise suggests that the text contains an antithesis, but it does not assume the contrast to exist between 8,23b and 9,1, but within 8,23b itself. The first clause of 8,23b pictures the tribulation, brought over the northern districts by an unspecified subject

---

23. In 2 Sam 6,22 we come across the same verbs, except that they are in the niphal.

24. The first option can be found in the *King James Version* ("…[he] did more grievously afflict her"), the second option in the *New Revised Standard Version* ("he will make glorious").

(God or the king of Assur); the second clause, in contrast, heralds the dawning of a hopeful future for these regions. For the people of the northern kingdom, overrun by the Assyrian armies, a glorious future is in store: the people who now wander in darkness will see a great light.

The translators of the LXX have abandoned the distinction between Israel and Judah and interpreted Isa 8,23b–9,1 as a description of the whole population of the Jewish land. This is particularly illustrated by the insertion of τὰ μέρη τῆς Ἰουδαίας. Thus the text no longer merely refers to the political situation in the eighth century but is given a wider implication. This is also evident from the fact that, through the use of vocatives and of the second person plural, the two verses have been formulated as an appeal.

The question now arises which selection Matthew makes from this wide spectrum. He does not side with the LXX translators, for Jesus leaves Judea, where John was active (3,1) and takes refuge in Galilee. The topographical names in Mt 4,15 link up with the list in the Hebrew text. The ambiguity of that text is straightened out by Matthew and solved in one particular direction. He opts for the second above-mentioned interpretation. Isa 8,23b–9,1 proclaims that the northern regions which were the first to be overwhelmed by a foreign superpower, will also be the first to share in the salvation. The temporal meaning of the pair of concepts הראשׁון / האחרון ("in the past" versus "in the future") fits in excellently with Matthew's interpretation: the future that is heralded in Isaiah, has in his opinion come about when in Galilee Jesus starts to preach of the kingdom of heaven.

In what way has Matthew woven the citation into the story he narrates? Before we can answer this question, we must first deal with two related topics: what exactly are the boundaries of the text in which the quotation has been incorporated and which function does this fragment fulfil within the entire composition of the first gospel?

As concerns the demarcation, the debate focuses on the question of whether 4,17 must be considered to form an integral part of the passage opening in 4,12. In the wake of Kingsbury and Bauer in particular, many exegetes regard this verse as a programmatic heading for the second part of Matthew's gospel (4,17–16,20), in which Jesus preaches the imminence of the kingdom of heaven[25]. In 16,21 the third part begins (16,21–

25. J.D. KINGSBURY, *The Structure of Matthew's Gospel and His Concept of Salvation-History*, in *CBQ* 35 (1973) 451-474; ID., *Matthew: Structure, Christology, Kingdom*, Philadelphia, 1975; D.R. BAUER, *The Structure of Matthew's Gospel: A Literary-Critical Examination*, Diss. Union Theological Seminary, Richmond, VA, 1985; = *The Structure*

28,20), in which the passion of Jesus is central. This last part is initiated
in 16,21 with a sentence that is closely related to 4,17. This proposition
for the overall structure of the book places a strong caesura between
4,16 and 4,17. This caesura however is extremely disputable, since ἀπὸ
τότε at the beginning of 4,17 has a connecting rather than a dividing
function (the same goes for ἀπὸ τότε in 16,21 and 26,16)[26]. I therefore
prefer to consider 4,17 to be an integral element of 4,12-17.

Also disputed is the precise place and function of 4,12–17 in the
structure of Matthew's gospel. In my opinion this brief segment forms
a kind of hinge between the prologue of the book (1,1–4,11) and the
following description of Jesus' activities in Galilee (4,18–16,12). This
idea is based on the observation that in 4,12–17 elements are mentioned which the reader is already familiar with, having read 1,1–4,11,
and that here at the same time themes are brought up which are not
developed until later[27].

These notes about the demarcation of 4,12-17 and the function of this
passage in the structure of the gospel as a whole demonstrate that the
quotation is woven into the narrated history in three different ways.
Firstly, the quotation forms a scriptural basis for the statement that Jesus
withdraws to Galilee (4,12ff). The introductory formula (4,13) indicates
that his departure for that district and his selection of Capernaum as his
home is a deliberate choice: he acts in this way in order to fulfil what
was prophesied in the Scriptures. Secondly, the quotation suggests that
Jesus' proclamation of the imminence of the kingdom can be represented as the rise of a great light. Thirdly, since the quotation is embedded in a passage which takes up important themes from the prologue and

of Matthew's Gospel: A Study in Literary Design (JSNT SS, 31), Sheffield, 1988. See
also the arrangement by J. GNILKA, Das Matthäusevangelium, 2. Teil (HTKNT, I/2),
Freiburg - Basel - Wien, 1988, p. 524: Vorgeschichte: 1,1–4,16; 1. Hauptteil: 4,17–
16,20; 2. Hauptteil: 16,21–25,46; Passion und Ostern: 26,1–28,20.

26. See F. NEIRYNCK, ΑΠΟ ΤΟΤΕ ΗΡΞΑΤΟ and the Structure of Matthew, in ETL
64 (1988) 21-59; = ID., Evangelica II (BETL, 99), 1991, pp. 141-182.

27. This can be substantiated as follows: a) Jesus' departure (4,12) forms a moment in
a continuous line which is prepared for in the prologue (2,12f: the magi leave; 2,14.22:
Joseph flees) and is followed up in 12,15; 14,13 and 15,21 (here, as in 4,12, Jesus is the
subject of the action); b) the many indications of place in 4,12-17 echo similar data in Mt
2, where the correspondences between 4,12-16 and 2,22-23 are particularly conspicuous;
c) the connection between 4,12-17 and the prologue is further shown by the reference to
John, already introduced in Mt 3, and by the fact that Jesus' message about the kingdom
of heaven corresponds literally with that of John (3,2; 4,17); d) as regards the connection
between 4,12-17 and what follows, the important role of Capernaum during Jesus's stay
in Galilee (4,13; cf. 8,5; 9,1; 11,13; 17,24) must be mentioned, as well as the fact that
the kingdom of heaven is a central theme in Jesus' preaching, which is also carried on
when he begins to teach his disciples about his suffering, death and resurrection in Jerusalem.

also anticipates themes which later on in the book will play an important role, it highlights matters which according to Matthew are characteristic of Jesus' ministry.

In Galilee, Capernaum becomes Jesus' new home base. The stories from Mt 8,2–9,34 are largely set in this town. It is also the last place which Jesus visits before he leaves Galilee to go to Judea (19,1); shortly before his departure he has another long interview with his disciples (17,24–18,35). In view of the more or less fixed connection between Capernaum and other topographical data (the house, the lake, the mountain) it is plausible that also a number of lengthy passages in which Capernaum is not explicitly mentioned, are also set in that town or its immediate vicinity (5,2-7,28 and 13,1-52). Capernaum is not mentioned anywhere in the Old Testament. The link with Isa 8,23b–9,1 is made on the basis of Naphtali, the region in which the town is situated.

In his new sphere of activity Jesus comes into contact with "the people (ὁ λαός) who sit in darkness". The term ὁ λαός is used twice in the prologue in connection with the description of Jesus' future ministry: he will save his people from their sins (1,21) and he will be the shepherd of the people of Israel (2,7). At the start of his ministry in Galilee, faithful to his mission, he focuses his attention on his people, on the lost sheep of the house of Israel (10,6; cf. 9,36; 15,24). To them he is a great light, and the people see that light (4,16), like the magi saw the rising star (2,2.9). Through the appearance of the star, the magi went on a journey, to the newborn king of the Jews. The people on the other hand are immobile: twice it is said that they are sitting in a dark and deadly region. The light itself sets itself in motion and comes to them: the light has dawned on them[28]. In continuation of 1,21 "sitting in darkness" refers to being trapped in sin, but this formulation also links up with 9,36 where the multitudes are described as sheep having no shepherd. In Jesus they find a new leader, one who enables them to leave the darkness and to become the light of the world themselves (5,14-16); whoever does not choose this road, will be thrown into "the outer darkness" (8,12; 22,13; 25,30). Jesus' new work area – in continuation of the LXX – is referred to as the Galilee of the gentiles. This description recalls the fact that this region repeatedly used to be overrun by foreign superpowers. As a result, Galilee had a mixed population. Although Jesus was sent to the lost sheep of the house of Israel, he also meets non-Jews in his wanderings through Galilee and in the neighbouring districts (e.g. 8,5-13; 8,28-34; 15,21-28). By means of another quotation from Isaiah, Mt 12,18-21 em-

---

28. Shortly before Jesus' death a darkness fell over the whole land, which lasted three hours (27,45).

phasises that the gentiles, too, look forward to his coming. All this forms the preparation of the final scene of the book, in which the risen Jesus sends out his disciples to all nations. All these connections serve to indicate that the quotation from Isa 8,23b-9,1 contains the main lines of the entire gospel in a nutshell.

III. THE TWO QUOTATIONS AND THE CHRISTOLOGY OF MATTHEW

After this analysis of the two quotations from Isaiah the question arises of how they are connected and what they contribute to Matthew's christology.

The connection can be clarified as follows. First of all there is a close connection between the two texts from Isaiah in their original context already. Within Isaiah they are in the same literary context, which can be read as a coherent text in the light of the many references to the Syro-Ephraimite war and the disastrous aftermath of that military operation. The turning point in Judah's uncertain fate is constantly related to the birth of a royal child that will guarantee the continuity of the house of David. Also in Matthew, their new literary context, the two texts from Isaiah remain closely connected. They are both applied to the redeeming ministry of Jesus, the son of David, in whom the history of Israel is fulfilled. We have observed that the semantic energy of the two citations is considerably enhanced when in our analysis we do not limit ourselves to the version of the LXX, but also give our full attention to the Hebrew text. Against that broader background it becomes clear that Matthew's interpretation of the two texts from Isaiah forms a new step in the ever colourful history of interpretation. As regards our first example, its development can best be visualised as a linear process: the representation of Isa 7,14 in the LXX forms a link between the Hebrew text and Mt 1,23. The second example does not lend itself very well to such a linear image. The formulation of Mt 4,15-16 has been influenced by the LXX, but in his interpretation of Isa 8,23b–9,1 Matthew links up with one of the two possible readings hidden in the Hebrew text. In this case it was a fascinating discovery that the segments from the original text which were not included by Matthew, were exactly the ones that must have had a guiding influence on his interpretation.

In which respect do the texts from Isaiah form an enhancement for the christology of Matthew? In answering this question I choose the name Emmanuel as my point of departure. This is not the name of Mary's child. By order of the angel the child is given the name Jesus. Emmanuel is a description more typical of his later ministry (cf. Isa 8,10: "for God is with us"): its nature is to make God's presence among his people perceptible. This presence is further elaborated in the second citation which I discussed in this contribution. It shows that Jesus is actively concerned with his people, who are in a crisis situation: they are bowed down by sin, afflicted by illness and abandoned by their leaders. From this nation he forges a new community that is also open to the gentiles.

Still, this does not round up the argument. The programmatic announcement that God will be present in Jesus, is followed later on in the book by statements of Jesus himself to his disciples in which he declares to be present in their midst when they overcome the tensions within their community and become reconciled (18,20: εἰμι ἐν μέσῳ αὐτῶν) and wherever in the world they preach what he taught them (28,20: ἐγὼ μεθ' ὑμῶν εἰμι). In these statements the speaker himself assumes the position which in 1,23 was reserved for God (μεθ' ἡμῶν ὁ θεός); he himself is the God who is with us. His community can be assured of his presence unto the end of the world (28,20), but when that moment has come, it will be revealed that this presence has taken a totally unexpected form: Jesus is present in the shape of a person who is hungry or thirsty, naked, or a stranger, ill or in prison (25,31-46). That Jesus is God-with-us, thus becomes an ethical imperative which inspires the disciples to show solidarity with people in distress just as Jesus himself did.

Tilburg Faculty of Theology   Wim WEREN
Academielaan 9
NL-5037 ET Tilburg

THE PHRASEOLOGY OF "KNOWING YHWH"
IN THE HEBREW BIBLE
A PRELIMINARY STUDY OF ITS SYNTAX AND FUNCTION

The idea of "knowing YHWH" is mentioned in a number of instances in the Hebrew Bible. As far as the Book of Isaiah is concerned, there are eight textual units in which this idea is expressed, four of which appear to be editorial in the sense that they are either a late redactional expansion (Isa 19,16-25; 52,3-6)[1] or *Wiederaufnahme* of an existing non-Isaian (36,1–39,8 → 1 Kings 18,13–20,19)[2] or Isaian text (60,1-22 → c. 1–55, especially c. 49)[3]. As a result, the majority of texts in Isaiah continuing the motif of "knowing YHWH" are part of that section of the book which is usually attributed to Deutero-Isaiah (41,20; 43,10; 45,3.6; 49,23.26)[4].

[19,21]   ונודע יהוה למצרים וידעו מצרים את יהוה ביום ההוא

[37,20]   וידעו כל ממלכות הארץ כי אתה יהוה לבדך

41,20   למען יראו וידעו וישימו וישכילו יחדו כי יד יהוה עשתה זאת

43,10-11   למען תדעו ותאמינו לי ותבינו כי אני הוא לפני לא נוצר אל
ואחרי לא יהיה אנכי אנכי יהוה ואין מבלעדי מושיע

---

* The following abbreviations are used in the present contribution (alphabetical order):
EAK, Expression of the Act of Knowing
ECK, Expression of the Content of Knowing
IF, I-Formula
IFl, I-Formula long form
IFs, I-Formula short form
pKY, phraseology of "Knowing YHWH"
RF, Recognition Formula

It is with pleasure that I dedicate this contribution to Wim Beuken. It was a privilege to work with such a faithful colleague and good friend.

1. Isa 19,16-25: cf. H. WILDBERGER, *Jesaja* (BKAT, 10/2), Neukirchen-Vluyn, 1978, pp. 729-730; A. SCHOORS, *Jesaja* (BOT, 9), Roermond, 1972, pp. 120-123. – Isa 52,3-6: cf. A. SCHOORS, *Arrière-fond historique et critique d'authenticité des textes Deutéro-Isaiens*, in *OLP* 2 (1971) 105-135, pp. 125-127.
2. Cf. H. WILDBERGER, *Jesaja* (BKAT, 10/3), Neukirchen-Vluyn, 1982, pp. 1369-1481 and the synoptic overview pp. 1484-1495. See also SCHOORS, *Jesaja* (n. 1), pp. 208-217.
3. Cf. SCHOORS, *Jesaja* (n. 1), pp. 354-360; W.A.M. BEUKEN, *Jesaja*. Deel III A (POT), Nijkerk, 1989, pp. 179-180.
4. K. ELLIGER, *Deuterojesaja* (BKAT, 11/1), Neukirchen-Vluyn, 1978, pp. 485-489 argues that Isa 45,1-7 "ist keine ursprüngliche Einheit, sondern wahrscheinlich eine redaktionelle Komposition, zu der wenigstens zwei Einheiten benutzt worden sind".

45,3   למען תדע כי אני יהוה הקורא בשמך אלהי ישראל

45,6   למען ידעו ממזרח שמש וממערבה כי אפס בלעדי אני יהוה ואין עוד

49,23   וידעת כי אני יהוה אשר לא יבשו קוי

49,26   וידעו כל בשר כי אני יהוה מושיעך וגאלך אביר יעקב

[52,6]   לכן ידע עמי שמי לכן ביום ההוא כי אני הוא המדבר הנני

[60,16]   וידעת כי אני יהוה מושיעך וגאלך אביר יעקב

The expression of the idea "knowing YHWH" occurs in a variety of patterns employing a particular type of phraseology. In addition to this, "knowing YHWH" is closely associated with the description of divine actions in the history of Israel[5], and in particular with the announcement of those actions which are going to take place.

Following W. Zimmerli, scholars usually label the Hebrew phraseology associated with "knowing YHWH" (hereafter: pKY) as recognition formula (hereafter: RF; *Erkenntnisformel*)[6]. The term "formula", how-

---

5. Cf. R. RENDTORFF, *Die Offenbarungsvorstellungen im Alten Testament*, in W. PANNENBERG (ed.), *Geschichte als Offenbarung* (Kerugma und Dogma, 1), Göttingen, ²1965, p. 65: "Wo ausdrücklich vom Erkennen Jahwes geredet wird, geschieht es im Zusammenhang mit seinem geschichtlichen Selbsterweis. Es ist deshalb nich verwunderlich, daß zunächst in der Exodustradition diese Formel gehäuft auftritt"; W. ZIMMERLI, *Erkenntnis Gottes nach dem Buche Ezechiel. Eine theologische Studie* (TB, 19), Munich, 1963, p. 49. See, moreover, B. LANG, *Ezechiel. Der Prophet und das Buch* (EdF, 153), Darmstadt, 1982, p. 96.

6. See, for example, WILDBERGER, *Jesaja* (n. 2), p. 1427 (*ad* Isa 37,20): "... also die formelhafte Wendung, die WZimmerli (...) als »Erkenntnisformel« herausgearbeitet hat... ". See, moreover, ZIMMERLI, *Erkenntnis Gottes* (n. 5), pp. 41-119; = ATANT 27, Zürich, 1954; = *Knowledge of God According to the Book of Ezekiel*, in ID., *I Am Yahweh*, Atlanta, GA, pp. 29-98; ID., *Das Wort des göttlichen Selbsterweis (Erweiswort), eine prophetische Gattung*, in *Mélanges bibliques rédigés en l'honneur de André Robert* (Travaux de l'Institut Catholique de Paris, 4), Paris, 1956, pp. 154-164; ID., *Ich bin Jahwe*, in *Geschichte und Altes Testament. FS A. Alt* (BHT, 16), Tübingen, 1953, pp. 179-205; ID., *Ezechiel* (BKAT, 13/1), Neukirchen-Vluyn, 1969, pp. 55-61; = *Ezekiel 1. A Commentary on the Book of the Prophet Ezekiel, Chapters 1–24* (Hermeneia – A Critical and Historical Commentary on the Bible), Philadelphia, 1979, pp. 37-40. Compare to G.J. BOTTERWECK, *»Gott erkennen« im Sprachgebrauch des Alten Testaments* (BBB, 2), Bonn, 1951. See, moreover, RENDTORFF, *»Offenbarung« im Alten Testament*, in *TLZ* 85 (1960) 833-838; ID., *Die Offenbarungsvorstellungen* (n. 5), pp. 21-41; F. GABORIAU, *Enquête sur la significaton biblique de connaître. Étude d'une racine*, in *Angelicum* 45 (1968) 3-43; ID., *La connaissance de Dieu dans l'Ancien Testament*, in *Angelicum* 45 (1968) 145-183; = *Le thème biblique de la connaisance. Étude d'une racine*, Paris, s.d. (Gaboriau actually takes over the data provided by Botterweck although not with the greatest of care); P. WEIMAR, *Untersuchungen zum priesterschriftlichen Exodusgeschichte* (FzB, 9), Würzburg, 1973, pp. 87-95; J.P. FLOSS, *Jahwe dienen – Göttern dienen. Terminologische, literarische und semantische Untersuchung einer theologischen Aussage zum Gottesverhältnis im Alten Testament* (BBB, 45), Bonn, 1975, pp. 566-589; F. HOSSFELD, *Untersuchungen zu Komposition und Theologie des Ezechielbuches* (FzB, 20), Würzburg, 1977, pp. 40-46; LANG, *Ezechiel* (n. 5), pp. 92-97; I.L. SEELIGMAN, *Erkenntnis Gottes und historisches Bewußtsein im Alten Testament*, in H. DONNER (ed.),

ever, does not appropriately cover the full range of the constructions involved since their structure and wording are not confined to one specific formulaic pattern.

Generally speaking, Hebrew pKY is made up of two primary constituents[7]:

– The grammatical formula ידע כי: the expression of the act of knowing in the strict sense of the word (hereafter: EAK; *Erkenntnisaussage*). This formula is linked to the mention or announcement of a divine action.

– A variable expression of the content of knowing (hereafter: ECK; *Erkenntnisinhalt*) which is either free or formulaic. In the latter case it represents the formula אני יהוה or the I-Formula[8], which has a short and long form (hereafter: IFs and IFl respectively).

The present paper will begin with a description of the form and setting of the pKY in the Hebrew Bible. In the second section I will then focus on the syntax and function of this phraseology.

I. The Form and Setting of the Phraseology of "Knowing YHWH"

1. *Form of the Phraseology*

The pKY: ידע כי (EAK: constant) + an expression of the content of the knowing (ECK: variable) appears roughly 150 times in the Hebrew

Beiträge zur alttestamentlichen Theologie. FS W. Zimmerli, Göttingen, 1977, pp. 414-445; J.L. SKA, *La sortie d'Égypte (Ex 7–14) dans le récit sacerdotal (P⁸) et la tradition prophétique*, in *Bib* 60 (1979) 191-215, pp. 207-208; W.H. BROWNLEE, *Ezekiel 1–19* (WBC, 28), Waco, TX, 1986, pp. 96-97; D. BODI, *The Book of Ezekiel and the Poem of Erra* (OBO, 104), Fribourg - Göttingen, 1991, pp. 297-305; C. LEVIN, *Erkenntnis Gottes durch Elijah*, in *TZ* 48 (1992) 329-342; J. STRONG, *Ezekiel's Use of the Recognition Formula in his Oracles Against the Nations*, in *Perspectives in Religious Studies* 22 (1995) 115-133.

7. See *THAT* I, col. 679-680; *TWAT* III, col. 501-502; RENDTORFF, *Offenbarungsvorstellungen* (n. 5), p. 37; ZIMMERLI, *Erkenntnis* (n. 5), pp. 88-107.

8. There is lack of unanimity with respect to the designation of the formula אני יהוה. In this regard, see WEIMAR, *Untersuchungen* (n. 6), pp. 88-89 n. 27: *Selbstvorstellungsformel/Selbstschilderung* (Zimmerli); *Selbstkundgabe* (Rendtorff); *Selbstbezeugungsformel*, but primarily *Heiligkeits-/Hoheitsformel*, respectively *Heilsgeschichts-/Huldformel* (Elliger); *Legitimationsformel* (Feucht); *Selbstpräsentation* (G. Lohfink). For a treatment of the I-formula, see cf. C. FEUCHT, *Untersuchungen zum Heiligkeitsgesetz* (Theologische Arbeiten, 20), Berlin, 1964, pp. 126-144 (p. 131: *Ich-bin-Aussage*); G. LOHFINK, *Eine alttestamentliche Darstellungsform für Gotteserscheinungen in den Damaskusberichten (Apg 9; 22; 26)*, in *BZ* nF 9 (1965) 246-257; ID., *Paulus vor Damaskus. Arbeitsweisen der neueren Bibelwissenschaft dargestellt an den Texten Apg 9,19; 22,3-21; 26,9-18* (SBS, 4), Stuttgart, 1965, p. 55; R. RENDTORFF, *Geschichte und Wort im Alten Testament*, in *EvT* 22 (1962), 621-649; W. ZIMMERLI, *»Offenbarung« im Alten Testament. Ein Gespräch mit R. Rendtorff*, in *EvT* 22 (1962) 15-31.

Bible, of which 76 times in the Book of Ezekiel[9]. The form of the pKY can be described as follows:

a) ידע כי + divine utterance from YHWH concerning himself (1st sing.) (107x)

(1) ECK is stereotypically formulated: IFs and IFl (96x). The form of the verb ידע is variable as is its subject.

* *weqataltí* (84x): subjects being
- Israelites (53x)
  IFs: Exod 10,2; 1 Kings 20,13.28; Ezek 6,7.14; 7,4.27; 11,10.12; 12,16.20; 13,9.14.21.23; 14,8; 16,62 (Jerusalem); 20,38; 22,16 (Jerusalem); 23,49; 24,24.27; 36,38
  IFs: Exod 6,7; 16,12; 29,46; **Isa 49,23.26; 60,16**; Ezek 5,13; 6,10.13; 7,9; 12,15; 15,7; 17,21; 20,42.44; 21,10; 22,22; 28,26; 33,29; 34,27.30; 37,13.14; 39,22.28; Joel 2,27; 4,17
- non-Israelites (34x)
  IFs: Exod 14,4; Ezek 29,6.16.21; 30,19.26; 32,15 (Egypt); Ezek 25,5.7 (Amon); Ezek 25,11 (Moab); Ezek 26,6 (Tyre); Ezek 35,9.15 (Edom); Ezek 28,23.24; 38,23; 39,6 (the nations)
  IFl: Exod 7,5; 14,18; Ezek 30,8.25 (Egypt); Ezek 25,17 (Philistia); Ezek 28,22; 36,23.36; 37,28; 39,7 (the nations); Ezek 21,10 (non-exclusive)
- objects
  IFs: Ezek 35,4; 36,14 (mountains); 37,6 (legs)
  IFl: Ezek 17,24 (trees); Ezek 35,12 (mountains)
* *yiqtol* (6x)
- בזאת תדע (1x)
  non-Israelites
  IFs: Exod 7,17 (Pharaoh)
- למען תדע (5x)
  Israelites
  IFl: Deut 29,5; Lev 23,43; **Isa 45,6**
  non-Israelites
  IFl: Exod 8,18 (Pharaoh); **Isa 45,3** (Cyrus)

---

9. Cf. ZIMMERLI, *Erkenntnis* (n. 5), pp. 41-78; compare with BOTTERWECK, *»Gott Erkennen«* (n. 6), pp. 15-17 and GABORIAU, *Le thème biblique de la connaissance* (n. 6), pp. 52-54. Errors: Botterweck: Ezek 7,14 → 7,4; 7,22 → 7,27; 21,16 → 21,10; 22,17?; Gaboriau: Ezek 7,14 → 7,4; 7,32 → 7,27; 21,16 → 21,10; 29,19 → 29,9; Zimmerli: Ezek 29,9 → 25,5. The enumeration provided by Botterweck and Gaboriau is incomplete. The following references are lacking in Zimmerli's enumeration: Exod 18,11; Josh 2,9; 23,13; Jer 32,8; Hos 2,10; 11,3; Jon 4,2; Ps 56,10; 119,75. Compare further with FLOSS, *Jahwe dienen* (n. 6), pp. 566-589.

* $q^e tol$ (imp. 1x)
  non-Israelites
    IFs: Ps 46,11
* $q^e tol$ (inf. 4x): with
  Israelites
    IFs: Jer 24,7
    IFl: Exod 31,13; Ezek 20,12.20
* $qat\bar{o}l$ (1x)
  human persons
    IFl: Jer 9,23

(2) The ECK is not stereotypically formulated (11x). The form of ידע
is variable and the subject is almost always the Israelites.
* $qatal$ (1x)
  Israelites: Hos 2,10
* $weqatalti$ (4x)
  Israelites: Jer 16,21; Ezek 14,23; Joel 2,27; Nah 2,4
* $yiqtol$ (6x)
  – למען תדע (4x)
  Israelites: Lev 23,43; **Isa 43,10; 45,6**; Jer 44,29
  – בעבור תדע (1x)
  non-Israelites: Exod 9,14 (Pharaoh)
  – לכן תדע (1x)
  Israelites: **Isa 52,6**

b) ידע כי + human utterance directed towards YHWH (2nd sing.) (15x).
  ECK is never stereotypically formulated. The form of ידע is variable
and its subjects are both Israelites and non-Israelites.
* $qatal$ (5x)
  – ידע (4x)
  Israelites: Judg 6,37; Jon 4,2; Ps 119,75
  non-Israelites: Job 42,2
  – בזאת ידע (1x)
  Israelites: Ps 41,12
* $weqatalti$ (2x)
  non-Israelites: 2 Kings 19,19 = **Isa 37,20**
* $yiqtol$ (6x)
  – וידע
  Israelites: 1 Kings 18,37
  enemies: Ps 83,19; 109,27
  – למען ידע
  Israelites: 1 Kings 8,43 = 2 Chron 6,33

– יודע (*Niphal*)
YHWH: 1 Kings 18,36
* $q^e tol$ (inf. 2x)
Israelites: 1 Kings 8,43 = 2 Chron 6,33

c) ידע כי + an utterance concerning YHWH (3rd sing.) (43x)

Here too we only encounter non-stereotypical formulations of the ECK. The form of ידע and the subject of "knowing" are variable.

* *qatal* (9x)
– ידע
Israelites: Judg 17,13; Ps 140,13; 2 Chron 25,16
non-Israelites: Exod 18,11; Josh 2,9; 2 Kings 5,15
– לא ידע
an Israelite: Judg 16,20
– זה ידע
an Israelite: Ps 56,10
– אני ידעתי
an Israelite: Ps 135,5
– עתה ידע
an Israelite: Ps 20,7

weqataltí (13x)
Israelites: Exod 16,6; Num 16,30; Deut 4,39; 7,9; 8,5; 9,3.6; 11,2; Josh 23,14; Zech 2,13; 4,9; 6,15
Zion: Zech 2,15

* *yiqtol* (11x)
– וידע
Israelites: Jer 32,8; 1 Sam 17,46.47
human persons: **Isa 41,20**
enemies: Ps 59,14
– ידוע תדע
Israelites: Josh 23,13
– בזאת תדע
Israelites: Num 16,28; Josh 3,10
– למען תדע
Israelites: **Isa 45,6**
non-Israelites: Exod 8,6; 9,29 (Pharaoh)

* *wayyiqtol* (4x)
Israelites: 2 Sam 5,12; Zech 11,11; 1 Chron 14,2; 2 Chron 33,13

*$q^e tol$ (imp. 3x)
Israelites: 1 Kings 10,10; Ps 100,3
human persons: Ps 4,4

*$q^e tol$ (inf. 3x)

– לדעת

Israelites: Deut 4,35

– למען דעת

Israelites: Josh 4,24; 1 Kings 8,60

d) Besides the standard EAK ידע כי we also find two examples of the construction ידע אשר (ידע + object clause introduced by אשר):

(1) ידע אשר + utterance of YHWH concerning himself (1st sing.) (formulaic)

yiqtol: למען אשר ידעו אני יהוה

Israelites: Ezek 20,26

(2) ידע אשר + utterance concerning YHWH (3rd sing.) (1x) (non-formulaic)

yiqtol: למען תדעון יפלה יהוה בין מצרים ובין ישראל

non-Israelites: Exod 11,7 (Pharaoh and his servants)

e) On a couple of occasions we find the pKY constructed with a direct object employing את: ידע את יהוה (*Akkusativaussage*)[10].

(1) The combination ידע + direct object + object clause:

ידע את יהוה כי + divine utterance of YHWH concerning himself (formulaic expression)

a human person: Jer 9,23 (*qatōl*: inf. abs.)

Israelites: Jer 24,7 (*q^e tol*: inf. cstr.)

(2) The expression ידע את יהוה: utterance of YHWH concerning himself (formulaic and non-formulaic)

* ידע אתי (formulaic): Jer 31,34 (*yiqtol*; subject: unspecified); Ezek 38,16 (למען + *q^e tol*; subject = the nations). Compare with Jer 4,22; 9,2.5; 22,16.

* ידע את יהוה (formulaic): Hos 2,22 (*weqataltí*; subject: Israel). Compare with Hos 5,4; 6,3; Hab 2,14

* ידע את (יהוה) (non-formulaic): Num 14,34 (*weqataltí*; subject: Israelites); Ezek 25,14 (*weqataltí*; subject: Edomites). Compare with Ezek 39,21 ראה (v. 22: ידע)[11]. Cf. also **Isa 45,4.5**; Jer 2,8; Ps 36,11; 79,6 (with suffix).

(3) A construction employing the term למען can be found in 1 Kings 8,43 (= 2 Chron 6,33): למען ידעו(ן) כל עמי הארץ את שמך (utterance addressed to YHWH).

---

10. ZIMMERLI, *Erkenntnis* (n. 5), p. 73 n. 48 and 49.

11. ידע/ראה: see, for example, Exod 14,4.18.31; 16,6; 1 Sam 14,38; 1 Kings 18,36. 37.39; Ezek 39,21. Cf. also *ibid.*, p. 15 n. 22 and p. 21 n. 31; *TWAT* III, col. 504, 507.

(4) There remains the pKY ‫ידע את יהוה‬: an utterance concerning YHWH (formulaic; IFl): **Isa 19,21** (*weqataltí*; subject: Egypt). Compare with Exod 5,2: ‫לא ידעתי את יהוה‬ (subject: Pharaoh). In Josh 4,24 we find a *qᵉtol* (inf.): ‫למען דעת כל עמי הארץ את יד יהוה‬.

In 2 Kings 5,8 and Ezek 33,33, the recognition of YHWH is closely associated with the recognition of the prophet[12]. Compare this with Num 16,28 and Ezek 2,5.

Conclusion

The phrase ‫ידע כי אני יהוה‬ is a formulaic expression of which the form *weqataltí* (‫ידע‬) + object clause ‫כי אני יהוה‬ (IFs or IFl) can be found 83 times in the Old Testament. In 49 places we find the Israelites as subject of this recognition of YHWH and in 34 places non-Israelites are the subject. This recognition formula in the strict sense of the word appears most frequently in the book of Ezekiel (69x) and a few times in Exodus (7x), 1 Kings (2x), Dt-Isa (1x) and Joel (1x). Ezekiel employs the formula in his judgement oracles (*Gerichtsworte*[13]) against Jerusalem and Judah (c. 1–24: 36x), in his oracles against the foreign nations (c. 25–32: 19x) and in his announcement of salvation for Israel (c. 33–39: 22x). With respect to the latter group of RFs, however, we also encounter texts which deal with YHWH's anger against the nations (c. 35, Edom and c. 38–39, Gog and Magog: 8x). The relationship between the recognition of YHWH and the judgement of Israel's enemies / salvation for Israel is likewise to be found in Exodus (5x), 1 Kings (1x), Dt-Isa (2x)[14], Trito-Isa (1x) and Joel (1x). In Exod 16,12 and 29,46 we find the RF (*weqataltí*) in association with the intervention of YHWH in Israel's favour. Compare also Exod 29 with 31,13 and Ezek 20,12.20.

The strict RF ‫ידע כי אני יהוה‬ can also be found a few of times in constructions with a particle of purpose + *yiqtol* (‫למען תדע‬: 5x / ‫בזאת תדע‬: 1x) or a *qᵉtol* (inf.) with ‫ל‬ (final meaning) (‫לדעת‬: 4x). The *yiqtol* con-

---

12. ZIMMERLI, *Erkenntnis* (n. 5), p. 77.
13. Cf. *ibid.*, pp. 44-45; RENDTORFF, *Offenbarungsvorstellungen* (n. 5), p. 38; SKA, *La sortie d'Egypte* (n. 6), p. 207.
14. See SCHOORS, *Jesaja* (n. 1), pp. 306-308; ID., *I am God Your Saviour: A Form-Critical Study of the Main Genres in Is. XL–LV* (SVT, 24), Leiden, 1973, pp. 89, 113, 119. – Where the nations are subject of the "knowing of YHWH" this does not mean that they partake of his salvation: cf. *ibid.*, p. 119: "The prophet explicitly deals with YHWH's salvific activity on behalf of Israel although the nations will be its witnesses. In the midst of their own ruin (Ex. XIV 4…), the Egyptians also came to know YHWH but no one would regard this as a kind of participation in his salvation. Similarly, Ezekiel proclaims that YHWH will be recognised in the destruction of Zion (Ez. XXVIII 22) without implying any level of participation in his salvation. These utterances are entirely theocentric and make no pronouncement on the salvific status of the pagan spectators".

struction is employed in Ezek 20,26 (אשר ידע אשר למען); Exod 7,17; 8,18; Lev 23,43; Deut 29,5; 1 Kings 8,43 = 2 Chron 6,33 and **Isa 45,3.6**. The *qᵉtol* construction is found twice in Ezekiel (20,12.20) and elsewhere in Exod 31,13; Josh 4,24 and Jer 24,7. The construction with *qatōl* (inf. abs.) occurs only in Jer 9,23[15]. Of the non-*weqataltí* forms, Exod 7,17; 8,18 (judgement for Egypt); Jer 9,23 (judgement for Judah); Jer 24,7 (vision: salvation for the exiles, judgement for the rest of Judah) and Ezek 20,26 (judgement) are associated with an announcement of judgement. **Isa 45,3.6** are part of a salvation and call oracle (Cyrus). Exod 31,13 and Ezek 20,12.20 relate the RF to the commandment on the Sabbath. Deut 29,5, in conclusion, is a parenetic reminiscence.

The non-formulaic pKY is constructed with *weqataltí* as well as *qatal*, *yiqtol* and *qᵉtol* (imp. and inf.). Thus the EAK, in the narrow sense (ידע כי), remains formulaic although the shifting use of verbal forms makes it much more heterogeneous. The ECK varies considerably[16]: no one can compare to YHWH (Exod 8,6; 9,14; 18,11; Deut 4,35.39; 7,9; 2 Kings 19,19; **Isa 37,20; 43,10; 52,6**; Ps 135,5; compare also with **Isa 45,6**) / YHWH is God (1 Sam 17,46; Ps 56,10; 59,14; 100,3; 2 Chron 33,13) / the land belongs to YHWH (Exod 9,29) / YHWH is in the midst of his people (Joel 7,27; compare also with Exod 8,18) / YHWH led Israel out of Egypt (Exod 16,6; Lev 23,43; Deut 11,2; compare also with Exod 6,7; 18,10f.; 29,46) / YHWH has given Israel the land (Deut 9,3.6; Josh 2,9; 3,10) / YHWH has sent… (Num 16,28.30; Zech 2,13.15; 4,9; 6,15; 1 Kings 18,36; 2 Kings 5,8.15) / YHWH is concerned for the welfare of his people (Deut 8,5; Josh 23,13f.) / the name of YHWH (1 Kings 8,43; Jer 16,21; Ps 83,19; 2 Chron 6,33) / the word of YHWH (2 Kings 10,10; Jer 32,8; 44,29; Zech 11,11) / the hand of YHWH (Josh 4,24; **Isa 41,20**; compare also with Exod 8,5) / YHWH has done this (Ezek 14,23; Ps 4,4; 20,7; 109,27; 135,5; 140,13; 1 Sam 17,47; 2 Sam 5,12; Judg 16,20; 17,13; compare also with Jer 9,23; Ezek 20,44; 28,22).

These non-formulaic expressions function in a context of judgement in which YHWH chooses salvation/judgement for Israelites and non-Israelites[17]. Salvation for the Israelites can be found in Exod 6,6; 18,10f.; Lev 23,43; Deut 2,6; Josh 23,13; 2 Sam 5,12; 1 Kings 8,43.60; 2 Chron 6,33 / Deut 4,35.39; 7,9; 8,5; 11,2; Josh 4,24; 23,14 / **Isa 41,20**; Ps 56,10; 135,5; Job 42,2 / Joel 2,27; Zech 2,15; 4,9; 6,15; Ps 20,7; 41,12; 1 Chron

---

15. On the *qatōl*-construction in Jer 9,23, see GK §113e, g and J.C.L. GIBSON, *Davidson's Introductory Hebrew Grammar: Syntax*, Edinburgh, ⁴1994, pp. 116, 123.

16. Cf. BOTTERWECK, *Gott Erkennen* (n. 6), p. 16; *TWAT* III, col. 503; ZIMMERLI, *Erkenntnis* (n. 5), pp. 74-78.

17. Judg 16,20; 1 Kings 18,36; Hos 2,10; Ps 4,4; 100,3; 119,75 do not express the theme of "knowing YHWH" as such.

14,2; 2 Chron 34,13 / Judg 6,37 and for non-Israelites in 2 Kings 5,15. Judgement for the Israelites can be found in Num 16,28.30; 2 Kings 10,10; Jer 16,21; 44,29; Ezek 14,23; 2 Chron 25,16; Zech 11,11; Mal 2,4 and for non-Israelites in Exod 8,6; 9,14; 11,7; Deut 9,3; Josh 3,10; 1 Sam 17,46f.; 1 Kings 20,13.28; 2 Kings 19,19; **Isa 37,20; 43,10; 52,6**; Zech 2,13, and for the enemy in Ps 59,14; 83,19; 109,27; 140,13.

2. *Formulaic Expressions*

As has been stated above, the recognition formula ידע כי אני יהוה is found in a short (IFs) and a long (IFl) form. The syntax of these RFs deserves closer investigation. The ECK of the IFs is articulated on the basis of a nominal clause (a). In the IFl, the expression אני יהוה is expanded in a variety of ways (verbs, nouns, participles, preposition) (b). In addition, the construction ידע כי אני יהוה can be more closely determined via an infinitive clause introduced by ב (c).

a) The short RF ידע כי אני יהוה

The short RF is a combination of the EAK in the strict sense (ידע כי) and the construction אני יהוה (IF) which may be considered an independent nominal clause[18] meaning "I am YHWH". What we have here is the so-called *Selbstvorstellungsformel* or *Selbstaussage* in which YHWH makes mention of his name. I do not wish to suggest here that an unknown god is making himself known by way of this formula. The phrase אני יהוה is rather an expression of superior divine power (*Imponierformel*)[19]. As noted above, I opt for the more neutral designation "I-Formula" (IF).

The short RF can be found 49 times in the OT, particularly in Ezekiel (42x) and elsewhere in Exod 7,17; 10,2; 14,4; 1 Kings 20,13.38; Jer 24,7 and Ps 46,11. On almost every occasion the *weqataltí* of ידע is employed (cf. above). In Ps 46,11 we find אנכי אלהים instead of אני יהוה and in Ezek 13,9; 23,49; 24,24; 28,24; 29,16 occurs the formula אני אדני יהוה[20]. The IFs אני יהוה is used as an independent formulation in Exod 6,2.6.8.29; 12,12 and Num 3,13.41.45.

---

18. ZIMMERLI, *Ich bin Jahwe* (n. 6), p. 181; RENDTORFF, *Offenbarungsvorstellungen* (n. 5), p. 32.

19. ZIMMERLI, *Erkenntnis* (n. 5), p. 58; LANG, *Ezechiel* (n. 5), p. 95; J. HOFTIJZER, *Die Verheißungen an die drei Erzväter*, Leiden, 1956, p. 22 n. 73; B. JACOB, *Mose am Dornbusch. Die beide Hauptbeweisstellen der Quellenscheidung im Pentateuch, Ex 3 und Ex 6, aufs Neue exegetisch geprüft*, in *Monatschrift für Geschichte und Wissenschaft des Judentums* 66 (1922) 11-33, 116-138, 180-200, pp. 187-189. See also above n. 8.

20. For a thorough study of the expression אני אדני יהוה, see J. LUST, *Traditie, redactie en kerygma bij Ezechiel. Een analyse van Ez. XX,1-26* (Verhandelingen van de Koninklijke Vlaamse Academie voor Wetenschappen, Letteren en Schone Kunsten van België; Klasse der Letteren, XXI/65), Brussel, 1969, pp. 71-94.

b) The long RF ידע כי אני יהוה + expansion

In similar fashion to the independent IF, the IF of the RF is also expanded in a variety of ways[21]:

– Verbal expansion: Ezek 5,13; 6,10; 17,21.24; 21,10; 22,22; 35,12; 36,36; 37,14. In **Isa 49,23** a relative clause with אשר is added to the IF (cf. also Gen 15,7). Compare further with the independent short IF in Num 14,35; **Isa 41,17; 42,6; 45,8**; Ezek 5,15.17; 12,25; 14,4.9; 17,24; 21,4.22.37; 22,14; 24,14; 26,14; 30,12; 34,34; 36,36; Nah 3,6.

– Nominal expansion: Exod 6,7 (+ *qotel*); 16,12; 29,46 (+ relative clause); Deut 29,5; Ezek 20,20; 28,26; 34,30; 39,22.28; Joel 4,17 (+ *qotel*). In each of these cases the IF is expanded using the nouns אלהיכם/ אלהיהם. In Ezek 39,7 an adjective is added. Compare with the independent formula in Exod 15,26; Lev 11,44; 18,2.4.5.21.30; 19,3.4.10.12. 14.16.18.25.28.30.31.32.34; 20,7.24; 21,12; 22,2.3.8.30.31.33; 23,22. 43; 24,22; 25,17.55; 32,27; Ezek 20,5.7.19; Zech 10,6. For the addition of a relative clause to the nominal expansion, see Lev 19,36; 25,38; 26,13; Num 15,41.

– Participial expansion: Exod 31,13; **Isa 45,3; 49,26**; Jer 9,23; Ezek 7,9; 20,12; 37,28; Joel 4,17. Compare with the independent formula in Lev 11,45; 20,8; 21,15.23; 22,9.16.32; Num 35,34; **Isa 27,3; 45,7.19; 61,8**; Jer 17,10.

– Prepositional expansion: Exod 8,18; Ezek 34,30. Compare with **Isa 60,22**.

These expansions of the RF exert an influence on the grammatical significance of the IF אני יהוה which, as I already noted, can be understood as a nominal clause. The short and long formulae are similar in terms of content[22]. The formula אני יהוה אלהיכם primarily means "I am YHWH, your God" and not "I YHWH am your God". Where verbal, and to a lesser extent participial expansions of the RF are concerned, the original grammatical structure of the IF is more easily disrupted. The expansion then loses its attributive function and becomes itself a predicate while the name of YHWH becomes an attribute of the subject of the RF[23]. See Ezek 20,12 where אני יהוה מקדשם: "I am YHWH who sanctifies you" becomes: "I, YHWH, sanctify you" and Ezek 17,21 where דברתי אני יהוה: "I am YHWH who has spoken" becomes: "I, YHWH, have spoken".

21. Compare also ZIMMERLI, *Erkenntnis* (n. 5), p. 42; BOTTERWECK, *Gott erkennen* (n. 6), pp. 15-16.
22. Cf. ZIMMERLI, *Ich bin Jahwe* (n. 6), pp. 181-184.
23. *Ibid.*, p. 183.

c) The RF ‫ידע כי אני יהוה‬ + infinitive clause with ‫ב‬

The RF is followed on 16 occasions by an infinitive clause introduced by the preposition ‫ב‬. In 14 cases, this adverbial modifier is associated with the IFs (‫אני יהוה‬): Exod 7,5; 14,18; Ezek 6,13; 12,15; 15,7; 20,42.44; 25,17; 28,22; 30,8.25; 33,29; 34,27; 37,13. In Ezek 5,13 and 39,28 the infinitive clause follows after an expanded IF (verbal and nominal expansion respectively); in Ezek 36,23 the formula ‫נאם אדני יהוה‬ is located between the IFs and the infinitive construction. With regard to the RF of the type ‫ידע את יהוה‬, the adverbial modifier is found in Ezek 38,16. Finally, the RF comes first in Ezek 24,24, 32,15 and 33,33. The infinitive construction with ‫ב‬ need not be exclusively temporal since it can equally well introduce an instrumental nuance[24].

The RF is found primarily at the conclusion of a divine utterance (see 3 below), forming the point at which a related speech of YHWH comes to an end. The RFs in which the IF is followed by an adverbial clause (infinitive with ‫ב‬) always come at the end of the divine utterance. We can distinguish two types:

– The RF with an infinitive clause concludes a speech of YHWH: Exod 7,5 (1-5); 14,18 (15-18); Ezek 5,13 (12-15); 15,7 (1-8); 25,17 (15-17); 30,8 (1-9); 33,29 (23-29); 36,23 (22-23); 39,28 (25-29); 38,16 (14-16); 24,24 (15-24); 32,15 (1-16); 33,33 (30-33). A further expansion introduced by *weqataltí* (Exod 7,5; Ezek 15,7; 30,8; 39,28) or *weyiqtol* (Ezek 5,13) sometimes follows after an infinitive clause

– The RF with an infinitive clause concludes a speech of YHWH but runs on into a second RF[25]: Ezek 6,13 → 14 (11-14); 12,15 → 16 (8-16); 20,42 → 44! (39-44); 28,22 → 23.24.26 (20-26); 30,25 → 26 (20-26); 34,27 → 30 (25-31); 37,13 → 14 (11-14). In each of these cases the first RF with infinitive clause is expanded with *weqataltí* (Ezek 6,14; 12,15f.; 20,43f.; 28,22f.; 30,25f.; 34,27ff.; 37,14), In Ezek 37,13 we find a double infinitive clause.

With respect to the infinitive clause which expands the RF we can distinguish three types according to location and relationship with the context of the RF:

24. ZIMMERLI, *Erkenntnis* (n. 5), p. 51.
25. *Ibid.*, pp. 51-52. According to Zimmerli, only Ezek 30,25/26; 34,27/30 and 37,13/ 14 are "pure" examples hereof. Cf. also ZIMMERLI, *Ezechiel* (n. 6), p. 59*: 6,13/14 and 28,23/24 are redactional. We consider these cases from a merely formal perspective, however, and not from a literary-critical perspective.

– [speech of YHWH] – [RF] – [infinitive clause]

The infinitive clause recapitulates the concluding words of the speech of YHWH or renders them anew in synonymous terminology. What we then encounter is a sort of "pincer device" or "sandwich structure" (pattern ABA') exemplified in the following texts: Exod 7,5; 14,18; Ezek 5,13; 15,7; 25,17; 33,29; 36,23; 37,13. Compare also Ezek 30,23.26. We encounter a complete recapitulation of the concluding words from the speech of YHWH in Exod 7,5 (with the exception of נטה יד instead of ונתן יד!); 14,18 and Ezek 33,29; 36,23; 37,13.

– [speech of YHWH] – [RF] – [infinitive clause]

The infinitive clause summarises the speech of YHWH or adds a concluding specification: Ezek 6,13; 12,15; 20,42.44; 28,22; 30,8; 30,25; 34,27; 38,16; 39,28. There is a connection between the speech and the infinitive clause at the level of content.

– [speech of YHWH] – [infinitive clause] – [RF]

The speech of YHWH comes to an end in the infinitive clause which introduces the RF as a motif of purpose (instrumental ב!): Ezek 24,24; 32,15; 33,33. Compare with the RF בזאת תדע.

3. Literary Setting[26]

As I pointed out above, the pKY is closely associated with a speech concerning the acts of YHWH either by YHWH himself or to YHWH or about YHWH by another. Zimmerli defines this association as *Erweiswort*. G. Fohrer, Hoßfeld and Lang are correct in noting, however, that the pKY is a "deutende Formel" and certainly not an essential device which transforms a speech into a *Erweiswort*[27].

According to Zimmerli, the normative location of the RF in the book of Ezekiel is at the end of the narrative of YHWH's intervention. Hoßfeld nuances this, however, and in line with his approach we can distinguish the following structures[28].

a) The pKY as a concluding formula:

– A non-expanded pKY as absolute end of a speech: Exod 10,2; 14,4; 16,12; 18,11; 1 Kings 20,13.28; (Judg 6,37; **Isa 37,20**; Jer 16,21);

26. Compare ZIMMERLI, *Erkenntnis* (n. 5), pp. 61-69; HOSSFELD, *Untersuchungen* (n. 6), p. 40.

27. ZIMMERLI, *Ezechiel* (n. 6), p. 58*; ID., *Das Wort des göttlichen Selbsterweis* (n. 6). See, however, E. SELLIN – G. FOHRER, *Einleitung in das Alte Testament*, Heidelberg, [10]1965, p. 449; HOSSFELD, *Untersuchungen* (n. 6), pp. 45-46; LANG, *Ezechiel* (n. 5), p. 95.

28. Cf. ZIMMERLI, *Erkenntnis* (n. 5), p. 45 and HOSSFELD, *Untersuchungen* (n. 6), p. 40.

Ezek 6,14; 7,24; 12,16.20; 13,23; 22,16; 23,49; 24,27; 29,16.21; 30,19.
26; 37,6 – as conclusion to a self-contained (small) textual unit within a
speech followed by a messenger formula which introduces a new section: Ezek 7,4; 25,5.7.11; 26,6; 28,24 (Zech 2,13) – as conclusion to
part of a speech after which there is a new commission or a repetition of
the original commission: Ezek 20,26.38; 24,24; 35,15; 38,23.

– An expanded pKY as a concluding syntagma (object clause and addition form one clause): Exod 6,7; 7,5; 8,18; 14,18; 29,46; Lev 23,43
(Josh 4,24; 1 Kings 18,37); **Isa 52,6**; Ezek 17,21; 20,20; 22,22; 28,26;
33,33 – as a concluding syntagma which begins with the pKY and has
subordinate clauses added thereto: Exod 11,7 (1 Kings 8,60; 2 Kings
19,19; **Isa 41,20**); Ezek 6,10; 21,4.10; 25,17; 33,29; 37,28; 38,16
(Zech 2,15).

b) The pKY as an introductory formula:

Exod 7,17; 16,6; 31,13; Num 16,28; Deut 11,2; Josh 2,9; 3,10; Ps
41,12

c) The pKY as a context formula:

Jer 9,23; 44,29; Ezek 13,14-16; 14,23; 15,7; 16,62; 17,24; 20,44;
25,14; 34,30; 36,23.36; 37,14; 39,28f.; Joel 2,27; Zech 4,9; 6,15;
etc..

d) Stringing (*Reihung*):

– connected stringing:
ב + infinitive + verbal clause + pKY: Ezek 6,7-10; 6,13-14; 12,15-16;
28,22-23(24); 30,25-26
ב + infinitive + verbal clause + pKY + *Gottesspruchformel* (נאם אדני
יהוה): Ezek 20,42-44; 34,27-30; 37,13-14
– non-connected stringing:
Deut 4,35.39; 9,3.6; 1 Sam 17,46.47; **Isa 45,3.6; 49,23.26**; Ezek
11,10.12; 13,9(.14); 13,21(.23); 29,6.9; 35,4.9; 39,6.7; 39,21.22.
23.

e) Independent pKY

Exod 8,6; 9,14.29; Deut 7,9; 8,5; 29,5; 1 Kings 8,43; **Isa 19,21;
43,10; 60,16**; Jer 24,7; Ps 4,4; 20,7; 46,11; 56,10; 59,14...; Ezek
5,13; 7,9; 14,8; 20,12; 30,8; 32,15; 35,12; 36,11; Joel 4,17; 2 Chron
6,33.

II. Syntax of the Phraseology of "Knowing YHWH"

1. *Introduction*

In a detailed excursus, J.P. Floß offers a study of the so-called "Wortstellungsschema in der Erkenntnisaussage"[29], meaning thereby the position of the verb in the verbal clause (in this case the pKY) and the interrelationship between consecutive verbal clauses (in this case clauses which precede the pKY)[30]. It is clearly of primary importance that we examine the way in which the pKY is syntactically related to its context. As a matter of fact, its syntactic relationship with what precedes is determinative of the function of the pKY. The pKY is normally seen as a motif of purpose: deeds of YHWH in history intended to let him be known/recognised[31]. Is it possible, however, to substantiate this claim from the perspective of syntax?

To this end an analysis of the place of the pKY in its context is necessary. Where possible I shall appeal to the results published in Floß' study although I feel limited by the fact that I cannot completely concur with his grammatical-syntactical approach. In a somewhat un-nuanced manner, Floß uses the Sumero-Akkadian terms *marû* and *ḥamtu* for the 'imperfect' and 'perfect' aspects respectively of the Hebrew verbal forms[32]. At the same time, he mingles aspect (syntactic category) with *Aktionsart* (lexical / semantic category)[33]. Furthermore, the elements of his *Wortstellungsschema* are over-simplified: *qatal*-x = x-*yiqtol* and

---

29. Floß, *Jahwe dienen* (n. 6), pp. 566-570
30. *Ibid.*, p. 299: "Die Studie W. Zimmerli's hat mich dazu angeregt, sämtlich von ihm aufgefürten Stellen einmal auf das Wortstellungsschema hin zu überprufen und zwar nicht nur die Erkenntnisaussage, sondern auch und vor allem die der EK voraufgehende Aussagen".
31. Cf. Zimmerli, *Erkenntnis* (n. 5), pp. 49-52; Schoors, *I am God Your Saviour* (n. 14), p. 119; Id., *Jesaja* (n. 1), p. 306; Floß, *Jahwe dienen* (n. 6), p. 299; cf. also the critique of Floß below.
32. Cf. W. Gross, *Zur Funktion von Qatal. Die Verbfunktionen in neueren Veröffentlichungen*, in *BN* 4 (1977) 25-38, esp. pp. 26-27. See also *Verbform und Funktion. Wayyiqtol für die Gegenwart? Ein Beitrag zur Syntax poetischer althebräischer Texte* (ATSAT, 1), St. Ottilien, 1976, p. 20. On the question of Hebrew verb form and function, see, moreover, A. Niccacci, *The Syntax of the Verbs in Classical Hebrew* (JSOT SS, 86), Sheffield, 1990; Id., *Lettura sintattica della prosa ebraico-biblica. Principi e applicazioni* (Studium Biblicum Franciscanum Analecta, 31), Jerusalem, 1991; M. Vervenne, *Hebrew Verb Form and Function: A Syntactic Case Study with Reference to a Linguistic Data Base*, in *Actes du second colloque international Bible et Informatique: Méthodes, outils et résultats* (Travaux de linguistique quantitative, 43), Paris - Geneva, 1989, pp. 605-640.
33. Cf. Gross, *Zur Funktion* (n. 32), p. 31.

yiqtol-x = x-*qatal*[34]. I consider it necessary, however, to distinguish between the Hebrew verb forms for the "perfect aspect": *wayyiqtol* (short form)-x or *qatal*-x // (*w*-)x-*qatal* and those for the "imperfect aspect": *w*-*qatal*-x or (*w*-)*yiqtol* (long form)-x[35]. Finally, Floß employs the pattern x-*yiqtol* for the *q*ᵉ*tol* imperative (e.g. Ezek 20,20) and infinitive (e.g. Ezek 24,24), an approach I feel obliged to reject[36]. Clearly, therefore, we must be on our guard against uncritical and simplifying generalisations in our analysis of the *Wortstellungsschema* of the pKY[37].

The idea that the pKY functions as a purposive construction in well-determined speeches of/concerning YHWH is challenged, among others, by Fohrer, Hoßfeld and Lang[38] according to whom the pKY is not used in such a *zielstrebig* way but rather functions emphatically in a text or has a concluding function at the end of a text. The pKY does not transform a divine utterance into a *Erweiswort*. It is an explanatory formula which indicates how the announced or narrated intervention of YHWH should be correctly understood, namely as an action *of* YHWH[39]. While one might question this critique of the pKY as a purposive construction it is our present aim to focus on the question whether the pKY expresses finality from the syntactical perspective.

2. *Syntactic Form and Setting of the pKY*

Floß is of the opinion that, if not expressed in a clearly determined construction (particle or infinitive of purpose), the purposive function of the pKY is rendered via its syntactic composition (*Wortstellung*)[40]. Zimmerli also sees the *weqataltí*, in connection, for example, with a series of *weqataltí* forms, as exhibiting the purposive character of the pKY, basing himself on those phrases which are drafted with a formal construction of purpose[41]. His conclusion, in other words, is not rooted in a thorough analysis of the syntax of the pKY as a whole.

---

34. *Ibid.*, pp. 29-30. Groß uses the specifications *qatal*-x / x-*qatal* / *yiqtol*-x / x-*yiqtol* but points out that in the last analysis such specifications, borrowed as they are from Arabic grammar, are ineffective in providing an accurate description of the Hebrew verbal system. See *ibid.*, p. 25 n. 1.

35. Cf. *ibid.*, p. 29. – Short form: e.g. *yaqtel*; long form: e.g. *yaqtîl*. See also GROSS, *Verbform* (n. 32), pp. 31-38.

36. Cf. ID., *Zur Funktion* (n. 32), p. 30.

37. *Ibid.*, p. 35: "Die Wortstellungsregeln unterliegen der Gefahr zu großen Verallgemeinerung".

38. SELLIN – FOHRER, *Einleitung* (n. 26), p. 449; HOSSFELD, *Untersuchungen* (n. 6), pp. 40-46; LANG, *Ezechiel* (n. 5), pp. 95-97. Compare with ZIMMERLI, *Erkenntnis* (n. 5), p. 14.

39. LANG, *Ezechiel* (n. 5), p. 95.

40. FLOSS, *Jahwe dienen* (n. 6), pp. 299, 585-590.

41. ZIMMERLI, *Erkenntnis* (n. 5), pp. 50-52.

According to Floß, in 121 cases the finality of the phraseology is exclusively rendered via the *Wortstellung*, to which extent we can speak of a *Wortstellungsschema*. With respect to the syntactic composition of the pKY he distinguishes the following: *qatal*-x (97), *yiqtol*-x (14x) and x-*qatal* (2x)[42]. Floß notes that on 113 occasions the position of the verb in the pKY is in agreement with that of the previous clause. He summarises these agreements in a schematic form:

- *qatal*-x + *qatal*-x (pKY) or x-*yiqtol* + *qatal*-x (pKY) (inversion)
- *yiqtol*-x + *yiqtol*-x (pKY) or x-*qatal* + *yiqtol*-x (pKY) (inversion)
- *yiqtol*-x + x-*qatal* (pKY) + *yiqtol*-x (inversion)

All forms of the pKY are held up against this pattern by Floß. The eight cases in which he does not see any agreement between the pKY and the previous clause (Exod 7,17; 14,4.18; 16,6; Num 16,28; Deut 4,39; 7,9[43]) lead him to draw a literary critical conclusion: there is no original cohesion.

I already noted above that Floß' syntactic theory requires some critical nuancing. In light of the fact that the schemas he maintains are far too simplifying, I would like to offer my own survey and briefly discuss the syntactic position and composition of the pKY in biblical Hebrew.

a) In two cases the pKY is an explicit purposive construction:

(1) Particle of purpose + *yiqtol*
- with בעבור: Exod 9,14
- with למען: Exod 8,6.18; 9,29; 11,7; Lev 23,43; Deut 29,5; Josh 4,24; 1 Kings 8,43.60; **Isa 41,20; 43,10; 45,3.6**; Jer 44,29; Ezek 20,26; 38,16; 2 Chron 6,33

According to Floß, the pKY in Exod 8,6 is a *Fremdkörper* which does not belong to the original context of 8,4-9[44]. He bases his opinion on an argumentation which is often difficult to follow: the *marû* (x-*yiqtol*) of v. 6e (= למען תדע) does not have the same logical function – namely the description of an action – as that of v. 5cd; the *ḥamtu* ויאמר כדברך (6d) has its *marû* pendant in v. 7 (*qatal*-x) and not in v. 6e. Floß mistakenly considers ויאמר כדברך (6d) as one single construction while it is in fact a *wayyiqtol* + a nominal clause with *qotel* (direct speech). The pKY introduced by למען connects to the nominal clause כדברך, of which the *weqataltí* of v. 7 is a continuation. It is striking that Floß sees problems

---

42. FLOSS, *Jahwe dienen* (n. 6), pp. 585-586. Floß also includes the imperative among the *yiqtol*-x.

43. *Ibid.*, pp. 586-598. "Daß ausgerechnet und ausschließlich in solchen literarischen Bereichen kein Wortstellungsschema vorliegt bzw. ein solchen gestört ist, in denen wir a priori mit literarisch zusammengesetzten Texten rechnen müssen, spricht für sich" (586).

44. *Ibid.*, pp. 574-575.

here while elsewhere he does not hold up constructions with למען against his *Wortstellungsschema*.

(2) ל-*qᵉtol* (inf.) (purpose): Exod 31,13; Deut 4,35; 1 Kings 8,43; Jer 24,7; Ezek 20,12.20; 2 Chron 6,33.

The pKY in each of these cases is considered a purposive construction since it is apparent from the syntax that it is connected as such to a preceding clause.

b) The pKY is constructed with a causal particle:

לכן + *yiqtol*: **Isa 52,6**[45]

c) The pKY is constructed with *qatal*:

(1) *qatal*-x: Josh 2,9; Ps 119,75; 140,13; Job 42,2; 2 Chron 25,16

(2) x-*qatal*: x is successively עתה (Exod 18,11; Judg 17,13; Ps 20,7), a personal pronoun (Judg 16,20; Hos 2,10; Ps 135,5), an emphatic particle (2 Kings 5,15), זה (Ps 56,10), בזאת (Ps 41,12).

There is no evident direct syntactic relationship here with a preceding clause. The pKY is constructed with *qatal* for the purposes of aspect, namely to express a punctual present (*perfectum declarativum*)[46]. In this case the pKY is not a purposive construction. For Ps 41,12 see below.

d) The pKY is constructed with *weqataltí*[47]

(1) *weqataltí*-x + *weqataltí*-x (pKY): Exod 6,7; 7,4-5; 29,46; Num 16,30; Deut 11,2; 1 Kings 20,28; Ezek 5,13; 6,6-7.8-9.12-13.14; 13,14. 23; 14,8; 16,62; 20,41-42.43-44; 22,16; 24,27; 25,7.14.17; 28,22.23; 29,9; 30,19.26; 33,29; 34,27; 36,11.23.35-36; 37,6.12-13.14; 38,23; 39,6. 21-22.29-30; Zech 2,13.15; 6,15; Mal 2,4.

The *weqataltí* pKY is normally part of a series of *weqataltí* forms (cf. Exod 6,7!) which it does not always conclude. In such stringing, the *weqataltí* is used independently as is also the case with the *wayyiqtol* (narrative)[48]. *Weqataltì* can express consecution[49]. According to Joüon,

45. Cf. SCHOORS, *Arrière-fond* (n. 1), pp. 125-127.

46. JOÜON – MURAOKA, §112f.

47. FLOSS, *Jahwe dienen* (n. 6), p. 585, mistakenly considers the verbal constructions in Exod 9,14 and Josh 3,10 to be *qatal*-x while in fact we are dealing with two *yiqtol* forms.

48. JOÜON – MURAOKA, §119f; R. MEYER, *Hebräische Grammatik*, Berlin, ³1966-1972, §101, 6c; S.R. DRIVER, *A Treatise on the Use of Tenses in Hebrew*, Oxford, ³1892, §§114 and 119. See, moreover, B.K. WALTKE – M. O'CONNOR, *An Introduction to Biblical Hebrew Syntax*, Winona Lake, IN, 1990, pp. 343-350, 455-563; NICCACCI, *The Syntax* (n. 32); ID., *Lettura sintattica* (n. 32).

49. JOÜON – MURAOKA, §119e and 169c, i; W. SCHNEIDER, *Grammatik des biblischen Hebräisch*, Munich, ²1983, §48.3.4.1; R.J. WILLIAMS, *Hebrew Syntax: An Outline*, Toronto, ²1976, §525.

the *waw*-inversivum is never used to express a nuance of finality[50]. Floß also speaks of "logische Folge" but does not appear to identify it with "finale Funktion" and "Zeilaussage"[51]. From a syntactical perspective, I do not consider the *weqataltí* pKY as a purposive form. It can, however, indicate succession or more precisely consecution and ought to be translated as follows: "so", "thus", "then".

(2) x-*yiqtol* + *weqataltí*-x (pKY): Exod 10,2; 16,12; Num 34,14; Judg 6,37; **Isa 49,23.26; 60,16**; Jer 16,21; Ezek 7,4.9.27; 11,10.12; 12,15. 16.20; 13,9.21; 14,23; 15,7; 17,21.24; 20,38; 21,10; 22,22; 23,49; 25,5. 11; 26,6; 28,24; 29,16.21; 30,8.25; 34,30; 35,4.9.12.15; 36,38; 37,28; 39,7; Joel 2,27; Zech 4,9.

The *weqataltí* (pKY) is the continuation of the preceding *yiqtol* and as a consequence bears a future significance. Moreover, I must insist that the *weqataltí* has consecutive meaning and does not express finality.

(3) *wᵉᵉeqtᵉlah*-x + *weqataltí* (pKY): Exod 14,4.17-18.

On two occasions the *weqataltí* is connected to a volitive, namely *wᵉᵉeqtᵉlah*-x (cohortative). This construction expresses succession: "then" in the sense that the succession of the preceding actions has reached its climax. In other words, there can be no talk of purpose or finality. According to Floß, there is no agreement in Exod 14,4.17-18 between the *Wortstellung* of the pKY and that of the preceding clause: *yiqtol*-x and *qatal*-x (pKY)[52]. The relationship between the motifs of "glory" and "knowing" thus creates a syntactic problem. The *Wortstellung* of the "glory" motif, however, does not agree with what precedes it either: *qatal*-x and *yiqtol*-x (pKY) (כבד) (note, however, 14,17-18: *yiqtol*-x + *yiqtol*-x!). According to Floß the two motifs interrupt the original *Wortstellungsschema*. He observes that Exod 14,1-2c.4c are related to one another at the levels of both syntax and content (v. 1: *yiqtol*-x; v. 2a-c: *yiqtol* (imp.!) + 2x *yiqtol*-x (nar.); v. 4c: *yiqtol*-x). The same

---

50. JOÜON – MURAOKA, §169i: "The Waw with an indirect volitive is used to indicate result as well as purpose, but the inversive Waw is not used except with consecutive force."; §119i: "But the fact that in some cases either a volitive or a *weqataltí* could be used does not justify the claim of certain writers that *w-qataltí* has in itself the meaning of purpose. To express purpose the indirect volitive is usually needed". Cf. also §119u: in 1 Sam 15,30 and 2 Sam 24,2, the context demands a final significance.

51. FLOSS, *Jahwe dienen* (n. 6), p. 299.

52. *Ibid.*, p. 569: "Darf man das nun als Gegenbeweis gegen unsere These ansehen, daß die Wortstellung der EK und die Wortstellung der voraufgehenden Aussage einander entsprechen? Die These käme dann zu fall, hätten wir es mit enen einwandfrei literarisch einheitlichen Text zu tun. Das ist aber vor allem für Ex 14,1-4 durchaus in der Forschung umstritten". Floß emplied what he has yet to prove as his argumentation: we do not find the *Wortstellungsschema* in Exod 14,4.17-18 / Exod 14,1-4.15-18 are not original units / thus the WS which Floß maintains is exact!

is true for v. 2d (x-*yiqtol*) and 3-4b (*qatal*-x) which, although the *Wortstellung* has changed, – probably in order to express a durative aspect –, ought to belong to 14,1-2c.

Floß continues with a summary of a few further difficulties concerning the motifs of "glory" and "knowing". Hardening and pursuit (v. 4ab) are carried out in v. 8, which is not the case with 'glory' and 'knowing' (v. 4cd). The object of the 'glory' and the subject of the 'knowing' are different in 14,4.17-18: Pharaoh and Egypt respectively (cf. 7,4-5). A concrete moment of action always precedes the pKY. נכבד, however, is an abstract theological term which itself requires some concretisation. Floß then refers to Lev 10,3; Isa 26,15; Ezek 28,22; 39,13; Hag 1,8 where one can find such a concretisation of the abstract and, according to his norms, a perfect *Wortstellungsschema*. Floß concludes that the "glory" motif in Exod 14,4.17 is a later addition to the pKY, perhaps under the influence of Ezek 28,22, and that the pKY itself did not originally belong to Exod 14,1-4,15-18[53].

Floß' arguments with respect to Exod 14,4.17-18 are not convincing. First of all, his continued application of an un-nuanced *Wortstellungsschema* does violence to the syntax of Exod 14,4.17-18. He only discusses Exod 14,4 and applies his conclusions mutatis mutandis to vv. 17-18, even although the latter verses exhibit a different *Wortstellung*. With respect to Exod 14,4.17-18 I refer to what I have outlined elsewhere[54]. I have suggested that the accumulation of the various verb forms and their mutual relationship bring about a climax resulting in the recognition of YHWH.

In addition, it is important to note that the fact that only "hardening" and "pursuit" (v. 4ab) are carried out in v. 8 and not "glory" or "knowing" (v. 4cd) is no reason to suggest that these latter motifs originally do not belong in the present context of the Sea Narrative. If one were to follow such a line of argument with respect to 14,17 one would have to insist that the "hardening" element is also alien to its context because there is only talk of "pursuit" in v. 23. "Revelation of glory" and "knowledge/recognition of YHWH" constitute the very point of the Sea Narrative which is ultimately a portrayal of the realisation of these mo-

---

53. *Ibid.*, p. 572: "EK ist also einfachhin in ihrer ezechielischen »Normalform« (qatal-x) in Ex 14,4.18 mit der Verherrlichungsaussage eingetragen worden, ohne die Wortstellung des ursprünglichen P-Kontextes zu berücksichtigen. Möglich war das deshalb und vielleicht aus auflösendes Moment, weil die Hand, die EK zusetzte, EK auch in P-Texten (Ex 6,7; 7,5) schon vorfand".

54. Cf. *The "P" Tradition in the Pentateuch: Document and/or Redaction? The 'Sea Narrative' (Exodus 13,17-14,31) as a Testcase'*, in C. BREKELMANS – J. LUST (eds.), *Pentateuchal Studies and Deuteronomistic History* (BETL, 94), Leuven, 1990, pp. 67-90.

tifs. In the view of the authors/redactors of our narrative, the hardening of Pharaoh's/the Egyptians' heart and his/their pursuit of the Israelites constitute the occasion for YHWH to manifest his glory through which the Egyptians – and also the Israelites (cf. 14,31!) – will come to know that YHWH is YHWH. Floß is too intent on applying the terms of his schema: promise – realisation.

I also note that the difference between the object of the "glory" motif and the subject of the pKY is proof of nothing. As a matter of fact, the object of נכבד includes more than just Pharaoh: his entire army is also part of the reference and, as such, it represents all Egyptians. Furthermore, the object of the "glory" needs to be related to the motif of "pursuit" of which Pharaoh is likewise the subject in v. 4 while in v. 17 it is the מצרים. We can state with confidence that Exod 14,4 and 14,17-18 came into existence via a stringing of more or less stereotypical formulas. It is not so much the logic of the speech that is important but rather its theological content and the climax to which it brings the text.

In conclusion, if Floß is of the opinion that Exod 14 lacks any concretisation of the abstract נכבד (subject YHWH) and that this is evidence of the non-originality of the connection between the "glory" motif (and the pKY) with the present context then he is going a little too far. Indeed one might ask whether the expression נכבד יהוה is as "abstract" to the Hebrew way of thinking as our modern translations tend to suggest. At the same time, it is not clear that other cases of נכבד יהוה are any more concrete. We might say of Lev 10,3, for example, that the notion of קדש is equally "abstract"; likewise, Ezek 28,22 is a quite analogous construction to Exod 14,4.17-18. In the last analysis, it is my opinion that the *Wortstellungsschema* of Exod 14,4.17-18 is no less "perfect" than that of Lev 10,3 and other texts. We are simply confronted with the fact that Floß once again applies his syntactic schema in a less than nuanced manner to the text in question.

(4) x-*qatal* + *weqataltí*-x (pKY): Deut 8,5; Ezek 29,6

The *weqataltí* can appear after a verb with past significance (Deut 8,5)[55], in which case it refers to a future act with an imperative nuance. The same is true for Ezek 29,6 where the preceding *qatal* functions as a present with a future significance[56]. From a syntactical perspective the pKY does not constitute a purposive construction in Deut 8,5 and Ezek 29,6.

55. JOÜON – MURAOKA, §119c.
56. *Ibid*, §112g.

(5) x-*qotel* + *weqataltí* (pKY): Josh 23,14; 1 Kings 20,13

weqataltí continues a participle with future significance and expresses succession/consecution ("then", "consequently")[57].

(6) x-*qetol* + *weqataltí*-x (pKY): 1 Kings 18,37; **Isa 37,20**.

weqataltí continues a volitive (imperative). Translations usually employ a purpose construction ("in order that") although *q^{e}tol* + *weqataltí* normally express succession[58]. In 1 Kings 18,37 and **Isa 37,20** we encounter a resultative clause: "as a result of which all nations/kingdoms of the earth will know that...".

(7) ב-*q^{e}tol* (inf.) +*weqataltí*-x (pKY): Ezek 24,24; 28,26; 32,15; 33,33.

weqataltí regularly follows an infinitive construction when it indicates succession ("then")[59], or more precisely: consecution ("as a consequence of which").

(8) nominal clause + *weqataltí* (pKY)

In Joel 4,17 *weqataltí* can have consecutive meaning: "As a consequence of which you will know...". Note the structure of Joel 4: YHWH's speech and that of the prophet alternate with one another (v. 12-13: YHWH / v. 14-16: prophet / v. 17: YHWH).

(9) temporal indicator + *weqataltí*-x (pKY): Exod 16,6 (cf. v. 7)

Floß cannot find his *Wortstellungsschema* in this verse and concludes, therefore, that the pKY in Exod 16,6 is a secondary interpolation[60]. The *waw*-apodosios, however, is used with equal frequency in temporal clauses, even after very short temporal indicators: cf. Exod 16,6-7; 17,4; Lev 7,16; 1 Kings 13,31; Prov 24,27 and compare with Gen 22,4 (*wayyiqtol*)[61]. From the perspective of syntax, therefore, there is no reason to separate the temporal indicator ערב from the *weqataltí* pKY.

(10) *wayyiqtol*-x + *weqataltí*-x (pKY): Deut 4,37-39; 7,8-9

According to Floß, the *Wortstellung* of the pKY does not correspond with that of the preceding clauses and the pKY is thus secondary[62]. After the description of YHWH's salvific acts in the past (*wayyiqtol*), a series of *weqataltí* forms in Deut 4,39 and 7,9 bring us once again into the sphere of the present/future. The *weqataltí*-pKY marks a new clause which, as conclusion or consequence, depends on what precedes it: "Thus you shall..." or "You know, therefore,...".

---

57. *Ibid.*, §119n: "near future" (cf. הנה).
58. *Ibid.*, §119l, m.
59. *Ibid.*, §119o.
60. FLOSS, *Jahwe dienen* (n. 6), pp. 572-573.
61. JOÜON – MURAOKA, §176f, g; GK §112oo.
62. FLOSS, *Jahwe dienen* (n. 6), pp. 299-300, 586.

e) The pKY is constructed with *yiqtol*

(1) *q^etol*-x (pKY) + x-*yiqtol* (pKY): Jer 31,34

The imperative constitutes a part of the main clause to which the x-*yiqtol* (pKY) is subordinate (כי-construction). There is, of course, no question of finality.

(2) Adverbial expression בזאת + *yiqtol*-x (pKY): Exod 7,17; Num 16,28; Josh 3,10 and cf. Ps 41,12 (*qatal*).

According to Floß the pKY disrupts the *Wortstellungsschema* in Exod 7,17 and Num 16,28[63]. Although Exod 7,17 exhibits structural similarity with Josh 3,10, Floß sees no difficulties with the latter text. It is my opinion, however, that there is no reason to consider the pKY of Exod 7,17 and Num 16,28 as secondary interpolations. The emphatic first positioning of the pKY ("By this you shall know...") intends to show that YHWH lets himself be known in his deeds. YHWH's intervention in history is not simply intended as a manifestation of his divinity. He lets himself be know by what he does. Here also, therefore, I prefer not to speak of the pKY expressing purpose.

f) The pKY is constructed with *w^eyiqtol*

(1) *weqataltí* x + *w^eyiqtol*-x (pKY): 1 Sam 17,46

The sequence *weqataltí* – *w^eyiqtol* normally does not express succession[64]. Pléiade's translation "pour que" (final) probably interprets the *yiqtol* of the pKY as an indirect jussive. While such a construction is not impossible, it is nevertheless rare after an indicative[65]. In my opinion, the *weqataltí*-x + *w^eyiqtol*-x construction in 1 Sam 17,46 clearly expresses the idea of consecution ("as a consequence thereof...").

(2) *yiqtol*-x/*w^eyiqtol*-x + *w^eyiqtol*-x (pKY): 1 Sam 17,47; Ps 83,19; 2 Kings 5,8. For 1 Sam 17,47, see discussion above on 1 Sam 17,46.

The *yiqtol* of the pKY in 2 Kings 5,8 may be an indirect jussive being employed after the direct volitive יבא נא. Such a relationship expresses finality as well as consecution[66]. In Ps 83,18-19 we encounter a series of

---

63. *Ibid.*, pp. 574, 576-577, 583.

64. JOÜON – MURAOKA, §119d: "This feature of succession is particularly evident where *w-qataltí* is avoided and replaced by *w-... yiqtol* when an expression of succession is not desired". – §119f: "A sequence of *w-qataltí* is not usually interrupted without a fairly strong reason".

65. *Ibid.*, §116e.

66. *Ibid.*, §116d and 168b. Cf. J. GRAY, *I & II Kings: A Commentary* (OTL), London, ²1970, p. 503: "Let him come to me *that* he may know that there is a prophet in Israel" (italics mine) and compare with T.R. HOBBS, *2 Kings* (WBC, 13), Waco, TX, 1985, p. 56: "Let the man come to me *and let* him know that there is a prophet in Israel"; M. COGAN – H. TADMOR, *II Kings: A New Translation with Introduction and Commentary* (AB, 11),

five *yiqtols* which function as jussives. The last form (וידעו) may be an indirect volitive (with energic *waw*) connected to the preceding direct volitive (with *waw* simplex) whereby purpose or consequence is expressed (see translations)[67].

(3) *q^{e}tol*-x/x-*q^{e}tol* + *w^{e}yiqtol*-x (pKY): 1 Kings 18,37 / 1 Kings 19,19

וידעו may be an indirect jussive following after a direct volitive (imperative) signifying finality or consequence[68].

(4) nominal clause + *weyiqtol*-x (pKY): Ps 59,14

The *yiqtol* of the pKY may be an indirect jussive following after a nominal clause, in which case the pKY is a purposive construction[69].

g) The pKY is constructed with *wayyiqtol*

wayyiqtol-x + *wayyiqtol*-x (pKY): 2 Sam 5,12; Zech 11,11; 1 Chron 14,2; 2 Chron 33,13. This syntactic relationship normally expresses succession[70]. With respect to the aforementioned texts, however, it is better to speak of consecution ("as a consequence thereof…") because the term succession is too general.

h) The pKY is constructed with *q^{e}tol* (imp.)
q^{e}tol-x: 2 Kings 10,10; 31,34; Ps 4,4; 46,11; 100,3.

i) The pKY is constructed with *qatōl*
qatōl + *w^{e}qatōl* Jer 9,23.

3. *Function*

I already noticed that according to Zimmerli the pKY, in general, functions as a purposive construction which he designates with the term *Erweiswort*. Floß maintains this position but attempts to provide it with syntactic foundations. Fohrer, Hoßfeld and Lang, in contrast, are of the opinion that the pKY should not be understood as a purposive construction. According to these three authors, the primary function of the pKY is emphatic, indicating that a particular act or deed is an act or deed of YHWH.

Garden City, NY, 1988, p. 61: "Let him come to me *and* he will learn that there is a prophet in Israel" (italics mine).

67. JOÜON – MURAOKA, §116d.
68. *Ibid.*
69. *Ibid.*, §116e. Cf. M. DAHOOD, *Psalms II: 51–100* (AB, 17), Garden City, NY, 1968, p. 66: "… exterminate and annihilate them, *that* they might know that God…" (italics mine), and compare with M. TATE, *Psalms 51–100* (WBC, 20), Waco, TX, 1990, p. 92: "… put an end to them so that they are no more, *and let* them know to the end…" (italics mine).
70. JOÜON – MURAOKA, §118c.

The study of the syntax of the pKY has shown that the opinions of the aforementioned scholars are in need of nuancing. Zimmerli's determination of the final character of the pKY is based more on intuition than on syntactic research. While Floß manages to overcome this methodological shortcoming, he himself falls into a number of further traps. Firstly, he employs an inaccurate *Wortstellungsschema* which he applies to every text as a sort of "master key". At the same time it is impossible to escape the impression that the hypothetical results of literary criticism have been used at the service of his syntactic research[71]. Finally, he is no less intuitive than Zimmerli when he insists that the final function of the pKY, if not evident in the use of an explicit purposive construction, can be deduced from the *Wortstellung* of the formula[72].

The fact that this latter position does not hold true can be seen from the results of my study which I summarise as follows:

– The pKY expresses clearly purpose when it is constructed with a final particle (cf. **Isa 41,20; 43,10; 45,3.6**) or a final infinitive [25x]. Besides this it is also possible to discern purposive significance in a number of rare syntactic patterns of the pKY: $(w^e)yiqtol$-x + $w^eyiqtol$-x [3x]; q^etol-x/x-q^etol + $w^eyiqtol$-x (pKY) [2x]; nominal clause + $w^eyiqtol$-x (pKY) [1x].

– On one occasion the pKY is constructed with a causal particle (**Isa 52,6**).

– The constructions בזאת + $yiqtol$-x (pKY) [3x] and בזאת + $qatal$-x (pKY) [1x] do not express finality. Their meaning is: YHWH lets himself be known in what he does.

– The pKY functions primarily as consequence (consecution). This is clear in the case of the $weqatalti$-x + $weqatalti$-x (pKY) pattern [43x]. It applies equally to the patterns x-$yiqtol$ + $weqatalti$-x (pKY) (cf. **Isa 49,23.26; 60,16**) [43x]; $wayyiqtol$-x + $weqatalti$-x (pKY) [2x]; nominal clause + $weqatalti$-x (pKY) [1x]; x-$qatal$ + $weqatalti$-x (pKY) [2x]. Furthermore, the patterns $(w^e)yiqtol$-x + $w^eyiqtol$-x (pKY) and q^etol-x/x-q^etol + $w^eyiqtol$-x (pKY) [2x] have either final or consecutive significance. Grammatically speaking, the combinations w^e'qt^elah-x + $weqatalti$ (pKY) (Exod 14,4.17-18), x-q^etol + $weqatalti$-x (pKY) (cf. **Isa 37,20**) [2x], ב-q^etol (inf.) + $weqatalti$-x (pKY) 4x) and x-$qotel$ + $weqatalti$-x [2x] normally express succession, but here too it is more accurate to speak of consecution.

– We also encounter the pKY in a few places without a direct syntactic relationship with the context. In this case it functions as a sort of con-

71. FLOSS, *Jahwe dienen* (n. 6), p. 569 n. 3.
72. See, for example, *ibid.*, pp. 299, 588.

fession [*qatal*; 14x] or command [*qᵉtol*; 5x]. Compare this with the pattern: temporal indicator + *weqataltí*-x (pKY) (Exod 16,6).

Fohrer, Hoßfeld and Lang are correct in suggesting that, in the case of Ezekiel, the pKY is less *zielstrebig*. The pKY has different functions in different contexts. We noted that it frequently has a consecutive significance. The boundary between purpose/finality and consequence is not always clear in Hebrew. Nevertheless, there is a difference between the pKY as purposive construction and as construction expressing consequence of an event. In the first case, YHWH's intervention is "degraded", as it were, to mere "material knowledge" which in itself possesses little value. If YHWH lets himself be known *in what he does*, however, then his intervention has actual value in itself. The recognition of YHWH *takes place* in what he does[73]. In other words, the pKY indicates that an intervention of YHWH is in fact an intervention of YHWH.

Groot Begijnhof 53   Marc VERVENNE
B-3000 Leuven

---

73. Cf. LANG, *Ezechiel* (n. 5), p. 96.

INDEXES

ABBREVIATIONS

AA	Alttestamentliche Abhandlungen
AASF	Annales Academiae Scientiarum Fennicae
ÄAT	Ägypten und Altes Testament: Studien zu Geschichte, Kultur und Religion Ägyptens und des Alten Testaments
AB	The Anchor Bible
ABD	The Anchor Bible Dictionary
ABRL	Anchor Bible Reference Library
ACEBT	Amsterdamse cahiers voor exegese en bijbelse theologie
AEM	Archives épistolaires de Mari
AJBI	Annual of the Japanese Biblical Institute
AnBib	Analecta Biblica
ANET	Ancient Near Eastern Texts Relating to the Old Testament, ed. J.B. Pritchard
ANL	Annua Nuntia Lovaniensia
AnOr	Analecta Orientalia
AOAT	Alter Orient und Altes Testament
AOT	Altorientalische Texte zum Alten Testament
ARM	Archives Royales de Mari. Textes cunéiformes
ASTI	Annual of the Swedish Theological Institute (Jerusalem)
ATANT	Abhandlungen zur Theologie des Alten und Neuen Testaments
AThDan	Acta Theologica Danica
ATSAT	Arbeiten zu Text und Sprache im Alten Testament
ATD	Das Alte Testament Deutsch
Aug	Augustinianum
AUSS	Andrews University Seminary Studies
BA	The Biblical Archaeologist
BAR	Biblical Archaeological Review
BBB	Bonner biblische Beiträge
BC(AT)	Biblischer Commentar über das Alte Testament
BDB	F. Brown – S.R. Driver – C.A. Briggs, A Hebrew and English Lexicon of the Old Testament
BEATAJ	Beiträge zur Erforschung des Alten Testaments und des antiken Judentums
BEvT	Beiträge zur evangelischen Theologie
BET	Beiträge zur biblischen Exegese und Theologie
BETL	Bibliotheca Ephemeridum Theologicarum Lovaniensium
BHS	Biblia Hebraica Stuttgartensia
BHT	Beiträge zur Historischen Theologie
Bib	Biblica
BibB	Biblische Beiträge
BiBod	Bibliotheca Bodmeriana
BiOr	Bibliotheca Orientalis

BibRev	Bible Review
BK(AT)	Biblischer Kommentar. Altes Testament
BN	Biblische Notizen
BogVest	Bogoslovni Vestnik
BO	Bibliotheca Orientalis
BOT	De Boeken van het Oude Testament
BS	Bibliotheca Sacra
BTrans	Bible Translator
BThSt	Biblical and Theological Studies
BWANT	Beiträge zur Wissenschaft vom Alten und Neuen Testament
BZ (NF)	Biblische Zeitschrift (Neue Folge)
BZAW	Beihefte zur Zeitschrift für die alttestamentliche Wissenschaft
BZNW	Beihefte zur Zeitschrift für die neutestamentliche Wissenschaft

CAT	Commentaire de l'Ancien Testament
CBET	Contributions to Biblical Exegesis and Theology
CBC	Cambridge Bible Commentary
CB OT	Coniectanea biblica. Old Testament Series
CBQ	Catholic Biblical Quarterly
CC SL	Corpus Christianorum. Series Latina
COT	Commentaar op het Oude Testament
CRB	Cahiers de la Revue Biblique
CRINT	Compendia Rerum Iudaicarum ad Novum Testamentum
CSEL	Corpus Scriptorum Ecclesiasticorum Latinorum
CTA	A. HERDNER, Corpus des tablettes en cunéiformes alphabétiques découvertes à Ras Shamra-Ugarit de 1929-1939

DBAT	Dielheimer Blätter zum Alten Testament
DBS	Dictionnaire de la Bible. Supplément
DCH	The Dictionary of Classical Hebrew, ed. D.J.A. CLINES, 1993-
DJD	Discoveries in the Judaean Desert
DSD	Dead Sea Discoveries

EB	Études Bibliques
EdF	Erträge der Forschung
EKKNT	Evangelisch-Katholischer Kommentar zum Neuen Testament
EncJud	Encyclopaedia Judaica
ErfTS	Erfurter theologische Studien
EstBíb	Estudios bíblicos
ETL	Ephemerides Theologicae Lovanienses
EurHS	Europäische Hochschulschriften. Reihe 23: Theologie
EvT	Evangelische Theologie
ExpT	Expository Times

FAT	Forschungen zum Alten Testament
FJB	Frankfurter Judaistische Beiträge
FOTL	The Forms of the Old Testament Literature
FRLANT	Forschungen zur Religion und Literatur des Alten und Neuen Testaments
FzB	Forschung zur Bibel

GB	W. GESENIUS – F. BUHL, Hebräisches und Aramäisches Handwörterbuch über das Alte Testament
GCS	Die griechischen christlichen Schriftsteller der ersten drei Jahrhunderte
GK	W. GESENIUS – E. KAUTZSCH, *Hebräische Grammatik*, Leipzig, ^{28}1909
GTA	Grundriße zum Alten Testament: Das Alte Testament Deutsch. Ergänzungsreihe
GTW	Grundriß der theologischen Wissenschaften
HAL	Hebräisches und Aramäisches Lexikon zum Alten Testament, eds. L. KOEHLER und W. BAUMGARTNER, neu bearbeitet von W. BAUMGARTNER *et al.*
HAR	Hebrew Annual Review
HAT	Handbuch zum Alten Testament
HB	Hebrew Bible
HBS	Herders biblische Studien
HCOT	Historical Commentary on the Old Testament
HK(AT)	Handkommentar zum Alten Testament
HSM	Harvard Semitic Monographs
HSS	Harvard Semitic Studies
HTKNT	Herders Theologischer Kommentar zum Neuen Testament
HTR	Harvard Theological Review
HTS	Harvard Theological Studies
HUCA	Hebrew Union College Annual
ICC	The International Critical Commentary
IEJ	Israel Exploration Journal
JAAR	Journal of the American Academy of Religion
JANES	Journal of the Ancient Near Eastern Society, Columbia University
JAOS	Journal of the American Oriental Society
JBL	Journal of Biblical Literature
JBT	Jahrbuch für biblische Theologie
JJS	Journal of Jewish Studies
JNSL	Journal of Northwest Semitic Languages
JPS	Jewish Publication Society
JPT	Jahrbuch für Protestantische Theologie
JQR	Jewish Quarterly Review
JSHRZ	Jüdische Schriften aus hellenistisch-römischer Zeit
JSOT	Journal for the Study of the Old Testament
JSNT SS	Journal for the Study of the New Testament. Supplement Series
JSOT SS	Journal for the Study of the Old Testament. Supplement Series
JSHRZ	Jüdische Schriften aus hellenistisch-römischer Zeit
JSJ	Journal for the Study of Judaism in the Persian, Hellenistic, and Roman Periods
JSS	Journal of Semitic Studies
JTC	Journal for Theology and the Church
JTS	Journal of Theological Studies

KAT	Kommentar zum Alten Testament
KatBl	Katechetische Blätter
KBANT	Kommentare und Beiträge zum Alten und Neuen Testament
KBL	L. KOEHLER – W. BAUMGARTNER, Lexicon in Veteris Testamenti Libros
KBS	Katholieke Bijbelstichting. Dutch Bible Translation (^{3}1995)
KHAT	Kurzer Hand-Kommentar zum Alten Testament
KEHAT	Kurzgefaßtes exegetisches Handbuch zum Alten Testament
KHC(AT)	Kurzer Hand-Commentar zum Alten Testament
KJ	King James Version
LAB	PSEUDO-PHILO, Liber Antiquitatem Biblicarum
LD	Lectio divina
MARI	Mari, Annales de recherches interdisciplinaires
MarTS	Marburger theologische Studien
MTU	Mitteilungen des Septuaginta-Unternehmens
MTZ	Münchener theologische Zeitschrift
MVEOL	Mededelingen en verhandelingen van het Voor-aziatisch-Egyptisch Genootschap Ex Oriente Lux
NAPS	J. FOKKELMAN, *Narrative Art and Poetry in the Book of Samuel*, Assen, 1981-1993
NBE	Nueva Biblia Española, Madrid, 1975
NBG	Bijbel: Nederlands Bijbelgenootschap (1951)
NBL	M. GÖRG – B. LANG (eds.), Neues Bibel-Lexikon, Zürich, 1988-
NCBC	New Century Bible Commentary
NICOT	The New International Commentary on the Old Testament
NIV	The Holy Bible: New International Version, Grand Rapids, MI, ^{9}1979
NEB	The New English Bible
NKZ	Neue kirchliche Zeitschrift
NovTSup	Novum Testamentum Supplements
NRT	Nouvelle revue théologique
NRSV	The New Revised Standard Version
NTAbh	Neutestamentliche Abhandlungen
NTT	Nederlands Theologisch Tijdschrift
OBC	Orientalia Biblica et Christiana
OBO	Orbis Biblicus et Orientalis
OLA	Orientalia Lovaniensia Analecta
OrAnt	Oriens Antiquus
OTA	Old Testament Abstracts
OTE	Old Testament Essays
OTL	Old Testament Library
OTM	Old Testament Messages
OTS	Oudtestamentische Studiën
PL	J. MIGNE (ed.), Patrologia Latina
POT	De prediking van het Oude Testament
PRU	Palais Royal d'Ugarit

QD	Quaestiones Disputatae

RAC	Reallexikon für Antike und Christentum
RAug	Recherches augustiniennes
RB	Revue biblique
RBén	Revue bénédictine
REB	The Revised English Bible
RechBib	Recherches bibliques
RevÉAug	Revue des études augustiniennes
RExp	Review and Expositor
RGG	Religion im Geschichte und Gegenwart
RHPR	Revue d'histoire et de philosophie religieuses
RivBib	Rivista biblica
RLA	Reallexikon der Assyriologie
RS	Rash Shamra
RQ	Revue de Qumrân
RSR	Recherches de science religieuse
RSV	Revised Standard Version
RTL	Revue théologique de Louvain

SB(i)	Sources Bibliques
SBAAT	Stuttgarter biblische Aufsatzbände Altes Testament
SBB	Stuttgarter biblische Beiträge
SBL DS	Society of Biblical Literature. Dissertation Series
SBL MS	Society of Biblical Literature. Monograph Series
SBL RBS	Society of Biblical Literature. Resources for Biblical Study
SBL SCS	Society of Biblical Literature. Septuagint and Cognate Studies
SBL SS	Society of Biblical Literature. Semeia Studies
SBL SP	Society of Biblical Literature. Seminar Papers
SC	Sources chrétiennes
SBS	Stuttgarter Bibelstudien
ScotJT	Scottish Journal of Theology
ScrHie	Scripta Hierosolymitana
SeL	Storia e letteratura
SESJ	Suomen eksegeettisen seuran julkaisuja, Helsinki
ShnatMiqr	שנתון למקרא ולחקר. Shnaton. An Annual for Biblical and Ancient Near Eastern Studies
SJOT	Scandinavian Journal of the Old Testament
SNT	Schriften des Neuen Testaments
SupRivBib	Supplementi alla Rivista Biblica
SSN	Studia Semitica Neerlandica
STANT	Studien zum Alten und Neuen Testament
StB	Studia Biblica
SVT	Supplements to Vetus Testamentum

TB	Theologische Bücherei
TBl	Theologische Blätter
TDOT	Theological Dictionary of the Old Testament
THAT	Theologisches Handwörterbuch zum Alten Testament

THKNT	Theologischer Handkommentar zum Neuen Testament
ThT	Theologisch tijdschrift
TLZ	Theologische Literaturzeitung
TOB	Traduction œcuménique de la Bible
TP	Theologie und Philosophie
TR	Theologische Rundschau
TRE	Theologische Realenzyklopädie
TRev	Theologische Revue
TSAJ	Texte und Studien zum antiken Judentum
TSHLRS	Texts and Studies in the Hebrew Language and Related Subjects
TSt	Theologische Studien
TTZ	Trierer theologische Zeitschrift
TUAT	Texte aus der Umwelt des Alten Testaments
TvT	Tijdschrift voor Theologie
TW	Theologische Wissenschaft
TWAT	Theologisches Wörterbuch zum Alten Testament
TynB	Tyndale Bulletin
TZ	Theologische Zeitschrift
UBL	Ugaritisch-Biblische Literatur
UF	Ugarit Forschungen
UTB	Uni-Taschenbücher
YES	Yale Egyptological Studies
VT	Vetus Testamentum
VuF	Verkündigung und Forschung
WBC	Word Biblical Commentary
WMANT	Wissenschaftliche Monographien zum Alten und Neuen Testament
WTJ	Westminster Theological Journal
WZKM	Wiener Zeitschrift für die Kunde des Morgenlandes
ZAH	Zeitschrift für Althebraistik
ZAR	Zeitschrift für Altorientalische und Biblische Rechtsgeschichte
ZAW	Zeitschrift für die alttestamentliche Wissenschaft
ZBK	Zürcher Bibelkommentar
ZDPV	Zeitschrift des deutschen Palästina-Vereins
ZEE	Zeitschrift für evangelische Ethik
ZKT	Zeitschrift für katholische Theologie
ZTK	Zeitschrift für Theologie und Kirche

INDEX OF AUTHORS

INDEX OF BIBLICAL REFERENCES

This index includes all references to Old and New Testament passages. For other ancient writings, see the Subject Index.

Special treatments of the passage concerned are marked by page numbers in bold printing.

SUBJECT INDEX

Ahaz 67, 69, 78, 80, 87, 91, 99-100, 113,
163, 450-452, 456
Anthropomorph(ism/ic) 27, 184
Apocalypse → Isaiah
Aram 59, 84, 99, 450, 453
Assonance 181, 315
Assyria(n) 12, 51, 57-58, 66, 68, 71, 77-
89, 91-93, 106, 111-113, 116,
132, 134, 146, 238, 390, 391-393,
400, 450-451, 453, 460

Babylon(ian) 10, 13-17, 29, 37, 45-46,
52, 58-59, 76, 86, 95, 101, 115,
117, 225, 232, 238, 247, 252, 257,
264, 319, 373, 377, 400, 404, 406,
422, 434, 441

Call Narrative → Isaiah
Canaan 345-346, 377
Chaldea 59, 400
Colometry 179-180, 325-329, 333
Versification 303-323
Covenant 35, 41-61, 252-254, 286
Book of the Covenant 93
Sinai Covenant 253
Cyrus 16, 42-43, 45, 47, 58-59, 68-69,
216, 225, 227-228, 232-233, 235,
238, 247-248, 267-268, 303-323

Damascus 59, 78-79, 82, 86-87, 91, 93,
135
David 47, 52, 82, 213, 309, 372, 453-455
Davidic covenant 41-61
Davidic figure 42, 47, 50
Davidic house (dynasty) 12-13, 14-15,
20, 34, 35-36, 42-43, 47, 49, 84,
91, 99, 451-452, 456
Davidic monarch(y) 43, 53, 55-57
Davidic rule 51-52
Deutero-Isaiah → Isaiah
Deuteronomic
Deuteronomic movement 15

Deuteronomistic 14, 79, 83, 85
Deuteronomistic History 9, 11-12, 14,
100, 105, 108, 112, 117, 213
Deuteronom(ist)ic school 78, 114-116
DtrP 115
Dispersion 10, 15-16, 380, 389-390, 393

Egypt 45, 57, 59, 76-79, 86-87, 88, 90,
92, 111, 113, 255, 375, 377, 390-
395
Emmanuel 99, 102, 163, 166, 171, 449-
450, 452, 455-456, 464
Ephraim 84, 93, 99, 453
Erkenntnis 139, 144, 204-205, 225, 227,
369
Erkenntnisformel → Recognition
Eschatology 87, 141, 223-249, 290, 299
Exile 27-29, 30, 53, 57, 83, 105, 108,
115, 216, 252, 307, 319, 373, 375,
380, 434, 441
Post-exilic 43, 58, 61, 79, 81, 83, 87,
89, 127, 247, 376, 380
Pre-exilic 111-112, 216, 239, 247
Ezekiel 14, 26, 367-382
Ezra 60-61

Form-criticism 133, 290-291, 296, 299-
301, 435
Gattung 299-300

Hezekiah 11, 13, 56, 67, 69, 71, 77-78,
82, 85, 87-88, 90, 92, 95, 97-98,
100-108, 110-111, 113-118, 213-
214
Canticle of Hezekiah 95, 97, 105, 117
History 223-249, 434, 450
Dates
735-732 B.C.E. 450
722/720 B.C.E. 104
703 B.C.E. 88
701 B.C.E. 8-12, 89-90, 112
598 B.C.E. 10, 13
587 B.C.E. 8, 9-10, 13-16, 89

BIBLIOTHECA EPHEMERIDUM THEOLOGICARUM LOVANIENSIUM

SERIES I

* = Out of print

*1. *Miscellanea dogmatica in honorem Eximii Domini J. Bittremieux*, 1947.
*2-3. *Miscellanea moralia in honorem Eximii Domini A. Janssen*, 1948.
*4. G. PHILIPS, *La grâce des justes de l'Ancien Testament*, 1948.
*5. G. PHILIPS, *De ratione instituendi tractatum de gratia nostrae sanctificationis*, 1953.
6-7. *Recueil Lucien Cerfaux. Études d'exégèse et d'histoire religieuse*, 1954. 504 et 577 p. FB 1000 par tome. Cf. *infra*, nos 18 et 71 (t. III).
8. G. THILS, *Histoire doctrinale du mouvement œcuménique*, 1955. Nouvelle édition, 1963. 338 p. FB 135.
*9. *Études sur l'Immaculée Conception*, 1955.
*10. J.A. O'DONOHOE, *Tridentine Seminary Legislation*, 1957.
*11. G. THILS, *Orientations de la théologie*, 1958.
*12-13. J. COPPENS, A. DESCAMPS, É. MASSAUX (ed.), *Sacra Pagina. Miscellanea Biblica Congressus Internationalis Catholici de Re Biblica*, 1959.
*14. *Adrien VI, le premier Pape de la contre-réforme*, 1959.
*15. F. CLAEYS BOUUAERT, *Les déclarations et serments imposés par la loi civile aux membres du clergé belge sous le Directoire (1795-1801)*, 1960.
*16. G. THILS, *La «Théologie œcuménique». Notion-Formes-Démarches*, 1960.
17. G. THILS, *Primauté pontificale et prérogatives épiscopales. «Potestas ordinaria» au Concile du Vatican*, 1961. 103 p. FB 50.
*18. *Recueil Lucien Cerfaux, t. III*, 1962. Cf. *infra*, n° 71.
*19. *Foi et réflexion philosophique. Mélanges F. Grégoire*, 1961.
*20. *Mélanges G. Ryckmans*, 1963.
21. G. THILS, *L'infaillibilité du peuple chrétien «in credendo»*, 1963. 67 p. FB 50.
*22. J. FÉRIN & L. JANSSENS, *Progestogènes et morale conjugale*, 1963.
*23. *Collectanea Moralia in honorem Eximii Domini A. Janssen*, 1964.
24. H. CAZELLES (ed.), *De Mari à Qumrân. L'Ancien Testament. Son milieu. Ses écrits. Ses relectures juives* (Hommage J. Coppens, I), 1969. 158*-370 p. FB 900.
*25. I. DE LA POTTERIE (ed.), *De Jésus aux évangiles. Tradition et rédaction dans les évangiles synoptiques* (Hommage J. Coppens, II), 1967.
26. G. THILS & R.E. BROWN (ed.), *Exégèse et théologie* (Hommage J. Coppens, III), 1968. 328 p. FB 700.
27. J. COPPENS (ed.), *Ecclesia a Spiritu sancto edocta. Hommage à Mgr G. Philips*, 1970. 640 p. FB 1000.
28. J. COPPENS (ed.), *Sacerdoce et célibat. Études historiques et théologiques*, 1971. 740 p. FB 700.

29. M. DIDIER (ed.), *L'évangile selon Matthieu. Rédaction et théologie*, 1972. 432 p. FB 1000.
*30. J. KEMPENEERS, *Le Cardinal van Roey en son temps*, 1971.

SERIES II

31. F. NEIRYNCK, *Duality in Mark. Contributions to the Study of the Markan Redaction*, 1972. Revised edition with Supplementary Notes, 1988. 252 p. FB 1200.
32. F. NEIRYNCK (ed.), *L'évangile de Luc. Problèmes littéraires et théologiques*, 1973. *L'évangile de Luc – The Gospel of Luke*. Revised and enlarged edition, 1989. X-590 p. FB 2200.
33. C. BREKELMANS (ed.), *Questions disputées d'Ancien Testament. Méthode et théologie*, 1974. *Continuing Questions in Old Testament Method and Theology*. Revised and enlarged edition by M. VERVENNE, 1989. 245 p. FB 1200.
34. M. SABBE (ed.), *L'évangile selon Marc. Tradition et rédaction*, 1974. Nouvelle édition augmentée, 1988. 601 p. FB 2400.
35. B. WILLAERT (ed.), *Philosophie de la religion – Godsdienstfilosofie. Miscellanea Albert Dondeyne*, 1974. Nouvelle édition, 1987. 458 p. FB 1600.
36. G. PHILIPS, *L'union personnelle avec le Dieu vivant. Essai sur l'origine et le sens de la grâce créée*, 1974. Édition révisée, 1989. 299 p. FB 1000.
37. F. NEIRYNCK, in collaboration with T. HANSEN and F. VAN SEGBROECK, *The Minor Agreements of Matthew and Luke against Mark with a Cumulative List*, 1974. 330 p. FB 900.
38. J. COPPENS, *Le messianisme et sa relève prophétique. Les anticipations vétérotestamentaires. Leur accomplissement en Jésus*, 1974. Édition révisée, 1989. XIII-265 p. FB 1000.
39. D. SENIOR, *The Passion Narrative according to Matthew. A Redactional Study*, 1975. New impression, 1982. 440 p. FB 1000.
40. J. DUPONT (ed.), *Jésus aux origines de la christologie*, 1975. Nouvelle édition augmentée, 1989. 458 p. FB 1500.
41. J. COPPENS (ed.), *La notion biblique de Dieu*, 1976. Réimpression, 1985. 519 p. FB 1600.
42. J. LINDEMANS & H. DEMEESTER (ed.), *Liber Amicorum Monseigneur W. Onclin*, 1976. XXII-396 p. FB 1000.
43. R.E. HOECKMAN (ed.), *Pluralisme et œcuménisme en recherches théologiques. Mélanges offerts au R.P. Dockx, O.P.*, 1976. 316 p. FB 1000.
44. M. DE JONGE (ed.), *L'évangile de Jean. Sources, rédaction, théologie*, 1977. Réimpression, 1987. 416 p. FB 1500.
45. E.J.M. VAN EIJL (ed.), *Facultas S. Theologiae Lovaniensis 1432-1797. Bijdragen tot haar geschiedenis. Contributions to its History. Contributions à son histoire*, 1977. 570 p. FB 1700.
46. M. DELCOR (ed.), *Qumrân. Sa piété, sa théologie et son milieu*, 1978. 432 p. FB 1700.
47. M. CAUDRON (ed.), *Faith and Society. Foi et société. Geloof en maatschappij. Acta Congressus Internationalis Theologici Lovaniensis 1976*, 1978. 304 p. FB 1150.

48. J. KREMER (ed.), *Les Actes des Apôtres. Traditions, rédaction, théologie*, 1979. 590 p. FB 1700.
49. F. NEIRYNCK, avec la collaboration de J. DELOBEL, T. SNOY, G. VAN BELLE, F. VAN SEGBROECK, *Jean et les Synoptiques. Examen critique de l'exégèse de M.-É. Boismard*, 1979. XII-428 p. FB 1000.
50. J. COPPENS, *La relève apocalyptique du messianisme royal. I. La royauté – Le règne – Le royaume de Dieu. Cadre de la relève apocalyptique*, 1979. 325 p. FB 1000.
51. M. GILBERT (ed.), *La Sagesse de l'Ancien Testament*, 1979. Nouvelle édition mise à jour, 1990. 455 p. FB 1500.
52. B. DEHANDSCHUTTER, *Martyrium Polycarpi. Een literair-kritische studie*, 1979. 296 p. FB 1000.
53. J. LAMBRECHT (ed.), *L'Apocalypse johannique et l'Apocalyptique dans le Nouveau Testament*, 1980. 458 p. FB 1400.
54. P.-M. BOGAERT (ed.), *Le livre de Jérémie. Le prophète et son milieu. Les oracles et leur transmission*, 1981. *Nouvelle édition mise à jour*, 1997. 448 p. FB 1800.
55. J. COPPENS, *La relève apocalyptique du messianisme royal. III. Le Fils de l'homme néotestamentaire*. Édition posthume par F. NEIRYNCK, 1981. XIV-192 p. FB 800.
56. J. VAN BAVEL & M. SCHRAMA (ed.), *Jansénius et le Jansénisme dans les Pays-Bas. Mélanges Lucien Ceyssens*, 1982. 247 p. FB 1000.
57. J.H. WALGRAVE, *Selected Writings – Thematische geschriften. Thomas Aquinas, J.H. Newman, Theologia Fundamentalis*. Edited by G. DE SCHRIJVER & J.J. KELLY, 1982. XLIII-425 p. FB 1000.
58. F. NEIRYNCK & F. VAN SEGBROECK, avec la collaboration de E. MANNING, *Ephemerides Theologicae Lovanienses 1924-1981. Tables générales. (Bibliotheca Ephemeridum Theologicarum Lovaniensium 1947-1981)*, 1982. 400 p. FB 1600.
59. J. DELOBEL (ed.), *Logia. Les paroles de Jésus – The Sayings of Jesus. Mémorial Joseph Coppens*, 1982. 647 p. FB 2000.
60. F. NEIRYNCK, *Evangelica. Gospel Studies – Études d'évangile. Collected Essays*. Edited by F. VAN SEGBROECK, 1982. XIX-1036 p. FB 2000.
61. J. COPPENS, *La relève apocalyptique du messianisme royal. II. Le Fils d'homme vétéro- et intertestamentaire*. Édition posthume par J. LUST, 1983. XVII-272 p. FB 1000.
62. J.J. KELLY, *Baron Friedrich von Hügel's Philosophy of Religion*, 1983. 232 p. FB 1500.
63. G. DE SCHRIJVER, *Le merveilleux accord de l'homme et de Dieu. Étude de l'analogie de l'être chez Hans Urs von Balthasar*, 1983. 344 p. FB 1500.
64. J. GROOTAERS & J.A. SELLING, *The 1980 Synod of Bishops: «On the Role of the Family»*. An Exposition of the Event and an Analysis of its Texts. Preface by Prof. emeritus L. JANSSENS, 1983. 375 p. FB 1500.
65. F. NEIRYNCK & F. VAN SEGBROECK, *New Testament Vocabulary. A Companion Volume to the Concordance*, 1984. XVI-494 p. FB 2000.
66. R.F. COLLINS, *Studies on the First Letter to the Thessalonians*, 1984. XI-415 p. FB 1500.
67. A. PLUMMER, *Conversations with Dr. Döllinger 1870-1890*. Edited with Introduction and Notes by R. BOUDENS, with the collaboration of L. KENIS, 1985. LIV-360 p. FB 1800.

68. N. LOHFINK (ed.), *Das Deuteronomium. Entstehung, Gestalt und Botschaft / Deuteronomy: Origin, Form and Message*, 1985. XI-382 p. FB 2000.
69. P.F. FRANSEN, *Hermeneutics of the Councils and Other Studies*. Collected by H.E. MERTENS & F. DE GRAEVE, 1985. 543 p. FB 1800.
70. J. DUPONT, *Études sur les Évangiles synoptiques*. Présentées par F. NEIRYNCK, 1985. 2 tomes, XXI-IX-1210 p. FB 2800.
71. *Recueil Lucien Cerfaux*, t. III, 1962. Nouvelle édition revue et complétée, 1985. LXXX-458 p. FB 1600.
72. J. GROOTAERS, *Primauté et collégialité. Le dossier de Gérard Philips sur la Nota Explicativa Praevia (Lumen gentium, Chap. III)*. Présenté avec introduction historique, annotations et annexes. Préface de G. THILS, 1986. 222 p. FB 1000.
73. A. VANHOYE (ed.), *L'apôtre Paul. Personnalité, style et conception du ministère*, 1986. XIII-470 p. FB 2600.
74. J. LUST (ed.), *Ezekiel and His Book. Textual and Literary Criticism and their Interrelation*, 1986. X-387 p. FB 2700.
75. É. MASSAUX, *Influence de l'Évangile de saint Matthieu sur la littérature chrétienne avant saint Irénée*. Réimpression anastatique présentée par F. NEIRYNCK. *Supplément: Bibliographie 1950-1985*, par B. DEHAND-SCHUTTER, 1986. XXVII-850 p. FB 2500.
76. L. CEYSSENS & J.A.G. TANS, *Autour de l'Unigenitus. Recherches sur la genèse de la Constitution*, 1987. XXVI-845 p. FB 2500.
77. A. DESCAMPS, *Jésus et l'Église. Études d'exégèse et de théologie*. Préface de Mgr A. HOUSSIAU, 1987. XLV-641 p. FB 2500.
78. J. DUPLACY, *Études de critique textuelle du Nouveau Testament*. Présentées par J. DELOBEL, 1987. XXVII-431 p. FB 1800.
79. E.J.M. VAN EIJL (ed.), *L'image de C. Jansénius jusqu'à la fin du XVIIIe siècle*, 1987. 258 p. FB 1250.
80. E. BRITO, *La Création selon Schelling. Universum*, 1987. XXXV-646 p. FB 2980.
81. J. VERMEYLEN (ed.), *The Book of Isaiah – Le livre d'Isaïe. Les oracles et leurs relectures. Unité et complexité de l'ouvrage*, 1989. X-472 p. FB 2700.
82. G. VAN BELLE, *Johannine Bibliography 1966-1985. A Cumulative Bibliography on the Fourth Gospel*, 1988. XVII-563 p. FB 2700.
83. J.A. SELLING (ed.), *Personalist Morals. Essays in Honor of Professor Louis Janssens*, 1988. VIII-344 p. FB 1200.
84. M.-É. BOISMARD, *Moïse ou Jésus. Essai de christologie johannique*, 1988. XVI-241 p. FB 1000.
84A. M.-É. BOISMARD, *Moses or Jesus: An Essay in Johannine Christology*. Translated by B.T. VIVIANO, 1993, XVI-144 p. FB 1000.
85. J.A. DICK, *The Malines Conversations Revisited*, 1989. 278 p. FB 1500.
86. J.-M. SEVRIN (ed.), *The New Testament in Early Christianity – La réception des écrits néotestamentaires dans le christianisme primitif*, 1989. XVI-406 p. FB 2500.
87. R.F. COLLINS (ed.), *The Thessalonian Correspondence*, 1990. XV-546 p. FB 3000.
88. F. VAN SEGBROECK, *The Gospel of Luke. A Cumulative Bibliography 1973-1988*, 1989. 241 p. FB 1200.

89. G. THILS, *Primauté et infaillibilité du Pontife Romain à Vatican I et autres études d'ecclésiologie*, 1989. XI-422 p. FB 1850.

90. A. VERGOTE, *Explorations de l'espace théologique. Études de théologie et de philosophie de la religion*, 1990. XVI-709 p. FB 2000.

91. J.C. DE MOOR, *The Rise of Yahwism: The Roots of Israelite Monotheism*, 1990. *Revised and Enlarged Edition*, 1997. XVI-445 p. *forthcoming*.

92. B. BRUNING, M. LAMBERIGTS & J. VAN HOUTEM (eds.), *Collectanea Augustiniana. Mélanges T.J. van Bavel*, 1990. 2 tomes, XXXVIII-VIII-1074 p. FB 3000.

93. A. DE HALLEUX, *Patrologie et œcuménisme. Recueil d'études*, 1990. XVI-887 p. FB 3000.

94. C. BREKELMANS & J. LUST (eds.), *Pentateuchal and Deuteronomistic Studies: Papers Read at the XIIIth IOSOT Congress Leuven 1989*, 1990. 307 p. FB 1500.

95. D.L. DUNGAN (ed.), *The Interrelations of the Gospels. A Symposium Led by M.-É. Boismard – W.R. Farmer – F. Neirynck, Jerusalem 1984*, 1990. XXXI-672 p. FB 3000.

96. G.D. KILPATRICK, *The Principles and Practice of New Testament Textual Criticism. Collected Essays*. Edited by J.K. ELLIOTT, 1990. XXXVIII-489 p. FB 3000.

97. G. ALBERIGO (ed.), *Christian Unity. The Council of Ferrara-Florence: 1438/39 – 1989*, 1991. X-681 p. FB 3000.

98. M. SABBE, *Studia Neotestamentica. Collected Essays*, 1991. XVI-573 p. FB 2000.

99. F. NEIRYNCK, *Evangelica II: 1982-1991. Collected Essays*. Edited by F. VAN SEGBROECK, 1991. XIX-874 p. FB 2800.

100. F. VAN SEGBROECK, C.M. TUCKETT, G. VAN BELLE & J. VERHEYDEN (eds.), *The Four Gospels 1992. Festschrift Frans Neirynck*, 1992. 3 volumes, XVII-X-X-2668 p. FB 5000.

SERIES III

101. A. DENAUX (ed.), *John and the Synoptics*, 1992. XXII-696 p. FB 3000.

102. F. NEIRYNCK, J. VERHEYDEN, F. VAN SEGBROECK, G. VAN OYEN & R. CORSTJENS, *The Gospel of Mark. A Cumulative Bibliography: 1950-1990*, 1992. XII-717 p. FB 2700.

103. M. SIMON, *Un catéchisme universel pour l'Église catholique. Du Concile de Trente à nos jours*, 1992. XIV-461 p. FB 2200.

104. L. CEYSSENS, *Le sort de la bulle Unigenitus. Recueil d'études offert à Lucien Ceyssens à l'occasion de son 90e anniversaire*. Présenté par M. LAMBERIGTS, 1992. XXVI-641 p. FB 2000.

105. R.J. DALY (ed.), *Origeniana Quinta. Papers of the 5th International Origen Congress, Boston College, 14-18 August 1989*, 1992. XVII-635 p. FB 2700.

106. A.S. VAN DER WOUDE (ed.), *The Book of Daniel in the Light of New Findings*, 1993. XVIII-574 p. FB 3000.

107. J. FAMERÉE, *L'ecclésiologie d'Yves Congar avant Vatican II: Histoire et Église. Analyse et reprise critique*, 1992. 497 p. FB 2600.

108. C. BEGG, *Josephus' Account of the Early Divided Monarchy (AJ 8, 212-420). Rewriting the Bible*, 1993. IX-377 p. FB 2400.
109. J. BULCKENS & H. LOMBAERTS (eds.), *L'enseignement de la religion catholique à l'école secondaire. Enjeux pour la nouvelle Europe*, 1993. XII-264 p. FB 1250.
110. C. FOCANT (ed.), *The Synoptic Gospels. Source Criticism and the New Literary Criticism*, 1993. XXXIX-670 p. FB 3000.
111. M. LAMBERIGTS (ed.), avec la collaboration de L. KENIS, *L'augustinisme à l'ancienne Faculté de théologie de Louvain*, 1994. VII-455 p. FB 2400.
112. R. BIERINGER & J. LAMBRECHT, *Studies on 2 Corinthians*, 1994. XX-632 p. FB 3000.
113. E. BRITO, *La pneumatologie de Schleiermacher*, 1994. XII-649 p. FB 3000.
114. W.A.M. BEUKEN (ed.), *The Book of Job*, 1994. X-462 p. FB 2400.
115. J. LAMBRECHT, *Pauline Studies: Collected Essays*, 1994. XIV-465 p. FB 2500.
116. G. VAN BELLE, *The Signs Source in the Fourth Gospel: Historical Survey and Critical Evaluation of the Semeia Hypothesis*, 1994. XIV-503 p. FB 2500.
117. M. LAMBERIGTS & P. VAN DEUN (eds.), *Martyrium in Multidisciplinary Perspective. Memorial L. Reekmans*, 1995. X-435 p. FB 3000.
118. G. DORIVAL & A. LE BOULLUEC (eds.), *Origeniana Sexta. Origène et la Bible/Origen and the Bible. Actes du Colloquium Origenianum Sextum, Chantilly, 30 août – 3 septembre 1993*, 1995. XII-865 p. FB 3900.
119. É. GAZIAUX, *Morale de la foi et morale autonome. Confrontation entre P. Delhaye et J. Fuchs*, 1995. XXII-545 p. FB 2700.
120. T.A. SALZMAN, *Deontology and Teleology: An Investigation of the Normative Debate in Roman Catholic Moral Theology*, 1995. XVII-555 p. FB 2700.
121. G.R. EVANS & M. GOURGUES (eds.), *Communion et Réunion. Mélanges Jean-Marie Roger Tillard*, 1995. XI-431 p. FB 2400.
122. H.T. FLEDDERMANN, *Mark and Q: A Study of the Overlap Texts*. With an *Assessment* by F. NEIRYNCK, 1995. XI-307 p. FB 1800.
123. R. BOUDENS, *Two Cardinals: John Henry Newman, Désiré-Joseph Mercier*. Edited by L. GEVERS with the collaboration of B. DOYLE, 1995. 362 p. FB 1800.
124. A. THOMASSET, *Paul Ricœur. Une poétique de la morale. Aux fondements d'une éthique herméneutique et narrative dans une perspective chrétienne*, 1996. XVI-706 p. FB 3000.
125. R. BIERINGER (ed.), *The Corinthian Correspondence*, 1996. XXVII-793 p. FB 2400.
126. M. VERVENNE (ed.), *Studies in the Book of Exodus: Redaction – Reception – Interpretation*, 1996. XI-660 p. FB 2400.
127. A. VANNESTE, *Nature et grâce dans la théologie occidentale. Dialogue avec H. de Lubac*, 1996. 312 p. FB 1800.
128. A. CURTIS & T. RÖMER (eds.), *The Book of Jeremiah and its Reception – Le livre de Jérémie et sa réception*, 1997. 332 p. FB 2400.
129. E. LANNE, *Tradition et Communion des Églises. Recueil d'études*, 1997. XXV-703 p. FB 3000.

130. A. DENAUX & J.A. DICK (eds.), *From Malines to ARCIC. The Malines Conversations Commemorated*, 1997. IX-317 p. FB 1800.
131. C.M. TUCKETT (ed.), *The Scriptures in the Gospels*, 1997. XXIV-721 p. FB 2400.
132. J. VAN RUITEN & M. VERVENNE (eds.), *Studies in the Book of Isaiah. Festschrift Willem A.M. Beuken*, 1997. XX-540 p. FB 3000.
133. M. VERVENNE & J. LUST (eds.), *Deuteronomy and Deuteronomic Literature. Festschrift C.H.W. Brekelmans*, 1997. XI-637 p. FB 3000.

ORIENTALISTE, KLEIN DALENSTRAAT 42, B-3020 HERENT